Public Relations Planning

Public Relations Planning provides students with an in-depth understanding of the steps involved in planning and executing a successful PR campaign. Taking a strategic approach to the subject, the author brings years of practical experience to the subject matter, helping students see how it all fits together in reality.

The book goes beyond an introductory discussion of the theory of PR planning, incorporating material from cutting-edge research in the field. A discussion of the psychological aspects of communication, material on in-house/employee communication, as well as a chapter dedicated to discussing how social media strategies fit into a PR campaign, give students a real edge when it comes to executing an effective campaign.

Plenty of global examples and a companion website featuring PowerPoint slides, a test bank, and answer key for end-of-chapter questions round out this excellent resource for students of public relations and corporate communication.

Edward T. Vieira, Jr. is Professor of Marketing and Statistics in the School of Business at Simmons University, USA.

Public Relations Planning

A Strategic Approach

Edward T. Vieira, Jr.

Routledge
Taylor & Francis Group

NEW YORK AND LONDON

First published 2019 by Routledge

711 Third Avenue, New York, NY 10017 and by Routledge

2 Park Square, Milton Park, Abingdon, Oxon, OX14 4RN

Routledge is an imprint of the Taylor & Francis Group, an informa business

Library of Congress Cataloging in Publication Data
A catalog record has been requested for this book

ISBN: 978-1-138-10516-4 (hbk)
ISBN: 978-1-138-10517-1 (pbk)
ISBN: 978-1-315-10188-0 (ebk)

Typeset in Bembo
by Swales & Willis Ltd, Exeter, Devon, UK

Visit the eResources: www.routledge.com/9781138105171

I dedicate this book to my lovely daughter, Kelsey, who was my steadfast source of encouragement.

Contents

PART II
Situational Analysis

5   Situational Analysis: Defining and Understanding the Public Relations Issue

PART III
Goals, Objectives, and Strategy 159

7 Strategy: Conceptualization, Goals, Objectives, and Central Message 161

8 Strategy: More on Public Relations Central Messaging 179

Preface

Public Relations Planning: A Strategic Approach is a practical real-world based and comprehensive book about the practice of public relations. Industry standards, best practices, and relevant applied research and theory inform it. Each component that comprises a public relations plan is addressed to provide the reader with a clear understanding including many real world and hypothetical examples. Each chapter stands alone, but also provides an integrated approach to the process of public relations and strategic communication.

The book carefully presents the development and implementation of public relations strategy informed by a situational analysis. The strategy then guides tactical decision-making for communications with stakeholders through the development of action plans. The process focuses on an understanding of the issue, publics, audience psychology, and the importance of maintaining relationships with stakeholders in a cost-efficient manner.

Public relations has clearly defined itself as a dynamic and evolving profession especially in the digital age. Changes in required skills, ability to execute with new technologies, and the globalization and diversification of the business climate in the past few years alone illustrate the need to consistently examine and re-examine public relations skills and update them to plan and provide the expertise needed to effectively implement strategic communication campaigns, a fact that is increasingly recognized in the communications industry. *Public Relations Planning: A Strategic Approach* is a response to this challenge.

The book is designed for practitioners in training or students who wish to develop an understanding of the systematic process of public relations and knowledge of its interdependent and moving components. Each chapter contains a real-world vignette relevant to the topic discussed, end-of-chapter questions, and a developing public relations case that unfolds through the book. The appendix contains over a dozen case studies across various topics with an emphasis on international strategic communications. Online resources include PowerPoint presentations of each chapter, end-of-chapter answer keys, an exam and answer key, and case study instructor notes.

There is a substantial chapter on social media surveying the major platforms. The relatively low cost and ability to adapt to specific publics and stakeholders make online tools an attractive and important option for the public relations practitioner.

Case Studies

The case studies are starting points and meant to represent real world scenarios in which the public relations practitioner has incomplete information and must further research an issue and its situation to make informed and effective decisions. The cases thus encourage the reader to seek more information in addition to that provided in the case. The assignment questions start the critical examination, strategy, and planning process. Many of the cases are international. They are different lengths and different levels of complexity. Some cases have a global focus or take place in a specific country or region of the world. It is for the instructor or student to decide on an appropriate application, given the pedagogical goal.

Chapter Summaries

The following are chapter summaries.

Chapter 1 – Introduction to Public Relations: Public relations is a strategic communication process that builds mutually beneficial relationships between organizations and their stakeholders. The exchange of ideas and free flow of information are fundamental to a representative democracy and capitalist economic system in the U.S.A and throughout most of the world. Accordingly, it is no wonder that the global public relations sector is a $19 billion industry comprising roughly 48,000 firms and upwards of 2 million practitioners worldwide. This chapter is an introduction to this book, which focuses on public relations strategy and planning centered on specific issues or challenges involving various publics. There is in-depth discussion about what is a situational analysis, the development of a public relations goal and informed strategy, objectives, tactics that are the means to achieving objectives, scheduling, budgeting, and assessment.

Chapter 2 – Professional Associations and Public Relations Code of Ethics: Why are ethics of paramount concern in the practice of public relations? A 2013 study about ethics violations by the Ethics and Compliance Initiative found that 41% percent of employees surveyed observed misconduct at work. Sixty percent reported that first-line supervisors, managers, or senior executives violated ethics codes. Sixty-three percent of respondents reported that they shared the misconduct. In a 2017 Washington Post article, North American and Western European executive "resignations" because of misconduct, rose from 4.6% of all departures to 7.8%. In Brazil, Russia, India, and China misconduct resignations went from 3.6% to 8.8%. These alarming trends call for attention to ethics; codes of ethics and conduct; and programs that foster ethical behavior. This chapter reviews types of ethics including best practices for the public relations professional as put forth by the International Public Relations Association (IPRA) and Public Relations Society of America (PRSA). There is also a review of public relations professional associations covering their missions as well as the various programs and opportunities offered. The organizations described are IPRA, PRSA, the Public Relations Student Society of America (PRSSA), International Association of Business Communicators (IABC), Canadian Public Relations Society (CPRS), and American Marketing Association (AMA).

Chapter 3 – Understanding Applied Theory and the Psychology and Behavior of Public Relations Stakeholders: A keen understanding of stakeholders and how they attend to messages, process information, think, feel, formulate attitudes, and behave is necessary for an effective public relations campaign. The emotional, cognitive, social, motivational, and behavioral aspects of individuals are some of the different types of psychology that come to mind when exploring messaging appeals that influence individuals. Applied theory supported by research, provides the framework from which the public relations practitioner can understand publics. This chapter covers these important topics and the major theories equated with them. The content builds an understanding through linking human psychology to public relations issue awareness, knowledge, and engagement as well as examining the potential for stakeholder advocacy and action. Through this understanding, the public relations professional engages in strategic communication that informs, persuades, and successfully mobilizes publics.

Chapter 4 – Public Relations Research: Public relations is about knowing the stakeholders, the issue, the situation, and building relationships with publics through strategic communications. This essential chapter provides an overview of research and touches upon types of research important to the public relations professional. The chapter also reviews key terms, public relations research topics, research designs, statistics in general, the importance of sampling and various sampling techniques, and key research techniques. The public relations practitioner uses research findings in several ways through the planning and implementation process including the pre-, during, and post-campaign periods. Information is garnered through the risk and issue management process (environmental scanning), from the situational analysis (defining the issue and identifying all relevant publics), and throughout the strategizing and planning phase. For the public relations practitioner, research has many purposes for internal organizational situations as well as external circumstances. In short, it allows for informed decision-making.

Chapter 5 – Situational Analysis: Defining and Understanding the Public Relations Issue: A situational analysis collects information relevant and necessary for the successful development and implementation of a public relations campaign. A key function of the situational analysis is to discover and sufficiently define the issue for the public relations professional. This chapter explains this critical function. The public relations issue is a problem or an opportunity, and sometimes both. Some issues are proactive based on advanced planning, and others are reactive requiring immediate attention in an environment of uncertainty as is the case of crisis communication. The situation is a public relations environment where the issue resides like a market for products, financial institutions, legislative branches of state and federal governments, and others. These environments define the situation for the public relations practitioner. Factors in a situation can operate to affect an issue or the issue can affect them. Sometimes more than one situation surrounds an issue. All these contexts involve the relevant publics and potentially other stakeholder groups.

Chapter 6 – Situational Analysis: Defining Stakeholders: A situational analysis collects information relevant and necessary for the successful development and implementation of a public relations campaign. A key function of a situational analysis is to discover and sufficiently define the relevant stakeholder groups for the public relations professional. This chapter explains this vital function. There are different kinds of groups. Their level of knowledge and involvement with an issue can vary among groups as well as within groups. The major kinds of public relations groups are stakeholders, publics, constituents, market segments, audiences, and internal/external types. Although definitions vary, there is general consensus on what constitutes each group. These groups comprise individuals including opinion leaders, organizations, and the news media. Ways of grouping publics usually include a combination of geographic, demographic, psychographic, behavioristic (including media habits), and motigraphic characteristics as well as incorporating their views about an issue and opinions of the organization communicating the issue. Along with the importance assigned to the public, these definitions guide the public relations practitioner's prioritization of the stakeholder groups.

Chapter 7 – Strategy: Conceptualization, Goals, Objectives, and Central Message: A strategic communication approach to public relations consists of strategy conceptualization and planning informed by goals, achieved through benchmarked objectives, executed using tactics and scheduling, and followed by evaluation whether ongoing or post-campaign. This process occurs in the context of budget limitations. As covered in this important chapter, the goal is to respond to an issue whether it is an opportunity or a challenge. Goal achievement happens through reaching objectives. There are overall objectives and those targeted at specific publics. The objectives along with characteristics of the publics guide the development of a central message or common thread that runs through all campaign messaging. The central message guides the public relations practitioner's tactical choices including message content and placement. For the public relations professional, the campaign is a seamless process to goal achievement.

Chapter 8 – Strategy: More on Public Relations Central Messaging: As covered in this important chapter, the public relations strategy includes a central message. The central message is the concrete manifestation of the public relations campaign central idea communicated to publics. Whether explicitly or implicitly, whether through direct communication or indirectly through other actions, each tactic includes at least some aspect of the central message. The public relations practitioner presents the same underlying message differently through multiple communication channels. In other words, the central message binds the strategic communication campaign. Stated in the public relations plan, it ranges from one sentence to a short paragraph. Central messaging applies to external and internal stakeholders or some combination of both. The central message is consistent with the organization's mission and values statements.

Chapter 9 – Public Relations Tactics' Toolbox: A tactic is a tool, task, or activity pursued to achieve an objective that is associated with a public relations' campaign goal, strategy, and objectives. Tactics tell a consistent narrative in accordance with the central message. Tactics also help create dialogue and establish relationships between and among publics and the organization. As covered in this essential chapter, tactics operate at the individual-, group-, or mass-communication level. Specific tactics are news/video/audio releases, media advisories, blog posts, interviews, search engine optimization, web banners, benchmark assessments, themed events, social shares and likes, email, texting, various promotions, public service announcements, and many other activities and tactics. The public relations professional makes decisions about which tactics to deploy based on stakeholder reach and cost. In choosing a tactic, the practitioner assesses its contribution to an objective through what is known about publics and society relevant to an issue wrapped in a situation that exists in time.

Chapter 10 – Social Media Tactics: In the United States, approximately 80% of internet users have at least one social media account. Ninety-five percent of Americans own cell phones, and of those, 77% are smart phones. Video streaming is the largest growing content delivery format. These trends continue to grow worldwide. Social media have become and continue to be central to keeping people connected, to informing them, and to building social capital that binds people. What exactly are social media? Social media provide a place where stakeholders communicate; collaborate; educate and learn; and entertain. Information takes the form of words, images, audio, and video. Social media tactics are the specific activities deployed to achieve public relations objectives. Developing these tactics requires an understanding of social media platforms and what they offer users as well as the public relations professional. This vital chapter surveys the key social media platforms and suggests best practices for deploying them in a strategic communication campaign.

Chapter 11 – Internal Messaging: Effective internal communication is vital for the success of a strategic communication campaign whether the target publics are primarily external or the focus is internal. Internal communication occurs among internal stakeholders as well as between them and the "organization." Internal communication serves to orient and indoctrinate, enhance morale and job satisfaction, communicate information about compensation and benefits, and facilitate organizational development and change. Stakeholders include consultants, volunteers, some shareholders, and interns working within the organizational structure but who are not employees. Internal public relations goes by various designations depending on the organization's structure and leadership's perspective about communication. Some of the names are internal corporate communications, corporate communications, internal communications, strategic communication, employee relations communications, and variations of these labels. This chapter also examines barriers to internal communication and suggests best practices.

Chapter 12 – Budgeting and Scheduling for a Public Relations Campaign: As covered in this chapter, strategizing, planning, executing, monitoring, and evaluating a public relations campaign requires financial resources from a limited pool of funds. To increase the likelihood of receiving these resources now and in the future, public relations practitioners must demonstrate that their expenditures will result in the expected outcomes. There are several budget systems available depending on the value ascribed to various aspects of a strategic communication campaign. Public relations campaign costs come in three varieties: personnel costs, administrative costs, and production and program costs. Scheduling tactics on a timeline and costing them so that optimal and effective combinations are deployed help assure the value of the public relations function. Campaign costs are affected by when messaging takes place, how often it occurs, and media placement. The cost per thousand exposures calculation is an excellent cost control tool to monitor cost efficiencies.

Chapter 13 – Public Relations Campaign Evaluation: As covered in this chapter, public relations campaign assessment is an evaluative research process that determines the effectiveness of a campaign by measuring outcomes such as level of awareness, understanding, attitudes, engagement, opinions and/or behaviors of a targeted audience or public against benchmarked objectives set relative to baseline measures. Evaluation occurs during an ongoing campaign or post-campaign. Evaluation is important for several reasons. First, it is necessary to determine campaign success. Second, results inform subsequent public relation practices leading to more cost-effective tactics. Third, it serves as the justification for future expenditures based on what is effective. Last and related to the third point, evaluation approximates public relations' contribution to the organization, which, in a highly competitive world where departments within organizations compete for limited resources, evidence-based outcomes can assure future commitment from senior management. One such campaign assessment calculation is advertising value equivalency. It is a standardized metric for placing a gross financial value on public relations efforts after deducting the cost of such efforts.

Chapter 14 – Putting It All Together – The Public Relation Campaign Plansbook: This chapter covers the components of a public relations campaign plansbook. It serves as a guide to campaign implementation. The plansbook is in Word format and later archived as a pdf file. Depending on the campaign complexity and level of detail, a plansbook is 10–75 pages and typically covers 6–24 months. The plansbook is a roadmap for the public relations campaign and contains the reasoning or justification for the plan. The planning and precampaign version of the plansbook is in the future tense. However, after the campaign concludes, the plansbook is edited to the past tense and archived for future reference. The final version includes assessment information.

Chapter 15 – Culture, Diversity, and Inclusion: As covered in this chapter, with the advent of new technologies, social media, and social movements that show promise for a more integrated and communicative world, understanding cultural diversity and inclusion are vital to reaching many stakeholders both locally and internationally. Diversity is based on race, ethnicity, gender, sexual orientation, socio-economic status, age, physical abilities and attributes, religious beliefs, political beliefs, or other ideologies. National origin and perceived behaviors such as different lifestyles, speech accents, culturally based practices, and values constitute diversity as well. Yet, a diverse culture is more than hiring quotas. It includes tolerance or a permissive attitude toward those persons who are different and, beyond tolerance, it is acceptance or thinking, feeling, and behaving in a manner respecting and consistent with diversity. This acceptance happens in small one-on-one relationships, in small groups, in large groups, in organizations, in sectors of society, and in an entire society. Inclusion involves actions associated with the acceptance of diverse beliefs, values, and acceptance. It occurs through programs designed to support and integrate diverse individuals in a group or organizational culture. Once inclusion occurs, a multicultural organization can thrive.

Chapter 16 – Global Public Relations: This chapter defines global public relations as a process involving efforts to communicate directly or indirectly with publics and stakeholders across national boundaries and from different cultures to convey messages that are informative, persuasive, and activate target behavior through various tactics and activities. Global public relations faces geographical, cultural, political, legal, socioeconomic, and communication challenges covered in this chapter. Three major reasons contribute to the value of global public relations and strategic communication. First, the ease with which people travel across countries using inexpensive modes of transportation provides opportunities to interact and learn about diverse people. Second, the division of the global economy into regions of comparative advantage based on low cost production, innovation, and professional services contribute to a highly interdependent world economy. Last, the advent of social media points to the importance of global communication. People throughout the world are aware of what is happening in the far corners of the planet and participate in world events. Global public relations shapes and plays an important role in people communicating and influencing agendas on a world-wide scale especially in marketing and other forms of strategic communication. The chapter also addresses barriers to world-wide effective communication and presents best practices.

Chapter 17 – Women in Strategic Communications: This chapter profiles five incredibly dynamic and successful women in careers where public relations or strategic communication play an important role. Their backgrounds and professions vary, but they share similarities. They are in the business of connecting with publics and stakeholders in different ways. These professionals are Carmen Baez, founder of PRxPR Fund and former President of DAS Latin America-Omnicom Group; Carlie Danielson, Strategy Lead at fuseproject; D. Josiane Lee, Recruitment Outreach Officer at the U.S. Department of State; Karen van Bergen, Chief Executive Officer of Omnicom Public Relations Group; and Lily Vautour, Social Media Manager at Boston Children's Hospital. These women are self-determined, highly motivated, and serve as an inspiration to strategic communication professionals.

Final Thought

Perhaps these final words are best left at the end of the book; however, I will share them now. For most of us, that which is worthwhile requires effort and sacrifice. A dream, an idea (even distant), or a goal becomes plausible through effort and tenacity. More tenacity makes it feasible. And even more tenacity makes it achievable, a reality! To the aspiring public relations professional, enjoy the ride!

Acknowledgments

I wish to acknowledge and thank Dr. Susan Sampson, Simmons University Associate Professor and Dr. Susan Grantham, University of Hartford Professor, for their advice, ideas, and support. I am fortunate to have them as dear friends and colleagues. Additionally, I wish to thank Carmen Baez, Karen van Bergen, Carlie Danielson, Josie Lee, and Lily Vautour for setting interview time aside from their busy schedules. Their insights contributed to the value of this book.

Part I

Introduction

Chapter 1

Introduction to Public Relations

For there is only one thing in the world worse than being talked about, and that is not being talked about.

(Oscar Wilde, 1891, p. 6)

Learning Objectives

To:

- Understand and define public relations.
- Explain what is propaganda.
- Describe the difference between symmetric and asymmetric public relations.
- Define glocalization.
- Describe the functions of public relations.
- List the types of public relations.
- Understand the relationship between public relations and marketing.
- Describe the roles of public relations and social media.
- Explain the four public relations models.
- Describe owned, paid, shared, and earned media.
- Understand the process of public relations.

Introduction

According to iExpert (2018), the global public relations sector is a $19 billion industry comprising roughly 48,000 businesses and upwards of 2 million practitioners, with almost half of its revenues going to salaries. The revenue breakdown by service category is 49.8% for general and full service public relations, 20.4% devoted to corporate and lobbying, 16.5% going to media relations, 7.5% to other, and 5.8% to event management.

The industries of operation are as follows: 34% of public relations for retail, 21.5% other client industries, 13.0% for the healthcare sector, 13.0% for information and telecommunications technology, 10.5% for banking and finance, and 8.05% for the automotive sector. Although these are global figures, retail accounts for 75% of the United States economy. The healthcare sector is growing especially considering the aging global population. Information and communications technology are becoming more and more critical for our interdependent world and will continue to do so in the future.

Figure 1.1 Because of Communications Technological Advancements, Including the Advent of Social Media, the World Is Smaller

The world is smaller today than it was ten years ago. People can easily travel virtually anywhere. Economies are more global. Communication technologies and social media have created a global village in which people from all corners of the world can learn about each other and communicate directly. People are exposed to diverse ideas and cultures. Communication plays an important role in fostering these trends. Public relations plays a central role in pluralistic cultures where the free exchange of ideas and debate take place.

The exchange of ideas and free flow of information is fundamental to a representative democracy and capitalist economic system. Informed citizens rely on information to vote for candidates. This process extends to policy making where voters can express their opinions in ways that support or oppose policies.

Like candidates, savvy consumers require information about products, services, or brands to make wise purchase decisions. Online brand reviews, product recalls, and independent consumer rating organizations provide information that aids consumers in the decision-making process.

Whether one is researching features and benefits of washer and dryer brands or positions of presidential candidates, the free flow of information is vital for the system to live up to its expectations. In both circumstances, public relations performs a critical role in providing information and a forum for the exchange of ideas and information.

So, what exactly is public relations? Although it is dynamic and evolving because of new and innovative ways of communicating, we can define public relations based on its key characteristics. The Public Relations Society of America defines public relations as "a strategic communication process that builds mutually beneficial relationships between organizations and their publics" (About Public Relations, 2017, para. 4). Along similar lines and considering the various types of public relations, **public relations** is perhaps best defined as a managed, researched, and planned process involving effort to communicate directly or indirectly strategically to publics of one or more persons or groups. Public relations efforts are routine, relational, or ad hoc in nature. The messages communicated are informative, persuasive, and/or compel a call to action through various paid or unpaid tactics. Ideally, previous messaging assessment informs future campaigns.

The focus of this book is public relations strategy and planning centered on a specific issue. However, public relations also performs a maintenance function in which it maintains and reinforces relationships with stakeholders over the long term. For instance, an unexpected event that brings negative publicity to a company and subsequent pressure from publics in opposition to the company, requires immediate action. Public relations agencies develop volunteer and fundraising campaigns for companies focusing not only at its employees, but the local communities in which the companies operate as well. Both situations can be short or long term or evolve into longer term or permanent programs. At the same time, organizations have long term relationships with employees and vendors. The support of these stakeholders is usually vital to the existence of organizations.

Public relations has been equated with propaganda. However, the two endeavors are different. **Propaganda** attempts to persuade based on appeals that are not supported by sound reasoning and/or evidence presented objectively. Propaganda makes use of exaggerated language, name calling, stereotypical labeling (directly or indirectly), fear tactics, euphemisms, and a host of other tactics to persuade individuals.

On the other hand, legitimate public relations makes use of warranted claims supported by evidence that fits the argument. Often these efforts are with the intention of establishing long-term relations with stakeholder groups. As discussed by Bobbitt and Sullivan (2014), public relations must provide choices that center on win/win possibilities.

In the past, whether in-person or mediated, interpersonal, small group, or mass, people assumed that communication was a natural and innate process and taken for granted. With the development of communication theories and advancements in technology, that changed. We began to question these assumptions. We discovered ways to make communication more cost and message effective. We developed and are still developing digital methods to measure and evaluate public relations' contribution to profit. The role of public relations as a management function is becoming more accepted as communication continues to evolve and management acknowledges the importance of its role in a pluralistic, social media world. With the growth of analytics and methodologies that measure online behaviors and public relations effectiveness, it is likely that the public relations manager as part of the dominant coalition (organizational decision-makers) will be commonplace.

This chapter defines public relations and describes the functions as well as types of public relations. We also discuss the relationships among public relations, advertising, integrated communication, and marketing and examine public relation practitioner roles in addition to public relations models. The discussion covers earned, paid, owned, and new media public relations. Finally, public relations is examined as a process of interdependent parts. In short, this chapter provides an overview of what is public relations and its place in the real world.

Asymmetric and Symmetric Public Relations

Asymmetric public relations campaigns can involve one-way or two-way communication. In either case, they are one-sided focusing on the "interests" of the organization. **Asymmetric public relations** can simply provide publicity framed to support an issue, the facts advocating a position, or an appeal with evidence to support a position. This perspective is usually short term, eliciting a desired response to an existential issue. The Press Agent/Publicity, Public Information, and Two-way Communication Asymmetric models examined in the Models of Public Relations section are asymmetric public relations approaches. The following are two examples of asymmetric public relations.

Yahoo waited two years before reporting a cybersecurity breach that occurred in 2014. A "state-sponsored" hacker procured the users' names, emails, telephone numbers, and encrypted passwords of more than 500 million Yahoo account holders. During the time between the hack and its reporting, Yahoo was negotiating its sale to Verizon for $4.8 billion, but kept the breach secret, which delayed the sale until it was finally announced in June 2017. Yahoo's credibility was damaged, which resulted in several law suits, delay in the acquisition, and the discovery of an even larger cyber-breach.

Equifax, the credit monitoring company, experienced a similar breach affecting 143 million individuals, but did not wait as long. The company was aware of a successful cyber-attack at the end of July 2017, but failed to communicate it until September of the same year. In the interim, the top three Equifax executives sold stock totaling $2 million. Equifax provided a verification website for users to check their breach status. The website included a hidden arbitration clause indicating that those consumers who utilized the breach service waive their rights to participate in a class-action lawsuit against Equifax. Currently, some law enforcement agencies are investigating how Equifax handled the situation. Clearly, both Yahoo's and Equifax's behaviors did not engender public trust.

On the other hand, **symmetric public relations** involves communication that is socially responsible and considers the positions of the various publics in a free-flow of information and give-and-take that are transparent, relational, and long term. Although perceived as ideal and likely impractical for some organizational structures, the Two-Way Symmetrical Model consists of five features (Wilson & Ogden, 2015). They are: (1) a long-term vision; (2) a commitment to community; (3) organizational values centered on people; (4) collective problem-solving; and (5) relationship building based on respect and trust in conjunction with the organizational mission. Let's look at an example.

AirBnb launched a new logo campaign in early 2014. The logo called "the Bélo," represents the essence of connection and a sense of belonging in an ever-expanding global village. The company produced a video that explained the reason for the new logo and branding strategy. Airbnb also developed an online application in which customers could create their own personalized Bélo using colors, lines, and backgrounds. For those current customers satisfied with the previous branding system, the company CEO, Brian Chesky, sent them an invitation to an exclusive online seminar where he personally explained the reason for the logo and brand change. Despite these efforts, a vocal, dissatisfied segment of customers were skeptical and expressed their displeasure by writing negative reviews. Tweets spiked as well. The Bélo was compared to animals, certain body parts, foods, transportation, and several unflattering objects. AirBnb embraced these comments, including those from customers who disagreed with the change. The company responded by creating and sharing with the public an infographic with the results. Eventually, dissatisfaction mitigated and the company continues to do well.

The Nature of Online Interaction

Public relations is constantly changing spurred by cultural, communication, and technological changes. The Internet transformed from Web 1.0 in which people received producer generated content in a top/down fashion to the advent of Web 2.0 and now Web 3.0. In Web 2.0, users and content producers interact in a transactional multidirectional and multi-spatial manner. User generated content emphasizes the needs, desires, and goals of the user influenced by the individual's cultural and environmental background. Web 2.0 provides an intriguing set of challenges for the public relations practitioner, who now must gain an understanding of stakeholder groups who often have subtle, but important differences. Web 3.0 moves us towards "computer to computer" interaction, more digital integration, increased artificial intelligence applications, and automated processes. It essentially provides us with more technological tools that collect and organize information so that society can benefit more from a Web 2.0 world.

The pluralism of the Web and opportunities for activism allow for **organic public relations,** which is public relations created, developed, and changed at the grassroots or user level, whether within an organization or externally. This type of public relations is alive and adopts like an organism does to survive and even thrive in its environment. An effective public relations professional understands the transactional nature of this process. **Transactional public relations** shapes public relations through the nature, direction, level, and multi-way communication of the interaction among publics. The dialogue steers the direction of the discussion and increases engagement, further increasing commitment and greater issue ownership.

Figure 1.2 Can Public Relations Be 100% Organic?

Glocalization

The nature of the public relations environment poses some interesting challenges including addressing the local environments' varied concerns. Yet, the organization's regional, national, or global goals are the primary focus. Developing an overall strategy with local tactics accounting for local conditions allays local concerns. For example, McDonald's created rice dishes in local Chinese markets and veggie burgers in India, where eating beef is culturally or legally prohibited. Accommodating the local culture is **glocalization**, which is a combination of the words "globalization" and "localization." In the case of brand promotions, the global brand name is differentiated to appeal to local markets.

There is also a glocalization trend in public relations agencies. Corella, Del Campo, and Toledo (2009) reported in one study that 64% of American public relations firms have alliances with international agencies. Table 1.1 contains more examples derived from Grigorescu and Zaif's research publication entitled, "The concept of glocalization and its incorporation in global brands' marketing strategies" (2017).

Keep in mind that glocalization can apply to many public relations functions such as events, copy, nature of persuasive appeals, and channels of communication.

Where Does Public Relations Start and Who Does It?

Where does public relations start? Individuals or organizations conduct the business of public relations in various forms and to varying degrees depending on a host of factors such as their mission, source of the issue, situational complexity, and available resources. A person, corporation, non-profit organization, special interest group, or governmental entity can conduct a public relations project, program, or campaign.

For instance, a student concerned about informing the public about FedLoan's dubious student loan practices may take to social media to inform others about the loan

Table 1.1 Glocalization Marketing Strategies

McDonalds sells the local dish called McMici, a local dish consisting of grilled ground meat rolls made from beef, lamb, pork, and spices. In India, the Maharajah Mac and Veggie McNuggets are offered. Mutton pies are available in Australia. In the Philippines, McSpaghetti is on the menu. Teriyaki Burger are sold Japan and the McLobster sandwich can be purchased in Canada.

Fanta soda offers Shokate in Romania, which is "elderflower juice," a traditional Romanian beverage. Green apple Fanta can be bought in China, as well as watermelon flavored Fanta in Spain and Portugal.

Lay's Potato Chips cheese-onions flavor is available in the United Kingdom. Lemon Lays is popular in Thailand and Seafood Lays is a hit in China.

Dunkin Donuts offers dry pork and seaweed donuts in China. Grapefruit coolatas are served in South Korea, mango chocolate donuts are a favorite Lebanon and Dunclairs are in demand in Russia.

Nokia cell phones offer an anti-dust keypad, to prevent cell phone damage caused by the heavy dust in regions of India.

Barbie in Japan differs from Barbie in the United States. In Japan, Barbie is tailored to the Japanese market. It is blond, has a round face, and large eyes.

company's activities. In its simplest form, the student is a special interest "group" formed to bring attention to this specific issue. On the other hand, a financially substantial corporation such as Equifax would launch a complex and expensive crisis communication campaign to address the hacking of millions of its client consumers' personal financial and social security records.

Where are public relations campaigns created? Although usually some work is outsourced, there are full-service public relations agencies that offer a wide range of services from research to public relations campaign plans development. Some full-service firms are Skyya Communications out of New York, Blast PR from California, and Landis Communications Inc. located in San Francesco. Additionally, boutique or specialty shops provide specialized services such as social media public planning, media buying, or strategy development. For example, all located in New York, Point Five specializes in graphic design, Brand Union provides branding expertise, and Critical Mention offers environmental scanning services.

Large organizations typically use multiple public relations agencies. Smaller organizations do the work in-house. Usually, the organization handles internal communication and hires one or more agencies for external public relations. Sometimes the in-house department, external agencies, or consultants share various responsibilities. The set-up is contingent upon the situation, urgency, expertise required, and available resources. For instance, BackBay Communications in Boston focuses on public relations for financial institutions. Jarrard Phillips, Cate, & Hancock from Tennessee concentrates on the healthcare sector. Smaller organizations deploy their own in-house public relations. These days, they focus on social media, especially Facebook, Twitter, Instagram, and Pinterest, depending on the nature of the organizational mission.

Functions of Public Relations

Another way of thinking about public relations is by function. What functions does public relations perform? Many of these tasks extend to different types of public relations; they overlap and are not neatly differentiated; and perform as part of the campaign process or as part of maintaining stakeholder relationships over the long term. Table 1.2 summarizes the major public relations functions.

The shaded area represents public relations functions whose primary purpose is to inform, persuade, or present a call to action. The remaining functions involve various basic tasks. Many of these activities are highly interrelated. For example, fostering diversity and inclusion in the workplace so that pluralism thrives involves change agentry. It includes elements of trust and relationship building as well as buy-in from the senior management and leadership.

Discovering an issue and planning a response in advance of its actualization requires environmental scanning, risk assessment, and issue management followed-up with a public relations plan and method for measuring effectiveness. The plan likely includes social media activities and usually incorporates news media tactics as well.

Typically, public relations involves informing, persuading, and calls for action, as well as providing the tactics for objectives. Tactics such as events, lobbying, and sales promotions, inform and persuade publics. News and social media aid crisis communication for such efforts as evacuating people or alerting them to impending developments.

Table 1.2 Public Relations Functions

Public Relations Functions	Purpose
Creating awareness, positive attitude, motivation, or call to action.	– Create a desirable psychological or behavior condition in the minds of internal or external stakeholders.
Change agentry.	– Facilitate change within the organization or externally such as implementing new training procedures for employees or a new return policy for company distributors.
Corporate image building.	– Promote the organization and its good deeds so that it is viewed positively by the public.
Generate publicity.	– Encourage awareness about the issue and organization through media coverage and social media feedback and sharing.
Develop loyal customer base.	– Foster company loyalty so that consumers develop a positive attitude toward brand, are repeat purchasers, and are brand advocates.
Establish trust, relationships, and support with stakeholders.	– The maintenance of internal and external stakeholder relationships.
Communicating social responsibility.	– Creating awareness and support for the organization internally and externally through its good deeds.
Counselling management/ leadership about issues.	– Senior management/leadership can make informed decisions when the public relations practitioner advises about situations and Issues affecting the company and its external and internal stakeholders/publics. Also, includes speechwriting.
Facilitate workplace diversity & inclusion.	– Communicate diversity and inclusion commitment and programs including promoting within the organization, networking opportunities, and active recruitment of diverse talent so that everyone thrives.
Organized public relations efforts.	– Develop, plan, implement, and execute effective public relations plans.
Risk and Issues management.	– Predict future situations or the impact of potential issues on the organization so plans can be made.
Situational analysis/ environmental scanning.	– As part of the risk or issue management function, monitor the internal or external environment for trends, changes, opportunities, or problems. This will inform future planning.
Raising funds or capital.	– Promoting the financial health of the organization so that credit raising capital terms are favorable.
Event management.	– Create, develop, and implement special in-person and/or online events that promote the issue and the message to garner support.
Evaluate public relations activities.	– Assess public relations success based on achieving objectives during and after the efforts in order to be effective presently and in the future.
Crisis communication.	– Inform and provide guidance for all publics affected by a crisis situation and issue with the intention to attenuate any negative effects.

Lobbying.	– In order to have a voice on public policy decisions, develop relationships with regulators, elected officials, other government administrators, and trade association groups.
Promoting products, services, and brands.	– Work with marketing and advertising to consistently promote company products, services, and brands so as to increase revenues and/or market share.
Media management.	– Develop relationships with media stakeholders both organizationally and individually with the intention of receiving favorable or, at least, neutral media coverage.
Social media management.	– Develop consistent content and manage the organization's social media activities across functions, departments, and divisions

Types of Public Relations

There are different emphases placed on various types of public relations based on the environment in which they primarily serve and types of stakeholders. Public relations can be corporate public relations, corporate communications, corporate relations, community relations, media relations, employee relations, governmental public affairs, publicist for the chief executive officer, legislature affairs (lobbying), industry relations, collective labor affairs, strategic communications, integrated communications, and financial relations. Table 1.3 provides a summary of the major kinds of public relations.

Table 1.3 Kinds of Public Relations

Public Relations Type	Description
Public Relations/Integrated Communications Strategic/ Communications/Corporate Communications/ Media Relations[a]	Public relations in general involving the full range of issues and stakeholders/publics.

Media are the primarily stakeholders/publics. Building relationships and providing information to the different media and influential representatives. |
| Public Affairs | Usually operates in a federal agency, state, or local government organization. Provides information to all relevant stakeholders/publics especially voters, taxpayers, and elected officials. Plays a critical crisis communication role during times of emergency. |
| Internal Corporate Communications | Responsible for all communication with employees, internal contractors, and interns. Gives information about policies, changes, benefits, and conducts projects, programs, and campaigns that foster morale, motivation, CSR. major organizational developments, and overall productivity. |

(continued)

Table 1.3 (continued)

Public Relations Type	Description
Community Relations	Typically, operates in larger organizations. The stakeholders/publics are the various groups in the local communities in which the organization conducts business. The key public depend on the specific issue and situation.
Employee Relations	A part of internal corporate communications, the focus is on messaging employees and concentrating on their issues and situations.
Industry Relations	Primary stakeholders/publics are competitors, vendors, trade associations, and other organizations in the infrastructure that support the company's mission.
Government Affairs/Legislative Affairs	The stakeholders/publics are governmental regulators, boards, officials, and elected officials who can have an impact on the organization's mission. The issue could be environmental, tax codes, tax credits, industry regulation, labor laws, trade regulations, and so forth.
Financial Relations	The primary stakeholders/publics are banks, investors, and specific individuals within those two sectors. These practitioners work closely with the organizational finance department.
Labor Relations	Organized labor and union officials are the key stakeholders/publics. This type of public relations is closely aligned with employee relations, but with a focus on collective bargaining and securing labor contracts and relationships with the union and rank and file membership.

[a] Social media are addressed within each form of public relations.

Public Relations and Integrated (Marketing) Communication

What is the relationship among public relations, advertising, and marketing? Are they the same? Are they separate and distinct? With the growth of digital technologies, the line that differentiates these areas has blurred. Let's start by defining each term.

Advertising is paid messaging. It is typically one-way communication and short-term geared toward selling brands, products, and services. In the past, it was primarily a mass media tool, reaching many audience members with a specific message. However, today it has evolved to where very specific market segments can be microtargeted. For example, searched sites are ranked through the deployment of search engine optimization tools. Specific ads also appear that appeal to the individual based on the search and other data collected about the person. Additionally, some forms of advertising encourage a limited amount of consumer engagement by encouraging ad click-throughs that link to online activities that further promote product sales directly or indirectly using public relations tactics. Common techniques such as these integrate advertising and public relations.

Because much activity is digitally based, especially with the increased usage of mobile applications, organizations can identify and group individuals with specific characteristics, attitudes, values, beliefs, and behaviors. This information allows us not only to microtarget groups, but also to engage individuals and establish longer term relationships with them by reaching out to them in ways that they prefer.

Marketing involves selling products, services, and/or brands to generate revenues, increase profits, and thus increase the value of an organization. Marketing activities concentrate on: 1) product development, 2) price points, 3) place or channels of distribution, and 4) promotion. These are the 4Ps of marketing. Together they constitute the "offering." The fourth P, promotion, includes public relations, advertising, personal selling, and any other communication with the marketplace about the brand, product, or service. Collectively, this coordinated effort is **integrated marketing communication (MARCOM)**. Integrated refers to consistent communication across channels, audiences, and functional area including customer relations management. It is less costly to keep current, repeat customers, than it is to acquire new ones.

This marketing trend toward relationship building not only increases the value of public relations, but also moves the nature of promotional marketing to a more personalized focus. Today and in the future, advertising or promotion is becoming more and more public relations-related. Organizations are also finding that communication integration also requires the coordination of and relationship building of internal groups. Because of these factors, there has been a trend toward relabeling MARCOM simply **integrated communication** or **strategic communication**. Both terms include all communication, internal as well as external, that is highly interdependent, coordinated, and consistent.

The relationship among marketing, advertising, and public relations is still unfolding. For now, we continue to use and adopt modes of operation that are message effective and cost efficient within the organizational structure as well as in the external environments.

Public Relations Roles

The public relations environment is constantly changing, creating challenges for the practitioner. The 2017 Global Communications Report by the UCS Annenberg Center for Public Relations found that long-term public relations growth is driven by content and digital technologies demanding specialized skills, talent, innovative ideas, and better measurement. Public relations professionals will need to stay current and regularly hone and adjust their skill sets to the latest technological tools, social trends, and market demands.

As covered in the "Think about This . . ." segment, public relations roles divide into five general categories (Vieira & Grantham, 2014). The roles are: senior public relations management/leadership, policy/operations management, brand specialist, internal communicator, and media specialist/manager.[1] The actual labels for these roles vary by organization. The senior public relations management position is the chief public relations officer or an internal communications practitioner is the corporate communications director. The senior public relations management/leadership and policy/operations management roles are clearly managerial involving longer term, strategic managerial decision-making. The brand specialist, internal communicator, and media specialist/manager roles are a blend of technical and managerial duties, with sometimes one role being dominant. The situation and nature of the organization define the dominant role. Managerial decision-making is typically day-to-day.

Figure 1.3 Public Relations Offers an Array of Career Opportunities

Senior public relations management/leadership individuals, some of which are consultants to the organization, have extensive experience and participate in strategic decision-making. These individuals span boundaries (reach out to various groups) among both internal and external stakeholders. Some responsibilities involve organizational image, product and services positioning, and public relations campaign evaluation.

Policy/operations managers have technical responsibilities as they relate to managing and developing strategic plans. Policy advisors have extensive experience. Their activities involve spanning boundaries by interacting with internal and external stakeholders. These managers marshal resources and assess aspects of the campaign before roll-out, during the campaign, and post-campaign. This information informs on-going and future campaign planning.

The third role is **brand specialist**. There practitioners are typically technicians, but sometimes perform some supervisory duties. They possess less experience than those fulfilling management roles. They are often involved with company brands, corporate image, or building the organizational brand with internal stakeholders.

Next, the **internal communicator** role consists of technical and managerial duties. This person has roughly the same number of years of experience as the brand specialist. The internal communicator is concerned with employee morale, motivation, and a variety of internal communications. Much of his/her communication is face-to-face.

The last public relations practitioner role is **media specialist/manager**. These individuals are involved with technical as well as managerial tasks. They have extensive experience. Their primary focus on external stakeholders especially the news media. They also consult with senior management about key stakeholders. These practitioners provide some strategic planning inputs especially about news media.

Social Media Role in Public Relations

The growing significance of social media as a flexible and efficient tool to reach both external and internal stakeholders forces us to examine social media roles. A study by Neill and Lee (2016) noted that previous research reported public relations practitioners within organizations manage upwards of 85% of social media activities. In their study, they discovered seven roles: social media technician, social listening and analytics, online media relations, policy maker, employee recruiter, internal social media manager, and policing.

The **social media technician** role develops and implements public relations tactics such as writing news releases and blog posts.

Social listening and analytics involve monitoring and interpreting social media communications and trends including deploying analytics, which is environmental scanning. Through this activity, opinion leaders are identified and news media activities surveilled. Additionally, the practitioner in this role measures social media effort effectiveness and helps develop problem detection protocols as part of risk and issues management.

The **online media relations** role comprises tasks and responsibilities such as developing relationships with opinion leaders including media professionals. The person in this role also pitches stories to news media representatives.

The public relations **policy maker** role develops policies and guidelines for how organizational members utilize social media, which can vary across departments and divisions.

Employee recruiter is a role by which the practitioner recruits people for positions throughout social media. This person shares information about the appeal of the organizational culture, fosters organizational pluralism, and supports diversity and inclusion in recruitment practices.

The role of **internal social media** is an internal communication function. The practitioner in this role writes content for the organizational intranet and internal social media. Likes, shares, comments, and other metrics measures employee engagement. This practitioner keeps employees informed of key developments and social events designed to maintain morale, motivation, and productivity.

Last, there is the **policing role**. In this role, the practitioner monitors organizational-related social media messaging for appropriateness that assures a positive public image.

Representation of these roles and the extent to which each influences the organization varies and changes according to circumstance, organizational culture, and resources available for public relations social media. In some cases, roles may be logically combined owing to similar required resources and talent availability.

Job Prospects for the Public Relations Practitioner

How do these public relations roles relate to the job market? According to the 2017 USC Annenberg Center for Public Relations Global Communications Report, the top sought after skills in public relation are writing, strategic planning, verbal communication, analytics, and search engine optimization.

In the United States, there are several public relations position classifications. They start at entry level public relations specialists with a median salary of $62,000 followed by more experienced senior specialists earning upwards of $114,000. Salary is based on the specialty and skill set sought. According to the Bureau of Labor Statistics, the job growth rate for these positions through 2024 is 6% per annum (Occupational Outlook Handbook, 2015).

Management and director positions median range salaries are between $110,000 and $150,000 with an anticipated growth rate of 7% (Occupational Outlook Handbook, 2015; Salary.com, 2017). Chief Public Relations Officers can expect to earn at the median $252,000. Compensation varies by location and size and nature of the organization.

Think about This . . .

In a 2014 *Public Relations Review* article entitled "Defining Public Relations Roles in the U.S.A. Using Cluster Analysis," Vieira and Grantham identified five public relations roles. The researchers collaborated with the Public Relations Society of America (PRSA) where 256 PRSA members who were practitioners completed a survey. Based on personal characteristics, modes of communication, management and technical functions, perceived level of strategic planning involvement, and attitudes about communication goals and public relations measurement, five public relations emerged. The roles were specifically labelled negotiator, policy advisor, brand officer, internal communicator, and press agent.

Findings revealed that public relations is a dynamic and evolving profession especially in the digital age. The ability to execute with new technologies, and the globalization and diversification of the business climate alone illustrate the need to consistently examine and re-examine public relations roles and responsibilities. This requires periodically updating roles to optimize the public relations function within organizations.

Ask yourself: Where do you see PR in the future? What new prominent roles may emerge?
Vieira, E. T., Jr., & Grantham, S. (2014). Defining public relations roles in the U.S.A. using cluster analysis. *Public Relations Journal, 40*, 60–68.

Models of Public Relations

Grunig and Hunt (1984) conceptualized four public relations models, which are Press Agent/Publicity, Public Information, Two-way Asymmetrical, and Two-way Symmetrical models.

Press Agent/Publicity Model

The **Press Agent/Publicity Model** is a one-way communication process. This approach creates extensive media coverage for an organization through persuasion, half-truths, publicity stunts, and other attention getting devices to gain media attention. These chosen activities persuade key publics based on experience or intuition, but not empirical testing beforehand.

Celebrities who hold extreme positions, engage in outlandish behaviors, and appear on such venues as American Idol or other celebrity participant reality-based programs hope that media coverage of them will increase their popularity and enhance their careers. P. T. Barnum exemplifies this viewpoint. He believed that any news coverage whether negative or positive was valuable because then the brand was in the minds of the consuming public. Although many of these public relations activities exist today, this framework emerged in the early 1980s before the availability of the Web and evolving nature of publicity.

Public Information Model

The **Public Information Model** is also a one-way communication approach. It deploys news releases and other techniques to distribute information. Generally, there is less concern for drawing attention and extensive news coverage. The goal is to disseminate information to stakeholder groups in a managed manner not informed by formal research.

This approach makes use of newsletters, brochures, email, social media, websites, and magazines with information about the organization, its key people, and, in some cases, products, services, and brands. The stakeholders receive content about the benefits of the brand, testimonials, and success stories at regular intervals.

Utility companies sometimes include fliers about energy efficiency with customers' bills. The IRS regularly issues press releases to explain changes to existing tax codes. In addition, there are nongovernmental organizations and special interest groups that release research study findings to inform the public and to provide information that can inform policy makers' decisions. In fact, some government regulators reply on these studies for policy development because the organization has the expertise and resources not available to government agencies.

Two-Way Asymmetric Model

The **Two-way Asymmetric Model** works to persuade stakeholders to embrace a specific attitude or behavior using one-sided arguments and based on what target publics value. Messages are also empirically pre-tested to predict efficacy. Additionally, post-campaign evaluation determines message effectiveness. The pre-testing and evaluation process provides feedback and hence two-way communication. However, because these types of organizations do not utilize much of their resources to measure responses from stakeholders, but focus instead on cost-efficiencies, there are limitations to measurement.

This perspective informs most corporate public relations. Many political candidates utilize the persuasive model as do governments to support their programs. For example, American military action in Iraq used two-way asymmetrical techniques to generate support for the war. Proponents for stiffer punishments and longer prison sentences advocate the same approach.

Two-Way Symmetric Model

The **Two-way Symmetric Model**, which is the most ideal and optimistic framework, employs communication between and among all publics. Back and forth negotiation

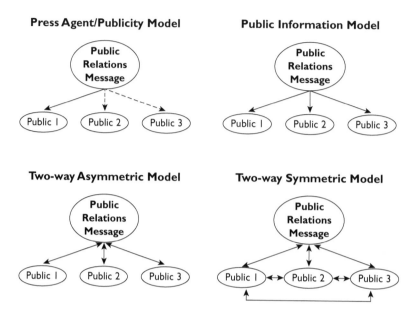

Figure 1.4 The Four Models of Public Relations

results in mutual understanding, resolved conflicts, and long-term agreements that respect the positions of all the publics. There is a free flow of information among the organization and its stakeholders in a manner desired by the various groups. Mutually arrived at agreements emerge. Messages are also empirically pre-tested to predict efficacy. During and post campaign message assessment occurs as well. The pre-testing and evaluation process provides feedback.

This model is useful when communicating within an organization because it helps employees feel valued and acknowledged as an essential stakeholder group. Investor relations as well as organizations in which human capital is highly dependent upon volunteers follow this approach. In these cases, success in large measure requires buy-in from these stakeholders.

Figure 1.4 illustrates the four models, each targeting three publics. The Press Agent/ Publicity Model is based on creating evocative publicity with the intention that the relevant public will receive and embrace the public relations message. There are no guarantees of exposure and favorable coverage because the public relations practitioner does not control publicity. In some cases, the message does not reach the public as depicted in the dashed arrows not touching any publics. The Public Information Model simply provides the informational message to each public. The single headed arrow represents planned and managed one-way communication. On the other hand, the Two-way Asymmetric Model and the Two-way Symmetric Model both require two-way communication, but the quality of the communication between them varies. In the case of the asymmetric model, the feedback is in the form of pre-testing and/or during or post-campaign feedback as characterized by the two-headed arrows. The symmetric model, however, also includes mutual resolution of the issue to the satisfaction of all relevant publics, which requires multiple directional communication not only with the organization, but also among the publics directly or indirectly through the public relations organization.

Owned, Paid, Shared, and Earned Media

The word "media" is plural. "Medium" is the singular form. **Owned media** are public relations' issue coverage and messaging that the organization owns. Owned media comprise created, owned, and disseminated organizational content such as expert endorsements, customer testimonials, employee stories, videos and blogs, and social media accounts.

Media paid for by the organization, but not owned are **paid media** such as Google AdWords or banners placed on various websites that are not organization owned. Public relations attempts to manage and communicate with various traditional and social media with the intention of obtaining favorable media coverage constitute **earned media**. For instance, a news release sent to the Associated Press that is subsequently covered by news media, a videos new release sent to the major networks and subsequently broadcast on the news, or an issue presented on social media that gains more discussion online, constitute earned media.

Publicity is a type of unpaid media coverage. The organization has no control over the content, where it appears or whether it is positive or negative. **Shared media** are publicity created by the sharing of content as the method of distribution. Word-of-mouth, opinion leaders (social influencers), Twitter, LinkedIn, Facebook, online reviews and rating,and any viral content are examples of shared media when distributed in the spirit of Web 2.0. However, paid and earned media coverage also use these social media platforms. It is important to note that shared media are becoming more and more social media activity-driven. Social networks serve as the channels of distribution reaching publics and stakeholders across the globe. Opinion leaders serve as the hub of social networks connecting many followers with others as well as sharing ideas and issues.

In the future, it is expected that the breakdown of media will be: Earned 31%, Owned 28%, Shared 24%, and Paid 15%. Increases in shared media drive most of the expected change (Global Communications Report, 2017).

Social Media as Two-Way Communication for Public Relations

In the past, civic engagement was highly associated with socioeconomic status. The Web has changed by opening the world to those from diverse backgrounds and incomes, thus, fostering increased participation in social issues (Smith, Schlozman, Verba, & Brady, 2009). Clearly, the internet and, especially, social media have created a pluralistic online environment.

According to Safko and Brake (2009), **social media** are:

> activities, practices, and behaviors among communities of people who gather online to share information, knowledge, and opinions using conversational media. Conversational media are web-based applications that make it possible to create and easily transmit content in the form of words, pictures, videos, and audios.
>
> (p. 6)

The two fastest growing digital tools are video and mobile. Why are they popular? People are busy and thus read less. Video is played, paused, and repeated. A person can listen to the audio and not focus on the video aspect. The cost of video production has dramatically decreased and many quality applications are free for personal computers, tablets, and cell phones. Individuals utilize their cell phone for more than communication. They manage their personal and professional lives with it. It is small, has relatively strong computing power, and millions of apps are available. For what it does, it is relatively inexpensive.

Table 1.4 represents a list of various social media by brand as well as generically.

Social media provide opportunities for diverse people to interact in a marketplace of ideas. These two conditions are ideal for activism to flourish and the self-mobilization of publics concerned about issues.

Platforms such as Facebook, Twitter, blogs, and the like offer a free flow of information, knowledge, and exchange of ideas, beliefs, and perspectives, which is the Two-way Communication Symmetric Model of public relations. Allowing diverse and contrary views may increase the veracity of the message through an open debate vetting process. Through dialogue, less compelling claims are invalidated. The strength of the public relations message, reputation of the organization, and its willingness to be open to diverse comments, not only maintain its credibility, but increases it through a two-stage process consisting of two groups of publics: opinion leaders and their followers, as well as other engaged publics.

Table 1.4 Examples of Social Media

Social Networking	Interpersonal
Facebook	Email
LinkedIn	Instant Messenger
Google +	WhatsApp
Qzone	Texting
ASKfm	Skype
Meetup	
WeChat	
Blogging	Video Sharing
Twitter	YouTube
Tumblr	Vimeo
Wordpress	DailyMotion
Blogger	
Image Sharing	Message/Forum
Instagram	Board
Snapchat	Reddit
Pinterest	IGN
Flickr	4chan
	Gaia Online
Audio Sharing	
Podcasts	
NoiseTrade	
Jamendo	

Figure 1.5 Opinions Leaders Are Effective Communicators

Social media influencers or **opinion leaders** are an intervening public. That is, they pass the public relations message along to their followers who are larger publics. They are trusted experts in a chosen field or simply have substantial social influence within their groups. It is this intervening public that directly or indirectly supports, is neutral, or opposes the message.

Social media can reach many publics especially those involved in an issue. However, using social media is not without its downside. There is less control of content. There is an increased probability of "trollish" behavior. **Trolling** is an activity in which the primary purpose is to post disparaging content about or relevant to an individual or organization to anger or damage the party's reputation. Chapter 10 covers suggestions for responding to this behavior.

The Process of Public Relations

A **process** is a systematic sequence of actions that produce something or achieve a targeted end. Most of the results are intentional, but some are unintentional. Understanding a process allows us to know *why* something happens, *how* it happens, and *what* happens. It is important to manage the process as best as possible by controlling the inputs and managing the interaction of inputs so that the outcomes or outputs are the desired results.

The public relations process is strategic communications activities operating at different levels of complexity. Smith (2013) differentiates among three fundamental kinds of public relations activities. The first is a public relations project. A **project** is a single public relations task such as developing a news release, a Twitter page, a video news release, planning an event, and so forth. It consists of one tactic or a small group of related tactics. It usually pertains to a single objective. Public relations **programs** achieve objectives linked to a goal on an ongoing basis. It typically focuses on a single public or stakeholder group. For instance, meeting regularly with unionized employees, maintaining social media channels with them, keeping them current about employee benefits, managing an employee BBQ, and other labor-related issues constitute a program. Other programmatic publics are the news media, regulators, and investors, each with tactics appropriate for messaging and maintaining relationships with them. Last, a public relations **campaign** is the systematic process in which a goal is reached through implementing tactics designed to achieve objectives relevant to an issue. A public relations campaign with the goal to reduce smoking or drinking and driving involves researching the problem or opportunity, strategizing (determine what must occur), implementing (doing it), and assessing the campaign (evaluate its effectiveness).

Public relations campaigns are issue specific targeting publics. Although projects and programs can be issue centered, they typically serve a routine or relational function geared to very specific stakeholder groups.

Kinds of Public Relations Campaigns

There are various types of public relations campaigns. First, there are **political campaigns**, which center on establishing and maintaining relationships among the various publics such as delegates, national, state, and local political leaders, boards of elections, elected officials, voters, and so forth. Depending on the scope of the campaign, the number of objectives and amount of complexity varies.

Second, there are **social campaigns**, which involve social issues such as domestic violence awareness and reporting, raising funds for disabled veterans, breast cancer awareness and support, Habitat for Humanity, Oxfam (global social justice and food for the poor), and many more. These campaigns create awareness, positive attitude, and present a call to action. **Marketing campaigns** sell goods, services, and brands to consumers. The iPhone, Nissan, Tide, Best Buy, and Office Max all have marketing campaigns to sell products and services. **Image campaigns** promote an organization's reputation, often by communicating the company's good deeds and corporate citizenship. Sometimes these campaigns successfully or unsuccessfully attempt to capitalize on an organization's expeditious and effective response to a crisis. Examples are the BP oil spill in the Gulf of Mexico, the Tylenol recall, or Turing Pharmaceuticals' price increase of Daraprim from $13.50 to $750.00. In sum, image campaigns attempt to increase or maintain an organization's positive image as well as mitigate negative publicity owing to a crisis.

A process involves various managed inputs that produce outcomes. Many of the components of this process are interdependent in cause and effect relationships, providing necessary and sufficient conditions for the public relations process to systematically continue, which moves from issue identification ultimately to outcomes derived from tactics, as depicted in Figure 1.6. Chapter 7 covers the process in detail.

The situational analysis comprises researching the situation, discovering whether the issue is a problem or opportunity, and determining the stakeholders. Informed by the situational analysis, a public relations strategy and plan consists of goals, overall objectives, and a central message followed by actions or programmatic plans for each public

The Process of a Public Relations Campaign

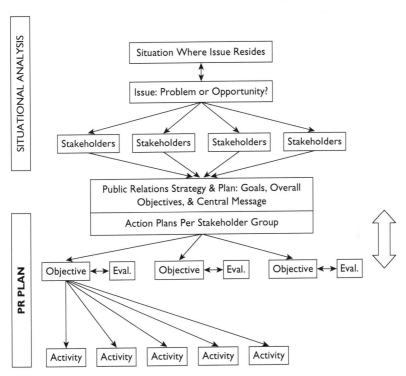

Figure 1.6 The Public Relations Process

including public relations objectives and an evaluation system. Project-based public relations activities achieve objectives. The bidirectional arrows indicate a feedback loop to accommodate adjustments made based on assessing the feedback during the campaign. This occurs in the case of overall objectives as well as individual action plan objectives, which are all measurable. It is important to note that situations change and thus issues can change, thus shifting the status and priority assigned to publics and objectives. The entire public relations campaign plan is the **plansbook**, saved in Word and later archived in pdf format. A plansbook size depends on whether the campaign is a proposal, in process, or post-campaign final version; its complexity; the level of detail; and the size of the appendix. It is usually 10–75 pages, typically covers 6–24 months, and may contain follow-up content.

Summary of Key Concepts

- Public relations typically involves building long-term relationships with stakeholders.
- Propaganda is persuasion not supported by warranted evidence.

- Symmetric public relations involves social responsibility; whereas, asymmetric public relations is based on one-way communication presenting only one side.
- Glocalization is a national strategy with a local focus.
- Public relations has various functions from lobbying to the creation of social media content.
- There are many types of public relations from various internal forms to external types.
- The relationship between public relations and marketing is fluid and contingent upon changes in technology and innovative applications of technology.
- Public relations roles are technical, technical/managerial, and managerial.
- The four models of public relations move from one-way communication to socially responsible two-way communication.
- Owned, paid, shared, and earned are the types of media coverage.
- Public relations is a process.

Key Terms

Advertising 12

Asymmetric public relations 6

Brand specialist 14

Campaign 22

Earned media 19

Employee recruiter 15

Glocalization 8

Image campaigns 22

Integrated communication 13

Integrated marketing communication 13

Internal communicator 15

Internal social media 15

Marketing campaigns 22

Media specialist/manager 15

Online media relations 15

Opinion leaders 21

Organic public relations 7

Owned media 19

Paid media 19

Plansbook 23

Policing role 15

Policy maker 15

Policy/operations management 14

Political campaigns 22

Press Agent/Publicity Model 16

Process 21

Program 22

Project 21

Propaganda 5

Public Information Model 17

Public relations 5

Publicity 19

Senior public relations management/leadership 14

Shared media 19

Social campaigns 22

Social listening and analytics 15

Social media 19

Social media influencers 21

Social media technician 15

Strategic communication 13

Symmetric public relations 6

Transactional public relations 7

Trolling 21

Two-way Asymmetric Model 17

Two-way Symmetric Model 17

Chapter Questions

1.1   Define public relations.

1.2   What is propaganda?

1.3   What is asymmetric public relations?

1.4   What is symmetric public relations?

1.5   Define Organic public relations.

1.6   What is transactional public relations?

1.7   Define glocalization and provide an example.
1.8   What general types of organizations use public relations?
1.9   Name three functions of public relations.
1.10   What are some types of public relations?
1.11   Define advertising.
1.12   Define integrated marketing communication (MARCOM).
1.13   Describe the senior public relations management/leadership role.
1.14   What is the policy/operations management role?
1.15   What is the brand specialist role?
1.16   What is the internal communicator's role?
1.17   Define the media specialist/manager's role.
1.18   Define the social media technician role.
1.19   What is the social listening and analytics role?
1.20   Define the online media relations role.
1.21   Define the policy maker role.
1.22   Define the employee recruiter role.
1.23   What is the internal social media role?
1.24   What is the policing role?
1.25   Describe the press agent/publicity model and offer an example.
1.26   Describe the public information model.
1.27   Define the two-way asymmetric model.
1.28   Define the two-way symmetric model.
1.29   Define owned media and provide an example.
1.30   Define paid media and offer an example.
1.31   What are earned media and offer an example?
1.32   What is shared media and provide an example?
1.33   Define publicity.
1.34   Define social media.
1.35   What are the two fastest growing digital tools?
1.36   Define social media influencers.
1.37   Define trolling.
1.38   Define the term process.
1.39   Define a public relations project and offer an example.
1.40   Define a public relations program and provide an example.
1.41   What is a public relations campaign?
1.42   Name four types of public relations campaigns.
1.43   What is a plansbook?

Note

1 These public relations role labels differ somewhat from the "Think about This . . ." segment.

References

Bobbitt, R., & Sullivan, R. (2014). *Developing the public relations campaign*. Boston, MA: Pearson Education.

Corella, M. A., Del Campo, A. M., & Toledo, J. A. (2009). The public relations industry in Mexico: From amateurship to the construction of a discipline. In K. Sriramesh & D. Vercic (Eds.), *The global public relations handbook: Theory, research, and practice* (pp. 676–703). New York: Routledge.

Global communication report. (2017). *USC Annenberg Center for Public Relations*. School for Communication and Journalism. Retrieved from annenberg.ucs.edu/ger17.

Grigorescu, A., & Zaif, A. (2017). The concept of glocalization and its incorporation in global brands' marketing strategies. *International Journal of Business and Management Invention, 6*(1), 70–74.

Grunig, J. E., & Hunt, T. (1984). *Managing public relations*. Belmont, CA: Wadsworth.

iExpert. (2018, May). *IBIS World*. Retrieved from www.ibis.com.

Neill, M. S., & Lee, N. (2016). Roles in social media: How the practice of public relations is evolving. *Public Relations Journal, 10*(2), 1–25.

Occupational Outlook Handbook. (2015, December 17). *United States Department of Labor: Bureau of Labor Statistics*. Retrieved from www.bls.gov/ooh/.

Public Relations Society of America. (2017). *About Public Relations*. Retrieved from http://apps.prsa.org/AboutPRSA/publicrelationsdefined/.

Safko, L., & Brake, D. K. (2009). *The social media bible: Tactics, tools, & strategies for business*. Hoboken, NJ: John Wiley & Sons.

Salary.com. (2017). Retrieved from http://swz.salary.com/SalaryWizard/layoutscripts/swzl_selectjob.aspx?txtKeyword=public+relations&txtZipCode=BOSTON%2C+MA.

Smith, A., Schlozman, K. L., Verba, S., & Brady, H. (2009, September). The internet and civic engagement. *Pew Internet. Pew Internet & American Life Project*. Retrieved from www.pewinternet.org/Reports/2009/15--The-Internet-and-Civic-Engagement.aspx.

Smith, R. D. (2013). *Strategic planning for public relations*. New York City: Routledge.

Vieira, E. T., Jr., & Grantham, S. (2014). Defining public relations roles in the U.S.A. using cluster analysis. *Public Relations Journal, 40*, 60–68.

Wilde, O. (1891). *The picture of Dorian Gray*. London, U.K.: Ward Lock & Co.

Wilson, L. J., & Ogden, J. D. (2015). *Strategic communications: Planning for public relations and marketing*. Dubuque, I.A.: Kendall Hunt Publishing Company.

Chapter 2

Professional Associations and Public Relations Code of Ethics

My biggest problem with modernity may lie in the growing separation of the ethical and the legal.

(Nassim Nicholas Taleb, 2010, p. 85)

Learning Objectives

To:

- Describe public relations organizations.
- Know about public relations certification and accreditation.
- Understand what are ethics, legality, and morality, and the differences among them.
- Understand and describe what are public relations code of ethics and code of conduct.

Introduction

Chapter 2 reviews some public relations professional associations including their missions as well as their public relations practitioner certification and accreditation programs. Additionally, the chapter discusses public relations ethics. A 2013 study about ethics violations by the Ethics and Compliance Initiative found that 41% percent of employees surveyed observed misconduct at work. Sixty percent reported that first-line supervisors, managers, or senior executives violated ethics codes. Sixty-three percent of respondents reported that they shared the misconduct (Ethics and Compliance Initiative, 2013). In a 2017 Washington Post article, North American and Western European executive "resignations" because of misconduct, rose from 4.6% of all departures to 7.8%. In markets such as Brazil, Russia, India, and China misconduct resignations went from 3.6% to 8.8% (McGregor, 2017). These alarming trends call for attention to ethics; codes of ethics and conduct; and programs that foster ethical behaviors.

Such statistics illustrate the importance of and need for ethics standards supported by the entire organization, including top management. The professional public relations associations have taken the lead to develop ethics programs and offer related resources to public relations practitioners. This chapter discusses these topics in greater detail.

Figure 2.1 Ethics Applies to All Organizational Members

Public Relations Associations

Essentially, there are two groups of public relations associations. The first category maintains a practitioner and student aim. The second group is more academic and scholarly concentrating on theory and research. We will focus on the professional category.

The professional public relations associations' goals center on improving and standardizing public relations practices through best practices, assessments, and adherence to a common code of ethics. Some of these organizations offer professional interest sections, local chapters, student chapters, accreditation programs, and their own periodicals.

Accreditation programs include content on ethics, applied public relations theory, and various other competency assessments in key public relations areas. Accreditation demonstrates a substantial degree of professionalism and is tangible evidence that one has achieved a high level of public relations knowledge and skills. For this reason, many organizations seek accredited public relations practitioners. Additionally, many accreditation programs require documented continuous professional development throughout one's career.

The professional associations that offer accreditation hold annual conferences and offer different levels of membership. Let's explore some of the associations in greater detail.

Public Relations Society of America (PRSA)

Founded in 1947, **PRSA** is the largest public relations association and is global. It reports a membership of more than 30,000. To quote its home web page: "PRSA offers its members innovative lifelong learning opportunities and professional development, celebrates innovation and excellence within the industry, upholds principles of ethics, and acts as one of the industry's leading voices" (About PRSA, 2017, para. 2).

Figure 2.2 Professional Association Accreditation Represents a Recognized Level of Competence

PRSA offers several professional interest groups where public relations professionals can network and engage at various levels on topics of shared interest. Topics include: Non-profit public relations, corporate communications, employee communications, entertainment and sports public relations, financial communications, public affairs and government, usage of technology in public relations communications, travel and tourism, and public relations education.

Additionally, PRSA has more than 100 chapters located in ten districts covering the entire United States. These chapters serve to help local members network through newsletters, local events, webinars, and other professional activities. Various programs with a local as well as national focus and international presence share job and career opportunities information. The local chapters also present awards and operate within the communities recognizing the achievements and contributions of members to their local communities. Additionally, there is a student community as well as opportunities for individual certification and accreditation as discussed below.

The Public Relations Student Society of America (PRSSA)

PRSA has an affiliated community for students. **PRSSA** has more than 300 chapters consisting of over 11,000 students and advisers located in the United States, Argentina, Colombia, and Peru (PRSSA, 2017, para. 1).

Focused on career exploration, PRSSA's mission is to prepare "the next generation of communication professionals with resources, networking events and mentorship opportunities" (PRSSA, 2017, para. 2). PRSSA offers students opportunities to enhance their public relations skill set through educational programs and the chance to build and maintain professional and peer contacts. Other tools are available that can aid in launching and developing a successful career in public relations.

PRSSA offer students the opportunity to compete in a national public relations competition. The Bateman Case Study Competition is PRSSA's national case study contest. Students apply their college education and internship experience to develop and implement a public relations campaign. Clients vary every year. Some public relations campaigns were: Student Veterans of America, Home Matters, Raising Awareness of the Consequences of Youth Bullying, United Way Worldwide, Ally Financial, the U.S. Census Bureau, "Hit the Books Running," "Safe Kids Buckle Up," and Habitat for Humanity.

PRSA Certification and Accreditation Programs

PRSA offers the **Certificate in Principles of Public Relations**, which is an acknowledgement designed to demonstrate a fundamental level of knowledge for graduates entering the public relations profession and related fields. The certification involves taking an online course and the successful completion of an online examination.

According to PRSA, earning the certification provides an advantage in the career market by demonstrating the individual's competency in key areas of public relations. Eligibility requires that a student must be a public relations or related field major and is within six months of graduation or no later than six months after graduation.

In addition to the Certificate in Principles of Public Relations, there is the **Accreditation in Public Relations (APR)** credential for experienced public relations professionals. APR certifies a public relations professional's desire to advance by staying current with best practices and developments, and maintaining professionalism, competency, and ethical principles. PRSA claims that the APR sets individuals apart from peers and positions them as leaders in the public relations industry (APR: Accredited in Public Relations, 2017). Essentially, the APR steps involve completing an online study course, followed by a panel Q&A review, and the completion of an examination. PRSA recommends that candidates possess at least five years of professional public relations experience before applying.

Last, there is the **Accreditation in Public Relations + Military Communication (APR+M)** for the practice of military public affairs. Like the APR, it facilitates ongoing professional development, which is transferrable to civilian public relations (APR+M: Accredited in Public Relations and Military Communications, 2017).

International Association of Business Communicators (IABC)

Formed in 1970, the **IABC** has more than 102 chapters worldwide consisting of over 10,000 members in more than 60 countries. As the name reveals, the focus is primarily internal public relations practiced globally.

IABC allows members to connect to

> a global communication network, stay informed about emerging trends and best practices, learn from top experts, gain recognition for your outstanding work and join a community of communication professionals around the world who are striving to be the best in the profession.
>
> (About Us, 2017, para. 5)

IABC grants several annual awards. Among them is The Gold Quill Award, which is for a public relations practitioner who demonstrates excellence in business communication.

IABC Student Chapters

Like most public relations associations, students receive benefits such as networking opportunities, conference participation, workshops designed to make them competitive in the marketplace, and exposure to internship and employment opportunities. IABC student members may join individually or set up chapters, which are more flexible compared to the other associations.

Global Communication Certification Council (GCCC) Certification Programs

The **GCCC certification programs** evaluate the business communication skills, knowledge, and experience of applicants. There is a required screening application process. Those approved take a certification examination. The areas covered are: Ethics, Strategy, Analysis, Context, Engagement, and Consistency. There is also a continued maintenance component requiring periodic testing.

American Marketing Association (AMA)

Established in 1937, the **AMA** is one of the largest marketing associations in the world, comprising over 30,000 professional, organizational, student, and academic members (AMA Membership Marketer, 2017). It has over 76 professional chapters in the United States, Canada, and Mexico. Recently, AMA has placed a greater emphasis on enhancing its presence in China and the surrounding countries. The AMA mission is to become "the most relevant force and voice shaping marketing around the world; an essential community for marketers" (About AMA, 2017, para. 4).

AMA membership offers resources designed to enhance careers such as networking events and tools (including local business resources); career postings, internship openings; webcasts; podcasts; an e-newsletter on the latest developments in marketing; industry and specialty publications; marketing communication toolkits; marketing management; leadership; public speaking opportunities; papers and guides on innovative marketing best practices; conferences and training; and research reports. Below is a description of the student chapter and AMA certification.

AMA Collegiate Chapters

There are more than 345 AMA collegiate chapters. They focus on professional development, community service, fundraising activities, hosting marketing and business speakers, etiquette dinners, career/resume workshops, among other activities. One such AMA-wide event is the annual International Collegiate Conference. The conference grants various awards and serves to provide marketing and trend information, cutting-edge knowledge and practices, as well as networking opportunities.

AMA Professional Certified Marketer (PCM) Program

Marketing certification demonstrates a marketing professional's competence and can provide a competitive edge in the job market. AMA offers two certifications (Professional Certified Marketer, 2017). One is the **PCM in Marketing Management**, which certifies competence in: Ethical Issues Affecting the Marketplace, Strategic Marketing, Understanding & Targeting the Marketplace, Value Creation, Value Capture, Value Delivery, Marketing Communication, and Marketing Evaluation.

The other certification is the **PCM in Digital Marketing**. This certification assesses competence in: Metrics & Conversions, Social & Community, Email Marketing, User Interface & Experience, Online Advertising, SEO, and Content Marketing.

Applicants must successfully complete a competency examination. The process starts start with a free practice examination to assess knowledge level followed by review of a study packet (which includes tutorials and videos) designed to prepare the individual for the competency exam. A minimum score of 80% or greater is necessary to pass the exam. Recertification occurs every three years.

Global Alliance for Public Relations and Communications Management

The **Global Alliance for Public Relations and Communication Management** consists of the world's major public relations and communication management associations and institutions. These organizations represent approximate 160,000 practitioners and academics around the world.

As published on its website:

> The Global Alliance's mission is to unify the public relations profession, raise professional standards all over the world, share knowledge for the benefit of its members and be the global voice for public relations in the public interest . . . The Global Alliance relies on the efforts of communication professionals to tackle common problems with a global perspective.
>
> (*Who We Are*, 2017, para. 1–2)

It operates on a project-by-project basis taking on endeavors aligned with its core mission and values through providing support in needed areas to its membership.

International Public Relations Association (IPRA)

Created in 1955, the **IPRA** has more than 10,000 members worldwide. To quote the association website:

> Today, IPRA is a worldwide organization with members in both established and emerging countries. A geographical representative Board and Secretariat in the UK govern the organization. IPRA represents individual professionals, not agencies or companies. IPRA is recognized as an international non-governmental organization by the United Nations and has been granted consultative status by the Economic and Social Council (ECOSOC).
>
> (About IPRA, 2017)

IPRA offers members career development services and publications that monitor trends and the latest developments in the international public relations environment. There are also member awards granted to those who demonstrate excellent in global public relations.

Canadian Public Relations Society (CPRS)

The **CPRS**, founded in 1948, is an association that practices public relations in Canada and abroad. It is a founding member of Global Alliance for Public Relations and Communications Management. Fourteen societies located in Canada comprise the CPRS. CPRS members strive to maintain the highest standards and to share the uniqueness of Canadian public relations (Canadian Public Relations Society Mission, 2017). Like other professional public relations associations, CPRS offers benefits to its membership such as scholarships, public relations awards, publications, workshops, career development guidance, networking opportunities, among other benefits.

CPRS Accredited in Public Relations (APR)

CPRS offers an accreditation credential. To qualify for APR, a candidate must be a CPRS member in good standing, have five years professional public relations experience, and have spent half of one's professional time involved in public relations. Candidate must also complete a self-assessment survey to discover whether one qualifies for APR. Next, applicants must submit sample work and successfully complete oral and written examinations. The entire process requires approximately one year.

Association for Education in Journalism and Mass Communication and Other Academic Associations

The Association for Education in Journalism and Mass Communication, International Communication Association, National Communication Association, and the American Advertising Federation among other associations have divisions or sections devoted to public relations. These largely academic associations focus on theory and scholarly research; however, they do offer some professional-oriented resources such as job postings, white papers, and applied research reports.

Think about This . . .

In a 2007 article in *PR Week* by Ted McKenna entitled "ESA calls firm's survey release 'unprofessional'," Hill & Knowlton (H&K), a New York-based public relations firm, was accused of unethical behavior by the Electronic Software Association (ESA), which is the trade organization representing the video and gaming industry.

According to ESA, to garner public relations business from them, H&K commissioned a study that gauged attitudes and beliefs about video game usage. The public relations firm reported that 60% of American consumers thought negatively about video games and believed that the industry should be government regulated. ESA also claimed that only the part of the study findings, which placed the gaming industry in a negative light, was released to the public. Against the backdrop of this

(continued)

(continued)

public sentiment, ESA alleges that H&K pitched for ESA's public relations business indicating that it could effectively address the negative public opinion about gaming which it happened facilitate in the first place.

H&K responded that the study was planned before their pitch to ESA. According to an H&K spokesperson,

> All surveys are intended to inform, provide insights, and stir debate . . . Ours is no different. We paid for the survey and own the data. We had always planned to conduct and publish a gaming survey in the fourth quarter and those plans were accelerated when the ESA invited us to meet with them earlier this year.

Ask yourself: Did H&K engage in unethical behavior? Did the fact that they decided to release the study findings earlier because of their ESA invitation to submit a proposal constitute unethical behavior? Explain your answer.

McKenna, T. (2007). ESA calls firm's survey release 'unprofessional.' *PR Week*. New York. Retrieved from www.prweek.com/article/1254693/esa-calls-firms-survey-release-unprofessional.

Public Relations Ethics

Before defining ethics, let's differentiate among the terms ethics, legality, and morality. Although these concepts can overlap, they are different constructs. **Ethics** are the moral principles governing or influencing professional conduct. They comprise a system of acceptable beliefs that control professional behavior. Ethics are the rules of conduct or moral principles of an individual or a group. These guiding rules are **deontological ethics**.

Figure 2.3 Ethics Are Influenced by Laws and Morality

Legality is the extent to which behaviors abide by the laws of a society. Society's institutions such as the legislature and executive branches of government or religious authorities influence laws. **Morality** is one's personal sense of what is "right" and what is "wrong."

Moral codes influence laws. However, in the eyes of some individuals, that which is legal is not always moral and that which is moral is not always legal. Ethics are, at least, guided by that which are legal and moral.

Moreover, different perspectives and in different cultures view ethics differently further complicating matters (Weil, 1994). These contexts are:

1) Duty to oneself informed by one's values and belief system;
2) Duty to one's client organization informed by the client's mission and value statements as well as a fiduciary relationship;
3) Duty to employer and one's responsibility to the employer;
4) Duty to one's profession that transcends other considerations; and
5) Duty to society and to what is entrusted to one.

"*I know you mean well, but each time you bring me one of these gifts I have to declare it to the ethics and compliance committee.*"

© PRIVATE EYE

Figure 2.4 Ethics Compliance Verification Is a Sure Thing, Assumptions Are Not

These duties represent **ethical relativism** where ethics shift over time and by situation. For instance, what if one's responsibilities to one's employer conflict with duties to society or to the profession? What if one's duties to one's employer conflict with one's responsibilities to a client? As we can see, ethics is a complex business interacting with legality and morality, while, at the same time, taking into consideration the situation and the relative importance of that situation.

Deontological ethics can change. Ethical relativism suggests that the nature of ethics and ethical priorities shift over time and under different circumstances. This implies that morality, values, and beliefs change over time and vary according to location.

Related to ethical relativism, actions can influence groups of people in different ways. **Teleological Ethics** focuses on the impact of behaviors on people. According to this perspective, if the consequences are positive, then the behavior is ethical. Although a practical perspective, there can be negative moral implications.

Public relations associations have attempted to address these and other ethical complexities by developing codes of ethics and codes of conduct that help guide ethical choices and behaviors, respectively. Over time, they have revised these codes. A **code of ethics** articulates the philosophical values of an organization; whereas, a **code of conduct** is the behaviors associated with a code of ethics. An ethical code is the framework of beliefs and values. A code of conduct is a set of guidelines for actions consistent with those ethics (Wood & Rimmer, 2003).

Violations of ethical and conduct codes are rarely clear cut and often involve gray areas. For example, faculty at a business school take pride in their principled leadership curricula; yet, the way they interact with their colleagues bears little resemblance to principled leadership. Is this ethical? In another example, a student once told me that she was paid very well for going into chatrooms from 7:00 pm to 10:00 pm Monday through Thursday to promote the wonders of a cosmetic line of products, even though she did not use the product line or personally find it appealing. This is an example of an asymmetric approach

Figure 2.5 What Is Truly Right or Wrong, Ethical or Not Ethical?

Figure 2.6 What Are We Willing to Do to Advance Our Careers?

to public relations known as astroturfing (or fake grassroots support). Paid people promote an issue or product to increase support and present the impression that the issue is highly popular, when, in fact, it may not be the case. Is this ethical?

One last example, the recall of Firestone tires was slow in coming even after 46 of the 148 deaths associated with the product. Firestone's resisted accepting responsibility and suggested that vehicle design was the cause of tire failure. Most of the defective tires came from a single plant that was the site of a work stoppage in which striking operators were replaced with inexperienced workers. The more likely truth was that lack of worker training contributed to the production of defective tires (Ford, Firestone Company Probes Blame Tire Manufacturing, 2000; McMillan, 2000). Was Firestone's handling of the crisis ethical?

Public Relations Codes of Ethics and Conduct

Public relations is used for "good" or for "bad" like many other resources in our society. In a representative democracy, officeholders are elected by the voters to represent the citizens' best interest. In principle, the election of a candidate to office is based on a citizenry who make informed voting choices. The process allows for access to accurate and sufficiently complete information. Thus, the process is based on a level of trust in the system. This process extends to consumers in a free market system. Consumers make purchase and consumption choices based on information, which also assume the free flow of accurate and complete information.

Voting and consumption choices are indispensable to free political and economic systems. For this reason, ethical guidance is important so that public relations practitioners do not lose sight of their pledge to do no harm to society (Corporate Watch UK, 2003). Part of the mission of public relations associations is to provide and promote codes of professional ethics and conduct. Since many of these codes overlap, we will describe the ethical codes from two associations, one with a United States focus and the other with an international scope. They are the PRSA and the IPRA.

Figure 2.7 Ethical Compliance Covers Several Areas

PRSA/PRSSA Codes of Ethics and Conduct

PRSA and PRSSA emphasize the importance of public trust and the aim of every public relations professional to serve the public good as critical reasons for operating ethically. The **PRSA Code of Ethics** represents the association's core values (Public Relations Society of America (PRSA) Member Code of Ethics, 2017). PRSA requires that members sign a **Code of Ethics Pledge** as well. The Code is as follows.

ADVOCACY: We serve the public interest by acting as responsible advocates for those we represent. We provide a voice in the marketplace of ideas, facts, and viewpoints to aid informed public debate.

HONESTY: We adhere to the highest standards of accuracy and truth in advancing the interests of those we represent and in communicating with the public.

EXPERTISE: We acquire and responsibly use specialized knowledge and experience. We advance the profession through continued professional development, research, and education. We build mutual understanding, credibility, and relationships among a wide array of institutions and audiences.

INDEPENDENCE: We provide objective counsel to those we represent. We are accountable for our actions.

LOYALTY: We are faithful to those we represent, while honoring our obligation to serve the public interest.

FAIRNESS: We deal fairly with clients, employers, competitors, peers, vendors, the media, and the general public. We respect all opinions and support the right of free expression.

(Public Relations Society of America (PRSA)
Member Code of Ethics, 2017)

These ethical principles inform the **PRSA Code of Conduct** and thus guide professional behavior.

FREE FLOW OF INFORMATION: Core Principle Protecting and advancing the free flow of accurate and truthful information is essential to serving the public interest and contributing to informed decision making in a democratic society.

- Preserve the integrity of the process of communication.
- Be honest and accurate in all communications.
- Act promptly to correct erroneous communications for which the practitioner is responsible.
- Preserve the free flow of unprejudiced information when giving or receiving gifts.

Figure 2.8 Pledge to Conduct Oneself Ethically and Professionally

COMPETITION: Core Principle Promoting healthy and fair competition among professionals preserves an ethical climate while fostering a robust business environment.

- Follow ethical hiring practices designed to respect free and open competition without deliberately undermining a competitor.
- Preserve intellectual property rights in the marketplace.

DISCLOSURE OF INFORMATION: Core Principle Open communication fosters informed decision making in a democratic society.

- Be honest and accurate in all communications.
- Act promptly to correct erroneous communications for which the member is responsible.
- Investigate the truthfulness and accuracy of information released on behalf of those represented.
- Reveal the sponsors for causes and interests represented.
- Disclose financial interest (such as stock ownership) in a client's organization.
- Avoid deceptive practices.

SAFEGUARDING CONFIDENCES: Core Principle Client trust requires appropriate protection of confidential and private information.

- A member shall: Safeguard the confidences and privacy rights of present, former, and prospective clients and employees.
- Protect privileged, confidential, or insider information gained from a client or organization.
- Immediately advise an appropriate authority if a member discovers that confidential information is being divulged by an employee of a client company or organization.

CONFLICTS OF INTEREST: Core Principle Avoiding real, potential or perceived conflicts of interest builds the trust of clients, employers, and the publics.

- Act in the best interests of the client or employer, even subordinating the member's personal interests.
- Avoid actions and circumstances that may appear to compromise good business judgment or create a conflict between personal and professional interests.
- Disclose promptly any existing or potential conflict of interest to affected clients or organizations.
- Encourage clients and customers to determine if a conflict exists after notifying all affected parties.

ENHANCING THE PROFESSION: Core Principle Public relations professionals work constantly to strengthen the public's trust in the profession.

- Acknowledge that there is an obligation to protect and enhance the profession.
- Keep informed and educated about practices in the profession to ensure ethical conduct.
- Actively pursue personal professional development.

- Decline representation of clients or organizations that urge or require actions contrary to this Code.
- Accurately define what public relations activities can accomplish.
- Counsel subordinates in proper ethical decision making.
- Require that subordinates adhere to the ethical requirements of the Code.
- Report practices that fail to comply with the Code, whether committed by PRSA members or not, to the appropriate authority.

(Public Relations Society of America (PRSA)
Member Code of Ethics, 2017)

IPRA Code of Conduct

IPRA developed a **Code of Conduct**, which affirms professional and ethical conduct by its public relations practitioner members worldwide. Its components are as follows.

(a) RECALLING the Charter of the United Nations which determines 'to reaffirm faith in fundamental human rights, and in the dignity and worth of the human person';

(b) RECALLING the 1948 'Universal Declaration of Human Rights' and especially recalling Article 19;

(c) RECALLING that public relations, by fostering the free flow of information, contributes to the interests of all stakeholders;

(d) RECALLING that the conduct of public relations and public affairs provides essential democratic representation to public authorities;

(e) RECALLING that public relations practitioners through their wide-reaching communication skills possess a means of influence that should be restrained by the observance of a code of professional and ethical conduct;

(f) RECALLING that channels of communication such as the Internet and other digital media, are channels where erroneous or misleading information may be widely disseminated and remain unchallenged, and therefore demand special attention from public relations practitioners to maintain trust and credibility;

(g) RECALLING that the Internet and other digital media demand special care with respect to the personal privacy of individuals, clients, employers and colleagues.

(Code of Conduct: IPRA codes, 2010)

The ethical principles inform the following behaviors:

1 Observance: Observe the principles of the UN Charter and the Universal Declaration of Human Rights;

2 Integrity: Act with honesty and integrity at all times so as to secure and retain the confidence of those with whom the practitioner comes into contact;

3 Dialogue: Seek to establish the moral, cultural and intellectual conditions for dialogue, and recognize the rights of all parties involved to state their case and express their views;

4 Transparency: Be open and transparent in declaring their name, organisation and the interest they represent;

5 Conflict: Avoid any professional conflicts of interest and to disclose such conflicts to affected parties when they occur;

6 Confidentiality: Honour confidential information provided to them;

7   Accuracy: Take all reasonable steps to ensure the truth and accuracy of all information provided;

8   Falsehood: Make every effort to not intentionally disseminate false or misleading information, exercise proper care to avoid doing so unintentionally and correct any such act promptly;

9   Deception: Not obtain information by deceptive or dishonest means;

10   Disclosure: Not create or use any organisation to serve an announced cause but which actually serves an undisclosed interest;

11   Profit: Not sell for profit to third parties copies of documents obtained from public authorities;

12   Remuneration: Whilst providing professional services, not accept any form of payment in connection with those services from anyone other than the principal;

13   Inducement: Neither directly nor indirectly offer nor give any financial or other inducement to public representatives or the media, or other stakeholders;

14   Influence: Neither propose nor undertake any action which would constitute an improper influence on public representatives, the media, or other stakeholders;

15   Competitors: Not intentionally injure the professional reputation of another practitioner;

16   Poaching: Not seek to secure another practitioner's client by deceptive means;

17   Employment: When employing personnel from public authorities or competitors take care to follow the rules and confidentiality requirements of those organisations;

18   Colleagues: Observe this Code with respect to fellow IPRA members and public relations practitioners worldwide.

IPRA members shall, in upholding this Code, agree to abide by and help enforce the disciplinary procedures of the International Public Relations Association in regard to any breach of this Code (Code of Conduct: IPRA codes, 2010).

Please note that this code consolidates and references the 1961 Code of Venice, the 1965 Code of Athens and the 2007 Code of Brussels.

Both the PRSA and IPRA ethical codes emphasize public relations credibility. Public relations is believable because there is a perception of trust and competence. The public relations professional has a sufficient level of expertise and/or experience. The public relations practitioner is trustworthy and thus honest, objective, fair, loyal to the client, and expected to hold propriety information confidential.

In sum, the practice of ethical behavior in public relations provides credibility, which assures publics that the message is accurate and sufficiently complete.

Summary of Key Concepts

- Public Relations associations are essentially professional and student-oriented or academic/scholarly centered, focusing on research.
- Public relations associations offer resources to members including a code of ethics and a code of conduct.
- Public relations associations offer practitioner certification and accreditation based on public relations professional experience and education. Accreditation usually requires continuous development throughout most of a practitioner's career.
- Although related, ethics, legality, and morality are different constructs involving complex factors that influence ethical decision-making.

- An open, democratic, and free market society requires the uninhibited flow of accurate and sufficient information to facilitate trust in its institutions. Public relations educates stakeholders about issues and situations, thus, contributing to an informed society.
- Public relations practitioners are guided by a code of ethics and code of conduct to insure the free flow of information.

Key Terms

Accreditation in Public Relations (APR) 30

Accreditation in Public Relations and Military Communication (APR+M) 30

American Marketing Association (AMA) 31

Canadian Public Relations Society (CPRS) Certificate in Principles of Public Relations 30

Code of Conduct 36

Code of Ethics 36

Code of Ethics Pledge 38

CPRS Accreditation in Public Relations 33

Deontological ethics 34

Ethical Relativism 36

Ethics 34

Global Alliance for Public Relations and Communications Management 32

Global Communication Certification Council (GCCC) Certification Programs 31

International Associations of Business Communicators (IABC) 30

International Public Relations Association (IPRA) 32

Legality 35

Morality 35

Professional Certified Marketer in Digital Marketing 32

Professional Certified Marketer in Marketing Management 31

Public Relations Society of America (PRSA) 28

Public Relations Student Society of America (PRSSA) 29

Teleological Ethics 36

Chapter Questions

2.1 What is the PRSA as opposed to the PRSSA?

2.2 What are the two general types of public relations associations and describe them?

2.3 What is the PRSA Certificate in Principles of Public Relations and what is required to attain it?

2.4 Describe the PRSA Accreditation in Public Relations (APR).

2.5 What differentiates the regular PRSA APR from the Accreditation in Public Relations + Military Communication (APR+M)?

2.6 What is the IABC?

2.7 Do the PRSA and IABC have student chapters?

2.8 What public relations areas are covered in the GCCC certification assessment process?

2.9 What is the approximate membership number of the AMA?

2.10 What certificates does the AMA offer and briefly describe them?

2.11 Describe the membership of the Global Alliance for Public Relations and Communication Management.

2.12 What is the mission of the Global Alliance for Public Relations and Communication Management?

2.13 Describe the IPRA.

2.14 What are the benefits of CPRS membership?

2.15 Name three academic public relations associations.

2.16 After reading the "Think about this . . ." article, did H&K engage in unethical behavior? Explain your reasoning.

2.17 Define ethics.

2.18 Define morality.

2.19 Define legality.

2.20 How might ethics become complex?

2.21 What are deontological ethics?

2.22 Why is a code of ethics important to public relations?

2.23 What is ethical relativism and provide a hypothetical example?

2.24 What is a code of ethics?

2.25 What is a code of conduct?

2.26 How are a code of ethics and code of conduct related?

2.27 Do public relations organizations maintain codes of ethics and/or conduct? Explain.

2.28 A company has a series of layoffs. In the interim, many talented employees are leaving making operations challenging. To mitigate departures, the internal communication director sends out a memo indicating that there will be no additional layoffs when she has evidence to the contrary. Is this behavior unethical? Explain your response.

2.29 What is teleological ethics?

References

About AMA. (2017). Retrieved from www.ama.org/AboutAMA/Pages/About.aspx.

About IPRA. (2017). Retrieved from www.ipra.org/.

About PRSA. (2017). Retrieved from www.prsa.org/about/about-prsa/.

About us. (2017). Retrieved from www.iabc.com/about-us/.

AMA membership Marketer. (2017). Retrieved from www.ama.org/membership/Membership-Benefits/Pages/Marketer.aspx.

APR: Accredited in Public Relations. (2017). Retrieved from www.praccreditation.org/apply/apr/.

APR+M: Accredited in Public Relations and Military Communications. (2017). Retrieved from www.praccreditation.org/apply/apr-m/.

Canadian Public Relations Society Mission. (2017). Retrieved from https://cprs.ca/aboutus/mission.aspx.

Code of conduct: IPRA codes. (2010, November 5). Retrieved from www.ipra.org/member-services/code-of-conduct/.

Corporate Watch UK. (2003 April). *Public relations and lobbying industry: An overview.* Retrieved from https://corporatewatch.org/content/pr-industry-overview.

Ethics and Compliance Initiative. (2013). *National Business Ethics Survey.* Retrieved from http://ethics.org/research/nbes/nbes-reports/nbes-2013.

Ford, Firestone company probes blame tire manufacturing. (2000, December 11). Retrieved from http://money.cnn.com/2000/12/11/recalls/firestone/.

McGregor, J. (2017, May 15). *More CEOs are getting forced out for ethics violations.* Retrieved from www.washingtonpost.com/news/on-leadership/wp/2017/05/15/more-ceos-are-getting-forced-out-for-ethics-violations/?utm_term=.25060e2a9ad3.

McKenna, T. (2007). ESA calls firm's survey release 'unprofessional.' *PR Week*. New York. Retrieved from www.prweek.com/article/1254693/esa-calls-firms-survey-release-unprofessional.

McMillan, A. F. (2000, August 9). *Handling the tire recall*. Retrieved from http://money.cnn.com/2000/08/09/recalls/q_tirerecall/.

Professional certified marketer. (2017). Retrieved from www.ama.org/events-training/Certification/Pages/us-pcm.aspx.

Public Relations Society of America (PRSA) *Member Code of Ethics*. (2017). Retrieved from http://apps.prsa.org/AboutPRSA/Ethics/CodeEnglish/.

Taleb, N. N. (2010). *The Bed of Procrustes: Philosophical and Practical Aphorisms*. (p. 85). New York: Random House Publishing Group.

The Public Relations Student Society of America (PRSSA) is the foremost organization for students interested in public relations and communication. (2017). Retrieved from www.prsa.org/about/about-prsa/affiliated-communities/prssa/.

Weil, V. (1994). *Professional ethics*. Handout from 1994 EAC Workshop. Center for the Study of Ethics in the Professions. Illinois Institute of Technology. Retrieved from http://ethics.iit.edu/teaching/professional-ethics.

Who We Are. (2017). Retrieved from www.globalalliancepr.org/who-we-are/.

Wood, G., & Rimmer, M. (2003). Codes of Ethics: What are they really and what should they be? *International Journal of Value-Based Management, 16*, 181–195.

Chapter 3

Understanding Applied Theory and the Psychology and Behavior of Public Relations Stakeholders

You never really understand a person until you consider things from his point of view.
(Harper Lee, 1960, p. 39)

Learning Objectives

To:

- Understand the importance and roles of self-esteem and motivations as drivers of action.
- Understand the nature of self-esteem and kinds of motivation.
- Describe human information processing.
- Know the process of decision-making including the key variables.
- Understand and describe the major persuasion theories and how they can inform public relations campaigns.
- Know the nature and role of opinion leaders in informing and in persuading.
- Understand the inter-relationships and sometimes interdependent nature of factors that influence decision-making and behavior.

Introduction

A keen understanding of stakeholders and how they attend to messages, process information, think, feel, formulate attitudes, and behave is necessary for an effective public relations campaign. The emotional, cognitive, social, motivational, and behavioral aspects of individuals are some of the different types of psychology that come to mind (pun intended) when exploring messaging appeals that influence human feelings, thoughts, values, beliefs, attitudes, and actions. Applied theory supported by research provides the framework from which we can understand stakeholders. So, what is a theory? A **theory** explains some phenomenon (e.g. individual or group behavior), the causes of the phenomenon (e.g. response to a persuasive appeal), and/or the likelihood of the phenomenon to reoccur.

Theories fall into micro-, intermediate-, and macro-analytic categories. Micro-analytic theories operate at the individual level such as how a person processes information or makes decisions. Intermediate-analytic theories operate at the interpersonal or group level such as dyads, small or large group, organizationally like opinion leader influence or the basis of some types of motivation. Macro-analytic theories are sociological in that they apply to all of society. One example is the Diffusion of Innovations theory

Figure 3.1 Theories Explain Individual Thought, Feelings, and Behaviors

or crowdsourcing. Many of these theories, although operating at different levels, share commonalities and may serve as building blocks for larger scale theories.

Research tests theories. The purpose of researching actual or potential stakeholder groups is to discover and segment group members for messaging in an effective and efficient manner. Understanding stakeholders informs strategy and execution development. Appealing to what is important to them increases the likelihood of convincing them to embrace the public relations central message. Thus, the appeal becomes about them and is consistent with their identity. Conversely, presenting a message contrary to what stakeholders hold dear will likely make them adversarial to the message. In sum, public relations professionals seek to understand stakeholders, predict their responses to issues and messages, and manage them through messaging and related activities with the intention of achieving desirable outcomes. This process is depicted in Figure 3.2.

This chapter provides a foundation for understanding the human mind and behaviors in the context of informing and persuading. It reviews proven human psychology and

Situational Understanding → Predicted Stakeholder Responses → Manage Stakeholders Responses → Expected Outcomes

Figure 3.2 The Process Inputs Are Stakeholder Involvement and Actions Based on Understanding and Predicting Their Responses to Public Relations Efforts. The Practitioner Manages the Interaction of the Inputs. The Outcomes Are the Results of the Process

behavior theories as they relate to public relations including how people in general receive and process messages; the roles of values and belief systems in forming opinions and attitudes; how appeal acceptance becomes action; and relevant media usage and habits.

What Drives People?

Different items drive people. Self-concept, self-esteem, and needs and desires motivate people. These psychological states activate behaviors. What follows is a discussion of theories that captures basic motivation.

Motivation is what drives a person to "act" in some manner after exposure to a stimulus. In other words, when exposed to a stimulus, the person approaches or avoids it. Acting in this sense can be psychological and/or behavioral. A person can decide to evaluate something favorably and act upon it. In another situation, that same person can assess something favorably and not act upon it. If no behavior happens, then there is no motivation to act, which is amotivation. There are different kinds and levels of motivation.

Motivation is different from **motives**, which are specific reasons (or causes for) why someone thinks, feels, or acts a certain way. Motives are situational and change. However, motivation and its nature are fundamental to an individual's personality. For instance, someone who strives to do her or his best in most undertakings is highly motivated. Someone who attempts his best at a *specific* task to win favor has a motive or specific reason for doing so.

Self-Esteem

If we feel that we are of value, then we may be more confident to act. The value that we place on ourselves is **self-esteem**. It is self-worth. It is the result of a self-evaluation resulting in what a person thinks of himself. Self-esteem develops after a person understand and defines herself. This descriptive process results in **self-concept**. It stands to reason that before a person can develop feelings of worth, that person must have information or self-awareness from which to base a self-evaluation.

These concepts are related from another perspective. It would be difficult for an individual to have high self-esteem, if lack of ability or lack of identity comprised her/his self-concept. Differentiating between the two concepts when communicating can impact message effectiveness. For instance, a public relations message might focus on the less threatening self-concept, leaving the stakeholders to draw conclusions about self-esteem. Concentrating communications on changes in self-concept-related behaviors while demonstrating the benefits to self-esteem might prove efficacious. In both cases, messaging advocating changes in opinions or behaviors is more effectual then judging those opinions or behaviors. Research has found these techniques to be successful.

According to theorists, one's ability to kayak as opposed to one's ability to engage in other water sports, or one's overall ability in life affects self-esteem. Thus, influences on self-esteem range from specific to global characteristics (O'Brien, Bartoletti, Leitzel, & O'Brien, 2006).

Individuals have low, moderate, or high levels of self-esteem. At the same time, the kind of self-esteem plays an important role as well. Self-esteem is secure or stable (Kernis & Paradise, 2002). **Secure self-esteem** is based on the individual's self-assessment, which is akin to task-involved activities. It does not require external validation. On the other hand,

Figure 3.3 People Want to Feel Good about Themselves

fragile self-esteem requires external validation from sources such as peers, parents, or some outside standard of excellence.

Let me illustrate the differences through an example. I installed a hardwood floor in my home because I wanted to learn this skill and experience this type of activity. I must confess that it was arduous work, but nonetheless, a worthwhile experience. A close relative visited us, noticed, and admired the new floor. The person commented that I did a fine job and should show it to my friends because they would be impressed. If that suggestion were a major reason why I completed the floor installation, then my self-esteem would be fragile, requiring regular reinforcement from others. However, driven by a need to learn and experience for my own sake even at the risk of doing a poor job demonstrates secure self-esteem.

Individuals can have different levels of self-esteem whether it is secure or fragile. Some research has found that persons with high levels of fragile self-esteem only take on tasks where they are likely to succeed. They do this to protect their self-esteem by embracing success. To these individuals, external parties cause failure: "I failed because the teacher doesn't like me" or "My program was not successful because everyone was not 100% committed." Understanding self-esteem can go a long way in constructing successful messages.

Maslow's Hierarchy of Needs

Maslow's Hierarchy of Needs Theory (Maslow, 1987) is a motivation framework based on the fulfillment of physical, psychological, and self-actualization needs. As we can see in Figure 3.4, at the base of the needs pyramid, there are **Physiological Needs**. These are the requirements of the human body such as food, water, sleep, and sensory gratification. Second, there are **Safety Needs**, which consist of the desires to stay free from danger and environmental threats. The third level comprises **Love/Belonging Needs**. These psychological needs are about giving and receiving human affection and identifying with others. Fourth, there are **Esteem Needs**. These are about the need to feel respected including the need to have healthy self-esteem and self-respect. People want to be accepted and valued by others. Esteem needs build on love/belonging needs. Last, there are **Self-Actualization Needs**. This is the highest level of needs in which individuals aspire to achieve their full potential and completeness as individuals.

Some motivation scholars have revised Maslow's model to incorporate two additional needs: the desire to know and understand and aesthetic needs (or the craving for beauty of various kinds).

Contrary to Maslow's initial conceptualization, many researchers posit that it is possible to operate at more than one level without the complete fulfillment of the previous level(s) of needs. For instance, an individual may lack regular shelter, but may have a loving relationship with another. A person may be highly respected, yet, have no meaningful personal relationships. Despite its imperfections, this framework has its value in persuasive messaging. Knowing where stakeholders stand in their needs hierarchy can assist in crafting messages that incorporate their needs. Someone who can barely acquire food and housing is less likely to be considering products or issue engagement that fosters self-actualization.

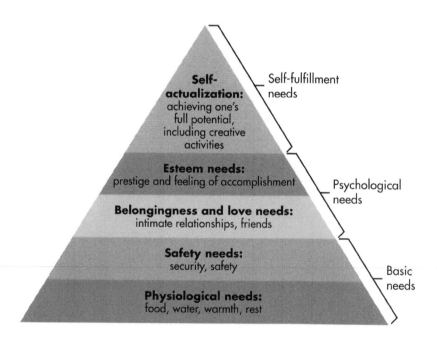

Figure 3.4 Maslow's Hierarchy of Needs

Self-Determination Theory (SDT)

Self-Determination Theory (SDT) (Ryan & Deci, 2000) is a conceptualization of motivation based on the fulfillment of three fundamental human needs along a continuum starting from amotivation (no motivation) to highly driven motivation, which is internally inspired. While reading this section, review Figure 3.5.

SDT distinguishes between intrinsic motivation (self-determining motivation) and extrinsic motivation (externally driven). The individual regulates both types of motivation. Although there are various definitions of motivation, according to SDT, "To be motivated means to be moved to do something" (Ryan & Deci, 2000, p. 54). Motivation is a conscious process where an individual, after exposure to an internal or external stimulus, is aware of why he/she decides to act or not to act. Motivational orientation is subjective and influenced by personal experience and personality factors. That is, one person may view a behavior as self-determining and another may perceive the same behavior as controlled by external influences.

More specifically, **intrinsic motivation** "is defined as the doing of an activity for its inherent satisfaction rather than for some separable consequence" (Ryan & Deci, 2000, p. 56). The valued act is congruent with that person's belief system. According to SDT, people possess universal needs that are self-determining and equate with intrinsic motivation.

The satisfaction of these needs can result in a high level of self-esteem. According to SDT, motivated people are satisfied, autonomous, competent, and have meaningful relationships in an enjoyable context. These motivations are self-determining and enabling.

Autonomy is the condition where a person willingly endorses and conducts a behavior. A perceived sense of control is reflective, mindful, and integrative. The level of autonomy can vary according to circumstance.

Another fundamental need is competence. **Competence** is the ability to effectively act and influence one's environment. A person may have different competencies employed under various circumstances such as sports skills, creative talents, or the ability to skillfully play the piano.

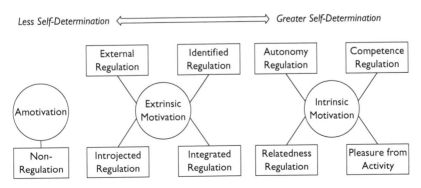

Figure 3.5 Self-Determination Theory Operates along a Continuum from Amotivation to Action that Is Fully Intrinsically Motivated

Figure 3.6 People Are Motivated by Passion

Last, there is a need for relatedness. **Relatedness** is the need to connect to and identify with one or more individuals at a personal level. This type of relationship is not based on peer-approval or some type of obligation, but exists because the individual genuinely derives pleasure from the relationship.

These needs can apply to an individual in general or can be situational, and are subjective. In sum, SDT has four requirements: (1) A sense of autonomy; (2) Perceived competence; (3) A sense of relatedness; and (4) Pleasure from participating in the motivated activity. The fulfillment of these needs results in psychological well-being.

Figure 3.7 The Happy Pill Works Wonders!

On the other hand, external considerations also drive people to act, which is **extrinsic motivation**. There are four levels of extrinsic motivation: Integrated, Identified, Introjected, and External.

Integrated regulation results from the most autonomous extrinsic motivation. It stems from an identification and congruence of the person's values and beliefs with the target behavior. The person integrates the behavior, but there is a lack of pleasure, inherent satisfaction, or self-initiated action as would be the case in intrinsic motivation. An appeal that frames the target behavior as fun can increase engagement in the issue.

Next, there is **identified regulation**, which is associated with the person identifying the behavior as having some instrumental value. For instance, if a student concludes that being competent and experienced in a boring subject is important to finding a desirable job upon graduation, then he/she will move closer to internalizing the behavior. Many persuasion campaigns attempt to move publics from this level of motivation to integration extrinsic motivation. Making a short-term sacrifice for a long-term benefit is the argument.

Third, **introjection regulation** involves greater extrinsic motivation and a controlling orientation. This regulation has been partially internalized, even though the individual does not consider it part of the integrated self. The behavior avoids guilt and shame. The approval of others is important. For example, in order not to stand out, a less motivated student might take a class assignment seriously because everyone else in the class does.

Last, **external regulation** has virtually none of the self-determining attributes. It is strictly externally driven. The person does not value the motivated act. The person may see him/herself as a "pawn" to external forces. The associated behavior involves engaging in an activity for the sake of some external reward.

When there is no intrinsic or extrinsic motivation to act, the person is in a state of **amotivation**. There is no regulation because motivation does not exist.

These days, companies and departments within companies must reduce costs. Budgets are cut and departments and functions merged to become more cost-efficient. Many managers feel that they are losing control of their departments. Such conditions can impact morale and individual performance.

How might an internal communications manager advise an operations executive on a forthcoming budget cuts announcement while attempting to maintain morale with department and division managers? Deploying SDT, the executive can provide managers with some degree of control over an issue. Let's assume that the departments must cut budgets by 10%. Top management communicates this requirement and leaves the decision-making cuts in the hands of the individual managers. The executive emphasizes her reliance on the managers' experience and good judgment. This approach serves to provide managers with a level of autonomy, while also acknowledging their competence, and allowing them to maintain relationships with their departments as they see best for the benefit of the organization.

Motivational Framework of the Values and Lifestyles (VALS)

The Values and Lifestyle typology (Strategic Business Insights, 2017) is a framework developed to group a population into eight market segments based on their values, beliefs, lifestyles, and expressive motivations.

The three expressive motivations are self-expression, values expressive, and achievement expressive. **Self-expression** involves communicating one's self-concept, self-identity, or who or what one identifies with. **Values expressive** is the communication of what one values; it is what is important to the individual. Last, there is expressing one's **accomplishments**. This relates to self-esteem and conveying one's worth. In marketing, pitching brands or products as status symbols satisfies this motivation. Some research has linked this expressive to the underground market demand for counterfeit high-end brands, which communicates success for those with limited financial resources.

Public relations communication can take advantage of this process by linking these expressives to messaging. Marketers link status with products by offering low end lines of high end brands such as entry level luxury vehicles. Second-hand clothing retailers often feature repurposed luxury brands. Remanufactured (or used) high end brands offered at a discount also satisfy these expressives to varying degrees depending on the person. There is a cottage industry that specializes in renting all sorts of high-end items for special events.

Cognitive Dissonance Reduction

Cognitive Dissonance Theory (Festinger, 1957) states that individual mental representations of a person's values, beliefs, attitudes, basis for decision-making, commitments, and behaviors tend to exist and operate in a state of harmony with one another. Disharmony causes psychological discomfort and motivates an individual to take action that restores harmony within the person's mental schema. The techniques for returning to harmony take many forms. This is known as **cognitive dissonance reduction**. There are three components to this process. They are the **focal element**, the **dissonant element**, and the **consonant element**. The focal element is the point of contention. The dissonant element is the disagreement. The consonant element is the basis of reconciliation for the inconsistency.

A person changes beliefs or behaviors depending on the importance of the issue and amount of discomfort. For example, let us say that a young couple with three young children need a car. They want to purchase a new Volvo because of its safety features. However, the monthly car payments would require a major adjustment to the household budget, which is likely to preclude the purchase of the Volvo, until the salesperson make her final pitch. She says, "I know that the monthly car payments might be more than what you want to pay. Yet, can you place a dollar value on the safety of your children?" This rationale causes the buyers to reprioritize their budget items resulting in their purchasing the Volvo.

In this example, the focal element is the purchase of the Volvo. The dissonance is that the car payment will be expensive. Not compromising the safety of their children is the consonant element (that which reduces dissonance). Table 3.1 depicts additional examples.

When I think about cognitive dissonance reduction, there is one example that comes to mind. Having been a professor for many years, I have had many students and have kept in touch with a few over the years. On more than one occasion, I recall lecturing a student or two on the dangers of smoking. In almost every case, the student retorted by saying that school is stressful and it was a temporary fix to get through graduation. After that, the smoking stops. Years later, speaking to the same students, some quit, others didn't. Some of the reasons given for smoking were: "I'm going through a stressful time," "I will when I get married and have kids," "I will when I find my dream job," or "It keeps me calm." These statements represent examples of cognitive dissonance reduction.

Table 3.1 Examples of Cognitive Dissonance Reduction

Focal Element	Dissonance Element	Consonant Element
She stated that the experimental task was fun.	She found the task dull and time consuming.	I was paid $100 for saying the task was fun.
He chose to buy the Honda over the Toyota.	The Toyota gets better gas mileage.	The Honda is more reliable, more stylish, and has more options.
My friend opposes abortion.	I favor choice.	My friend cannot go against his religious beliefs and besides, I agree with him on most issues.
My friend voted for George W. Bush.	I am a registered Democrat.	Bush protected us against terrorists and maintained America's prestige abroad.

Adapted from Eagly, A. H., & Chaiken, S. (1993). *The psychology of attitudes.* New York City: Harcourt Brace College.

Inconsistent ideas or behaviors residing in one's mind can be a source of consternation and the inspiration for what motivates one to restore consonance. Individuals use many techniques to maintain consistent mental thoughts and feelings. Marketers often persuade customers to purchase products and services in the context of cognitive dissonance reduction. When the goal is to change existing attitudes or behaviors, cognition dissonance (and its reduction) is a tool that can provide justification to buy something or to engage in any other type of behavior.

A concept related to cognitive dissonance is **post-purchase cognitive dissonance or buyer's remorse**. After spending more than anticipated for a home, car, vacation, or some other item, the consumer needs to rationalize the purchase. Marketers are aware of this process especially for higher priced products. In the case of buying a home, the real estate agent might provide additional positive information about the home to the buyer even after the purchase to reinforce it and thus reduce any potential buyer's remorse.

A different take on cognitive dissonance involves the dissonance between people knowing that they should exercise but do not do so for various "reasons." Marketers take advantage of people's insecurities about appearance and body image. Although not motivated to walk the treadmill, some individuals relieve the dissonance by purchasing so-called miracle products such as fat blockers, diet supplements, cellulite creams, and even low-carb beer. These alternatives to exercise provide easy choices by aligning consumer beliefs and behaviors, if only on a temporary basis.

Cognitive dissonance reduction also applies to organizations. Companies can capitalize on their strengths. An employee who has invested years in an organization and forged meaningful relationships with coworkers, is less likely to leave an organization (Gass & Seiter, 2007). People find reasons to stay.

In short, cognitive dissonance and the desire to reduce it provide opportunities for public relations practitioners to offer solutions that bridge the gap between beliefs that are inconsistent with behaviors, thus creating cognitive harmony.

Figure 3.8 Cognitive Dissonance Reduction Allows Us to Live a Noncontradictory and Happy Life

The Nature of Information Processing

To communicate with people requires an understanding of how they process information. **Information processing** involves knowing about something, understanding it, and developing knowledge about it, which implies a degree of mental involvement. All information processing is cognitive and affective. **Cognitions** are thoughts or a rational awareness of oneself, others, or one's environment. **Affects** are emotions (feelings) and moods. Affects are all that remain after we account for rational processing. **Emotions** are intense, focused, and short-term. **Moods** are less intense emotions, less focused, and enduring. Emotions can change a person's attitude toward something or someone. Specific moods place individuals in a state that allows them to be receptive to ideas or specific persons. As we can see, all awareness or information processing thus involves thinking and/or feeling. In most instances, we experience some level of both. This framework is what we refer to as dual information processing.

We will cover two dual processing models. One is the Affective Reason Involvement Model and the other is the Heuristic Systematic Model.

Affect-Reason-Involvement Model

The **Affect-Reason-Involvement (ARI) Model** (Buck, 1988) posits that all information processing consists of a combination of emotional and analytic (rational) mental activity. The level of each of these dimensions together constitutes the level of information processing involvement. This model describes the relationships among affect, reason, and involvement, arguing that both affective and rational processing are important determinants of individual message engagement.

According to Buck, Chaudhuri, Georgson, and Kowta (1995),

> One way to interpret the Affect-Reason Continuum is by situations in which the relative influence of affect and reason vary. We assume that affect has a role in all situations, while the influence of reason varies from zero (in situations ruled wholly by passion) to high levels (in situations where 'mindful' systematic analysis is paramount). However, even in the latter, highly mindful situation, affect retains influence, thus the relative influence of affect never falls to zero.
>
> (p. 441)

Figure 3.9 illustrates the ARI Model in specific situations. According to the model, situational information processing can be primarily emotional as in the case of circumstances of passion along a continuum to a chemistry lecture, which is mostly rational. All information processing situations contain an underlying emotional dimension, whether it is the satisfaction derived from understanding a chemistry lecture to the relief associated with a suspicious stranger leaving an elevator. As the model illustrates, the nature and level of information processing are contingent upon the circumstances. It is important to note, that according to the ARI Model, both kinds of processing usually occur, with emotions always present. In fact, an individual can rationally assess emotional responses to specific situations.

ARI research suggests that optimizing the level of emotional and cognitive processing in persuasive messages increases the probability of the individual becoming involved and engaged with the message, thus increasing the likelihood of compliance with an appeal. Messages that are emotion, whether because of their novelty or uniqueness, and messages that are personally relevant or potentially important to the person, increase the likelihood of involvement. It stands to reason that a message that optimizes both types of processing would stimulate attention and maximize message involvement. This increases the chances that stakeholders will embrace a message and comply with a call to action. For example, appeals that provide the attributes of a product or brand, which is an analytic or "thinking" consideration, can also demonstrate the benefits of the attributes, which are typically emotionally based. Think of a car that is reliable, is safe, has great gas mileage, and low repair

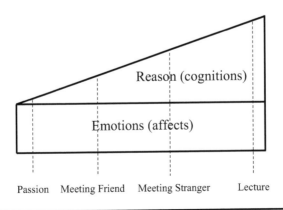

Figure 3.9 Affect-Reason-Involvement (ARI) Model

costs – these are largely practical attributes. Now add benefits such as cost savings, the car's sex appeal, attention-getting style, and how it communicates success. This car has it all! There is likely to be greater involvement in considering this vehicle as opposed to one that is practical, but a bit boring, or one that is exciting, but highly impractical.

Heuristic Systematic Model

The **Heuristic Systematic Model (HSM)** is an information processing framework that explains how people receive and process persuasive messages. Message are heuristically or systematically processed (Chen & Chaiken, 1999).

Systematic processing is comprehensive and analytic. This path includes processing information relevant to the persuasive message. Conclusions about the validity and merits of the appeal form after an argument evaluation in conjunction with the individual's existing knowledge.

Heuristic processing is not as comprehensive as systematic processing and utilizes a limited amount of information relying on mental shortcuts and simple rules to make evaluations. The assessment process incorporates heuristic cues such as credible sources of information. Sources include trusted and competent experts. General consensus offers agreement about the assessment implying "correctness." The decision-making process considers pre-existing beliefs and attitudes consistent within the context under consideration, notwithstanding nuances and other contextual differences.

Often both types of processing operate and contribute to the decision-making process. They can act independently and interdependently with each other.

HSM provides opportunity points for public relations practitioners to impact decision-making. For the systematic processing route, providing logically presented information is effective. Information should be straightforward and easily available. The heuristic processing path provides opportunities for practitioners to communicate the identity and positions of supportive opinion leaders and social influencers as well as relevant stakeholder endorsements. Opinion leaders are discussed below.

Understanding: The Challenge of Listening

Conveying a simple message appears straightforward. Let's test this statement with a simple exercise. Take out a piece of paper or on your digital device answer the following questions. So that we can mimic the real world, do not spend too much time processing the question. Answer it as though your heard it in passing on television or the radio. Number the questions from #1 onward. Do not view the answers until after you answer the questions.

1   How many members of each species did Moses take aboard the ark?
2   If you take two apples from three apples, how many do you have?
3   How many outs are there in an inning of baseball?
4   Can a man in South Carolina marry his widow's sister?
5   If a farmer lost all but nine of his seventeen sheep, how many would he have?
6   Does England have a fourth of July?
7   A clerk in a butcher shop is six feet tall. What does he weigh?
8   How many two cent stamps are there in a dozen?

9   What was the president's name in 1970?

10 You are a Baby Bull. You have been away from home a long time and are in need of loving. To whom would you go, Mama Bull or Papa Bull?

11 A plane crashes on the border between the United States and Canada. In which country would you bury the survivors?

12 How many months have 28 days?

Answers:

1   None. Moses didn't take any animals on an ark. Noah did. (1, 2)

2   Since you took two, you have two. You do not have: $3 - 2 = 1$. (1, 3)

3   There are six, three for each team. Three outs are for each team during an inning of baseball. We tend to focus on what is personally relevant such as our team. (2)

4   No. If he has a widow, then he's dead. (3)

5   Nine since he lost all but 9. The farmer does not have: $17 - 9 = 8$. (1, 3)

6   That depends on what you refer to. If it denotes Independence Day or a proper noun like Fourth of July, then the answer is no. On the other hand, if it refers to the July 4th or the fourth day in July, then the answer is yes. (2)

7   He weighs meat. Don't read too much into it. The answer is right before you. (1)

8   There are 12 two cent stamps in a dozen. A dozen means 12. The answer is not $12/2 = 6$. (1, 3)

9   It is the current president assuming that he/she was alive in 1970. The question was not who was the president in 1970. At that time, it was Richard Nixon. (2)

10 You would go to Papa Bull. There are no "Mama" bulls. (2)

11 Neither side. One does not bury survivors. (3)

12 All of the months have at least 28 days. (1, 3)

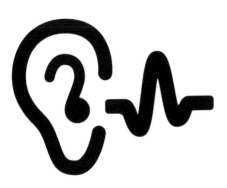

Figure 3.10 Getting a Message Across Can Be Harder than We Think

How did you do? The incorrect answers to these questions may be related to three conditions. 1) When we hear familiar words or phrases, we often judge prematurely. 2) Cultural background influences listening. 3) Poor listening habits is problematic even in the simplest listening situations. The end of each answer notes the conditions that apply to the questions. As we can see, even communicating simple messages can be challenging. Misunderstanding sound bites and 30 second commercials are common.

The Overall Process of Decision-Making

McGuire (1968, 1989) developed a model of persuasion that captures the key variables in the decision-making process in progressive stages. Although modified, his model serves as the basis for the process described below.

The practice of public relations involves communicating with stakeholders. Before we start our discussion about the decision-making process, we define communication terms starting with what is communication. **Human communication** is the process by which a sender encodes and transmits information that a receiver decodes. The information received may or may not be intentional, which leads to our next term. What is effective communication? **Effective communication** is the overlap of the sent message with the received message. The greater the overlap, the less miscommunication. Figure 3.11 depicts this relationship. Poor listening practices as well as personal and cultural filters can cause misunderstanding.

The shaded area labeled **Mutual Understanding** is that part of the message understood as intended by the sender.

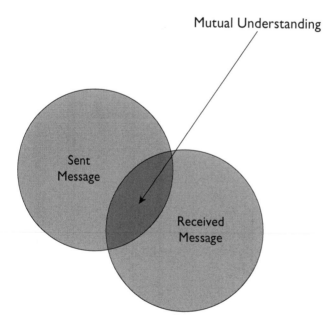

Figure 3.11 Effective Communication Is about Mutual Understanding

Persuasion or **persuasive communication** is intentional communication aimed at forming or changing an attitude and/or behavior in an individual, group of stakeholders, or organization(s). An **attitude** forms after an individual who is exposed to an item, person, idea, product, service, or any other type of object, either accepts or rejects it (Eagly & Chaiken, 1993). The acceptance or rejection of the object is the attitude. For instance, a person may accept ads promoting the merits of GMC trucks and reject those ads promoting the benefits of Dodge trucks or prefer donating to one charity over another. Attitudes, which are pre-existing, are based on reason, emotions, and/or habitual or reinforcing existing behaviors.

Figure 3.12 represents the decision-making process from a public relations communication perspective. The process starts at the **learning stage**. First, **reach** is the number of stakeholders **exposed** to a message over a given time. Stakeholders cannot be aware of an issue, develop a favorable attitude toward it, and act unless they process the message. A message serves no purpose unless stakeholders are aware of it. Media planning is responsible for message placement and scheduling in which the greatest number of stakeholders see it in a cost-efficient manner.

Message **attention** is a precursor to information processing and message awareness. Attention-getting messages contain personally relevant and novel content. In the case of websites, using varying color schemes, font types and sizes, images, video, and manipulating the degree of symmetry in the layout can hold stakeholders' attention and increase the likelihood of engagement. Different layouts can be pre-tested using focus groups in naturalistic and controlled settings.

Factors such as circadian rhythms can affect attention-getting tests. **Circadian rhythms** are 24-hour physiological cycles that every human being possesses. For example, "night people" would be most alert at night, whilst "morning people" are more alert during the earlier parts of the day. For this reason, when studying message attention, in order to generalize to a public, it is important to have a representative sample of the target public.

Once drawn to a message, stakeholders process the content. Depending on the level of involvement, issue awareness increases. **Awareness** is knowing about the topic followed

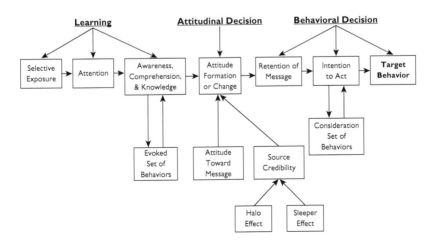

Figure 3.12 The Decision-Making Process

Figure 3.13 Often, We Have More than One Course of Action

by **comprehension**, which is an understanding of the issue and situation. Subsequently knowledge develops. Arguably, **knowledge** is more than having information and understanding; it is the ability to be aware of what the issue means, apply information and context to it, and envision its potential. In the case of a persuasive appeal that calls for action, knowledgeable stakeholders are aware of their choices and the consequences of each one. The choices in a situation are a person's evoked set. An **evoked set of behaviors** are potential actions.

Armed with knowledge, a stakeholder evaluates the message and available options. This is the **attitudinal decision** stage. It leads to the formation of a new attitude, a change in an existing attitude, or the continuation of a predisposition. The change is usually consistent with existing values, beliefs, attitudes, and behaviors that change the status quo. In cases in which a person considers making a major attitudinal change, a compelling argument must be made that accounts for and suggests a course of action for adjusting the person's mental state as to restore consistency. Strong attitudes supported by core values are difficult to change. This is known as **attitudinal inertia**. Those individuals who are open to change are likely to shift attitudes.

Other considerations during the attitudinal decision stage are attitude toward the message, source credibility, the Halo Effect, and the Sleeper Effect.

The execution of the message and message source credibility are factors that influence attitude toward the message. Professionally produced messages are more effective than poorly produced messages. Messages that are emotional yet not too busy tend to increase information processing and the likelihood of attitude formation. Highly busy and emotion

Figure 3.14 The Source of an Appeal Can Affect whether a Person Accepts It

messages cause audience members to tune out because there is too much to process. Slow messages with little emotion are boring because there is insufficient novelty. Other message characteristics such as extreme language and exaggerated claims discount message validity.

Perceptions of the source influence message receptivity. The message source is the sponsor or the presenter of the message. **Source credibility** is believability. It consists of three dimensions. The first is source **trustworthiness**. Trusting the source can be based on two factors. The source's reputation or personal experience with the source demonstrates trust. The second dimension is competence. **Competence** is education/training and/or experience with the issue. Last, source charisma influences favorability. **Charisma** is subjective and consists of personality attributes, energy level, and general likability. Charismatic individuals can affectively and cognitively empathize with audience members. **Affective empathy** is the ability to feel and understand the emotions and moods of another. **Cognitive empathy** is the ability to think like and understand what another person thinks. Figure 3.15 illustrates the components of credibility.

The **Halo Effect** is a source of credibility. It is a type of cognitive bias that extends a favorable assessment of a person in one area to one or more other areas. For example, an opinion leader is perceived to have an equal competence across an array of products because she provided sound advice on the purchase of major appliances.

Last, the Sleeper Effect can impact attitudes about issues. The **Sleeper Effect** is a delayed increase in the impact of a salient persuasive message because of doubts in

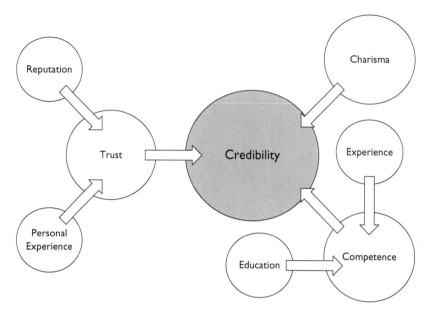

Figure 3.15 Components of Source Credibility

the source's credibility. Over time, as the connection between the message and source weakens, the audience member remembers and embraces the message without thinking about who said it. For instance, Candidate A runs a negative ad about Candidate X citing facts and a compelling argument not to support Candidate X. An undecided voter who views the ad would have been convinced by it had it not come from the opposing candidate. Over time, however, the voter forgets the source of the message but remembers the arguments and decides to not support Candidate X.

Some public relations campaigns' primary goals stop with attitude formation or change. Others seek to activate behavior. The last group of considerations involve whether to comply with a call to action. This is the **behavioral decision** stage. A well-received and remembered message inspires action. Three to ten **exposures** to a message fosters retention. In instances of new products, brands, or ideas more exposures are necessary to effectuate recall. Message channels should vary, but the central message must be consistent.

What follows message retention and a favorable attitude is the placement of the message's choices in the stakeholder's **consideration set of behaviors**, which are those choices viewed by the person as acceptable options from which to act. For example, if someone considers traveling to Boston from New York City, there are a few transportation options such as car, airplane, train, bus, hitchhiking, and walking. This is the evoked set. A mode of transportation that a person would seriously consider is part of the consideration set. Knowing the stakeholder's preferred choices increases the likelihood of message compliance by focusing on the consideration set.

The **intention to act** will activate once there is a gap between what is desired or needed and what is actual. The selected action generally comes from the consideration set of behaviors. The outcome is the **target behavior**. McGuire and others have examined this process as reoccurring incorporating reinforcement and feedback loops. Suffice to say, this version provides public relations with a litany of opportunities to influence the decision-making process.

More on Attitudes, Decision-Making, and Behaviors

There are decision-related theories applicable to public relations publics. These theories account for motivational factors that influence attitudes and decision-making. We will cover Rokeach's Theory of Beliefs, Values, and Attitudes, the Theory of Reasoned Action, the Theory of Planned Behavior, Social Judgment Theory, and the Transtheoretical Model of Change. We will also examine Uses and Gratifications theory, which is a framework for understanding an individual's media usage.

Rokeach's Theory of Beliefs, Values, and Attitudes

Rokeach's Theory of Beliefs, Values, and Attitudes, the Theory of Reasoned Action, the Theory of Planned Behavior build starting from the first theory which lays the foundation for the subsequent approaches. According to the **Theory of Beliefs, Values, and Attitudes** (Rokeach, 1968), behavior is based on attitudes, which core values and beliefs influence. **Values** are core beliefs about what is important in life. They guide our lives. **Beliefs** are inferences about ourselves and the environment. There are two types of values. **Terminal values** are desirable end states based on important individual beliefs. They are also goals to which people aspire during throughout life. Wisdom is a terminal value. **Instrumental values** refer to modes of behavior that help people along the way to achieving terminal values. Broad-mindedness is an instrumental value that leads to wisdom. Individuals strive to maintain consistent values, beliefs, and attitudes.

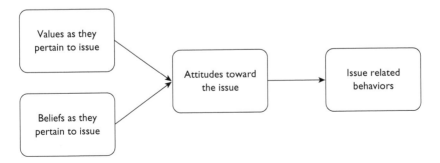

Figure 3.16 The Theory of Beliefs, Values, and Attitudes

From a public relations perspective, an effective appeal must tap into the values and beliefs that support an issue and ultimate stakeholder behavior. For example, someone who values security because the world is a dangerous place and full of crime will likely advocate greater support for law enforcement, longer sentences for crimes, see a need for home security systems, and support the right to bear arms. In cases where cognitive dissonance or attitudinal inertia exists, messaging techniques that shape the values and beliefs around an issue can result in individuals embracing an appeal.

Theory of Reasoned Action

The **Theory of Reasoned Action** (Fishbein & Ajzen, 1975) extends the Theory of Beliefs, Values, and Attitudes to include social factors that include emotional aspects of decision-making. Specifically, subjective norms are part of the model. **Subjective norms** are how we perceive others (e.g. peers, friends, family members, and professionals) and how society expects us to behave. These social factors influence attitudes and behaviors.

Therefore, as we can see in Figure 3.17, attitudes and subjective norms influence intention to behave in a certain way, and, in turn, intentionality becomes action. There are external factors that come into play such as individual demographic and personality attributes. Moreover, attitudes are based on beliefs that lead to certain outcomes and the probability of those outcomes occurring, which affects choices as well.

Perceptions about others' expectations about our actions influence the process. The weight assigned to these beliefs depends on the person's motivation to comply with these expectations. For instance, if the referent is important to the person, then there is an increased likelihood of compliance. Attitudes and subjective norms together predict the level of intentionality to act and any subsequent related behavior.

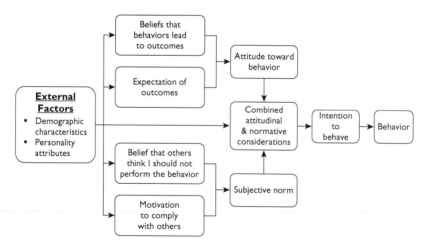

Figure 3.17 The Theory of Reasoned Action

Adapted from Bettinghaus, E., P., & Cody, M. J. (1994). *Persuasive communication*. Orlando, FL: Harcourt, Brace.

Think about This . . .

In a 2015 *Professional Safety* article entitled "Audience Analysis: Taking Employees from Awareness to Understanding," Dunn discusses how a 2003 combustible dust explosion at a pharmaceutical plant, which killed several workers, was due to a lack of understanding of the risk involved. Had the employees not only been aware of the risk, but also understood the dangerous relationships between dust buildup and production materials, the tragedy could have been avoided. Such incidents prompted Occupational Safety and Health Administration in 2012 to update its hazard/risk communications' regulations that extend giving workers the right to know and understand the hazards and risks.

To effectively increase awareness and understanding of potential hazards requires understanding the affected audiences and how best to communicate with them while considering their level of information, knowledge, and communication channels best suited to reach them. As pointed out by Dunn (p. 30), audience analysis is a tool to develop "information that effectively communicates hazards across a spectrum of risk communication formats." Appropriate audience-centered formats include face-to-face training, written documentation, videos, and/or web-based training. The article also noted the importance of regularly conducting audience analyses so that organizations can stay current and act quickly and effectively should the need arise.

Ask yourself: Can you think of other audience analysis factors?

Dunn, C. K. (2015). Audience analysis: Taking employees from awareness to understanding. *Professional Safety*, November, 30–34.

Theory of Planned Behavior

The **Theory of Planned Behavior** is a follow-up to the Theory of Reasoned Action (Ajzen, 1991). It adds behaviors that are not fully under the person's control. In other words, the theory posits that attitudes toward behavior, subjective norms, and perceived behavioral control, together shape an individual's behavioral intentions and behaviors.

Acting requires perceived control. The person must have the ability and resources necessary to carry out a behavior. For example, a student may register for a course, providing that she has the time, it fits into her schedule, and she has financial resources to enroll in the course. Simply having a positive attitude toward the course and knowing that her parents and peers would approve of her taking the course are not sufficient. She must have the time and funds to pay for the course. Figure 3.18 depicts the process.

Transtheoretical Model of Behavioral Change

The **Transtheoretical Model of Behavioral Change** (Prochaska & DiClemente, 2005) is a theory of behavior based on change over time. It is a system for behavioral change or action starting from before the person considers the behavior to the completion of the behavior, whether a single event, action, or behavior over time. The process involves six

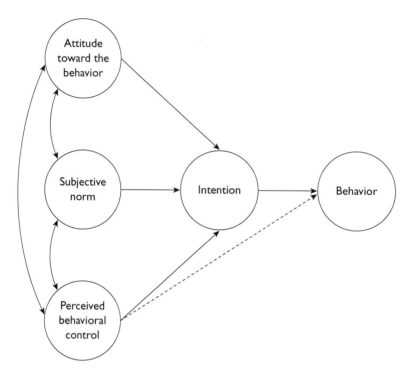

Figure 3.18 The Theory of Planned Behavior

stages which are Precontemplation, Contemplation, Preparation, Action, Maintenance, and Termination. The healthcare and marketing fields apply the model.

At Stage 1: Precontemplation involves individuals who do not intend to engage in the target behavior within six months. They may not be aware of the need to change or engage in any action. Messaging encourages individuals to think about the positive aspects of changing behavior. They may think and feel about the negative effects on others because of inaction. At this stage, individuals usually underestimate the benefits of changing, overestimate the costs. Therefore, being aware of the benefits, including the impact on others, is important in messaging.

At Stage 2: Contemplation individuals plan to start the target behavior within six months. While they are now usually more aware of the benefits of changing, their cost/benefit assessment is a wash. This ambivalence about changing can postpone target action. However, they think about the behavior because they have learned that they can benefit from it. They learn more about the benefit of the behavior from other sources. Public relations efforts can focus on providing information, endorsements, and testimonials about the target behavior.

At Stage 3: Preparation involves readiness. Stakeholders are ready to act within 30 days. They tell others of their intention to act. They may tell colleagues, friends, and family.

Table 3.2 Application of the Stages of the Transtheoretical Model of Behavioral Change

Attribute/Stage	Precontemplation	Contemplation	Preparation	Action	Maintenance	Termination
Standard time	More than 6 months	In the next 6 months	In the next month	Now	At least 6 months	Any time
Action & intervention	New video streaming service	Ambivalent	Intend to subscribe	Subscribe	Continued subscription	Drop the service
Information source	Reviews, news coverage, social media	Reviews, news coverage, social media, friends	Friends, company information	Friends, company information	Friends/family, social media, programming	Stress, technical issues, lack of new programming & company support

Public relations tactics to address this stage include encouraging persons to seek support from those important to them as well as suggested start dates, ideas for preparation, and inspiration including positive imagery (visions of success).

Stage 4: Action is behavior. The behavior is in motion and continues for at least six months. Individuals strengthen their engagement and learn tactics for their continued success.

Stage 5: Maintenance is about keeping it up. If there is habit formation, no behavioral extinction occurs (**extinction** is the termination of the requested behavior). From a public relations perspective, providing information that covers potential pitfalls to continued success can go a long way in educating people and maintaining the behavior. Credible sources of support are effective. Sources with similar values and beliefs associated with the target behavior can help assure continued behavior. For example, opinion leaders known for certain political views endorse candidates with similar views and promote those candidates to audiences with similar perspectives.

Stage 6: Termination means the behavior ceases, at least temporarily. This occurs when the person stops the behavior. Depending on the situation, public relations messages can encourage people to start again and provide support where needed.

Uses and Gratifications Theory

If not exposed to the message, stakeholders will not have the opportunity to evaluate it. Thus, knowing the media usage, habits, and patterns of publics is necessary to reach them. Using specific communication channels says something about the sender and message. For example, high-tech ideas communicated in high-tech media reach high-tech stakeholders. As McLuhan said, "The medium is the message" (1964, p. 1).

Uses and Gratifications Theory attempts to explain why and how people, groups, and society in general actively seek out and use media to satisfy needs. It is an audience-centered approach focused on the psychological and social reasons why people use media (Katz, Blumler, & Gurevitch, 1973). Uses and gratifications theory argues that people examine and evaluate various types of media to accomplish their goals. They actively seek out certain media and certain content to obtain specific gratifications. They return to the medium for repeated gratification until they are no longer satisfied by the medium.

Reasons for Using Media

The reasons for media usage and satisfaction fall into four broad categories: Entertainment; Interaction and Personal Relationships; Personal Identity; and Surveillance and Information. Gratification can involve one or more of these reasons. Let's explore them.

Entertainment

Media provide diversions for people to temporarily escape their normal day. Entertainment usage can help to:

- escape or divert from problems and stress;
- relax;
- receive cultural or aesthetic enjoyment;

- fill time;
- be an emotional release;
- cause sexual arousal.

Interaction and Personal Relationships

Social interaction grows using social media. The media also offer the opportunity to develop personal relations with others through social media and common interests. Through media, people form parasocial relationships. A **parasocial relationship** is when someone follows another in the media, and learns a great deal about the person. The person extends emotional energy, interest, and time; yet, the object of attention is unaware of the person's existence. For instance, there are people who follow certain celebrities, know a great deal about those celebrities, and communicate about them on social media as though they are friends. In fact, some of my students are devotees of the Kardashians.

Personal Identity

Personal identification is an important and powerful link between individuals or between an individual and an object that exemplifies values, beliefs, and attitudes. This type of identification fulfills a need to belong to something, to share a commonality. It can play a major role in self-concept construction. People identify with characters in movies. During the 1970–80s, I recall seeing interviews with boxers who indicated that the first "Rocky" movie was the reason why they became fighters. Identification through the media can help:

- find reinforcement for personal values;
- find models of behavior;
- identify with valued others (in the media);
- develop a sense of belonging;
- gain insight into one's self and others;
- find a basis for conversation and social interaction;
- have a substitute for real-life companionship;
- help carry out social roles;
- enable one to connect with family, friends, and society.

Surveillance and Information

Media help to inform and educate people. Monitoring and scanning news-related media that cover and provide information about topics, situations, government, and society in general perform a surveillance function. In this regard, the media help to:

- provide advice on practical matters, opinions, and choices;
- satisfy curiosity and general interest;
- learn and self-educate;
- gain a sense of security through knowledge.

These uses can overlap. For instance, media use can include personal relationships and personal identity at the same time. Surveillance and entertainment can occur concurrently.

Characteristics of Those Who Use the Media

Uses and gratifications theory makes five key assumptions about the process.

1   The audience is active and goal directed.
2   Linking needs gratifications to a specific media rests with the audience member. The individual is the active player. Audience members' needs and desires influence what media cover and media coverage affects the audience as well. Interaction and satisfaction among individuals exists as well. Crowdsourcing, blogs, personal website, product/service review, and a host of social media are examples.
3   The media compete with other sources to provide gratification. There are numerous platforms that offer social media engagement. Cable companies are integrating more and more functionality in their services. There are many ways to access programming. Media services are customized. Virtual reality and holographic technologies are taking the promise of products to a new level.
4   People are aware of their own use, interests, and motives. Media flexibility and product customization accommodate unique individual needs. This is the case with online shopping and product recommendations based on purchase, browsing, search, and other online behaviors.
5   The audience makes value judgments of media content. Individuals decide whether using a specific medium is valuable and these evaluations shift over time. Section 3.7 covers the role of social influencers in this process.

Fear Appeals

People respond to messages that deploy fear to alleviate negative emotions. A **fear appeal** is a persuasive message that attempts to arouse fear through the threat of an existential danger or harm to effectuate behavior. It presents a risk and vulnerability to the risk, and suggests protective action. Some research has discovered that the more compelling fear appeals work better.

However, there are disadvantages to fear appeals. Depending on the nature of the fear, people might avoid the message. The fear argument causes the person to adopt the opposite position because the message is so upsetting, which operates to reduce cognitive dissonance. Rejection sometimes is based on questioning the source's credibility (trust and/or competence). Sometimes, **third person effects** come into play. People tend to think that a mass media message applies more to others rather than to them. The more distant the person from the predicted situation, the stronger the third person effect. The effect weakens when people known to the individual fall victim to the concern in the appeal such as the occurrence of unplanned pregnancy, drinking and driving arrest, or failure to use an antivirus program on one's computer resulting in a loss of important files. In these cases, the message hits close to home.

Opinion Leaders and Diffusion of Innovations

Opinion leaders are individuals who people consult for their opinions or advise on a topic, often in a specialized area. As influential individuals sharing similar characteristics, they:

- influence others' attitudes and behaviors;
- are in a specific social network whether formal or informal;
- are effective communicators;
- possess charisma;
- are perceived as being very knowledgeable in their field;
- have extensive experience about the topic of expertise;
- are trusted by those who follow them;
- have access to extensive information in their field;
- are innovators or early adopters of innovations in their area of expertise.

As we can see, opinion leaders have credibility. They are trusted, possess expertise, and are liked. There are different ways to distinguish opinion leaders. We can view opinion leaders as formal or informal. **Formal opinion leaders** are those leaders in professional positions such as tax assessors, safety engineers, physicians, or union leaders. They are in structured roles of authority. For instance, a prospective home buyer asks a real estate agent about local communities that have lower property tax rates or a patient asks a physician to recommend a specialist. **Informal opinion leaders** are not in a formal position. The basis of their relationship with followers is informal, social, and less structured. In social media, informal opinion leaders are **social influencers**. Informal opinion leaders can provide opinions on a single or range of topics. They can be average individuals or celebrities. For example, people seek advice about what type of cell phone service to purchase or what brand of automobile to buy. Some followers have a parasocial relationship with an opinion leader and simply take the person's lead on issues because the followers identify with the opinion leader. In other cases, the Halo Effect comes into play. People assume that an opinion leader is credible across a wide array of issues and topics.

Sponsorship links is a way to differentiate opinion leaders. Those given consideration for their position about a topic are **change agents**. Although there is a potential conflict of interest, at least in principle, these opinion leaders are committed to their opinions. In marketing, a person that comes closest to being a change agent is a **brand ambassador**, who is a person hired by an organization to represent a brand in a positive light. There is an intriguing point about change agents. Because they present themselves as objective sources of information, people perceive them as bona fide opinion leaders. During the persuasive process, the audience typically forgets the sponsorship link.

In financial markets an opinion leader is a **market maven**. This is someone with extensive knowledge about financial markets and who is well connected. He or she has enjoyed investment success. Thus, a market maven's opinions are credible, trusted, and valued.

As we can see, understanding opinion leaders and how they influence beliefs, attitudes, and behaviors of followers can provide public relations professionals with opportunities to persuade such followers through their opinion leaders. Winning over one opinion leader can translate into winning over many followers.

New products, manufacturing techniques, product variations, ways to deliver products, ways to package products, new brands, different and new ideas, attitudes, new practices, behaviors, and so forth are collectively known as **innovations.** The dissemination of innovations is the **diffusion of innovations** (Rogers, 1995). This framework also examines how the spread of something occurs, why it spreads, and at what rate. As depicted in Figure 3.19, the innovation spreads in a pattern among five specified groups of people.

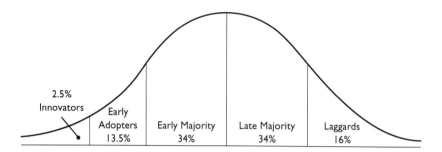

Figure 3.19 Diffusion of Innovations Curve

Innovators are venturesome. These are the first persons to engage an innovation whether it is support for a new candidate, a new technologically advanced device introduced in the market, or some new policy or approach to a societal challenge. Innovators are willing to take risks, they have high social status, they have financial resources, and they are knowledgeable about an innovation. Innovators constitute 2.5% of the population.

Early adopters are respected people who place great value in this attribute. This group represents 13.5% of the population. They consist of a high percentage of opinion leaders. Early adopters have social status, more financial resources, greater education, and are vanguard in their perspective. They are more discreet in adoption choices than innovators. They accept less risk than innovators and are deliberative in their choice of innovations.

Early majority are deliberative. This is one of the two largest groups comprising 34% of the population. The early majority wait significantly longer than the innovators and early adopters before adopting an innovation. Because they are thoughtful in decisions to adopt, they require time and adopt just before the average person does so. They tend to possess above average social status, are in contact with early adopters, and seldom hold positions of opinion leadership. They serve as the connection to the other groups.

Late majority members are skeptical. These persons adopt an innovation after the average person. These people approach the innovation with a high degree of skepticism and caution. Peer norms play an important role in adoption. Individuals in this group generally have below average social status, limited financial resources, are in communication with others in their group and in the early majority group, and have little opinion leadership. They account for 34% of the population.

Laggards are traditional and hold 16% of the population. These people are the last to adopt an innovation. There is no opinion leadership. Laggards usually have an aversion to change agents and are suspicious of innovations. They believe in existing tried and true practices, products, brands, and ideas. They are of low social status, of very limited financial resources, have a local focus, and mostly interact only with family and close friends.

The successful diffusion of an innovation requires certain conditions. Table 3.3 depicts these five requirements.

Two examples come to mind when thinking about diffusion of innovations: car door panels and e-readers. Early vehicle door panels consisted of stitched leather, various fabrics, and wood trim. The stitches were clearly visible. Over time this changed; door panels were made from injection molded plastics and some type of carpet-like fabric. The early injection molded panels had a stitch design in the panels to simulate stitching that did not exist.

Table 3.3 Requirements for Successful Adoption

Compatibility	Innovation should be compatible with the consumers' lifestyles, values, and beliefs.
Trialability	People are more likely to adopt an innovation if they can experiment with it prior to purchase.
Complexity	A product that is easy to understand will be chosen over more complex products.
Observability	Innovations that are easily observable are more likely to be adopted.
Relative Advantage	Product should offer an advantage over its competitors.

Eventually, vehicle manufacturers did away with the stitch look. This practice suggested that vehicle manufacturers transitioned to the new design by phasing out the old panel in a series of steps that would not disrupt consumer mental models of what constituted the interior of a car.

The second example is the e-book reader. Some competing brands mimicked traditional book features such as having the outside case of the e-reader designed as a book. Other e-readers screens appeared to have a paper texture and made a paper page turning sound when moving to the next page. Here, again, e-reader manufacturers considered consumer psychological factors and what would smooth the diffusion of e-readers into the marketplace.

Putting It All Together

These theories collectively explain the decision-making process as it relates to public relations and persuasive communication. They introduce key psychological frameworks relevant to public relations and persuasion.

We discussed how values, beliefs, and attitudes influence behaviors. The process involves assessments based on experience and other weighted factors in the decision-making process at the cognitive and emotional levels. Decision-making also includes relational factors. These perspectives remain relatively stable through active mechanisms such as cognitive dissonance reduction, reinforcement dynamics, and other personality variables that drive the level and nature of an individual's motivation to act.

Summary of Key Concepts

- Theory can help predict attitudes and behaviors.
- People with similar attributes think, feel, and likely act similarly in many situations.
- Self-esteem and motivation can drive people to act for different reasons.
- The kinds of self-esteem and motivation stakeholders possess call for different types of public relations messages.
- Human information processing and decision-making consists of three collective stages each with its own considerations.
- Decision-making involves learning, attitudinal decisions, and behavioral decisions.
- People decide based on their values, beliefs, attitudes, and previous behaviors.
- Opinion leaders inform and influence stakeholders' thoughts, feeling, and behaviors.
- Dynamics that impact attitudes are message construction, source credibility, the Halo Effect, and the Sleeper Effect.

Key Terms

Chapter Questions

3.1   What is a theory?
3.2   What is the key purpose of researching stakeholders?
3.3   What is motivation?
3.4   Define self-esteem.
3.5   Define self-concept.
3.6   What is secure self-esteem?
3.7   Define fragile self-esteem?
3.8   What is Maslow's Hierarchy Needs Theory?
3.9   List and explain Maslow's Hierarchy Needs.
3.10 What is self-determination Theory?
3.11 Define intrinsic motivation and extrinsic motivation and provide examples of each.
3.12 What are the four components of Self-determination theory and explain them?
3.13 What are the types of extrinsic motivational regulation and describe each one?
3.14 Define amotivation.
3.15 What are the VALS three types of motivations and provide an example of each?
3.16 Define Cognitive Dissonance Theory.
3.17 Define cognitive dissonance reduction.
3.18 What are the three elements of the cognitive dissonance reduction process? Explain
      each one
3.19 What is another term for post-purchase cognitive dissonance?
3.20 Define cognitions.
3.21 Define affects.
3.22 Define emotions.
3.23 What are moods?
3.24 What is the Affect-Reason-Involvement Model?
3.25 Define the Heuristic Systematic Model (HSM).
3.26 What are the two types of processing involved in the Heuristic Systematic Model
      (HSM) and briefly explain each of them.
3.27 Define human communication.
3.28 Define effective communication.
3.29 What is persuasive communication?
3.30 What is an attitude?
3.31 What are the three major stages in the overall decision-making process?
3.32 What are the components of source credibility?
3.33 What are the two types of empathy and explain them?
3.34 What is the Halo Effect?
3.35 What is the Sleeper Effect?
3.36 What is a consideration set of behaviors?

3.37   Define the Theory of Beliefs, Values, and Attitudes.
3.38   Define the Theory of Reasoned Action.
3.39   What is the Theory of Planned Behavior?
3.40   Define the Transtheoretical Model of Behavioral Change.
3.41   What is Uses and Gratifications Theory?
3.42   Who are opinion leaders?
3.43   What is the Diffusion of Innovations?

References

Ajzen, I. (1991). The theory of planned behavior. *Organizational Behavior and Human Decision Processes*, *50*(2), 179–211.

Bettinghaus, E. P., & Cody, M. J. (1994). *Persuasive communication*. Orlando, FL: Harcourt, Brace.

Buck, R. (1988). *Human motivation and emotion*. New York City: Wiley.

Buck, R., Chaudhuri, A., Georgson, M., & Kowta, S. (1995). Conceptualizing and operationalizing affect, reason, and involvement in persuasion: the Ari model and the CASC scale. In F. R. Kardes & M. Sujan (Eds.), *Advances in Consumer Research Volume 22* (pp. 440–447). Provo, UT: Association for Consumer Research.

Chen, S., & Chaiken, S. (1999). The heuristic-systematic model in its broader context. In S. Chaiken and Y. Trope (Eds.), *Dual-Process Theories in Social Psychology*, (pp. 73–96). New York: The Guilford Press.

Dunn, C. K. (2015). Audience analysis: Taking employees from awareness to understanding. *Professional Safety*, November, 30–34.

Eagly, A. H., & Chaiken, S. (1993). *The psychology of attitudes*. New York City, N.Y.: Harcourt Brace College Publishers.

Festinger, L. (1957). *The theory of cognitive dissonance*. New York: Harper & Row.

Fishbein, M., & Ajzen, I. (1975). Belief, attitude, intention, and behavior: An introduction to theory and research. Reading, MA: Addison-Wesley.

Gass, R. H., & Seiter, J. S. (2007). *Persuasion, social influence, and compliance gaining*. New York City: Pearson.

Lee, H. (1960). *To kill a mockingbird*. Reprint 1988. New York City: Grand Central.

Katz, E., Blumler, J. G., & Gurevitch, M. (1973). Uses and gratifications research. *The Public Opinion Quarterly*, *4* (37), 509–523.

Kernis, M. H., & Paradise, A. W. (2002). Distinguishing between secure and fragile forms of high self-esteem. In E. L. Deci & R. M. Ryan (Eds.), *Handbook of Self-Determination Research* (pp. 339–360). Rochester, NY: The University of Rochester Press.

McGuire, W. J. (1968). Personality and attitude change: An information-processing theory. In A. G. Greenwood, T. C. Brock, & T. Ostrom (Eds.), *Psychological foundations of attitudes* (pp. 171–196). San Diego, CA: Academic Press.

McGuire, W. J. (1989). Theoretical foundations of campaigns. In R. E. Rice, & C. K. Atkins (Eds.), *Public communication campaigns* (pp. 43–65). Newbury Park, CA: Sage.

McLuhan, M. (1964) *Understanding media: The extensions of man*. London: Signet Books.

Maslow, A. (1987). *Motivation and personality* (3rd ed.) New York City: Harper & Row.

O'Brien, E. J., Bartoletti, M., Leitzel, J. D., & O'Brien, J. P. (2006). Global self-esteem: Divergent and convergent validity issues. In M. H. Kernis (Ed.), *Self-esteem: Issues and Answers. A sourcebook of current perspectives* (pp. 26–35). New York City: Psychology Press.

Prochaska, J. O., & DiClemente, C. C. (2005). The transtheoretical approach. In J. C. Norcross and M. R. Goldfried (Eds.), *Handbook of psychotherapy integration* (pp. 147–171). New York City: Oxford University Press.

Rogers, E. M. (1995). *Diffusion of innovations.* New York City: The Free Press.

Rokeach, M. (1968). Beliefs, attitudes, and values: A theory of organization and change. San Francisco, CA: Jossey-Bass.

Ryan, R. M., & Deci, E. L. (2000). Intrinsic and extrinsic motivation: Classic definitions and new directions. *Contemporary Educational Psychology, 25,* 54–67.

Strategic Business Insights. (2017). *About VALS.* Retrieved from www.strategicbusinessinsights.com/vals/about.shtml.

Chapter 4

Public Relations Research

Without data you're just another person with an opinion.
(W. Edwards Deming, reported in Stoica & Ivan, 2016, p. 225)

Learning Objectives

To:

- Describe the different types of analytics.
- Understand and define public relations research.
- Explain the various ways to categorize research.
- Understand the concepts of internal validity, external validity, and reliability.
- Discuss the various aspects of experimental research.
- Know the difference between statistical and census data.
- Describe the uses of public relations research.
- Describe the numerous research designs and sampling strategies.
- Understand the basics of focus group and internal communication audit research.

Introduction

A 2017 University of Southern California (USC) surveyed of 875 public relations executives about the state of public relations in the world today (Global Communications Report, 2017). They reported that there is a growing need to recruit talent adept at conducting research and analytics. Seventy-five percent indicated that analytics will continue to grow and be more important; whereas, 49% of respondents expressed concern for hiring more research expertise. These areas are critical to measure and evaluate public relations campaign success.

Total reach, impressions, and content analysis measure outcomes. The most common measurements reported by respondents are counts of followers, followed by reach, and counts and classification of interactions such as likes or comments. Brand perception or return on investment measurement are seldom deployed. Participants reported little research on tracking sentiment, social listening, and real-time monitoring of conversations, and shifts in attitudes or behaviors. This is not surprising because understanding and measuring the psychological impact of a campaign requires skills more complex than simply reviewing automated counts and reach numbers.

According to Fred Cook, the Director of the USC Center for Public Relations, "Measurement remains the holy grail in the PR industry . . . Everyone agrees that it's a huge growth opportunity but few seem to have figured out an integrated approach to determining the real return on investment for communications" (Global Communications Report, 2017, p. 10). In fact, studies have cited that the lack of measurement and linkage to effectiveness and profitability have prevented public relations management from entering the circles of the dominant coalition, those at the top who make the key decisions (Grantham, Vieira, & Trinchero, 2011). It stands to reason that public relations will play a more prominent role in organizational decision-making once its contribution is measurable and assessable. Research and analytics are paths in this direction.

This chapter provides an overview of research and touches upon types of research relevant to public relations. It also reviews key terms, public relations research topics, research designs, statistics in general, the importance of sampling and various sampling techniques, and key research techniques.

Some Definitions

Let's define key research terms. **Analytics** "is an encompassing and multidimensional field that uses mathematics, statistics, predictive modeling and machine-learning techniques to

Figure 4.1 Analytics Explains Much of What We Do

find meaningful patterns and knowledge in recorded data" (SAS, 2017, para. 1). Massive amounts of digital data are available for analysis and the volume continues to grow. The basic kinds of analytics are descriptive, predictive, and prescriptive. **Descriptive analytics** discovers, describes, and detects patterns and trends in the data. **Predictive analytics** utilizes data to develop models that forecast future behaviors and events. **Prescriptive analytics** combines the other two and adds data-driven decision-making to the mix, including calculating the probabilities of success for alternative courses of action and risk evaluation.

What is public relations research? **Public relations research** is a set of techniques and principles for systematically collecting, recording, analyzing, and interpreting data that can inform decision makers about public relations including outcome evaluation, the organization itself, and the environments in which public relations operates. These formal principles and guidelines help assure that both internal- and external-oriented research findings are objective, valid, and reliable.

Research's degree of complexity varies. It determines the chances of certain behaviors occurring such as purchasing habits or media activities. It involves pre-testing messages, monitoring and assessing an ongoing public relations campaign for necessary adjustments, and evaluating campaigns after they are over. All of these activities constitute **formal research**.

Informal research is less complex, less structured, usually exploratory, and typically it is not conducive to measurement. "Analysis" is subjective. It can provide insights that lead to formal research. A conversation, an email, a small group discussion during lunch, a conversation with an expert, or a simple Google search are examples of informal research. This type of research is of limited use, not highly accurate, and limited to the sources of the collected information. The research practitioner must take care not to generalize to an entire public.

Figure 4.2 Water Cooler Talk Can Be Informal Research

The distinction between formal and informal leads us to another comparison which is the difference between quantitative and qualitative research. **Quantitative research** is the exemplar of formal research including **statistics**, a type of applied mathematics, used specifically for analyzing sample data. A **sample** consists of data derived from small groups of people or other sampling units that are representative of the larger population of interest. A **population** comprises all members of a group. In public relations research, populations are stakeholders or publics. They consist not only of people but also include organizations so that the total number of public members can vary from a handful to millions. Last, quantitative studies use objective techniques. However, the interpretation of results is, in part, subjective based on experience, judgment, and expertise.

On the other hand, although planned and systematic, **qualitative research** does not involve statistics or numbers, but, at most, some basic tabulations. For the most part, the techniques used are not quantitative. There is a large degree of subjectivity. Focus groups and open-ended interview research are examples.

What makes quantitative research objective? Quantitative research must possess internal and external validity as well as reliability. Validity provides accuracy. **Internal validity** assures that the intended items are actually measured. This can become challenging when measuring concepts such as intrinsic or extrinsic motivation, brand loyalty, or love. We usually measure these constructs by asking questions about the topic or some aspect of it. If, for example, a respondent consistently answers questions about brand loyalty, and this pattern follows through all those persons responding to the questionnaire, then it is likely that the results accurately represent what respondents think about loyalty.

External validity assures the accurate application of sample results to the entire target public. Thus, it is critically important that the sample represent a target public. For example, if findings from a representative sample reveal that most employees are interested in more pension plan options, then we extend this finding to all employees as likely being the case.

Reliability provides statistical consistency. Think about a reliable thermometer. If I take eight temperature readings between 8:00 and 8:01 am, all of them should be nearly identical. The similar (or nearly identical) readings demonstrate that the thermometer is consistent and does not require calibration. For instance, if a sample of people responded to a series of questions about their typical media habits twice during a given week, a reliable set of questions would yield essentially similar results for both sets of measurement, which suggests reliability. Statistics offers methods for determining the degrees of validity and reliability, which are beyond the scope of our discussion.

Validity and reliability are of concern when conducting experimental research. An **experiment** is exposing a sample to a condition and recording responses. The **setting** is the environment in which an experiment takes place. There are two types of settings. A **laboratory setting** allows the researcher to control the experimental environment and manage the experimental condition. Experiments provide internal validity. At the same time, people may not behave naturally in a controlled setting. An alternative approach is to conduct the experiment in a **naturalistic setting**. In this case, the experiment is realistic because the phenomenon is likely to take place in its natural environment. However, it is often difficult to control other factors that might affect how they respond in the experiment. Distractions or other activities can impact responses. So, although the results represent their true responses under realistic conditions, it may be difficult to discover what unaccounted factors, if any, contributed to their responses.

One final topic is about the nature of data collection. Data or research can be primary or secondary. **Primary research** means gathering the data firsthand such as having people complete a questionnaire or measuring productivity. **Secondary research** or data is using previously collected data. Data available from the United States Census Bureau, existing organizational records, or through any number of private companies such Arbitron, Nielsen, Claritas, Acxiom, and various aggregated industry reports are secondary sources.

Both types of research have merits. Secondary research data is usually easily accessible, less expensive than collecting primary data, and often used by public relations practitioners with limited resources (generally, public relations departments spend 3–5% of their budget on research) as well insufficient research expertise. By the same token, primary data can be specific to an organization's public relations needs and is especially suitable for pre-testing messages using qualitative research such as focus groups or informal approaches that might include some basic summary tabulations. Campaign evaluation can be primary- or secondary research depending on the research aim. Tracking polls that gauge attitudes about an issue over time if conducted by the organization, are a source of primary data. On the other hand, similar existing polling data from other organizations are secondary data. Evaluative research is the topic of Chapter 13.

The Process of Reification

How do we go from an idea inside someone's mind to a measurable research finding? We do so through reification. **Reification** is the process of taking something abstract and making it concrete or measurable. For example, what is "work satisfaction?" We can define it abstractly by giving it a conceptual definition. Through reification, we can define it concretely; that is, we can provide a measurable definition of work satisfaction, which can then be subject to quantitative analysis. A conceptual definition for work satisfaction includes level of job gratification. A measurable definition of work satisfaction may combine measures of: happiness, reward, discovery, helping others . . . These components are questions and collectively measure work satisfaction in a comprehensive way.

For instance, "How happy am I at work": respondents would answer this question by selecting one of five possible answers: ranging from 1 = not at all through 5 = intensely happy. The same would apply to rewarding work, learning new things, helping others at work, and so forth. In this example, such questions together measure work satisfaction because they cover all the major aspects of what constitutes a satisfying work experience.

Sample Data vs. Census Data

Sample data come from a sample or small representative group of a public and thus are subject to statistical analysis. On the other hand, **census data** are information derived from an entire public or population. For instance, an internal public might consist of all employees in the finance department of a company. It might comprise a dozen or so special interest groups concerned about gun control. If 90% or more of the data come from the target public, then it is reasonable to assume that the data are census. Census data analysis is simpler than that of statistical analysis. The Sampling Issues section discusses this topic further.

Uses of Research in Public Relations

The public relations planning process including pre-, during-, and post-campaign deploy research as well as risk and issue management (environmental scanning), for the situational analysis (define the issue and identify all relevant publics), and throughout the strategizing and planning phase. Specific uses and purposes of public relations research are to:

- scan the environment as part of the risk and issue management function (crisis prevention and discover opportunities);
- identify the public relation issue and situation;
- define, understand, and prioritize stakeholders and publics;
- strategy development;
- message pre-testing;
- stakeholder relationship maintenance;
- identify communication channels for effective and efficient messaging;
- monitor the competition;
- influence public opinions and attitudes;
- generate favorable publicity;
- assess campaign effectiveness;
- minimize campaign costs.

Through these activities, public relations research reduces uncertainty and increases predictability.

Basic Types of Research Design

There are various research designs. The types covered in this chapter are by no means comprehensive. A **study design** is the strategy and plan that specifies the methods for collecting and analyzing data. One way to classify designs is by the nature of the data. From this perspective, designs fall into three broad categories: survey, experimental, and observational. Survey or questionnaire data provided from research participants has subjective as well as objective responses depending on the nature of the question. Experimental studies collect data relevant to an experimental condition via questionnaires. Observational studies offer a wider variety of sources. They can be researcher recorded behaviors, secondary economic or financial data, content analysis, web surfing data, and so forth. Observational research is typically objective.

These designs often share similar attributes. For instance, an experimental study may involve questionnaires and include recorded observations. Research can be exploratory, descriptive, evaluative, or cause–effect oriented. Research goals, objectives, target public characteristics, accessibility to a representative sample, and available study resources shape research design. We will discuss survey, experimental, observational, as well as related research designs.

Survey or Self-Report Research Design

A **survey research design** is based on questionnaires given to a sample to complete for analysis that might uncover some phenomenon or pattern. For instance, if a social service

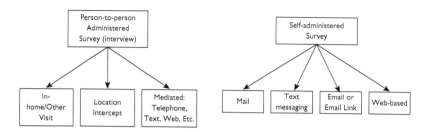

Figure 4.3 Survey Design Study

agency suffers from high social worker turnover, surveying the staff on their work conditions might reveal the causes of the high turnover.

A **survey design** approach implies subjective responses. For instance, if you ask employees whether they think that their supervisors are too strict, some might answer yes while others indicate no. An employee may claim to be a hard worker, which may vary from perceptions of the employee's supervisor. Thus, survey studies likely measure participant perceptions.

Survey differentiation rests with the mode of data collection. There are two basic types of survey data collection. As depicted in Figure 4.3, some surveys are person-to-person administered and others are self-administered.

Person-to-Person Administered Questionnaire

Surveys completed in-person are **person-to-person administered questionnaires**. Some are technology mediated using digital devices with applications such as Skype, telephone, Google Plus, and many other platforms. A person-to-person method has a higher response rate compared to self-administered questionnaires. A major drawback of this method is that persons may not provide candid answers to sensitive questions especially when the researcher is face to face with the survey participant.

Examples are special U.S. Census studies and door-to-door polling. Work interviews and mall intercepts are other examples. A mall intercept is where someone approaches a mall customer and invites the person to participate in a survey, which consists of a brief interview in which the participant answers questions recorded on a tablet or clipboard.

Self-Administered Survey Questionnaire

A **self-administered survey** involves respondents completing questionnaires on their own time. They have questionnaire access. Participants answer questions using any of the following formats: hardcopy (returned via mail), text message, email, text message-linked, or web-based questionnaires using services such as Qualtrics and Zoomerang.

Compared with person-to-person data collection methods, respondents tend to be more candid with these more private modes of data collection. The text messaging format or link is ideal for short mobile-based questionnaire. Email survey invitations follow a similar approach to that of text messaging. On the down side, the response rates are lower than person-to-person questionnaire recruitment and data collection methods.

Figure 4.4 Questionnaires Can Be Administered in Different Ways

Experimental Research Design

An **experimental design study** introduces a condition in a laboratory or field (natural) setting and tests to determine whether the condition affects the study participants in some way. Thus, the study focuses on the presence or absence of a condition and establishes whether there is a cause and effect relationship at least in the short term. The condition is known by various names such as **treatment, manipulation,** or **stimulus.** Generally, participants complete a questionnaire that sets a baseline. This is the **pre-test**. Then, participants experience the experimental condition followed by answering another questionnaire, which usually includes the pre-test questions or some form of them. This is the **post-test**. To determine whether there are differences between them, there is a pre-exposure and post-exposure measurement comparison. If they are different, then exposure to the treatment likely had an effect. For example, a researcher measures students' attitude toward binge drinking before they watch a number of videos describing the dangers of such a behavior. After the exposures, they respond again to the same questions. A difference intimates that the videos had at least a short-term impact. No difference suggests that the ads were ineffective. In other words, differences suggest an effect.

Cause and Effect Relationship

Experimental studies measure possible cause and effect relationships between two or more variables. A **variable** is something measured that changes or varies such as age, attitude, belief, or some behavior. An **independent variable** influences a **dependent variable**. For example, do different persuasive appeals affect attitude formation? The persuasive appeal style is the treatment, cause, or independent variable. The change in attitude is the effect or dependent variable. We can introduce another independent variable such as gender, which may also influence attitude change. These studies can become quite complicated involving multiple independent and dependent variables.

Lab Experiment

As previously discussed, a **lab experiment** occurs in an artificial setting such as a laboratory. It is highly structured, which makes it much easier to manage factors that can affect results. For example, a marketing company seeks to determine whether newly developed video ads increase Brand A's appeal. In this experiment, a sample of people visit a theater setting in which each participant has a tablet. Before and after watching each ad, the individuals record their attitude toward the brand as well as answer questions about the ad. Findings would apply to the target population if the sample represents the population and the controlled experimental environment is free from other factors that would influence results. The major drawback of a lab experiment is the artificial setting, which may not simulate real-world conditions.

Field Experiment

A **field experiment** occurs in a **natural setting** where the experimental treatment exists in real life. There is less structure and there is less control. Accounting for external factors is challenging. Extending the above example, participants are also asked questions about Brand A between segments of their program, during commercial breaks, and before and after ad exposure.

Figure 4.5 Experimental Designs Are Only Limited by Our Imagination

Manipulation Check

Another important component of an experimental design is the **manipulation check**, which is a test that determines the saliency of the experimental condition. The condition must be sufficiently strong so that study participants notice it. In the marketing example, recall of the ads or details about the ads are indicators that participants were aware of the different ads.

External Influences

There are potential external influences on the dependent variable that are not part of the study. Sometimes researchers are unaware of them. These are **extraneous variables** because they are external and not part of the study. In the persuasion example, since the focus is style, variables such as pre-existing beliefs as well as attitudes toward the topic of the appeal are extraneous factors. Using various techniques of statistical adjustments, the analysis considers and accounts for identified extraneous variables.

Managing the Effects of Unaccounted for Extraneous Variables

It is not always possible to know all extraneous variables in an experimental study. Although not identified, usage of a control group can help uncover the effects of unknown variables in a study. The control group is a sample measured along with the experimental group. If the treatment made a difference, then there should be a difference between the pre- and post-treatment groups, and there should not be a difference between the pre- and post-control groups. A similar difference between the two pre-treatment groups (experimental and control) and the post-treatment groups (experimental and control) suggests that unknown extraneous variable(s) and not the experimental treatment is responsible for the difference.

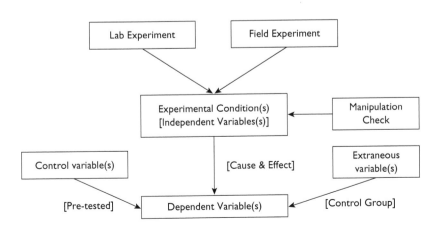

Figure 4.6 Experimental Design Study

Observational Research Design

Observational research is the observation, collecting, and recording of data from people, objects, and events in a systematic manner by human and/or digital methods. The observer does not question any people. Personal observation, digital observation, audit, content or interaction analysis, and trace analysis are the major methods of observation. Let's cover these methods. Figure 4.8 summarizes observational designs.

Personal Observation

Personal observation is a method in which the researcher interacts, observes, and records behavior. For example, an observer might document wait times in a hospital emergency room. A researcher might observe and record individuals negotiating terms of an agreement. The observer is vigilant about being objective. In **structured observations**, the researcher records specific observations (collects specific data). For instance, the observation may involve recording how many times a person looking toward the left during a conversation. In **unstructured observations**, everything that occurs is recorded. There are **disguised observations** in which case the participants do not know that they are being observed. For example, the researcher may observe participants engaged in an activity through a one-way mirror. If participant know that they are being observed, then it is an **undisguised** observation. Last, observations may occur in a **natural** or **lab setting**.

Digital Observation

Digital observation requires a device rather than an individual to record observations. Observation may include video or audio recordings, Internet traffic and behavior, eyes-on-screen tracking, response latency devices, vehicle traffic counters, devices that record individual physiological responses, and so forth. For example, the functional MRI (fMRI) measures brain activity by recording the flow of blood to different areas of the brain. The fMRI discovers what areas of the brain are more active during exposure to stimuli. Responses are compared to different stimuli. Eyes-on-screen studies can determine what website content initially draws people's attention and what content keeps them involved.

Content Analysis

Content analysis examines communication content. It systematically studies words, the relationships among words, themes, images, and the overall message. Organizations can content analyze messages posted on an internal discussion board or blog to develop a sense of how organizational members think and feel about the organization. Literature on new medical products can be content analyzed to determine whether they show promise and warrant further investigation. Companies can content analyze competitors' websites to learn about how competitors position or reposition their brands. Studying the content of social media communication and interaction help us understand what is important to publics, how these publics spend their free time, identify social influencers, and so forth.

Computational approaches rely on **manifest content analysis**, which counts actions, words, and co-occurrence of words. For instance, an analysis might seek to determine how many times do specific emotional words co-occur with the words "leadership" and

Figure 4.7 A More Complete Picture of a Public Emerges by Combining Different Observational Modes of Data Collection

"children." **Latent content analysis** is a technique that examines implicit messages and themes. For example, research might look for patterns in the relationships among television stereotypical characters, ethnicity, and gender.

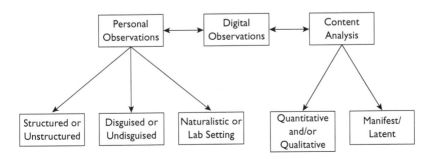

Figure 4.8 Observational Study Design

There are others ways to view research design. The following discussion briefly covers some approaches.

Single Time vs. Multiple Times Designs

Some research designs collect data at a single point in time, while others collect data more than once, sometimes within a brief period or sometimes over several years.

Cross-Sectional Design

A **cross-sectional study** design involves collecting data from a sample at a single point in time. It is a snapshot in time. For example, a satisfaction questionnaire sent to discharged hospital patients is a cross-sectional study and is meant to measure satisfaction responses at that single time as it pertains to the last hospital stay. This type of research describes and establishes associations among variables, but cannot address cause and effect relationships.

Longitudinal Design

Generally, **longitudinal** study designs incorporate collecting data from the same sample over a period (usually at least three times). Typically, it is the same kind of data and the analysis is meant to detect changes or trends over time. For example, pollsters may wish to monitor whether individuals who voted for presidential Candidate X continue to support her. Researchers may wish to learn whether children's media habits influence how they respond to stress as young adults. What follows is a discussion of the major types of longitudinal designs.

A **panel study** entails collecting data from the same sample over time whether they are persons, devices, records, or some other type of data source. This is a **within-subjects design** because the purpose is to examine for consistency or change within the person over time. For instance, monitoring the same group of children's cell phone usage from junior high school through and including college is a panel study. The key drawback is response bias. Over time, people simply answer the same way regardless of change. Over time, there is also the issue of attrition. For whatever reason, people drop out of the study.

As represented in Figure 4.9, a **tracking study** involves collecting data over time from the same people and replacing those who leave the study with others from the same sampling frame. A **sampling frame** is a source of data such as specific telephone lists, email lists, Facebook friends, Twitter followers, LinkedIn connections, voter lists, type of registration list, property ownership list, all the machinery output records from a manufacturing facility, or list of companies. Although not all the original individuals participate in the entire study, those replaced come from a sampling frame critical to the study goal. For example, marketing researchers may monitor the change in new brand awareness by drawing from a customer cell phone list and surveying customer samples during an ad campaign, including replacing those participants who are nonresponsive.

If a tracking study focuses on a similar group of individuals who share a specific experience during the same time, then it is a **cohort study**. For example, a researcher may survey social issue awareness in children starting from ages 5 to 9 and then follow this group for 30 years asking the same questions every five years from samples drawn from the same sampling frame.

Longitudinal study designs often suggest cause and effect relationships. Cost and time requirements are drawbacks. Over time, other variables come into play that can affect the study. For this reason, careful planning to anticipate and control for such situations is necessary.

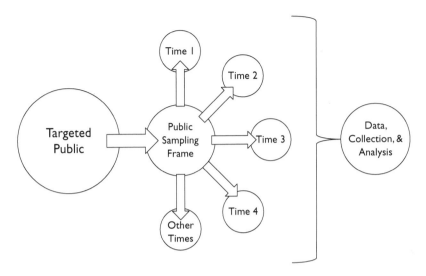

Figure 4.9 Process of a Tracking Study

Mixed Research Designs

Many times, the nature of the study requires a combination of research designs. This is a **mixed research design**. For example, some designs combine the focus group and survey designs. First, focus groups provide depth by delving into an issue. Results inform survey development. Inversely, focus groups may follow survey data collection because some findings might require further exploration. Focus group data is an expeditious approach to addressing questions in survey results.

In some experimental designs, pre-test survey and personal observation work together. Participants complete a pre-test survey that collects basic demographic and control data. Then, researchers observe and record participant behaviors before and after exposure to an experimental treatment. The treatment can be background music, a program on a television in a room, a public relations message, slogan, or just about anything else. There are many combinations of study designs suitable for various types of research.

Case Studies

A **case study** is primarily a qualitative research approach.

> A case study is an intensive examination, using multiple sources of evidence (which may be qualitative, quantitative or both), of a single entity which is bounded by time and place. Usually it is associated with a location. The "case" may be an organization, a set of people such as a social or work group, a community, an event, a process, an issue or a campaign.
>
> (Daymon & Holloway, 2002 , p. 105)

In public relations research, relevant cases provide insights about the issue. The similarity may be the issue, dealing with a specific type of public, government regulatory conditions, a specific type of media plan, and so forth. The case provides success- and failure-related insights that help develop all or part of a public relations campaign. Most case study reports are available online through websites such as those of libraries, professional associations, consultant firms, and academic institutions.

Think about This . . .

The *Institute for Public Relations Board of Trustees* published the "Top 10 Public Relations Research Insights for 2016," based on information collected from communications-related organizations. The insights are (p. 1):

- Millennials are more concerned about their work reputation than any other generation
- Few top leaders are very effective at both strategy and execution
- More Americans are using Twitter and Facebook as a news source
- Managing change effectively within corporations is critical to business success
- The "Internet of Things" will influence and shape the global economy
- Reducing gaps between top leaders and employees will strengthen leadership communication and results
- Adaptability is crucial to organizational success in a fast-changing global market
- Diversity within the workplace correlates to improved market share
- The public relations industry must work harder to grow and develop a diversified workforce
- Measurement and organizational listening are vital in strategic communication

Ask yourself: How can public relations usage facilitate these trends? State specific examples.

Kochhar, S. (2016). Top 10 Public Relations Research Insights for 2016. *Institute of Public Relations Board of Trustees*. Gainesville, FL. www.instituteforpr.org.

Research Goal and Questions

Research Goal

Quantitative research is a systematic, logical, and well-organized process, which starts with a goal. A **research goal** is what we intend to achieve by conducting a study. An issue that requires informed decision-making inspires goals. It further guides the research process.

Some goals examine existing topics from different perspectives. Some explore new topics. Bobbitt and Sullivan (2014) name four broad categories of public relations research goals. They are: 1) attitudes, beliefs, and opinions; 2) existing knowledge and level of issue involvement; 3) media habits; and 4) consumer habits and decision-making. These areas can apply at the individual or organizational level. Other types of goals involve risk assessment, finance, competitive messaging, comparative competitive advantage, or any number of ones centered on Porter's Five Powers (1998): 1) competition in the industry; 2) potential of new entrants into the industry; 3) power of suppliers; 4) power of customers; and 5) threat of substitute products or innovations.

The following are a few examples of research applications:

- An organization seeks to know why there is high employee turnover in some of its customer service districts.
- A marketing department wants to know the extent of consumer demand for a new product under development.
- A company considers whether to acquire a competitor and its customer list or take another approach in a move to increase market share. Feasibility research that explores these options helps identify the most attractive strategy to increase market share.
- Other research explores the costs and benefits of capital equipment upgrading while considering long-term marketing opportunities.

Research Questions

Developing carefully framed research questions about the issue and later accurately answering these questions starts the situational analysis process. These questions guide the design of a study, selection of sampling strategy, and planned statistical analyses, which all address objectives and ultimately achieve the research goal. Most of the time, a study has more than one question each addressing a specific aspect of the goal. For example, let us assume that a company's productivity is trending downward. A research goal to discover why employees are underperforming would seek answers to questions such as the following. Is there a connect between employee motivation and job performance at the company? Have there been changes in management/leadership, and, if so, are these related to the underperforming areas? Are employees satisfied with their work environment? These questions represent key areas of what might affect productivity. They involve the collection of specific data necessary to answer these questions, which collectively address the goal.

The Interconnected Parts of Research

As we can see, after defining the public relations research issue, there is goal development. The collective answers to the questions through collecting data from a representative sample of the target publics takes us to the goal, which is the information required to create and execute an informed and effective public relations campaign. Figure 4.10 depicts this process.

Sampling Issues

Statistical analysis is based on a sample of the target public rather than the entire population representing the public. It often involves more than one public. **Sampling** is the activity associated with selecting sampling units from a population under study. Ideally, a sample should represent the target public as best as possible. There are precise sampling methods designed to assure a representative sample and others are less precise.

Sampling offers benefits not afforded to census-based studies. First, the costs of collecting data from an entire public or population might be prohibitive. For example, the U.S. Constitution mandates census data collection every ten years. According to the Congressional Research Service, the decennial U.S. census in 2010 cost an estimated $15 billion. If the U.S. Census primarily relied on sample data, the cost would be substantially less. Second, there is the issue of timeliness. Surveying an entire population can be time consuming. Although the 2010 U.S.

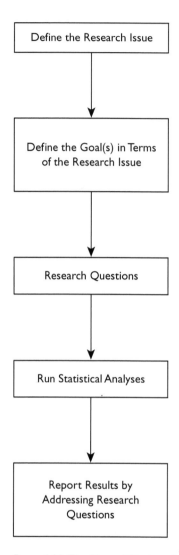

Figure 4.10 The Flow of Goals and Questions in Quantitative Research

Census data collection phase required 12 months, preparation takes years. For 2020, preparation began in 2011. Representative sample data can be collected in a fraction of the time. Last, collecting census data can be impractical. For instance, in an experimental design study of Millennials, it would be highly unlikely that a team of researchers could recruit all or most of this population to participate in a study requiring exposure to some experimental condition. Yet such an experiment is possible with a representative sample of Millennials. We can see that statistical studies offer a variety of benefits not available to population-wide data collection methods.

As noted in the Introduction, sampling is the selection process of a representative small group of a target public. For instance, a public might be 18–24 men on the West Coast of all ethnicities, religious traditions, incomes, who are full-time enrolled in community colleges.

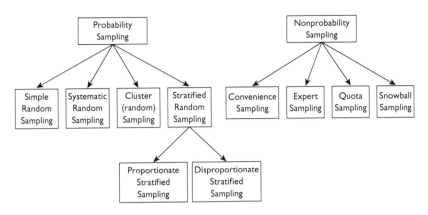

Figure 4.11 Sampling Strategies

The male is the basis of analysis. The population may consist of 2 million. For example, think about privately owned quick service restaurant chains in the United States with at least 50 locations. The basis of analysis is the restaurant chain. Articulating the basis of analysis assures appropriate data collection in a format conducive to statistical analysis.

For sampling purposes, the origin of the data is important. Will the data come from survey respondents, credit records, machinery output, drug trials, etc.? The data collection method must be true to the definition of the target public. For instance, credit records of undocumented workers may not yield the extent of their economic impact on the economy since many of these workers may not use credit cards. Figure 4.11 depicts the various sampling approaches.

Probability Sampling

Probability sampling techniques help assure that a sample truly represents the target public. Using random selection techniques guarantees an equal probability of selection for each source of data. Probability sampling methods each have their advantages and disadvantages. Below is a description of the four major probability sampling approaches: simple random, systematic random, cluster (random), and stratified random.

Simple Random

Every sampling unit has an equal chance of selection when utilizing the **simple random sampling** techniques. A **sampling unit** is the individual source of data such as a person. This method is simple, easy to implement, and provides a level of random selection. The primary disadvantage of simple random sampling is the presence of hidden data patterns or ordered conditions in the list or sampling frame, which creates bias in the data and thus reduces randomness. If the list consists of ordered levels of credit worthiness for example (most credit attractive to least), then a data pattern may be present, and thus the sample may not represent the entire population (full distribution of credit worthiness).

Systematic Random

When using **systematic random sampling**, every sampling unit has a known and equal chance of selection as in the case of the simple random approach. However, the methodology varies and is more complex than simple random sampling. This method overcomes some of the pitfalls of simple random sampling because sampling unit selection comes from the full range of the population or sampling frame, which more closely represents the entire public.

Cluster (Random)

Clustering sampling often draws sampling units from natural clusters such as geopolitical locations like states, company departments, neighborhood blocks, people who shop on certain days, and so forth. The clusters are mutually exclusive and collectively exhaustive subpopulations. Random sampling and clustering methods are often combined. The major benefit of this technique is that if the clusters represent the publics, researchers can avoid sampling the entire population, which will be cost-effective and time efficient. The cluster definitions and criteria for inclusion must match the publics. If the cluster definitions do not match the data, findings will not represent the target public.

Figure 4.12 Samples Items Are Like Snowflakes, No Two Are Exactly Alike

Stratified Random

Stratified random sampling segments the publics into sub publics or strata based on homogenous characteristics, which are important to the study. These characteristics are stratification variables with different levels. Once the strata (and level) combinations are determined for each subgroup, then a representative sample is drawn from each. The process has the following requirements:

1   the publics are divided into homogenous strata;
2   the strata must be mutually exclusive and exhaustive;
3   the individual sources of data are assigned to only one stratum;
4   random samples are drawn from each stratum; and
5   the samples from each stratum are combined into a single sample representative of the target public.

This approach is like multiple layered clustering where there are multiple combinations of sample data that possess homogeneous characteristics. For example, the stratification variables may be age and income in which there are four age groups and five income levels thus providing 20 strata. Based on simple or systematic random sampling, samples are drawn for each stratum or subpopulation sampling unit. If the size of each stratum in the target population is known, then the stratum is drawn proportionately, which is **proportionately stratified sampling**. For instance, in a sample of 700 participants, if 35–44-year-old persons, whose incomes are $50,001–75,000, consisted of 10% of the target population, then a sample of 70 would be required for this group. Table 4.1 depicts a **disproportionately stratified sampling** approach. In this case, all stratum sample sizes are equal regardless of their known proportions in the population.

The stratified random sampling method assures representativeness in the sample. The key drawback relates to its strengths. Inaccurate development of stratification variables and levels reduces the representativeness of the sample.

Nonprobability Sampling

In addition to probability sampling, we have nonprobability methods. **Nonprobability sampling** is a subjective technique based on the judgment of the researcher. There are no assurances that each source of data has an equal chance of selection and the representativeness

Table 4.1 Stratified Random Sampling

Stratified Random Sampling by Income/Age in Years	18–34	35–44	45–65	Over 65	Totals
0 – $25,000	35	35	35	35	140
25,001 – $50,000	35	35	35	35	140
50,001 – $75,000	**35**	**35**	**35**	**35**	**140**
75,001 – $125,000	35	35	35	35	140
Over $125,000	35	35	35	35	140
Total	175	175	175	175	700

of the sample remains the judgment of the researcher rather than an objective measure. For these reasons, nonprobability sampling-based findings cannot be generalized to the target public. There are the four major types of nonprobability sampling methods: convenience, judgmental, quota, and snowball.

Convenience

Convenience sampling is based on selecting sources of data that are readily available. Convenience samples include students, co-workers, family members, and other social group members such as Facebook and Twitter. These sources of data are easy to access. There is no random component to selection and the sample often does not fully represent the target public. The main advantage of a convenience sample is that it is easily and quickly accessible. The main disadvantage is limited generalizability at best.

Judgmental

A **judgmental sample** consists of experts. For example, if a study goal is to predict when a cure for cancer will likely occur, the researcher may ask the top leading oncologists and oncological researchers in the world. A company may interview its top clients to discover their opinions about a new product or service. Judgmental sampling has the benefit of being quick and cost-effective, but limited to a narrow public.

Quota

Quota sampling is a special case of judgmental sampling involving two-stages. First, categories of characteristics are the basis for selection. These categories attempt to assure representative sampling. Second, characteristics or combinations of them are assigned quotas. For example, the researcher may wish to collect data from 60% women and 40% men because it represents the breakdown in a public. A benefit of quota sampling is that the proportion-based quotas represent the target public. Since expert selection is in the hands of the researcher's judgment, findings only apply to the sample.

Snowball

Snowball sampling involves selecting an initial group of participants using random sampling techniques. The initial participants, in turn, identify other target public members for recruitment. This process continues until recruitment of a sufficient number of participants occurs. Snowball sampling applies to hard to reach small and unique target publics. For example, if the U.S. Census Bureau wants to collect economic data about undocumented workers, it might use snowball sampling. The researchers would initially locate workers receptive to providing data and ask those workers to identify others who might be willing to "talk." This sampling method is effective to recruit victims of unreported domestic violence, workers who operate in some aspect of the underground economy, or people who live off the grid. Keep in mind, although that initial group selection deployed random sampling, subsequent referrals will likely possess characteristics like those who referred

Table 4.2 Advantages and Disadvantages of Sampling Strategies

Sampling Strategy	Advantages	Disadvantages
Simple Random	• Simple and easy to use • Provides a level of random selection • Can generalize from sample to target public	• Data patterns can create bias • Elements may not contain full range of values • Probability statistical analysis can be compromised
Systematic Random	• Relatively simple and easy to use • Provides a level of random selection • Less likely to have data pattern bias • Can generalize to the target public	• Data patterns can create bias • Elements may not contain full range of values • Probability statistical analysis still can be compromised
Cluster (random)	• Can provide a level of random selection • Can be time saving and cost-effective • Specific publics can be targeted • Can generalize from sample to target public	• Defining clusters can be challenging especially as they relate to the target public • Sometimes clusters are homogeneous thus compromising statistical analysis
Stratified Random	• Provide the most precise random selection • Can be time saving and cost-effective • Specific publics can be targeted • Can generalize from sample to target public • Smaller samples are possible	• Defining strata can be challenging especially as they relate to the target public • Number of strata can become challenging resulting in a larger sample size

them and thus there is limited generalizability. Tables 4.2 and 4.3 list the advantages and disadvantages of the various sampling strategies.

The Focus Group and the Internal Communication Audit

Focus group research and internal communication audits represent qualitative and quantitative/qualitative ways for gathering useful information. Focus groups provide data from both internal and external publics. The internal communication audit can deploy many research techniques, both formal and informal including focus groups. Let's start with focus groups.

Table 4.3 Advantages and Disadvantages of Sampling Strategies

Sampling Strategy	Advantages	Disadvantages
Convenience	• Quick and cost-effective	• No random selection • Usually sample does not represent the public • Generalization is limited often to the sample
Expert	• Quick and cost-effective	• Can only generalize to a narrow public
Quota	• Quick and cost-effective • Of the nonprobability methods, it comes closest to being a representative sample	• No random selection • Defining quota groups can be challenging especially as they relate to the target public • Generalization is limited to defined groups and often to the sample
Snowball	• Can access hard to reach publics	• No random selection • Elements may not represent the target public • Generalization limited to the sample

Focus Groups

A **focus group** is an assembly of 8–12 people who meet to discuss an issue. They represent a target public. A researcher and assistant moderate the session with the purpose to gain knowledge and insights about what a public perceives about an issue or situation. Typically, focus groups occur in person, but are also mediated through video conferencing applications such as Go-To-Meeting, VC, or Skype. Focus groups meetings also take place in participant homes. This approach allows for interaction and the exchange of ideas in a naturalistic setting. Terry Hopper, former Regional Vice President of Sales for Pabst Blue Ribbon beer reported that this approach is highly effective because people tend to respond spontaneously and more openly in a natural setting (personal communication, September 17, 2017).

The meeting is recorded. Before the session, participants sign a form agreeing to the recording and to having their input used in reports. Refreshments and compensation are often provided. The session usually lasts 1–4 hours.

The information collected from focus group sessions can be used for many purposes such as pre-testing public relations messages or action words; gauging sentiment, knowledge, and involvement in an issue; assessing needs; testing public relations strategies; determining media habits or other behaviors; evaluating the effectiveness of a campaign; and so forth.

According to Krueger (1994), under the following circumstances, focus group usage is appropriate to:

- explore the depth and nuances of opinions regarding a situation or issue;
- understand different perspectives about an issue;
- understand what factors influence opinions or behavior toward an issue;
- test materials, messages, or slogans;
- test reactions to actual or proposed products, services, or actions;
- inform the design of a large study or help understand its results;
- learn about publics by observing their interactions.

Focus Groups are not appropriate when:

- sensitive information from the participants is involved;
- statistical analysis is generalized to relevant publics as a whole;
- the participants are emotionally or politically charged;
- confidentiality is required;
- the aim is to force participants to agree.

A **moderator** and an **assistant moderator** conduct focus groups. The moderator leads the discussion, keeps the conversation flowing, and takes a few notes to remember comments used later in the discussion. This person facilitates the group session. The assistant moderator takes thorough notes, operates the recording device (video/audio or only audio), sets up the physical or virtual meeting place, addresses all logistical concerns, responds to unexpected interruptions, and keeps track of time.

Figure 4.13 A Focus Group Session Is an Excellent Opportunity to Deeply Explore an Issue

Let's highlight some key aspects of focus group research. Participants are told that their opinions are valuable because they are the "experts." The facilitator and other staff are there to learn from them. This gives participants a sense of purpose and helps eliminate any barriers that may arise because of differences among participants and focus group staff.

The moderator should be neutral and welcome all comments pertaining to the topic discussed, exploring related but important subjects, yet, at the same time, keeping participants from straying off topic too much. It is a delicate balance to encourage dialogue about relevant topics but not constrain the discussion so that participants do not feel held back.

The moderator, who often uses a series of organized prompts that encourage discussion of topics germane to the issue, should start the discussion with general topics about the issue rather than to explore more specific items. This process may require the moderator to connect topics about the issue to keep discussants on track. Another technique is the usage of probes. Some examples are: Would you explain further? Would you give me an example of what you mean? Would you add more to that? Is there anything else that might help us understand? Please describe what you mean. I don't understand—would you mind explaining further? Does anyone see it differently? Has anyone had a different experience? Tables 4.4 and 4.5 represent a focus group session outline for a fictitious energy drink called "All Boost."

Table 4.4 Focus Group All Boost Session Outline (Part 1)

BREAK THE ICE (5 minutes)

- Thanks and welcome
- Nature of a focus group (informal, multiway, all views acceptable, disagree)
- There are no right or wrong answers—all about finding out what people think
- Audio and video recording
- Colleagues viewing
- Help self to refreshments
- Going to be talking about All Boast
- Questions or concerns?

INTROS and WARM-UP (5 minutes)
Like to go around the room and introduce yourselves . . .

- First name
- Best thing about drinking All Boost
- Worst thing about drinking All Boost

ALL BOOST USAGE (15 minutes)

- I'd like to understand a bit about how you typically use your All Boost . . .
- How many times a day do you drink it?
- What are some of the most common types of occasions you drink it?

BRIEFLY EXPLORE

- If we were to take away your All Boost from you, what difference would that make to your life?

BRIEFLY EXPLORE
PAST ALL BOOST PURCHASES (15 minutes)

- How you actually went about the process of choosing All Boost, and second, any criteria you had for selecting sports drinks . . .

Table 4.5 Focus Group All Boost Session Outline (Part 2)

PAST ALL BOOST SELECTION PROCESS
- So, thinking first only about how you went about choosing your All Boost, not any features you wanted, how did you go about choosing One?

EXPLORE PROCESS
PAST ALL BOOST CRITERIA
- Ok, so now tell me what you actually looked for in an All Boost?

EXPLORE
USAGE OF ALL BOOST FEATURES (20 minutes)
- Thinking now about All Boost features, I'd like to start by making a list of all the features you can think of—anything All Boost can do, etc.
- We'll talk in a minute about which features you actually like, but I want to start with a list of everything your All Boost has.

EXPLORE
DESIRED FEATURES (10 minutes)
- Are there any features your All Boost doesn't have but you wish that it did?

EXPLORE
MOTIVATIONS FOR DRINKING (20 minutes)
- You've all been invited here because you drink All Boost...
- What motivated you to drink All Boost?

EXPLORE
- What do you think are some of the reasons that people would drink All Boost?

EXPLORE
- What were ALL the factors involved in that decision?
- What was the single biggest reason?

EXPLORE
CLOSING EXERCISE (10 minutes)
- Finally, I'd like your creativity for a few minutes—to come up with ideas...
- Don't worry about whether it's a good idea or a bad idea.
- The only word I'm going to ban is "free"!
- Supposing an All Boost manufacturer wanted to encourage you to buy tomorrow...
- What could they do?
- Just call out anything at all that occurs to you—obvious, profound, serious, silly, whatever...

EXPLORE and REFINE
- Thank the respondents and close the session.

What aspects of focus group research are reported? Krueger (1994) suggests the following components in the focus group report.

1   *Cover page*: This includes the title, names of those receiving the report, the names of the researchers, and the submission date.
2   *Executive summary*: The summary should be no more than two pages and should include the major findings.

3   *Table of contents*: The APA style guide provides an example.

4   *Statement of the issue, key questions, and study methods*: Contains a brief discussion including recruitment method, discussion prompts, and sizes and number of focus groups.

5   *Findings*: They are organized by key questions in bullet summary form.

6   *Summary of themes*: Discuss the discovered key motifs of the focus group results. Organize them by logical linkages to themes.

7   *Limitations or alternative explanations*: Different interpretations of the findings are noted as well as any possible weaknesses in the research.

8   *Appendix*: This might include quotations from participants relevant to the key questions or themes.

There are many online resources available that offer protocols and best practices for focus group research.

Internal Communication Audit

Organizations that consider feedback from their members are dynamic systems. A dynamic system is one in which existential and historical feedback play important roles in the functioning of the system. Internal communication audits provide this feedback. Today, many organizations are being financially pressured to find more efficient and cost-effective ways to operate. Internal organizational communication audits provide insights about intra-organizational communication as well as shedding light on other aspects of organizations.

So, what exactly is an internal communication audit? An **internal communications audit** is internal research regarding some aspect of the organization and its stakeholders. The focus is on discovering communication effectiveness and perceptions and behaviors of internal stakeholders about an issue. There are various types of audits: some are simple and informal involving casual conversations with a handful of employees; some are formal and highly structured audits. The level of audit complexity is contingent upon the size of the organization, the degree of hierarchical structure, and the intricacies of the issue and situation in which it resides.

The Two Purposes of an Internal Communication Audit

The audit covers two general areas of concern. First, it uncovers the formal and informal channels of communication within the organization. The formal hierarchical structure for communication and the actual modes of communication often differ. It is typically a matter of degree. Understanding how people communicate within an organization offers insights and opportunities for improving communication effectiveness in a cost-efficient manner. For instance, intra-organizational communication using social media such as Facebook may be more appropriate then setting up a private and internally managed intranet for a number of reasons. First, there are costs involved in constructing and maintaining a private website. Second, employees are more likely to stay current because they are familiar with Facebook. Last, social media platforms offer analytics so that organizations can examine employee interactions and take advantage of any opportunities to improve communication.

The second function of an audit is to uncover opinions, attitudes, beliefs, other psychological factors, or behavior about stakeholders concerning an issue. This includes uncovering stakeholder degree of engagement with the issue as well as level of knowledge. For example, if a company is merging with another entity, then it is important to know what the employees of both companies think and feel about the merger so that issues are allayed to facilitate a smooth transition. If employee turnover is on the rise, an audit can uncover the reasons and solutions devised to rectify the situation. To discover best practices, audits uncover and compare communication effectiveness among departments or business units, which are subsequently incorporated in the formal organizational structure. Last, asking employees for their feedback also sends the message that they have valued opinions and contribute to the organizational mission.

Issues Covered in an Internal Communication Audit

Internal communication audits deal with many issues. What follows is a description of some key groups of issues.

Communication items. The distribution of formal written policies; the position of communication among management priorities; management support of communication based on functional areas such as marketing, finance, manufacturing, and quality assurance; the connections of communication to other staff functions; operational issues; and centralized vs. decentralized communication are areas where stakeholder feedback can increase better communications within the organization.

Existing communication programs. What are the formal and informal methods for communicating downward, upward, and laterally throughout the organization? Tactics considered are interpersonal, in-person, printed materials (annual reports, fact books, histories, news releases, and brochures), video streaming, audio media, and special events (annual meetings, open houses, etc.). Additional media are Internet, intranet, email, voicemail, digital publications, bulletin boards, PowerPoint, teleconferencing, texting, memos, decks, reports, and correspondence.

Meetings. Opinions about in-person or remote meetings. Meeting frequency, content, format, effectiveness, and duration are considered.

Objectives and goals. Do short-term and long-term objectives match goals? Are established objectives accurate measures of goals? An audit can elicit answers to these questions from relevant stakeholders.

Connections between internal and external stakeholders. An audit can examine the connections among internal and internal stakeholders relative to the organizational mission. For example, does an organization have the core competencies and scalability (financing lined up) to develop and effectively market a new product line? Are there sufficient external agency talent and budget available to launch a social media awareness campaign espousing the benefits of a product or service?

Organization, staffing, and compensation. Are the organizational structures; duties and responsibilities of positions; and salary levels comparable to other organizations in the same or similar sector? Employee perceptions of these considerations can impact productivity and organizational effectiveness.

Attitudes and opinions. Opinions and perspectives about various organizational practices and policies can be queried by an audit. For instance, a merger, acquisition, change in employee benefits or hiring practices, recruitment for community outreach and other programs, employee attribution, and morale are all topics an audit addresses.

Figure 4.14 A Communication Audit Helps Us Know and Understand More about Our Business

The Internal Communication Audit Professional

Who conducts an internal communication audit? Someone with effective interpersonal skills, who understands the issue and situation sufficiently to reach out to stakeholders that represent their groups, can execute a simple, informal audit. In a relatively small company, essentially everyone can potentially participate. For an extensive audit, bringing in a third-party consultant divorced from the issue offers advantages.

A seasoned consultant has a broad frame of reference gained through education and experience working with many, and varied types of organizations on diverse communication research projects. The consultant brings a level of expertise that optimizes the audit.

Second, an outside consultant brings an objective and fresh perspective to the situation. Individuals may be more inclined to offer candid responses if they think that there is no hidden agenda or predisposition about the issue.

This relates to the third point. When a third party conducts an audit, participants are more likely to participate and be forthright in their responses because of the expectation of confidentiality and, in some cases, anonymity. As we can see, consultant credibility can help assure accurate audit findings. For this reason, it is important that stakeholders are aware of the caliber of the party conducting the audit. Commitment from senior management as well as involvement from the membership of the relevant stakeholder/public groups are critical.

Steps of an Internal Communication Audit

Although the stages involved to execute an audit vary, the following steps and descriptions as represented in Table 4.6 provide an overview of the process.

Step 1: Hold planning meetings. During these meetings, the researchers determine audit objectives, identify question areas, plan an approach, and develop a schedule for the various data collection methods and phases of the project.

Step 2: Conduct top management interviews. Determine management's attitudes and beliefs about communication, as well as pinpoint communication problems in any management area. Senior management buy-in is critical. Interviews usually include the chief executive officer, heads of the various operations: communication, personnel, marketing, finance, and representatives from other key management and functional areas. Interviews are recorded and transcribed.

Step 3: Collect, inventory, and analyze communication material. The researchers collect, inventory, and analyze representative samples of all existing communication vehicles and programs, such as orientation packets, publications, audiovisuals, benefit summary plan descriptions, and representative memos whether in hardcopy or digital formats.

Step 4: Conduct employee interviews. Individual interviews or employee focus groups are valuable to discuss the organization's communications and other issues. The members of each focus group should be from the same functional area to reduce anxiety and foster engagement. Each focus group should be from a different functional area to enable the researcher to collect a representative sample of opinions across organizational areas. Usually, focus groups provide the opportunity to identify issues for further investigation. These interviews or focus group sessions are recorded.

Step 5: Develop a questionnaire. Interviews and focus group findings inform questionnaire development. It consists of specific questions related to communication areas identified during the planning meeting, management interviews, focus groups and individual employee interviews. A newly designed questionnaire can be pilot tested to assure question clarity.

Step 6: Administer a survey. Questionnaires are administered via hardcopy, email and link, website, social media, or text message. Response rates vary according to degree of issue engagement and knowledge.

Table 4.6 Internal Communication Audit Steps

1) Hold planning meetings.
2) Secure senior management buy-in.
3) Conduct interviews with internal stakeholder groups (e. g. employees).
4) Conduct focus groups with internal stakeholder groups.
5) Collect and analyze available organizational materials.
6) Prepare and administer surveys of relevant and representative stakeholder groups.
7) Analyze and summarize responses for all data collection methods.
8) Communicate results to management/employees (write report).

Step 7: Analyze and summarize responses. Collected data are summarized. The data should be held in the strictest confidence. There are various software applications for tabulating and running analyses such as SPSS, Excel, SAS, Minitab, and so forth.

Step 8: Communicate results to management and employees in a timely manner. The findings are communicated candidly and quickly. In addition to a written report, PowerPoint decks are an efficient and expeditious method for delivering presentations. Using PowerPoint, a deck consists of slides with bullet points and a detailed outline of the presentation in the notes area of the slides. Some decks also include details (sometimes with links) of the presentation in an appendix that follows the main presentation.

Lastly, a follow-up audit or ongoing monitoring may be necessary. For instance, in the case of a merger, management may wish to monitor employee perceptions throughout the transition process to pre-empt potential barriers to a smooth change. This not only has operational benefits, but has relational benefits as well. Knowing that management is concerned with the rank-in-files' opinions can motivate these stakeholders to behave in a manner that supports the transition.

Summary of Key Concepts

- There are descriptive, predictive, and prescriptive kinds of analytics.
- Public relations research can be formal or informal.
- Public relations research is viewed in different ways.
- Quantitative research allows us to have internal validity, external validity, and reliable results.
- Experimental research can occur in a lab or naturalistic setting.
- Statistical data comes from a representative sample of a target public.
- Census data comes from the entire target public.
- Public relations research is used for both internal and/or external related issues and situations.
- Numerous research designs and sampling strategies are available depending on the resources available, complexity of the situation, and degree of preciseness of findings required.
- Focus group research is an effective exploratory form of research involving both internal and external stakeholders.
- Internal communication audit research deploys a wide range of data collection tools extending across quantitative and qualitative methods.

Key Terms

Chapter Questions

4.1   Traditionally, how has public relations effectiveness been measured?
4.2   Define analytics.
4.3   Define the three types of analytics.
4.4   What is public relations research?
4.5   What is informal research and provide examples?
4.6   Describe quantitative research?
4.7   Define a population in research terms.
4.8   Define qualitative research.
4.9   What is internal validity?
4.10 What is external validity?
4.11 What does reliability offer?
4.12 What are the two types of experimental settings?
4.13 Describe primary and secondary research.
4.14 What is reification and provide an example?
4.15 Define sample data.

4.16 Define census data.

4.17 At least what percentage of a population is required to be considered census data?

4.18 Name four uses of public relations research?

4.19 In general, what does research do for public relations?

4.20 Define study design.

4.21 What is a survey design?

4.22 Describe two types of survey designs and provide examples.

4.23 What is an experimental research design?

4.24 Define the term "variable" and offer some examples.

4.25 What is a lab experiment and give an example?

4.26 What is a field experiment?

4.27 Define manipulation check.

4.28 Define observational research and list the major kinds.

4.29 Describe the various types of personal observational studies.

4.30 Define the two types of content analysis and offer examples.

4.31 What is a cross-sectional study and provide an example?

4.32 What is a longitudinal study?

4.33 What is a tracking study and how does it relate to a sampling frame?

4.34 Define mixed research design and provide an example.

4.35 What is a case study?

4.36 Define research goal.

4.37 Define sampling.

4.38 What is probability sampling?

4.39 What is nonprobability sampling?

4.40 What is focus group research?

4.41 Define an internal communication audit.

References

Bobbitt, R., & Sullivan, R. (2014). *Developing the public relations campaign*. Boston, MA: Pearson Education.

Daymon, C., & Holloway, I. (2002). *Qualitative research methods in public relations and marketing communications*. New York: Routledge.

Global communication report. (2017). *USC Annenberg Center for Public Relations*. School for Communication and Journalism. Retrieved from annenberg.ucs.edu/ger17.

Grantham, S., Vieira, E. T., Jr., & Trinchero, C. (2011). Are we practicing what we preach? Perspectives on public relations evaluation from practitioners. *Public Relations Journal, 5*(3), 1–19.

Kochhar, S. (2016). Top 10 Public Relations Research Insights for 2015. *Institute of Public Relations Board of Trustees*. Gainesville, FL, www.instituteforpr.org.

Krueger, R. A. (1994). *Focus groups: A practical guide for applied research*. Newbury Park, CA: Sage.

Porter, M. E. (1998). *Competitive strategy: Techniques for analyzing industries and competitors*. New York: Free Press.

SAS. (2017). *What is analytics? Analytics*. Retrieved from www.sas.com/en_us/insights/analytics/what-is-analytics.html .

Stoica, M. I., & Ivan, M. L. (2016). Using data envelopment analysis in healthcare for estimating birth rate efficiency. *International Journal of Scientific & Technology Research, 5*(4), 225–229.

Part II

Situational Analysis

Chapter 5

Situational Analysis
Defining and Understanding the Public Relations Issue

Einstein is reported to have said that if he only had one hour to solve a problem he would spend 55 minutes defining the problem and the remaining 5 minutes solving it routinely.

(Robert J. Greene, 1986, p. 68)

Learning Objectives

To:

- Understand what is a public relations issue.
- Differentiate between a problem and an opportunity.
- Understand, describe, and differentiate between reactive and proactive issue recognition.
- Define what is crisis management.
- Describe the different types of crises.
- Understand and explain different types of risk and issues management and why they are important.
- Explain what is environmental scanning.
- Understand and explain the steps for defining a public relations issue.

Introduction

The two key aspects of a public relations situational analysis are (1) discovering and sufficiently defining the issue and (2) defining the stakeholder groups that are relevant to the issue. This chapter addresses the issue and the next chapter covers stakeholders.

Understanding a public relations' situation is critical. A **situation** is a public relations environment such as the market for products, financial institutions, legislative branches of state and federal governments in which the public relations issue exists, and others. These environments define the situation, which consists of a host of potential interdependent variables. Factors in a situation can operate to affect an issue or the issue can affect them. Sometimes more than one situation surrounds an issue.

One aspect of the situational analysis involves defining the public relations issue whether it is a problem or an opportunity or both. This is the reason for the public relations campaign. The goal addresses the issue and, at least indirectly, guides everything else that follows. Issue definition also requires an understanding of context and the identification of the relevant stakeholder and their role concerning the issue. If past behavior is a sound predictor of future behavior, then knowing the history associated with the issue can help define it.

Figure 5.1 Issues Can Be Problems or Opportunities

Before we continue further, we will define key terms. An **issue** is a matter of concern for an organization. It is a public relations internal organizational or external environment problem or opportunity. A **problem** is the difference between a desired situation and the actual situation. It can have a negative impact on an organization in one or more ways and it involves stakeholders. A problem can threaten an organization's ability to realize its mission or goal. For example, a state government wants a new pension plan to be successful. For this to happen, funding requires 45% employee participation. However, only 25% participate. The gap is 20%. Not filling the gap will call the pension plan's success into question, which is a problem.

Reactive and Proactive Issue Recognition

Recognizing and addressing issues can be unplanned or deliberative so each are arrived at from different circumstances. How an organization confronts an issue can be reactive and uncertain, or proactive with a margin of predictability.

Reactive Issue Recognition

Some public relations situations are unanticipated and require immediate action. In the case of crisis management and communication, before taking sound, quick action, the problem must be clearly identified. **Crisis management** is a reactive approach to a largely out of control problem often laden with uncertainty. A **crisis** consists of unplanned events that have the potential to disrupt normal organizational operations and endanger the mission.

Seamless and follow-up communication is crucial in crisis management situations. For example, on Saturday, January 13, 2018, the Hawaii Emergency Management Agency inadvertently dispatched a cell phone alert mistakenly warning of an incoming ballistic missile attack in the wake of an already tense situation between the United States and North Korea. Authorities revoked the alert 38 minutes after the broadcast.

Because of the error, confusion and alarm plagued Hawaii. The panic resulted in 2.5 times the typical medical emergency calls, over 5,000 calls to the Honolulu Police Department, a heart attack, numerous hospitalized people due to falls from people running, and two known vehicle accidents. There were reports of children going down manholes, stores closing their doors to people seeking shelter, and cars driving at high speeds.

This example emphasizes the importance of redundancy apparatuses and timely updates for crisis management systems. The mistaken alert as well as the untimely correction resulted in damage, injuries, and expenses that could have been worse.

Figure 5.2 How an Organization Handles a Crisis Can Be a Matter of Survival

There are different ways to categorize crises. Although many of these crises overlap, the following is an attempt to highlight some of the key types (Lerbinger, 1997; Management Study Guide, 2017).

Allegations of Discrimination and Prejudice Crisis: This crisis occurs when there are allegations about the organization being involved in practices that foster discrimination and prejudice in the workplace. This crisis can lead to legal and civil actions, the departure of talented employees, stymied organizational activities, and revenues may suffer.

Bankruptcy Crisis: This pertains to an organization becoming financially unstable in which it cannot pay its creditors and other parties. The future becomes uncertain, employees may leave, and other companies may refuse to do business with the organization.

Confrontation Crisis: This crisis arises from organizational in-fighting whether formal or informal or from external conflict. Organizational members may attempt to damage morale by circulating ill-found rumors about the company or brand, become uncooperative, less motivated, and eventually boycott or strike the organization. Employees disobey superiors and make demands and issue deadlines for those demands. Such a protracted situation often endangers the organization. Many of these issues are due to lack of effective communication. For instance, the Chicago area tainted Tylenol containers were an attempt to hurt the company. The Nike boycott owing to its overseas labor practices is another example.

Crisis due to Workplace Violence: Violent acts constitute beating employees, sexual assault, and other physical acts on the premises.

Crisis of Deception: Deception involves management intentionally tampering with data and information so that they can make unfounded fake promises and ill-advised commitments to customers. Conveying inaccurate information about the organization and products leads to this situation. Whether or not they rise to the level of illegality, it challenges the organization's ethics. An example is VW's falsification of the emissions readings in their diesel engine vehicles.

Crisis of Internal Malevolence: This crisis pertains to employees, including management, engaging in criminal activities to fulfill their job requirements. False rumors about stocks, sabotaging operations, over-billing customers, and falsifying records or tax documents are instances of malevolence. Job pressures and unrealistic job expectations can encourage these types of activities. Management may conduct illegal activities such as bribery, passing on propriety information, and so forth.

Crisis of Organizational Misdeeds: Misdeeds occur when management make decisions knowing the harmful consequences of their actions towards stakeholders. Superiors turn a blind eye and allow the implementation of deleterious policies designed to produce quick results. Short-term issues prevail at the expense of broader longer-term goals. These misdeeds raise questions about the organization's values.

Natural Crisis: These crises are natural events generally beyond the control of humanity. Tornadoes, earthquakes, hurricanes, landslides, tsunamis, floods, and droughts are examples of natural disasters.

Smoldering Crisis: Management ignores the initial signs of an impending crisis. The crisis thus smolders until it fully blossoms and is out of control. One instance of a smoldering crisis was General Motors' reluctance to acknowledge and address the ignition switch defect in its vehicles. Other examples are the Chernobyl nuclear disaster and the ExxonMobil Valdez oil spill.

Sudden Crisis: This type of crisis occurs suddenly and at short notice. The situation is often out of the organization's control. An example is BP's Deepwater Horizon oil spill.

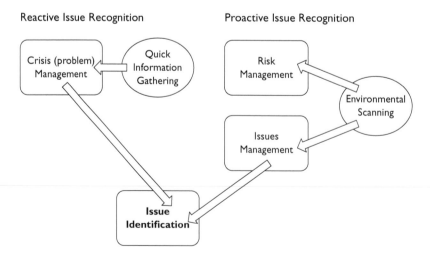

Figure 5.3 The Issue Identification Process

Technological and Accident Crisis: A technological crisis is the result of a failure in technology. Equipment failure, power loss, industrial accidents, corrupted software, and software safety vulnerabilities cause technological crises.[1] These types of crises are becoming ever more complex to diagnose and address owing to the complicated nature and interdependent relationships of the different facets of our technological world.

Proactive Issue Recognition

While surveilling the environment and relevant stakeholders on a regular basis to prepare for potential situations, opportunities and problems present themselves. This allows the public relations practitioner to identify and respond to situations before they become unmanageable. This process calls for two types of management.

Risk management identifies and develops plans for responding to uncertain situations that, yet, have not become issues that impact an organization. There is coordination across departments within an organization. This work involves calculating the probability of a situation becoming an issue. For example, practitioners may surveil potential legislation that might have a negative impact on a company's profits.

A current risk management topic is climate change. Insurance companies regularly assess the probability of catastrophic weather conditions occurring so that they can forecast and plan for future claims payouts. The Department of Defense conducts climate change risk assessments and management as a matter of national security. Extreme weather can threaten military bases and limit access to vital resources necessary to defend the country. The various Defense Department sections share information and resources, including public affairs, to plan and to communicate action plans during such events as Hurricane Harvey.

Figure 5.4 Issue Management Addresses a Situation Before It Becomes a Crisis

Although risk management can provide more analysis, once a risk management concern materializes, it becomes an issue and a matter for **issues management**, which is a long-term proactive and systematic approach that monitors, anticipates degree, and evaluates issues that could impact the organization positively or negatively. Response planning uses this information. Think about the legislation example above. If the legislation in the example were to become law, then it would become a concern for issue management.

The risk and issues management process allows time to optimize decision-making. For example, over the years, trends have developed about employment opportunities for individuals covered under the Americans with Disabilities Act (ADA). Vanguard organizations consider ADA requirements in their plans for future facilities, thus saving financial resources over the long term as well as being able to capitalize on this pool of talented human capital.

Other trends center on social issues, the environment, and sustainability. Organizations such as Habitat for Humanity and Maxwell House coffee; Dove and breast cancer prevention; and Product RED and fighting AIDS in Africa, partner with other organizations to engage different social issues. These affiliations enhance an organization's image in the public's eye.

Think about This . . .

In a 2011 *PR Week* article entitled "Without Solid Comms, Occupy Wall Street Lacks Staying Power," Bernadette Casey wrote that the Occupy Wall Street movement could not sustain itself because of its inability to leverage its initial momentum into a clear strategic and credible core message. The article suggested that Occupy Wall Street's failure to develop a central message resulted in the movement protestors viewed as a group of the "disenfranchised" with no clear goal, which eroded the movement's credibility.

Casey suggested that third party credible groups such as politicians, trade groups, and businesses could have provided support and credibility to the movement. The lack of these vital partnerships only weakened it.

An April 2018 visit to the web page http://occupywallst.org/about/ revealed little current activity but numerous references to 2011 activities. It appears that Casey's assessment was accurate.

Ask yourself: As a public relations professional, what advice would you have given the Occupy Wall Street movement? What groups would you have approached to become advocates and voices for the movement?

Casey, B. (2011). Without solid comms, Occupy Wall Street lacks staying power. *PR Week, 14*(12), 24.

Environmental Scanning

I opened this chapter discussing the importance of understanding the situation. Keeping abreast of the situation requires regularly scanning the environment. "**Environmental scanning** is the acquisition and use of information about events, trends, and relationships in an organization's external (and internal) environments, the knowledge of which would assist management in planning the organization's future course of action" (Choo, 2001, pp. 1–2). It is a function of risk and issue management.

I would add that regularly scheduled scanning not only identifies situations (e.g. events and trends) and issues, but also provides valuable information about how they can affect organizational stakeholders. The importance of the issue centers on its potential impact on the organization's mission and key stakeholders.

Further, environmental scanning is intra-organizational and/or externally focused. Situational complexity affects the level of scanning, which ranges from informal one-on-one discussions to highly involved methods such as the Scan by SBI described later in this chapter.

Why is environmental scanning important? According to Abels (2002),

> All organizations need to monitor at some level what goes on in their environments and recognize their strengths and weaknesses in relation to it. The importance of environmental information depends on the degree to which the success of the organization itself depends on its environment. In the business literature, this dependency of the organization on its environment is referred to as perceived environmental uncertainty (PEU). Gordon and Narayanan (1984) identified factors that determine PEU. These factors include the nature of the society, economic stability, legal stability, political constraints, the nature of the industry, the customer base, and the nature of the organization.
>
> (p. 1)

Figure 5.5 Environment Scanning Detects Situations that Can Become Issues

One approach to environmental scanning consists of surveilling six separate sectors, which are political, economic, social, technological, legal and environment (PESTLE). Another schema is based on Porter's Five Forces. These five areas explain why different industries sustain different levels of profitability. The five forces are competition in the industry, potential of new entrants into an industry, power of suppliers, power of customers, and threat of substitutes.

Some experts recommend quarterly environmental scans for organizations of any size. Whether an environmental scan uses PESTLE or Porter's Five Forces, information from the scan can help organizations take advantage of opportunities before competitors do, address threats before they become major problems, and adjust organizational strategy to meet changing demands in the marketplace.

Albright (2004) lists a number of informational sources for scanning. The **internal information sources** are:

- personal contacts
- internal reports
- conference papers
- marketing-related information
- any research
- internal memos
- committee/meetings
- sales staff
- other managers
- other employees
- internal databases.

The **external information sources** are:

- personal contact
- journals/magazines
- books
- newspapers
- professional conferences/meetings
- radio, televisions, and internet
- professional colleagues
- customers
- secondary research such as benchmarking reports
- commercial databases.

Environmental scanning can take different forms. This chapter will focus on one method primarily useful for external scanning and another used for organizational members. Chapter 4 covers additional research methodologies.

Text network analysis (TNA) (Vieira & Grantham, 2017) is a content analysis method that takes large amounts of text and distills meaning from words in relation to other words, clusters of words, and the entire text under examination. This method is based on network principles and weighs word importance based on its location in the text and its connections to other words. TNA has the potential for extensive usage in public

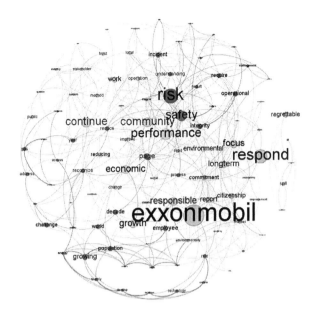

Figure 5.6 Text Network Analysis Is a Self-Contained World of Organized Words that Present Central Messages

relations research including big data applications. It is applied to speeches, social media such as Twitter and Facebook, blogs, books, discussion forums, reports, and as well as observational and interaction analysis. TNA can identify social influencers in social media as well as discover what topics those leaders influence. Results are quickly generated.

Figure 5.6 is a word network depiction of Rex Tillerson's introductory letter to ExxonMobil's Corporate Citizen Report for 2012 (Grantham & Vieira, 2018).

The **internal communication audit** is a useful research method to uncover organizational issues. There are two key components. First, there is an examination of the formal and informal ways employees communicate. The formal hierarchy does not often represent the full story of internal communication. It does not include conversations at the proverbial water cooler. Second, a communication audit gauges what employees think and feel about an issue such as attitudes about a forthcoming merger, the state of morale in the organization, beliefs about the organization's leadership, and many other internally related issues or challenges. If properly conducted, an internal communication audit can identify an issue and the opinions of stakeholder groups about that issue.

To be effective, a third party should conduct the internal communication audit. This is important for a number of reasons. First, in principle, a third party has no hidden agenda or conflicting self-interest. Second, a third party brings a fresh perspective to the issue compared to those who are part of the organization and in the fray of things. Third, organizational members are more likely to express their true responses to an objective third party who holds feedback in confidence. Consequently, the communication audit report holds a degree of credibility.

The methods for collecting this information vary and usually involve techniques depending on the urgency to define and address the issue. An audit involves interviews, focus groups, TNA, and combinations of these data collection methods. Regularly scheduled communication audits are a valuable internal environmental scanning tool, including interim truncated versions focusing on "watch items."

Issue Identification Steps

The process of issue identification should include the issue and sub-issues as well as prioritizing the relevant stakeholders by their importance to the organization and the impact of the issue on them. Keep in mind, that problems may also offer opportunities. For example, in a case where counterfeit iPhone chargers were sold in China, Apple took advantage of not only removing the fake Apple chargers from the market, but also brought those who turned in the chargers to the Apple store as new customers thus increasing its customer base in China. In another example, the IBM On Demand program not only provides software solutions to local communities, but also increase awareness of its product line in those communities.

Although the problem statement is 1–2 sentences, the following situational analysis steps provide a clear understanding and identify the key aspects of a public relations issue. The information discovered informs campaign development and planning. The weight of each item is contingent upon the situation, gravity of the issue, and time constraints. Not all aspects play a role in all situations. Differentiating key aspects of the issue and its symptoms are supported with evidence.

1 *Identify the key issue whether a problem and/or opportunity. (a) Indicate any problem components, (b) where it is occurring or occurred, and/or (c) when it started.* Provide a brief history of the organization as it relates to the issue. How does the issue impact the organization and its mission? The issue may involve legislation affecting the organization's product line. The competition may have launched a new brand extension that competes with the organization's core line. A company may be experiencing high turnover. The acquisition of a competitor may open new markets for the company's expanded product and brand lines. A competitor's product recall may provide opportunities to increase market share. The issue can positively or negatively impact the organization's mission and competitiveness. Its effects on the organization should be determined from a standpoint of its stakeholders as well as the mission.

(a) *If any, indicate the issue's components.* Some issues are multifaceted, which requires addressing all the components to develop an effective response. Sometimes the public relations professional must coordinate efforts with other departments and organizations. For instance, recalling a defective product necessitates not only the dissemination of the recall notice, but a termination of all product distribution and promotions by contacting distributors, wholesalers and retailers, and sometimes governmental agencies. The successful coordinated effort of all parties will help assure recall compliance.

(b) *Discover where the issue is occurring.* Ascertaining the birth of the issue may help reveal its root causes. The location and degree of the issue affect public relations planning. Different demographics and different geographic locations often need customized messaging for the various stakeholder groups. Where the issue is prevalent and where it is not might reveal important information such as clues as to ways to enhance or mitigate issue support.

(c)   *Indicate when the issue started.* Knowing when an issue started may help determine the cause and other interdependent factors. The circumstances at the time when the issue manifested itself may have changed. The issue may have changed. A fluid situation demands careful attention especially in crisis situations where an event was unanticipated.

2   *Determine the cause(s) of the issue.* Uncover the key reasons for the issue's existence. The issue may have started because of a convergence of items that singularly would not cause it, but together, they trigger it. They are like the grooves in a key that together at that very moment can unlock a door. For example, workers usually do not strike for a single reason. The factors that cause a strike can be low wages, cuts in benefits, and poor working conditions, topped by a personnel incident that causes workers to act.

3   *Identify stakeholders and learn what role they play regarding the issue.* Is the issue important to them? Are they important to the issue? Prioritize them based on these two points. The public relations function is about communicating to stakeholders in a manner that will result in an attractive issue outcome. Identify the stakeholder groups. Understand their roles in the issue from their perspective and from the viewpoint of the organization. Prioritize them based on their importance in achieving the public relations goal. This step is the topic of the next chapter.

4   *Do any symptoms of the issue affect the stakeholders?* Often issue symptoms can impact stakeholders either in a positive or negative manner. For instance, workers on strike in one facility results in increased overtime at another facility. These dynamics can affect perspectives on the issue.

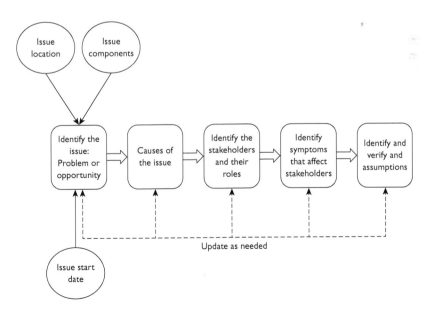

Figure 5.7 Update the Process as New Information Becomes Available, Which Requires Revised Information and New Analysis along These Steps

5   *If important, discover and verify any assumptions.* Consider assumptions that are potentially important to the issue or public relations campaign; assumptions by stakeholders as well as the public relations team. Solutions to the issue are often based on these assumptions because most decisions are imperfect owing to incomplete information. So, necessity often requires assumptions. At some level, assumptions should be "verified." Experience or common sense informs verification. Stakeholder false assumptions brought to light about an issue can change issue dynamics. Assumptions can change over time. New circumstance can invalidate an assumption.

6   *Keep the information current and update as needed.* Again, we live in time and situations change over time. Information becomes dated and stakeholder positions change.

Chapter 6 covers stakeholder analysis in greater detail.

Reporting Issues

The situational analysis starts with a brief history of the organization and situation including the issue. Next, systematically cover the nine steps as noted in the section immediately above, one at a time each under its own heading. These steps present a complete understanding of the issue.

Issue Definition Example

The following is an application of the issue definition steps as it pertains to Nike's overseas employment practices years ago.

1   *Identify the key issue as a problem and/or opportunity. a) Indicate the issue, b) where it is occurring or occurred, and/or c) when it started.* **Mostly during 1994 to 1997, Nike ran sweatshops overseas, which inspired human rights groups to launch an anti-Nike campaign**. Allegedly, the company underpaid, overworked, and mistreated employees. **As the news media began covering the story, over time**, the campaign **gained traction (see stakeholder groups)**. The negative publicity could have potentially resulted in customers boycotting Nike products thus impacting revenues.

2   *Determine the cause(s) of the issue.* Nike's competitors engaged in similar labor practices. Why was Nike singled-out? (1) Nike was the largest sports footwear brand and **widely recognized globally**. (2) The **media reported high profile endorsement contract for large amounts of money juxtaposed with low wages** for overseas factory workers. (3) Initially **Nike executives ignored the issue** because they thought it would dissipate. To the contrary, it gained momentum. (4) With the **advent of the internet, the Nike story disseminated expeditiously**. In short, the perception of Nike was that of the great, big exploiter of low-wage workers for the sake of profits.

3   *Identify stakeholders and learn what role they play regarding the issue. What choices do they have concerning the issue?* The stakeholders, in order of "net" importance to Nike, are **customers, students and their organizations, stockholders (especially institutional), human rights groups, employees in overseas factories, factory owners/managers, news media, those holding the endorsement contracts, governments, and other vendors**. Keep in mind, since it affects many other publics given its dissemination of stories and information about the issue, the intervening media public is on the list. In any case, Nike's customers were the key stakeholder group. They included students,

many of whom were committed to social issues and participated in college-based human rights organization chapters and events. Second, institutional investors were concerned about their public image and being associated with a company that exploits its workers. Third, international human rights organizations with resources to monitor, research, and report abuses to the news media and other interested parties were an organized and formable stakeholder group. Fourth, any genuine effort to alleviate worker abuses would involve the workers. Their participation and public testimony to fair labor practices were crucial. Fifth, if meaningful reform were to take place, factories needed to cooperate and commit to reform. Negative publicity could affect their relationship with other footwear customers. Sixth, the news media needed to be convinced so that they might report objectively and favorably about Nike's efforts. Seventh, any endorsement withdrawals would fuel negative publicity. Nike's negative publicity could impact celebrities, who endorsed the brand. They were concerned about being associated with Nike's reported labor practices, and thus they risked damaging their personal brand. They would need to be convinced of Nike's commitment. Eighth, dubious labor practices could facilitate government investigations exploring violations of labor and other laws. Because of this, government regulators were relevant. Last, Nike's vendors were concerned about being guilty by association. Allaying their concerns was important. Practitioners may prioritize these stakeholder groups differently for valid reasons. This case simply serves as an example.

4   *Do any symptoms of the issue affect the stakeholders?* **Inaccurate perceptions of the issue and situation that imply company insensitivity to the workers' plight** could negatively affect profit and stock value.

5   *If important, discover and verify any assumptions.* Assumptions serve as the basis of perception and perception becomes reality. The human rights groups, news media, and public **perceived that Nike owns and operates the overseas factories, which was not the case. The factories were under contract with Nike**. Their operations and practices varied.

6   *Keep the information current and update as needed.* Nike took steps to alleviate the labor practices of its contractors including investing in the local communities where it operated overseas. **The situation improved over 6–12 months**.

An Example of Environmental Scanning: The Scan by SBI

There are firms that provide online environmental scanning services. Some firms provide comprehensive and customized services while others offer software solutions with varying degrees of customer service. SBI's **Scan** environmental spanning product is one such example.

Scan is a continuous, multidisciplinary process that globally harvests seminal events in the chaotic external environment in which businesses operate. In successive steps, the Scan process identifies underlying currents likely to have an impact on future developments. Scan strives to provide early alerts about emerging issues that so far haven't found recognition in the business community.

Scan's approach distills chaotic and unstructured events into focused and structured early alerts, which enable clients to influence changes proactively and obtain a head start on emerging threats and opportunities.

(SBI, The Scan Process, 2017, para. 1–2)

Scan follows systematic steps as illustrated in Figure 5.8.

Step 1: General scanning identifies dynamic and uncertain environments.

Step 2: A Scan multidisciplinary team proactively and continuously searches for events, signs of change, disruptions, and unusual factors where change can happen. These factors include consumer behavior, government regulations, politics, business processes, cultural events and trends, public opinion, and scientific and technology developments, which are like the PESTLE framework and reported in abstract form.

Step 3: Experts attend monthly "Scan" meetings on the three major global market continents to ascertain patterns among industries, geographical regions, topics, and their impact on organizations, markets, and industries.

Step 4: Topic experts evaluate and condense these developments into monthly "Signals of Change" reports so that this information provides usable insights for clients across industries, functions, and fields.

Step 5: Scan provides customized "Signals" to clients focusing on specific issues and goals. Additional services are available through SBI Consulting Services.

In sum, monthly abstracts of the current situation from key information sources, a report on the top 12 monthly environmental patterns, a report on the top six Signals of Change, a synopsis of the monthly Scan topic experts' discussion, and conclusions from the monthly meeting are the deliverables (Scan Services, 2017).

Other companies that offer different types and levels of environmental scanning include infoAnalytics, Inc., Just the Facts, Inc., Marketing Analytics International, Inc., McKinsey & Company, SIS International Research, and TrendSource.

The Scan Concept: The Scan Process

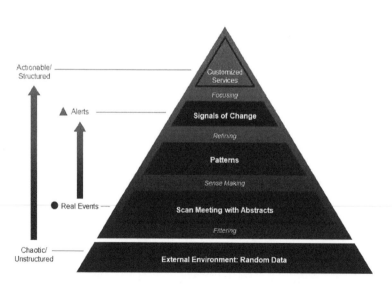

Figure 5.8 SBI's Scan Process. Special Thanks to SBI Scan Director Martin Schwirn for Providing This Illustration

Some Final Thoughts

Don't be a "solution" in search of a problem. Organizational members in general, even within the public relations function, develop new tools that seem to apply to everything or are accustomed to using the same issue-related practices. Each situation may have similarities, but they also have differences, whether nuanced or stark. So that there are optimal solutions to the problem, defining the problem is based on objective, evidence supported reality. Social media do not define every public relations issue. Negative publicity is not always associated with lobbying. The uniqueness of the situation informs issue definition and ultimately the development of solutions. In sum, these public relations factors related to issue identification and definition are an excellent start to understanding and practicing strategic public relations.

Summary of Key Concepts

- The public relations issue is either a problem or opportunity.
- A public relations problem can become an opportunity.
- Issue recognition can be reactive or proactive.
- Crisis issues are largely reactive situations.
- Crises come in different varieties.
- Risk and issues management provide a heads up about what issues may be developing and thus are important so that contingency planning can take place.
- Environmental scanning is a tool that provides advance warning and information about issues and trends.
- Problem definition consists of nine considerations.

In the Case of Canyon Ranch . . . Introduction of the Issue

Canyon Ranch is a world destination health spa and hotel resort established in 1979. Its mission is to create a place where people turn their "healthiest thoughts" into lifestyle habits through wonderful experiences while enjoying a relaxing vacation. The company has expanded with two destination resorts one located in Lenox, Massachusetts and the other in Tucson, Arizona as well as two SpaClubs all in the United States. The resort attracts 17,000 visitors annually. The focus of this case is the Lenox location.

The Health and Healing department, which sets Canyon Ranch apart from its competitors, is a potential source of growth; yet, it was underperforming. Canyon Ranch intends to increase sales of the Health and Healing department at the Lenox location, while continuing the same level of quality and premium level of service at its spa, fitness center, salon, and hotel services, all of which face strong competition.

The Canyon Ranch public relations campaign centers on promoting the resort and its programs with an emphasis on health and healing services. The promotional campaign is a 12-month effort directed at key publics.

Key Terms

Crisis 116

Crisis management 116

Environmental scanning 120

External information sources 122

Internal communication
   audit 123

Internal information sources 122

Issue 116

Issues management 120

Problem 116

Risk management 119

Scan™ 127

Situation 115

Text network analysis (TNA) 122

Chapter Questions

5.1   What is an issue and provide an example?

5.2   What is a problem and offer an example?

5.3   Define crisis management.

5.4   Define a crisis and offer an example.

5.5   Define what is an allegation of discrimination and prejudice crisis.

5.6   What is a confrontation crisis?

5.7   What is a crisis of internal malevolence?

5.8   Define what is a smoldering crisis.

5.9   What is a sudden crisis?

5.10   What is reactive issue recognition and provide an example?

5.11   What is proactive issue recognition and provide an example?

5.12   What is risk management?

5.13   What is issues management?

5.14   Define a situation.

5.15   Define environmental scanning.

5.16   Why is environmental scanning important?

5.17   What is PESTLE?

5.18   What are Porter's Five Forces?

5.19   Name five internal sources of information.

5.20   Name five external sources of information.

5.21   What is text network analysis?

5.22   What is an internal communication audit?

5.23   What are the six aspects for defining a public relations issue?

5.24   What is SBI's Scan product?

Note

1 Contrasting views of high reliability theorists vs. normal accident theorists address the debate about whether we can safely harness technology.

References

Abels, E. (2002). Environmental Scanning. *Bulletin of the American Society for Information and Technology*, February/March, 16–18.

Albright, K. S. (2004). Environmental scanning: Radar for success. *The Information Management Journal*, May/June, 38–44.

Casey, B. (2011). Without solid comms, occupy wall street lacks staying power. *PR Week,* *14*(12), 24.

Choo, C. W. (2001). Environmental scanning as information seeking and organizational learning. *Information Research,* 7(1), 1–37.

Grantham, S., & Vieira, E. T., Jr. (2018). Do external events influence subsequent social responsibility (SR) messaging? *Applied Environmental Education & Communication,* *17*(3), 266–279.

Greene, R. J. (1986). *Creatively managing your mind.* Educational Transactions of the 8th Annual IAQC Spring Conference (pp. 62–68). Published by International Association of Quality Circles. (Verified with scans; thanks to Don MacDonald and the Harvard Business School, Baker Library).

Lerbinger, O. (1997). *The crisis manager: Facing risk and responsibility.* Mahwah, NJ: Erlbaum.

Management Study Guide. (2017). *Crisis management: Types of crises.* Retrieved from www.managementstudyguide.com/types-of-crisis.htm.

Scan Services. (2017). *Strategic Business Insights.* Retrieved from www.strategicbusinessinsights.com/scan/services.shtml.

The Scan Process. (2017). *Strategic Business Insights.* Retrieved from www.strategicbusinessinsights.com/scan/process.shtml .

Vieira, E. T., Jr., & Grantham, S. (2017). A new content analysis methodology appropriate for CSR communication. Final editing. In A. Lindgreen, J. Vanhamme, F. Maon, & and R. Watkins (Eds.), *The use and effectiveness of CSR communications through digital platforms: A research anthology.* London: Routledge.

Chapter 6

Situational Analysis
Defining Stakeholders

I was talking to one of the writers about our target audience, and he was insulted that I used that term. But if you're given $60 million to make a film, you'd better know who your target audience is. That's who's going to pay back the bills you run up.

(Michael Bay, Diamond, 1996, para. 5)

Learning Objectives

To:

- Understand who are stakeholders.
- Differentiate what are stakeholders, internal vs. external stakeholders, publics, intervening publics, audiences, constituents, and market segments.
- Explain the role of opinion leaders and media as intervening publics.
- Describe the basis for differentiating stakeholders in terms of an issue.
- Understand the considerations for prioritizing publics.
- Describe the underpinnings for segmenting stakeholder groups by common characteristics.
- Write-up profile of publics.

Introduction

The purpose of the situational analysis is to understand and describe the issue and the relevant publics. The **situation** is the environment in which an issue exists. As discussed in the last chapter, part of defining an issue involves discovering and sufficiently defining the publics pertinent to the issue. A keen understanding of an organization's stakeholders and especially of its publics informs an effective public relations campaign. This chapter defines stakeholders, publics, and other groups. Also covered are prioritizing publics and writing up profiles. We start by examining different ways of thinking about stakeholders.

Public Relations Target Groups: Who Are They?

From a public relations perspective, we are concerned with communicating to the various groups important to an issue and organization. These groups may be important now or in the future. Initially, organizationally related groups may not be a concern; however, once they mobilize around an issue, then they become a focus of concern.

Figure 6.1 Trust Is the Foundation of Stakeholder Relationships

There are different kinds of groups. Their level of knowledge and involvement in an issue can vary among groups as well as within their group. The major kinds of public relations groups are stakeholders, publics, constituents, market segments, audiences, and internal/external types. Although definitions vary, there is general consensus on what constitutes each group. As the discussion progresses, you will see why the term "stakeholder" captures the relationship aspect of groups to the organization and that "public" is more about the connection of groups to an issue.

Stakeholders

Stakeholders can be individuals or organizations. In either case, they comprise a group with shared characteristics. Stakeholders have an ongoing relationship with the organization. The organization affects them and they affect the organization. They possess varying amounts of knowledge about an issue depending on the issue. Stakeholder issue engagement varies as well. Suffice to say, the key point is that they have some type of connection to the organization and will likely be involved with issues that concern them. The priority assigned to them concerning an issue is based on their importance to the organization and level of issue involvement.

For example, a list of hospital stakeholder groups typically includes the following:

- patients
- physicians
- nurses
- administrators
- patient family and friends
- support and technical staff
- professional associations/accreditation organizations
- board of trustees
- state regulators
- insurance carriers

- vendors and suppliers
- contractors
- affiliations
- donors.

Although these groups may not be involved or concerned with every major hospital-related issue, there is a connection with some aspect of the hospital. For instance, an internal campaign to raise organizational morale would not involve state regulators, insurance carriers, vendors and suppliers, contractors, affiliations, and donors, but would focus on employees.

Publics

A **public** consists of individuals or organizations with shared interests and attributes. Publics mobilize or self-organize around an issue and, therefore, exist for the duration of the issue. A stakeholder group that mobilizes because of an issue is a public who is involved with an issue. This public understands the issue and wants to address it. Publics can be communities, **special interest groups (SIGs)**, and other groups with a cause. A SIG is a community within a larger organization who shares an interest in advancing a

Figure 6.2 Activism Comes in Many Forms and for Many Reasons

specific area of knowledge. Community members cooperate and often produce solutions within their particular expertise as it relates to an issue.

Publics thrive in environments conducive to activism. Activism is the core element of publics. **Activism** is the creation and maintenance of a shared collective identity among individuals for a time with the intention to influence a problem, causing an entity to act through engagement of various sorts.

For example, because of a crisis such as the BP Deepwater Horizon oil spill in the Gulf of Mexico, publics emerged such as the formation of environmental and other groups engaged in the cleanup. Some publics were initially stakeholders, while others had no connection to the organization until the issue materialized and then they organized in response to it. As a public, the connection is around an issue.

To compare, stakeholders typically maintain long-term relationships with an organization. Publics are usually short-term focused, but can become institutionalized resulting in stakeholder status. A company may create a permanent position on an advisory board for a SIG human rights representative to place an objective eye on its extensive overseas labor operations triggered by negative publicity about isolated instances of questionable labor practices.

Key publics are of paramount importance for a public relations campaign. These are publics necessary to achieve the public relations goal.

In 1982, eight Tylenol murders resulted from someone lacing acetaminophen capsules with potassium cyanide in the Chicago area. Johnson & Johnson, who owned the Tylenol brand, responded quickly by warning the public and removing Tylenol capsules from retail shelves. The publics were:

- retail consumers
- retailers
- manufacturing
- media
- marketing department
- wholesalers
- law enforcement
- department of health authorities
- vendors.

In this case, the noted publics would play a key role in removing the product from the market, informing other publics about the tainted product, and preventing additional injuries or deaths. All aspects of marketplace distribution and communication were involved including consumers, retailers, wholesalers, and authorities. The retailers and wholesalers were critical because the product had to be immediately removed from the shelves.

Internal and External Stakeholders

Internal stakeholders are groups within an organization. They can be employees, contract workers, or volunteers. For example, sale associates, customer service representatives, members of a specific department, line supervisors, managers, division heads, and so forth all have a stake in the organization. Categorizing internal publics is easier than external ones because there are a finite number of public members and they are readily identifiable.

Internal publics are likely to be issue focused regardless of many of their geographic, demographic, and psychographic characteristics. Therefore, knowing their attitudes, beliefs, and other perceptions about an issue are vital. Human resources departments use informal and formal techniques to collect information that leads to distinguishing internal publics. Chapter 4 discusses specific information gathering techniques.

External stakeholders are external publics such as customers, vendors, competitors, distributors, wholesalers, banks, franchisees, government regulators, potential employees, media, voters, trade associations, labor unions, nongovernmental organizations (NGOs), SIGs, and any other group that affects the organization or that the organization affects.

Often public relations campaigns involve both internal and external publics. For instance, externally a product recall includes publics such as the customers who own the product, media to get the word out, as well as retailers, wholesalers, and distributors in the channels of distribution; internally, publics include those responsible for returns and storage, product credit, and are responsible for customer service throughout the process.

Another example concerns corporate social responsibility (CSR). Larger CSR programs include a CSR officer or coordinator and the relevant internal parties such as volunteer recruitment, donations, services/products provided, as well as external publics related to the CSR effort whether special interest groups, nongovernmental organizations, local communities, customers, and vendors. The Xerox Foundation's Community Involvement Program has enabled 13,000 employees to participate in over 800 community-based programs. Since 2010, Target has donated more than $1 billion worth of books, school supplies, food, and field trips to students and schools across the United States and the world. These endeavors require the participation of both internal and external publics.

News Media as a Stakeholder

The news media, like opinion leaders, is an intervening stakeholder. They provide information to the public about the issue. Media serve to persuade individuals to support or oppose an issue through its opinion/editorial activities and the framing of issue coverage. Over time, the media have moved from first level agenda-setting, in which they report what is important, to second level agenda-setting, where they report in a manner that affects how people think or feel about an issue (Sones, Grantham & Vieira, 2009).

Public relations practitioners such as the media relations manager maintain long-term relationships with members of the news media. They provide media with information both on and off the record that affects news coverage in a way that generates favorable publicity toward the organization.

Opinion Leaders as a Public

An intervening public can inform other publics about an issue. The extent to which this public is perceived as objective and knowledgeable provides a degree of credibility. Other publics rely on intervening publics for their information about an issue and base their opinions on this information. Here again, like the news media, the opinion leader's recommendations and how he or she presents information influences attitudes about an issue.

Opinion leaders are an intervening public for both internal and external publics. They are a credible source of information for others. Opinion leaders are formal or informal. **Formal opinion leaders** are in professional positions such as tax assessors,

Figure 6.3 An Opinion Leader's Position on an Issue Extends to Followers

safety engineers, physicians, or union leaders. They are in structured roles of authority. A prospective home buyer asking a real estate agent about local communities that have lower property tax rates or a physician asked to recommend a specialist are examples of formal opinion leaders exercising their influence. **Informal opinion leaders** are not in a formal position. The basis of their relationships with followers is informal, social, and less structured. In social media, informal opinion leaders are **social influencers**. Informal opinion leaders can provide opinions on a single or range of topics contingent upon the nature of the opinion leader.

They can be average individuals or celebrities. For example, a person is sought for advice on what type of cell phone service to purchase based on her self-taught technical expertise. For the public relations practitioner, a neutral opinion leader, or better still, winning over opinion leaders is an objective. Having a social influencer in the organization's corner translates into winning over others as well.

Constituents

Constituents are a stakeholder group. According to Hallahan (2000), **constituents** are "groups (such as voters) that an organization serves and to whom the organization is ethically and legally responsible" (p. 501). Constituents usually relate to stakeholders or publics served by a governmental entity that provides goods or services to segments of the population. For example, voters whose children attend public schools are a constituent. They expect quality education provided in a safe environment. Should expectations fall short, they would pressure elected officials to address any deficiencies. Other examples of services are bridge and road repairs, sufficient law enforcement in neighborhoods, and the maintenance of parks and recreational facilities.

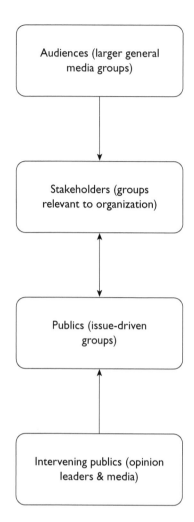

Figure 6.4 Public Relations Types of Groups

Figure 6.4. The bidirectional arrow between stakeholder groups and publics indicates that once stakeholders become issue active, they become a public. Keep in mind, some mobilized publics had no prior connection to the organization until the issue came into existence.

Market Segments

A **market segment** is a specific defined market of consumers or potential customers for a product, brand, or service. For example, a market segment for smart cell phones might be 18–22-year-old undergraduate university students in the U.S.A. comprising 14 million people. Attributes based on their personal characteristics; ability to buy; psychology (values, beliefs, and attitudes); lifestyles; media habits; and other behaviors are the bases for market differentiation. Although the focus is typically short term, there is a trend toward establishing longer-term relationships with consumers.

Audiences

An **audience** is a group of people exposed to a media message at a given time. They are usually larger than the number of members constituting a target public. So, reach does not represent only those members of a public exposed to a message at a given time. It pertains to the entire audience, even those exposed who are not members of the target public.

Think about This . . .

In a 2006 Institute for Public Relations Gold Standard white paper entitled "Prioritizing Stakeholders for Public Relations," Brad Rawlins presented four steps for prioritizing stakeholders in the context of a public relations-related situation. The first step focuses on identifying stakeholders, which can be done by discovering their control and authority over the organization; how essential they are to the organization; their common interest, shared values and beliefs with other stakeholders; and the nature of their involvement with the organization.

Step two involves prioritizing stakeholders according to their attributes. There are different kinds of the "stake" in stakeholders. Some stakeholders have ownership in the organization, others are economically dependent on the organization, in some cases, the organization may be dependent on other stakeholders, and some stakeholders are interested in seeing that the organization is socially responsible. The level of power, legitimacy, and urgency play an important role in advocating these types of stakes.

The third step prioritizes stakeholders by their level and nature of their involvement with the situation. Their engagement and level of support influence how they communicate in the context of the situation. They can be advocate, dormant, adversarial, or apathetic stakeholders.

As we can see, stakeholders can be prioritized by first defining them by their relationship to the organization, the stakes they have in the organization, and the level and nature of their engagement in the organization.

Ask yourself: Can you think of an actual or hypothetically situation in which to prioritize stakeholders? What factors might cause public relations practitioners to change priorities?

Rawlins, B. (2006). Prioritizing stakeholders for public relations. Published by the *Institute for Public Relations*. Retrieved from www.instituteforpr.org.

Defining Stakeholders by Shared Characteristics

The definition of stakeholders includes various criteria. This section describes appropriate ways to differentiate them. We will examine the basic differentiating categories followed by specific frameworks from which to segment. Specifically, external stakeholders are appropriate for this approach.

By segmenting relevant stakeholder/public members by shared attributes, we can predict the likelihood of how they will respond to messages. Ways of grouping stakeholders usually includes a combination of geographic, demographic, psychographic, behavioristic, and motigraphic characteristics. The classification includes similar media usage habits as well, which is helpful for determining media outlet placement.

Geographic

Geographic segmentation is defining a group based on physical location such as city, county, state, region, facility where someone works, department, company division, or some other boundary. The Nielsen Company has geographical regions of the United States organized by designated market areas (DMAs). The system combines geography and number of homes with television sets.

> A DMA region is a group of counties that form an exclusive geographic area in which the home market television stations hold a dominance of total hours viewed. There are 210 DMA regions, covering the entire continental United States, Hawaii, and parts of Alaska. The DMA boundaries and DMA data are owned solely and exclusively by The Nielsen Company.
>
> (Nielsen, 2013, para. 3)

For 2017 (Nielsen, *Local Television Market Universe Estimates*, 2016), the three largest DMAs are New York (7,348,620 TV homes, 6.41% of the population); Los Angeles (5,476,830 TV homes, 4.78%); and Chicago (3,463,060 TV homes, 3.02%). The three smallest DMAs are Glendive (4,370 TV homes, < 1%); North Platte (14,370 TV homes, 1.3%); and Alpena (16,010 TV homes, 1.4%).

Demographics

Demographic segmentation is a classification based on gender, age, educational background, marital status, ethnicity, religion, race, occupation, position within organization, functional position, position/job within an organization, income, and the like. For example, a demographic segment is all men and women, 18–24 who are undergraduate students in Canada of all ethnic backgrounds and religions, not married, with incomes less than $20,000 per year. Another example might be all human resource managers in the service sector in companies with more than 1,000 employees located in the United Kingdom. Sometimes researchers combine geographic and demographic segmentation.

Psychographics

Geographic and demographic types of segmentation are based on attributes not associated with psychological characteristics. **Psychographic segmentation** is based on defining publics according to lifestyle, values, beliefs, attitudes, and personality characteristics. The Strategic Business Insights VALS (About VALS, 2017) segments individuals by values, attitudes, and lifestyles into eight categories. VALS assists in producing message content. Using the eight types schema helps the public relations practitioner to effectively frame a message in the content of a public's values and belief systems. The Myers Briggs Type Indicator (MBTI) differentiates persons by personality and how they process information and make decisions (MBTI Basics, 2017). The MBTI assigns individuals into one of 16 categories based on their mental activities and provides a guide for message construction.

VALS

The **VALS** is a classification system of people based on an individual's primary motivation. One or more of three self-expressive motivations drive people. They are ideals, achievement, and self-expression. People identify with them. They also serve as the basis from which people make sense of the world. For instance, individuals motivated by ideals are likely moved by a call to action that somehow relates to his/her ideals such as a sense of doing what is right. Those motivated by achievement gravitate to a position or behavior that signals their success to others. Expressing achievements promotes and reinforces self-esteem. Last, messages that allow them to express themselves and their identity draw their attention.

The nature of primary motivation fulfillment and the degree of their achievement are contingent upon the availability of resources such as financial, time, access, and so forth. For this reason, in addition to psychographic information to assure consistent and successful messaging, it is essential to know demographic attributes.

The VALS comprises eight types of individuals based on their primary motivations, values, beliefs, and lifestyles, as well as accounting for the resources available to them.

Innovators

Innovators are successful, complex, in-charge people with high self-esteem. They possess all three primary motivations, which may exist at different levels. They have abundant resources. They are change agents (and can be opinion leaders) and are highly open to new ideas and

Figure 6.5 Lifestyles Are a Window to What People Value

innovative technologies. Challenges attract innovators. They purchase high-end products and brands, which include niche products and services. As a matter of self-expression, image is important to Innovators because it functions as an expression of taste, independence, and personality. These people are also well-established or emerging leaders in different sectors of society.

Thinkers

Ideals motivate **thinkers**. They are satisfied, mature, and comfortable in their lives. As the name suggests, they reflect on their lives and society. Thinkers value order, knowledge, and responsibility. Many of them are well-educated and informed about the world. Thinkers have a moderate level of respect for current institutions of authority and social norms; however, they are receptive to new ways of doing things. They have resources. Thinkers are generally conservative and pragmatic in their outlook. They make decisions that tend to be practical with long-lasting value.

Achievers

Goal-driven activities motivate **achievers**. They are committed to career and family. The center of their social life is family, worship, and work. They are conventional people who live conservative lives. Achievers respect authority and the status quo. They tend to be politically conservative. Consensus, predictability, and stability, closeness to others, and self-discovery are important to them. Achievers value an image that supports the establishment, prestige brands, products, and services that demonstrates their success to others. Time management is important to them owing to their frenetic schedules.

Experiencers

Self-expression drives **experiencers**. They are young, impulsive, and enthusiastic about new possibilities. They like variety, excitement, enjoying the new, the offbeat, and the risky. Their activities include exercise, sports, and social activities. Experiencers tend to spend a larger amount of their resources on fashion, entertainment, and socializing. They want to be cool. If the received message offers an opportunity for experiencers to show that they are cool, they will likely attend to it.

Believers

Ideals motivate **believers**. These are conservative and conventional individuals with concrete beliefs based on traditional, established codes for family, religion, community, and country. They rely on the tried and true. Believers follow established routines. They are predictable because they prefer and purchase familiar products and reliable brands that are American made. Typically, they are loyal to a specific brand. Winning this public to an issue would require linking them to tradition.

Strivers

Achievement drives **strivers**. This fun-loving public is trendy and attracted to fads. They seek peer approval. Money and materialism define their success. Strivers typically do not possess a sufficient amount of financial resources to meet their desires. They purchase higher-end products and brands to project a favorable impression about their status. Shopping is a social event for strivers. They often lack the education or training to advance their jobs or increase their income; thus, it is difficult for strivers to improve their lot. They prefer name brand clothing available at thrift stores. Appealing to impression management would be effective with this segment. Connecting a call for action with status would increase the likelihood of compliance.

Makers

Makers focus on self-expression. They communicate to the world about themselves and their experiences by building a house, raising children, and repairing a car. They are practical individuals who have constructive skills and believe in self-sufficiency. They have traditional families, do practical work, and engage in physical recreation. Makers are suspicious of innovations and big business. They respect government and organized labor. At the same time, they resent government intrusion on individual rights. They are unimpressed by material possessions other than those that serve a practical purpose. They focus on basic, functional items. Makers buy economical, value products, and have no interest in luxury brands. Appeals to this public should focus on functionality and value.

Survivors

Survivors are just that—survivors. This public has few resources and perceives the world as too fast and rapidly changing. Their focus is more on Maslow's lower level needs such as safety and security. They do not have any primary motivation. Survivors tend to be cautious. They will purchase their favorite brands especially when they are on sale, recycled, or repurposed.

Myers Briggs Type Indicator (MBTI)

The **MBTI** is a typology based on personality as represented by four mental habits. It profiles publics according to their preference for interacting with others (introvert or extrovert), how they process information (intuitive or sensor), the human element of decision-making (thinker or feeler), and the nature of their decision-making in the world (judger or perceiver). There are 16 MBTI types based on one of two types for each of the four mental habits. Defining publics by the MBTI can provide insights about a person's personality and aid the construction of messages that appeal to a specific personality type.

Extroversion or Introversion: Preferred Interaction with Others

According to MBTI research, there are approximately 50% extroverts (E) and 50% introverts (I) in the world. This mental habit focuses on the flow of an individual's energy. An **extrovert**'s energy flows outward. This person is outgoing and tends to think out loud. Extroverts are comfortable in crowds of strangers and enjoy introducing themselves to strangers. American culture values extroversion. On the other hand, an **introvert**'s energy flows inward. This type of person does not think out loud. Introverts prefer an agenda beforehand so that they can process the information in advance. They are comfortable around small groups of people who they know. Typically, theorists are introverts and salespeople are extroverts. Japan and the United Kingdom value introversion.

Intuitive or Sensor: The Nature of Information Processing

Sensors (S) comprise 55% of the world and intuitives (N) consist of 45%. **Sensors** are tacticians, operators, line supervisors, and managers. They are detail driven and concerned with planning with execution. They focus on concrete, sensory tasks. This segment thinks about the past, present, and matters that are practical. If one were selling an electric drill to a sensor, one would emphasize the features of the product such as price, warranty, number of speeds, reliability, durability, and so forth. An **intuitive** is a strategist, a leader. This is a big picture person who integrates the various aspects of an endeavor and inspires organizational members to what they can achieve. He/she is a visionary and future-oriented. Selling a drill to an intuitive would be most effective by focusing on the benefits, the holes. In other words, intuitives are concerned about the benefits derived from a product or a position. Engineers are sensors, while intuitives are strategic planners.

Feelers or Thinkers: The Nature of Decision-Making

Thinkers consist of 50% of the population and 50% are feelers. Although **thinkers** may consider the human impact of a decision, their decisions are based on logic and data. Decision-making considers financial costs and efficiency. The human impact is not in the decision-maker's calculation. **Feelers** factor the human cost in their decision. Harmony is an important consideration. Social workers are feelers and accountants are thinkers.

Judgers or Perceivers: Decision-Making in the World

Judgers are 55% of the world and perceivers consist of 45%. **Judgers** value order, planning, and decisive decision-making. They prefer information for decision-making presented in bullet form and will not hesitate to decide on an issue. Judgers do not let decisions linger. **Perceivers** require a thorough review of detailed information and research to make the "perfect" decision. Perceivers sometimes become trapped in nuances, and are often viewed

Table 6.1 The MBTI Types

ISTJ (12%)	**ISFJ** (8%)	**INFJ** (4%)	**INTJ** (6%)
Doing what should be done	A high sense of duty	An inspiration to others	Everything has room for improvement
ISTP (4%)	**ISFP** (4%)	**INFP** (4%)	**INTP** (4%)
Ready to try anything once	Sees much but shares little	Performing noble service to help society	A love of problem-solving
ESTP (3%)	**ESFP** (5%)	**ENFP** (8%)	**ENTP** (5%)
The ultimate realists	You only go around once in life	Giving life an extra squeeze	One exciting challenge after another
ESTJ (12%)	**ESFJ** (8%)	**ENFJ** (5%)	**ENTJ** (6%)
Life's administrators	Hosts and hostesses of the world	Smooth-talking persuaders	Life's natural leaders

Note: The percentages represent MBTI type estimates of the population.

Source: *Types*. (2016). *Changing Minds: Jungian Type Inventory*. Retrieved from http://changingminds.org/explanations/preferences/mbti.htm.

as procrastinators. In messaging to judgers, focus on the key points. Appeals to perceivers should include a great deal of information or at least provide the option to access more information.

The MBTI categories consist of 16 combinations of these four mental habits. Table 6.1 depicts the types. As we can see, introvert, sensor, thinker, and judger (ISTJ) and extrovert, sensor, thinker, and judger (ESTJ) each comprise the largest percentages (12%). These individuals tend to be practical and detail oriented. They are comfortable making data-driven decisions.

VALS and MBTI

We've heard the expressions that "Birds of a feather flock together" and "Opposites attract." So, which is it? The answer depends on what is the basis for the comparison. The VALS are about values, beliefs, and lifestyles. Individuals without such commonalities, would not "flock together." On the other hand, the MBTI is about personality-related mental habits. In this case, opposites may very well balance their relationships with others such as an introvert and extrovert, the planner and the spontaneous person, the visionary at work and those that will make that vision a reality, and the balance between organizational optimization and compassion.

The success of an organization may well be due to this delicate balance. It is in the interest of the public relations practitioners to uncover these relationships and involve these publics in the service of goal achievement whether internally, externally, or both.

Behavioristic

Behavioristic segmentation categorizes publics predicated on behaviors or behavioral responses to a message. Depending on the situation and issue, responses vary. The number of instances of behavioral compliance of an appeal, the status of the person complying, the readiness stage, and, in the case of marketing, product or brand loyalty are all components of behavioristic segmentation.

Let's discuss loyalty. **Loyalty** is devotion to a product, service, brand, or cause. It has three parts. First, loyalty requires a favorable attitude toward the organization or object of concern. Second, repeated pro-organizational or object behavior is a component of loyalty. For instance, a repeated action would be donating to a specific charity every year. Last, those loyal toward an organization become advocates for that organization. They spread positive word-of-mouth; they post favorable online reviews about the organization or brand for example. **Hardcore loyalty** is always being loyal to a single organization according to the definition described above. **Split loyalty** is loyalty to more than one organization.

Motigraphics

According to Maddock (2000), **motigraphics** is a method to discover, define, and measure human motives and desires. Motives are situationally based reasons for moving us to certain thoughts, feelings, and/or actions. "Without motigraphics, the marketer knows only two-thirds of what he or she needs to know about his or her customer . . . With motigraphics, demographics, and psychographics, the marketer knows it all" (pp. 5–6).

Maddock suggests that persons, places, and time orientation motives; spiritual, physical, territorial, and sexual survival motives; adaptation motives, expectation/resolution

Figure 6.6 People Are Motivated for Different Reasons

motives, and play motives are all drivers of behavior. Individuals with shared combinations of these motives form the basis of this segmentation approach.

Not only knowing and understanding a public's motives, but incorporating message content that speaks to these motives, will be effective to bring about support and action for a public relations message. For example, a campaign goal that allays concern about a company merger may find that one motive for being apprehensive about it is job security. Employees think that the merger will result in departmental consolidations and budget cuts. Addressing these issues early will make the transition less stressful for employees in both organizations. Chapter 3 covers motivation from various perspectives.

Data Resources for Segmenting Publics

There are many secondary and primary sources for segmenting the population. Below is a brief listing of some of the companies that offer a variety of services.

Market Research Insights (MRI)

Arbitron

Acxiom

Claritas

ESRI

Experian

MAPINFO

As illustrated in Figure 6.7, geographic segmentation helps the practitioner to determine the various venues for public relations activities on the basis for classification of publics. Defining publics by psychographics and motigraphics can assist in developing messages that will involve and move publics toward the public relations goal. Behavioristic information determines which media outlets publics visit so that those communication channels carry the public relations message.

Defining Public Relations Groups by Relationship to the Organization, Issue, and Shared Characteristics

In a 2006 Institute for Public Relations Gold Standard white paper entitled "Prioritizing Stakeholders for Public Relations," Rawlins (2006) presented four steps for defining stakeholders or publics in the context of a public relations issue based on level of knowledge and on degree of issue engagement. The following steps are a modification of Rawlins' framework.

There are different kinds of "stakes" in stakeholders. Some stakeholders have ownership in the organization, others are economically dependent on the organization, and the organization is dependent on some stakeholders as well. The level of power, legitimacy, and urgency play an important role in advocating on the part of these perspectives. The *first step* focuses on identifying stakeholders by discovering their control and authority over the organization; identifying the dominant coalition; and learning how essential stakeholders are to the organization and vice versa.

Does the group have a long-standing relationship with the organization? How important is the group to the organization? How important is the organization to the group? Whether it had a relationship with the organization prior to its formation, if the group is primarily issue-driven, then it is a public. Stakeholder relations with the organizations are typically more complex because of the existence of a prior and ongoing relationship.

The publics' engagement and their level of support influence the public relations message. *Step two* categorizes the publics into groups relevant to changing attitudes in favor of the campaign message. They are advocate stakeholders, dormant stakeholders, adversarial stakeholders, and apathetic stakeholders (Rawlins, 2006).

Advocate stakeholders are active publics in support of the campaign message. They embrace the message and advocate for it. Messages to this group are often a call to some type of action in support of the campaign. For example, advocates for drug rehabilitation programs would convince other publics and would also move to find resources available to reduce illicit drug use in the community.

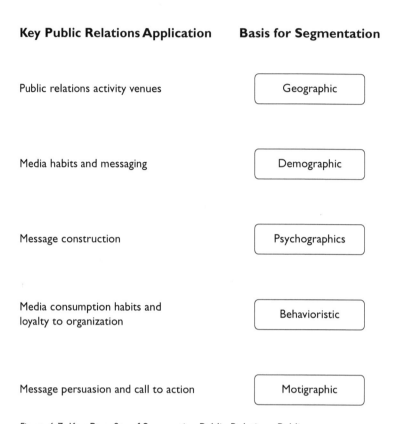

Key Public Relations Application   **Basis for Segmentation**

Public relations activity venues   Geographic

Media habits and messaging   Demographic

Message construction   Psychographics

Media consumption habits and   Behavioristic
loyalty to organization

Message persuasion and call to action   Motigraphic

Figure 6.7 Key Benefits of Segmenting Public Relations Publics

Dormant stakeholders are not ready to become involved. They may be unaware of the issue. The degree of knowledge varies, but is not at a point where it increases engagement. As a latent public, they may not know how to deal with the problem or they may think that it is not a concern. They might require more information including content that addresses barriers to involvement. Dormant stakeholders are receptive to change and willing to make concessions. They do have potential to become engaged in a manner consistent with the public relations goal.

Adversarial stakeholders are active publics opposed to the public relations message. They are the opposition, resistant to change and concessions, and are typically defensive. Converting these publics to supporters is difficult. However, an effective approach is to present the issue and message in a win–win context. They need concessions if there will be any chance of winning them over. In the drug problem example, an adversarial stakeholder group opposes addressing substance abuse, thinking that it is a burden on taxpayers and a matter of individual responsibility. Perhaps they might be more receptive if the message indicated that the overall financial burden to taxpayers would be minimal because of available drug rehabilitation resources and the positive impact of less drug-related crimes. Examples should support the argument such as reduced incarceration, fewer resources needed for law enforcement, and so forth.

Apathetic stakeholders are the apathetic publics. They either do not care or do not acknowledge the problem's existence. Providing information and an invitation to participate in addressing the problem might prove useful. This group is more likely to change in favor of the campaign appeal and make concessions once the dormant stakeholders become involved.

The *third step* is to define stakeholders by the level and nature of their involvement with the issue and situation. Level of knowledge involves awareness, understanding, beliefs, attitudes toward the issue, and a degree of engagement. Involvement can be situational or enduring depending on the issue, organizational commitment, and personal relevance. These stakeholders fall into four groups: active publics, aware public, latent public, and apathetic publics (Grunig & Hunt, 1984).

An **active public** is a group that is highly immersed in the situation possessing extensive knowledge of an issue. People for the Ethical Treatment of Animals (PETA) in laboratory testing is an example of an active public. Human rights groups monitoring governmental activities in the Sudan or Somalia are also active publics. These publics are aware of the issue. Messaging should focus on directly alleviating their concerns.

Aware publics are groups that know an issue and its relevant consequences. However, they are not organized to act on an issue. They have knowledge of the problem and are involved to the extent that they recognize the problem. For instance, town officials may know that there is a drug problem in their local community. They may know the statistics. Yet, they do not know what state and federal programs exist or how to go about accessing these programs. The public relations message would focus on providing detailed information for addressing the issue perhaps including a call to action.

A **latent public** is a group of individuals that know the issue exists, but they do not see it as a problem or opportunity. Latent publics have little knowledge and low levels of involvement. The objective with this public is to increase knowledge and engagement. Taking the drug problem example, messaging would need to include information supporting the existence of the drug problem including numbers, percentages, ranking, and evocative anecdotal content. By increasing awareness, problem recognition will occur, which will spur a desire to learn more and engage the issue.

Last, we have the **apathetic public**. This public knows that the problem exists, but does not consider it important. This is the most difficult public to persuade. The best approach to reach them is to monitor their attitudes and beliefs for changes that may make them receptive to messaging. In the case of the drug problem, should something drastic occur to warrant their attention, then the likelihood of persuasion will increase (Smith, 2013).

Step four involves profiling stakeholders according to their attributes. Learn their common interest and shared values and beliefs. For example, some stakeholders are interested in seeing that the organization is socially responsible or that there are dividends paid. This step defines the groups by geographic, demographic, psychographic, behavioristic, and motigraphic factors. In sum, individuals are segmented by common attributes so that a common message can be communicated to them geared to achieving the target outcome.

Keep in mind, some stakeholder groups may not be active publics at a given time. Considering the dynamic nature of public relations, situations change, and stakeholders can easily become engaged publics. These types of circumstances can warrant modifications to public relations planning and tactics.

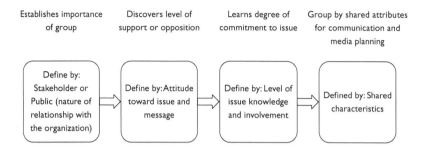

Figure 6.8 The Process for Defining Public Relations Target Groups

As we can see, their relationship to the organization, their attitude toward the issue and message, the level and nature of their engagement and knowledge about the organization, and their shared group characteristics define publics. Figure 6.8 illustrates the components for defining target public relations groups. First, practitioners discover the publics' attitude toward the issue, followed by their degree of involvement and level of issue knowledge. Next, their values, beliefs, demographics, and media habits are the basis of their profile. Their engagement and knowledge is managed to support or oppose an issue. These bases for defining public relations target groups are necessary to develop and execute a successful campaign.

Choice Benefit Analysis

Sometimes because of the nature of the situation and publics, an assessment of the choices available to stakeholders about the issue sheds light on how best to message them. One way to approach this evaluation is through a public choice benefit analysis (CBA). The matrix table includes the key choices to a public(s)—located in the rows and the key benefits of each choice placed in the columns. Each cell is rated on a 5-point scale. One (1) denotes less of the benefit and 5 represents more of the benefit. Choices can have similar ratings.

Ratings are based on objective and/or subjective scores. For example, a brand that has high ratings from participants that are consistent with high ratings from independent, external sources, is likely an objective measure. On the other hand, in a target public in which perceptions lack evidence and are opinion based, then ratings are subjective. Scores are identified as objective or subjective by using an asterisk.

Table 6.2 represents a CBA for undergraduate candidate preference in a national election. In this example, the preference is largely subjective based on perceptions on the noted benefits. Candidate A is the candidate of choice because of a score of 40 compared to Candidates B and C with scores of 22 and 24, respectively. Candidate A differentiates herself from the others especially concerning the issues of student loans, foreign policy, positions on social programs, and healthcare policy as noted in the grayed-out areas.

Table 6.2 Choice Benefit Analysis Matrix

Undergraduate College Student 18–24 Years

Benefits/ Choices	Party Member	Position on Student Loans Support	Position of Tax Policy	Policies to Support Small Businesses	Economic Philosophy	Foreign Policy	Stand on Social Programs	Healthcare Position	Immigration	Total
Support Candidate A	5	5	4	3	5	5	4	5	4	40
Support Candidate B	3	1	3	5	3	1	2	1	3	22
Support Candidate C	4	2	5	4	3	1	1	1	3	24

Supported by these findings, Candidate A might emphasize her positions on student loans, foreign policy, social programs, and healthcare perhaps comparing her positions on these issues to those of the opposition. To take advantage of popular issues. The candidate links matrix topics where there is strong support to the other issues.

A specific CBA matrix applies to one or more publics. If publics share many commonalities, they may have identical CBAs. Moreover, there will likely be overlapping benefits and scores among publics.

Although formats are consistent within a matrix, there are various ways to format a matrix. Alternatively, sometimes scores are based on ranking benefits based on the number of choices provided. In the example, there are three that would be rank ordered as first, second, and third. The various formats each have their strengths and weaknesses.

Prioritizing Stakeholders/Publics

According to the following criteria, prioritize public relations' publics:

1   The importance of a public to the organization, which carries double the weight of the other criteria.
2   The importance of the organization to a public, which can mobilize dormant stakeholders.
3   The importance of the issue to a public, which can also mobilize them.
4   Whether a public agrees with the campaign message.
5   The cost effectiveness of reaching a public.
6   Lag time required to reach a public.

In short, the combination of prioritized publics must best achieve the public relations goal and objectives while minimizing costs. The optimal solution results from rank ordering the public by importance with 1 indicating the most important public on a specified criterion. The lowest total scores represent the highest priority publics for the issue in question. The rating can be based on qualitative and/or quantitative measures. It is important to note that situations change and thus issues can change, thus shifting the status and priority assigned to publics.

Table 6.3 is a suggested format for prioritizing public relations groups. For illustrative purposes, scores are based on a hypothetical situation. Internal and external sources such as public relations practitioner expertise, the heads of various organizational departments associated with the groups or issue, upper level management, external experts, the public or stakeholder groups, and other sources influence scores.

Although most groups are publics, a public relations strategy may consider specific stakeholder groups that are marginally engaged in the issue to account for unexpected situational changes that could enhance their status in terms of the issue.

The example in Table 6.3 concerns the Tylenol recall. The left-most column identifies publics. As we can see, the lowest total scores are for retail Tylenol customers, retailers, the news media, and wholesalers. These are the most important publics; they are the key publics and address the immediate danger of the Tylenol situation. They are clearly important to Johnson & Johnson, the maker of Tylenol. As you can see in the table, the publics important to Johnson & Johnson carry a double weight because they are more significant than other publics to the issue and organization. This amplifies the differences between the most and least important publics.

Table 6.3 Prioritizing Stakeholder Groups

Tylenol Recall Prioritized Publics' Scores

Group/Priority	Type	Group import to organization	Organization Import to group	Importance of issue	Message agreement	Cost effective PR	Time effective	Prioritized Score
Retail customers	Public	1 × 2 = 2	8	1	1	9	9	30
Retailers	Public	2 × 2 = 4	3	4	2	8	8	29
News media	Public	3 × 2 = 6	6	6	3	5	4	30
Wholesalers	Public	3 × 2 = 6	4	5	4	6	6	31
Other distributors	Public	4 × 2 = 8	5	7	5	7	7	39
Vendor (mfg.)	Public	6 × 2 = 12	1	8	6	4	5	36
Authorities	Public	7 × 2 = 14	7	2	7	2	1	33
Shareholders	Public	8 × 2 = 16	2	3	8	3	3	35
Insurance carrier	Public	9 × 2 = 18	9	9	9	1	2	48

Focusing on key publics may not be the most cost-efficient or effective approach. The required financial resources may be beyond what is available in the budget and the lead time may be a challenge. In the Tylenol example, the lead-time scores are misleading because the highest scores essentially represent a handful of telephone calls, unlike involved communication with other publics.

Examples of Publics' Profiles

The point of a public relations campaign is to inform, persuade, and sometimes present a call to action. Unless there is sufficient information about the publics, it will be difficult to speak to them in a convincing voice. Defining a public requires the following components.

- geographic location;
- demographics (including an approximate number of individuals);
- indication of the priority ranking;
- indication of whether their attitudinal status is advocate, dormant, adversarial, or apathetic;
- identification according to their level of issue knowledge and degree of engagement;
- psychographics.

The amount of reported information depends on the situation. Some issues will also require the following data about publics as well:

- behavioristics; and
- motigraphics.

An internally based campaign includes organizational publics.

Let's take the Tylenol recall example once more. For illustrative purposes, we will only cover the key publics: retail customers, retailers, news media, and wholesalers in the context of 1982. Therefore, online-based considerations are not included.

Retail customers. These are the end-users of Tylenol. Although the crisis occurred in the greater Chicago metropolitan area, the market consists of all users and potential users in the United States spanning across demographic and psychographic characteristics, representing 40 million[1] people.

Retailers. There are approximately 300,000[1] Tylenol retailers in the U.S. including some pharmacy chains, independent pharmacies, and various big, medium, and small box chains.

News media. The news media public consists of the top American news wire services, which are the Associated Press, United Press International, Bloomberg News, Dow Jones News, and ZUMA Press. This public also includes CNN, FOX, MSNBC, NBC, CBS, ABC, and HLN. Also, the top circulating newspapers are in this public: *USA Today, The New York Times, The Wall Street Journal, Los Angeles Times, New York Post,* and *Chicago Tribune.*

Wholesalers. Wholesalers purchase Tylenol from the company for resale. There were approximately 10,000[1] Tylenol wholesalers in the U.S.

Not all publics require a full definition owing to the situation and specific circumstances. In general, a hypothetical and comprehensive example of a defined public is as follows. Let's consider a hypothetical public for a stop-smoking public service announcement campaign in Canada.

The key public is 5 million, 18–34-year-old men and women in Canada. They are regular or social smokers who enjoy smoking despite the cost. Consumption ranges from 1 pack per week to 3 packs per day. They are aware of the risks of smoking but think they will be fine for now possibly through cognitive dissonance reduction behaviors based on various justifications for smoking.

They tend to be VALS Makers and Survivors. Some of them communicate to the world about themselves and their experiences by building a house, raising children, and repairing a car. They live in a traditional family, do practical work, and engage in physical recreation. They are suspicious of innovations and big business. They respect government and organized labor. At the same time, they resent government intrusion on individual rights. They focus on basic, functional items. Makers buy economically and have no interest in luxury brands. The Survivors within this public have fewer resources than the Makers.

They prefer short, simple messaging in bullet-like formatting. Because of their ages, this public tends to be heavy users of social media and mobile apps. Texting is a major form of communication for them. They tend to watch series-based programming on their smart phones. The split between intrinsically motivated and extrinsically motivated is equal. In both cases, they focus on issues that are economically and functionally practical.

Stakeholders by Organization Type

Certain stakeholder groups are more conducive to non-profit, for-profit, or governmental organizations. Of course, there is overlap among some of the groups across the three sectors. Table 6.4 highlights this breakdown.

For corporations, shareholders, investors, and customers are essential stakeholders. In the case of non-profit organizations, volunteers and donors are significant stakeholders. Last, in the government sector, elected officials, taxpayers, voters, and related agencies are key stakeholders.

Table 6.4 Stakeholder Group by For-Profit, Non-Profit, and Governmental Organizations

For-Profit	Non-Profit	Government
Shareholders/investors	Contributors/donors	Taxpayers/voters
Customers/consumers	Client/consumers	Elected officials
Employees	Volunteers	Related gov't agencies
Suppliers	Employees	Employees
Financial institutions	Members	Community activists
Elected officials	Suppliers	News and social media
Activists	Elected officials	Educational institutions
Educational institutions	Activists	Lobbyists
News and social media	News and social media	Suppliers
Competition	Board of trustees	Activist
Board of directors	Businesses/corporate foundations	

Source: Modified from Straubhaar, J., LaRose, R., & Davenport, L. (2015). *Media Now: Understanding media, culture, and technology.* Boston, MA: Wadsworth (p. 327). These lists are by no means exhaustive. They are meant to provide a sampling of stakeholders relevant to the designated organizational type.

Summary of Key Concepts

- A public relations campaign plan is about communicating with stakeholders about an issue with the intention to persuade or present a call to action.
- Target public relations groups are defined in different ways.
- Stakeholders, internal vs. external stakeholders, publics, audience, constituents, market segments, and intervening publics are groups affected by a public relations campaign.
- There are clear roles for opinion leaders and media as intervening publics.
- There are multiple ways to differentiate publics based on an issue.
- Shared characteristics are the basis for defining stakeholders.
- Publics are prioritized according to criteria.

In the Case of Canyon Ranch . . . the Publics

Women customers. Women represent 75% of Canyon Ranch customers. The average woman is 47 years old and from an upper-middle and upper income household. She is fit, active, and values high quality service and is willing to pay for it. She has refined taste. Being the core customer base, these women are vital to Canyon Ranch's success. Fifty-five percent of this market segment are returning guests. Additionally, there are new female customers, who represent an untapped source of customers. Approximately 12 million women in the United States comprise this demographic.

Men customers. While they are the minority at Canyon Ranch, the average male customer is in his early fifties, married with adult children, and comes from an upper-middle and upper income household. Many men arrive at Canyon Ranch with their spouse or significant other; however, there is a large number who visit alone looking to get away and are drawn to health services, including nutrition, exercise physiology, movement therapy, behavioral health, and lifestyle choices as opposed to others who prefer traditional spa services. Many would find the Health and Healing services an attractive option at Canyon Ranch. Some male customers will be new to the Canyon Ranch experience, which provides Canyon Ranch with an opportunity to start their experience in the Health and Healing services department. There are approximately 11.8 million men in the United States with this profile.

News media. The media consists of general news broadcast media of the four major TV networks in the top ten designated market areas in the U.S.A. as well as the top three in reach networks in health-, spa-, travel-, and business-related areas such as Bloomberg and CNBC. Additionally, included are the top three radio stations by weekly listenership in each of the top ten DMAs. The major business, health, health spa, vacation, and travel magazines and websites by reach that target upper-middle and upper income households are included.

Corporate customers. Corporate customers are those organizations that purchase Canyon Ranch packages for their executives. This campaign focuses on Fortune 500 companies.

Travel agents and agencies. There are approximately 105,000 travel agents in the United States alone. Of those, 3,000–5,000 are luxury destination vacation agents. Eighteen percent of Canyon Ranch's referrals are from such travel agents.

Key Terms

Achievers 142
Active public 149
Activism 135
Adversarial stakeholder 148
Advocate stakeholder 148
Apathetic public 149
Apathetic stakeholder 149
Audience 139
Aware public 149
Behavioristic segmentation 145
Believers 142
Constituents 137
Demographic segmentation 140
Dormant stakeholder 148
Experiencers 142
External stakeholders 136
Extrovert 143
Feeler 144
Formal opinion leader 136
Geographic segmentation 140
Hardcore loyalty 145
Informal opinion leader 137
Innovators 141
Internal stakeholders 135
Introvert 143

Intuitive 144
Judger 144
Key publics 135
Latent public 149
Loyalty 145
Makers 143
Market segment 138
MBTI 143
Motigraphics 145
Opinion leader 136
Perceiver 144
Psychographic
  segmentation 140
Publics 134
Sensor 144
Situation 132
Social influencer 137
Special interest group (SIG) 134
Split loyalty 145
Stakeholders 133
Strivers 142
Survivors 143
Thinker 142
Thinkers 144
VALS 141

Chapter Questions

6.1 Define the term situation.
6.2 What is the primary public relations function?
6.3 Regarding the issue, what can vary among stakeholders?
6.4 Define stakeholder and provide an example.
6.5 Define public and provide an example.
6.6 Define key public.
6.7 What is an internal stakeholder and offer an example?
6.8 Define external stakeholder and provide examples.
6.9 What is a SIG and provide an example?
6.10 Define and name two intervening publics.
6.11 Define opinion leaders and offer an example.
6.12 What is a formal opinion leader and provide examples?
6.13 Define informal opinion leader and provide an example.
6.14 Define social influencer and provide an example.
6.15 Define constituent and provide an example.
6.16 Define market segment.
6.17 Define audience and provide an example.
6.18 What is geographic segmentation?

6.19   What is demographic segmentation?

6.20   Define psychographic segmentation.

6.21   Name two psychographic frameworks.

6.22   What is the basis for VALS?

6.23   How many types does VALs provide?

6.24   Define MBTI.

6.25   Name each of the MBTI paired four mental habits and briefly describe them.

6.26   Define behavioristic segmentation and provide an example.

6.27   Define loyalty.

6.28   Define hardcore and split types of loyalty and provide an example of each one.

6.29   Define motigraphics.

6.30   According to Rawlins, name the four types of stakeholders.

6.31   According to level of knowledge and degree of engagement, what are the types of publics?

6.32   What are the criteria for prioritizing publics?

6.33   Provide a write-up of a hypothetical public.

6.34   What factors might cause public relations practitioners to change priorities?

6.35   Define activism.

Note

1   This amount is estimated for 1982.

References

About VALS (2017). *Strategic Business Insights.* Retrieved from www.strategicbusinessinsights. com/vals/about.shtml.

Diamond, J. (1996, June 16). One director who's proud to be called commercial. *The New York Times.* Retrieved from www.nytimes.com/1996/06/16/movies/one-director-who-s-proud-to-be-called-commercial.html.

Grunig, J. E., & Hunt, T. (1984). *Managing public relations.* New York: Holt, Rinehart & Winston.

Hallahan, K. (2000). Inactive Publics: The forgotten publics in public relations. *Public Relations Review, 26*(4), 499–515.

Maddock, R. C. (2000). *Motigraphics: The analysis and measurement of human motivations in marketing.* Westport CT: Quorum Books.

MBTI Basics. (2017). *The Myers & Briggs Foundation.* Retrieved from www.myersbriggs.org/ my-mbti-personality-type/mbti-basics/home.htm?bhcp=1.

Nielsen. (2016). *Local television market universe.* The Nielsen Company.

Rawlins, B. (2006). *Prioritizing stakeholders for public relations.* Published by the Institute for Public Relations. Retrieved from www.instituteforpr.org.

Smith, R. D. (2013). *Strategic planning for public relations.* New York: Routledge.

Sones, M., Grantham, S., & Vieira, Jr., E. T. (2009). Communicating CSR via pharmaceutical company web sites evaluating message frameworks for external and internal stakeholders. *Corporate Communications: An International Journal, 14*(2), 144–157.

Straubhaar, J., LaRose, R., & Davenport, L. (2015). *Media Now: Understanding media, culture, and technology.* Boston, M.A.: Wadsworth Publishing.

The Nielsen Company. (2013). *Nielsen DMA Regions.* Retrieved from http://www.nielsen. com/intl-campaigns/us/dma-maps.html.

Types. (2016). Changing Minds: Jungian Type Inventory. Retrieved from http://changingminds. org/explanations/preferences/mbti.htm.

Part III

Goals, Objectives, and Strategy

Strategy

Conceptualization, Goals, Objectives, and Central Message

The tragedy in life doesn't lie in not reaching your goal. The tragedy lies in having no goal to reach.

(Benjamin Mays, 2011, p. 222)

Learning Objectives

To:

- Understand how public relations goals and objectives are linked.
- Know the types of goals and objectives.
- Understand and develop the components of a public relations objective.
- Understand that objectives are the basis for assessing a public relations campaign.
- Describe what is a public relations strategy and what does it involve.
- Know the importance of a public relations central message.

Introduction

Today Web 3.0 continues to change the business of public relations. Advancements in communications and other technologies such as social media, analytics, and marketing research, make planning and execution easier, more standardized, timelier, and cost-efficient. There is a growing cadre of specialty firms that offer competing services to implement or evaluate campaign activities. What drives the success or failure of these marshalled resources is sound strategy informed by timely information. Strategy is the heart of public relations and is where the value is added. Whether it is strategic counsel provided by an agency or internally developed, it is vital to the success of a public relations campaign.

Strategy development occurs after the situational analysis is complete. This chapter discusses the development of goals, objectives, and overall strategy. The next chapter is devoted to creating a central message strategy.

Albert Einstein allegedly said, "No challenge can be solved from the same level of consciousness that created it." Public relations solutions require requisite variety. **Requisite variety** indicates that resources equal to or greater than that which caused the challenge are required to meet the challenge. In other words, solving problems requires greater flexibility than that inherent in the problem.

Figure 7.1 Critically Thinking about What Needs to Be Done Results in a Strategy and Plan

A public relations strategy consists of two parts. First, it requires a sound rationale for the overall planning and actions. Second, the conceptualized strategy, informed by the campaign goal, guides central message development and selection of communication channels. A campaign plan includes a brief statement justifying strategic recommendations. The sample public relations campaign in Chapter 14 demonstrate the connections between rationale and plans.

Let us start with the first point. A public relations campaign strategy's purpose is to effectively and systematically communicate to stakeholders to change or to reinforce an existing condition. It begins with the development of a sound strategy. Consistent with the organization's mission, **strategy** is the reasoning behind an overall framework of a public relations plan including goals, objectives, and a central message.[1] The situational analysis research provides all of the information and data necessary to develop the strategy, including defining the issue and key stakeholders and publics.

Figure 7.2 summarizes a public relations campaign planning process. The process consists of interrelated and, in some cases, interdependent components. In fact, ongoing monitoring and evaluation assures detection and adjustment to underperforming areas of the campaign.

Since public relations' campaigns focus on groups of people who have a connection to the organization, we will collectively refer to them as stakeholders. Additionally, **tactics** and **execution** are the means by which we achieve objectives. They are the individual messages, ads, events, or other activities associated with realizing objectives.

The Public Relations Integrated Strategy and Planning Process

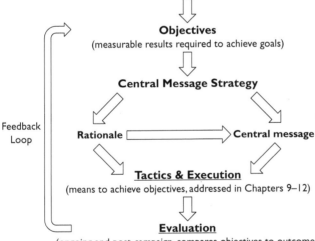

Mission Statement
(guides all organizational activities)

⇩

Situation Analysis
(research and analysis needed for strategic planning;
addressed in Chapters 4–6)

⇩

Strategy

Focus: Issue- Problem or Opportunity
(a campaign may involve one or more of these situations;
addressed in Chapter 4)

⇩

Goals
(generally, what is expected to be attained or achieved)

⇩

Objectives
(measurable results required to achieve goals)

⇩

Central Message Strategy

Feedback
Loop   **Rationale** ⟶ **Central message**

Tactics & Execution
(means to achieve objectives, addressed in Chapters 9–12)

⇩

Evaluation
(ongoing and post-campaign, compares objectives to outcomes,
addressed in Chapter 14)

Figure 7.2 The Process of Public Relations Planning

Strategy Development

As noted above, a strategy is the overall approach, emphasis, and general plan for the public relations campaign. Called "glocalization," public relations strategies are often "broad" with a local focus. Public relations projects or programs that have no clear message strategy lead to unguided tactics. Unguided tactics can easily lead to a disjointed and ineffective campaign. As we shall see in Chapter 14, strategy guides action plans that target various publics. Taking advantage of similarities within publics allows for effective

Figure 7.3 Tactics Are the Pieces of a Puzzle that Together Achieve Objectives and Goals

and cost-efficient planning and implementation. One last point, buy-in from senior management is critical. Without the support of those who control the organization, a public relations goal will be difficult to achieve. We start with the public relations goal.

Public Relations Goals

After the public relations issue identification process, a goal or set of goals is developed. A **goal** is a general statement of purpose. It is what the public relations campaign will attain or accomplish in relation to the issue under consideration. Achieving the goal will result in addressing the issue whether it is a problem or taking advantage of an opportunity. One to two sentences describe the issue. A goal, aligned with the organization's mission, is the positive version of the issue (Wilson & Ogden, 2015).

Although the degree of detail varies, a goal typically begins with "To . . ." A goal has a single aim whether it pertains to a profit, non-profit, or any level of governmental issue. One to three goals drive a campaign. Goals should not conflict with each other.

Table 7.1 contains a number of public relations internally and externally centered goals. Notice that increasing employee morale and increasing volunteer rolls are internal public relations goals. These two goals could very well fall under the profit, non-profit, or government designation.

The next step is translating the public relations goals into actionable and measurable results or objectives.

Public Relations Objectives

Measurable **objectives** must be met to achieve the public relations goal. They must be accurately measurable outcomes so that they can clearly contribute to the goal. Objectives refer

Table 7.1 Examples of Profit, Non-Profit, and Government Public Relations Goals

Goal Type	Goal
For-profit	To increase employee morale.
	To substantially increase customer satisfaction ratings.
	To minimize negative publicity of the latest product recall.
	To increase social media presence.
Non-profit	To maintain current level of donor contributions.
	To increase awareness of organization's mission.
	To maintain and enhance relationships with nongovernmental organizations (NGOs).
	To increase volunteer lists through volunteer word-of mouth.
Governmental	To decrease substance abuse.
	To increase citizen usage of social service programs.
	To increase awareness of need for reading literacy.
	To increase awareness as a tourist attraction.

to the outcomes and not to public relations tactics or activities. For instance, if the goal is to increase awareness, then linked objectives are realistic, adequately measurable, and provide a level of awareness. The objectives are thus specific operational guides that allow us to measure and evaluate the campaign. **Benchmarks** are the expected outcomes for each objective. We compare benchmarked objectives with actual campaign outcomes to determine the degree of campaign effectiveness. In sum, objectives provide the following benefits (Fill, 2009).

1   They provide direction and an action focus for all those participating in the activity.
2   They provide guidance to a variety of tactical decisions so that they are consistent with goals.
3   They determine the period in which the activity is to be completed.
4   They communicate the values and scope of the activity to all participants.
5   They serve as a means to evaluation tactics.

As we can see, objectives provide value from the beginning of the public relations planning process all the way through post-campaign evaluation.

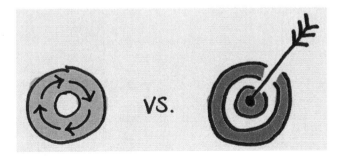

Figure 7.4 Experience of the Organization, Competition, or Industry Inform Benchmarks, Which Are Aspirational and Achievable

There are four categories of benchmarked objectives. They are exposure, information, persuasion, and behavioral, which are measured before, during, and after a campaign.

Exposure objectives are the number of stakeholders reached or the number of message exposures. In the case of news media objectives, it includes the target news media coverage. Traditionally, measures are number of news article clippings, mentions on the radio or broadcast television, and event attendance for example. Today, social media plays an important role in message exposure such as the number of Facebook friends, Twitter followers, email list, LinkedIn connections, media impression, and various online content analysis. Exposure objectives are especially important when promoting little known or new "products" such as innovative brands, new services, ideas, persons, programming, or candidates. Exposure is necessary in order to raise awareness about the issue. Creating awareness during the early days of Uber, Hello Fresh, Blue Apron, Tesla, Zipcar, robot carpet and floor vacuum cleaners, and the Square occurred first through exposure. Exposure is primarily a media management function. In other words, selecting media outlets where the target publics frequent is necessary to facilitate exposure.

Information objectives involve creating awareness and knowledge about an issue through repeated contact, assessed using awareness and recall surveys. Individuals are asked if they remember the item. On average, 3–10 exposures facilitate message recall. Exposure can occur through different medium vehicles such as news media, text messaging, radio, and social media. The effectiveness of drawing attention, creating awareness, and knowledge about an issue involves deploying message attention-getting devices. Drawing on novelty and personally relevant content are effective means to gain attention. Some examples of successful attention-getting campaigns were the reintroduction of the Star Wars trilogy in the late 1990s utilizing a mysterious, curiosity appeal (Carroll, 2000), free Brexit tattoos offered in London, Reebok's transformation of bus stops into mini gyms, a Giant Monopoly board in Trafalgar Square, and the Anti-aGin Young in Spirit campaign to name a few (Leigh, 2016).

Persuasion objectives focus on attitudes toward the issue. Positive attitude formation or positive attitude change through persuasion contributes to **organizational equity**, which is the reputation of the organization. Positive brand equity contributes to credibility. Once there an awareness of the issue, understanding or knowledge about the issue has the opportunity to grow. Rational and/or emotional factors provide positive support. Persuasion is more likely to occur in those persons who do not harbor a strong negative attitude toward the issue or message. The greatest opportunity exists with those persons who are "on the fence" and thus could either support or oppose the issue. Surveys measure attitudes as well as Facebook "Likes," product/service reviews, measures of word-of-mouth, other types of postings, and so forth. Some of the top brands with the greatest positive brand equity are Apple, Google, Microsoft, Amazon, IBM, and VISA.

As we can see, persuasion occurs through awareness and issue knowledge, which likely increases engagement and the target behavior.

Behavioral objectives are targeted actions facilitated by the public relations campaign. Like growing awareness and knowledge, behavior is engagement. Not all campaigns include a call to action. For those that do, it is challenging. A smaller percentage

Figure 7.5 Objectives Are the Outcomes that Take Us to the Goal

of those publics who are aware convert to positive attitude, and an even smaller amount move to actual behavior (Snyder et al., 2004).

As covered in Chapter 13, behaviors such as sales, new product inquiries, and product option choices are measured and assessed on an ongoing basis throughout a campaign. In the case of branded products, brand loyalty defined as positive attitude toward the brand, repeat purchases, and brand advocacy contribute to sales behavior and are measurable behaviors.

Nielsen offers a service that provide weekly scanned sales figures. According to the Nielsen website, "With presence in more than 100 countries, Nielsen collects sales information from more than 900,000 stores within our worldwide retail network—including grocery, drug, convenience, discount and e-commerce retailers—who, through cooperation arrangements, share their sales data with us" (The Nielsen Company, 2017, para. 2).

Remember, a benchmarked objective is what we want the target stakeholder group to think, feel, or do, OR what we must do to get them think, feel, or do something that helps achieve the public relations goal. A benchmarked objective includes an objective, a quantifiable and expected outcome for that objective, a specific timeline, and can identify a target public for the objective. Many times, objectives operate in a hierarchical structure. Some objectives are met before subsequent ones are reached, especially behavioral ones. For example, a plan for disseminating information about a new benefits package at a university to encourage enrollment would first include awareness as well as understanding about the new benefits before a call for action to enroll.

Think about This . . .

A 2016 *Houston Chronicle* article entitled "Goals and Objectives in PR Campaigns" by Neil Kokemuller examines four key public relations goals and their importance.

The first goal is developing relationships. This goal helps build long-term connections and relationships with key stakeholders such as customers and the local communities where the organization operates. Community involvement and charitable giving foster strategic relationships. The second goal, akin to task-related activities, is raising awareness such as product and brand awareness. This goal enhances recognition in the marketplace.

The third one, another task-related goal, centers on creating positive brand equity or a desirable attitude toward the brand, as well as promoting the brand or organization. Last, informing audiences is a reputation goal. For example, providing stakeholders with a free regularly distributed newsletter not only informs them but also creates and maintains awareness, positive attitude, and goodwill toward the organization. These four goals can work together toward creating a positive organization and brand image.

Ask yourself: How might you apply these goals toward a specified well-known brand or organization? How can these goals apply to a non-profit organization and its mission?

Kokemuller, N. (2016). Goals and objectives in PR campaigns. *Houston Chronicle*. Retrieved from http://smallbusiness.chron.com/goals-objectives-pr-campaigns-21010.html.

Required Components of Public Relations Objectives

An objective answers the four Ws of a public relations campaign. *What* do we want to achieve and to *what* degree? *Who* do we want to target? *When* will it be done?

Therefore, a clear, precise, and complete objective must contain four parts: (1) What do we want to achieve? In other words, what is the general objective? The anticipated result falls into one of the four types of objectives as discussed above. (2) Who do we want to target? A defined target stakeholder group. Base the group on the criteria set forth in Chapter 6, which includes demographic and psychographic characteristics as well as the approximate count of the public. (3) When will it be done? The expected outcome requires a timeline and deadline. Reaching the objective progressively and on time may be necessary for other aspects of the campaign to move forward. (4) To what degree? That is, what is the benchmark? It must be precise so that it leaves no room for interpretation. It is quantifiable. Specific numbers or percentages to express expected and actual results are used. Note the timeline and size of the public as well. For example, in "Increase volunteerism *to 25% of the 5000 employees* who are 18–34 years old *during the next 6 months*," the 25%, 6 months, and count of 5,000 are concrete quantitative aspects of the objective.

Other considerations include creating objectives that are attainable, cost-efficient, and mission-driven. Realistic objectives are attainable. Yet, they must be sufficiently challenging so that their achievement makes a difference. They must also reflect the available resources, which are not limitless. Finally, objectives are consistent with the organization's mission and values statements.

"I have some specific, unknown objectives
for you to achieve."

Figure 7.6 Unless Objectives Are Precise, then Their Value Is Limited

Table 7.2 depicts examples of the four categories of public relations objectives along with the four required components. Notice that there is sufficient information in order to measure and evaluate each objective. The specific measurable outcome, expected outcome, target public (including size of the group), and timeline are stated. As we can see, an objective contains sufficient detail to measure and evaluate it.

Table 7.2 Types of Public Relations Objectives

Objective Type	Objective	Components
Exposure	To receive HealthCare One media mentions on 120 web sites during the next 12 months reaching 10 million households.	Outcome: media coverage. Benchmarks: 120 websites. Stakeholders: Websites reaching 10 mil. HHs. Timeline: 12 months.
Awareness	During 2018, increase the My Sales Deals app awareness 30% in the 18–24-year-old college student market of 16 million.	Outcome: Increase brand awareness. Benchmarks: 30% awareness. Stakeholders: 16 mil. 18–24 college students. Timeline: During the year2018.

(continued)

Table 7.2 (continued)

Objective Type	Objective	Components
Persuasive	To build support from the top 100 social influencers for the Let's Meet social media platform with the next 18 months.	Outcome: Build support. Benchmarks: Top 100. Stakeholders: Social media influencers. Timeline: 18 months.
Behavioral	To have 35% of the 25–54-year-old 12,000 workers enroll in an employer-sponsored pension plan over the next 5 years.	Outcome: Pension plan enrollment. Benchmarks: 35%. Stakeholders: 12,000 25–34-year-old workers. Timeline: 5 years.

Note: The organizations noted are fictitious.

As a rule of thumb, a campaign may have 1–3 goals and each goal usually has 1–6 overall objectives. On average, each public has at least 2–3 objectives. Situations and issues vary as do their goal and objective requirements. Table 7.3 represents examples of goals and their objectives.

Table 7.3 Comparing Goals and Objectives

Goal	Objectives
To increase employee morale.	• During next 2 months, 75% of 1,000 employees will attend community meetings about morale and related issues. • During the community meetings over next 2 months, 30 employees will submit reasons why they think morale is low. • Over next 3–6 months, 90% of 500 manufacturing employees will become aware of company concern for their work well-being. • Over the next 6–8 months, 40 employees will submit suggestions for improving morale. • Over the next 18 months, employee turnover will decrease to 1% from 5% in each of the manufacturing departments totaling 500 people.
To increase inquiries about brand ambulatory aids in the seniors' market.	• Over the first 6 months, receive positive media coverage in the top 10 by circulation periodicals for senior citizens (65+ years old). • Over the next 2 years, increase positive attitude toward the brand to 30% in the 30 mil. senior citizens' market. • Over 6 months, 20% of inquiries for top 50 in sales durable medical equipment suppliers that carry the brand, will be about the brand ambulatory aids.

To maintain and increase relationships with nongovernmental organizations (NGOs).	• Over two years, company inquiries about ambulatory aids will increase to 25% of all calls and email inquiries. • Over 3–4 months, the executive directors of the top 75 NGOs based on budget will be aware of our initiatives to strengthen ties. • Within 12 months, an additional 5–10 new joint projects will be signed with some the 75 top NGOs. • Over the next 18 months, increase the number of affiliated NGOs from 12 to 22.

As we can see in Table 7.3, unlike, a goal, which is a general statement of purpose, an objective is specific. The objectives are organized in a natural progression moving toward the goal. In the ambulatory aids case, the objectives start with exposure in the media to positive attitude, followed by behaviors as captured by the two inquiry objectives from general ambulatory aids to the specific brand. Depending on the circumstance, objectives do not always follow this progression. Each situation has its unique characteristics.

Setting the Public Relations Objective

Achieved outcomes assures the campaign's success. To determine benchmarks requires knowing the baseline for each objective. The **baseline** is the actual starting point of an objective before the campaign intervention. Benchmarking serves as a reference point from which to develop the anticipated outcome of an objective. For example, if 20% is the current level of elderly daycare programs awareness in a given community, then 20% is the baseline. The objective formulation accounts for the baseline, but it is not expressed as a percentage (or fraction) of the baseline. The objective stands alone. Thus, in our example, the goal is to increase elder daycare awareness. Since the baseline is 20%, it would need to be greater than this percentage. The objective may be to increase the awareness level to 35%, which represents a net gain of 15 percentage points. The objective would also contain a description of the specific public and timeline.

Note that a percentage point increase is different from a percent increase. There is a *15-percentage point increase* moving from 20% to 35%. However, the *percent increase is 75%* because 15% represents a 75% of 20% (.20 × .75 = .15).

Overall and Stakeholder Public Relations Objectives

A public relations campaign contains **global objectives** that apply to all targeted publics. **Action plan objectives** pertain to individual publics. "To increase positive brand equity over the next year starting on 6/1/18 to 30% of the 10 million customers who are aware of Brand A" is an example of a global objective. An action plan objective might involve the same type of objective but indicate different percentages because of the nature of existing brand perceptions and public characteristics.

Keep in mind, each public relations public has unique characteristics, and, at the same time, they may share similar objectives. The objective may be set higher for those publics

Figure 7.7 Benchmarks for Global Objectives Equal the Total Benchmarks of the Action Plan
Objectives

who are more receptive to the message. For instance, the expectation of support for candidate Donald Trump was greater in the Midwest than on the East and West coasts. Focusing on the electoral votes, the objectives would be higher in certain swing states compared to other states.

Situations vary. One public's benchmark may be to increase positive attitude by 20%; whereas, a second public's benchmark calls for a 35% increase. In this case, the latter public's support plays a more important role in the public relations campaign and the achievement of global objectives. Perhaps they have a higher conversion rate from a favorable attitude to behavior or they are more likely to act expeditiously compared to the former public or all other publics. The latter public serves to generate a cascade of support for the issue.

The Case of News Media Public Relations Objectives

Media objectives are a special type of objective because they serve a key purpose. They relate to exposing the message to stakeholders thereby creating awareness through publicity. **Publicity** is unsponsored and unmanaged coverage of an issue in the media. Thus, the public relations team does not control positive or negative coverage.

The media are important because they are an intermediate stakeholder serving to reach other publics. Media objectives are overall campaign objectives unless the media are specific to a target public. This is so because their effect crosses over to more than one public. The following is an example. "To achieve neutral or positive coverage about the ABC firm and XZY company merger in the top 6 circulating newspapers in the 10 largest designated market areas (DMAs) during 2018 representing a reach of 25 million."

Central Message Strategy

The second major component of a public relations strategy is the central message. This message drives the issue's narrative by telling a story that engages and wins over publics. The **central message** is the key message that appeals to stakeholders. It is the big selling idea, central thesis, or central motif of the campaign. The situational analysis research guides central message development. It is present in some form in all direct and indirect campaign communication and actions. The central message is the common thread that runs through and connects all aspects of the campaign. Message presentation varies, but the central theme remains consistent. Think of the central message as the **creative road map** of the campaign guiding the creative in all messages and related activities.

The central message can be simple, represented by one sentence, or it can contain multiple components stated in a paragraph with bullet points including a secondary message, a structural hierarchy, and slogan or tagline. Table 7.4 presents a number of simple central messages.

Figure 7.8 All Tactics or Public Relations Activities Are Consistent with the Central Message. Effective Tactics Stay on the Creative Road to Success

Table 7.4 Examples of Simple Central Messages and Rationales

Organization	Simple Central Messages	Rationale
Google	Contributing financially toward fighting Ebola, which will go a long way toward eradicating this disease.	Motivate people to donate money to fight Ebola by appealing to their humanity and the fact that Google would match every $1 with $2.
Orchard Pig Cidar	Be happy on Blue Monday and spread the word.	Increase brand awareness by generating interest around their hashtag with the hashtag #BlueMonday as well as integrating other social media.
Buchanan's Scotch Whiskey	Latino cultural pride is key to unlocking true greatness.	Develop a new generation of customers who take pride in their heritage, and to embrace this pride as a key to achieving greatness by linking Buchanan's to this celebration.
The Naval Criminal Investigative Service (NCIS)	NCIS encourages and welcomes women and minorities to apply for special agent positions where there are numerous career opportunities and benefits, including the opportunity to travel.	Increasing awareness, positive attitude, and interest in what NCIS has to offer will increase the number of women and minority applicants.

On the other hand, Table 7.5 illustrates a more complex approach to central messaging.

Table 7.5 Examples of Complex Central Messages

Organization	Central Message
Volvo	Volvo's safety features will be communicated by focusing on the features and benefits of (1) accident prevention (anti-lock brakes, special steering system, etc.) and (2) damage mitigation (side airbags, panels in doors, etc.) to passengers and vehicle.
Toyota Corolla	The Toyota Corolla central message will communicate the following groups of features and demonstrate the benefits (e.g. convenience benefit of some interior features and appeal benefit of a stylish looking vehicle) of the features to the target audience:

1) Reliability: dependability, warranty, and track record (ratings)
2) Low cost operation: great value & competitively priced, fuel economy (MPG), low maintenance, and track record (ratings)
3) Safety: high crash test ratings, vehicle stability control system, front and side curtain airbags
4) Interior & exterior features: Interior- Comfort, style, upgraded cloth/ velour, headroom/legroom, storage space, CD player, remote entry and Exterior (Style)-Mica paint, redesigned/refined exterior.

Walmart	Walmart respects its individual employees and will launch programs and initiatives that support the goal of a more diversified workforce. The company will take the following actions: (1) A diversity and inclusion officer will be hired with a staff (2) Walmart will require diversity and inclusion training for all employees. (3) The company will proactively seek women and minorities for managerial positions. (4) Walmart will offer tuition reimbursement programs for all employees. (5) The company will monitor, assess, and take actions to assure that women and minorities are representative at all levels of the organization. (6) Walmart will proactively seek women and minorities for management training at recruitment-related events. In short diversity and inclusion will be fully integrated in the organization.

Not all complex central message subpoints are necessarily included in each tactic. Individual messages convey natural combinations of the subpoints that appeal to publics. For example, a message about the Toyota Corolla may emphasize interior features and the low cost of maintenance in a slice of life ad, while another message may focus on the overall benefits of the vehicle's attributes. Additionally, the entire central message is often artfully incorporated in communications or events. Chapter 8 delves into the central message.

Slogans and Taglines

A **slogan** is a catch phrase using between one and a few words that capture the essence of the central message. It is fluid and changes over relatively short periods because it pertains to a brand, product, campaign, or limited area of an organization. For instance, "Change is in the air" was specifically for the iPad in 2014. Sometimes slogans include a **jingle** or catchy music such as the Kit Kat "Give me a break" short song associated with the brand and its central message. Throughout the years, McDonalds has created various jingles associated with its evolving slogan, tagline, and brand.

Except for one difference, a slogan and tagline are similar. A **tagline** applies to the entire organization, everything the organization does, and all of its brands. It captures the mission and identity of the organization. For instance, Apple developed the tagline "Think different," which exemplifies all things Apple including the iPad. Some other taglines are ExxonMobil: "Energy lives here," Merck: "Inventing for life"; U.S. Army: "Be all that you can be;" and DeBeers: "A diamond is forever."

Specific campaigns develop slogans and a tagline is longer term applying to the brand or organization. As long as they are consistent with the central message and organizational mission, some campaigns deploy existing taglines. Table 7.6 depicts the relationship between message and slogan/tagline.

In Table 7.6, we can see that each slogan/tagline cleverly encapsulates the main message of the campaign. "5 for the Fight" reflects the $5 requested donation to fight cancer. "Save money. Live better." Captures the essence of the Walmart message.

Pre-testing Central Messages and Slogans

Samples of stakeholder groups in a controlled setting can evaluate various central messages and taglines on a host of measures such as compatibility with the organization, attractiveness,

Table 7.6 Examples of Central Messages and their Slogans/Taglines

Organization	Central Message	Slogan/Tagline
Utah Jazz & Qualtrics	Cancer affects more than the person suffering from the disease. A small donation of $5.00 will help find a cure so that less people are hurt by this illness.	"5 For The Fight."
Hilton Hotels	The new Hilton Honors rewards program is easy to use, provides extra rewards for its VIP customers, is flexible, and can be used with Hilton's many partners.	"We are Hilton. We are Hospitality."
Walmart	We help our shoppers live better because we deliver low prices on the brands they trust, in an easy, fast, and one-stop shopping experience.	"Save money. Live better."
	Nike is committed to corporate social responsibility and is working toward changing management policies and improving the quality of life in Southeast Asian communities including its employees.	"Just do it!" (No specific slogan for this campaign)

credibility, and persuasiveness before implementing strategy. This is **pre-testing**. Pre-testing findings inform message strategy. The study settings include focus groups, completing surveys in person, personal interviews, and various online forms of data collection. Central messages can also be pilot tested in specific locations with target publics based on screening criteria. Chapter 4 covers pre-testing.

Summary of Key Concepts

- A public relations strategy consists of two parts: strategy conceptualization and strategy statement.
- A goal is the intended purpose of a public relations campaign.
- Objectives are the means by which goals are achieved, they are measurable, and they are the basis for assess campaign success.
- There are four general types of objectives.
- Objectives have four required components.
- Objectives are the basis for assessing a public relations campaign.

In the Case of Canyon Ranch . . . the Strategy

Goal

The goal is to increase sales in the U.S. market of Canyon Ranch's Health and Healing services at the Lenox location by integrating the spa, fitness, and salon services as well as Hotel as a total healthy vacation experience while maintaining total brand saliency.

Expected Outcomes

Overall Objective 1: By the end of the 12-month campaign, raise awareness and knowledge of Canyon Ranch's Health and Healing services to 90% of its existing customer list.

Overall Objective 2: By the end of the 12-month campaign, increase Health and Healing services sales by 30% and overall sales by 5%.

Overall Objective 3: By the end of the 12-month campaign, experience a 5% increase in new visits and a 15% increase in repeat visits to Health and Healing.

Central Message

Canyon Ranch is dedicated to developing and offering a full range of customized health wellness services especially health and healing designed to meet client needs in a high quality, responsive all-inclusive resort environment.

Key Terms

Action plan objectives 171
Baseline 171
Behavioral objectives 166
Organizational equity 166
Central message 173
Creative road map 173
Execution 162
Exposure objectives 166
Global objectives 171
Goal 164
Information objectives 166
Issue 000

Jingle 175
Media objectives 172
Objective 164
Persuasion objectives 166
Pre-testing 176
Publicity 172
Requisite variety 161
Slogan 175
Strategy 162
Tactics 162
Tagline 175

Chapter Questions

7.1   Define what is a public relations strategy.
7.2   What are the two components of a public relations strategy?
7.3   What are tactics or execution?
7.4   What is the meaning of the statement: "Strategies are often 'broad' with a local focus"?
7.5   What is a public relations goal and provide an example?
7.6   What is the public relations issue?
7.7   What is an objective and provide an example?
7.8   Define exposure objective and give an example.
7.9   What is an information objective and provide an example?
7.10 Define persuasion objective and offer an example.
7.11 What is organizational equity?

7.12   Define behavioral objective and offer an example.
7.13   What are the four components of a public relations objective?
7.14   How many goals might a typical public relations campaign have?
7.15   Typically, how many overall objectives might a goal have?
7.16   What is a baseline and provide an example.
7.17   What is a global objective?
7.18   What is an action plan objective?
7.19   What is a media objective and provide an example?
7.20   What is the central message and provide an example?
7.21   What is the creative road map of the public relations campaign?
7.22   What is a slogan and provide an example?
7.23   What is a tagline and offer an example?
7.24   What is a jingle and provide an example?
7.25   What is pre-testing?
7.26   What is a benchmark?

Note

1 Some public relations campaigns include a slogan or tagline.

References

Carroll, M. T. (2000). *Popular modernity in America: Experience, technology, mythohistory*. Albany, NY: State University of New York Press.

Fill, C. (2009). Marketing communications: Interactivity communities & content. Boston, MA: Pearson.

Kokemuller, N. (2016). Goals and objectives in PR campaigns. *Houston Chronicle*. Retrieved from http://smallbusiness.chron.com/goals-objectives-pr-campaigns-21010.html.

Leigh, R. (2016). *2016 in review – Top 20 PR campaigns and stunts of the Year*. Retrieved from http://prexamples.com/2016/12/2016-in-review-top-20-pr-campaigns-and-stunts-of-the-year/.

Snyder, L. B., Hamilton, M. A., Kiwanuka-Tondo, J., Fleming-Milici, F., & Proctor, D. (2004). A meta-analysis of the effects of mediated health communication campaigns on behavior change in the United States. *Journal of Health Communication, 9*, 71–96.

The Nielsen Company. (2017). *Solutions Retail Management*. Retrieved from http://www.nielsen.com/us/en/solutions/measurement/retail-measurement.html .

Wilson, L. J., & Ogden, J. D. (2015). *Strategic Communications: Planning for Public Relations and Marketing*. Dubuque, IA: Kendall Hunt.

Chapter 8

Strategy
More on Public Relations Central Messaging

Anyone in art school can paint a portrait of a Paris Café. However, only the truly talented can paint the same picture and make one go out of one's way to eat there.

(Tom Ong, Dougherty, 2015, para. 7)

Learning Objectives

To:

- Know what are the central idea and the central message of a public relations campaign.
- Understand and describe a positioning strategy.
- Describe the different kinds of central messages.
- Understand and describe what are slogans, taglines, and jingles.
- Describe what is repositioning and why it occurs.

Introduction

Public relations strategy includes a central idea expressed through a central message. The **central idea** is the conceptualization or overall theme of a key message, which is the central thesis or motif. The **central message** is the concrete manifestation of the public relations campaign central idea communicated to publics. Whether explicitly or implicitly, whether through direct communication or indirectly through other actions, each tactic includes the main message. The same underlying message presented differently through multiple communication channels, is the key to effective public relations communication. The central message is the common thread that passes through all varied communications with stakeholders. In other words, the central message binds a campaign. Stated in the public relations plan, its length is from one sentence to a short paragraph. Central messages apply to external and internal publics or some combination of both. Messages are consistent with the organization's mission and values statements.

The situational analysis research, including identifying the campaign issue; whether the issue is a problem or opportunity; and clearly defined publics, inform central message development. One such tool used to understand publics as they relate to the issue and/or situation is the choice benefit analysis (CBA) matrix, discussed in Chapter 6. Information from a CBA informs messaging by focusing on the benefits of the advocated position.

Figure 8.1 The Central Message Is the Magic Needed to Say the Same Thing in
Different Ways

Assume a situation where two hospitals are merging to increase cost efficiencies. The central idea (strategy) focuses on allaying a range of concerns about the merger. The central message addresses these concerns by celebrating the contributions and value of all stakeholders in both hospitals throughout the years. The message further emphasizes a tradition of service at both facilities, and their moving forward with this tradition and their shared strong common spirit of service in the future. In this case, the central message operates to reduce concerns about the merger by underscoring the positive past and how it transfers to an optimistic outlook about the merger and future.

As depicted in Figure 8.2, the central message flows from the issue and goal. They are interrelated and influence messaging.

Figure 8.2 From Issue Discovery to Central Message

Figure 8.3 Positioning Serves as a Reference Point for Moving Forward

Many practitioners add another layer called the **positioning strategy** or **statement**, which is a general statement of how an organization wants its stakeholders to view an issue, but is more general than the central theme. A positioning strategy is typically a strategic marketing function and serves to inform all aspects of marketplace strategies. To minimize confusion, we will focus on the central message strategy because it is the basis for a public relations plan that centers on communicating with publics about an issue.

There are different kinds of central messages. Some contain parts that appeal primarily to emotions; while, other appeal to reason, and still many appeal to both.

Kinds of Central Messages

Like the goal, the central message provides a response to the public relations issue. A central message should contain two to four main points. The main points can include subpoints. There are several types of central messages (or appeals) sometimes combined in a campaign. They vary by public relations campaign goal and target stakeholders. Below is a review of some general kinds of central messages. The list is by no means exhaustive.

Attributes and benefits. Some central messages focus on the characteristics and benefits of an issue. The issue may be a position, service, product, brand, or organization. The characteristics appeal to the rational part of the mind. In the case of a drill, the product attributes are the price and features such as speed, design, and construction. The ability to drill a hole to place a hook to hang paintings or secure a shelf are benefits. These benefits activate emotional processing. A social services agency offers specific services (the characteristics) resulting in benefits from receiving the services. Participation in educational programs that bring about feelings of accomplishment and satisfaction, child daycare services that free up primary caregivers to pursue personal or professional goals are examples of characteristics and benefits.

Price and quality. This type of message emphasizes quality for the price. The benefit of compliance outweighs the cost. Walmart advertises that it offers quality products that are competitively priced. In fact, Walmart's tagline is "Save money. Live better." BestBuy will match a competitor's lower price on a specific brand and model number. Some companies offer an additional discount after price matching. Consumer Reports often recommends generic brands not only because of their quality but also because of low price points or associated cost. Price is not always monetary. It can also involve investing time to derive some benefit. For example, the benefits from participating in a free workshop facilitated by an expert outweighs the length of time required to complete the activity.

Application. This type of messaging concentrates on demonstrating product usage to stakeholders. One recent example is the usage of IBM's Watson business analytics service. IBM's central message presents the usage of Watson across various industries small to large companies in real world applications. At the local level, this may involve testimonials and stories from actual customers attesting to their success owing to Watson. Internally, testimonials support the usage of a new set of best practices in different operations of a business or non-profit organization are examples of a central message centered on application of the issue or what the organization offers.

Think about This . . .

Some brand messaging is indirect through product lines. A 2010 *Advertising Age* article by Emily Bryson York entitled "KFC's Stunts Make Nightly News, But Do Nothing to Stop Sales Slide," which cited KFC as an example of how lack of a consistent product line and message can have a detrimental impact on sales.

KFC, formerly known as Kentucky Fried Chicken, changed its name to its initials and then back to its previous name and again back to KFC, changed its secret recipe, and replaced its signature chicken sandwich with another sandwich. Additionally, the company ran promotions that created demand that the company failed to accommodate, only causing more customer dissatisfaction and confusion. In the article, York quoted branding consultant Denise Lee-Yohn, "They (KFC) don't have a clear identity anymore, and I think that's hurt them." These blunders, along with the lack of a clear and consistent brand positioning strategy have resulted in continued market share losses. Closing more U.S. restaurants, KFC continues to struggle today.

Ask yourself: How might KFC effectively position itself and develop a consistent central message about its brand and products? What suggestions might you offer?

York, E. B. (2010, April 19). KFC's stunts make nightly news, but do nothing to stop sales slide. *Advertising Age.* Retrieved from http://adage.com/article/news/fast-food-kfc-s-stunts-stop-sales-slide/143359/.

Product class. Competition among brands may come from outside the product class (e.g. brands of cars, tablets, running shoes). In this case, it is important to understand expected product benefits. For example, why do people primarily drink milk? Is it for the calcium or as a beverage to complement consumption with another food product? In the case of transportation, going from Boston to New York City can occur using different modes of transportation. One can take a bus, train, plane, drive a vehicle, hitchhike (not recommended), or even walk (if one is not in a hurry). Each has its merits. Understanding the relevant stakeholders will inform the development of a central message that considers choices and the importance of specific benefits associated with those choices.

Product user, service user, or affiliation. This central message aims to create a link between stakeholders and the organization whether it is a product, brand, service, organization, or other affiliation. The goal is to establish and strengthen the stakeholders' identification with the organization. Early Apple laptop users experienced this connection when Apple had less than 10% of the market. Most graphic design practitioners would only use Apple computers. Another example would be the U.S. Marine Corp., "The Few. The Proud," in which the central message is that the Marine Corp. is an exclusive club, with high physical standards and values. It's not for everyone.

Compared to competition. This type of message emphasizes comparisons with the organization's major competitors, which can extend across product class. The comparison may involve objective measures assessed by a third party. This process extends across different contexts in which a decision is a response to the appeal. There have been ad campaigns that deploy this approach. Comparisons among brand paper towel absorption properties is one example. Another is the Eveready and Duracell batteries' long-lasting performance comparison. Last, Avis positioned itself against the largest car rental company at the time, Hertz, claiming that they try harder because they are number two.

Unique selling proposition. This approach involves offering something unique, which is not available from other parties. The message emphasizes one or two unique aspects of the offering and evidence to support the claim. For example, FedEx guarantees overnight delivery of packages covering a large geographical area. Domino's delivers fresh, hot pizza to your door in 30 minutes or less or it's free. Staples offers a price match program, plus 10% off the difference. Mast Brothers Chocolate offers high quality gourmet products precisely crafted through every step of the process. The company pays attention to detail, meticulous craftsmanship, innovation, and inspirational simplicity. Tom Shoes donates a pair of shoes to a child for every pair the company sells. These brands offer a uniqueness that is central to their identity and message.

Cultural symbol. A message centers on creating a new or using an existing cultural symbol, which is usually a person, object, or idea that represents what stakeholders value and believe. There is a connection between the symbol and appeal. Politicians often use celebrities or place themselves juxtaposed to such symbols hoping that the symbol's goodwill will increase their support. The Ford Mustang and Mr. Clean are iconic symbols developed by marketers. More recently, we see "Flo" the Progressive Insurance spokesperson or "Bob" from Bob's Furniture stores located in the Northeastern United States. Ronald McDonald, Burger King, and The KFC Colonel are other examples.

Strong organizational cultures have their own cultural symbols such as Steve Jobs, Bill Gates, Al Gore (in the environmental and sustainability community), and many others. These individuals exemplify the organization's values and culture.

Figure 8.4 Cultures Have Their Own Symbols with Ascribed Meaning

Borrowed interest. A variation of cultural symbol is the borrowed interest approach. Borrowed interest draws attention and interest to the message because of a well-known person, object, or idea. For instance, Shaquille O'Neal promoting the Ring Floodlight Cam security systems or Tiger Woods promoting Buicks. A celebrity or leader promoting volunteerism for a specific charity is another example. In these cases, the key strategy is to have the appeal of the attention getter rub off on the overall message, issue, or organization.

Product recall. This specific type of central message is self-explanatory. Depending on the nature of the recall, the message may have components directed not only the product recall, but also the procedures and support necessary to successfully execute the recall campaign. Coordinating messaging minimizes conflicting communications. In other words, a recalled product should not be promoted at the same time. Examples of recalls have been cars, a Black & Decker coffee maker, and a Samsung cell phone. In the case of the Black & Decker coffee maker, the central message focused on messaging that would assure compliance, while at the same time, mitigate adverse publicity. In the coffee maker example, successful product recall campaigns cover two areas: (1) inform customers on how to return the product, which also requires a sufficient internal return system, and (2) minimize negative publicity about the recall. Both concerns necessitate communicating with internal as well as external stakeholders and publics.

Fear appeals. Fear messaging is based on dire consequences for noncompliance, thus exploiting fear and anxiety caused by the message. This is a type of risk communication. Fear exposure is a function of level of fear communicated and repetition of the fear message. Anti-smoking campaigns, stop illicit drug usage appeals, and anti-drunk driving messages make use of fear to deter action by explicitly presenting the consequences of engaging in undesirable behavior.

Sometimes people avoid exposure to strong fear appeals because exposure causes psychological discomfort. The most effective fear appeals present moderate levels of fear and a simple solution for addressing the problem. Fear messages are effective on those stakeholders with low self-esteem and who find the message significant and relevant to them. A credible message source also strengthens the efficacy of the message.

Crisis communication. The Institute for Crisis Management defines a crisis as "Any issue, problem or disruption which triggers negative stakeholder reactions that can impact the organization's reputation, business, and financial strength" (Institute for Crisis Management, 2017, p. 1). Crises can be internal as well as external. A crisis message contains the following components.

- An emotionally charged situation emerges in which the message shows concern for the stakeholders. Support from the organization helps people cope.
- The message addresses the key stakeholders' apprehensions about the circumstances.
- The message provides evidence to support how people's concerns such as safety and the likelihood of reoccurrence are addressed. This requires a balance between understanding the needs and worries of the stakeholders and simply presenting the facts.
- Communication is candid and honest.
- Messaging provides follow-up and updates.

The central message should be accurate and communicated expeditiously. Under crisis conditions, sometimes miscommunication occurs and becomes the basis of what people believe, independent of facts. For this reason, an accurate, clear, and disseminated central message to all stakeholders during a crisis is important. Under these circumstances, stakeholders who do not make informed decisions can make the situation worse. In the late 1990s, the media reported that Nike mistreated its workers in Asia. There was a tremendous amount of negative news coverage and many rumors circulated, some of which were inaccurate. Nonetheless, inaccurate media coverage fueled animus toward Nike. Nike's crisis communications set the record straight by responding with evidence dispelling ill-informed opinions. Like product recall campaigns, publicity plays a vital role in crisis communications.

Internal organizational action. An appeal directed at organizational members comes in many forms covering a wide range of topics. Some central messages are persuasive such as convincing employees to make charitable contributions or persuading them to volunteer their time for a social cause. Other messaging focuses on increasing employee morale or productivity.

One such successful example is the IBM On Demand Community. This initiative allows employees access to 140 software tools so that they can provide tools and assistance to local schools and community organizations on a volunteer basis. The central and sub-messages of the On Demand campaign center on the following points:

- informing publics of IBM's commitment to volunteering;
- learning how to be an IBM volunteer;
- developing solutions for local communities;
- learning what tools are available;
- receiving volunteer training;
- getting answers to questions;
- submitting volunteer hours and recognizing employees; and
- submitting feedback.

The program has operated for nearly 15 years throughout the world and continues to do so today with the participation of employee, retirees, and community-partner stakeholders.

Figure 8.5 Corporate Social Responsibility Can Take Many Forms

Corporate social responsibility (CSR). This type of central messaging concentrates on corporate social responsibility communication as a process that inherently is about good deeds performed by an organization relative to its various stakeholders (Sones, Grantham, & Vieira, 2009). CSR messages include demonstrating how benefits are shared between the organization and society. The appeal can take two general forms. First, it can pertain to a social cause itself such as advocating support for a bill or a call to action concerning a social issue. Second, it might center on the organization's specific involvement in a social cause (Du, Bhattacharya, & Sen, 2010); for instance, Maxwell House's participation in Habitat for Humanity or Dove's efforts to raise awareness about early cancer detection and support for cancer survivors.

A CSR central message emphasizes the importance of the social issue. In the case of corporations, the cause should not relate to the company's business because doing so raises suspicion and potentially damages credibility. Du and colleagues (2010) put forth other message content required in CSR messaging: 1) commitment to the cause, 2) the impact the organization has or will have on the cause, 3) why it engages in a social cause, and 4) the CSR fit with the organization and its mission and values.

Slogans and Taglines

Often a catchy slogan or tagline that captures the essence of the central message accompanies messaging. A **slogan** is a catch phrase using between one and a few words. It is fluid and changes over relatively short periods of time because it pertains to a specific campaign or area of the organization. A slogan can include a **jingle** or catchy music such as the Kit Kat "Give me a break" short song, which also is associated with the central message and issue.

Figure 8.6 Slogans Evolve Over Time

On the other hand, a **tagline** applies to the entire organization, everything it does, and its brands. It encapsulates the mission and identity of the organization. For instance, ExxonMobil's tagline is "Energy lives here." The company's central message is about meeting the world's energy needs so that everyone can benefit and have an improved quality of life.

The point to remember about slogans and taglines is that slogans pertain to a specific campaign and a tagline is longer term and applies to the entire organization. Chapter 7 provides more information about slogans and taglines.

Repositioning the Central Message

Repositioning a central message involves revising a central message to fit current market or internal environmental needs. There are essentially two reasons for repositioning.

First, sometimes messages are simply ill-conceived requiring a new message. Second, over time a message becomes less effective. Situations change, competitors react, consumers' perceptions change, mergers occur, trends move markets and society in different directions, new products and brands enter the market, demographics shift, and technology is forever changing. Any one or combination of these conditions can cause a decline in revenues, less services utilized, or diminished brand equity. Repositioning helps get the situation back on track.

For instance, MTV has reinvented itself over the years moving from essentially a music video channel to a lifestyle source of information and engagement. Target has also shifted its message with greater emphasis on price competitiveness, concentrating more on lower price points including its own value product lines. Some changes have been unsuccessful like Kmart's attempt to move upscale. In this case, preconceptions became an enduring reality to the detriment of Kmart.

In general, brand extensions and product extensions take advantage of sales opportunities in new markets by borrowing the positive equity of the brand. Coca-Cola, Hallmark cards, Starbucks, Disney, Domino's and libraries in general are examples. For instance, Domino's once was Domino's Pizza, specializing in pizza. Currently, pizza is the anchor to a host of nonpizza prepared foods and hence the current name "Domino's." This strategy allows Domino's to expand its market to those consumers who may want greater variety in their food choices. Libraries have expanded their services to include more programs such as literacy, children's programs, rental items in addition to books, and any number of special interest activities.

In addition, unanticipated opportunities cause changes in messaging. A product recall, a new market opening, the acquisition of a new service or product line, a new brand extension, the need to effectuate cost efficiencies, executive scandal, and egregious organizational practices are reasons to cause a revision in the message.

Some Thoughts from a Pollster

A political pollster, Frank Luntz, in his book, *Words that Work: It's Not What You Say, It's What People Hear* (2008), provides insights based on his many years of research.

According to Luntz, the public relations practitioner must empathize with the stakeholder because what the individual perceives constitutes his or her reality. This reality is based on the stakeholder's deepest thoughts and beliefs. The person must first understand through his/her personal life's filters, and then relate to the message at some level.

Table 8.1 Corresponding Issues, Goals, Central Messages, and Slogans/Taglines

Type of Public Relations Campaign	Issue	Goal	Central Message	Type of Central Message	Slogan/Tagline
Crisis and Marketing	Fake iPhone chargers in China are exploding, hurting and killing people	Stop circulation of counterfeit iPhone charger in China	Trade in the fake iPhone charger, no questions asked and buy the real deal at Apple store for half price	External stakeholder call to action	"Think Different"
Organizational	Walmart suffered from gender discrimination and inequality	Eliminate gender discrimination and inequality at Walmart through a realignment of the company culture	Walmart is dedicated to implementing policies that foster salary and job advancement gender equality	Internal organizational stakeholder (employees including management) action	"Save money. Live better."
Marketing	There is low awareness of the BMW Z3 Roadster	Increase the Z3 Roadster recognition	The Z3 is an exhilarating experience providing by BMW through German innovative design, sports performance, and made in the USA.	Inform customer/ consumer stakeholders of new product	"Made by BMW"
Marketing	Tropicana juice sales have not reached their potential	Increase Tropicana Pure Premium juice sales	Tropicana juice enhances health because it contains potassium and thus is ahead of its competitors	Unique selling proportion offer lo customer stakeholders	"Not from Concentrate" "100% Pure Florida Squeezed Orange Juice"
Organizational and Corporate Social Responsibility	Increase the number of volunteer hours for the On Demand Community (ODC) program	Increase employee awareness and participation in the ODC	ODC highlights IBM's reputation for philanthropy. ODC sets it apart from its competitors by combining the strengths and skills of its employees with the power of IBM's technologies and solutions. ODC volunteers have resources to aid communities.	Inform and call for action	"our values, your skills, real impact" "Our values at work"

Based on his experience, Luntz recommends ten best practices for effective communication:

1   Use small words. Certain words evoke people.
2   Use short sentences. Keep it simple and understandable.
3   Credibility is as important as philosophy. Source trust, competence, and likability are vital to message believability.
4   Consistency matters. Conflicting messages damage credibility.
5   Novelty offers something new and draws attention to the message.
6   Sound and texture matter. Appealing to the senses increases involvement in the message.
7   Speak inspirationally. Stakeholders want to be positive, so inspire them.
8   Ask a question. Get the stakeholder to think about the message.
9   Provide context and explain relevance. Why is this message relevant and important to the stakeholder?
10   Visual imagery matters. Visuals inspire and are remembered.

Putting It All Together with Some Examples

The goal is usually the opposite of the issue because it is a solution to the issue. The central message and slogan are the manifestation of the public relations central idea. The goal informs the central idea. The central message is a structured, communication manifestation of the central idea. Table 8.1 provides some examples of sets of these components.

The first case is an example of a combination of a crisis communication and marketing public relations campaign. While trying to stop the purchase and usage of counterfeit Apple chargers that exploded resulting in injury and death in some cases, the company also saw an opportunity to bring these consumers into the Apple fold. If consumers turned in the counterfeit product at an Apple store, they received a large discount on a genuine Apple charger. Apple anticipated an increase in retail traffic, exposing these potential customers to the Apple line, while reducing the number of fake chargers in the marketplace.

The fourth example attempted to differentiate Tropicana premium orange juice from its competitors by emphasizing that the juice contains potassium which is healthy for one's heart. Communicating this product attribute enhanced the perceived quality of Tropicana in the eyes of consumers.

Walmart has had a cultural realignment challenge for years. It centers on bringing about gender equality in the Walmart workplace. The Z3 campaign was about increasing not only brand awareness but also the "Made by BMW" brand. Last, the IBM On Demand global program, which has been highly successful and continues today, managed to increase the involvement of employees assisting non-profit and governmental entities in their local communities.

Summary of Key Concepts

*   The central message communicates the central theme.
*   The central message is what guides all communication with stakeholders in a public relations campaign.
*   There are numerous types of central messages for internal and external stakeholders.
*   Sometimes central messages include a slogan, tagline, or jingle.

- A slogan is campaign specific.
- A tagline is more permanent and usually organization-wide.
- A central message revision occurs when circumstances change or new opportunities arise.

In the Case of Canyon Ranch . . . the Central Message

The Central Message: For its clients, Canyon Ranch is dedicated to developing and offering a full range of customized health wellness services especially health and healing designed to meet their needs in a high quality, responsive all-inclusive resort environment. Messaging emphasizes:

1 having available a multidisciplinary team of outstanding physicians and other health and healing specialists;
2 through the usage of a cutting-edge customer relations management system, providing personalized services for each client;
3 offering health and healing services; spa, fitness, and salon services; and top shelf lodging second to none in a seamless process;
4 offering the health and healing services as the cornerstone of the unmatched Canyon Ranch experience;
5 Canyon Ranch offers the best for the best.

Key Terms

Application 182
Attributes and benefits 181
Borrowed interest 184
Central idea 179
Central message 179
Compared to competition 183
Corporate social responsibility 187
Crisis communication 185
Cultural symbol 183
Fear appeal 185
Internal organizational action 185
Jingle 187

Positioning strategy 181
Positioning statement 181
Price and quality 182
Product class 183
Product or service user and affiliation 183
Product recall 184
Repositioning 188
Slogan 187
Tagline 188
Unique selling proposition 183

Chapter Questions

8.1 What is a central message?
8.2 What is a positioning statement?
8.3 Describe what is a central message based on attributes and benefits. Provide an example.
8.4 Describe what is a central message based on price and quality. Provide an example.
8.5 Describe what is a central message based on application. Provide an example.

8.6   Describe what is a central message based on product class and provide an example.

8.7   Describe what is a central message based on user or affiliation and offer an example.

8.8   Describe what is a central message based on comparison with the competition and offer an example.

8.9   Describe what is a central message based on unique selling proportion and provide an example.

8.10   Describe what is a central message based on cultural symbol and offer an example.

8.11   Describe what is a central message based on borrowed interest and offer an example.

8.12   Describe what is a central message based on product recall and offer an example.

8.13   Describe what is a central message based on fear appeal and offer an example.

8.14   Describe what is a central message based on crisis communication and offer an example.

8.15   Describe what is a central message based on internal organizational action and offer an example.

8.16   Describe what is a central message based on corporate social responsibility and provide an example.

8.17   What is a slogan and provide an example?

8.18   What is a jingle and offer an example?

8.19   What is a tagline and provide an example?

8.20   Define central message repositioning.

8.21   What are the ten best practices that Luntz suggests for effective communication?

8.22   What are the two main reasons for repositioning the central message?

8.23   What is the typical length of a central message?

References

Dougherty, T. (2015, February 15). *The elegance of Starbucks flat white.* Quoted Tom Ong. Retrieved from www.stealingshare.com/elegance-starbucks-flat-white/page/11/.

Du, S., Bhattacharya, C. B., & Sen, S. (2010). Maximizing business returns to corporate social responsibility (CSR): The role of CSR communication. *International Journal of Management Reviews, 12*(1), 8–19.

Institute for Crisis Management. (2017, April). *ICM Annual Crisis Report.* Denver, CO: Institute for Crisis Management (ICM).

Luntz, F. I. (2008). *Words that work: It's not what you say, it's what people hear.* Boston, MA: Hachette Books.

Sones, M., Grantham, S., & Vieira, E. T., Jr. (2009). Communicating CSR via pharmaceutical company web sites: Evaluating message frameworks for external and internal stakeholders. *Corporate Communication: An International Journal, 14*(2), 144–157.

York, E. B. (2010, April 19). KFC's stunts make nightly news, but do nothing to stop sales slide. *Advertising Age.* Retrieved form http://adage.com/article/news/fast-food-kfc-s-stunts-stop-sales-slide/143359/.

Part IV

Planning

Key Stakeholder Tactics and Action Plans

Chapter 9

Public Relations Tactics' Toolbox

A brand is no longer what we tell the consumer it is – it is what consumers tell each other it is.
(Scott Cook, Founder of Intuit, Hardoon & Galit, 2013, p. 133)

Learning Objectives

To:

- Understand what is a tactic and provide examples.
- Explain tactics as individual-, group-, and mass-level messaging.
- Understand and select tactics for different conditions.
- Describe what is message framing.
- Understand and know key psychological dynamics that impact message interpretation.
- Describe compliance gaining strategies.
- Know the Toulmin Model of Argumentation.

Introduction

A **tactic** is a tool, task, or activity pursued to achieve an objective that is associated with a public relations' goal, strategy, and objective. Effective tactics are creative, cost-efficient, draw attention to and are consistent with the central message. For example, if a promotional campaign focuses on increasing awareness of a new and innovative cell phone charger by emphasizing its ease of use and style design, tactics might include producing and distributing short videos featuring the charger in use, accentuating its design. Charger users would likely post reviews and testimonials about the product. Guided by a creative strategy, other tactics would also communicate the merits of the charger.

As the example illustrates, tactics tell a contextual story. In choosing a tactic, the practitioner assesses its contribution to an objective through what we know about publics: individuals, groups, organizations, and society in general relevant to an issue wrapped in a situation that exists in time. Tactics also help create dialogue and establish relationships between and among stakeholders and the organization. Moreover, assessment tools are tactics listed in the overall evaluation section and specified in each action plan. In other words, an assessment activity is itself a tactic. Last, the information for a tactic is located in an activity brief that details each tactical activity including execution dates, target public information, messaging content, images, storyboards, and scheduling. The activity brief located in the appendix assures that the tactic is appropriate for the campaign goal.

This chapter focuses on groups of public relations tactics available to the practitioner to these ends. Because of their importance in society and to public relations, the next chapter solely examines social media tactics. This chapter examines types of tactics, considerations for choosing tactics, message frames, and message construction. First, we start with general ways of viewing tactics.

General Ways of Looking at Tactics

There are different ways to consider tactics. Tactics are formal and informal; external and internal; explicit and implicit; and involve measurement of their effectiveness.

Especially relevant to internal organizational interaction, there are formal and informal methods of communication. Chapter 4 discusses an internal communication audit whose goal is to discover the formal and informal ways organizational members communicate. The audit also helps identify informal opinion leaders within an organizational structure.

Figure 9.1 Internal Organizational Communication Involves Groups of Different Sizes Operating for Numerous Reasons

This type of situational analysis might uncover more effective and cost-efficient ways for internal communication by learning how members communicate informally. Sometimes the proverbial water cooler place for gossip is an effective approach to start.

Tactics are directed at internal organizational stakeholders such as employees who serve in various capacities as well as external stakeholders such as customers, vendors, regulators, NGOs, various activists and so forth. Although internal groups can be easier to manage, this is not always the case especially today where social media's reach is ubiquitous. Chapter 5 discusses internal conditions that can potentially spiral out of control if not managed sufficiently early during the situation.

Next, some tactics are explicit while others are implicit and communicated through policies, rules, and actions. We are familiar with emails, postings, ads, and other forms of messaging. Yet, non-communication or specific behaviors whether organization-wide or individuals-focused can speak volumes. For instance, a manager asserts that employees' opinions and input matter. Yet, that same manager does not respond to suggestions or requests to meet. What might we conclude about this manager? The manager's sincerity is called into question by his/her own actions. This dynamic can operate at an organizational-wide scale. For example, an organizational merger will likely raise concerns about lay-offs. How both parties to the merger address or do not address this concern sends a message to employees or, at the very least, leaves room for speculation. This same process can easily apply to product recalls or situations that rise to crisis levels because of management's failure to proactively address an issue.

Last, tactics include activities required to measure the effectiveness of public relations activities. These tactics can range from surveying publics to web analytics to themed event attendance and media coverage that compare outcomes to quantifiable clear benchmarked objective operating on a timeline. Chapters 7 and 13 cover this topic.

Types of Tactics

Public relations includes many activities and tactics that complement each other in a manner geared to achieve the objectives of a campaign. Table 9.1 lists the major public relations tactics. The nature of the engagement with the target publics is the basis for grouping tactics (Wilson & Ogden, 2015). Keep in mind that many of these messaging tactics overlap. Because of the important engagement function that they perform, they are discussed separately.

The first level of engagement is the most persuasive. It is **individual-level messaging**, providing an appeal geared to the identified individual using tactics such as personal emails, telephone calls, personal meetings, and private messaging through the various social media platforms. This level of messaging provides the opportunity for two-way transactional communication and involvement.

Second, identifying publics for communication, which targets groups that have a shared interest or other commonality, is **group-level messaging.** Tactics include blogs, special interest groups and published materials, meetings of those who share common interests, and so forth. People are active participants in a collective dialogue among themselves, generate content, disseminate information, and increase issue knowledge with audience members.

Last and at the other end of the spectrum, is **mass-level messaging** in which stakeholders are undifferentiated. These tactics include news releases, media advisories, public

Table 9.1 Groups of Tactics by Nature of Messaging

Individual-Level Tactics

Direct message	Publicist
One-on-one meeting	Speech writing
Interview	Virtual reality (VR)
Lobbying	
Ongoing media relationships*	
Internal counseling	

Group-Level Tactics

Social media (See Chapter 10)	Brochures/handbooks	Campaign evaluation*
Conference & Event*	Tours/briefing	
CD/DVD*	Partnership/program development	
Specialty magazine	Report on diversity & inclusion	
Specialty newsletter	Situational analysis (incl. scanning)*	
Annual report	Background information/research*	

Mass-Level Tactics

Banner	Media advisory	Brand promotional content
Public service announcement*	Pitch letter	Website*
Podcast*	Fact sheet	Signage
Video*	Press kit	Sponsorship*
Advertising* (can be micro-targeted)	Magazine	Celebrity endorsement/mgmt
News release	Newsletter	Retail activity/ exhibition
Video news release	Opinion/editorial piece	
Audio new release	Product literature*	

* Initial contact is the basis of this classification. Some messaging can micro-target publics. Tactics can transition into other categories. For instance, event attendees may be followed-up with private meetings. Undifferentiated messaging can result in individual- or group-level activities.

service announcements (PSA), cable and network television, and billboards to name a few. Communication is one way. It is usually top down and content is informational.

The tactics used depend on the public relations strategy and objectives of a public's action plan. For instance, appealing to opinion leaders involves persuading them not only to support a position but also to advocate for the position. On the other hand, to increase issue knowledge and engagement, targeting publics through common interests at a group-level is effective. In situations where the objective's focus is general awareness and building a basic level of knowledge, then mass-level messaging would be an efficient approach. As messaging moves from individual to undifferentiated, the individual stakeholders become less distinguishable. Moreover, tactic types can overlap or transition into other kinds of tactics. For instance, event attendees may be followed up with private meetings. Mass messaging may result in subsequent individual- or group-level activities. There are entire chapters and books written about these various communication tactics. Since our focus is strategy and planning for public relations, this section simply highlights key considerations for each type of messaging.

Individual-Level Messaging

Individual-level messaging is the most persuasive public relations tactic, but not the most cost-efficient. The transmission of the message is controlled and, although responses are not controlled, the transactional nature of the interaction can be managed to a degree. For instance, elected officials can frame the government's response to a public challenge, but cannot control how constituents react to the message. For individual messaging tailored to the individual to be effective, the recipient must feel that the sender is communicating with him/her directly. Last, direct messaging is effective to persuade opinion leaders who then become credible issue advocates. The following are brief descriptions of some individual-level tactics deployed to engage publics.

Direct Written Messages

Identified parties receive direct messages. They can take the form of traditional mail, emails, and text messaging. Since there is a direct link with an identified stakeholder, this type of messaging is costly but persuasive. Private messaging can occur through the various social media platforms well, which allows the professional to pretest or run the message by others to maximize its effectiveness.

One-on-One Meeting

One-on-one meetings can take various forms and can be formal or informal. Public relations practitioners meet with stakeholders to engage them and elicit support for important issues. At such meetings, the public relations professional presents a case often supported with evidence including why the issue is important to the stakeholder. For example, a local candidate may meet with various community leaders individually to garner their support for the candidate and the positions that the candidate represents. One-on-one meetings provide the opportunity for instant feedback and clarification; therefore, the practitioner must be well prepared and versed on the issue and possible challenges to the message owing to this immediacy.

Interview

One-on-one interviews are usually between a media representative and the public relations practitioner. They can be in-person, on the telephone, or by way of a video call. The practitioner's greatest asset is credibility. In other words, the interviewee knows the issue, is succinct and forthright so that trust is established, and should communicate confidence and clarity during the interview. If possible, request topics and questions in advance of the interview including the interviewer's sources of information. Agree in advance about the length and location of the interview. Assure that there is an understanding of what is and what is not on the record.

Will the interview be recorded? If so, will the recording be hand notes, an audio device, and/or videotape? For videotaped interviews, dress professionally to communicate credibility.

With the information available, plan so that the interview serves to support the public relations' issue. Consider the following items:

1   What? State the issue concisely.
2   To what end? Be aware of the importance of the issue to stakeholders and to the organization.
3   Who? List the individuals, publics, and stakeholders involved.
4   Timeline? Indicate all important time considerations.
5   Where? Are there significant geographical locations, especial local areas?
6   History? Does the organization have a history (especially public relations) on this issue?
7   Credibility? Is the organization perceived credible? If so, in what way?
8   Organizational expectations? Note the organization's goals especially pertaining to the interview.
9   Motives and intentions? The interviewee should summarize his/her motives for becoming involved in the issue.

Lobbying

Lobbying is a public relations function. Entry level public relations practitioners are not likely to assume lobbying duties. This sensitive function is the charge of seasoned professionals. Depending on the nature of lobbying, some lobbyists are lawyers, scientists, government relations specialists, former government officials, or individuals with expertise in an area. In 2016, lobbyists spent over $3 billion in the United States advocating for positions. In 2017, the average lobbyist salary for local, state, and national efforts was nearly $110,000. The top 10% earned $200,000+.

What exactly is a lobbyist? A **lobbyist** is a person who attempts to influence the voting on legislation or the decisions of government officials by meeting directly with officials or staff to make a case. Sometimes, officials depend on lobbyists such as trade association representatives to provide industry research that aids in their decision process. This might involve the testimony of experts or the availability of data. As we can see, a lobbyist focuses on building relationships with government officials to defeat, help pass, or amend proposed legislation, policies, or rules to the benefit of the organization or group the lobbyist represents. Federal law requires lobbyists to register before engaging in activities. States and local municipalities have regulations, which vary by location.

Ongoing Media Relationships

Public relations practitioners maintain relationships with **gatekeepers** and others who decide what news stories to cover. The news influences an organization's reputation. Depending on how news media frame reporting, the audience develops a positive, negative, or indifferent attitude toward an organization or issue.

News reporters seek stories that engage readers and audience members. They are skeptical about public relations efforts that attempt to clearly frame stories in a favorable or unfavorable light. For the same reason, organizations want fair media coverage and assume that if they maintain positive relationships with news professionals, their coverage will be fair if not favorable. Yet, the news media's credibility rest on perceptions of "objective" coverage. Often, these perspectives can conflict with the practitioner's messaging and goals causing strained relationships among the parties involved. Against this reality, it is important to know that although media coverage will not always be desirable, maintaining and understanding others' positions will benefit an organization in the end. The public relations practitioner realizes that being credible and earning the respect of news media professionals require timely responses (even if answers to media questions are not provided), being forthright, and treating journalists and reports with professional courtesy and respect. Actions can speak louder than words in this type of relationship and environment.

Internal Counseling

Generally, the internal counseling role of the public relations professional involves providing advice to management about policies, relationships, and messaging. There are different levels of the advisory role. At the **advisory-only** role, management or staff are under no obligation to follow any advice provided by the practitioner. Next is the **compulsory-advisory** position. In this role, the decision-makers must listen to the public relations professional. The third kind of counseling is **concurring-authority**. In this case, the approval of public relations takes place before communication occurs. If there are differences between the communication creator and public relations professional, no action occurs. Only upon agreement can messaging transpire. In cases of trademark and other content of a propriety nature, sometimes the legal department must approve content. Johnson & Johnson and its many divisions follow this approach. Last, **command-authority**, usually granted to legal departments, allows them to edit or change content to meet legal liability concerns with or without the consent of public relations. This can hamstring public relations efforts and mitigate messaging effectiveness by making communications adhere to more "legalese" framing.

Publicist

A **publicist** is a professional who deals with the placement of stories in the news media. This person often represents specific individuals as opposed to a **press agent**, whose function is to find unusual news angles and plan themed events that draw media attention. Publicists can operate internally within an organization, work at an agency, or operate alone. An external publicist receives a monthly fee for advising and representing clients such as celebrities or high-profile business executives. Some publicists advise or prepare news releases or statements on behalf of clients, write speeches or prepare presentations, prepare clients for interviews, provide social media communication advice, offer research on the client's social presence, and advise on attire for special events. A successful publicist provides positive publicity for the client whether individual or organization.

Speech Writing

Public relations practitioners write speeches as well whether it is for an organizational administrator, company executive, or celebrity. There are four types of speeches. In **impromptu speech** requires no preparation. A **manuscript speech** is reading the speech word for word from a podium or teleprompter. If presented well, it can be effective. A **memorized speech** is simply a speech presented from memory. Last, an **extemporaneous speech** is one given with some preparation. In a sense, it is a combination of the other methods and can be highly effective.

Before giving a speech, acquiring information about the venue is critically important, including anticipated number of audience members, their views about the issue, media coverage, who is sponsoring the event, and audiovisual capabilities.

Speeches generally follow a standard outline such as the one below.

1   an *introduction* that draws and connects with the audiences;
2   statement of the *main purpose* of the speech including a *preview* of the speech;
3   two to four main points supported by evidence such as facts, examples, or anecdotes;
4   a *conclusion* through restatement of the overall theme and main points;
5   if appropriate, a compelling question or statement to end.

For an extemporaneous speech, the speaker should sufficiently know the content and may very well follow an outline on index cards. Reading per verbatim from paper, a digital device, or PowerPoint slides diminishes a speech's effectiveness. The audience wants to know that the speaker is committed to the topic. The speaker's command of the issue demonstrates this. The mantra is "Be prepared, be prepared, and again be prepared."

Finally, various speakers' bureaus provide expert speakers available to talk about numerous topics such as fossil fuels, green energy, foreign policy, the state of healthcare around the world, and many more subjects. Since many of these speakers promote a position, they often do not charge to give a speech. Some notable bureaus are the American Program Bureau, Washington Speakers' Bureau, Keppler Speakers, and Macmillan Speakers.

Virtual Reality

With easy access to broadband and digital technologies, online-based innovative tools are available such as **Virtual reality** (VR) worlds. Some headsets simulate places and conditions throughout the world that otherwise would be inaccessible to most people. Stories unfold in a virtual world that provides an audio-visual compelling presence supporting or opposing an issue. "Being there" takes on new meaning. VR can raise awareness about conditions throughout the world and place a face on these conditions. The virtual setting exposes journalists to issues in a realistic way not heretofore experienced. Potential customers experience innovative products through VR. The possibilities are limited by the imagination of public relations practitioners.

Group-Level Messaging

Tactics at the group level combine attributes of individual- and mass-level messaging. The publics and stakeholder groups are typically defined and differentiated. Therefore, messaging targets each community or group comprising the public. This is a popular venue for the public relations practitioner and for activism efforts as well. For example, individuals concerned about the environment follow a blog about environmental sustainability. The average level of awareness, knowledge, and perhaps advocacy about environmental issues is likely to be greater with these audience members as opposed to news broadcast directed at the general population. Audiences based on commonalities or issue affiliation are likely to mobilize as well as provide feedback, comments, and share content, lending themselves to crowdsourcing and viral marketing techniques. Constructing effective messages is straightforward for identified publics. However, there is less control over feedback and responses to the message. A public might take the issue and run with it positively or negatively, or it might gain no traction.

Event

Themed events are conferences, annual meetings, celebrations, workshops, dinners, recruitment fairs, contests, and competitions. Event management not only involves the planning and organizing of an activity, but also its promotion. It is important to keep the venue size in mind because over promoting an event can result in turning people down, which often has an adverse impact on the public relations goal. Events are local, regional, national, and international, each with its unique and common set of considerations. Events can be in-person, online, or a combination of both. For example, in South Berwick, Maine we have an annual Strawberry Festival in which local vendors sell crafts, people eat strawberry shortcake, and local musicians perform. Boston hosts many regional events such as the Boston Flower & Garden Show. Automobile manufacturers hold shows for rolling out their new models for the forthcoming year. These events can be national and international in scope. Mountain Dew launched its highly successful online DEWMocracy contest in which artists submitted bottle designs, voted by the DEWMocracy community. The winning designers received graphic design commissions.

The following are suggestions typically addressed during event planning and promotion (Smith, 2013).

1   Is the event relevant to the target publics and the public relations goal?
2   Will the event garner media attention and publicity?
3   Does the scheduled date and time for the event conflict with any other major events or holidays?
4   Will the event program maintain participants' involvement?
5   Is the event theme appropriate and inclusive? Will any stakeholder groups oppose it?
6   If the event is outdoors, is there a contingency in case of inclement weather?
7   Focusing locally, are there any nearby concurrent activities that might draw from the event's attendees?
8   Will the host city or facility provide planning assistance or value-added options such as free parking or shuttle service?

Many of the public relations tactics and tools used for messaging and promoting an issue involve promoting special events.

CD/DVD

Some people prefer information in a tangible format such as CDs, DVDs and the cloud. Their attractiveness is the ability to store and present content using multi-modalities such as images, videos, audio, pdf, and so forth in an interactive digital environment. Some organizations present information to donors, investors, and potential customers on these media.

Specialty Magazine (Periodical)

There are thousands of offline and online magazines and websites devoted to special, and, in some cases, narrow topics. Some are non-profit and others are for-profit. Most readers possess knowledge of the topic and engage at various levels. **Specialty periodicals** can take the form of magazines, trade journals, and organizational magazines. Some examples are *Motor Trend, Aviation Week & Space Technology, Money, The Chronicle, Consumer Reports, America's Civil War, The African Executive, Le Commerce du Levant, FinanceAsia,* and *New Civil Engineer.* Complete articles or ready-to-publish news releases are sent to highly specialized magazines that appeal to very specific publics.

Specialty Newsletter

Newsletters are informal publications in hardcopy or digital format designed to provide information to stakeholders at regular intervals. Corporations use newsletters to communicate with employees and other stakeholders as well as non-profits and trade associations. Some media celebrities or organizations regularly produce newsletters about specialty topics. Sentences are short and to the point.

Annual Report

The Securities and Exchange Commission requires American companies that issue stock to provide **annual reports**. Some annual reports are simple while others are elaborate using color illustrations and graphics. The report contains information about a company or organization including the names of officers, their salaries, financial statements, narratives about the company's performance, social responsibility statement, and independent auditor's certification about the veracity of the report. Typically, the annual report is available in hardcopy and online at the corporate website in pdf format for download. Some companies also provide quarterly reports. The legal, financial, and public relations departments of an organization approve the annual report. Shareholders, other investors, banks, brokers, and other financial parties are key stakeholders interested in reviewing annual and quarterly reports. Last, in the United States, non-profits are required to submit annual reports to the Internal Revenue Service.

Brochure and Handbook

Brochures and handbooks are organizational publications that focus on a topic of interest. For example, **brochures** are about recruiting, brand and product lines, services, a social issues, or some other aspect of an organization. They are often for external usage. Sentences are short and to the point. Complex issues presented in smaller digestible parts keep the reader engaged. A brochure can range from one to 30 pages and the topic can be destination weddings to recruiting donors for a blood drive.

By the same token, **handbooks** are more involved and usually for internal usage. They often contain policy statements, statistics, and other facts about the organization or topic. Trade associations, universities/colleges, and corporations frequently develop and distribute various kinds of handbooks. They often specify procedures for various activities and duties including a hierarchy for reporting. Examples are faculty policy manuals and the Zappos Employee Handbook. Effective handbooks consist of the following characteristics:

1   They are engaging.
2   They use colors and visuals.
3   They communicate organizational culture.

4   They explain the reasoning and benefits behind organizational rules.
5   They include notification about topics subject to legal compliance such as the Americans with Disabilities Act and other relevant laws.

Press Tour and Briefing

A **press tour** is a visit and tour of an organization. The purpose is to increase an organization's visibility and build relationships with the news media. The key to a press tour is to provide newsworthy information about an issue relevant to the organization and stakeholders. Introducing something novel in addition to being personally relevant increases the likelihood that the message will draw media's attention. For example, a production facility that has expanded and created new jobs in an area with a high unemployment rate is newsworthy. A non-profit experiencing a tremendous spike in volunteerism and donor contributions is also newsworthy. In both examples, the news angle serves multiple purposes. It bolsters organizational image, communicates the organizations' contributions to society, and might very well increase sales and volunteerism respectively.

A press tour ends with a briefing in which the public relations representative answers additional questions or provides more information about the issue and organization in a press conference setting. The key to conducting a press tour and briefing is preparation. The practitioner should anticipate questions and prepare answers. Knowing the news media's concerns and focusing on them in advance aids in preparing satisfactory responses.

Partnership Program Development

Public relations' core activity is building relationships with stakeholders through the development of strategic partnerships in which an organization, public, or other organization work together on a campaign to bring about mutual beneficial outcomes. Partnerships differ based on the degree of shared involvement in the issue. Alliances and coalitions are types of partnerships.

An **alliance** is an informal and loosely structured relationship between or among organizations. An example is the alliance between Starbucks and the NAACP, which both work together to promote the goals of social and economic justice.

A **coalition** is a similar relationship with greater structure and specificity. For instance, in Kenya, communities build coalitions around decentralized institutions leading to the successful implementation of specific water sector reforms.

Both types of partnerships aim to establish relationships with individuals or groups that share common values and concerns. Stakeholders form partnerships for the following key reasons:

1   There is some identification among the groups.
2   There is a shared ideology, value, or belief system.
3   There are pragmatic considerations to mutual benefit such as job security, social programs, etc.

In all three cases, there is a commonality. Sometimes these partnerships enhance the organizational image of one or more members of the partnership especially between a partner with little social presence and one widely recognized.

Situational Analysis

An important tactic of the practitioner is conducting a situational analysis prior to developing a public relations campaign. Understanding the issue and challenges facing the organization's position on the issue in the context of the relevant environments is important whether the issue resides within the organization, externally, or in both places. Identifying and prioritizing publics according to their importance to the organization and the importance of the issue to them is a significant component of this research. Discovering stakeholder media habits guides the placement of messaging as well. Chapters 5 and 6 cover this function in detail.

Monitoring the relevant environments prior to the identified need for a public relations response is also a situational analysis function. This occurs through risk and issue management and tactics. Risk tactics involve scanning the environment for potential issues warranting attention. Contingencies are developed using issue management and tactics for closely monitoring identified issues.

Campaign Evaluation

Another public relations practitioner function is a campaign effectiveness assessment. Evaluation occurs at the end of the campaign or as a process of monitoring, evaluating, and adjusting throughout the campaign. In the latter case, progress reports provide updates and precede the post campaign report. Chapter 13 covers ongoing, summative, and formative types of evaluation. Ongoing evaluation requires prorated benchmarks for different measurement points during the campaign. These benchmarks serve as the basis of evaluation. There are many data collection tools available such as weekly sales data, surveys, tracking studies, social media measures, content analysis, total impressions, message recall, inquiries, media coverage, and other measurement tools.

The assessment occurs in two general areas. First, to what degree are the target publics exposed to the message? In other words, have they seen the message? Are they aware of the issue? These data refer to channel placement, exposure, and reach issues. Second, whether the message was persuasive refers to message construction and effectiveness. Was the message appealing? Did it shift opinions? Thus, both types of these assessments areas operate in unison and offer a picture of message reach and effectiveness.

Mass-Level Messaging

Mass-level messaging provides an immediate and effective impact. Mass-level messaging can take the form of other media coverage, which is less controlled by the practitioner and through using social media tools such as creating an active YouTube channel and Twitter feeds where the organization manages the content and timing of messaging. The following are several useful guidelines.

1   Know media contacts and their requirements for covering a story.
2   Provide materials for the target media market and audiences. Materials should consist of intriguing, relevant solid news.
3   The newsworthy materials should be relevant to the local community that the media outlet services. Sometimes "local" is a specialty topic with audience members across a wide geographical area.

4   The submitted material should be ready-to-use because it contains the story, is written in the style of the news media outlet, and is relevant to the audience.

5   In the event of an interview, select organizational executives who are knowledgeable in the subjective area and are dynamic speakers. For this role, interviewees will need coaching.

6   Use news conferences sparingly for genuine newsworthy developments. Alternatively, consider using news releases, statements, and the interview format when more appropriate. Remember, reports and journalists are busy as well.

Banner and Other Web Ads

A banner ad is a form of online advertising embedded on a web page. It is usually rectangular. Banners attract page visitors to a website by linking to the website of the advertiser. By clicking onto the banner, the visitors go to the advertiser's site. The advertiser pays the hosting website based on impressions and click-throughs. Click-through rates range from .14% to .28%. Monitored traffic happens in real-time.

There are different banner designs. Types include animated, rotating, scrolling, pop-up, pop-under, drop-down, interstitial, floating, corner peel, unicast, push-down, fixed panel, and XXL box banner.

Animated banners have a fixed number of loops in GIF format. Audio is available. In the case of product banners, features are demonstrated. They tend to have higher click-through rates.

Rotating banners switch between two pages every 10–15 seconds. They are used for high traffic sites. The refresh content is appealing, which gives publishers more impressions to sell.

In a **scrolling** banner, the ad scrolls through banner space like a billboard every 10–30 seconds.

A **pop-up** banner displays in a new browser window according to a fix size with the intention of not disrupting the visited page.

A **pop-under** is a banner that displays after the browser window closes according to a fix size, which makes identifying with the previously visited page less likely.

A **drop-down menu** banner enables viewers to choose which site area to visit before clicking through.

An **interstitial** banner opens in a new browser window as the destination page loads. They often contain large images, a streaming presentation, and extra applets that enhance the use of display, graphics, and human interaction.

A **floating** banner appears after a viewer first lands on the web page. It then floats on or around the page for up to 30 seconds or more. These banners may move over a desired mouse click location sometimes hindering accessibility to page content thus frustrating visitors. They have a high click-through rate.

A **corner peel** banner partly displays (also called peel banners, page peels, or magic corners) in the corner of a web page. Once the user moves the mouse over the animation peel in the top corner (usually the right), the animation peels over the web page displaying the entire ad. These types of banner ads are not annoying to most viewers.

A **unicast** advertisement usually runs in a pop-up window playing a video like a television commercial, up to 30 seconds. They generate a high click through rate.

Push-down banners expand to almost a full screen upon loading a page. Some publishers require the ad to collapse after a certain time (usually 7 to 10 seconds). The viewer may then click to re-expand the banner and read the content. Other website hosts allow the advertiser to keep the ad expanded, requiring the viewer to click to collapse it.

A **fixed panel** banner appears on the website. The panel (measuring 336 x 860 pixels) rolls to the top and bottom of the page as the user scrolls up and down.

Finally, there is the **XXL box** banner, a colossal sized (468 x 648 pixels or more) banner used by prominent advertisers for brand awareness. This massive advertisement can comprise several pages and video.

Public Service Announcement (PSA)

PSAs are messaging that focuses on the public good. They come in different formats, but typically take the form of audio (radio) spots or video for impact. They are pre-recorded and produced for broadcast or they are spot announcements in which the talent delivers the PSA live. They normally run 30 to 60 seconds. Medium vehicles such as radio, television, and cable stations donate air time to PSAs.

Podcast

A **podcast** is an online audio posting accessible for listening. Public relations messaging via podcasts can be listened to, re-winded, and saved for future usage. Many individuals listen to podcasts while commuting, a function previously dominated by broadcast radio. Podcast content includes music genres, general interviews, specialty interviews, and presentations about many topics. Chapter 10 covers podcasting in depth.

Video

Video usually includes motion graphics and audio. Some video are animations or rely heavily on special effects. An idea for a video starts at the storyboard phase. A **storyboard** consists of key scene shots framed in drawing or photo format; direction for camera angles, types of cuts, transitions, and sound effects; and a voice script. The size of the storyboard varies based on the video length. For example, 8 to 12 frames are standard for a 30–60 second production. Movies contain hundreds of storyboard frames.

The storyboard and script provide the instructions for the actors, director, and camera people. For example, the numbered frames contain the length of time for the scene and specific sound effects. The voice script includes voice direction such as "speak enthusiastically" or "voice trails off to silence."

The produced video then moves into the post-production editing phase, which entails cutting and sometimes reshoots. The selection of the resources required to produce the video are contingent on budget, time schedule, and client requirements.

Advertising

Traditional advertising is a mass communication approach to messaging audiences. It utilizes many medium vehicles such as television, radio, print and digital periods, podcasts, banners, flyers, newspapers, and many other outlets. Public relations and marketing practitioners use traditional mass media to reach undifferentiated audiences. However, with technological advances and sophisticated research and data collection methods, marketers and communicators now micro-target specific audiences, which mitigates waste coverage. Micro-targeting is highly effective and efficient for online activities such as web searches that place ads and email messaging customized to individual users.

News Release

A new release is a basic public relations tactic. The public relations practitioner writes the **news release**, which is a story given to gatekeepers for coverage in local, regional, national, and international news media. The practitioner submits general and specialty topic news releases to the relevant editors, news directors, reporters, newspapers, magazine, radio stations, and television stations. Associated Press, Reuters, Canadian Press, United Press International, and many other news wire services receive releases. Most of these services charge a fee. Some news release topics are sports events, consumer information, features, prepared statements, business, economic, research, and social issues.

Video News Release

Television gatekeepers receive **video news releases**, which are video formatted news releases. They are typically 30 to 90 seconds long with narration, interviews, and other information. They often include **video B-rolls**, which are unedited video shots and sound bites related to the news topic. The broadcast station edits the content to meet their reporting and time scheduling needs. Video news releases ready-for-broadcast are **mat releases**. There are two kinds of video news releases based on subject matter. First, the topic reflects a current news situation. Second, the topic is a human-interest story called an **evergreen release**. Designed to allow publishers to stream live coverage to television, websites, and social media platforms from one source, Reuters rolled out its Reuters Connect platform for multimedia publishers in 2017.

Audio News Release

An **audio news release** is a sound bite news story for radio news media. The audio news release, general news release, and the video news release have a common goal—to inform the news media about an issue. Radio stations welcome this tactic. They are commonly 30 to 60 seconds. LifeScan One Touch Testing Supplies uses audio news releases aired on the Radio Health Journal, which is a nationally syndicated health program reaching over 3 million listeners in 90% of the top radio markets including New York, Chicago, Boston, and Washington, D.C. They provide stories related to testing, including the latest brand innovations, and quality of life benefits.

Media Advisory

A **media advisory** or **media alert** informs the news media of forthcoming newsworthy events. Unlike a news release, the advisory describes the accommodations available to news media professionals during the event such as photography and filming opportunities including lighting and sets, but does not include the level of topic information provided in a release. The journalists or reporters must attend the event to get the "scoop."

Pitch Letter

A **pitch letter** draws attention to an event. Sent to an editor or producer, it often accompanies a media advisory or fact sheet. The personalized letter justifies why an event warrants news coverage by emphasizing its novelty or relevance to the media's audience. There are directories and databases that contain the names and contact information of news gatekeepers such as the PNA News Media Directory and Easy Media List.

Fact Sheet

To provide an overview to news reporters, a **fact sheet** summarizes the key points about an event, issue, product, or organization. The following are fact sheet best practices.

- Do not include too many facts. Cite those that support and add value to the message.
- Only cite one source to support facts. If sources and citations turn a fact bullet into a convoluted paragraph, then place the sources in a footnote.
- Present facts systematically and logically to build and support the organization's message. Make it easy for the reporter to see what the facts corroborate.

In sum, strike a balance among the points of the fact sheet and guide the reader to the desired conclusions while not losing them in unnecessary details.

Press Kit

A **media kit** consists of materials about an issue or organization to support an organization's position. It goes to news media outlets or is accessed online depending on the content. It is in hardcopy and more often is available in digital form on an organization's website. It contains a cover letter that previews its contents, news releases, fact sheets, and other items such as background information, product information, the benefits of products and services, demonstrated product usage, product samples, images, schedules, brochures, reports, newsletters, promotional materials, and any other material germane to the issue and situation. In general, the press kit (also called media kits) links to public relations campaigns, product launches, or the organization. **User kits** and **consumer kits** are specifically associated with products or brands.

Airbnb, which hosts an online marketplace and hospitality service for individuals to lease or rent lodging including vacation rentals, apartment rentals, homestays, hostel beds, or hotel rooms, has an effective press kit. The kit includes the latest news related to Airbnb, press releases, links to their blogs, contact information, and media content including founder headshots, community photos, product screenshots, logo files, corporate video, annual report, and other interesting information. Airbnb's focuses on the personal side of business and encourages the news media to cover the human side of the company.

The social media site Pinterest's press kit includes resources that build relationships with reporters and journalists. Materials include media downloads such as logo and product image files, photos of the Pinterest workplace, videos, and management biographies. In the kit, Pinterest invites anyone to write a story about them.

Magazine

Magazine issues are available less often than newspapers. They are typically weekly or monthly runs in hardcopy and increasingly in digital format. There are approximately 7,300 magazines in the United States. Some are general interest while other are specialty periodicals. The top three magazines by total reach in the United States (Statista, 2017) are *ESPN* the magazine (123 million), *People* (83 million), and *Forbes* (981 million). Two measures influence magazine reach. First, there is the number of subscribers called **circulation**. Second, there is the **pass-along rate**, which is the number of total readers exposed to a magazine (passed from person-to-person who are typically not subscribers). For example, although a dentist's office subscribes to a single copy of a magazine, many patients read it. Pass-along rates range from 2 to 6. In other words, 2 to 6 people read some of the magazine.

Magazine editors are always looking for good stories that draw their readers. The story idea must be relevant to the subscribers and offer something unusual or novel to draw them to the content. The content focuses on current issues or a feature relevant to the readers. The following are ways to submit ideas or stories.

- Submit a story to the editor asking that the magazine have it written and covered.
- Send a written request and outline to the editor offering to write and submit the complete article upon approval.
- Simply submit a complete article for publication.
- Submit a news release in ready-to-publish format.

Newsletter

Newsletters are informal publications in hardcopy or digital format designed to provide information to stakeholders at regular intervals. Typically, they are used for internal organizational communication.

A company newsletter serves to:

1   inform employees of their company's organization, mission, and policies;
2   apprise employees of position openings, benefits, and career advancement opportunities;
3   announce policy changes and developments about issues;
4   recognize employee contributions to the mission as demonstrated in work-related achievements.

Non-profit organization newsletters function to:

1   recognize volunteers;
2   acknowledge the financial support of members and donors;
3   foster additional support beyond membership dues;
4   recruit new members, sponsors, and donors;

5   increase awareness of the organization's mission;
6   maintain credibility among all stakeholders.

Opinion Editorial Piece

An **opinion editorial** (op-ed) piece is opinion content sent to a news media outlet gatekeeper espousing an issue or position. Editorials can be letters to the editor or a submission to the op-ed page. Public relations practitioners write editorials for others who sign the piece. Editorial pieces appear in local, regional, national, or international newspapers, magazine, radio, television, and online. Media outlets provide equal coverage for opposing views about serious topics important to the public. Best practices include the following.

- Write a clear headline, which the editor will likely change because of space constraints.
- Hook the reader in right away with an anecdote. Humor is effective. Connect the narrative to the issue or organization. End the piece with something memorable perhaps linked to the initial humor.
- The ideal length for op-eds is between 800 and 1000 words.
- Tell a story and advocate a position supported by evidence. Start with the story, then provide evidence.
- Note whether the writer expresses his/her own opinion or that of the organization.
- Submit op-ed pieces to relevant publications. The overall audience must be interested in the topic.
- Timely submit editorials. Current issues in the news media are likely to draw audience members. Pitch pieces linked to seasonal events four weeks ahead of time. Keep holidays in mind and submit editorials tied to a holiday early before the flood of submissions from others.

Brand Promotional Content

In many organizations, the public relations department is involved in the production of product/brand promotional content copy. The department attends to copy and grammar, consistency with the brand style guide, and any other considerations deemed appropriate before dissemination. The goal is to present a consistent message (integrated communication) in a professional manner that supports the position, the issue, and organizational mission.

Website

Organizational websites serve multiple purposes. Relative to public relations, they provide information to the public as well as to news media outlets. Organizations use web analytics to monitor site activities and profile individuals who visit the site. Website developers use this information to supply content desired by visitors in a user-friendly way.

Prominent and easy to access content communicates what an organization values. Therefore, navigation is important. Website structure and labeling provide a navigation friendly environment. Some navigation development suggestions are to:

- use key phrases rather than generic terms such as "products" to describe navigation tools because they optimize searches and they inform visitors;
- do not use format-based navigation because labels such as "video" or "photo" do not provide the nature of the subject-matter. Visitors seek specific information;
- minimize the use of drop down menus. Research indicates that visitors do not like them because they interrupt information processing such that visitors must refocus, which they find annoying;
- limit the number of menu items to seven because people have limited information processing capacity. If they feel overwhelmed, they will likely leave the site;
- note that the order of website navigation is important. Generally, individuals easily remember items at the beginning and end of lists. Examining the site's web analytics informs placement decisions;
- do not forget website navigation on mobile devices. Mobile device usage continues to grow. Mobile sites make use of the **hamburger icon**, which is three short horizontal lines that represent a menu. Place it in the top right of the mobile website.

Signage

Signage is outdoor and indoor signs that communicate the public relations campaign message. One typical outside sign is a billboard. Non-profit and for-profit organizations deploy billboards as a means for messaging. Traditional billboards are static; that is, the billboard serves as a base for the installation of painted panels. However, more billboards are converting to digital signs that run multiple ads cycling for several seconds each. Some digital billboard includes audio as well. Digital signs draw attention and offer the opportunity to accommodate more advertisers. Authorities regulate the size and usage of billboards.

Mobile billboards are popular in Europe and Asia. Research reveals that mobile billboards have an 82% recall rate, which is probably owing to its prominent presence in those regions. Some billboards are on bicycles, buses, trucks, and cabs.

Inside signs come in all sizes and types. Some are hardcopy while others present digital content. Some big box stores maintain flat screen displays at registers which promote various products. Overall, the trend is for digital signage.

Sponsorship

Sponsorship provides financing, personnel, and other resources necessary to implement a program. Effective sponsorships are those that link the sponsored program and the sponsoring organization's mission. NASCAR is sponsor driven (pun intended). Sponsors include Chevrolet, Ford, Featherlite Trailers, MACK (trucks), Mobil 1, Goodyear, and Monster Energy. Maxwell House sponsors Habitat for Humanity. Budweiser sponsors the Super Bowl and Snickers sponsors little league baseball. In these cases, there is a natural connection between the sponsor and the partner.

Celebrity Endorsement and Management

A **celebrity endorsement** is a comment by a celebrity who supports an issue that an organization promotes. These endorsements draw media attention and garner public support for an issue. For four years, actor Neil Patrick Harris has pitched Heineken Light beer, using his personal brand of humor with the "lighter" side of the brand. Charlize Theron has promoted Dior for years. LeBron James signed a lifetime contract with Nike. Celebrities who have at least a connection to products and brands are effective. Theron's sophisticated look is consistent with Dior. James basketball superstardom links to Nike sports footwear and sports gear.

Celebrity endorsements are effective in the non-profit sector. Celebrities raise awareness and financial support for many charitable causes. For example, in 2017, Chance the Rapper, raised over $3 million for schools in Chicago. Colin Kaepernick, an athlete-activist pledged to donate $1 million to various charities including Meals on Wheels. He sparked a national conversation about police brutality and racial injustice. After a tragic bombing at her concert, Ariana Grande organized the One Love Manchester concert to benefit victims and families of the Manchester, England terrorist attack raising over $2.6 million. Through the years, celebrities such as Jami Gertz, Herb Alpert, and Mel Gibson have raised millions of dollars for charities and foundations.

Exhibition

Public relations professionals deploy **exhibitions** and various trade shows to target stakeholder groups. These are events where organizations inform and promote issues, products, services, cause, and other organizational positions. Exhibitors rent space and pay a registration fee to participate. Attendees usually pay to attend as well. Each venue has its requirements and some "booth" locations are more desirable and costlier than others. Depending on the nature and size of the exhibition, planning varies. Consider the following when preparing to exhibit, some of which will not apply to every exhibition.

In order of priority, answer these questions and plan accordingly.

- Has the situation or issue changed? If so, how?
- Who are the specific publics?
- What is the central message theme and planned experience?
- Will the same engagement tactics work for each target public or must they be customized? If they vary, then develop an experience for each public.
- What is the outreach plan for each public? How will the conversation start with each public? Indicate the tactics including social media.
- What are the objectives such as creating awareness, favorable opinions, knowledge, engagement, issue advocacy, and other behaviors?
- Assign public relations staff by function or target public. Base the assignments on the event, target publics, and types of engagement.
- For booth staff, create an engagement road map, complete with transitional conversations for directing a visitor to the appropriate organizational professional.
- If activities occur away from the booth, plan a follow-up so that the connections continue. Assign individuals responsible for follow-up.
- Consider tactics such as VIP events, talks, workshops, and creating exciting attention getting activities.
- Develop a follow-up plan for after the exhibits ends. Send thank you notes soon after and contact the relevant individuals or organizations within one week after the exhibition depending on the circumstances. This gives them time to return and settle down in their organization. Wednesday and Thursday are the best days, either earlier or later during the day.

Think about This . . .

Public relations practitioners are looking at how to use virtual reality (VR) as a tool to engage and build stakeholder relationships. In a 2016 article in *Public Relations Tactics* entitled "A New Reality: 6 Ways VR can transform Public Relations," Kara Alaimo makes a strong case for its usage by emphasizing six points.

1   VR revolutionizes the way we tell stories. Public relations professionals tell a story in a 360-degree space in which viewers become immersed in the story and can explore intriguing aspects of the issue at their own pace. For instance, one can experience driving a sports car down the autobahn or walking in the Roman Colosseum.

2   VR puts audiences in the shoes of other people. When an audience member can delve into aspects of a story, the potential to empathize increases especially in an emotional context. For example, one can closely experience a local community plagued by unsafe drinking water or experience the consequences of driving while under the influence of alcohol.

3   Its audiences are captive. VR requires active participation. Use of a headset stimulates the senses. The need to focus limits the opportunity to multi-task (so far).

4   VR provides a different presentation platform for the news media. Reporters can explore the various aspects of an issue and revisit those aspects to enhance their understanding. They thus have the option to report in greater depth.

5   VR offers advantages over physical meetings. For use anywhere and anytime, VR has no bounds. VR also provides detailed audience data unlike physical meetings. For instance, eye, facial, and "movement" tracking are easily recorded.

6   Innovative brands associate with VR. Innovative brands draw young and tech-savvy potential customers.

Ask yourself: Can you think of other ways to use VR to engage and build relationships with stakeholders? Think about non-profit as well as for-profit situations.

Alaimo, K. (2016). A new reality: 6 ways VR can transform Public Relations. Public Relations Tactics, January, 13. www.prsa.org/Intelligence/Tactics/Articles/view/11364/1121/A_New_Reality_6_Ways_VR_Can_Transform_Public_Relat.

Choosing Tactics

There are several factors to consider when selecting public relations tactics for a given public. Keep in mind that the selection of public relations tactics is informed by the characteristics of the targeted stakeholders. First, the situational analysis reveals the media habits of the stakeholders. Practitioners find stakeholders at the places where they seek information and communicate with other parties. Second, the medium selected influences the meta-message or the message in the context of the communication channel, situation, and audience. For instance, a crisis communication message requiring immediate attention utilizes channels that convey the message directly and quickly in a one-way manner to the affected publics such as broadcast news and mobile news reports. In turn, audience members share the information thus reinforcing this process. This two-stage approach disseminates the information quickly and then relies on audience members to spread the word further, thus helping assure message penetration. In other instances where the goal is to build and grow support in constituencies, group level and individual opinion leader-level messaging are effective.

The third point relates to the second. Organizational communication controls one-way top-down communication identified as coming from the organization. Depending on the nature of the message, some audience members may question the credibility of the source. To a degree, a transactional communication environment mitigates lack of trust. Being responsive and sincerely forthright when addressing feedback from audience members can allay credibility concerns. Additionally, having audience responsiveness shape future dialogue fosters an element of trust. Selecting tactics that allows for this process to occur can be beneficial.

Fourth, as discussed in Chapters 7 and 8, the central message moves forward in different ways to, within, and among publics. This approach minimizes audience message fatigue resulting in message habituation and desensitization. This dynamic also applies to message channels. It is effective to communicate messages using a variety of tactics and channels that consistently reinforce the central message. For example, promoting an issue whether it is gun-control, support for a referendum, volunteerism, or promoting a brand communication involves support from opinion leaders, favorable news coverage on the issue, a website providing issue information, an email distribution list, and social media analytics-driven ads.

Fifth, the central theme, goal, and objectives guide message content. The specific tactic chosen to deliver the message must be conducive to the content. For instance, promoting a sporty vehicle for the young at heart using video that demonstrates the sports car in action in various life situations where people are having fun appeals to younger consumers. Using this same approach to promote life insurance or printers would have limited effect.

Sixth, effective messaging is also consistent with the values and beliefs of the target audience while considering their level of issue awareness, knowledge, attitude, and degree of advocacy. This means being able to have cognitive and affective empathy for the target public. Know what they think about the issue. Know what they feel about the issue. This knowledge informs the public relations practitioner's development of content, message production, and placement. Again, consider the meta-message or related elements of messaging: central message, audience, content, message production, channel of communication, and medium vehicle.

Seventh, the scheduling of tactics must support the achievement of objectives and ultimately the public relations goals based on a timeline so that there are approximately three to ten message exposures on average per public member. In the case of social media, the time of day across time zones can impact tactics' effectiveness. Chapters 10 and 12 cover scheduling considerations.

Eighth, similar tactics often apply to more than one public. For example, special mall events promote the iPhone 8, 8 Plus, and X to more than one public. By the same token, some tactics are unique to specific publics such as tactics focusing on AARP (American Association of Retired Persons) members or promoting credit card membership to university students.

Last, as a rule of thumb, two to six tactics are sufficient to achieve an objective. Circumstances may dictate other requirements. For instance, considering the media coverage and interest in Apple's annual meeting, it is a single objective event/tactic, especially in anticipation of a new product rollout. Of course, such an event involves a checklist of logistical and other requirements.

These nine considerations vary in importance depending on the situation, issue, and nature of the campaign. A well-informed public relations practitioner optimizes messaging choices to maximize effectiveness in a cost-efficient manner.

Framing Messages

Before we discuss message framing, let's briefly review the psychology of tactics. Through the situational analysis, the public relations tactician learns the public's degree of issue awareness and knowledge, attitudes, level of involvement, and potential issue advocacy. Additionally, understanding how people process information and make decisions from their perspective informs not only message content and framing, but message construction and placement. Chapters 3 and 6 discuss numerous frameworks for classifying publics according to common characteristics and interest so that tacticians efficiently and effectively design messages that appeal to the target publics. One less discussed aspect of message development and testing involves human chronobiology, which is the field of biology that examines cyclic phenomena in individuals and their adaptation to solar and lunar related rhythms.

Circadian Rhythms

We hear individuals describe themselves as night people or morning people, indicating that they prefer to stay up late or rise early respectively. Generally, this preference for a specific time of day refers to **Circadian Rhythms**, which are 24-hour internally activated physiological cycles experienced by many forms of life including human beings.

The hypothalamus part of the brain controls circadian rhythms. Although an internal function, environmental factors such as lightness, darkness, body temperature, and other conditions can also influence these cycles. For example, at night, the brain sends a signal to the body to release a chemical called melatonin, which makes the body tired and thus facilitates sleep. There are numerous reasons why individuals do not follow normal sleep patterns, some of which involve environmental conditions such as lifestyle at a given stage in life, stress, lighting, etc.

Although non-normal body rhythms causing fatigue during the day can influence level of alertness and attentiveness to messages, general patterns do emerge. These patterns inform public relations messaging in two ways.

First, the time of day message pretesting occurs influences attention-getting measurement. Most research reveals that people are most alert between 11:00 am and 3:00 pm accounting for food digestion from lunch. Exposing focus group participants to messages during peak attention times provides the optimal effect of the message. This leads to the second point. If possible, conduct message testing during the time of day that the message is intended to be disseminated. Keep in mind that messages scheduled for distribution during non-peak periods may require additional attention-getting content to draw audience members to the message.

What Is Framing?

To **frame** a message is to "select some aspects of a perceived reality and make them more salient in a communicating text, in such a way as to promote a problem definition, causal interpretation, moral evaluation, and/or treatment recommendation for the item (or issue) described" (Entman, 1993, p. 52). In other words, message framing involves selecting content and presenting it in a manner that presents a specific position. Messages can make use of text, images, audio, and video production. This section covers types of appeals, properties of visual communication, the effects of colors and music in messaging, and several production considerations.

Visual Communication

There are different ways to examine images. The properties of images relate to signs. A **sign** is "any mark, bodily movement, symbol, token, etc., used to indicate and to convey thoughts, information, comments, etc." (Messaris, 1997, p. viii). Three categories of signs exist, which are the icon, index, and symbol. Often these categories overlap. Contextual characteristics such as text captions and object presentation within depictions, all of which influence producing meaning in images, guide the classification.

The simplest are the icons. **Iconic Signs** are artifacts of an object. They are explicit representations of something such as a photo or drawing of a clearly identified item.

Figure 9.2 contains three iconic signs. They clearly represent two individuals shaking hands. The photograph is the most perfect representation.

Indexical Signs are images that resemble some aspect of reality. They provide a physical trace to a cause and effect relationship in many but not all cases. Their influence on individuals is based on their connection to the person's life experiences. For example, a bullet hole indicates that a gun was discharged, smoke is an index of fire, tire tracks on a road suggest that a vehicle drove on the road, and a weathervane provides the direction of the "invisible" physical wind. Understanding the image requires seeing a logical connection, which is a cognitive, and sometimes, emotion process. The interpretation rests on uncovering the physical relationship between the object or event in the image and that which is implicit based on what one knows.

Additionally, manipulated indexical signs evoke emotions so that an image does not have to be a perfect match with what it represents. For instance, a group of roses shaped like a heart signifies love or passion. A picture of a house with smoke from the chimney, flowers in the front yard, and children playing nearby connote a home.

In its purest form, Figure 9.3 is an indexical sign. The damaged vehicle is an index of the consequence of some distraction during driving.

Providing more information than the image in Figure 9.3, Figure 9.4 depicts the potential consequences of driving distractions. The image focuses on broken glass with images of

Figure 9.2 Iconic Signs Represent Identified Objects

What do you do while driving?

Figure 9.3 The *Cause* Is Doing Something while Driving; the *Consequence* Is an Accident

the types of distractions responsible for the broken glass representing a windshield. The cell phone, being a major distraction, is in the center of the image pointing to the car accident. The other distractions prompt drivers to think about kinds of driving distractions: Which distraction is likely to cause the viewer to have an accident? This image is more likely to remain in a person's mind compared to a text warning because it encourages information processing and causal linkages.

The image in Figure 9.5 is a stark reminder that cigarette smoking is dangerous to one's health. The morphed alive face changing into a skeleton evokes more of a response compared to a text indicating the fatal dangers of smoking. Viewers develop all sorts of negative feelings associated with smoking based on what they know.

Symbolic Signs are arbitrary conventions such as stop signs or words. Providing that a person has knowledge of the symbols, their meaning is largely straightforward. Sometimes a word has multiple definitions that give way to an array of meanings.

As we can see, images possess the property of **syntactic indeterminacy**, which indicates that meaning ascribed to an image is implicit and subjective. In some cases, images convey meaning that individuals would not venture to articulate explicitly. This property allows for greater interpretation of images and meaning allowing for greater audience awareness.

Let's consider two examples. As illustrated in Figure 9.6, how do people view a politician visiting factory employees? Some people interpret the situation as the politician supporting factory workers; whereas, other may simply see another politician trying to garner votes. Observers' preconceptions of the politician inform the interpretation.

As depicted in Figure 9.7, think of an image of a president signing a new tax bill into law. A president surrounded by white men in suits as opposed to a diverse group of

Same Outcome

Figure 9.4 Driving Distractions Come in Different Forms but with the Same Dire
Consequences

"average" people leaves different impressions. In both cases, the images are photographs depicting explicit events that serve as proof of evidence that the events occurred. This format lends greater credibility to the message.

Visual communication allows us to convey implicit messages. Text or image editing in conjunction with the visual message cues the audience to a desired interpretation. Left as vague, submits the image to broader interpretations. The approach is based on the intention of the message.

How would you like to grow old?

Figure 9.5 The Deadly Effects of Cigarette Smoking

Figure 9.6 How Would You Perceive of this Image?

Lovemarks

Lovemarks is a framework for classifying product or brand based on the amount of love (positive emotions) and respect (assessed quality) for it (Roberts, 2005). The system classifies items or issues by low and high levels of these two consumer assigned properties.

There are four types of items. Brands that consumers have a passing passion for are **Fads**. They are highly loved, but have little respect. Mood rings and trendy apparel are

Figure 9.7 Could This Have Been Framed for Broader Appeal?

examples of fad items. Younger, trend sensitive publics find fad items appealing. **Products** possess low levels of love and respect. They are low cost, low involvement products that typically serve to fill the gap where needed products are lacking. Examples are staples such as milk, bread, socks, and shoe laces. The target publics or markets are everyone. **Brands** are highly respected, but not loved. Loyalty is based on product reliability, reputation, and features. Warranties, customer service, and easy access are important aspects of brands. For instance, reputable appliance brands such as Kenmore, Whirlpool, and GE, and Michelin and Continental tires are respected brands. The market segment consists of savvy, willing,

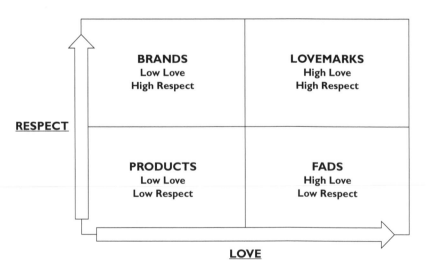

Figure 9.8 Lovemarks Are Beyond Brands

and able consumers. **Lovemarks** are items loved and respected by their market segments, who tend to identify with the item, are loyal customers, and have a passion for the item. The connection is both emotional and rational. Product quality and reliability assure trust. Examples are Starbucks, Apple products, and one's college/university alma mater. Lovemarks are the ultimate "product" placement in the consumers' collective mind. Figure 9.8 illustrations these categories in relation to each other.

Whether it is a product or a public relations issue, where publics stand along these four categories clarifies their likely emotional and rational attitudes about the issue. Using the Lovemarks schema, public relations practitioners can frame messages that appeal to stakeholders including moving them from one category to a more advantageous view of the issue or product.

Compliance Gaining Strategies

Compliance Gaining Strategies (CGS) are techniques used to persuade an individual or group to think a certain way or to engage in a target behavior (Marwell & Schmitt, 1967). CGS can be short- or long-term oriented involving interpersonal or nonpersonal relationships.

Relational factors influence CGS effectiveness. Factors include the level and direction of dominance (boss or subordinate relationship), intimacy (family and personal relationships), resistance (the anticipated amount of resistance to the strategy), personal benefit (the greatest benefit derived by the recipient), rights (the degree to which the request is perceived as warranted), relational consequences (short- and long-term effects on relationships), and apprehension (because associated with an intense situation the person finds strategies that mitigate anxiety as attractive).

Coupled with the nature of the relationship among individuals and/or groups, the kind of influence over others plays a role in assuring compliance (French & Raven, 1960). Some types of power tend to go hand in hand with certain relationships. Reward (promotion and raises), coercive (fire, demotion, and other forms of punishment), expert (competence and experience), legitimate (authority and position), and referent (personal relationships) types of influence are the basis of control over others.

After considering the nature and basis of the relationship between the influencer and the target publics, there are several CGS available, which are often combined. The following is a list of CGS and examples (Gass & Seiter, 2007).

- **Altruism:** "Out of the kindest of your heart, would you please let me go and not give me a ticket, please." "Please join me in volunteering to help those in need. It's the right thing to do for all of us."
- **Aversive stimulation:** "I am taking your cell phone away from you until you do your homework every night." "Until everyone completes the reimbursement paperwork correctly, there will be no reimbursements."
- **Debt:** "I've given you rides in the past. Now, I need you to return the favor." "When you needed time off, I was always accommodating. Now I need you to work this weekend."
- **Liking:** "You've done well in school and have been a go-getter. When do you plan to visit graduate schools and plan for the GREs?" You take an employee to lunch and praise her contribution to the company's mission. On the way back from lunch, you ask her to head a new task force because she can get it done right.

- **Moral appeal:** "It is morally wrong for you not to do your best in college especially when your parents are paying for your education." "We have a responsibility to be informed voters keeping society and our fellow human beings in mind when voting."
- **Negative altercating:** "You tell Mike to explain to his children when he punishes them because only a callous person would not do so." "Not signing the green petition is irresponsible and the act of someone who does not care about future generations."
- **Negative expertise:** "If one does not graduate from a reputable college with a STEM degree, one will have difficulty finding a well-paying position." "Employees who don't participate in the workshop will have difficulty justifying why they should be promoted."
- **Negative interpersonal relatedness:** "If you are the only member of your family not participating in the charity dinner, your family might think less of you." "If you don't stand up to the polluters, what will your neighbors and family think of you?"
- **Negative self-feeling:** "If you are the only member of your family not participating in the charity dinner, your family might think less of you *and how then will you feel?*" "If you don't stand up to the polluters, *will you be able to live with yourself?*"
- **Positive altercating:** "A student who appreciates the sacrifice made by his/her parents to pay for college, will not hesitate to do his/her best in school." "Anyone who cares about the future and people will without a doubt sign the green petition because it is the responsible thing to do."
- **Positive expertise:** "Because one graduates from a reputable college with a STEM degree, finding a highly desirable job that pays well will be relatively easy." "Employees who participate in the workshops will be career fast-tracked in the company."
- **Positive interpersonal relatedness: esteem:** "Your family will think very highly of you for participating in the charity dinner" "By standing up to the polluters, your neighbors and family will know that you care about the community."
- **Positive self-feelings:** "You will feel a sense of pride and accomplishment because you played a major role in organizing the charity dinner." "You will have a tremendous feeling of reward because you stood up to the polluters."
- **Pregiving:** A person invites a neighbor to lunch with the hope that he will be invited to a dinner party at that neighbor's home. A person buys charity cookies from a colleague's child hoping that the colleague will reciprocate in the future.
- **Promise:** "If you do well in school, I will buy you your dream cell phone." "If you take on this additional responsibility for the next year, I will advocate for your promotion citing this additional work."
- **Threat:** "If you fail that test, then you will not be able to use the car." "If the project is not completed on time, there may be lay-offs."

These examples clearly illustrate CGS. Often though, they are subtle, but still make the point.

Toulmin Model of Argumentation

The **Toulmin Model of Argumentation** is a usable and useful framework for constructing a persuasive argument about an issue. As rendered in Figure 9.9, the Toulmin Model consists of six key components. The **claim** is the argued statement. It is what we ask the audience to believe or agree to. For instance, "The budget needs to be reduced." or "You are always late for class!" Unlike a claim, an **assertion** is a statement not supported with evidence. A strong **argument** consists of how well the following parts link together.

Data are the facts or evidence used to support or prove the claim. So, data or grounds, are the evidence offered to provide reasons for accepting the claim. Evidence comes in the form of statistics, expert opinions, examples, explanations, descriptions, and narratives. For example, "the number of wins during a season" or "the previous year's economic figures" are data.

A **warrant** is the reasoning or logical connection between the claim and the data. It is the satisfaction of the relationship between the claim and the data. That is, it is how well the data support the claim. For example, in the claim "The team's near perfect record will virtually guarantee them the championship," the claim is: "The team will win the championship," the data are: "near perfect record," and the warrant is the record which proves the claim that the team will likely win the championship.

Notice that the claim is not an absolute statement. It indicates that the record would "virtually" or likely assure them the championship. This approach adds an element of realism and credibility to the claim. Research indicates that a recipient or reader often discounts absolute statements or extreme language because the individual becomes suspicious. For this reason, the usage of qualifiers makes the claim more persuasive. A **qualifier** is a statement that limits the strength of the claim. It presents the claim to be generally true with some realistic exceptions. For example, the claim "You are late for class all of the time!" can be disputed by simply providing one or more instances in which the person was not late. A qualified claim would read "You are late for class most of the time!"

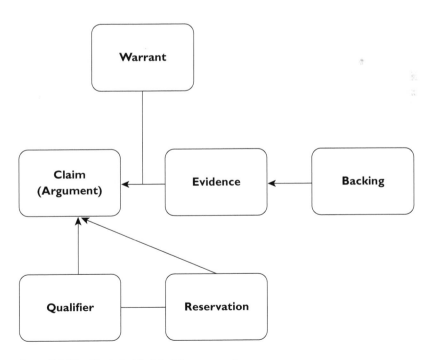

Figure 9.9 The Toulmin Model of Argumentation

The Toulmin Model of Argumentation comes in two forms: single-sided and two-sided arguments. The single-sided simply presents one side of the argument, which may work well with some audiences. The two-sided approach includes an additional component that serves to inoculate audience members against counterarguments toward the claim. A **reservation** is the rebuttal or acknowledgment of counterarguments to the claim. Think of it as a special type of qualifier. It addresses objections and questions to immunize or neutralize the audience against counterarguments. For example, "*Although it will cost more in the short run,* we should increase our training programs. In the long term, productivity will significantly improve." This technique is most effective when counterarguments are not salient. In cases where the counterargument is strong, a single-sided approach may be appropriate.

In some cases, a very skeptical audience may challenge the relationship between the data, claim, and warrant. This is often the case when addressing controversial issues. Additional evidence reduces resistance by strengthening the warrant or the link between the data and the claim. Thus, **backing** is reinforcement that assures the legitimacy of the warrant.

Keep in mind, an unsupported statement is an assertion. A statement supported with evidence is a claim. A warranted statement strongly supported with evidence is an argument.

The Toulmin framework is an effective method for presenting a position including elucidating the flaws in positions counter to the claim. It is important to present an argument supported by evidence, yet, in a manner that is understandable. Much of the research suggests that individuals can reasonably process between two and four main points about an argument.

Satisfaction Model

There are studies that compare appeals that make promises in exchange for engagement in a target behavior such as buying a product, voting for a candidate, or advocating a position. For participating in the requested behavior, there is at least an implicit promise in return, whether it be product performance, elected officials developing specific policies, or the benefits of taking a position, respectively. No matter what the promise, individuals typically assume that there is a bit of exaggeration in the promise. In the case of products, **puffery** overstates product performance.

One meta-analytic research project, which was an examination that combined the results of multiple findings and analyzed the data collectively, studied potential relationships among ad message promise, actual perceived performance (or the expectations set by promotional efforts), and consumer satisfaction ratings for similarly priced products. The study examined four conditions, which were (1) low promise/low performance, (2) high promise/low performance, (3) high promise/high performance, (4) low promise/high performance. Figure 9.10 depicts these quadrants. The level of promise is on the vertical axis and actual perceived performance is on the horizontal axis.

There is the unremarkable situation in Quadrant 1, the consumer does not expect much from the product, which is consistent with advertising or lack thereof. Quadrant 2 illustrates how satisfaction suffers when performance is grossly exaggerated. Excessive puffery can have a deleterious impact on future sales because of negative word-of-mouth and diminished repeat purchases. In Quadrant 3 and as expected, if the product is advertised as being a superior performer and delivers on the promise, then consumers are happy. Quadrant 4 results in very happy consumers because product performance exceeds expectations. Although this

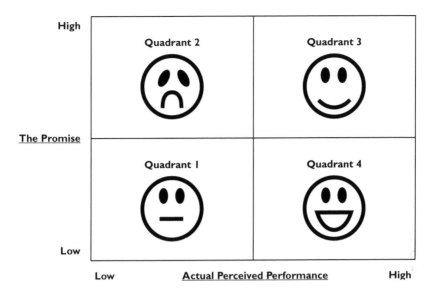

Figure 9.10 The Advertised Promise Sets Consumer Expectations for Perceived Product Performance. The Relationship between the Promise and Expectations Determines Consumer Product Satisfaction

approach appears attractive, it is problematic in the longer term and may result in lost sales because those who might have purchased and been satisfied with the product, do not buy it initially because of the under-advertised product benefits. In other words, the consumer does not consider the product because of lack of advertising or a perception that it will not satisfy the individual's requirements.

So, what does this mean for product/service advertisers and public relations professionals? Public relations practitioners typically message about an issue. Here too, there are often benefits or a promise associated with issue support or compliance with a call to action, whether it is implicit or explicit. Before deciding on which of the four options to deploy, it is of value to consider consumer psychology and expectations. People expect the product to perform as advertised; however, they also anticipate that some puffery occurs. It is a matter of degree. Cognitive dissonance reduction may come into play as well (See Chapter 3).

Notwithstanding these factors, if puffery were measured as a percentage of delivered performance, some experts hold that no more than 10% puffery would not negatively influence consumer expectations. I am not advocating for such a practice, but merely describing how this dynamic operates. Of course, there are other contextual factors that complicate this process such as functional, financial, and social risks associated with product usage, the state of the competition, and household or individual income, for example.

Fear Appeals

A **fear appeal** is a persuasive message to effectuate behavior that attempts to arouse fear through the threat of an existential danger or harm. It presents a risk and vulnerability

Figure 9.11 Understanding What Features of a Fear Appeal Prompt Publics to Respond Increases the Likelihood of Compliance.

to risk, and suggests protective action. The level of fear in an appeal can take two forms: the intensity of the appeal and message repetition. People respond to messages that deploy fear to alleviate negative emotions associated with such fears. They decide whether to comply based on four factors. First, the person judges the severity of the presented threat. For instance, will there be unacceptable results from realization of the threat? Second, how vulnerable is the person to the threat. In other words, what is the likelihood that the threaten materializes? Third, is the proposed response to the threat effective? For example, will wearing seatbelts reduce the amount of injury should a driver become involved in a vehicle accident? Last, is the compliance behavior practical (cost of compliance)? For instance, do the financial, social, time, or other expense provide a benefit that exceeds the cost of compliance? Additionally, owing to the nature of responses to threatening messages, experts recommend placing a call to action close to the identified threat.

Message Construction

The central message guides public relations communication. Tactical messaging presents the central message in different ways. All the messages contribute to unfolding the story, whether it is drinking and driving kills people, Product A is great value for the money, or donating to a cause will make the world a better place for everyone. Knowing and understanding the following aspects of message construction will assist in developing effective public relations messages.

Content and Video Production

In addition to content, video producers must decide on the amount of pacing in a video. **Pacing** is the number of cuts in a video of a given size. A **cut** is the transition or change from one camera sequence or shot to another. Since video is an effective method for presenting emotional content and pacing is a production component for presenting emotional content, we discuss low and high levels of emotional content.

I conducted a study that compared combinations of brand commercials that varied by amount of pacing and level of emotional content. There were low and high levels of each feature. The combinations of the two characteristics in each of the four ads were (1) low pacing/low level of emotional content, (2) low pacing/high level of emotional content, (3) high pacing/high level of emotional content, and (4) high pacing/low level of emotional content. One hundred individuals participated in this study. Participants were asked whether they remembered what occurred in the ad and whether they had a favorable opinion of the brands soon after viewing each of the commercials, one week later, and two weeks after seeing the ads.

After exposure to the ad as well as one and two weeks later, participants remembered the commercial with low pacing and a high level of emotional content. They also had a more favorable opinion of the brand compared to the other ads. There were no differences in recall or favorability among the other three ad conditions. These findings suggest that greater recall occurs in highly emotional videos if the viewer has the capacity to process the information. Low pacing allows the viewer to do so. Higher pacing and a high level of emotional causes information overload. Exceeding information processing capacity causes information loss and often individuals lose interest and do not continue message engagement. The less emotional conditions were unremarkable resulting in little attention devoted to the ads. Further, the remembered ad also had a significantly higher favorability rating compared to the other brands. These findings intimate that emotional content draws attention; however, production features must account for information processing constraints and message recall in order for viewers to develop a favorable attitude toward the brand.

The Meaning of Colors across Cultures

There has been a great deal of research about the effects of colors on a person's psyche. Colors influence whether some individuals attend to a message. They can also affect a person's mood. They remind people of the time of year and certain traditions. In fact, colors in the dining area influence what meals people order in a restaurant and how much they eat. Moreover, the meaning and impact of colors on people vary by culture. In a global marketplace, knowing and understanding the role of colors is an important consideration. Let's examine how various cultures perceive specific colors (Briggs, 2017; Kroulek, 2016; Wang, 2015).

Black

In many countries, black represents sophistication and formality. At the same time, it also symbolizes death, evil, mourning, magic, fierceness, illness, bad luck, and mystery. In the Middle East, it represents both rebirth and mourning, and, in Africa, the color black connotes age, maturity, and masculinity. In Eastern societies, black is popular among young boys. It is associated with good health and prosperity. In Japan, black symbolizes mystery and feminine energy. Indians relate the color black with evil, rebellion, or death.

Blue

Blue has many meanings across the world from depression to loyalty to trust. In Western society, blue often means feeling melancholy or "having the blues." At the same time, blue is a calming and soothing color engendering authority, security, and trust. In North America, many financial institutions and hospitals, which are sectors where trust and security are especially important, contain blue in their name or logo. In the West, blue also represents masculinity and the birth of a boy. On the other hand, in China, blue is a feminine color. In many Middle Eastern countries, blue symbolizes safety and protection, and connotes of heaven, immortality, and spirituality. Catholicism in some countries equates the color with hope, good health, and the Virgin Mary, depicted wearing a blue robe and headscarf. Jewish culture associates blue with holiness and divinity. In Hinduism, it is the color of the god Krishna, who symbolizes love, joy, and destroys pain and sin.

Green

Green embodies ecology, environmental awareness, and nature. In Western cultures, green symbolizes freshness, spring, money, inexperience, jealousy, and greed. Green is the national color of Ireland. It exemplifies good luck, leprechauns, shamrocks, and St. Patrick. In Eastern and Asian societies, green means new and eternal life, new beginnings, fertility, youth, health, and prosperity. Mexico selected green for its flag to symbolize independence.

Orange

In some Western cultures, orange represents all things fun. It epitomizes curiosity, trying new things, and creativity. In the Netherlands, orange characterizes wealth; yet, in the Middle East, it connotes mourning. In many Asian cultures, orange means courage, happiness, love, and good health. In Indian cultures, it is a symbol for fire. Saffron, an orange colored spice, represents luck and something sacred.

Pink

In general, pink reduces violent behavior and makes people feel calm and in control. In Western cultures, pink is associated with femininity, love, romance, caring, tenderness, and the birth of a baby girl. In Japan, pink is more masculine than feminine. In Korea, it epitomizes trust. Until more recently, pink was not a recognized color in China. Western influence has caused an increasing awareness of the color in China. In fact, the word for pink in Chinese translates to "foreign color."

Purple

In many cultures, purple is associated with royalty, wealth, power, exclusivity, and fame. For many centuries, purple clothing was expensive and became a status symbol among kings, queens, and other rulers, which contributed to the color's perception of exclusivity. In some countries, purple signifies death and grieving. In Thailand and Brazil, people mourn the death of a loved one by wearing purple with black. Some people in Brazil believe it is unlucky to wear purple when not attending a wake or funeral service.

Red

In India, red is a powerful color. It holds important meanings. Red represents fear and fire, wealth and power, purity, fertility, seduction, love, and beauty. It is also associated with marriage, in part, manifested by the red henna and powder on a married woman's hands. In South Africa, red equates with mourning, and the red in the country's flag symbolizes the violence and sacrifices made during the struggle for independence. Traditional Chinese wear red to celebrate the New Year, as well as during funerals and weddings. It is meant to celebrate important dates and bring luck, prosperity, happiness, and a long life to people. For Thai people, red represents Sunday, which relates to Surya, a sun God, who was born on that day. Many Thai honor Surya by wearing red on his birthday each year.

White

In Western nations, the color white represents purity, elegance, peace, and cleanliness. In some Asian countries, white symbolizes death, mourning, and misfortune, and is worn at wakes and funerals. Peruvians associate the color white with angels, good health, and time. In the Middle East, white means purity and mourning. Ethiopians think of illness when exposed to the color white.

Yellow

In France and Germany, yellow means jealousy, betrayal, weakness, and contradiction. During the tenth century, the French painted the doors of traitors and criminals yellow. The Chinese equate yellow with pornography. For instance, the Chinese term for "yellow picture" or "yellow book" refers to pornographic content. In many African nations, yellow signifies individuals of high rank because of its close resemblance to gold. In Japan, yellow exemplifies bravery, wealth, and refinement. In Thai culture, yellow is the lucky color for Monday.

Music in Messaging

Music affects a person's mood. Depending on the music, it can elevate, excite, calm, and slow down individuals. For example, retail environment studies incorporating pop songs for background music found links to impulsive buying. Unfamiliar music tends to make shoppers lose track of time. In retail liquor stores, playing classical background music is linked to an increase in higher priced wines. These studies suggest that music does impact human psychology and behavior. The sections below examine the effects of music on the brain through engaging emotions; memory; attention; and learning and neuroplasticity (Goldstein, 2017). By understanding the ways music engages the brain and mind, public relations practitioners can produce effective multimedia messages for digital formats.

How Does Music Engage the Brain?

Emotion

Research suggests that music stimulates affects through specific pathways in the brain. At an early age, a child exposed to music smiles because music engages and uplifts moods such as children dancing to a rhythm and becoming full of joy. Moreover, when a mother sings a lullaby, the bond between child and mother solidifies. Additionally, listening to music spikes emotions, resulting in a rise in dopamine, which is a neurotransmitter produced in the brain that helps control the brain's reward and pleasure centers. Listening to music is also a physical experience because the hormone oxytocin is released during musical exposure just as it does when individuals hug or kiss. In short, it regulates social interaction and sexual reproduction starting from maternal–infant bonding and milk release, to empathy, generosity, and, once an adult, through sexual activity.

Our understanding of how music affects the psyche is leading to innovative ways to utilize music and the brain to emotionally connect people. Studies have found that music as a form of communication increases emotional understanding in autistic children. These children identify specific songs or pieces of music to express how they feel emotionally at a point in time. Music coupled with content reinforces a public relations message from an emotional perspective. Calls for action to rectify a dire situation supplemented with stark music so that both cognitive and affective information processing occurs increases the likelihood of message engagement.

Memory

People remain connected to their lives through music associated with them and their experiences. In one study, researchers found that the brain associates music and memories. Familiar songs that are related to deep, meaningful past experiences activate emotionally salient episodic memories. Music connected to the past reinforces messages associated with those memories.

As discussed in the case of emotions, music provides environmental support for human attachment as well as facilitates the release of neurotransmitters that further reinforce emotional bonds between and among people. In the case of memories, music accesses those strong memories affiliated with specific songs or musical pieces.

Attention

According to studies, some forms of music such as instrument pieces, draw an individual's attention and involvement. They hold attention and intensify information processing in a flow of consciousness state. By the same token, other types of music or songs distract people from performing tasks. In the case of songs, listeners become inundated with information provided not only by the music, but the lyrics as well. Thus, depending on the intention, music can engage or distract from message content.

Learning and Neuroplasticity

Neuroplasticity is a physical process in the brain in which it reorganizes itself by forming new neural connections throughout life. This is usually due to normal learning or learning in response to brain damage. Music acts like a catalyst to facilitate learning through rewiring the neural pathways in the brain which reestablish the connections among thoughts and feelings. One important function of public relations is to inform and increase issue understanding. Music can be incorporated in messaging to increase issue knowledge. The last two points address the role of music to draw attention to the message as well as aid in increasing issue understanding and knowledge, both public relations objectives.

Why Is Music Attractive?

A study suggests three main reasons why music draws people (Schafer, Sedlmeier, Stadtler, & Huron, 2013). The first involves cognitions and centers on self-awareness. Music helps people learn more about themselves on rational and emotional levels. They assess emotions rationally as well. Along these lines, music helps define, refine, and reinforce a person's self-concept. Second, music helps individuals connect socially and identify with a culture. The type of music and how others relate to it provide a common thread and sense of community. Last, music stirs emotions and creates moods through physiological and experiential processes. Music activates feelings related to past experiences associated with specific songs or pieces of music. These feelings become longer lasting moods. Music linked to communications that fulfill these human needs and desires motivates audience members to comply with a message or call to action.

Summary of Key Concepts

- Tactics are tools, tasks, and activities used to achieve public relations objectives.
- Tactics focus on individuals, groups of individuals, or are undifferentiated concentrating on everyone.
- Publics and stakeholders are individuals, groups, organizations, and/or society.
- Specific tactics are more effective under different conditions.
- Message framing involves selecting content and presenting it in a manner that informs and/or persuades.
- Framing considers various frameworks informed by psychology to develop effective messages.
- Numerous compliance gaining strategies individually or in combination target behavior activation.
- The Toulmin Model of Argumentation is a method for producing a compelling message.

In the Case of Canyon Ranch . . . Action Plan for Corporate Clients

Corporate customers are those organizations that purchase Canyon Ranch packages for their executives. These are Fortune 500 companies. There may be more than a single point of contact in the top 500 based on the company's organization structure and operational policies. The executive and human resources departments are logical starting points.

Strategy and Primary Message: Corporations want to know how the Canyon Ranch experience will benefit their key performing employees. Position the experience as a health and wellness experience that will rejuvenate employees and their motivation to be effective and productive professionals. They will be reenergized. Promote the central message and be sure to communicate that Canyon Ranch handles everything and there is little investment other than the cost of the experience which will yield an appealing ROI through better performing executives.

(continued)

(continued)

Objective 1: By the end of the 12-month campaign, have on-site visits with 150 of the Fortune 500 companies.

Tactic 1: Send digital communications, make personal calls, and meet with higher probability prospects.

Tactic 2: Provide a complimentary one-night stay to a designated decision-making so that she/he experiences Canyon Ranch.

Tactic 3: Follow-up with a telephone call and email with all prospective representatives, and, if possible, their potential visitors, focusing on their needs.

Objective 2: By the end of the 12-month campaign, open accounts where at least 3–5 executives from 50 of the Fortune 500 stay at Canyon Ranch within 12 months of the campaign.

Tactic 1: Offer one complimentary visit for every specified number purchased packages to Canyon Ranch.

Tactic 2: Follow-up after the visit with a telephone call and email focusing on their experience and needs.

Tactic 3: Seek approval and implement a link to Canyon Ranch with the host client company. The link or content should focus on the central message as it relates to meeting individual client needs. Possibly provide testimonials. Praise the client company for providing Canyon Ranch services to its community.

Tactic 4: Monitor the progress of achieving corporate client marketing benchmarked objectives.

Key Terms

Chapter Questions

9.1   What is a tactic and provide an example?
9.2   What are the levels of tactics and provide an example of each type?
9.3   Define what is a lobbyist.
9.4   What is a gatekeeper and provide an example?
9.5   Describe the authority associated with the public relations internal counseling role.
9.6   What is a publicist?
9.7   What is a press agent?
9.8   Describe the different types of speeches.

9.9   What is a public relations event?
9.10   What is a specialty periodical?
9.11   What is a newsletter?
9.12   Define what is a press tour.
9.13   Define what is an alliance and provide an example.
9.14   What is a coalition and offer an example.
9.15   Name three types of banners and describe them.
9.16   What is a PSA?
9.17   What is a podcast?
9.18   What is a storyboard?
9.19   What is a news release?
9.20   What is a video news release?
9.21   What is a video B-roll?
9.22   What is a mat release?
9.23   What is an evergreen release?
9.24   Define audio news release.
9.25   What is a media advisory?
9.26   What is a pitch letter?
9.27   Define fact sheet.
9.28   What is a media kit?
9.29   Define pass-along rate.
9.30   Define circulation.
9.31   What is a newsletter?
9.32   Define opinion editorial.
9.33   Define Circadian Rhythm.
9.34   What is message framing?
9.35   What is a "sign"?
9.36   Define the three types of signs.
9.37   Define syntactic indeterminacy.
9.38   Define Lovemarks.
9.39   Define Compliance Gaining Strategies.
9.40   What is the Toulmin Model of Argumentation and list its components?
9.41   What is puffery?
9.42   What is a fear appeal?
9.43   Define pacing.
9.44   Define what is a cut.
9.45   Define neuroplasticity.

References

Alaimo, K. (2016). A new reality: 6 ways VR can transform Public Relations. Public Relations Tactics, January, 13. Retrieved from www.prsa.org/Intelligence/Tactics/Articles/view/11364/1121/A_New_Reality_6_Ways_VR_Can_Transform_Public_Relat.

Briggs, O. (2017, January 26). What colors mean in other cultures. *Huffington Post*. Retrieved from www.huffingtonpost.com/smartertravel/what-colors-mean-in-other_b_9078674.html.

Entman, R. (1993). Framing: Toward clarification of a fractured paradigm. *Journal of Communication*, 43(4), 51–58.

French, J. P., & Raven, B. (1960). The bases of social power. In D. Cartwright & A. Zander (Eds.), *Group dynamics* (pp. 607–623). New York: Harper & Row.

Gass, R. H., & Seiter, J. S. (2007). *Persuasion, social influence, and compliance gaining.* Boston, MA: Pearson.

Goldstein, B. (2017, December 27). Music and the brain: The fascinating ways that music affects your mood and mind. *Conscious Life Magazine.* Retrieved from www.consciouslifestylemag.com/music-and-the-brain-affects-mood/.

Hardoon, D. R., & Galit, S. (2013). *Getting started with business analytics: Insightful decision-making.* New York: CRC Press.

Kroulek, A. (2016, December 21). An international marketing cheat sheet: color meanings around the world. *Kinternational.* Retrieved from http://www.k-international.com/blog/color-meanings-around-the-world/ .

Marwell, G., & Schmitt, D. R. (1967). Dimensions of compliance gaining behavior: An empirical analysis. *Sociometry, 30,* 350–364.

Messaris, P. (1997). *Visual communication: The role of images in advertising.* Thousand Oaks, CA: Sage.

Roberts, K. (2005). *Lovemarks.* Brooklyn, NY: powerHouse Books.

Schafer, T., Sedlmeier, P., Stadtler, C., & Huron, D. (2013). The psychological functions of music listening. *Frontiers in Psychology, 4,* 1–33.

Statista. (2017). *Reach of popular magazines in the United States in November 2017 (in millions).* Retrieved from www.statista.com/statistics/208807/estimated-print-audience-of-popular-magazines/.

Wang, C. (2015, April 3). Symbolism of colors and color meanings around the world. *Shutter Stock.* Retrieved from www.shutterstock.com/blog/color-symbolism-and-meanings-around-the-world.

Wilson, L. J., & Ogden, J. (2015). *Strategic Communications.* Dubuque, IA: Kendall Hunt Publishing.

Chapter 10

Social Media Tactics

Social media is not just a spoke on the wheel of marketing. It's becoming the way entire bicycles are built.

(Ryan Lilly, Edwards, 2017)

Learning Objectives

To:

- Understand the growing importance of social media in today's global society.
- Define and explain what are social media.
- Discuss the various types of social media and the primary purposes they serve society.
- See the potential uses of social media for public relations messaging.
- Explain why social media are about relevance, trust, and engagement.
- Describe social media best practices.

Introduction

In the State of Social Media 2016 study, businesses responded to a survey indicating the main reasons why they use social media. The breakdown of answers was: 85% to create and increase brand awareness, 71% to engage various communities, 61% to distribute content, and 54% to generate sales leads and sales (Read, 2016). At work, employees are likely to use social media to take a mental break from work, make professional connections and maintain those relationships, find information that helps solve work challenges, build personal relationships with co-workers, and learn about someone with whom they work (Olmstead, Lampe, & Ellison, 2016). In a recent Pew Research Center study, 67% of Americans receive their news from social media (Shearer & Gottfried, 2017). They reported Reddit, Facebook, Tumblr, Instagram, LinkedIn, and WhatsApp as sources of news. The platforms increasingly used as news sources over the last two years are Twitter, YouTube, and Snapchat.

In the United States, approximately 80% of internet users have at least one social media account. The number is greater for women and younger people. Ninety-five percent of Americans own cell phones, and of those, 77% are smart phones (Greenwood, Perrin, & Duggan, 2016). Video streaming is the largest growing content delivery format. In fact, 61% of individuals aged 18 to 29 report that the primary way they watch television is via streaming services (Horrigan & Duggan, 2015). These trends continue to grow worldwide. As we can see, social media have become and continue to become central

Figure 10.1 More People Are Relying on Mobile Devices for News

to keeping us connected, to informing us, and to building the social capital that binds us (Putnam, 1995).

What exactly are social media? **Social media** are digital platforms that afford people, groups, communities, and organizations to not only communicate but also to interact in a dynamic and transactional way that allows for the creating and sharing of information, knowledge, beliefs, values, and opinions through informal and/or formal dialogue. In short, social media provide a place where stakeholders communicate; collaborate; educate and learn; and entertain (Safko & Brake, 2009). The information takes the form of words, images, audio, and video. **Social media tactics** are the specific activities deployed to achieve public relations objectives. Developing these tactics requires an understanding of social media platforms and what they offer users. This chapter covers the current major platforms available.

The Social Media Communication Process

The social media process and what makes it effective are ideal for organic public relations. Today, users generate content and interact in a transactional free flow of information and dialogue. Activities emphasize the needs, desires, and goals of the participant influenced by cultural and environmental factors. Social media are social; they are about relationships among people, groups, communities, and organizations. These parties provide content. Based on the relationships of the source of social media content with other parties, there is a degree of trust and an assumed level of issue understanding.

Credibility

In short, social media communication is effective when stakeholders find the source of the message credible. **Credibility** is believability, which consists of three dimensions. The first is **trustworthiness**. Trusting the source can be based on two factors. The message source's

Figure 10.2 Social Media Continues to Grow in Importance

reputation and integrity contribute to trust. The second dimension is competence. Issue knowledge affects perceptions of source **competence**. Last, source charisma influences favorability. **Charisma** is subjective and consists of personality attributes, energy level, and general likability. Charismatic individuals empathize with audience members thus increasing their connection and persuasiveness with them. Unlike traditional advertising, public relations focuses on building a longer-term relationship with stakeholder groups. This emphasis requires an element of trust between the organization and stakeholders, which is the adhesive that binds these relationships.

Loyalty

Loyalty is a characteristic of a positive relationship between two parties. It is devotion to a product, service, brand, person, group, organization, or cause. It has three parts. First, loyalty requires a favorable attitude toward an organization or brand for example. Second, repeated pro-organizational behavior is a component of loyalty. For instance, a repeated action would be donating to a specific charity every year. Last, those loyal toward an

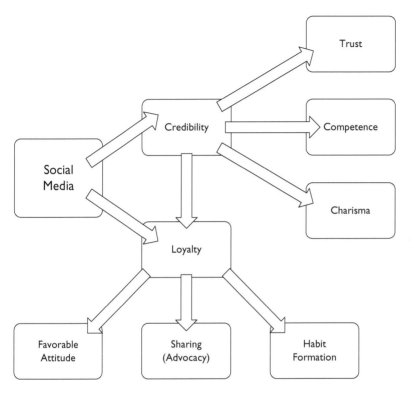

Figure 10.3 The Social Media Process Leading to Loyalty and Engagement Is Ideal for the Practice of Public Relations

organization or brand are advocates for it. They spread positive word-of-mouth; they post favorable content about it.

Figure 10.3 depicts the connection between social media credibility and loyalty. Credible messages leave the door open for relationship building. Stakeholders advocate for the message through likes, sharing, and other positive behaviors.

Networks of online followers and social media influencers disseminate information. "Regular" people share information and pass it along through crowdsourcing, online reviews, and numerous personal social media platforms. Through social media, the basis of credibility is often personal, perceived as objective, and there is an identification or connection with the sources of information. Similarly, social media influencers are credible individuals or parties because of their expertise, trust, celebrity, or identifiability with followers at some level. What follows is a discussion of the dissemination of information by parties, including social media influencers.

Spreading the Word, Spreading the Behavior

Online reviews, blogs, and various kinds of crowdsourcing share content and often call for action. Product and service reviews, addressing social issues on blogs, and other efforts to share content and compel action start and shape trends as well as give birth to social movements that impact our local communities and, in some cases, shake the core of our social structures. The local Parent Teacher Associations using social media influence school policies and facilitate changes that enhance the quality of education during a child's formative years. The Arab Spring resulted in the toppling of dictatorial regimes in part due to Twitter. These are average people deploying social media, doing extraordinary things, and sometimes, in the process, leaders are "born."

The collective knowledge of the group takes on a credible strength of its own. In the case of issues or product reviews, readers process them in their minds (or use websites that do it for them) and decide whether to develop a favorable opinion. The genuineness of people sharing what they know is a powerful impetus for change.

A key online sharing activity phenomenon that has become a tool to disseminate information and encourage behaviors is crowdsourcing, which comes in various forms. Initially crowdsourcing was described as ". . . taking a function once performed by employees and outsourcing it to an undefined (and generally large) network of people in the form of an 'open call'" of some form of action (Howe, 2006, p. 1). There is no consensus on what exactly constitutes crowdsourcing. This book defines **crowdsourcing** as building knowledge and engagement through the collective efforts of a group in response to a call for action to address a situation or achieve a goal. The nature of a crowdsourcing group depends on the goal of the activity. Communication primarily takes place online using social media and other forms of contact. Crowdsourcing does not always constitute employees of an organization. The group consists of individuals, other groups, and/or organizations. The group may or may not be anonymous. The crowdsourced group may be homogeneous or heterogeneous. Heterogeneous crowdsourcing mitigates groupthink and generates new ideas for innovative products and services.

The general term crowdsourcing has specific applications such as crowdfunding, crowdvoting, crowdlabor, and crowdideation among others. **Crowdfunding** focuses on generating funding for an endeavor through investments or donations. **Crowdvoting** generates support such as "likes" or "votes" for a position on an issue. **Crowdlaboring** concerns recruiting individuals, groups, or organizations to engage in some action such as volunteering for a social cause. **Crowdideation** engages parties to develop ideas and innovations about an issue, product, or service. For example, Dell's "Idea Storm" program encourages parties to submit innovative ideas to improve its products, services, and other aspects of the company. To date, the company has received well over 10,000 submissions and continues to do so today. These efforts deploy different types of crowdsourcing to various degrees depending on the circumstances and goals.

Social Media Influencers

A **social media influencer** is a type of opinion leader who exerts influence in social media spaces. Others perceive this person, group, or organization as a trusted and objective third party. The basis of influence may be emotional, and/or cognitive relying on the party's level of expertise or topic knowledge. In short, a social media influencer is credible in the eye of followers.

One way to gauge the impact of a social media influencer is by determining the number of followers that a person has in any given social media platform. Keep in mind that the definition of followers varies depending on the social media.

Figure 10.4 Social Media Provide an Environment Where Public Relations Can Reach Its Potential

In 2017, the top ten Facebook accounts according to following are professional soccer player, Cristiano Ronaldo, 117 million; singer and dancer, Shakira, 104.5 million; actor, Vin Diesel, 101.6 million; Coca-Cola, 99.3 million; professional soccer team, FC Barcelona, 94.5 million; professional soccer team, Real Madrid CF, 92.4 million; rapper and actor, Eminem, 91.4 million; professional soccer player, Lionel Messi, 87 million; singer, Rihanna, 81.9 million; and YouTube, 81.5 million.

As of 2017, the most followed Twitter accounts are singer, Katy Perry, 105.9 million; singer, Justin Bieber, 103 million; former U.S. president Barack Obama, 96.4 million; singer, Taylor Swift, 85.6 million; singer, Rihanna, 81.1 million; The Ellen Show, 74.9 million; singer, Lady Gaga, 73.3 million; YouTube, 70.3 million; singer and actor, Justin Timberlake, 62.8 million; and Twitter, 62 million.

As of the first quarter of 2017, the YouTube accounts with the most subscribers were video gamer, PewDiePie (Felix Kjellberg), 55 million; comedian and musician, HolaSoyGerman (German Garmendia), 31.2 million; video gamer, ElRubiusOMG (Ruben Doblas Gundersen), 23.5 million; comedy duo, Smosh (Ian Hecox and Anthony Padilla), 22.6 million; video gamer, VanossGaming (Evan Fong), 20.2 million; video gamer, Fernanfloo (Luis Fernando Flores), 20 million; comedian, NigaHiga (Ryan Higa), 19.3 million; beauty consultant, Yuya 17.8 million; comedian, Whinderssonnunes (Whindersson Nunes), 17.7 million; and video gamer and voiceover artist, Vegetta777 (Samuel de Luque), 17.3 million.

Some of the LinkedIn person and group accounts with the most followers are Richard Branson (13.2 million), Bill Gates (12 million), Jeff Weiner (7.4 million), Arianna

Huffington (6.6 million), Jack Welch (6.2 million), India (51 million), Workplace Leaders (Chinese, 41 million), Self-promotion (Chinese, 40 million), Prospective Media (huxiu. com, 40 million), and Leadership & Management (27 million).

Huffington Post, Mashable, Techcrunch, Buzzfeed, Business Insider, Gizmodo, Lifehacker, The Verge, Engadget, and The Daily Beast are among the most popular blogs in 2017.

As we can see, most of the top Facebook, Twitter, YouTube, and blog accounts provide entertainment/celebrity-related and news functions; whereas, LinkedIn has a professional focus.

Social Media Platforms

Over time the distinction between what is an application and what is a platform has blurred. Some experts define these terms based on usability, while others define them from a technical perspective. Applications are specialized software and platforms that are expandable. A **platform** consists of software (and sometime hardware) which interfaces with other independent applications. That is, a platform, which often has its own applications, runs with other applications in a seamless manner providing greater functionality thus offering an expandable software environment. At the same time, some applications are scalable in that they possess some of the characteristics associated with platforms, but not to the same degree. We can be sure that technological developments and advances will shift the usages and technical definitions of these tools over time.

The following is a list of some of the most popular social media platforms. It is by no means exhaustive and serves as a sample of what is available to the public relations practitioner. Most of the reported figures are as of mid-2017. The descriptions are by social networks, video sharing, image sharing, audio sharing, interpersonal messaging, blogging, message board/forum, Wikis, and search engine optimization (SEO).

The indicated number of active users is an approximation because there is no clear consensus about what constitutes an "active" user (i.e. number of visits, duration of visits). Moreover, some analytics are based on active users per month while others are over different time periods. When available, this chapter reports user data from the relevant social media website. In cases of inconsistent data, averages are reported. Keep in mind that social media figures and statistics are fluid and can substantially change in a relatively short period of time.

Although verification is nearly impossible, most social networking platforms require users to be at least 13 years old. These platforms provide free membership. Some offer premium memberships or additional services or tools for a fee.

General Social Networks

A **social network** is a place where parties connect much of which is online. They are comprised of people, groups, and/or organizations, who share a commonality or purpose. They communicate, interact, share information, and socialize in various ways. Their identification or basis for connection with other parties in the network is specific or more broadly based.

The descriptions of the social media below are meant to provide an overview of the main features of platforms with large numbers of active users. Virtually all of them offer options to integrate across social media places, offer analytical tools, and accommodate third party applications. Many of them allow users to import contacts from other platforms.

These sites focus around aspects of life such as personal, professional, and other interests using somewhat different social interaction models. Some empathize different aspects of the social experience while others offer a little bit of everything. In any case, the descriptions serve as a starting point for understanding how these major social media platforms might fulfill a public relations need.

Facebook

Facebook is an online social network site consisting of over 2 billion members. Arguably, for some users, it serves as a "hub" for other social media platforms. The minimum age to join Facebook is 13 years old. Users create free accounts and then develop pages using a host of template tools. Members set the level of access to their information by others. They share messages, videos, photographs, images, and other content. They create or join groups as well as follow individuals, groups, and organizations.

There are three types of Facebook accounts available to users. They are profile, group, and page members.

A **Facebook profile** represents a single individual. It is for non-commercial use. It contains as much information that the person wishes to provide. The profile includes a personalized description of the person and shared images, stories, content, and experiences. The profile owner can post his/her status and life events on a timeline. Users can add and message friends, view friends' statuses on their news feed, and share personal updates. Profiles accepted into one's Facebook social network are **friends**. Depending on privacy settings, friends have access to different levels of each other's content. They have the opportunity for public or private two-way communication. Profile owners can "like" content from other profiles and Facebook pages. A **like** is an expression of favorability or approval.

Facebook groups are smaller communities within Facebook. These parties share common interests and express their views. Groups exist for a common cause, issue, or activity to organize and plan; discuss issues; and share content. Groups are based on narrow or more broad interests across many areas such as work, geography, family, peers, teammates, and people with similar interest. Many organizations use Facebook groups as a place where work teams collaborate and share project information.

Groups have three privacy options. The **public setting** allows anyone to join. The **closed setting** option requires a member to add the prospective member. Last, the **secret setting** requires an existing member to add the prospective member. Only current or former group members can see a secret group's home page. To be a group member, one must have an individual Facebook profile.

Last, there are **Facebook pages**. A page allows public figures, businesses, organizations, fans, and other entities to create an authentic and public presence on Facebook. Those who qualify for a page must meet specific criteria. Everyone on the internet has access to them. However, to create a page requires a Facebook account. There are six category templates for Facebook pages: Local Business or Place; Company, Organization or Institution; Artist, Band, or Public Figure; Entertainment; Brand or Product; and Cause or Community. These categories offer features not available in profiles, but are conducive to the page's topic such as specific analytics and filters. People can stay connected by following the page's news feed, becoming a fan of the page, and liking content. Companies use Facebook pages to raise brand awareness, offer sales promotions, keep fans apprised of new product developments, and build a central fan base.

Think about This . . .

In 2010, the trade periodical *Candy Industry* reported the 360-degree rollout of M&M's Pretzels in which Mars, the producer of M&Ms, combined traditional marketing techniques with social media. The Mars marketing department spent one-year planning and executing their 360-marketing campaign. It was the largest in reach and dollars spent in the history of the company.

They tested the waters by pre-launching a "save-the-date" teaser campaign on their Facebook page, which comprised 700,000 followers. Friends could sign-up for a free sample of M&M's Pretzels. In three days, all the samples were "sold out." The campaign also made extensive use of Orange, the M&M character in a series of television commercials. Additionally, Mars partnered with MSN and developed a program called "Behind the Shell," which featured a series of three-minute videos about various topics such as fashion, food, music, and sports. These segments incorporated Orange and M&M's Pretzels.

The M&M's Pretzel campaign was highly successful. In fact, in 2012, the National Confectioners' Association reported the campaign as one of the most successful candy launches ever.

Ask yourself: Today, what other combinations of traditional public relations and social media might be effective to promote M&M's Pretzels?

Twisting a product rollout 360 degrees. (2010, September 21). *Candy Industry*. Retrieved from www.candyindustry.com/blogs/14-candy-industry-blog/post/83395-innovation-investment-go-hand-in-hand.

Facebook allows for different types of relationships between and among its three kinds of communities: friends, followers, and fans. Friends and followers take place between two personal profiles. The level of access is contingent upon the person's privacy settings. Fans involve personal profiles following pages. Group membership is another relationship where profile pages interact in a private group setting. Last, people can join Messenger to communicate with Facebook members, fans and followers, an activity especially relevant to public relations.

Once a Facebook profile user likes a page, that person becomes a fan. Fans receive updates and news from the page regularly on their profile. **Fan** status is a one-sided relationship with news communicated to the fan from the Facebook page. Content from the fan's profile does not flow to the page. The **follower** status allows one who follows a profile to see posts without having a two-sided relationship or friend's status. It is a type of "fan" setting for personal profiles. Although it too is one sided, there are differences. There are two relationship settings. Either people who are friends are the only persons who can follow a personal profile or anyone can follow a personal profile. Depending on the privacy setting of the followed person, access and communication vary.

Facebook's focus is to increase network traffic. In accordance with company guidelines, Facebook monitors usage to assure that personal profiles, pages, and groups optimize engagement. Those individuals who do not initially qualify for a Facebook page can enhance their visibility by increasing the number of personal profile followers until they meet the page criteria at which point they can create a Facebook page and take advantage of the added features.

Figure 10.5 Social Media Offers Many Options to Suit Individual Needs and Wants

LinkedIn

LinkedIn is a social network focusing on all thing professional and career development related. It consists of 500 million members worldwide. There are two levels of membership. The basic membership is free and there is a paid premium membership as well. There are two types of relationships among LinkedIn members. **Connections** are two-way relationships between two people. Connected parties see each other's shares and updates on their homepages. Messages are easily sent between connections. **Followers** maintain a one-way relationship with those parties they follow. They see a followed person's homepage posts and articles, but the followed person cannot see the follower's posts as would be the case with a connection. Followed users are individuals, groups, or large organizations.

LinkedIn provides opportunities to make new professional contacts as well as reestablish contact with old colleagues, professors, former class colleagues, and others deemed appropriate as part of one's professional network.

LinkedIn has several key features. The home page feed is the news feed. It displays posts from connections and those followed. The home page contains options to share the user's professional life and development. There are some customization features. The "My Network" section consists of all connections and invitations to connect. There is a "Jobs" section that lists daily posted positions. There are also job search features and tools. Moreover, individuals can write and post professional recommendations, which appear on both the recommender's and recommendee's pages. A LinkedIn profile can serve as an interactive résumé or link to or on a resume. LinkedIn also offers many educational programs such as online workshops. There is an internal private messaging system for connecting, which accommodates attachments. Additionally, members can participate in special interest groups, which is an effective way to connect with professionals who have similar interests as well as to stay current on a topic. There are opportunities to blog and to publish articles. The platform interfaces with other social media such as Twitter.

Google Plus

Google Plus (Google+) is a social networking service from Google consisting of 150-200 million active users. The social media platform integrates all Google services. The key social features are Circles, Hangouts, Google Photos, and Gmail. Google+ focuses on personalizing communication and sharing with smaller groups rather than large numbers of users. However, Google+ users can elect to make their feeds visible to everyone, including those who do not have accounts. Hangouts offers video chat and instant messaging. Ten users are the maximum number of group participants. There are live broadcasting and archive options through YouTube Live. Google's parent company owns YouTube. Google Photos is an image sharing program interfaced not only with Google+, but also with other social network platforms such as Facebook and Instagram. Google+ integrates with Gmail and a suite of other cloud applications.

Qzone

Qzone is a social networking service developed by Tencent, a Chinese company. It has over 610 million active users. Qzone allows users to share photos, watch videos, listen to songs, write blogs, maintain diaries, and engage in a host of other activities. Home pages can be customized. However, most Qzone tools must be purchased unless a user buys a Canary Yellow Diamond subscription.

WeChat

WeChat is another Tencent company. The platform integrates instant messaging and social entertainment with 938 million active users. If provides free text and multimedia messaging in real-time. WeChat offers photo sharing, gaming, sticker gallery, and other services. It is primarily a place where users seek entertainment as a shared experience.

QQ

QQ is a Tencent social networking platform that has 861 million active users. The platform's instant messaging, which offers features and services, is popular among young Chinese members. The messaging options are text, video, pictures, and stickers. Users can decorate their personalized avatars, chatting bubbles, and profile photo widgets. There are also interactive entertainment applications centered around programming such as comics, literature, and gaming. There is a mobile payment application called QQ Wallet for online shopping and banking. This platform allows users a great deal of customization in how they communicate, incorporating an entertainment dimension as well as providing options for online financial activities.

Video Sharing

YouTube

With the growth of video and mobile video, it is no surprise that YouTube is the world's largest video-sharing social network site. There are an estimated 1.5 billion active users. Videos sharing occurs through different ways such as through email and general social networking sites. Many YouTube videos go viral resulting in many views reaching 100s of millions of people throughout the world. Users can make playlists of their favorite videos, create a channel to which they can upload their own videos, comment about videos, like videos, and subscribe to other users' channels. If they meet YouTube's criteria, videos and channels can be monetized. For channels, a user must have at least 10,000 views to run ads.

Vimeo

Vimeo is a video sharing platform with 35 million registered members, 240 million monthly visitors, and 735 million monthly views. Most of the members use Vimeo to share and promote their work. The focus is on artistic work. People comment on the videos. A premium subscription is available for those members who desire greater functionality, which gives them more resources to highlight their work. Moreover, videos production is available on Vimeo. Some of the tools available are: Enhancer (adds a music track many of which are free), Video School (tutorial on how to create the videos), Music Store (Music tracks available for purchase), Creative Commons Videos (videos eligible for legal usage), and Tip Jar (optional tool that allows viewers to tip those who created videos). Members can create video channels and rent full-length movies for a fee. Members with shared interests can join groups. Recently, the company acquired Livestream, which gives members live broadcast and archives capabilities. The cross-platform analytics provides user data across platforms in real-time.

DailyMotion

DailyMotion is a free video sharing website mostly used by international audiences. The site reports 300 million users and 3.5 billion videos watched per month. Playlists and channels and monetized content options are available. In 2017, DailyMotion added a new feature, the Library, which is a dashboard page that enhances the DailyMotion experience.

Mostly Image Sharing

Pinterest

Pinterest is a free visual social network site comprised of 200 million users and over 100 billion pins. **Pins** are visual bookmarks consisting of images and/or video about a topic, which upload or link to a board. By clicking onto the image or video, the viewer goes to the source of the visual. Pins are saved on **boards** or other places where they are available for viewing as collections. Boards can be about any subject. Users can comment on pins and boards.

Pinterest has different types of pins. Pinterest sells **Buyable Pins**, which are about products. **Picked for You Pins** are recommended pins based on the boards a user creates. **Promoted Pins**, which are based on a user's Pinterest behavior including comments, are those marketed by advertisers. Pinterest members can follow other members so that those following news and posts appear on the follower's board feed. **Re-pinning** allows sharing on one's board, on shared other social media, and embedded in websites, blogs, and emails. Much of Pinterest's success is owing to the visual nature of content. Because images require less information processing effort and provide the opportunity to easily incorporate novelty and other attention getting devices, they draw people.

Instagram

Instagram, owned by Facebook, is an image and video social network online community of more than 800 million users. Users must be at least 13 years old. Although primarily designed for mobile devices, it functions on computers. On their profiles, users can share up to ten photos and videos in one news feed post. Profiles can be set to different levels of access. Followers see postings of those users whom they follow. Users can comment, like, private message, and tag images. **Tagging** is the act of identifying photos or some other content by placing key descriptive terms in the metadata part of a photo. It makes searching for photos as well as people in photos easier. For instance, if one had a photo of a beloved dog named Jack, one would tag it "Jack." Because the photo's name or tag is Jack,[1] it is easily located in a search. Videos are only 3 to 15 seconds long. The platform also offers Instagram Stories, which allows users to share photos and videos as a slideshow. Stories disappear after 24 hours and do not appear on the user's profile.

Why is Instagram popular? First, Instagram, through its Filters tool and other options, makes taking, editing, and enhancing photos easy. Second, Instagram is for people on the go and designed to capture in-the-moment experiences.

Snapchat

Snapchat is a mobile device messaging and social network platform with approximately 255 million users, many of which are young. Membership is free. Users send messages, photos, and videos up to 10 second in length where the emphasis is on interacting in the present. Photos and videos essentially disappear up to 10 second after viewing. These self-destructing messages, photos, and videos are **snaps**. **Multisnaps** allows users to record up to 60 seconds posted in at most 10-second snaps. The platform offers tools to customize snaps. Each day, hundreds of millions of photos and videos are shared. Users have a news feed to post images and videos viewed by others as a story clip, which disappear after 24 hours.

Flickr

Flickr is a photo and video sharing social network site which has 90 million users. This is another highly popular photo-sharing website. Typically, users share high quality images, especially by photographers or people who enjoy photography as art. The platform operates on mobile devices, home computers, and various software application. Flickr offers images and videos sharing on website, RSS feeds, email, and blogs.

Users create profiles in which they can display up to 25 photos. Members use features as Photostream, which is public photo portfolio. Additionally, users can use the Albums tool to organize and share pictures with family and friends. Members can **fave** or mark photos that they like. The photo owner receives notice when a picture becomes a fave (favorite). It then is viewable on the person's fave folder. Galleries allow users to display up to 50 photos from other users. Members join groups, which are communities centered around a central topic or common interest. They share or participate in group discussions. Like other platforms, members import contact lists from Facebook, Yahoo, or Gmail as well as tag images.

Audio Sharing

Americans spend almost four hours daily consuming audio content 2017 (Edison Research and Triton Digital, 2017). The sources of audio content and their percentages are AM/FM

Radio (54%), Owned Music (15%), Streaming Audio (15%), SiriusXM (7%), TV Music Channel (5%), Podcasts (2%), and Other (2%).

Podcasts

A **podcast** is a recorded audio program such as a radio show, lecture, or book reading that is available on the Internet for download and listening using a digital device. Sixty-seven million Americans listen to podcasts monthly. The average listener subscribes to 6 podcasts. Eight-five percent listen to the entire podcast. Anyone can create a podcast. The quality of production varies by producer. Some of the most popular podcasts are This American Life (*This American Life*/Serial), The Daily (*The New York Times*), Up First (NPR), RadioLab (WNYC Studios), and Stuff You Should Know (HowStuffWorks). Their unique global monthly downloads range from 21 to 107 million.

Most podcasts are free to download and keep. Access requires registration on the service site. However, there are premium versions of some podcast sites that charge a fee for additional features such as access to archived recordings. Donations, sponsorships, and ads support podcasts.

NoiseTrade

NoiseTrade is a free cross-platform entertainment social network for artists to share their music and books with subscribers and fans consisting of 1.3 million subscribers of which over 500,000 are active users. Subscribers provide contact information and agree to be on an email distribution list in exchange for free access to music. Members create profiles, comment on music, and indicate their favorite albums. Fans are encouraged to tip their favorite artists. Advertisers and sponsorships support the platform.

Jamendo

Jamendo is a free music sharing social network. It provides over 500,000 songs from 40,000 independent artists. From its inception, there have been 300 million downloads from over 100 countries. There is a comprehensive choice of music genres, free downloads and streaming are unlimited for personal use, and there are options for download formats. Additionally, Jamendo offers commercial music licensing for retail background music and other nonpersonal usages for a fee. Features include playlist generation, radio station access, user reviews of albums, an album rating system, discussion forums, sharing, and liking options.

Interpersonal Messaging

Interpersonal communication is synchronous or asynchronous communication between two individuals or small groups of no more than 20–25 parties. Voice telephone, mobile texting, various messenger applications, and video messaging are the major types of interpersonal communication. It is difficult to classify these modalities as discrete ways to communication because they are often a blend of more than one combined with social networking platforms as well as stand-alone systems with nuanced features. Below is an attempt to provide an overview of what is available.

Email

Companies such Google, Yahoo, Microsoft (Outlook), Apple, and others offer free email accounts often combined with other services. There are 3.7 billion email users in the world. Two hundred and sixty-nine billion emails are sent and received each day (The Radicati Group, Inc., 2017). Most of the growth comprises personal communication.

There are two basic methods for building email lists. One approach is simply building a list from existing contacts. Constant Contact offers services to aid in this process. For those who do not have existing or sufficiently large lists and require such lists on short notice, there are companies that sell opt-in email lists usually at a rate of per 1000 email addresses. Some companies offer options to filter lists down to specific attributes. Each filter adds to the cost per thousand addresses typically at $5 per filter. General email lists start at $50–60 cost per thousand (CPM). Some lists cost as high as $160 CPM. InfoUSA, Dunhill International, KPI Analytics, Experian, and many of the large demographic data firms are examples of companies that provide email distribution lists.

Instant Messaging

Instant messaging is a broad term referring to applications in which people send text messages. Some applications offer additional features such as customization of layouts, accommodations for images, audio and video recordings, calling, embedded games, and other features. Additionally, one can send money and share emojis and stickers. There is also an option to automatically share one's location. Many of the social networking platforms described in this book include an instant messaging application. The largest messaging tools by number of active users are Facebook's WhatsApp (1.3 billion), Facebook's Messenger (1.2 billion), Skype (300 million), and Snapchat (178 million).

WhatsApp

WhatsApp operates on smartphones, tablets, and personal computers. WhatsApp is available for iPhone, Android, BlackBerry, Nokia, and Windows devices. The application accommodates voice-recorded messages, syncs directly to mobile devices connected to WiFi, and shares the user's location. The application allows free phone calls to other WhatsApp users. The user's mobile number serves as the identifier. WhatsApp is compatible with SMS and MMS formats for individual and group text messaging. There is also a "Moments" feature, which allows for sharing life's moments captured in photos and videos.

Facebook Messenger

Although Messenger is an instant messaging service owned by Facebook, it is separate from Facebook, but often used together. Messenger operates on a wide array of digital devices. It also operates well with third party applications. It offers a wide selection of features. Users send customized text messages, images, and videos, including side effects, emojis, stickers, and GIFs. Delivered receipts, read receipts, and timestamps are available. Messenger collects a user's content and keeps it in a single place so that locating a specific file is easy. Texts archiving is an appealing feature. Recorded voice and video call communication is available. The application automatically connects to WiFi, which saves consuming data plan quotas. Through Messenger, the user can send (or request) money to/from others by using a debit card. While in group messaging, users can play games and share locations. Contacts can use the Scan Code feature, which automatically allows a user to add someone to Messenger with all pertinent information without having to manually input it. In addition to these highlights, Messenger offers other options described on its website.

Mobile Texting

Mobile devices are the fastest growing communication sector. Most texting happens through mobile phones, which offer a plethora of features. There are basic phones, essentially used for voice calling and basic texting of limited size. There are also smartphones, which provide many more features including the ability to send long text messages. As of mid-2017, there were over 6.5 million smartphone applications available. Android is the largest offering 2.8 million apps followed by Apple with 2.2 million.

There are two cell phone protocols. Basic texting uses the Short Message Service protocol (SMS), which operates on most cell phones. **SMS** messages are between 70 and 160 characters. Longer messages split into smaller parts before transmission. Multimedia Messaging Service (MMS) offers greater functionality. Using **MMS**, messages can be longer and include media rich content such as pictures, video, and audio content. As of 2017, there are 5.3 billion active cell phones subscriptions worldwide of which 2.75 billion are SMS phones and 2.55 billion are smartphones deploying MMS (Ericsson Mobility Report, 2017).

Video Communication

There are several major video communication platforms. Although many messaging applications offer video chat, those featured below specialize in video communication.

Skype

Skype, owned by Microsoft, is a service that allows parties to send and receive high-quality free texts, voice calls, and video calls around the world with other Skype users. Free group video chat for up to 25 connections is available. Most digital devices accommodate Skype. Usage requires registration. The company also offers paid premium services for those who wish to call devices not using the Skype platform. One paid feature is "Translate," which is a real-time talk translation application. There are over 300 million active members.

Viber

Viber is a free instant messaging and calling application. It has more than 900 million active users in 193 countries. There is no registration process. Users' telephone numbers operate as the Viber ID, which seamlessly integrates with one's address book. Users send text messages, stickers, photos, videos and doodles, as well as make HD-quality phone and video calls. Viber also operates on personal computers and tablets. Group chat is available.

Blogging

What is a blog? A **blog** (web log) is a web page usually on a host site maintained by an individual or party for regularly posting content in a specified format. Posts include opinions, commentaries, thoughts, and ideas, or an unfolding situation. Most blogs offer news and content on a specific subject, while others are essentially personal journals. They contain photos, graphics, audio (music), video, and links. Some blog platforms allow for customized blog pages. Entries are displayed in reverse chronological order. They can be re-blogged. Depending on the blogger's settings, readers can make comments about posts. Some blog services accommodate many plug-ins thus increasing functionality, while others do not. A **plug-in** interfaces an external application to various platforms or other applications to extend capabilities of those platforms or applications. **Extensions** are native computer code that extends a specific application's functionality. The difference between a plug-in and an extension lies in the interface with the platform or application. To the user, they both result in increased functionality.

There are various types of blogs. Some blogs are podcasts or **audioblogs**. There are also **vlogs** or video blogs. **Liveblogs**, as the name suggests, occur in real-time; they are subsequently archived. Blogs are personal or business related. Business blogs are used for internal or external communication. Sales engagement, marketing, branding, internal management, and public relations activities use blogs. Some companies have question blogs or **qlogs**. With this type of blog, readers can submit a query through a comment, submission form, or email, which is followed up by a company response. **Linklogs** are blogs consisting of short posts with links to other blogs. **Tumbleblogs** are media rich blogs and **bloghoods** are blogs located in the same geographical area. In short, there are many specialty blogs in the blogosphere. Most blogs are for personal usage and some contain advertising such as banners and other types of promotions supported.

B2C organizations that blogged 11 or more times per month received more than four times as many leads compared to those that blog only 4–5 times per month (An, 2017). **Compounded blog** posts have increased traffic and engagement over time (think of this like compounded interest on savings). They hold value because their utility extends over the long term. Such posts comprise over 10% of all blog posts and are responsible for at least 38% of all blog traffic. As of the end of 2017, there are approximately 500 million blog accounts throughout the world. What follows is a description of the major blogging sites.

Tumblr

Tumblr is one of the most popular blogger platforms. It is free. As of late 2017, there were a reported 381 million Tumblr blogs and billions of blog posts. Tumblr offers seven types of blogging features to create anywhere from simply blogs to multimedia ones. The platform has an active community of bloggers and readers.

Tumblr provides a user-friendly live feed, including blog posts from those followed. Creating a qlogs is an option and tumbleblogs can be highly customized. There is an option to schedule postings at a specific date and time. Private messaging and sharing are available. Reblogging is available. Posts can be liked as well. Tumblr operates well on many digital devices and operating systems. The analytics are easy to use and interpret.

Twitter, Micro-blogging

Twitter is a micro-blogging platform consisting of 330 million monthly active users worldwide. Membership is free. **Tweets** are short blog posts no more than 280 characters. Links and images in tweets are taggable. Key words using #hashtags make searches easy and tweets can include the @twitter name of other community members. Users can retweet and like others' tweets. Users can follow others on the home feed page.

Twitter pages address specific topics or subjects in general. Users provide updates about friends, family, scholars, journalists, and experts. A key advantage of Twitter is that it offers easily processed, limited information about a subject of interest. Information about social movements, humanitarian efforts throughout the world, and sports events can easily be disseminated, to foster their activities. Twitter users share moment-by-moment updates of anything imaginable. Social influencers and celebrities use Twitter to maintain their presence with their fan base. Twitter users advertise, promote, and participate in marketing-related events and activities. In short, Twitter is a valuable social network platform for both content providers as well as consumers of information.

WordPress

WordPress is an online platform for creating websites and blogs. In 2017, more than 409 million people viewed 16 billion pages each month. The site reported 41.7 million new posts and 60.5 million new comments each month. WordPress offers a wide array of plug-in tools. Like most sites, the platform is compatible with most digital devices. WordPress offers many of the tools available to other blogging sites such as Weebly, Wix, Squarespace, Ghost, TypePad, Joomla, Medium, and Blogger.

Message/Forum Board

Discussion forums are boards usually centered around a specific discussion topic. Users read and respond to posts and comments. Forums foster and build online communities of people with similar interests. Some discussion subjects are travel, gardening, motorcycles, vintage cars, cooking, social issues, music artists, and many more. Discussion groups or newsgroups are forums. Communication is asynchronous. Below is a discussion of some of the major discussion forums.

Reddit

Reddit is a discussion board in which users post links and share them with others. As of 2017, Reddit had 234 million unique monthly visitors. Images, videos, and articles serve as links. Typically, larger groups have subcommunities called **subreddits**. They share topics within the broader subject area. Users comment and vote on links. To quote Reddit's About page, "Reddit bridges communities and individuals with ideas, the latest digital trends, and breaking news (… okay, and maybe cats). Our mission is to help people discover places where they can be their true selves, and empower our community to flourish" (Reddit *About*, 2017, para. 1).

Gaia Online

Gaia Online is a popular free forum of worldwide communities. There are 23 million registered users (mostly teens), and one million posts made daily. Users must be at least 13 years old. The topics discussed focus on anime, games, comics, sci-fi, fantasy and others. Members have access to free games. The site also sells collectible items of interest to teens.

Meetup: From online to in-person

Meetup is an online social networking website that arranges offline group meetings in various physical localities around the world. Meetup helps members find and join groups with common interest such as hobbies, social issues, politics, books, games, movies, health, pets, careers and so forth. Meetup has 36 million members in over 100 countries. The site collaborates with more than 65,000 organizers involving over 307,000 Meetup Groups. On average, 50,000 Meetups occur each week.

The service is free for individual members. Organizers pay a fee. The site locates groups and arranges a place and time to meet. The individual group organizers define group membership requirements. Meetup offers meeting templates from which organizers can choose. The application provides the following services: 1) meeting scheduling and automated notices to members invited to attend; 2) assignment of leadership responsibilities and access to the group data; 3) the capability to accept RSVPs for an event; 4) create a file archive for group access; 5) post event photos; 6) coordinate communications between group members; and 7) group polling and results reporting. Other communication services are available as well.

Wikis

A **wiki** is akin to an online, collaborative encyclopedia that specializes in a specific topic or may be more general such as Wikipedia. Other wikis are Wikibooks, Wikileaks, Wikimedia Commons, and Wikinews. All the wiki sites together generate approximately 16 billion-page views per month. Users can add, edit, or modify (update) content entries through a browser. Content generators encourage page links of related material. In short, wikis involve an ongoing process of development and collaboration that continuously modifies content. Of course, there is concern about the quality of Wiki content and the intentions of those generating and editing material.

Search Engine Optimization (SEO)

SEO is the practice of optimizing the visibility of web pages as well as making user searches as relevant as possible. From a public relations perspective, knowing how to optimize visibility about an issue is important for creating awareness and knowledge about the topic. Some of the major search engines are Google, Google Scholar, Dogpile, Yippy, DuckDuckGo, and Bing.

Selecting Social Media

Selecting which social media to deploy involves keeping the public relations goal and objectives in mind, understanding how people engage, knowing social trends, and uncovering the social media usage and habits of target demographics.

The campaign goal as expressed in objectives informs the selection of social media vehicles. For instance, a campaign goal to increase the number of volunteer hours at a non-profit organization would require the achievement of objectives leading to increased volunteerism.

Figure 10.6 Some Search Engine Algorithms Change Multiple Times in a Single Day

Public relations focuses on effective communication and issue engagement. The social media process ideally provides engaging and relevant messaging that draws attention and issue involvement from a perceived trusted source with no known hidden agenda. This results in issue awareness and knowledge that facilitates more engagement and support through advocacy. In short, the process is about *relevance, trust, knowledge, engagement,* and *advocacy.*

Relevant or unusual (novel or new) messages draw publics. A person will spend time thinking about a message if it is a trusted source. The relevance of a message and trust toward the message source are the building blocks for increasing issue awareness and knowledge, which leads to engagement and the opportunity for advocacy. Figure 10.7 renders this process.

Social media offer a rich set of options to support this process. They allow practitioners to create dynamic multi-modal messages that appeal to our senses. People learn primarily in one of three ways. Visual individuals learn by looking, seeing, viewing, and watching. Auditory learners learn by listening, hearing, and speaking. Kinesthetic persons tend to learn by experiencing,

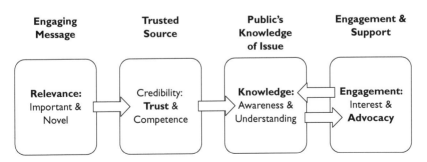

Figure 10.7 As Illustrated by the Feedback Loop, Engagement Facilitates Greater Knowledge and Increases the Likelihood of Advocacy

moving, and doing. Individuals retain roughly 10% of what they see, upwards of 40% of what is seen and heard, and 90% of what is seen, heard, and experienced in some way. This suggests that public relations communications that contain engaging media rich components will more likely involve audience members compared to any single modality.

Although related, what one learns is not exactly what one processes. For example, the senses account for the following amount of information input: 83% – Sight, 11% – Hearing, 4% – Smell, 2% – Touch, and 1% – Taste (Hurt, 2012). Of content remembered, 83% is visual, 11% is audio, and 50% is visual and auditory. As we can see, when examining research on the senses, what draws people to a message, what they remember, and what they learn are not equally affected by the senses.

A risk and issues management situational analysis involves monitoring the external environments. Specifically, social media usage trends are another important consideration when selecting mediums. Usage varies by demographics. The popularity of social media shifts over time. Once MySpace was the most popular social media platform until overtaken by Facebook. Other platforms such as ooVoo and Vine are no longer available. Video delivers more content today. Mobile is the fastest growing video channel. Television as a news source is on the decline; whereas, online news seeking is increasing. By spring 2017, 45% of American adults were getting news from their mobile device, which is up from 36% in 2016 and 21% in 2013 (Bialik & Matsa, 2017). Older adults drive this trend. Roughly 67% of those individuals who are 65 years old and older get news on a mobile device and for those aged 50 to 64, it is 79%. Understanding trends helps the public relations practitioner learn what social media vehicles publics use and when they use them.

Relevance, Engagement, and Advocacy

Individual, groups, and organizations visit and use social media sites that are relevant to them. In conjunction with the social media best practices discussed below, communication tools available in platforms and applications encourage social media engagement and issue advocacy. To develop a sense of public relations engagement and support for issues,

Table 10.1 Consistent and Frequent Postings Results in More Likes and Followers. Approximately 90% of a Post's Likes and Comments Occur within the first 12–24 Hours of the Post.

Social Media Relationships and Behaviors	Relevance	Support	Engagement
Visit	x		
Active user, member, & subscriber	x		
Like. Thumbs up. favorite, fave		x	
View, click on posts or other content			x
Comment			x
Mention			x
Friend, connection			x
Follower, fan			x
Share, moment			x
Reshare, retweet, repin, repost, reblog			x

Note: Tinted areas indicate greater applicability.

practitioners assess likes, fans, retweets and other ways to communicate that convey opinions. Table 10.1 provides an overview of the various ways available to interact with others.

Today, public relations social media tactics and activities do not operate in a vacuum. One social media tactic can feed others in a multi-directional loop exposing stakeholders to the message at various places. Although the central message remains the same, effective tactical messages meet the needs or desires of specific stakeholder groups in a social context that speaks to and engages them. We are more likely to engage publics by using many of the tools available to communicate and interact with them. Undoubtedly, some tactics will be more effective than others. Through experience and monitoring, optimal tactical choices will yield the most productive outcomes. Now we turn to best practices.

Social Media Messaging Best Practices for Public Relations

Select a diverse number of social media networks to reach your publics. Some social media choices are more appropriate than others depending on the demographics and the target public members' opinions about the issue. Successful and popular social media tend to be easy to use incorporating different communication modalities. Additionally, it is important to know that social media measurement and assessment can take different forms.

Moreover, the **meta-message** context is important. It is the message (text, images, audio, and video), channels of communication, and context of the message including the source, topic, mode of delivery, and any other characteristics associated with the message which all contribute to its interpretation. The senders or receivers of the message are individuals, groups, publics, stakeholder, organizations, or society. For example, sometimes email content is misunderstood; whereas, in-person communication of the same content is clearer. Some examples of ambiguous email text are: "I don't mean to be critical but . . ." "It doesn't really matter, but . . ." "It's only because I care that I tell you this . . ." "Guess I'll have to do it by myself from now on . . ." "I don't mean to be negative, but . . ." As opposed simply to words in emails, the words along with accompanying expressions or gestures from the sender, increase clarity and reduce misinterpretation. Social media platforms have attempted to mimic in-person interaction by incorporating the availability of emoticon, emojis, live video chat, and other tools.

There are many general practices deployed to optimize the use of social media in public relations campaigns. They center on increasing issue awareness and knowledge, engagement, and advocacy. The following attempts to provide groupings of useful best practices. They are not exhaustive, but are meant to survey what is available to the public relations practitioner.

Know the Social Media Where Your Target Publics Work or Play

Know the demographics for the social media platform. In a Pew Research Center Report (2017), 59% of U.S. Instagram users were between 18 and 29 years old and 31% were 30 to 49 years old. More than 36% of online adults aged 65 and older have Facebook accounts. Sixty-nine percent of women and 67% of men use Facebook. The highest percentage of social media users have incomes of at least $75,000. They also have at least some college education. Knowing user demographic information aids in the development of social media strategies and tactics designed to reach specific publics.

Figure 10.8 Emoticons Come in all Shapes and Sizes

Text-Based Messaging

Text consists of words and symbols, both constituting language. Text messaging and emails are largely comprised of words and are interpersonal. Texting makes wide use of message shortcuts such as OMG for oh my God and LOL for laugh out loud, and images. In addition to adding clarity, these language devices emphasize points, account for nonwritten modes of communication, mimic spontaneous human expressions, and work best with limited text space. Figure 10.8 depicts some common expressions.

The practice of cutting and pasting the same text across media or repetitively in the same platform damages credibility because readers perceive that it is an impersonal message serving an agenda. Since a reader is devoting time to read text, it should be fresh and add value in some form, whether it is an insightful product review, new information about an innovative product launch, or information about a forthcoming sale on a high demand brand. As discussed in Chapters 7 and 8, public relations messaging centers on conveying the central message in ways that appeal to target publics.

In the case of email, personalize the message. In the email field, the person's name should appear. A personalized subject line will increase the likelihood of the receiver opening the email. The same holds true for the salutation as well. Including an image draws the reader into the content.

MailChimp and Constant Contact are companies that offer automated email services. They offer user-friendly online templates for designing email layouts. MailChimp is free for up to 8,000 emails sent per month. The user uploads the email distribution list in Excel. By formatting the relevant data fields, the sender can personalize the email label, subject line, and salutation. There is also an opt-in/out feature. Progress reporting, click-through rates, and overall analytics are useful as well. Constant Contact offers similar and additional features.

Let's focus on email design best practices (Constant Contact, 2017). The goal of design is to create an email that draws the recipient's attention so that the person opens it, reads and understands it, and acts upon it such as clicking on a link.

- Select a recognizable "From" name. People open emails sent from others they recognize such as the organization's name, the sender's personal name, or a combination of both. For example, my From field might read "Ed, your former marketing professor."
- Choose a branded "Reply" email address that presents a professional appearance. A branded domain name is effective like JohnDoe@ABCIndustries.com.

- Focus on the subject line. It should be personalized, eye-catching, and provide a compelling reason to open the email. The optimal length for personal computers is 40 characters and 32 for mobile devices. Four to seven words are best.
- Since most emails are opened on a mobile device, be sure to use a responsive mobile template. This will assure that the email adapts to the size of the viewing screen.
- Brand the email. If available, include a clickable and recognizable logo, photo, or some other image at the top of the message. This practice conveys the source of the message.
- Any colors should match or complement those used in the logo or image. Limit the number of colors to four. Too many colors present the content as disorganized and challenging to read. Select a different color for the headline, body, links or buttons, and background. Keep the background color lighter than the font colors.
- Use no more than two font styles or sizes to avoid the email appearing overwhelming and unprofessional. Deploy one size for headlines and the other for the copy of the email.
- One to three images per email is optimal and increases the likelihood of a click-through. Select images that are consistent with the overall feel of the email. Include an image description in case the email client disables image viewing.
- Consistent with business writing, keep the amount of content concise especially for mobile devices. Keep the message short and clear leading to a call for action. Aim for no more than 20 lines of text or approximately 1,200 characters. Keep in mind that a shorter email has a higher click-through rate.
- Incorporate one main and clear call to action. Place the call at the beginning of the email. Because readers have short attention spans, avoid the need to scroll down to the call to action.
- Keep links limited to 1–3. Research indicates that this amount optimizes click-throughs.
- Add relevant social media links. What is known about the target public's social media habits informs social media placement.

Blogging

The goal of bloggers is to drive traffic to a web site so that individuals will read their content. To achieve this aim, bloggers post, text, images, videos, and links to a topic. They also rely on their content's likes and shares, which further extends their reach. Monetized blogs generate revenue for the blogger. There are several best practices that will increase traffic (Gunelius, 2017).

- Writing should be grammatically correct and organized effectively. Present content in a manner that facilitates return visits.
- Post regularly in not too lengthy intervals. Readers like a regular and constant feed of information about a topic including updates. Search engines likely detect frequent posts so keep the narrative going. Of course, this approach is contingent upon the public relations goal.
- Related to the previous point, the probability of showing up on search engines results increases by submitting the blog address to major search engines. Be sure to use carefully chosen key words.

- Create a **blogroll**, which is a list of links to other blogs and sites located on the blog homepage. When the owners of the links discover their links to a blog, they will likely reciprocate by linking the blog link to their site, which will increase traffic to both blogs.
- Use the **trackback** tool, which informs a blogger when his/her site appears as a link in a post.
- Respond to comments left on the blog. Do not cut and paste the same response, but customize it to the comment, which conveys that readers are valued.
- Also, leave meaningful comments on other blogs including a link to one's blog.
- Create a **RSS feed** button on the blog so that followers will receive new post updates.
- Links in a blog are important contributors to traffic. Other bloggers, followers, and readers are likely to investigate sites connected to them in some way. This may lead them to become new followers or to promote links to the blog.
- Tag posts using key words. Doing so will increase the chances of detection by general search engines and by blog search engines like BlogSearchEngine.org.
- Submit posts to **social bookmarking** sites, which are social media sites that maintain lists of web addresses by subject from "all" users for future access. Digg, StumbleUpon, and Reddit are examples of these sites.
- Optimize pages for search engines to find them. Include relevant keywords and links but do not overload posts with too many keywords. Doing so is spamming, which can de-optimize search results rankings or flag a blog for removal from results.
- Tagging images increases SEO especially for image searches.
- Consider having well-known guests post on one's blog or write a post on another's blog. This technique provides access to the other's readers and possibly new followers.
- Link other social media network platforms, websites, and email to the blog. Announce and promote posts or guests on various social media platforms to attract interested individuals.
- Nominate oneself and others for the various blog awards. This will increase visibility, reciprocity, and drive traffic.

Image

Images include static visuals like drawing, emoticons, emojis, avatars, and photos. An image conveys meaning difficult to achieve through words. As discussed in Chapter 9, there are three kinds of images. **Symbols** are arbitrary conventions like stop signs or words. Providing that a person has knowledge of the symbols, they are largely straightforward. Sometime a word has multiple definitions which gives way to an array of meanings. **Iconic Signs** are artifacts of an object. They are explicit representations of something such as a photo or drawing of someone. **Indexical Signs** are images that resemble some aspect of reality. Their influence on individuals is their connection to the person's life experiences. For example, smoke signifies a fire or tire tracks on a road suggest that a vehicle drove on the road. Understanding the image requires seeing a logical connection between what is in the image and one's mental representations of reality, which is a cognitive, and sometimes, emotion process. The interpretation rests on uncovering the relationship based on what one knows. Moreover, such images can evoke emotions. Their meaning can vary among individuals based on presentation. For instance, a football player giving a beautiful flower to a child provides different meaning compared to the same player on the field tackling someone.

Images possess the property of **syntactic indeterminacy**, which indicates that the meaning ascribed to an image is implicit and subjective. In some cases, images convey meaning that individuals would not venture to articulate explicitly. This property allows for greater interpretation of images and their meaning and wider audience reach.

Let's consider two examples. Consider a politician standing outside of a factory shaking hands with employees, which can be viewed in different ways. Some people interpret the situation as the politician supporting factory workers; whereas, others may simply perceive it as another politician trying to garner votes. Observers' preconceptions of the politician inform the interpretation. Think of an image of a president signing a new tax bill into law. An observer might draw different conclusions watching the president surrounded by white men in suits as opposed to a diverse group of "average" people.

When preparing images for social media usage keep the following in mind (Englander, 2017).

- Effective usage of images varies by social media space. For example, Instagram images with more background space are more popular. The converse is true for Pinterest. On Instagram, blues draw more attention. On Pinterest, reddish-orange performs better.
- Do not develop too many objectives, which will confuse users. Develop one or two objectives that will guide image selection. Driving traffic, increasing audience participation, and garnering followers are some objectives. For instance, if the objective is to increase involvement, an image with an absorbing quotation or intriguing fact will draw users. A curiosity appeal is effective to boost click-through rates.
- Images that resonate draw stakeholders. Any graphics should be consistent with the public's profile developed during the situational analysis stage of the campaign.
- Background images can effectively draw the attention of social media users. Many images are available online for free. Google image searches offer filters to include specific types of images, specific size ranges, usage requirements (free to use), and other filters. Services such as Getty Images, Think Stock, iStock, and PixaBay offer free or fee-based image usage plans.
- Brand images with text such as incorporating a log and web address. However, be mindful that some social media platforms such as Facebook limit the amount of text in an ad image for example.
- Recommended image size varies by platform, by location within the social media site, operating system (iPhone or Android), and format (jpeg or png). For instance, for a profile picture, the recommended image specifications are: for computers, 170 x 170 pixels; for smartphones, 128 x 128 pixels; and for other feature phones 36 x 36 pixels. For cover photos, the minimum is 400 x 150 pixels. Specifically, the suggested sizes are: for computers, 820 x 312 pixels and 640 x 360 pixels for smartphones. Facebook recommends jpg and png formats.

Video

Video includes motion graphics such as only video, audio/visual, and GIFs. They can be curated or produced. Studies found that the optimal video length to hold attention is 60–90 seconds, which is based on the **Environmental Monitoring Attention Cycle** in individuals (Meadowcroft, 1996). At the end of the 60–90 second cycle, people break attention and then refocus to continue attending to the stimulus (i.e. video). Although this occurs for a moment, it is an opportunity for distraction away from the message. Thus, keeping the video length to no more than a 60–90 second cycle increases the likelihood of holding audience attention. In fact, Boston's Children Hospital's Social Media department has a policy that posted videos cannot be longer than 90 seconds. Viewers tend to watch shorter videos in their entirety.

Successful video messaging follows the formula:

Camera + Storytelling + Creativity + Messaging/Sharing.

The following are some suggested best practices for deploying video in social media (Llewellyn, 2017).

- Video tells a story. Be sure that the video adequately does this in an intriguing manner. Appeal to curiosity, compassion, and emotions so that people stay for the entire story.
- Pre-test videos. Have a small group of people view the story. Viewers remember and accurately recount videos that tells a story.
- Whenever possible, use **native video uploads**, which is uploading a video directly in a social media site as opposed to linking it from such sources as YouTube. Native videos play automatically and are the first detected in social media network searches. They are higher quality compared to linked videos.
- Most people do not have the sound turned on when viewing videos. Ideally, viewers also understand the story without audio. However, adding a note in the caption or text about the content will help clarify the video's message.
- Test the duration of the video at different lengths to discover which length is optimal for the audience. Remember the 60–90 second rule. Length will be subject to the platform's requirements. Testing and monitoring the various versions' analytics will shed light on the most effective video durations.
- Consider short 10–20 second **teaser videos**, which are shorter versions of a longer video. Teasers draw attention, spike curiosity, and increase traffic to the full videos and web site.
- Live Streaming is an option. This feature is available on Facebook Live Videos, Instagram Live Videos, and Twitter (or Periscope). Live streaming draws viewers, offers live demonstrations, or serves a Q&A session function. Future viewing is an option through archiving.
- Tag videos, which will make them easier to find.
- Share videos more than once. However, be sure that sufficient time passes between the interval sharing times to mitigate video fatigue.
- Re-purpose videos across platforms. Edit them or use different teaser videos to draw users to the web site. This too will minimize video fatigue. Remember, central messaging is about conveying the same message differently.

Executed effectively, these techniques increase sharing and traffic to profiles.

Timing

Scheduling public relations activities on social media is critical. Because social media are global, they involve many time zones and different media usage habits. Particularly important are time of the day and days of the year. Holidays and vacation times vary. There are numerous reports and studies easily available online that provide media habits about populations such as peak usage times during the day. These resources inform the social media professional when to schedule messaging.

For example, early mornings are the best time to tweet to get clicks-throughs. Evenings and late night are the best times for total engagement. The most effective tweet times vary by area of the world. In the United States, noon is the most popular time to tweet. In Europe, it is 10:00 am and in Asia and Australia, it is 8:00 am – all local time.

Search Engine Optimization

Search engine optimization (SEO) requires certain conditions to maximize search placement. Search engine algorithms change over a relatively short period of time. Google changes its search algorithm at least 500 times per year. What might be optimal one week, may not be so the following week. The discussion below provides suggested practices (Gunelius, 2016; Fishkin, 2017), but does not cover the technical aspects of SEO.

- Keywords should be relevant to the post or page.
- Investigate the popularity of keywords by researching usage utilizing tools like Wordtracker, Google AdWords, Google Hot Trends, or the Yahoo! Buzz Index. Each of these sites provides a snapshot of keyword popularity at any given time.
- Select one keyword phrase per page. Some more general search terms are highly used so create keywords that are sufficiently specific. This will place the blog or web page higher on the search results list. For instance, if a blog is about celebrating Green Day in South Berwick, Maine, then incorporate the key terms "South Berwick, Maine Green Day" rather than simply "Green Day."
- Make keyword phrases 2–3 words each. Most keyword searches are 2–3 words so mimicking actual searches optimizes placement.
- Place the main keywords in the page title, subtitles, headlines, or blog post. Creating subtitles provides additional opportunities to insert keywords.
- Incorporate a keyword phrase in the body of the content. Use the phrase at least twice in the first paragraph of a post within the first 200 words and as many times as possible after without stuffing the space. **Stuffing** involves repeating keywords many times, which is considered spamming. Keywords should not be more than 2–3% of the total content. **Keyword density** is the percentage of stuffing.
- Create links that use keywords. Search engines place linked keywords higher in search results. Moreover, the text close to links weighs more than other text on a page, which is an option for keyword placement should link placement be unavailable.
- Use keyword phrases in images along with image filenames and captions.
- Do not use block quotation tags. In HTML code, "< text >" is the coded format for long quotations.
- If possible, keep the web site simple to avoid slow loading pages. This optimizes search rankings.
- Incorporate keywords in the meta description and the meta keywords tags. Hidden in the page's code, these tags help search engines find relevant pages.

Select Social Media Best Practices

The following are some highlighted best practices for specific social media platforms (Collins, 2017).

Facebook

- Keep Facebook posts between 40 and 80 characters, but not longer than 120 characters, especially when posing a question. Questions perform well on Facebook; they prompt discussion among other parties.
- Keep hashtags to a minimum. According to Facebook, they do not enhance engagement. Use them for visual emphasis.
- Images or videos added to posts, on average, increase engagement 2.3 times.
- In general, the ideal image size for a Facebook post is 1200 x 900 pixels.

LinkedIn

- Keep posts between 75 and 100 characters for business stakeholders and 100 to 125 characters for consumer publics.
- Consumer publics will likely engage when posts have less than 128 characters because this length minimizes cutoffs across platforms.
- Exclamation points perform well on LinkedIn.
- The ideal image size for posts is 1200 x 627 pixels.

Pinterest

- Keep the title board length less than 26 characters.
- Create keyword-rich board descriptions between 75 and 150 characters.
- Pin 5–10 times spread throughout the day.
- Keep image sizes around 736 x 1102 pixels.

YouTube

- Keep video lengths between 60 and 90 seconds.
- Create video titles no more than 70 characters.
- The maximum video description should be no more than 5,000 characters. Ideally, 1,200–3,000 characters are effective. Keep the most important information within the first 150 characters. Shorten the balance of text using the "Show more" option.
- Write video titles and descriptions that are keyword-rich.
- Use subtitles because they can enhance traffic by 19%.
- In the video description, include the website address, any social media channels, a strong call to action, and a link to subscribe to the video channel.
- Mobile comprises 40% of video views, so keep them mobile-friendly.
- Post videos during peak viewing times.

Summary of Key Concepts

- Social media are quickly becoming the dominant source of information for many people throughout the world. More and more individuals are seeking their news, other information, and services from mobile devices.

- Social media are more than sharing information. They are also about common identity, community building, and activism.
- Social media uses are open to the imagination. Because social media are becoming more integrated, communication easily expands across many boundaries.
- The free flow of social media communication and content sharing creates an environment conducive to public relations activities.
- Social media users focus on what is relevant to them and share content from trusted sources. These conditions feed engagement and advocacy.
- Social media best practices have similarities and differences based on several factors.

Key Terms

Chapter Questions

10.1   Define social media.

10.2   What are social media tactics?

10.3   Define credibility.

10.4   What are the three dimensions of credibility?

10.5   Define loyalty.

10.6   What are the three attributes of loyalty?

10.7   Define crowdsourcing.

10.8   Name four types of crowdsourcing and describe them.

10.9   Define social media influencer.

10.10 What is a social media platform?

10.11 Define social network.

10.12 Name the three types of Facebook accounts.

10.13 Define Facebook group settings.

10.14 What is the difference between Facebook fan and follower relationships?

10.15 What is a LinkedIn connection?

10.16 What is a Pinterest pin?

10.17 What is a Pinterest board?

10.18 Describe different Pinterest pins.

10.19 What is tagging and provide an example?

10.20 What is a snap?

10.21 Define multisnap.

10.22 What is a Flickr fave?

10.23 Describe what is SMS.

10.24 Define MMS.

10.25 What is a blog?

10.26 Describe four types of blogs.

10.27 What is a compounded blog post?

10.28 Define subreddit.

10.29 Define wiki.

10.30 Concerning public relations, what are the five parts of the social media process?

10.31 Define meta-message.

10.32 Define blogroll.

10.33 Define trackback.

10.34 Define RSS feed.

10.35 What is a social bookmark and name some web sites that offer bookmarking?

10.36 Define what is a symbol.

10.37 What are indexical signs?

10.38 What are iconic signs?

10.39 Define the image property of syntactic indeterminacy.

10.40 What is the Environmental Monitoring Attention Cycle?

10.41 Define native video upload.

10.42 Define teaser video.

10.43 Define keyword stuffing.

10.44 Define keyword density.

Note

1 In Windows 10, where there is a "Tag" field, right-click, select "Properties," and then "Details" to tag an image.

References

An, M. (2017). State of inbound 2017. *Hotspot*. Retrieved from https://blog.hubspot.com/marketing/state-of-inbound-marketing-and-sales-research.

Bialik, K., & Matsa, K. E. (2017, October 4). Key trends in social and digital news media. *FactTank: News in the Numbers*. *Pew Research*. Retrieved from www.pewresearch.org/fact-tank/2017/10/04/key-trends-in-social-and-digital-news-media/.

Collins, A. (2017). The ultimate social media best practices 2017 [Infographic]. *Bonfire Marketing*. Retrieved from https://thinkbonfire.com/blog/social-media-best-practices-infographic/.

Constant Contact. (2017). How to design the perfect email newsletter. *Best Practices Guide*. Retrieved from www.constantcontact.com/features/email-newsletter-design-tips.

Edison Research and Triton Digital. (2017). *The podcast consumer* 20. #PodCon17. Retrieved from www.edisonresearch.com/.

Edwards, M. (2017, March 6). 26 awesome social media statistics to back up your strategy. *My Social Game Plan*. Retrieved from http://mysocialgameplan.com/social-media-marketing/26-social-media-statistics-strategy.

Englander, A. (2017, February 21). 5 tips for creating more effective images for your social media campaigns. *Social Media Today*. Retrieved from www.socialmediatoday.com/social-business/5-tips-creating-more-effective-images-your-social-media-campaigns.

Ericsson Mobility Report. (2017). Stockholm, Sweden: Ericsson. Retrieved from www.ericsson.com/en/mobility-report/reports.

Fishkin, R., et al. (2017). The beginner's guide to SEO. *Moz*. Retrieved from https://moz.com/beginners-guide-to-seo.

Greenwood, S., Perrin, A., & Duggan, M. (2016). Social media update 2016. *Pew Research Center*. Retrieved from www.pewresearch.org.

Gunelius, S. (2016, October 19). Search engine optimization tips. *Lifewire*. www.lifewire.com/top-search-engine-optimization-tips-3476668.

Gunelius, S. (2017, June 1). 20 ideas for writing a blog post. *Lifewire*. Retrieved from www.lifewire.com/ideas-for-blog-posts-3476726.

Horrigan, J. B., & Duggan, M. (2015). Home broadband 2015: The share of Americans with broadband at home has plateaued, and more rely only on their smartphones for online access. *Pew Research Center*. Retrieved from www.pewinternet.org/2015/12/21/home-broadband-2015/.

Howe, J. (2006, June 2). Crowdsourcing: A Definition. *Crowdsourcing*. Retrieved from http://crowdsourcing.typepad.com/cs/2006/06/crowdsourcing_a.html.

Hurt, J. (2012, May 23). Your senses are your raw information learning portals. *Velvet Chainsaw Consulting*. Retrieved from https://velvetchainsaw.com/2012/05/23/your-senses-your-raw-information-learning-portals/.

Llewellyn, G. (2017, April 6). Facebook video advertising – creative best practices. *Smart Insights*. Retrieved from www.smartinsights.com/social-media-marketing/facebook-marketing/facebook-video-advertising-creative-best-practices/.

Meadowcroft, J. (1996). Attention span cycles. In J. H. Watt and C. A. Vanlear (Eds.), *Dynamic patterns in communication processes* (pp. 255–273). Thousand Oaks, CA: Sage.

Olmstead, K., Lampe, C., & Ellison, N. B. (2016). Social media and the workplace. *Pew Research Center*. Retrieved from www.pewresearch.org .

Putnam, R. D. (1995). Bowling alone: The collapse and revival of American community. *Journal of Democracy* 6(1), 65–78.

Read, A. (2016, November 14). The future of social media [and how to prepare for it]: The state of social media 2016 report. *Buffer Social Blog*. Retrieved from https://blog.bufferapp.com/social-media-2016 .

Reddit. (2017, December 4). *About*. Retrieved from https://about.reddit.com/.

Safko, L., & Brake, D. K. (2009). *The social media bible: tactics, tools, & strategies for business*. Hoboken, NJ: John Wiley & Sons.

Shearer, E., & Gottfried, J. (2017). News uses across social media platforms 2017. *Pew Research Center*. Retrieved from www.pewresearch.org .

The Radicati Group, Inc. (2017). *Email statistics report, 2017–2021*. Retrieved from www.radicati.com/.

Twisting a product rollout 360 degrees. (2010, September 21). *Candy Industry*. Retrieved from www.candyindustry.com/blogs/14-candy-industry-blog/post/83395-innovation-investment-go-hand-in-hand.

Chapter 11

Internal Messaging

The most important thing in communication is to hear what isn't being said.
(Peter Drucker, Bill Moyers Interview, 1988, para. 43)

Learning Objectives

To:

- Know what is an organization and organizational culture.
- Explain organizational communication.
- Understand and describe rational, natural, and open organizations.
- Understand centralized vs. decentralized organizations.
- Describe different internal stakeholder groups.
- Understand organizational goals and types of internal communication.
- Describe the channels of internal communication.
- Understand the key barriers to internal communication.
- Understand and describe internal communications best practices.

Introduction

Effective internal communication is vital for the success of a public relations campaign whether the target publics are primarily external or the focus is internal. What is internal communication? It refers to communication to and among internal stakeholders as well as between these stakeholders and the "organization." Stakeholders include consultants, volunteers, some shareholders, and interns working within the organizational structure but who are not employees per se; yet, they function internally and interact with employees. Thus, although most organizational communication involves employees, there are other internal participants.

Internal public relations communication goes by various designations depending on the organization's structure and leadership's perspective about communication. Some of the names are internal corporate communications, corporate communications, internal communications, strategic communication, employee relations communications, and variations of these labels.

According to Conrad and Poole (2013), **organizational communication** is "generally defined as a process through which people, acting together, create, sustain, and manage meanings through the use of verbal and nonverbal signs and symbols within

Figure 11.1 Organizational Communication Involves Two or More People Communicating in Different Ways

a particular context" (p. 5). The process of people collectively ascribing meaning and the context affecting meaning differentiates communication that is solely interpersonal from that which is organizational. As Conrad and Poole point out, there is a history of past communications, there is of course the present, and there is an expectation for future communication in the context of specific organizational situations. Like criteria for defining publics as discussed in Chapter 6, the level of issue and situational knowledge and degree of engagement vary whether the issue is about a forthcoming merger, change in top leadership, change in pension plans, re-organization, ethical standards concerns, employee behavior/practices, or new procedures for customer relations management.

A point of change is a point of stress by all those affected by the change. Budget cuts cause uncertainty and threaten job security. Employees no longer assume employment for life as was the case in the past. Global shifts based on comparative advantage and technological developments such as robotics and artificial intelligence necessitate constant adjustments and responses to these changes, making employment uncertain. Employees have become "free agents." Expectations about future employment have changed from the past.[1] Whether voluntarily or forced to leave a job, people are less optimistic about finding a comparable or meaningful new position (Weaver, 2015). These trends clearly indicate that during times of major change, keeping employees informed about developments is beneficial for assuring a stable workplace and workforce.

This chapter will cover what is an organization, organizational culture, types of internal stakeholders, internal goals and types of communication, barriers to effective internal communication, best practices, and the role of social media in internal communications.

What Is an Organization?

An **organization** is a structured environment in which individuals have assigned job tasks that are grouped and coordinated in the service of a mission. The structure includes work specialization, departments, a hierarchy of authority, a specified number of individuals who report to supervisors, and designated decision-making authority (Robbins & Judge, 2017). Ideally, the organization and employees share compatible goals that minimize conflict between and among them.

For example, in a hospital there are numerous internal stakeholders. There are nurses, physicians, various support staff, administrators, maintenance engineers, certified nursing aids, and others. The shared mission is high quality and cost-effective patient care. Each type of employee has his/her expected tasks or specialization as a healthcare provider, supervisors in each department are responsible for people reporting to them, and there are higher level decision-makers in charge of each department. The hospital is an organization impacted by its organizational culture.

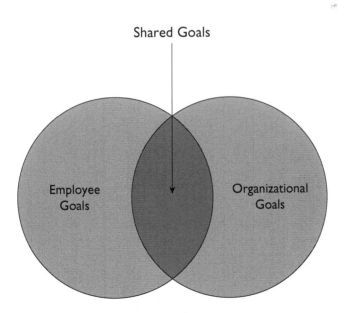

Figure 11.2 Goal Compatibility is Crucial to Organizational Success

In fact, the lubricant that oils the machinery of an organization is its culture. The organizational culture influences its members. **Organizational culture** is the collected deposit, passing down, and learned knowledge (history), experience, beliefs, values, attitudes, meanings, lexicon, communication (ways of interacting), hierarchies, artifacts, and material objects acquired by an organization while fulfilling its mission during its collective existence. In this context, culture affects how people perceive, organize, communicate, and learn at the organizational level. Culture thus affects organizational members' behaviors.

General Types of Organizations

There are different ways to categorize organizations. For our purposes, we will classify them according to rational, natural, or open systems (Scott, 1998). They are often a combination of all three and can vary by department, another organizing unit, or time and context.

Through the systems framework, stakeholders and publics are identified, defined, and prioritized so that central message development optimizes reaching goals. More specifically, the three-system typology focuses on how stakeholders communicate, the types of opinion leaders operating in the organization, what drives individual and organizational goals, and how and why members behave the way they do.

A **rational system**, as conceptualized by Scott is one in which an organization is highly formalized in pursuit of organizational goals and its mission. In a rational organization, the formal hierarchy provides the structure. Informal mechanisms are inconsequential. The goals are that of the organization and accountability is clear. The contact points are set forth and easily determined because they are the official channels of communication. The stakeholders are all internal. This is the most straightforward type of organization for public relations practitioners. For example, military organizations are perhaps a more extreme version of rational systems. Soldiers follow strict formal hierarchies. There is no tolerance for deviation from the formal structure. Rules are in place and there are prescribed ways to communicate, which follows the chain of command.

From a **natural system** framework:

> Organizations are collectivities whose participants are pursuing multiple interests, both disparate and common, but recognizing the value of perpetuating the organization as an important resource. The informal structure of relations that develops among participants provides a more informative and accurate guide to understanding organizational behavior than the formal.
>
> (Scott, 1998, p. 27)

In this structure, organizations maintain two hierarchies, the formal and the informal. The informal structure is the key source of communication and dominates the culture (Grunig, 2001). Informal opinion leaders wield a high degree of influence. Ascertaining the key publics and individuals becomes more challenging because of the dual nature of the environment and the importance of informal interaction. The stakeholders are all internal. These types of organizations are at an intermediate level of complexity for the practitioner to serve, especially since determining and assuring that individual and organizational goals are mutually compatible is a challenge.

Organizations that focus on team work and creative output are examples of natural systems such as ad agencies and think tanks. In an ad agency, tensions materialize between creative people, who drive the artistic process, and account executives and clients, who focus on marketing goals and objectives such as increased revenues and market share. For marketers, it is about selling, not winning Clio Awards.[2] Crisis situations where expeditious responses preclude following the formal communication channels and universities in which creativity and ideas are more important than formal structure are other examples of natural systems.

An **open system** involves independent activities linking changing stakeholder groups, both internal and external, to mutual benefit. The internal groups are dependent on continued interaction with the external environments where they operate. Thus, an open organization is not isolated and there are interdependent internal and external stakeholders. Identifying publics and their relationships is challenging not only because they are both internal and external, but also because they shift. Messaging must stay current and adjust accordingly. This situation is the most complex type of organizational structure.

An example of an open system is government, which receives inputs from employees, citizens, legislatures, courts, other government entities, companies, NGOs, and SIGs. The Public Broadcasting Service (PBS) is also another example. PBS receives funding from government, and relies on voters' support, volunteers, high-profile supporters, and private donors. In open systems, because the environment is dynamic and key publics and stakeholder groups change, revisions to messaging and even strategy must stay current.

Level of Control

Organizations vary in degree of control (centralized vs. decentralized decision-making). Some adhere to a strict hierarchical structure, while others are free flowing. The nature of the business guides the organizational structure. "Predictable" or repeated process organizations are conducive to hierarchical structures in which decision-making and communication follow an expected pattern. This is a **centralized** system. A centralized system

Figure 11.3 Degree of Control Can Vary for Various Reasons

has the potential to be subject to a high degree of red tape. **Decentralized** systems are fluid, crisis-related, or creative organizations. In these workplaces, the individuals have greater discretion and decision-making options, as well as increased opportunity for two-way communication with others in lateral positions, in higher management/leadership roles, and in the rank and file.

Internal Stakeholders

There are numerous internal stakeholder groups. The following listing comprise types of stakeholders, many of which overlap.

- Interns
- Contract workers
- Supervisors/Management
- Senior management
- Public relations department
- Departmental staff
- Administrative staff
- Finance staff
- Strategic planners
- Board of directors (or trustees)
- Shareholders both major individual and institutional
- Sales staff
- Customer service staff
- Marketing Department

An organizational chart helps identify stakeholders. Figure 11.4 represents a 2012 chart of the Federal Express (FEDEX) company. At the top, are the Chief Executive Officer (CEO) and Board of Directors. Below them, are the Chief Financial Officer, Chief Information Officer, Vice-President for Human Resources, Vice-President for Marketing and Communications (including Public Relations), and Feeder Companies' CEOs (other FEDEX companies that contribute to the mission). There are also various other vice-presidents. Next, are the senior managers of the various FEDEX departments, which consist of team leaders and finally each FEDEX organizational member who is responsible for carrying out his or her specific duties.

With the advent of digital technologies, the FedEx logistical system is highly automated and efficient. The company operates on a "management by exception" basis as indicated by the function of the team leaders, who head the FedEx small problem teams. Their main function is to address and rectify relatively small issues that happen during the process of package delivery.

Goals and Types of Internal Communication

There are different reasons for developing a public relations campaign. Goals can be about increasing morale, reducing turnover, increasing volunteerism, informing employees about forthcoming negative media coverage, new product roll-outs, informing members about mergers or acquisitions, improving communication, transparency issues, inspiring

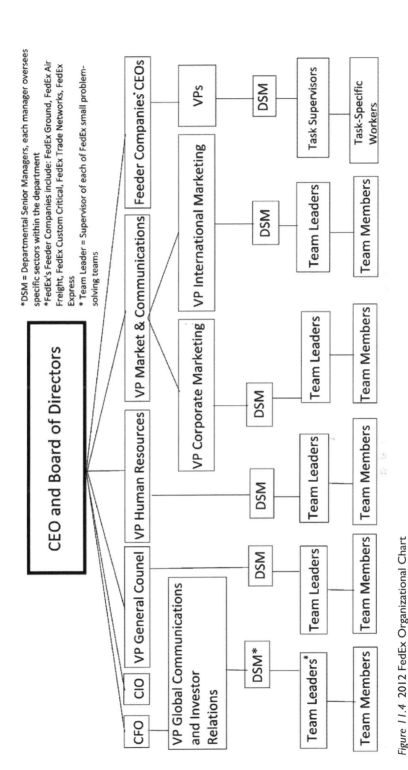

*DSM = Departmental Senior Managers, each manager oversees specific sectors within the department
*FedEx's Feeder Companies include: FedEx Ground, FedEx Air Freight, FedEx Custom Critical, FedEx Trade Networks, FedEx Express
* Team Leader = Supervisor of each of FedEx small problem-solving teams

CEO and Board of Directors

CFO | CIO | VP General Counel | VP Human Resources | VP Market & Communications | Feeder Companies' CEOs

VP Global Communications and Investor Relations

VP Corporate Marketing | VP International Marketing | VPs

DSM* | DSM | DSM | DSM | DSM | DSM

Team Leaders* | Team Leaders | Team Leaders | Team Leaders | Team Leaders | Task Supervisors

Team Members | Team Members | Team Members | Team Members | Team Members | Task-Specific Workers

Figure 11.4 2012 FedEx Organizational Chart

Figure 11.5 Goal Compatibility Is Not Only Between Organization and Individual, but Also Among Individuals

the organization, advising the CEO on a current issue, lobbying for legislation, seeking feedback on reorganization or cost-cutting measures, and many others. Chapter 1 covers the many functions of public relations both internal and external.

For an organization to operate effectively and efficiently, individual members' goals cannot significantly conflict with those of the organization. In fact, their mutual goals and shared vision of the organization help make everything run smoothly. In the case of a volunteer organization, the shared mission, values, and beliefs play an important role especially since these members are contributing their time for no financial consideration.

Terms associated with internal communications vary such as employee relations, corporate communications, union relations, employee relations communications, internal communications, and internal affairs communications, among others.

The types of internal communication depend on the basis for categorizing them. What follows is a discussion about the four broad functional areas of internal communication, the effectiveness of implicit communication, the concept of auto-communication, and a description of the various channels of internal communication.

Internal Communication by Function

Papa, Daniels, and Spiker (2008) found that many of the standard internal communication topics fall into four functional categories. The first is **orientation and indoctrination**. This type of communication exposes new employees to the procedures and practices of the company. They also operate to foster organizational norms. Orientation can occur more than once should a person change positions internally or accept additional duties.

The second area is **morale and satisfaction**. Effective follow-up and responsive communication between and among organizational members fosters morale and job satisfaction. Acknowledgement of achievements and information about opportunities for advancement play a role in members' morale.

Another role is communication about **compensation and benefits**. This area becomes challenging in a multicultural organization because of the variety of expectations of what constitutes benefits. The importance assigned to employee benefits may vary according to motivation and level of need. For instance, in some cultures, family-related lifestyle benefits take precedence over personal health maintenance programs.

Finally, **organizational developments and change** is another communication function. The acquisition of other companies, downsizing, merger activity, relocation of facilities, and new major product innovation are examples of developments and changes. Employees appreciate advance notice about such developments.

No Communication that Speaks Volumes

Written, visual, and/or in audio forms are types of **explicit communication**. Explicit messaging is clear, leaving little room for interpretation. For instance, if a company provides clear and thorough information on its new pension contribution or guidelines for office-related expense reimbursement, then there is likely to be less misunderstanding. Anticipating concerns and questions beforehand and presenting clear responses increases credibility.

Implicit communication is indirect, more complex, and influenced by an individual's perceptual filters. An organization's policies, practices, and operations convey directly and sometimes indirectly what it values. If an organization claims that it values its employees, but then freezes wages, cuts benefits, expects people to work longer hours, and is inattentive to employee needs, then the claim becomes dubious. Organizations that value employee feedback acknowledge comments.

Auto-communication

Communication that influences the sender is **auto-communication** (Hagen, 2008). For instance, a public relations practitioner responsible for communicating information about

Figure 11.6 Facial Impressions Can Convey Intentional and Unintentional Messages

a company merger would also be concerned about the impact on her/himself. Therefore, the communicator's perspective affects the message content in some way whether in the selected material provided or message framing. In this case, content might include merger topics relevant to the sender.

This is especially so when it comes to corporate reputation. Organizational members typically know their workplace better than outsiders and are thus able to construct more complex and insightful viewpoints and assessments of the organization. This informed perspective can make them more effective when communicating about the organization to publics.

Internally, auto-communication does not only affect the communicator, but can extend across the organization especially with corporate social responsibility (CSR) messaging. Research has found that conveying CSR efforts to external stakeholders has a positive influence on the organization's reputation with internal as well as external stakeholders (Morsing, 2006). The connection to socially responsible acts motivates organizational members to achieve goals and reinforce the mission. The successful recruitment of talent linked to CSR programs helps recruitment efforts because many prospective employees want to affiliate themselves with an organization that has an active CSR agenda. Starbucks, Apple, and IBM have well known CSR programs that contribute to their corporate citizenship image.

Channels of Internal Communication

Communication channels can be one-on-one, small group, large group, or organization-wide using a host of technologies. Messaging includes asynchronous and synchronous (in real-time) methods. Depending on the size of the audience, synchronous communication permits interaction. Typically, a group of no more than 20 people is optimal to assure an equal opportunity for participants to express their views. With larger groups, the opportunity for live feedback diminishes. Table 11.1 lists various static and dynamic channels of communication.

Table 11.1 Static and Dynamic Channels of Communication

Channels of Communication
Static Communication
All printed materials E-newsletter Email Texting Voice mail Company intranet Social media
Dynamic Communication
Telephone Social media Live meeting & presentation Videoconferencing

Barriers to Internal Communication

There are barriers to internal communication and the operation of an organization. Technology, red tape, culture, and groupthink are four potential road blocks to messaging.

Technology

The structure of the organizational system should integrate the technological tools necessary for employees to effectively communicate. Tools include email, social media, company intranet, and others that are practical for the organization, which may also include face-to-face or video conferencing for team-based projects or for a remotely based workforce. These options are important because they can foster the regular flow of information and interaction in an easily accessible manner.

I recall a situation in which a program director wished to create an online space so that graduate students and alums could access information such as news about the program, news about fellow students, and general program materials. I suggested that she simply use social media such as Facebook or Twitter because people frequent these spaces and they are cost-effective modes of messaging. She decided to create a special website that required a user ID and password. The project was relatively costly and few students and alums accessed it. Eventually, it was closed. As we can see, sometimes managers are unaware of optimal technology choices and the appropriateness of channels for the intention at hand.

An important component about digital communication is the ability to send messages and information quickly and ahead of situations requiring advanced notice and planning. Public relations practitioners need messaging mechanisms in place if they are going to communicate in a timely and effective manner. Updated contact information and organized lists are necessary to reach publics about time-sensitive issues.

Last, technology provides us with the ability to have synchronous communication. Synchronous communication with stakeholders is especially important when conveying bad news, when calling for immediate action, or when attempting to persuade opinion leaders.

Red Tape

Red tape is a term that has a negative connotation. It refers to the perception of an over-abundant number of steps or requirements necessary to operate in some way. In organizations, these steps involve multiple levels of approval that must be met before proceeding to the next step, which can be a timely and frustrating process. Different time zones and work shifts, varied practices across organizational units, and cultural differences add to the complexity. Examples are the steps one must take to register a vehicle at a department of motor vehicles, completing the paperwork for a research grant registering as a lobbyist, and seeking approval for public relations events.

Much of the red tape empirical research focuses on governmental organizations. A study by Kaufmann and Tummers (2017), found that red tape had a negative impact on both organizational clients as well as employees, which can lead to loss of revenue as well as contribute to high employee turnover. Another study about governmental organizations found that red tape had a deleterious influence on organizational performance, and that political and culture pressure can reduce the negative impact of red tape on organizational

Table 11.2 The Meaning of Nonverbal Gestures across Cultures

Nonverbal Behavior	Taboo in Indicated Area
Blinking your eyes	Impolite in Taiwan
Folding your arms over your chest	Disrespectful in Fiji
Putting your hands in your pockets	Impolite in Malaysia
Waving your hands	Insulting in Nigeria & Greece
Thumbs up gesture	Rude in Australia
Tapping two index fingers together	In some areas of Europe, sleeping together or a request for it
Pointing with the index finger	Impolite in Middle East & China
Bowing to a lesser degree than your host	Implies superiority in Japan
Insert thumb b/w index and middle fingers of fist	Obscene in southern Europe
Using left hand to eat or shake hands	Impolite in Malaysia, Indonesia, & some Arab nations
Pointing at someone with your index and middle fingers	In Africa means wishing evil upon someone
Resting your feet on a table or chair	Insulting in Middle Eastern nations
The back side of the peace or victory two fingers	In the UK denotes the middle finger

performance (Pandey & Moynihan, 2006). These studies point out some of the pitfalls associated with too many controls. In both studies, the findings suggested that a happy medium leads to smooth performance and positive outcomes.

Cultural Barriers

There are numerous **cultural barriers**, which can be misinterpreted and hinder effective communication. Nonverbal gestures or actions can be misunderstood because of cultural differences. The same words, phrases, symbols, actions, and colors can have different meanings in different cultures. Chapter 16 on global public relations covers these differences. Table 11.2 lists some potential areas for misunderstanding.

Cultural barriers occur within an organization. Groupthink is a manifestation of a strong culture that can endanger an organization's mission. A discussion of it follows.

Groupthink

Groupthink is the belief that one's group, culture, or organization is infallible, always "right," and should never be questioned (Janis, 1982). Janis posited nine typical symptoms of groupthink.

1   **Illusion of Invulnerability**: Because the group is special, everything will work out.
2   **Examining few alternatives**: Since the group is special, alternatives beyond what they represent are unnecessary.
3   **Belief in Inherent Morality of the Group**: The group has a firm belief in the moral righteousness of its cause.
4   **Collective Rationalization**: There is a collective mindset about being rational supported with selective information that confirms the group's positions.

5   **Out-group Stereotypes**: The group engages in stereotyping outsiders by vilifying and presenting them as evil, threats, biased, and spiteful.

6   **Self-Censorship**: The group avoids outside expertise. There is pressure to conform to the group's values and beliefs about situations and issues. Consequently, there is resistance to criticize the group.

7   **Illusion of Unanimity**: Individual members seek self-validation from others within the group to justify their positions and actions.

8   **Direct Pressure on Dissenters**: There are strong efforts to protect the group from negative views or inconsistent information.

9   **Self-Appointed Mindguards**: The "mindguards" protect the group's leader from others with opposing views.

The first two symptoms demonstrate the group's overconfidence in their capacities. The next two symptoms represent their narrow-mindedness. The last five characteristics pertain to pressure to conform. The increased presence of symptoms increases the likelihood of groupthink and faulty decision-making.

Groupthink exists when there is **high group cohesiveness** and little disagreement. The process of **deindividualization** occurs, which is a condition in which group cohesiveness dominates individual freedom of expression and identity. A second cause of groupthink centers around **structural faults**. Group structure precludes the communication of objective information; thus, decisions become less informed and careless. Finally, the **situational context** is a third major cause of groupthink. Highly stressful time-sensitive external environmental factors can foster stress and anxiety where the group seeks sure solutions

Figure 11.7 Groupthink Maintains Unity through Consistent Group Centered Communication

and uncertainty reduction. The confidence exuded by groupthink provides psychological relief to organizational members.

Janis (1982) suggests several ways to combat groupthink.

1   Appoint a devil's advocate to force everyone to think about contrary perspectives.
2   Encourage members to critically evaluate the group's position.
3   The group leader should not make her/his position known before the group members individually assess the issue.
4   Establish independent groups or sub-groups within the organization.
5   Include outsiders to participate in the group's activities about the issue.
6   Recruit new members with fresh views about the organization and issue.
7   Collect anonymous feedback from group members.

Walmart has had its groupthink-related challenges. Through continuous efforts over several years, the company has been realigning its culture to place both men and women on an equal footing concerning internal job promotions and equal pay. The company has endeavored to identify current female employees for promotion and recruit women externally for management positions.

Another example was the Challenger Space Shuttle disaster. There were warning signs that the shuttle launch was unsafe. Yet, determined to have a successful timely liftoff, these signs did not deter the shuttle management. They felt that their teams and systems were the best in the world and, thus, nothing would go wrong. The result was a tragic loss of life. More recently, a similar situation transpired with the Deepwater Horizon BP oil spill in the Gulf of Mexico.

Internal Communication Best Practices

There are different ways to view internal communication best practices. We focus on communication to manage organizational change. Woodall (2006), suggests the following practices.

1   *Communicate content.* Regular communication about ongoing issues is important especially updating the "whys" and "whats" of issues. For instance, if healthcare insurance options are under company review, periodic updates about the review progress will reduce uncertainty and stress.
2   *Manager/supervisor focus.* These stakeholders are critical because of their role in the formal organizational structure. Employees go to them for information. Uninformed managers and supervisors will only contribute to uncertainty and worry, especially if the change is substantive.
3   *Storytelling as communication.* People relate to a narrative. Telling a story about a forthcoming change including the why and when framed in a manner that reinforces desired behaviors is effective. If presented as an unfolding story, the change will make sense to employees.
4   *Leverage digital technology.* Social media, mobile apps, and other communication technologies measure attitude and engagement; collect other forms of feedback; and keep the goal's achievement always in sight, adjusting where necessary.
5   *Define and know the relevant publics.* Engage in empathy. Understand what publics need, what they know, their level of engagement about the change issue, and how to reach, inform, and persuade them to behave in a manner consistent with the public relations goal.

6   *Budgeting.* Allocate approximately one third of financial resources to programming with the remaining devoted to salaries. Additional resources should come from other internal funding sources where there is shared benefit.

Deploying best practices together take advantage of synergies. For example, tell the story of change including the whys and whats in terms of what is important to the various stakeholders. Start with the managers and keep everyone updated regularly. Take advantage of social media and other platforms where employees congregate.

Think about This . . .

In a July 2017 *Institute for Public Relations* blog post entitled, "Can We Just Play Nice? The Challenge of Toxic Employees and Importance of Followership," Peter Smudde discusses toxic employees and ways of dealing with them by knowing the core types of organizational members.

Troublesome employees exist at any organizational level and can hold formal leadership or management positions. At the management level, they can have a coercive impact on the organizational culture from the top down, undermining internal communications and morale.

Typically, management focuses on converting the problematic employee to at least an average performer. If all else fails, avoid or fire the person.

Smudde references Kellerman's book *Followership* (2008), in which she describes five types of followers (employees):

- Isolators are detached people who are unaware of their leaders' actions and what is going on to fulfill the mission. If invited, these followers can provide healthy skepticism.
- Bystanders are observant of what is going on but do not participate very much if at all, effectively adopting a neutral stance on everything and, thereby, giving tacit support for leaders and their activities. These followers can be engaged by giving specific invitations to do so in ways that play to their strengths or areas of expertise.
- Participants are engaged in some way, including favorable attitudes toward leaders and making contributions to the cause. Because of their involvement in things, these followers can contribute well, for example, when asked to assess pros and cons, risks, and benefits.
- Activists have strong feelings about their leaders and the mission in which they are engaged, contributing great amounts of time and effort to the cause, even if that means changing processes, policies, plans, leadership, etc. These followers are solid self-starters and willing to identify challenges on their own as well as take on new challenges.
- Diehards have the greatest degree of passion, dedication, and loyalty to the group, its leaders, and the mission in which all are engaged, including being willing to give their professional lives to the cause that consumes them to ensure success. These followers possess a very deep passion for the cause and the organization, making them especially predisposed for doing whatever it takes for success. (Smudde, 2017, para. 8).

(continued)

(continued)

The article points out that understanding organizational members can go a long way to address toxic individuals before they have a deleterious effect on the organization. Identifying, defining, and communicating with these persons in ways that they understand and find appealing can produce an enriching organizational environment that is fulfilling to all those concerned.

Ask yourself: Can you think of a situation in which a toxic employee's negative perspective about an organization affected others and endangered the mission? Consider categorizing such a person according to one of the "followers" designations. How might you reduce the negative perspective of this person?

Kellerman, B. (2008). *Followership: How followers are creating change and changing Leaders.* Cambridge, MA: Harvard Business Review Press.

Smudde, P. (2017, July 18). Can we just play nice? The challenge of toxic employees and importance of followership. *Institute for Public Relations.* Retrieved from www.instituteforpr.org/can-just-play-nice-challenge-toxic-employees-importance-followership/.

Internal Communication Audit

An **internal communication audit** is a type of internal research that can take many forms. It serves two purposes. First, it discovers how organizational members in fact communicate in the organization. This is compared to the actual communication channels with the formal and suspected informal ways that employees communicate. Adjustments to communication channels based on audit findings can result in cost savings. An audit performs a second function that is more issue oriented. It can collect employees' thoughts and feelings about morale, employee turnover, compensation, benefits, a merger, an acquisition, a new product line, the major competition, and other issues. In sum, an internal communication audit collects information about where employees "talk" to each other as well as what they talk about including their attitudes about something that is going on in the organization.

As covered in Chapter 4, the audit can be casual relying on informal emails, discussions, and word-of-mouth information. It can also be formal, involving focus groups, online surveys, interviews, and company records. External consultants with the requisite competencies conduct formal audits. An impartial third party brings no hidden agenda, is objective, and employees are more likely to speak candidly to an outsider, who, they suspect, will keep sources of information confidential.

Depending on the size of the establishment, the entire organization or a representative sample participates in the audit. Internal communication audits are conducted on an ad hoc basis or regularly to uncover perceptions and developments. The length of an audit depends on its goals, scope, and complexity. A write-up can range from 1–2 pages to over 100 pages.

Intranet and Social Media

Employees have tools available, and sometimes in combination, with which to communicate. Some of these tools are: email, telephone, instant messaging (texting), forums,

Figure 11.8 An Internal Communication Audit Tells Us What Really Is Going On

blogs, and social media such as Twitter, LinkedIn, Facebook, YouTube, Pinterest, and Instagram among others.

Social media communication disseminates information and spreads the word. Social media content represents employee sentiments on specific issues as well as their level of engagement and knowledge about an issue.

In her 2015 article "7 Ways to Use Social Media for Employee Communications," Taurasi describes seven social media platforms that enhance employee communication. The first platform is **Yammer**. This application allows the sharing of information through organization-wide to localized team boards. Yammer is easy to use and a mobile app is available. Employees can communicate in real time; thus, it is immediately responsive and can reduce the number of asynchronous communications.

Company information is on **Facebook** including images and video. Facebook serves as a hub for the other social platforms. On Facebook, companies share ad hoc projects, providing linked information, changes in company policies, training opportunities, position postings, and calls to action. Information about employee volunteer activities and corporate citizenship activities are specific usages.

Twitter is another social media communication tool. Employers tweet publicly and privately sharing a short burst of information within an employee network or with the entire organization. According to Taurasi (2015),

> Big brands, like Google and Starbucks, use Twitter to engage and inspire employees, and provide a glimpse of what it's like to work at these companies. Other employers, like the Massachusetts Institute of Technology, through its @MITWorkLife handle, promotes work-life content and professional development events and more on Twitter.

(para. 9)

Figure 11.9 Although It May Not Be Evident, People Talk

LinkedIn functions as a company intranet. Public relations practitioners manage groups of employees so that they can share information about internal activities and make announcements as well as increase and maintain morale, pride, and motivation.

Company blogs post information about human resources topics such as benefits, training, diversity, and inclusion programs. Blogs serve a Q&A function by allowing readers to benefit from individual questions and responses to those questions.

Remote Access is an excellent approach to train employees in multiple locations in a cost-effective and timely manner. Periscope and Meerkat are remote access tools for product training and live focus group activities. These types of platforms allow people to watch live or recorded videos.

YouTube videos, which are archivable, is a powerful social media video tool.

Using a private YouTube channel, organizations can store training videos produced live or beforehand. Through these videos, the public has a glimpse of an organization and what it does. Viewers can leave comments or questions below the video area.

Summary of Key Concepts

- An organization has structure and people. An organization's culture is the oil that keeps the structure's "machinery" running smoothly.
- Organizational communication is formal or informal. It can be explicit or implicit.
- Organizations are rational, natural, or open systems, and more often a combination of them. The system varies over time and within areas of the organization.
- There is organizational centralized or decentralized decision-making authority.

- There are different internal stakeholder groups.
- Organizational goals vary as do types of internal communication.
- There are a variety of channels of internal communication.
- There are barriers to internal communication.
- Internal communications best practices help assure successful strategic communication.

Key Terms

Auto-communication 279
Centralized organization 275
Compensation and benefits
    communication 278
Cultural barriers 282
Decentralized organization 276
Deindividualization 283
Explicit communication 279
Groupthink 282
High group cohesiveness 283
Implicit communication 279
Internal communication audit 286
Morale and satisfaction
    communication 278

Natural system 274
Open system 275
Organization 273
Organizational communication 271
Organizational culture 274
Organizational change and
    development communication 279
Orientation and indoctrination
    communication 278
Rational system 274
Red tape 281
Situational context 283
Structural faults 283

Chapter Questions

11.1   Define organizational communication.
11.2   What is a stressful time in an organizational environment?
11.3   Is employment for life at the same organization common today as it was years ago?
        If not, explain why.
11.4   Define organization.
11.5   What is organizational culture?
11.6   What is a rational system?
11.7   What is a natural organization?
11.8   What is an open organization?
11.9   What is a centralized organization?
11.10   What is a decentralized organization?
11.11   What are other names for internal communication?
11.12   According to Papa, Daniels, and Spiker (2008), what are the functions of internal
        communication? Briefly explain each function.
11.13   Define explicit and implicit types of communication and provide an example of
        each.
11.14   What is auto-communication and offer an example?
11.15   What is organizational red tape and provide an example?
11.16   What is groupthink?
11.17   What is deindividualization?
11.18   What is structural fault?
11.19   Name three internal communication best practices and explain each one.

11.20 Define internal communication audit.

11.21 Name three social media platforms appropriate for internal communication and explain why.

11.22 What is the optimal group size to assure that each member has an opportunity to communication?

11.23 Explain Groupthink's collective rationalization.

11.24 Name five ways to combat Groupthink.

11.25 What is remote access?

11.26 How can technology become a barrier to internal communication?

Notes

1 Findings: "Compared with workers in 1977 and 1978, workers in 2010 and 2012 expressed significantly less job security. They were more afraid of losing their jobs (11.2 percent versus the earlier 7.7 percent) and were less likely to think that they could find comparable work without much difficulty (48.3 percent versus the earlier 59.2 percent)" (Weaver, 2015, para. 12).

2 The Clio Awards are annual awards that recognize creative and innovative excellence in advertising, design, and communication.

References

Conrad, C., & Poole, M. S. (2013). *Strategic organizational communication in a global economy.* Malden, MA: Wiley-Blackwell.

Grunig, J. E. (2001). *The role of public relations in management and its contribution to organizational and societal effectiveness.* Speech delivered in Taipei, Taiwan, May 12, 2001.

Hagen, O. (2008). Seduced by the proactive image? On using auto communication to enhance CSR. *Corporation Reputation Review, 11*(2), 130–144.

Janis, I. L. (1982). *Groupthink: Psychological studies of policy decisions and fiascoes.* Boston, MA: Houghton Mifflin.

Kaufmann, W., & Tummers, L. (2017). The negative effect of red tape on procedural satisfaction. *Public Management Review, 19*(9), 1311–1327.

Kellerman, B. (2008). *Followership: How followers are creating change and changing Leaders.* Cambridge, MA: Harvard Business Review Press.

Morsing, M. (2006). Corporate social responsibility as strategic auto-communication: on the role of external stakeholders for member identification. *Business Ethics: A European Review, 15*(2), 171–182.

Moyers, B. (1988, November 17). *Peter Drucker: Father of Modern Management* (Interview with Peter Drucker). Moyers and Company. A world of ideas. Retrieved from http://billmoyers.com/content/peter-drucker/ .

Pandey, S. K., & Moynihan, D. P. (2006). Bureaucratic red tape and organizational performance: testing the moderating role of culture and political support. In G. A. Boyne, K. J. Meier, L. J. O'Toole Jr., and R. M. Walker (Eds.), *Public service performance* (pp. 130–151). Cambridge, U.K.: Cambridge University Press.

Papa, M. J., Daniels, T. D., & Spiker, B. K. (2008). *Organizational communication: Perspectives and trends.* London: Sage.

Robbins, S. P., & Judge, T. A. (2017). *Organizational behavior.* Boston, MA: Pearson.

Scott, W. R. (1998). *Organizations: Rational, natural, and open systems.* Upper Saddle River, NJ: Prentice Hall.

Smudde, P. (2017, July 18). Can we just play nice? The challenge of toxic employees and importance of followership. *Institute for Public Relations*. Retrieved from www.instituteforpr. org/can-just-play-nice-challenge-toxic-employees-importance-followership/.

Taurasi, L. (2015, July 6). 7 Ways to Use Social Media for Employee Communications. *Care@work*. Retrieved from http://workplace.care.com/7-ways-to-use-social-media-for-employee-communications.

Weaver, C. N. (2015, January). Worker's expectations about losing and replacing their jobs: 35 years of change. *Monthly Labor Review*. United States Department of Labor, Bureau of Labor Statistics. Retrieved from www.bls.gov/opub/mlr/2015/article/workers-expectations-about-losing-and-replacing-their-jobs.htm.

Woodall, K. (2006). The future of business communication. In T. L. Gillis (Ed.), *The IABC handbook of organizational communication* (pp. 514–529). San Francisco, CA: Jossey-Bass.

Part V

Budgeting and Evaluation

Chapter 12

Budgeting and Scheduling for a Public Relations Campaign

Don't tell me what you value, show me your budget, and I'll tell you what you value.
(Former Vice President Joseph Biden, *New York Times*, 2008, para. 17)

Learning Objectives

To:

- Describe the three major types of public relations campaign costs.
- Understand the purpose of a contingency fund.
- Describe the types of budgeting methods.
- Explain the major scheduling strategies.
- Know what is a Gantt chart.
- Understand the concept of reach.
- Identify the major components of a master schedule and budget document.
- Understand, describe, and know the value of cost per thousand (CPM).

Introduction

On average, organizations spend from 3% to 10% of their revenues on marketing. Public relations accounts for 3–5% and social media activities receives 2%. For example, a corporation with $1 billion in revenues typically spends between $30 million and $100 million on marketing. Based on a $100 million marketing budget, a company spends $3 million to $5 million on public relations and $2 million on social media. Typically, 60–70% covers administrative costs and approximately 30% includes programming and production costs (Bobbitt & Sullivan, 2014).

Many organizations define the relationship among marketing, public relations, and social media differently. This makes setting benchmarks challenging at times. For instance, some organizations include public relations as part of marketing. Others consider it a separate strategic management function. Social media face a similar situation. They are part of marketing, public relations, and other programs.

Additionally, these percentages vary based on the size of an organization, the nature of its business, and characteristics of the issue at hand. Non-profit organizations spend less. Larger organizations spend less. New technologically-based products or brands spend more on public relations. The baseline level of brand equity also affects marketing budgets. A well-recognized brand will devote resources to "reminder" messaging which focuses on keeping the brand in the consumers' collective mind; whereas a new product with little equity will need to work harder by creating awareness, positive attitude, and, ultimately, purchase behavior.

Strategizing, planning, executing, monitoring, and evaluating a public relations campaign requires financial resources in which various departments are vying to procure. To increase the likelihood of receiving these resources now and in the future, public relations practitioners must demonstrate that their expenditures result in the expected outcomes. Scheduling tactics on a timeline and costing them so that optimal and effective combinations are deployed help assure the value of the public relations function. A **tactic** is a specific public relations activity designed to help achieve an objective. Examples are news release, media advisory, Twitter account, Facebook page, online or in-person event, lobbyist efforts, conducting a set of focus groups, internal memo, and email project.

This chapter examines types of budgets; types of campaign costs; scheduling strategy and practices, including Gantt charts; as well as a common method to standardize costs for comparative and evaluation purposes.

Types of Campaign Costs

There are three kinds of public relations campaign costs. They are personnel, administrative, and production/program costs as well as a set-aside contingency fund.

Personnel Costs

Personnel costs are allocated time for permanent and temporary staff, hired consultants, and/or freelancers to perform specialized functions. Personnel costs are the billable hourly rates multiplied by the number of hours estimated and assigned to a project or a campaign. For full time staff, the rate includes indirect costs such as benefits and employment taxes, which add an additional 28% to 40% to the base rate, thus, providing the total compensation cost (Bureau of Labor Statistics, 2017). Agency expertise, freelance, and internal billable rates vary from $25/hour to $500/hour, depending on the size of the organization, location of activities, and specific tasks.

Administrative Costs

Administrative costs cover general support expenses such as stationery supplies, photocopies, other office supplies, rental cars, and travel including lodging and per diem. In some cases, included are agency or organizational fixed or overhead costs such as facility leasing, insurance, security, and parking space leases, which are all prorated and charged to the campaign.

Production and Programming Costs

Production and program costs directly relate to the public relations campaign communication activities other than support personnel costs. They are all that goes into messaging including what it costs to design, produce, and disseminate messages including the costs of event planning, management, and execution. They include the development, production, and release of news releases and videos, as well as media advisories. Nonsupport persons such as celebrities or sports figures compensated for attending an event are program costs.

In short, all the direct expenses associated with the messaging to publics constitute production and program costs.

Contingency Fund

A **contingency fund** is set aside and available when there is a need for campaign adjustments. This occurs for the replacement of ineffective tactics or if an unexpected opportunity presents itself. Five to ten percent of the total cost serves as the contingency fund. For example, for a $10,000 budget, a 10% contingency is: $10,000 X 10% = $1,000. The final total budget is $11,000. As the overall budget increases, at some point, the percentage decreases.

Final Budget

The personnel, administrative, production/programming costs, and contingency fund constitute the total estimated budget for a public relations campaign. For an internal budget, a 10–20% **service fee** is the cost assigned to an internal "client." Using the $11,000 example above, at 15%, the fee is $1,650. Therefore, the total campaign cost is $12,650. In the case of an agency budget for a client, the **handling fee** is 15–20%. This fee covers purchasing and managing the various aspects of the campaign. At 20%, the handling fee is $2,200 and the total budget is $13,200.

Finally, public relations planning relies on the total budget allocated to achieve the campaign goal. It requires a balance between achieving objectives to reach the goal and not exceeding the allocated budget. Therefore, choices involve operating in a cost efficient manner with limited resources.

Types of Budgets

A **budget** consists of the financial resources and allocations to activities necessary to implement a public relations campaign. It includes costs from the beginning of the campaign, at the situational analysis stage, and throughout the campaign including the evaluation phase. Once the situational analysis is complete, the budget can be adjusted to accommodate newly discovered information. An experienced practitioner has a sense of financial requirements and will often come close to knowing what amount of financial resources will be necessary to implement a campaign.

There are various approaches to public relations budgeting. Along with the parameters set by senior management, these approaches are the bases for determine the size of the budget. The most appropriate method depends on the nature of the campaign, issue, and organization. The basis of the tabulations varies. For example, the percentage-of-sales method, based on a percentage of revenues, applies to sales, donations, grant, and other measures. Competitive-comparison, co-op only budgeting, cost–benefit analysis, objective-benefit budgeting, opportunity–cost analysis, past-spending, percentage-of-sales, units-of-sales, month-to-month budgeting, stage-of-life-cycle budgeting, subjective budgeting, and zero-based budgeting are key methods for setting budgets. Budgeting systems can be customized to fit an organization's needs and some approaches are used in combination. Most of them share characteristics and are not mutually exclusive. Table 12.1 lists the major budgeting systems.

Table 12.1 Type of Public Relations Campaigns Budgets

Budget Methods
Competitive-comparison
Co-op Only budgeting
Cost–benefit analysis
Objective-based budgeting
Opportunity–cost analysis
Past-spending
Percentage-of-sales
Unit-of-sales
Month-to-month budgeting
Stage-of-life-cycle budgeting
Subjective-budgeting
Zero-based budgeting

Competitive-comparison

Competitive-comparison is budgeting based on the amount of spending by competing organizations for similar campaigns. The main competition, all competitors, or only those that are like the organization, serve as the baseline. Armed with this information, the practitioner can decide whether to match, increase, or decrease spending.

Keep in mind, this approach is imprecise because estimates are dependent upon educated guesswork and available industry and professional association data. Additionally, most situations vary. For example, market share affects promotional dynamics and positive brand equity may be based on a market segment with diverse media habits. In the case of non-profit organizations, the mission and affiliations bring varied resources and commitment to a campaign grounded in diverse values and beliefs requiring an array of messaging, some less costly and others costlier. Finally, across the competition, goals and strategies vary and publics differ. These factors make an accurate comparison challenging.

One approach designed to develop a fair comparison is competitive contrasting adjusted for market share whether it is in numbers of volunteers, corporate sponsors, or total market sales. This approach weighs the budget items, then adjusts them accordingly.

Co-op Only Budgeting

Co-op only budgeting primarily operates in a corporate setting. Its basis is limiting the budget size to cooperative (co-op) advertising support dollars from a vendor such as a manufacturer or an intermediary. In the non-profit sector, it might be a sponsor, special interest group, or professional association. For example, some malls have merchants' associations whose primary purpose is to pool resources to draw traffic to the malls. The mall owners often match promotional dollars, and retain control of local advertising and promotional events. Many healthcare brands offer promotional arrangements to their wholesalers and retailers.

Cost–benefit analysis

Cost–benefit analysis compares the cost of the campaign to the anticipated outcomes. This method optimizes benefits in relation to associated costs. For instance, a promotional

Figure 12.1 Budgets Are Tools that Help Us Manage Expenses

campaign, which cost $120,000 generating $1 million in sales of which $300,000 is profit, is a desirable outcome because profit exceeds cost by $180,000 ($300,000–$120,000). Discussed in the next chapter, the advertising value equivalency (AVE) approach calculates the benefits from public relations efforts.

There are disadvantages to this method. First, there is no linkage to objectives. Second, the analysis requires ongoing and post-campaign analysis to assure meeting expectations. Third, if the benefit is the basis of financial planning, then the actual budget must be based on the anticipated outcomes. Overstated expectations may result in an underperforming campaign.

Objective-Based Budgeting

Objective-based budgeting starts with the campaign's overall objectives, followed by the tactics needed to achieve them. The budget is based on the cost of executing the planned tactics. Prioritization or the removal of objectives and tactics can occur if the actual budget exceeds the available resources. Alternatively, practitioners can develop creative ways to achieve the objectives such as forming alliances with other organizations who are committed to the issue and who have access to needed resources. Using more online channels of communication may be more cost effective as well.

Objective-based budgeting has one major pitfall. Psychological objectives like awareness and positive attitude are difficult to link to the organization's goals. It is challenging to quantify their contribution especially when these objectives often operate in a hierarchical or step-building progressive process in which they ultimately manifest themselves in a behavioral way, such as purchasing products, voting for a candidate, engaging in volunteer work, and so forth. Objective-based budgeting encourages new and creative ways to engage publics in cost-efficient ways.

Like all budgeting, there are constraints. Owing to the hierarchy of interdependent objectives, this type of budgeting is most suitable from a communication perspective, which is the approach adopted throughout this book.

Opportunity–cost analysis

Opportunity–cost analysis, which is related to objective-based budgeting, is dependent upon objectives and weighs the costs of alternative combinations of tactics necessary to achieve specific objectives. The intent of this method is to attain objectives in a cost-effective manner. For example, an objective to increase trade journal awareness and positive attitude about a new, innovative product occurs through tactics such as online presentations, live, in-person events, in-person visits or interviews, and personal telephone calls, among other approaches. While any or a combination of these tactics will achieve the objective, costs and degree of effectiveness vary. Including tactics relevant to the objective requires a trade-off between cost and an assessment about the probability of success.

Past-spending

Past-spending planning is based on the costs of similar previous campaign budgets, employing the same benchmarks and objectives, and assuming successful outcomes. Adjustments account for inflation.

Percentage-of-sales

Percentage-of-sales is the most common budgeting method utilized by organizations that market products and/or services. It is based on a percentage of sales, revenues, donations, or profit of a previous period, so that the budget links directly to a metric. Budget adjustments occur for special circumstances such as unanticipated marketing opportunities, a precipitous decline in fundraising success, or new product promotions while considering past performance and industry standards.

There are criticisms of the percentage-of-sales method. If sales or donations decline, there is a reduction in the subsequent public relations budget when there should be increased expenditures. Also, subscribers to this approach assume that there is a linear relationship between public relations efforts and sales, which may not be the case. Product life cycles, competitive actions, shifting demographics, and other external environmental conditions influence revenues. For example, Uncle Ben's Original Converted Rice (20-minute rice) brand sales were declining because of changes in market demographics from older traditional rice consumers to on-the-go professionals, who were looking for a quick and easy way to prepare meals. The company developed a line of Uncle Ben's microwavable rice-based meals. Creating brand awareness for this new product required a significant increase in advertising and promotional expenditures.

Unit-of-Sales

Unit-of-sales budgeting is a variation of the percentage-of-sales technique. It is based on the number of units sold. For example, for each unit sold or for each volunteer recruited, a set amount of funds is committed to the campaign for the subsequent year. The criticisms of the percentage-of-sales approach apply to the units-of-sales method. Additionally, increases in units sold do not necessarily reflect profitability if sales prices are close to or below costs.

Month-to-Month Budgeting

Public relations **month-to-month budgeting** is based according to what resources are available rather than a long-term, planned approach. This technique is common in organizations that view public relations as an expense rather than as an investment in the future. The lack of planning associated with month-to-month budgeting limits efforts to the here and now. Limited resources preclude taking advantage of opportunities.

Stage-of-Life-Cycle Budgeting

Stage-of-life-cycle budgeting is based on the progression of an issue in conjunction with objectives. For instance, new issue exposure precedes creating awareness, knowledge, and attitude formation. These objectives require repeated messaging over time. Once there is issue knowledge and engagement, then it is a matter of relationship maintenance. Early on, there are resource requirements not needed during the maintenance stage. Moreover, the compliance rate for a call to action is less than the rates for psychological objectives. Getting people to do something is harder than making them aware of something. Therefore, increasing behavioral compliance requires greater resources.

Subjective Budgeting

Subjective budgeting is based on practitioner expertise and experience. This type of budgeting considers objectives, but it is a qualitative process. The practitioner who sets the budget often uses features from other budgeting techniques. Two major disadvantages are apparent. First, there is no clear, systematic rationale for the budget. Second, if the connection to the organization's mission is unclear and subjective, there are limitations to evaluation.

Zero-Based Budgeting

Zero-based budgeting starts from zero. Resources are allocated based on prioritized objectives and tactics within those objectives. The elimination of less important objectives and tactics occurs when budgetary resources are exhausted. During the planning process, innovative, less costly tactics designed to be effective and to save money replace previous assigned tactics. In zero-based budgeting, although past budgets and campaigns are insightful, the budget starts from scratch (zero) and then moves forward. There are variations of this approach. Zero-based budgeting has one major pitfall. It is primarily based on financial considerations. The progression of communication objectives is secondary.

Think about This . . .

In 2014, Theresa Wendhausen, the branding and communications officer for First Bank and Trust located in Wisconsin, wrote an article entitled "Guidelines for Formulating a Public Relations Budget" for the trade publication *ABA Banking Marketing and Sales*. Wendhausen emphasized the significance of accounting for all public relations stakeholders when formulating a budget. Based on her banking experience, she listed the following budget considerations:

- Know the populations of the towns and counties where each branch is located.
- Know the number of branches in each defined community.
- Know how many customers each branch serves.
- In each defined area, know how many schools, school districts, hospitals, golf courses, and sports teams are located.
- Know your competition in the defined area.

Being aware of these facts and identifying potential stakeholders, and building relationships with them, can go a long way in successfully meeting public relations' goals and objectives. For this reason, it is important to include them in the budget.

Ask yourself: Identify other public relations opportunities to build and enhance an organization's image? Do some of these relate to the list of budgeting considerations in this article?

Wendhausen, T. (2014, October 1). Guidelines for formulating a public relations budget. *ABA Banking Marketing and Sales*. Retrieved from www.thefreelibrary.com/Guidelines+ for+formulating+a+public+relations+budget.-a0384967941.

Scheduling

Scheduling Strategy

Three factors contribute to determining a scheduling strategy. They are 1) where is the public in terms of the issue (which informs the second consideration), 2) whether there is a hierarchy of objectives, and finally, 3) the nature of the issue.

First, **frequency** is the number of times the public relations practitioners send a message in a set time. The number of times individual audience members receive a message during a given period is **exposures** or **impressions**, which is a function of audience size. The number of unique individuals or households exposed to a message over a period is **reach**. A person needs 3 to 10 message exposures before remembering it. Those people who are familiar with the issue require fewer frequencies and some of those individuals new to an issue will require a frequency rate closer to ten times. The exposure occurs through a variety of channels such as interpersonal communication, video, news story, email, and social media.

The second point relates to the first. If a public has low issue awareness, then awareness and knowledge must be created before issue comprehension can be achieved. Less awareness requires more messaging to assure increases in knowledge and engagement.

Figure 12.2 Scheduling Involves Communication-Related and Budgeting Considerations

The effort devoted to creating understanding and knowledge depends on the level of issue and situation complexity. In the case of a highly informed and involved public, public relations tactics focus on developing favorable attitudes and fostering target behaviors.

In addition to a public's level of knowledge, attitude, and degree of engagement, there is the nature of the issue. Some issues are ad hoc, while others are seasonal, depending on the time and region of the country. Some are cyclical. Air conditioners are not marketed during the winter and snow blowers are not promoted during the summer in Canada and most parts of the USA.

A **scheduling strategy** is the systematic, time-oriented placement and frequency of message planning by communication channels to achieve campaign objectives during a specified timeline. Flight, continuous, and pulsing are the basic strategies. Figure 12.3 illustrates them.

Flighting. Messaging transpires only at certain times of the year because of the seasonal nature of an issue (or product) such as selling snow blowers, selling Cadbury Easter eggs, or recruiting volunteers to work at various summer festivals.

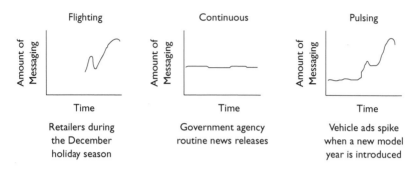

Figure 12.3 Scheduling Strategies

Note: Campaign start and end dates vary and are not required to follow a calendar year. Messaging typically takes different forms.

Continuous. This is messaging that maintains the same consistent schedule throughout the year such as promoting laundry detergent, food staples like milk and bread, and awareness of the importance of taking medications regularly according to the prescribed time.

Pulsing. Messaging is continuously scheduled with spikes (a combination of continuous and flighting) such as promoting issues or products that are regularly used, but more so during certain times of the year, such as new model year vehicles, furniture and appliance sales, or efforts to raise charitable donations especially during holidays.

Gantt Chart

Gantt charts depict public relations scheduling, which provide an easily understandable and organized overview of the timelines for objective-based tactics. Gantt charts can be simple or relatively detailed incorporating project management techniques. They are for assigning and scheduling tasks associated with tactics and objectives. Our focus is on scheduling tactics.

So, what exactly is a Gantt chart? A **Gantt chart** is a horizontal bar chart designed as a management tool to coordinate, track, and manage the flow of tasks from start to completion. There are four types of relationships among tactics.

First, there is **Finish to Start**. This means that a tactic cannot start before its predecessor ends. It also can start later than the end of the previous tactic. For example, persuasive tactics must come before calls to action. Once publics develop a positive attitude, then there is an increased likelihood of their engaging in the desired behavior such as voting for a candidate, donating to a charity, or becoming more productive at work.

Next, there is **Start to Start**. In this case, the tactic cannot start until the preceding tactic starts, but it does not have to be at the same time because they are interdependent tactics. Increases in awareness requires exposure to the message and issue tactics. While exposure occurs, awareness begins to build. In a communication campaign, it is common for awareness, increased knowledge, and positive attitude to occur before completing awareness tactics.

Third, there is **Finish to Finish**. In this case, a tactic cannot end before the preceding one ends, but it can end later. For instance, a call to action does not end while the campaign continues to persuade people to act because the target action follows persuasion to act.

Last, there is the **Start to Finish** relationship in which the tactic cannot end before the preceding one starts, which may end later. For example, tactics that build issue knowledge cannot end before a public's exposure to the issue followed by awareness building.

These relationships among scheduled tactics operate best for clearly differentiated tasks. Public relations objectives and tasks overlap. Despite this, a Gantt chart is useful to schedule events and tactics because it offers a visual overview of campaign activities, which is available to aid in planning and execution. A Gantt chart easily reveals inconsistent scheduled tactics or incompatible tactical connections with hierarchical objectives.

Figure 12.4 is a Gantt chart. The scheduling information comes from the "Public Relations Campaign Master Budget and Schedule for 7/1/17 to 8/31/18" comprising Table 12.2. In this example, there are two objectives for the same public over the course of the campaign. Depending on the size of the campaign, an actual Gantt schedule can be far more extensive.

Notice that each of the two groups of tactics start with an estimated time frame by objective, which serves as a reference for the activities. The start and end dates for the tactics vary. Depending on the campaign, Saturdays, Sundays, and holidays may or may not be included in the schedule. In this example, all tactics operate within the objectives' timelines.

These objectives have a hierarchical relationship because creating iPhone X awareness and knowledge precede positive attitudes and favorable opinions. In some campaigns, objectives overlap so that awareness and attitude objectives' tactics operate concurrently and reinforce each other. In the case of the iPhone X, advertising and other marketing activities integrate within a public relations framework.

Single event tactics such as the roll-out and conferences span over time. This is because these events require planning and take place on the last day of the Gantt bar. The post-event clean-up and packing are implicit in the schedule. However, some charts account for post-event time.

It is important to know that message placement, message frequency, and the timing of frequencies are executed within the constraints of a budget; because of this, cost effectiveness is also a crucial consideration.

Objectives, Scheduling, and Budgeting

Decisions involving which channels of communication to use, when, and at what time messaging takes place require an understanding of the collective mind and behaviors of the target publics. The situational analysis and practitioners' experience inform these decisions. Objectives with budgetary constraints in mind guide messaging. Adjustments to objectives and schedules occur during the campaign because of changes in the operating environments, miscalculation, new opportunities, changes in publics, and changes in the situation or issue. Remember that achieving benchmarks within the budget and according to a schedule is a measure of success.

Within a communication framework, objectives can be organized in several ways. One approach often used in advertising is by designated market areas (DMAs), which is a propriety system owned by Nielsen based on the number of American television homes assigned to geographical areas. There are 210 DMAs in the USA. In 2017, the largest was

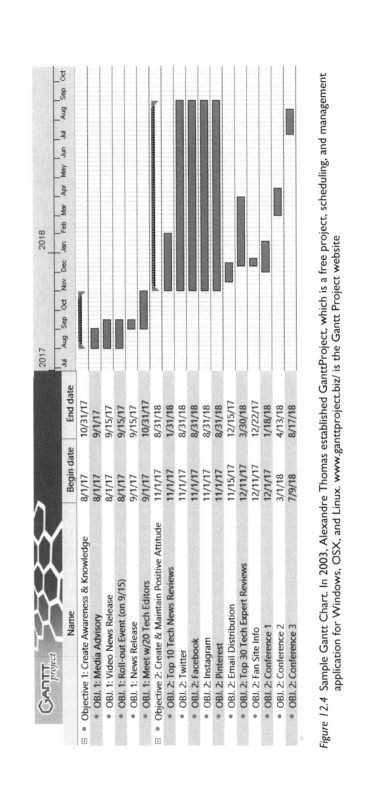

Figure 12.4 Sample Gantt Chart. In 2003, Alexandre Thomas established GanttProject, which is a free project, scheduling, and management application for Windows, OSX, and Linux. www.ganttproject.biz/ is the Gantt Project website

New York City consisting of nearly 7.5 million TV homes and the smallest was Glendive, M.T. with 4370 TV homes (Nielsen, 2016). In the case of DMAs, publics inform the organization of communication objectives. For instance, all market mavens in New York City may be slated for awareness and positive attitude objectives.

Keeping track of a major campaign is challenging. The Public Relations Campaign Master Budget and Schedule is a useful tool. It is the key working document that contains scheduled activities, the cost of these tactics, and how they connect to objectives. The data for total campaign reach and cost calculation come from this document. The master budget and schedule integrate in Excel or Access so that Gantt charts, schedules, and estimated costs can be calculated in relation to specific objectives.

Table 12.2 is a sample partial master budget and schedule. We can see the relationship between the budget and schedule. Chapter 14 contains an example as it would appear in an actual public relations campaign plan. Note that the scheduling information appears in the Figure 12.4 Gantt chart. As we can see, the public and objectives are identified along with the relevant tactics. Included are the timeline for the objectives and tactics as well as the number of impressions and cost. The average number of message exposures per person is **average frequency**.

For example, from 11/1/17 to 8/31/18, the expectations are for messaging through tweets to reach 10 million exposures at a cost of $15,000. This campaign will cost nearly $6.2 million and garner over 106 million impressions or exposures. Based on the 43 million public members, this is nearly an average of 2.5 frequencies per person in an ideal world. Some audience members' exposure will be more than 2.5 messages, the degree to which persons pay attention or even remember a message will vary and some of the coverage will reach nontargeted audience members. As we can see, applying average frequencies to the total target public is a gross number or, at best, a general guide unless there is a concentrated and manageably small group.

Standardized Costs

Being able to standardize costs for public relations tactics allows us to set benchmarks and compare costs across the various activities so that we can choose cost-effective tactics while, at the same time, meet our objectives. Standardization makes cost comparisons manageable. Cost analysis occurs across campaigns where potential trends are discoverable. Keep in mind though, the most cost-efficient communication channel is not necessarily the most effective. Different publics and even within publics vary in their media habits, which necessitates a variety of channels to reach a sufficient number of public members. The costs of these channels vary as well.

One common standardization approach is **cost per thousand (CPM)**. This technique permits us to compare costs per 1000 exposures of a message in different communication channels or in total. The quality of the exposures varies as do the costs. Some exposures have little impact, while others create awareness, knowledge, and a favorable opinion. The average frequency can also influence a public. Higher frequencies assure awareness and recognition. CPM does not include the contingency allowance, advertising value equivalency, personnel costs, or administrative costs. It comprises only the production and program costs, which is a straightforward comparison.

Table 12.2 Master Budget and Schedule

Partial Public Relations Campaign Master Budget and Schedule for 7/1/17 to 8/31/18

Public: The top half of all 18–34 year old people by personal or family income in the USA and Canada totaling 43 million

Objective 1: From 7/3/17 to 10/31/17, create awareness and knowledge for the new iPhone X in 75% of the target public

Tactic description:[a]	Dates	Public Exposures	Forecasted total tactic cost
Media advisory for launch conference	8/1/17–9/01/17	–	$1,500
Video news release for media & YouTube	8/1/17–9/15/17	30 million	$7,500
Rollout Event (on 9/15)	8/1/17–9/15/17	20,000	55,000,000
News release	9/1/17–9/15/17	10 million	$1,500
Meet with top 20 technology editors[b]	9/1/17–10/20/17	15 million	$110,000
	Objective/Public subtotal	55,020,000	$5,120,500

Public: The top half of all 18–34 year old people by personal or family income in the USA and Canada totaling 43 million

Objective 2: From 11/1/17 to 8/31/18. create and maintain positive attitude in 40% of the target public

Tactic description:	Dates	Public Exposures	Forecasted total tactic cost
Top 10 tech media to write reviews[b]	11/1/17–1/31/18	2 million	$20,000
Twitter presence	11/1/17–8/31/18	10 million	$15,000
Facebook iPhone X page	11/1/17–8/31/18	30 million	$25,000
Instagram presence	11/1/17–8/31/18	2 million	$5,000
Pinterest presence	11/1/17–8/31/18	2.2 million	$5,000
Select Apple email lists w/follow-up	11/15/17–12/15/17	2.5 million	$75,000
Top 30 tech experts to write reviews (blogs)	12/11/17–3/31/18	1.5 million	$20,000
Provide information to top 10 fan sites	12/11/17–12/2 2-17	1 million	$10,000
Presence three major technology conferences[b]	12/1/17–1/18/18, 3/1/18–4/14/18, 7,9/18–8/18/18	60,000	$900,000
	Objective/Public subtotal	51,260,000	$1,075,000
	Campaign total	**106.280.000**	**$6.195.500**

Note: This is a hypothetical market for the iPhone X.
[a] The assumption is that these activities fall within the responsibility of public relations.
[b] There will be a concentration of opinion leaders.

Going back to Table 12.2, we can calculate CPM by individual tactic, public, or for the entire campaign. The Public Exposures are the number of times the message was received or delivered in a period followed by the total tactic cost.

The formula is:

Total production and program cost X 1000

Number of exposures

Returning to our tweets example, 10 million exposures cost $15,000. CPM is:

= $15,000 X 1000

10 million

= $15,000,000

10 million

CPM = $1.50

Thus, in this hypothetical example, a CPM that equals $1.50, means that the cost to produce and deliver 1000 messages using this tactic is $1.50. In 2017, the CPM for social media was: $4.00–$6.00 for Instagram; $5.00–$7.00 for Facebook; $28.00–$30.00 for LinkedIn; and $4.00–$7.50 for Twitter.

For the iPhone X example, the CPM is $58.29 or 5.8 cents per message. This CPM formula standardizes costs by multiplying the total cost by 1000 and then dividing it by the total number of exposures.

In sum, CPM is a cost control device. It is an efficient method for comparing the cost of a given tactic over time, for comparing the costs of a specific tactic deployed in different campaigns, and for comparing a tactic's cost against benchmarks.

Summary of Key Concepts

- Personnel, administrative, and production/programs are the three types of public relations campaign costs.
- A contingency fund, which is typically 5–10% of the campaign budget, is set aside for adjustments while public relations efforts are in progress.
- There are various budgeting methods often combined. Objective-based budgeting works well in public relations campaigns.
- Flighting, continuous, and pulsing are the major scheduling strategies.
- A Gantt chart provides an effective overview of a campaign schedule.
- Reach is the number of a public's members exposed to a message in a period.
- Publics, objectives, tactics, timelines, reach, and costs are the major components of a master schedule and budget document.
- Cost as cost per thousand (CPM) is an efficient method for comparing the cost of a specific tactic over time, with different campaigns, or against benchmarks.

In the Case of Canyon Ranch . . . the Schedule and Budget

Because wellness services are in demand year-round, the campaign adopted a continuous scheduling strategy as demonstrated in the following Gantt chart.

Partial Public Relations Campaign Master Budget and Schedule for 1/1/19 to 12/31/19

Gantt Chart

Name	Begin date	End date
Objective 1: Achieve 90% knowledge of health and healing services for …	1/1/19	12/31/19
Redesign the Canyon Ranch website	1/2/19	1/2/19
Develop and implement a mobile app	1/2/19	1/2/19
Develop and implement blog	1/2/19	12/31/19
Create and maintain social media presence	1/2/19	12/31/19
Email blast to existing female customers	1/1/19	3/1/19
Follow-up email blasts, with a hardcopy mailer	3/2/19	4/2/19
Run ongoing email and texting tracking studies	1/1/19	12/31/19
Objective 2: 25% increase in health and healing sales from existing fem…	1/1/19	12/31/19
Personal selling paired guests	1/1/19	12/31/19
Suggest personalized plan	1/1/19	12/31/19
Benchmark tracking	2/28/19	12/31/19

The budget is $500,000 and contingency allocation is $25,000. The CPM is $3554.

Key Terms

Chapter Questions

12.1   Typically, what percentage of the marketing budget is allocated to public relations?

12.2   What are the types of campaign costs?

12.3   Define contingent fund.

12.4   What kinds of fees are associated with internal public relations or agency management?

12.5   Define budget.

12.6   Define competitive-comparison budgeting.

12.7   What is co-op budgeting and give an example?

12.8   Define cost–benefit analysis budgeting and provide an example.

12.9   What is objective-based budgeting?

12.10 Define opportunity-based analysis budgeting and give an example.

12.11 Define past spending budgeting.

12.12 What is percentage-of-sales budgeting?

12.13 Define unit-of-sales budgeting and give an example.

12.14 What is month-to-month budgeting?

12.15 Define stage-of-life budgeting and offer an example.

12.16 What is subjective based budgeting?

12.17 What is zero-based budgeting?

12.18 Define scheduling strategy.

12.19 What are the three scheduling strategies and describe them?

12.20 What is a Gantt chart?

12.21 What are the four types of relationships in Gantt charts and briefly describe them?

12.22 What is reach?

12.23 Define CPM.

12.24 What is the CPM formula?

12.25 What is a tactic and provide examples?

References

Biden, J. (2008, September 15). Biden's Remarks on McCain's Policies. *New York Times. Politics Section.* Retrieved from www.nytimes.com/2008/09/15/us/politics/15text-biden.html?mcubz=3.

Bobbitt, R., & Sullivan, R. (2014). *Developing the public relations campaign: A team-based approach.* Boston, MA: Pearson Education.

Employer costs for employee compensation–June 2017. (2017, September 8). News Release. Bureau of Labor Statistics. U.S. Department of Labor.

Nielsen. (2016). *Local television market universe.* The Nielsen Company.

Wendhausen, T. (2014, October 1). Guidelines for formulating a public relations budget. *ABA Banking Marketing and Sales.* Retrieved from www.thefreelibrary.com/Guidelines+for+formulating+a+public+relations+budget.-a0384967941.

Chapter 13

Public Relations Campaign Evaluation

Measuring engagement and engaging consumers are two sides of the same coin.

(David Penn, Lloyd, 2013, para. 4)

Learning Objectives

To:

- Understand and explain the evaluation process.
- Describe public relations campaign benchmarked assessment.
- Explain the components of a public relations objective.
- Know the types of campaign objectives.
- Understand how objectives are interrelated.
- Describe the objective process.
- Describe methods for linking outcomes to the organization.

Introduction

The primary purpose of a public relations campaign is to communicate a central message to people who are members of a public or stakeholder group to achieve a stated goal. Evaluating whether a campaign is successful involves comparing expected outcomes to actual outcomes. **Outcomes** are indirect or direct influences on one or more publics that occur because of public relations efforts. Anticipated outcomes are measurable or benchmarked objectives within an allocated budget. This means that cost efficiencies are part of planning.

So, how do we define public relations evaluation? The Commission on Measurement and Evaluation of Public Relations defines evaluation as:

> A form of research that determines the relative effectiveness of a public relations campaign or program by measuring program outcomes (changes in the level of awareness, understanding, attitudes, opinions and/or behaviors of a targeted audience or public) against a predetermined set of objectives that initially established the level or degree of change desired.
>
> (Stacks & Bowen, 2013, p. 7)

Figure 13.1 Benchmarked Assessments Apply to Many Aspects of a Public Relations Campaign

Evaluation is a systematic research process grounded in principles of scientific inquiry and statistical soundness. Therefore, it is a credible approach for assessing a campaign.

Evaluation is important for several reasons. First, it is necessary to determine campaign success. Second, results inform subsequent public relation practices leading to more cost-effective tactics. Third, it serves as the justification for future expenditures based on what is effective. Last and related to the third point, evaluation approximates public relations' contribution to the organization, which, in a highly competitive world where units within organizations compete for limited resources, evidence-based outcomes can assure future commitment from senior management. Let's start with the topic of transparency.

Transparency

Because methods for linking public relations efforts to quantitative measures, profitability, and cost reduction are imprecise, there is an element of subjectivity in the evaluation process. Expectations to succeed sometimes cloud judgments for any number of reasons including career advancement, meeting client expectations, and the agenda of senior management. These dynamics cause a tension between the organization's interests and a truthful assessment of outcomes. The public relations practitioner walks a fine line between reality and the ideals of the dominant decision-makers. According to Place (2015),

Because many practitioners experience stringent client expectations and fast-paced timelines, they may be subject to unique industry, culture, and power dynamics (Place & Vardeman-Winter, 2013) that prioritize misinterpreting or inflating evaluation results to bolster an organization's financial health or deflect blame on organizational decision-makers.

(p. 130)

The nature and amount of data available complicates evaluation. The extracting of data from massive databases utilizing such practices as data mining to distill data and uncover quick results does not always yield accurate findings or it simply tells part of the story. Yet, the attractiveness of timely evaluation is appealing. The issues of transparency, credibility, and accountability are important and contribute to the legitimacy of the public relations role in an organization. The practitioner must carefully navigate this terrain.

When to Evaluate Public Relations

Evaluation happens pre-campaign, during the campaign, and/or post-campaign. **Pre-testing evaluation** involves gauging reactions to a message prior to communicating it. The presentation format varies. For example, focus group participants, who represent the key publics, rate different versions of a message. Focus groups also provide feedback about buzz words associated with issues and situations. Other types of pre-testing involve having participants rate messages or topics on a tablet in a theater-like setting using a perception analyzer dial application that records participants' sentiments at different times during the message presentation.

Next, there is **ongoing evaluation**. Using this approach, the practitioner monitors and assesses a campaign underway to detect ineffective tactics and address them in time to make a difference for the balance of the campaign. For ongoing evaluation that involves any aspect of the campaign, there are comparisons between results and benchmarks. Effective reach and message persuasiveness are the two key areas monitored and assessed. Specifically, tracking studies measure changes in issue awareness and attitude development throughout the course of a campaign. Ongoing evaluation is practical for campaigns nearly one year and longer in length. Evaluation occurs weekly, semi-monthly, monthly, or quarterly. Nielsen, TradePulse (a company that partners with Nielsen), and Acxiom provide up-to-date data on defined population segments from measures of awareness, attitude information, social listening, and media usage to habits over time.

Last, there is post-campaign evaluation, which comes as summative and formative. **Summative evaluation** determines whether the campaign was successful by comparing the benchmarked objectives with the actual outcomes. **Formative evaluation** describes how the information gathered during the summative phase benefits future campaigns. Uncovered trends, lessons learned, what is effective, what is not effective, and what media are cost-efficient are addressed through formative feedback. A large complex organization incorporates all forms of evaluation and social listening and analytics specialists, who monitor and interpret social media communications and trends. Online services such as *Howsociable, LexisNexis Social Analytics, Hootsuite*, and *Mention* monitor brand presence on social media. Finally, at this point, the post-campaign results in the plansbook are in past tense.

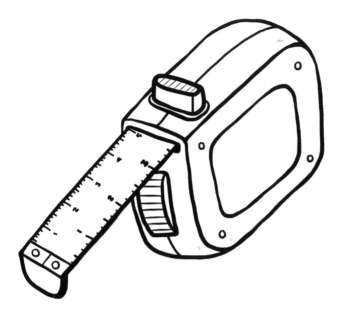

Figure 13.2 Measurement Takes Many Forms

Characteristics of Public Relations Measurable Objectives

Objectives are the means in which we achieve our goals. From an evaluation perspective, objectives provide what is necessary to measure aspects of the campaign that ultimately indicate goal achievement. Thus, collectively they measure whether a campaign is successful. Because of this, it is important that the objectives accurately represent what constitutes goal achievement. Second, a cost-efficient approach to goal achievement prevails since there is no endless supply of financial resources. This means that the total paid and owned media do not exceed the estimated cost of earned media. It thus is a rough and indirect measure of contribution to profit. Below is a detailed explanation of some of these topics.

Basis for Establishing Measurable Objectives

What is the basis for setting quantitative targets for objectives? It starts with the **baseline**, which is the current level of an objective. The baseline is based on past performance, industry data, or some other source of information. For instance, if the percentage of positive opinion about an issue at the start of a campaign is 20%, then the baseline of support is 20%.

On the other hand, a **benchmark** is part of an objective. It is the expected outcome. A benchmark is realistic, given available resources, but, at the same time, it is aspirational. Research such as history and performance; competitors' best practices; other information from the competition; internal expertise; case studies; academic research publications; consultants; industry reports; and professional association research findings and data inform benchmarking.

Figure 13.3 There Are Numerous Resources Available to Aid Benchmarking

Baselines and benchmarks are quantitative metrics expressed as a percentage or some other numeric value. They are objective and quantitative assessed values. In short, a benchmark is an expected outcome informed by an existing baseline and other information.

Components of a Clear Measurable Objective

Objectives are the expected outcomes required for a successful public relations campaign. They are precise and quantitatively measurable. An objective contains four parts: 1) A specific, target benchmark. The benchmark must be precise so that it leaves no room for interpretation. Benchmarks can be exposure-, information-, persuasion-, and/or behavioral-related. 2) A defined target public. The defined group is based on the criteria set forth in Chapter 6, which includes demographic and psychographic characteristics as well as the level of issue knowledge, degree of issue engagement, and approximate size of the target public. 3) Campaign objectives have deadlines so that a specific timeline for achieving the outcome is necessary. To reach other benchmarks essential for a successful campaign requires reaching the objective on time. 4) Parts of the objective must be quantifiable so that they are measurable. Measurable results are reported in specific numbers or percentages. For example, "Increase volunteerism to *25% of employees* 18–34 years old *during the next 6 months*," indicates a measurable target of 25% over the next 6 months.

Based on Table 13.1, Figure 13.4 illustrates answers to the four Ws questions of a public relations campaigns. *Who* do we want to target? Answer: Millennials as described in the figure. *What* do we want to achieve and to *what* degree? Answer: Positive opinions shared by 40% of Millennials in the USA. *When* will it be done? Answer: From 1/1/18 to 12/31/18.

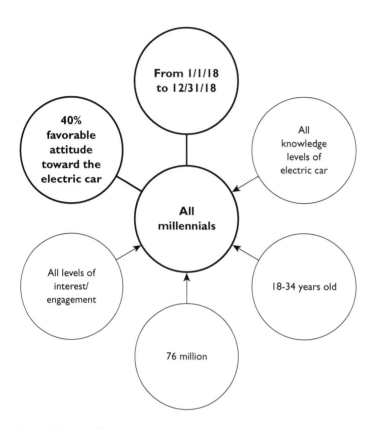

Figure 13.4 An Objective Answers the Four Ws of a Public Relations Campaign. *Who* Do We Want to Target? *What* Do We Want to Achieve and to *What* Degree? *When* Will It Be Done?

Types of Public Relations Measurable Objectives

Objectives must be accurate. An objective is a concrete version of a goal. For instance, if a goal is to increase awareness, then reaching the set forth objectives will represent goal achievement. They are thus specific operational guides and benchmarks for measuring, reaching, and evaluating campaign success. There are four categories of objectives. They are exposure, information, persuasion, and behavior. Measurement occurs before, during, and after the campaign ends depending on the length of the operations.

Exposure objectives are outcomes that expose stakeholders to a message. Traditionally, exposure measurement consisted of the number of news article clippings or event attendance for example. Today, social media and digital technologies play an important role in effectuating message exposure such as the number of Facebook friends, Twitter followers, email list, texting, LinkedIn connections, media impression, and various other analytics. Exposure objectives are especially important when promoting little known or new "products" such as innovative brands, new services, ideas, persons, new programming, or candidates. They are necessary to raise awareness about an issue. Creating awareness during the early days of Uber, Hello Fresh, Blue Apron, Tesla, Zipcar, carpet and floor vacuum cleaner robots, and the Square occurred first through media coverage. Exposure is primarily a news and social media management function. In other words, selecting news media outlets and social media platforms that target publics frequent are critically important to facilitate exposure.

Information objectives are outcomes that create awareness and knowledge about an issue through memorable messaging. Often measurement transpires through awareness and recall survey data collection where individuals respond to questions of message or issue recall. The effectiveness of drawing attention, creating awareness, and increasing knowledge about an issue requires using attention getting techniques that keep people engaged. Drawing on novelty and personally relevant information are effective to gain attention. Some examples are the reintroduction of the Star Wars trilogy in the late 1990s which utilized a mysterious, curiosity appeal; free Brexit tattoos offered in London; Reebok transforming bus stops into mini gyms; the existence of a Giant Monopoly board in Trafalgar Square; and the Anti-aGin Young in Spirit campaign, to name a few.

The role of information objectives is important in non-profit campaigns developed to increase awareness and understanding about an issue such as regular breast screenings for cancer or any number of preventive activities designed to promote healthy lifestyle habits. Nongovernmental organizations that inform the public about genocide and violence against peoples in other countries is another example. In these cases, information objectives serve to educate publics about an issue.

After publics develop an understanding and knowledge, they then form an opinion or attitude about an issue. Persuasive objectives influence the process between informing and attitude formation. Thus, **persuasion objectives** are outcomes that form or shape attitudes toward the issue by using some form of appeal based on rationale and/or emotional considerations. Persuasion is more likely to occur in those persons who do not harbor a strong negative attitude toward an issue. The greatest opportunity exists with those individuals who are "on the fence" and, thus, they are open to persuasion. The types of data collection that measure persuasion are surveys, Facebook "Likes," product/service reviews, measures of word-of-mouth, various other postings, and so forth. Some of the top brands with the greatest positive brand equity are: Apple, Google, Microsoft, Amazon, IBM, and VISA. Table 13.1 is an example of ongoing benchmarking for a 12-month campaign.

Table 13.1 Ongoing Objectives of a Public Relations Campaign

Timeline	1/1/18–3/31/18	4/1/18–6/30/18	7/1/18–9/30/18	10/1/18–12/31/18
Target Public	Millennials (76 million)	Millennials (76 million)	Millennials (76 million)	Millennials (76 million)
Objectives	Favorable opinion of electric car: 31%	Favorable opinion of electric car: 33%	Favorable opinion of electric car: 36%	Favorable opinion of electric car: 40%

Note: In 2017, there are an estimated 76 million Millennials, aged 18–34, in the United States. The baseline is 30% and the objectives are the benchmarks during the course of the campaign according to the noted timeline

The baseline is 30% and the objectives are the progressing benchmarks during the campaign according to a timeline. The expectation is that the increase over the baseline moves to 40% of the 76 million Millennials in the USA by the end of the campaign. Early on, the objective progresses slowly; however, gains increase at a greater rate during the second half of the campaign. This is owing to the cumulative effect of messaging on memory. People are likely to recall and develop opinions after 3 to 10 exposures to an issue that occurs through various channels such as email, event, news coverage, social media, and so forth.

Behavioral objectives are behavioral outcomes. Like awareness and knowledge, behavior is action-driven engagement. Not all campaigns include a call to action. This objective is the most difficult to achieve. A small percentage of awareness stakeholders convert to positive attitude, and an even smaller amount move to actual behavior (Snyder et al., 2004).

Behaviors such as sales, new product inquiries, and product choices are measured and assessed during and after a campaign. Brand loyalty defined as positive attitude toward the brand, repeat purchases, and brand advocacy contribute to sales behavior and are measurable.

Nielsen offers a service that provides weekly scanned country-wide sales figures. According to the Nielsen website, "With presence in more than 100 countries, Nielsen collects sales information from more than 900,000 stores within our worldwide retail network—including grocery, drug, convenience, discount and e-commerce retailers—who, through cooperation arrangements, share their sales data with us" (The Nielsen Company, 2017, para. 2).

Remember, a measurable objective is what we want a target public to think, feel, or do. For example, a plan for disseminating information about a new benefits package at a university and encourage enrollment includes increasing understanding as well as awareness of the new benefits. Table 13.2 represents some additional examples. As we can see, there is a natural progression to organizing objectives moving toward the goal. In the ambulatory aids case, the objectives start with exposure to positive attitude, followed by behaviors as captured by the two inquiries' objectives moving from general ambulatory aids questions to specific brand queries. Depending on the circumstance, objectives do not always follow a progression. Each situation has unique characteristics.

Although not always the case, a general rule of thumb calls for 4 to 6 overall measurable objectives to achieve a goal. Goals can vary per public because of differences in level of issue knowledge, degree of engagement, attitude toward the issue, and other factors.

Note that objectives and tactics are not the same. Objectives guide tactics and are the basis for evaluation. Tactics are specific public relations activities that range from creating and disseminating a media advisory to composing a social media post to organizing and holding an in-person or online event. Depending on the size of an activity and complexity of a public relations campaign, a single event can leave such a major impact that it alone functions as an objective. An event held at a large stadium for a new product launch is an example. Moreover, assessment tools are tactics listed in the overall evaluation section or specified in each action plan. In other words, an assessment activity is itself a tactic. Typically, 2–6 tactics are sufficient to achieve an objective.

"Return on Investment" Objective

There is much debate in public relations about whether financial metrics are useful to calculate **return on investment (ROI)**. In public relations, ROI has different definitions

Table 13.2 Goals and Corresponding Measurable Objectives

Goal	Objectives
To increase employee morale.	• During next 2 months, 75% of employees will attend community meetings about morale and related issues. • During the community meetings over next 2 months, 30 employees will submit reasons why they think morale is low. • Over next 3–6 months, 90% manufacturing employees will become aware of company concern for their work well-being. • Over the next 6–8 months, 40 employees will submit suggestions for improving morale. • Over the next 18 months, employee turnover will decrease to 1% from 5% in each of the manufacturing departments.
To increase inquiries about brand ambulatory aids in the seniors' market.	• Over the first 6 months, receive positive media coverage in the top 10 by circulation periodicals for senior citizens (65+ years old). • Over the next 2 years, increase positive attitude toward the brand to 30% in the senior citizens' market. • Over 6 months, durable medical equipment suppliers that carry the brand will see a 40% increase in inquiries about ambulatory aids. • Over two years, company inquiries will increase to 25% of company mailing list.
To maintain and increase relationships with nongovernmental organizations (NGOs).	• Over 3–4 months, personally contact the executive directors of the top 75 rated NGOs based on budget • Over 6 months, generate joint projects with an additional 5–10 of the 75 top rated NGOs. • Over 12 months, submit proposals in response to RKPs to 4–8 of the top 75 NGOs. • Over the next 18 months, increase the number of affiliated NGOs from 12 to 22.

Note: Metrics denotes types of measurement. Exposure and informational (creating awareness) benchmarks go hand-in-hand because exposure to an issue through messaging is necessary to become aware of the issue. Often, target behaviors are the ultimate goal of the campaign.

and measurement approaches. Some models incorporate financial measures with communication objectives (Watson & Noble, 2014).

As a financial measurement, ROI is:

$$\frac{\text{Gross profit} - \text{Investment in public relations campaign}}{\text{Investment in public relations campaign}} \times 100$$

The challenge in using this approach centers on differentiating what amount or percentage of profit comes from public relations efforts. In the case of non-profits, it is more complicated. Additionally, outcomes must be defined in financial terms whether they are an increase in revenue, cost reduction, or some explicitly nonfinancial measure such as increased number of volunteer workers or increased awareness.

Arguably, **advertising value equivalency (AVE)** is the closest standardized metric for placing a gross financial value on public relations efforts after the costs of related public relations activities are deducted. It estimates return on investment. Essentially, the AVE places an advertising dollar value on outcomes owing to public relations efforts, especially media coverage. So, it is a dollar value (for our purposes, value is the cost of coverage had it been paid) on all relevant publicity. It is the monetary value of earned media. During the 2016 presidential campaign, candidate Donald Trump's media coverage value was estimated at $5 billion (Le Miere, 2016, November 9) far outpacing the $958 million spent by the candidate, Republican Party, and various political action organizations (Narayanswamy, Cameron, & Gold, 2017, February 1). This would place the campaign's AVE at over $4 billion.

Let's say that *Time* features a one-page story about the new Apple iPhone X, including images and a description of what the product offers users. If a full-page color ad typically costs $200,000, then the AVE is $200,000. An important consideration is the accuracy of media monitoring and cost assignment. Overreporting inflates the AVE and underreporting underestimates it.

Additionally, how costs are calculated; the assumption that all public relations efforts are measurable as publicity outcomes; news coverage is more credible and thus more effective than company-sponsored ads; spillover of integrated marketing communication influences occur; there is existing brand equity value; public relations practitioner's time and labor costs for AVE-related activities are additional costs; and other marketing-related activities make a precise assessment of AVE challenging. Far from perfect, it is an approximate financial metric and may be viewed as a gross ROI.

A modified ROI would substitute the total AVE for profit. This would provide a campaign ROI. **ROI-AVE**s is part of a formative evaluation to examine campaign comparisons and discover trends. For example, assume that a public relations campaign cost $1 million and the AVE was $200,000. The ROI-AVE would be:

$$= \frac{\$1,200,000 \; - \; \$1,000,000}{\$1,000,000}$$

$$= \frac{\$200,000}{\$1,000,000}$$

$$= .20 \times 100 = \mathbf{20\%}.$$

The expenditure of $1 million for this campaign yielded a 20% ROI-AVE. In other words, public relations efforts provided a 20% return on investment as measured in the value of additional exposure to the message provided by publicity. There may be instances where the nature of the campaign may not lend itself to AVE such as internal communications or campaigns focused on interpersonal communication. In those cases, ROI-AVEs warrant careful scrutiny.

Overall Objectives and Individual Public Action Plan Objectives

A relatively simple campaign, program, or project contains only a general plan and tactics. For example, a public relations American Association of Retired Persons "Awareness of

Benefits" campaign directed at men and women 55+ years old would likely have the same objectives for both groups and thus the entire campaign. This campaign does not include action plans for individual publics.

Most public relations plans include action plans for each public. An **action plan** is that part of the campaign plan designed for a specific public. The overall campaign strategy and objectives inform it. An action plan identifies the public that it covers, includes objectives, and specifies tactics.

Let's start with objectives. First, there are overall objectives, which pertain to the entire campaign, and then there are objectives for individual publics presented in the various action plans. The later accommodates differences and nuances among the publics. For instance, a campaign designed to improve healthcare literacy across a broad population consists of diverse publics. Appeals to them vary according to their healthcare needs. Elderly people have a unique set of needs and challenges; families with minor children have a different set of medical concerns; and young single people have their perspective about healthcare. Each one of these publics differ in their level of need, involvement, and knowledge about healthcare. More awareness is likely necessary for younger people. For primary caregivers, healthcare literacy about children is important. In the case of the elderly, transportation to healthcare facilities is a concern.

Interdependent Nature of Objectives and Publics

The dynamic nature of some public relations environments, the connection of objectives to publics, the hierarchy of objectives, and nature of measurement are kept in mind when planning and executing a campaign.

First, publics are groups of people or organizations that share some commonality about an issue and environment in which the issue exists. Practitioners identify, define, and prioritize publics in this context, never losing sight of the public relations goal. Changes in an issue, an issue's environment, or any of the publics, requires consideration. Decreases or increases in campaign budgets or other resources, organizational scandal, or some other crisis, changes in organizational leadership, the entrance or exit of a major competitor, technological developments, regulatory changes, domestic or international political events, and social trends, all affect how a campaign proceeds. For example, a political candidate, who was a frontrunner until she slipped in the polls so that her campaign became inconsequential, is not likely to warrant serious attention from the leading candidate's communications director. A new corporate CEO shifts a company's social responsibility from education literacy to sustainability. These are changes that affect public relations tactics.

Second, objectives fit the target public. To use an extreme example, a series of events targeting 18–24-year-old persons sponsored by the AARP, which is an association for older adults, is not an optimal use of resources. Focusing on promoting a host of Apple high-end phone accessories to low income households or to people 70+ years old for their personal usage are not dollars well spent.

Additionally, messaging focuses on publics who are undecided or open to possibilities. However, individuals with firm beliefs and opinions are either supporters, who do not require convincing, or opponents, who will not be convinced. In both cases, resources are better spent elsewhere where minds can be changed and actions can be facilitated. One exception are loyal supporters who serve as advocates. These individuals are often opinion leaders who create buzz about an issue and generate support. Getting them more engaged increases support.

Third, persuasion occurs first through issue awareness, followed by opinion formation, engagement, and behavior. These steps assume a rational process, which is not always the case. Personal experiences influence individuals as well as their professional and social environments including news and social media exposure. Some of these experiences stir emotions and frustrations, which cannot be discounted. Additionally, the level of knowledge associated with opinions varies. As we can see, a hierarchy of objectives varies based on a public's collective characteristics.

Last, is the nature of measurement. It is challenging to measure communication objectives that capture what a person thinks, feels, knows, and intends to do. Getting individuals to think about something is easier than getting them to do something about it. Yet, even though behavioral objectives are more difficult to achieve, they are straightforward. We can easily measure financial donations, event attendance, purchases, and votes, as well as the number of social media impressions, click-throughs, and "Likes." Analytics provides the public relations practitioner with all sorts of data, especially web-based. Despite refinements and innovations, there is no holy grail of measurement for the entire public relations process, from exposure to contribution to profit. Until a more effective methodology exists, we will rely on tools such as surveys, the present state of analytics, and ROI-AVE.

Think about This . . .

A 2013 article entitled "In Search of Meaningful Measurement," published in Public Relations Tactics by Beverly Payton, discusses the role of measurement in campaigns. The article notes the important links among research, goal-setting, and measurement. Meaningful measurement requires "communication objectives that answer the who, what, when, and how much the PR program is intended to affect" (p. 17).

Data is a competitive advantage. Yet, organizations struggle with implementing useful measurement metrics for a variety of reasons such as budgetary constraints, the perspective that public relations is not a significant component of the marketing plan, and the lack of understanding of what informative measurement entails. Payton covers examples that support measurement programs that take simple and affordable steps with the goal in mind to show how public relations affects business results and ultimately profit.

Ask yourself: What types of measurements are available and what can be assessed? When and why should campaign evaluation measurement occur?

Payton, B. (2013, December 17). In search of meaningful measurement. *Public Relations Tactics*. Retrieved from www.prsa.org/searchresults/view/10429/1086/conference_recap_measurement_matters_a_lot_but_how.

Assessment Process

Once the strategy and planning process is complete, including the identification of overall and action plan objectives, the public relations campaign starts. Monitoring objectives occurs throughout the campaign at periodic intervals or after it ends. Quantified benchmarks, hierarchical objectives, cost comparisons using costs per thousand, and financial return on the public relations investment are factors in the assessment process.

1) What constitutes success? Some strategists might consider outcomes within 1.5% of the objective, while others might evaluate outcomes based on a range of values referenced from the benchmark. For example, a successful campaign may be one in which a benchmark set at 15% with a 1.5 percentage point range demonstrates positive attitude in a public when the actual outcome is between 13.5% and 16.5%. Scalability constraints dictate that more is not always better. A conference attendance target of 15,000 attendees, which is the maximum capacity of the venue, is best benchmarked at 12,000–15,000 because those extra people who show up beyond the first 15,000 people will be refused entrance. Rejecting people at the door, would have a negative impact on the event. In sum, benchmarks in general must be realistic, yet they also function to inspire.

2) How does a benchmarked objective relate to its baseline? The calculation of the benchmark starts by considering the baseline. For example, what does a 25% increase in awareness mean? The percentage is the benchmark and not a percentage change in the baseline. Thus, if the baseline is 10%, then the benchmark is to increase awareness to 12.5% (.10 x 1.25) of the target public, which provides clarity because it stands alone without the need of other numbers from which to determine the meaning of a percentage increase.

3) There is often a hierarchy or ordering of objectives that requires a sequence in which specific objectives occur before reaching subsequent ones. Insufficient levels of antecedent objectives contribute to falling short on the final objectives. For instance, fostering a positive attitude about an issue follows knowing that an issue exists. Thus, providing information about an issue is a precursor to a favorable attitude toward it.

4) As covered in Chapter 12, CPM aids summative and formative evaluation whether applied to specific tactics or some other grouping such as social media, publics, or objectives. These standardized cost points are compared to other campaigns, over time, or against external benchmarks. Since the allocation of personnel and administrative costs can vary, CPM comparison is based on production and program costs only.

5) An approximate financial value of a campaign offers an overall approach to summative and formative evaluation. The difference between campaign cost and financial value of the campaign is the worth of the earned media for all the outcomes. The AVE or ROI-AVE approaches inform cost/benefit and return on investment analysis. Avoid double counting overall outcomes with individual action plan results.

Table 13.3 is an example of benchmark and outcome comparisons for an ongoing campaign. The ongoing percentages represent progressing outcomes throughout the campaign. As we see, except for the third quarter, where there are three, within each quarter, there are two tracking measurement time points. This is so because the largest anticipated gain is between the third and fourth quarters, and it is in the third quarter where the last

Table 13.3 Ongoing Objectives and Outcomes of a Public Relations Campaign

Timeline	1/1/18–3/31/18	4/1/18–6/30/18	7/1/18–9/30/18	10/1/18–12/31/18
Target Public	Millennials (76 million)	Millennials (76 million)	Millennials (76 million)	Millennials (76 million)
Objectives	Favorable opinion of electric car: 31%	Favorable opinion of electric car: 33%	Favorable opinion of electric car: 36%	Favorable opinion of electric car: 40%
Ongoing	Tracking 2/1:30.1% 3/15:30.75%	Tracking 5/1:31.8% 6/15:32.8%	Tracking 7/30:34.0% 8/30:35.0% 9/30:36.0%	Tracking 11/1:38.0% 12/15:39.8%

Note: In 2017, there are an estimated 76 million Millennials, aged 18–34, in the United States. The baseline is 30% and the objectives are the benchmarks during the course of the campaign according to the noted timeline. The ongoing percentages represent outcomes.

opportunity rests to make effective adjustments before the campaign ends. Other campaigns track at different, more, or less time points. This example is meant to illustrate that there is logic behind evaluation depending on the circumstances. The first measurement result is 30.1% and the last (post-campaign) measurement yields 39.8%, which is close to the final benchmark of 40%.

Keep in mind that objectives and their corresponding outcomes can be exposure, information, persuasion, and/or behavioral.

Steps in the Evaluation Process

Figure 13.5 illustrates the public relations evaluation process. Objectives start with establishing a baseline value and, based on inputs, developing benchmarks that are the anticipated outcomes. Communication, behavioral, and organizational goals as well as cost reduction contributions are the basis of evaluation.

Larger campaigns are monitored, assessed, and adjusted, if necessary. At the end of the campaign, there is a summative evaluation. To learn and discover best practices or propose changes in future campaigns, formative evaluation compares summative outcomes to previous ones. CPM and ROI-AVE comparisons across different and past campaigns are useful.

Benchmark Metrics

There are a variety of metrics available to assess benchmarks. Table 13.4 lists types of objective. The list is by no means exhaustive, but serves to provide a sampling of ways to measure benchmarks.

Metrics are ways to measure something. Exposure and informational (creating awareness) benchmarks go together because exposure to an issue is necessary to become aware of it. Often, behaviors are the last kind of objective in a hierarchy of objectives.

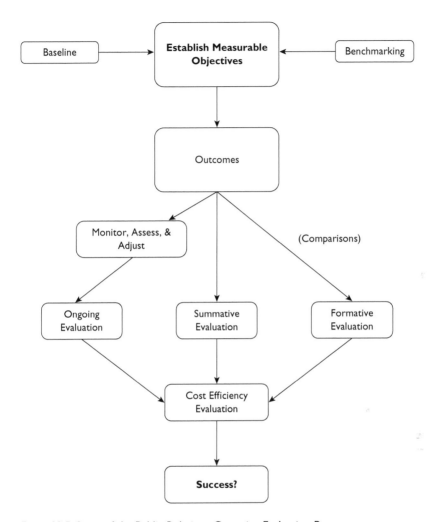

Figure 13.5 Steps of the Public Relations Campaign Evaluation Process

Similar measures for more than one type of benchmark exist depending on the reasoning and purpose for the objective. Google Analytics, Twitter Analytics, and Facebook Analytics are readily available social media evaluation tools used to measure objectives. Buffer, Viralwoot, Quintly, Cyfe, and Rival IQ are examples of third party applications that measure social media effectiveness as well. Some of these applications integrate data across various social media platforms so that a more comprehensive and accurate picture exists to evaluate campaign efficacy.

Remember that achieving benchmarks within the budget and according to a schedule is a measure of success.

Table 13.4 Benchmark Metrics for Objectives

Benchmark	
Exposure	**Metrics**
	Impressions
	News media stories
	Event attendance
	Favorable media editorials
	Emails distributed
	Interviews to media
	Press conferences
Information	**Metrics**
	Survey (including internal communication audits)
	Request for more information
	Click through rates
	Web page posts
	Mall intercepts
	Retweets
	Event attendance
	Web searches
	Various secondary data social media
	Presence scores
	Online reviews
	Number of press conferences
Persuasion	**Metrics**
	Survey (including internal communication audits)
	Content analysis
	Interviews
	Likes
	Mentions
	Supportive emails
	Supportive text messages
	Click through rates
	Focus groups
	Positive online reviews
Behavioral	**Metrics**
	Sales inquiries
	Coupon redemptions
	Sales
	Votes
	Registrations
	Subscriptions
	Repeat purchases
	Adoption rates
	Brand advocacy mentions
	Volunteer signups
	Total dollars raised

Summary of Key Concepts

- The evaluation research process is systematic and borrows from scientific principles.
- Public relations campaigns assessment occurs during and/or after a campaign.
- Public relations objectives have four components: Benchmark, timeline, defined public, and quantifiable measures for assessment.
- Public relations objectives relate to exposure, information, persuasion, and behaviors.
- AVE and ROI-AVE are approximate methods for financially linking public relations outcomes to the organization.
- Objectives are often sequential and interdependent.

In the Case of Canyon Ranch . . . Benchmarks and Evaluation

The goal of this 12-month promotional campaign is to primarily increase sales in the U.S. market of Canyon Ranch's Health and Healing services at the Lenox location by integrating the spa, fitness, and salon services and the hotel as a total healthy/wellness vacation experience while maintaining total brand saliency within the allocated budget.

By the end of the campaign, success will be achieved if the following are reached: an awareness and knowledge of Canyon Ranch's health and healing services increase to 87.5%–92.5% of the existing customer list; a health and healing services sales increase by 27.5%–32.5% and overall sales grow by 2.5%–7.5%; and a 2.5%–7.5% increase in new visits and a 13.5%–17.5% jump in repeat visits.

Note: Most measures are expressed as percentage increases because the baseline data were not available to the author.

Key Terms

Advertising value equivalency
  (AVE) 322
Baseline 316
Behavioral objective 320
Benchmark 316
Exposure objective 318
Formative evaluation 315
Information objective 319

Objectives 317
Ongoing evaluation 315
Outcome 313
Persuasion objective 319
Pre-testing evaluation 315
Return on investment (ROI) 320
ROI-AVE 322
Summative evaluation 315

Chapter Questions

13.1   Define public relations outcome.
13.2   Describe public relations evaluation.
13.3   Why do public relations practitioners walk a fine line between reality and senior management's ideals?
13.4   Define pre-testing evaluation.

13.5   What is ongoing evaluation?

13.6   Define summative evaluation.

13.7   Define formative evaluation.

13.8   Name some firms that monitor brand awareness in social media.

13.9   What is a baseline?

13.10 Define benchmark.

13.11 What are the four parts of an objective and describe them?

13.12 What are the four categories of objectives and briefly explain each one?

13.13 Define return on investment (ROI).

13.14 What is AVE?

13.15 What is the point of the article entitled, "In Search of Meaningful Measurement"?

13.16 What is meant by a hierarchy of objectives?

References

Le Miere, J. L. (2016, November 11). Did the media help Donald Trump win? $5 billion in free advertising given to president-elect. *International Business Times*. Retrieved from www.ibtimes.com/did-media-help-donald-trump-win-5-billion-free-advertising-given-president-elect-2444115.

Lloyd, S. (2013, January 25). Measuring engagement and engaging consumers are two sides of the same coin. *Qualtrics*. Retrieved from www.qualtrics.com/blog/research-quotes/.

Narayanswamy, A., Cameron, D., & Gold, M. (2017, February 1). Election 2016 Money raised as of Dec. 31. *Washington Post*. Retrieved from www.washingtonpost.com/graphics/politics/2016-election/campaign-finance/.

Payton, B. (2013, December 17). In search of meaningful measurement. *Public Relations Tactics*. Retrieved from www.prsa.org/searchresults/view/10429/1086/conference_recap_measurement_matters_a_lot_but_how.

Place, K. R. (2015). Exploring the role of ethics in public relations. *Journal of Public Relations Research*, *27*, 118–135.

Place, K. R., & Vardeman-Winter, J. (2013). Hegemonic discourse and self-discipline: Exploring Foucault's concept of bio-power among public relations professionals. *Public Relations Inquiry*, *2*, 305–325.

Retail Measurement. (2017). *The Nielsen Company*. Retrieved from www.nielsen.com/us/en/solutions/measurement/retail-measurement.html.

Snyder, L. B., Hamilton, M. A., Kiwanuka-Tondo, J., Fleming-Milici, F., & Proctor, D. (2004). A meta-analysis of the effects of mediated health communication campaigns on behavior change in the United States. *Journal of Health Communication*, *9*, 71–96.

Stacks, D. W., & Bowen, S. A. (2013). *Dictionary of public relations measurement and research*. Retrieved from www.instituteforpr.org.

Watson, T., & Noble, P. (2014). *Evaluating Public Relations: A guide to planning, research, and measurement*. London: Kogan Page.

Part VI

Putting It All Together

Chapter 14

Putting It All Together

The Public Relation Campaign Plansbook

The history of PR is . . . a history of a battle for what is reality and how people will see and understand reality.

(Stuart Ewen, Diggs-Brown, 2012, p. 38)

Learning Objectives

To:

- Learn the key characteristics and components of a standard public relations campaign plansbook.
- Explain how parts of the plansbook link together to provide the big picture of the campaign.
- Be able to identify the important parts of a public relations campaign from the example in this chapter.

Introduction

The entire public relations campaign plan is the **plansbook**, which is also a guide to implementation. The plan is in Word format and later archived as a pdf file. A plansbook size[1] depends on whether the campaign is a proposal, in process, or post-campaign final version; its complexity; the level of detail, and the size of the appendix. It is usually 10–75 pages, typically covers 6–24 months, and may contain followed-up content. The plan is a roadmap for the public relations campaign and contains the reasoning or justification for key components. The degree of justification included in the narrative is contingent on any specific reporting requirements as well as whether the plan is presented in-person where it is likely that the "why" questions will be asked and answered face-to-face instead of in writing.

The planning and precampaign version of the plansbook is in the future tense. However, after the campaign concludes, the plansbook is edited to the past tense and archived for future reference. Information such as the actual cost per thousand and advertising equivalency evaluation data are incorporated in the final version after the close of the campaign.

Keep in mind that the exact format may vary based on organizational requirements and preferences. However, using sufficient headings not only helps organize the plan, but also aids the reader in understanding how the components of the campaign connect creating the big picture.

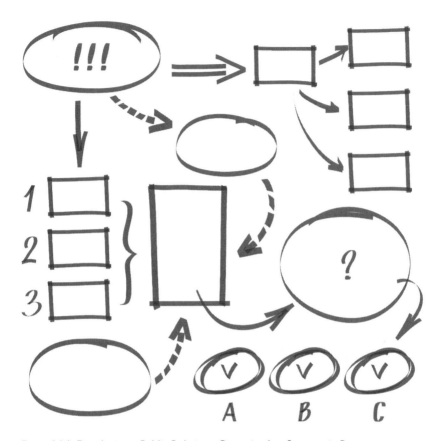

Figure 14.1 Developing a Public Relations Campaign Is a Systematic Process

The sections below describe the parts of a public relations campaign plan followed by a sample, annotated plansbook – the Deepwater Horizon Incident.

Executive Summary

The **Executive Summary** contains an overview of the plan. Usually, it is the last part completed. One page long, the executive summary begins by stating the campaign goal in 1–2 simple sentences. The sections follow the public relations campaign outline using headings and subheading that summarize the key publics, strategy, central message, key tactics, and outcomes. The Table of Contents follows the executive summary.

Situational Analysis

The **Situational Analysis** contains information about the issue in the context of the related situation as well as identifies and prioritizes stakeholder groups relevant to the issue. It is the result of researching the issue and situation. This section contains: A brief history of

Figure 14.2 Public Relations Campaigns Involve Multiple Publics

the organization and situation; whether the issue is a challenge or opportunity; competitive issue analysis (CIA), if necessary; and the profiles of the publics and/or stakeholders groups.

It is important to understand the target publics. **Public** definitions include the approximate number in the population, their rank in importance and why, their level of issue awareness, knowledge, and engagement, and if appropriate, their media habits. The Action Plans section discusses how the overall central messages may be adjusted to accommodate publics based on what was discovered about them.

Strategy

The public relations **strategy** contains a goal, overall benchmarked objectives, and a central message. Sometimes the strategy includes a brief justification supported by evidence typically from the situational analysis. In other cases, the reasoning for the strategy is discussed during its presentation to the leadership.

Again, the **goal** is 1-2 sentences. It addresses the issue and is clearly stated.

The overall quantified objectives include timelines, benchmarks, and target publics. They usually number from 1-6.

The strategy includes the overall **central message**. This message has something that appeals to each public.

Action Plans

Unlike traditional advertising, a public relations campaign has a broad strategy, but local focus geared to various stakeholder groups. Specific aspects of a public relations plan may speak more to one public as opposed to another.

Figure 14.3 A Campaign Plansbook Is Based on Sound Reasoning Which Is Supported with
Evidence

Therefore, an **action plan** focuses on a specific target public, and a campaign usually
has multiple actions plans. Each public has an (action) plan unique to its characteristics
including their levels of issue awareness, knowledge, and engagement as well as any pre-
dispositions toward the issue, situation, and/or organization. Although the central message
applies to the entire campaign and all publics, it typically may emphasize certain points
when directed at a specific public. Taking these considerations in mind, this is why each
public has its own plan of action.

The public is defined not only as it was in the situation analysis such as level of issue
knowledge and opinions as they relate to goal achievement, but also in terms of messaging
reach and effectiveness. That is, other characteristics that inform message development and
appeal are described. For example, if the goal is to increase sales in home security systems,
the publics or market segments are defined in terms of their attitudes toward home security systems, VALS type including perspectives about law enforcement and crime, what
they value and believe, and media habits as well as other attributes that might influence
receptiveness toward purchasing such a product and service. Attractive messaging appeals
to what the public values.

Next, there are **benchmarked objectives** directed at specific publics. They may overlap with overall objectives but should not be double counted for planning or assessment purposes. Like the overall objectives, they are comprised of timelines and benchmarks. Typically, an action plan has 2–3 objectives, but may vary.

A **tactic** is a tool, task, or activity deployed to achieve an objective, which is associated with a public relations' goal, strategy, and objectives. Objectives are achieved through the execution of specific tactics. Each objective typically has 2–6 tactics depending on the level of objective complexity. Tactics are the individual messages or activities directed at a public such as news releases, social media shares, blog posts, in-person events, interviews, trade show participation, data collection and evaluation such as surveys, assessment tools, and many more. Effective tactics are creative, draw attention, are cost-efficient, and are consistent with the central message.

Tactics must fall within the allocated budget, effectively convey the message, reach the appropriate public, and prescribe how assessment is executed. Some messaging tactics are more suitable for some publics, but not for others based on a public's opinions, level of issue knowledge, and personal attributes. For example, a public relations plan that advocates tax cuts for the middle class might appeal to a personal sense of morality and justice to those in the social work field. However, to an upper income/wealthy business person, such tax cuts might appeal to self-interest because greater spending would result in more business activity and increase in stock values; thus, eventually benefiting those in business. In both cases, different appeals toward the same goal are effective – tax cuts for the middle class.

Activity briefs are details about the action plans. Found in the appendix or included in the action plan, each **activity brief** provides details about each tactical activity such as execution dates, target public information, messaging content, images, storyboards, scheduling, and assures that the tactic is appropriate for the campaign goal. In short, an activity brief is the set of instructions for a given public relation tactic that falls within an action plan and helps the public relations tactician keep a strategy focus. A quick online search will reveal numerous activity brief layouts.

Think about This . . .

In 2013, Janelle Hawthorne wrote an article in PR Week entitled, "Fantasy Fragrance Messaging Celebrates 10 Years of Britney," which covered the effectiveness of a public relations campaign that promoted the Britney Spears/Elizabeth Arden fragrance line. The fragrance franchise was celebrating its ten year anniversary. The public relations strategy was to make the fans feel that they were a part of the celebration thus becoming customers and advocates for the brand. A chalk artist was hired for the promotion. He visited areas around major publishing houses and media outlets in New York City where free fragrance samples were distributed to visitors. The expectation was that employees and visitors of the nearby businesses would share the event on social media.

Many of the media outlet editors and executives posted comments about the art and a number of outlets covered the event. The budget was $12,000. As of 2013, the fragrance continues to grow.

> *Ask yourself: What other promotions would you recommend to the franchise? Can you think of other effective public relations tactics that can be implemented for no more than $12,000?*

Hawthorne, J. (2013). Fantasy fragrance messaging celebrates 10 years of Britney. *PR* Week, November, 45. Retrieved from www.prweek.com/article/1274222/fantasy-fragrance-messaging-celebrates-10-years-britney.

Scheduling

A **scheduling strategy** is the systematic, time-oriented placement and frequency of message planning by communication channels to achieve campaign objectives. Anticipated costs and return on investment play a role in selecting where the messaging will be placed, at what time(s), and how often.

Figure 14.4 Scheduling Involves Message Placement, Frequency, and Timing within Budgetary Constraints

Budgeting

Budgets support public relations campaigns and are determined using any number of methods. Scheduling and budgeting decisions are represented in a single table so that easy comparisons can be made, which leads to the next section on evaluation.

Evaluation

Campaign assessment can occur ongoing during implementation and post campaign depending on the duration and complexity of it. Actual outcomes are compared to benchmarked objectives.

Cost per thousand (CPM) analysis determines the cost of the total campaign or a specific medium outlet as measured by cost per thousand exposures to the message. This approach serves two purposes. As an ongoing assessment tool, practitioners can determine if they are within the budget for objective timelines. Second, we discover the level of cost-efficiencies over time and any cost trends by comparing previous campaigns' CPMs with post-campaign figures. Moreover, during the ongoing or post-assessment, a CPM analysis might provide the opportunity to discover more cost-effective communication outlets by comparing various CPMs. In other words, CPM serves a cost control function.

On the other hand, **advertising value equivalency (AVE)** is a method to estimate gross return on investment. The AVE places an advertising dollar value on outcomes owing to public relations efforts, especially media coverage after deducting the costs of facilitating such coverage.

Figure 14.5 Achieving Benchmarks within Budget and On Time Is a Measure of Success

Conclusion, References, and Appendix

In the conclusion, state the campaign plan's main strategy and anticipated outcomes in no more than ½ page. The reference section comprises information about cited sources in the plansbook. The appendix includes activity briefs.

Public Relations Campaign Plan Outline

Executive Summary

Table of Contents

I   Introduction

II   Situational Analysis

> Brief history of the organization and situation

> Issue whether a challenge or opportunity

> Competitive issue analysis (CIA), if necessary

> Profile publics and/or stakeholders

III Strategy: Goals, Overall Objectives, and Central Message

> Goal

> > Inverse of challenge or address opportunity

> Overall Objective 1

> > Reasoning

> Overall Objective 2

> Overall Objective 3

> Overall Objective 4

> Overall Objective *i*

> Central Message

> > Reasoning, compare to CIA, if necessary and pre-testing results, if conducted

> > If appropriate, slogan/tagline

IV   Action Plans for Publics

> Define Public 1 for Messaging

> > Strategy and primary message, which relates to central message

> > Objective 1

> > Tactic 1

> > Tactic 2

> > Tactic 3

Tactic 4

Tactic *i*

Objective 2

Objective 3

Objective *i*

Define Public 2 for Messaging . . .

Define Public *i* for Messaging . . .

V   Scheduling & Budgeting

Scheduling

Scheduling strategy (reasoning)

Gantt chart

Master Schedule & Budget

Budgeting

Budget strategy

Budget for Personnel, Administration, & Production

Cost per thousand

Contingency Fund

Master Schedule & Budget

VI   Evaluation

Post-Campaign Assessment

Public 1 Benchmarked Objective 1

Public 1 Benchmarked Objective 2

Public 2 Benchmarked Objective 1

Public 2 Benchmarked Objective 2

Public *i* Benchmarked Objective 1

Advertising Value Equivalency

VII Conclusion

Half-page Summary Paragraph

VIII References

IX   Appendix

NOTES: Some adjustments and verb tense edits after the campaign. *i* equals more of an item.

Figure 14.6 The Campaign Outline Serves as an Effective Checklist for What Is Required

The Canyon Ranch Public Relations Campaign Plansbook

The following example is a proposed public relation campaign plansbook based on marketing wellness services offered at the Canyon Ranch Health Resort as well as broadening its appeal to other market segments without sacrificing the exclusive and high-status image of the brand. Keep in mind that a post campaign Executive Summary would be edited to the past tense and include Outcomes in place of Expected Outcomes. The Evaluation section would include actual outcomes instead of anticipated results. Last, the sample below only contains post-campaign evaluation measures and not ongoing campaign benchmarks.

Executive Summary

This is a 12-month promotional public relations campaign plan for Canyon Ranch Health Resort located in Lenox, Massachusetts, U.S.A. The budget is $500,000.

ISSUE

The health and healing department, which sets Canyon Ranch apart from its competitors, is a potential source of growth; yet, it was underperforming. Canyon Ranch intends to increase sales of the health and healing department at the Lenox location, while continuing the same level of quality and premium level of service as its spa, fitness center, salon, and hotel services, all of which face strong competition.

GOAL

The goal is to increase sales in the U.S. market of Canyon Ranch's health and healing services at the Lenox location by integrating the spa, fitness, and salon services as well as Hotel as a total healthy vacation experience while maintaining total brand saliency.

EXPECTED OUTCOMES

Overall Objective 1: By the end of the 12-month campaign, raise awareness and knowledge of Canyon Ranch's health and healing services to 90% of its existing customer list.

Overall Objective 2: By the end of the 12-month campaign, increase health and healing services sales by 30% and overall sales by 5%.

Overall Objective 3: By the end of the 12-month campaign, experience a 5% increase in new visits and a 15% increase in repeat visits.

KEY PUBLICS

Women customers: Existing and new clients,

Men customers: Existing and new clients,

News Media,

Corporate customers, and

Travel agents and agencies.

CENTRAL MESSAGE

Canyon Ranch is dedicated to developing and offering a full range of customized health wellness services especially health and healing designed to meet client needs in a high quality, responsive all-inclusive resort environment.

Table of Contents

I. Introduction

The Canyon Ranch public relations campaign centers on promoting the resort and its programs with an emphasis on health and healing services. The promotional campaign is a 12-month campaign directed at key publics.

II. Situational Analysis

Brief History of the Organization and Situation

> This is the story of the situation.

Canyon Ranch is a world destination health spa and hotel resort established in 1979. Its mission is to create a place where people turn their "healthiest thoughts" into lifestyle habits through wonderful experiences while enjoying a relaxing vacation. The company has expanded with two destination resorts one located in Lenox, Massachusetts and the other in Tucson, Arizona as well as two SpaClubs all in the United States. The resort attracts 17,000 visitors annually. This campaign focuses on the Lenox location.

Canyon Ranch has three departments or groups of serviced offered to visitors. They are: spa, fitness, and salon services; the hotel; and health and healing, which sets Canyon Ranch apart from the competition, has growth potential, but is underutilized.

Over a short period, the company grew rapidly because of the high volume of returning customers and referrals. Canyon Ranch is among the most reputable spas in the industry because of its attention to detail and guest needs. The selection of services and the innovative health and healing department set it far above the competition. Customer service representatives build profiles of customers before their first visit so that they can offer a personalized experience to suit individual needs and desires.

Canyon Ranch has an Information Technology system custom-made to manage the property, accounting, reservations, scheduling appointments, and payroll, all in a relational database. The data and customer relations management (CRM) system maintains records of services and products each customer purchased while at the resort. It includes a pre-visit survey designed to customize the guest experience as well as post-visit feedback tools.

Issue

> The issue picks up at the end of the story.

The health and healing department, which sets Canyon Ranch apart from its competitors and is a potential source of growth, was underperforming. Canyon Ranch intends to increase utilization sales of the health and healing department.

Canyon Ranch thus must expand and develop the health and healing department while continuing the same level of quality and premium level of service as its spa, fitness, salon, and hotel services.

In sum, the company must integrate its growing array of products and services under its one brand, including customer relations management, quality, service operations, and marketing efforts in a consistent manner. Greater incorporation of health and healing will increase its competitive advantage; increase services and customer satisfaction; and generate new revenue streams.

Profile Publics and/or Stakeholders

These are the market segments.

The main target market segments are upper-class, middle-aged men and women with teenage or young adult children, a high household income, who possess a strong interest in fitness, health, and well-being. The following are the publics in order of priority.

Women customers. Women represent 75% of Canyon Ranch customers. The average woman is 47 years old and from an upper-middle and upper income household. She is fit, active, and values high quality service and is willing to pay for it. She has refined taste. Being the core customer base, these women are vital to Canyon Ranch's success. Fifty-five percent of this market segment are returning guests. Additionally, there are new female customers, who represent an untapped source of customers. Approximately 12 million women in the United States comprise this demographic.

Men customers. While they are the minority at Canyon Ranch, the average male customer is in his early fifties, married with adult children, and comes from an upper-middle and upper income household. Many men arrive at Canyon Ranch with their spouse or significant other; however, there is a large number who visit alone looking to get away and are drawn to health services, including nutrition, exercise physiology, movement therapy, behavioral health, and lifestyle choices as opposed to others who prefer traditional spa services. Many would find the health and healing services an attractive option at Canyon Ranch. Some male customers will be new to the Canyon Ranch experience, which provides Canyon Ranch with an opportunity to start their experience in the health and healing services department. Approximately 11.8 million men in the United States fit this profile.

News media. The media consists of general news broadcast media of the four major TV networks in the top ten designated market areas in the USA as well as the top three in reach networks in health-, spa-, travel-, and business-related areas such as Bloomberg and CNBC. Additionally, included are the top three radio stations by weekly listenership in each of the top ten DMAs. The major business, health, health spa, vacation, and travel magazines and websites by reach that target upper-middle and upper income households are included.

Corporate customers. Corporate customers are those organizations that purchase Canyon Ranch packages for their executives. This campaign focuses on Fortune 500 companies.

Travel agents and agencies. There are approximately 105,000 travel agents in the United States alone. Of those, 3,000-5,000 are luxury destination vacation agents. Eighteen percent of Canyon Ranch's referrals are from such travel agents.

III. Strategy: Goals, Overall Objectives, and Central Message

The goal addresses the issue.

Goal

To primarily increase sales in the U.S. market of Canyon Ranch's health and healing services at the Lenox location by integrating the spa, fitness, and salon services and the hotel as a total healthy/wellness vacation experience while maintaining the total brand saliency.

Central Message

> This is the reasoning for the central message.

Rationale for the Central Message: Despite the intense competition for destination health spa resort clients, Canyon Ranch has a competitive advantage. It offers a full range of high quality services that include a spa, full host of fitness options and salon services, lodging accommodations, with a focus on an extraordinary array of health and healing services. The wellness resort is a one-stop all-inclusive destination that provides a total health vacation experience or holistic wellness approach – it is a getaway second to none. To make it more satisfying to each client, Canyon Ranch's CRM system allows staff to customize and make suggestions to clients once they arrive whether they are first time visitors or repeat guests.

Canyon Ranch provides an integrated highly personalized healthy getaway, which will be demonstrated by showing the benefits of these services, followed by presenting images of the facilities and then content highlighting what is available including a subtle call to action. Canyon Ranch's clients have financial resources. They are paying for an experience, a benefit that is largely emotional. Because of this, messaging will emphasize Canyon Ranch as a luxury experience that aligns with the individual customer's identity and lifestyle. It starts with health and healing services.

The Central Message: For its clients, Canyon Ranch is dedicated to developing and offering a full range of customized health wellness services especially health and healing designed to meet their needs in a high quality, responsive all-inclusive resort environment. Messaging will emphasize:

1) Having available a multidisciplinary team of outstanding physicians and other health and healing specialists.
2) Through the usage of a cutting–edge customer relations management system provide personalized services for each client.
3) Offer health and healing services; spa, fitness, and salon services; and top shelf lodging second to done in a seamless process.
4) Offer the health and healing services as the cornerstone of the unmatched Canyon Ranch experience.
5) Canyon Ranch offers the best for the best.

Overall Objectives

> Awareness & knowledge is the objective and achieving 90% is the benchmark, which is based on an existing baseline percentage.

> The overall objectives are presented before the central message because they are strategic rather than individual action plan oriented.

Overall Objective 1: By the end of the 12-month campaign, raise awareness and knowledge of Canyon Ranch's health and healing services to 90% of its existing customer list.

Overall Objective 2: By the end of the 12-month campaign, increase health and healing services sales by 30% and overall sales by 5%.

Overall Objective 3: By the end of the 12-month campaign, experience a 5% increase in new visits and a 15% increase in repeat visits.

IV. Action Plans for Publics

> Achieving action plan objectives will result in reaching the overall objectives.

For this promotional campaign there are five key publics.

Action Plan for Women

Women represent 75% of Canyon Ranch customers. The average woman is 47 years old from upper-middle and upper income households. She is fit, active, and values high quality service and is willing to pay for it. These women have refined tastes. Although they are the reason for visiting the resort, some women are accompanied by a significant other. Being the core customer base, they are vital to Canyon Ranch's success. Fifty-five percent of this market segment are returning guests. Additionally, there are new female customers, who represent an untapped source of customers. Approximately 12 million women in the United States comprise this group.

> The central message follows the identification of the public and precedes the objectives because they are more tactical in action plans.

Strategy and Primary Message: The message will focus on providing services and products that meet their individual needs starting with health and healing services. They can take advantage of the professional experts who will customize and meet their requirements. Images of a similar demographic will be depicted enjoying the services and benefits of Canyon Ranch starting with health and healing. Peaceful images of the facility will be presented as well. Appeals will link visits to seasons or times of the year where a woman might want to getaway. The CRM system will uncover which profiles are more open to new and novel services and products, those interested in traditional methods, and the health circumstances of guests- all so that the staff develop personalized plans and appeals that emphasize services with health and healing serving as the cornerstone of the experience. Messaging will give them a reason to schedule a visit at Canyon Ranch. It might also relate to a guest special expert who will be available only during certain dates. Last, for those women accompanied by someone, depicting couple activities and services appealing to a significant other would be beneficial.

Objective 1: By the end of the 12-month campaign, achieve 90% knowledge of health and healing services for existing female customers and 100% for new female customers.

> The details of each tactic are in the activity brief for each tactic located in the plansbook appendix.

Tactic 1: Redesign the Canyon Ranch website so that it centers on health and healing.

Tactic 2: Develop and implement a mobile app that allows clients to see suggested services in advance of their visit.

Tactic 3: Create a blog centered on health and healing and how they are interdependent with the spa, fitness, salon, and the overall resort experience at Canyon Ranch. The message must be indirect and framed as informative.

Tactic 4: Because these people are busy, create a social presence (Facebook, Twitter, & Instagram) but be selective and limited in messaging. Respond within 24 hours to any inquiries.

Tactic 5: Email all existing female customers with a reminder of the offerings of the health and healing department. The email will illustrate subtly the advantage of combining or supplementing their previous services with the health and healing. This will be effective because it will reinforce not only brand image, but also the importance of health and healing activities.

Tactic 6: Follow-up email blasts with a hardcopy mailer.

Tactic 7: Regularly send text messages or emails with 1–2 questions to tracks level of awareness and knowledge about health and healing as well as track blog analytics.

Objective 2: By the end of the 12-month campaign, there will be a 25% increase in health and healing sales from existing female guests and a 45% increase in first time clients.

Tactic 1: Personal selling to individual guests paired with an expert based on CRM client data.

Tactic 2: Develop and suggest a personalized plan for services, starting with health and healing and products.

Tactic 3: Track benchmark objective progress on an ongoing and regular basis.

Action Plan for Men

The average male customer is in his early fifties, married with adult children, and comes from an upper-middle and upper income household. Many men arrive at Canyon Ranch with their spouse or significant other; however, there is a large number who visit alone looking to get away. They find health services, including nutrition, exercise physiology, movement therapy, behavioral health, and lifestyle choices attractive. Many would find the health and healing services an attractive option. Some male customers will be new to the Canyon Ranch experience, which is an opportunity to start their experience with health and healing. There are approximately 11.8 million men in the United States in this market segment.

Strategy and Primary Message: The message will focus on providing services and products that meet their individual needs starting with health and healing. They can take advantage of the professional experts who will customize an appropriate program. Depict images of this demographic enjoying the services and benefits of Canyon Ranch. Present peaceful images of the facility as well. Appeals will link visits to seasons or times of the year where a man might want to getaway. The CRM system will uncover which profiles are more open to new and novel services and products as well as those focusing on traditional wellness with health and healing serving as the cornerstone of the experience. Messaging will give them a reason to schedule a visit at Canyon Ranch. Link the Canyon Ranch experience to concrete benefits such as health and positive on performance in general. Associate the benefits of health and well-being with sports and sports figures. Relate these benefits to guest experts who might visit the resort during specified dates. Although these men are the reason for visiting the resort, significant others sometimes accompany them. Position Canyon Ranch as an experience that can meet both their needs.

Objective 1: By the end of the 12-month campaign, achieve 85% knowledge of health and healing services for existing male customers and 100% for new male customers.

Tactic 1: Redesign the Canyon Ranch website so that it centers on health and healing.

Tactic 2: Develop and implement a mobile app that allows clients to see suggested services in advance of their visit.

Tactic 3: Create a blog centered on health and healing and how they are interdependent with the spa, fitness, salon, and the overall resort experience at Canyon Ranch. The message must be indirect and framed as informative.

Tactic 4: Because these people are busy, create a social presence (Facebook, Twitter, & Instagram) but be selective and limited in messaging. Respond within 24 hours to any inquiries.

Tactic 5: Email all existing male customers with a reminder of the offerings of the health and healing department. The email will illustrate subtly the advantage of combining or supplementing their previous services with the health and healing. This will be effective because it will reinforce not only the brand image, but also the importance of the health and healing activities.

Tactic 6: Follow-up email blasts with a hardcopy mailer.

Tactic 7: Regularly send text messages or emails with 1–2 questions to tracks level of awareness and knowledge about health and healing as well as blog track analytics.

Objective 2: By the end of the 12-month campaign, an increase of 20% in health and healing sales from existing male guests and an increase of 50% for first time clients.

Tactic 1: Post special events and programs on Twitter. Use this platform as a news channel. Include videos and actionable information. Use key hashtags.

Tactic 2: Develop a personalized plan for suggested services, starting with health and healing services and products for all male visitors.

Tactic 3: Personal selling to individual guests paired with an expert based on CRM client data.

Tactic 4: Track benchmark objective progress on an ongoing and regular basis.

Action Plan for News Media

The media consists of the four major TV networks in the largest ten designated market areas (DMAs) in the USA as well as the top three in reach networks in health-, spa-, travel-, and business-related networks such as Bloomberg and CNBC. Additionally, include the top three radio stations by weekly listenership in each of the largest ten DMAs. Include the major business, health, health spa, vacation, and travel magazines and websites by reach that target upper-middle and upper income households. Also, target the Sunday newspaper magazines in the three largest circulating newspapers in the top ten DMAs.

The major TV broadcast media outlets are: NBC, MSNBC, CNN, CBS, ABC, Fox, Bloomberg, and Travel Channel.

Target market websites include Airbnb.com, bankrate.com, CBS.com, CBSNews.com, CNBC.com, Cnet.com, CNN.com, ESPN.com, Fox News, Hotels.com, Hotwire.com, HuffPost.com, LivingSocial.com, MSNMoney.com, NBC.com, NBCSports.com, NYtimes.com, PBS.org, and websites for The Weather Channel, The Street, Travelocity, USA Today, Weather Underground, wsj.com, Yahoo Finance, Fine Living Network, and Yahoo News.

Target market magazine and blogs are *Clean Eating Magazine, Eating Well Magazine, Real Simple Magazine, Natural Solutions Magazine, Alternative Medicine Magazine, Herb Quarterly, Nutrition Today, Organic Spa, Experience Life, Yoga, Healthy Living, Men's Health, Men's Journal,* and *Senior Fitness.*

Strategy and Primary Message: Messaging should present the central theme in a manner that draws attention to the media outlet's audience. Human interest or unusual and effective aspects of Canyon Ranch's services and products hook gatekeepers and audiences. Provide sufficient content that both activates emotions and cognition information processing. Describing special services or programs is effective. Provide images and videos as well. The cornerstone should be Canyon Ranch's health and healing benefits. Present these in sound bites. News professionals are busy, so, make their adopting the story easy. Appealing media coverage of Canyon Ranch will create knowledge and engagement in the target markets.

Objective 1: By the end of the 12-month campaign, hold interviews, receive favorable media coverage, and/or place a feature story in the top three largest reach local TV broadcast markets in the largest 10 DMAs.

Objective 2: By the end of the 12-month campaign, hold interviews, receive favorable media coverage, and/or place a feature story in the top three reach networks or programs on health-, spa-, and travel- topics.

Objective 3: By the end of the 12-month campaign, hold interviews, receive favorable media coverage, and/or place a feature story on Bloomberg, CNBC, and Fox Business.

Objective 4: By the end of the 12-month campaign, hold interviews, receive favorable media coverage, and/or place a feature story on the top three radio stations by weekly listenership in each of the largest ten DMAs.

The following tactics apply to all news media objectives.

Tactic 1: Create and disseminate via email and other digital forms: a media kit, news release, and video news release.

Tactic 2: Offer press tours of the Canyon Ranch facility in Lenox.

Tactic 3: Provide stories describing how individuals' lives improved because of the Canyon Ranch experience.

Tactic 4: Provide news media interviews especially during morning shows.

Tactic 5: Distribute through the news wire a release about the "new" and benefits of Canyon Ranch's health and healing services.

Tactic 6: Regularly comment on blogs about topics related to health and healing and present Canyon Ranch positively and subtly.

Tactic 7: Pitch the health and healing angle to personal media contacts.

Tactics 8: Run content analysis and analytics to measure success of news media coverage plan.

Action Plan for Corporate Customers

Corporate customers are those organizations that purchase Canyon Ranch packages for their executives. These are Fortune 500 companies. There may be more than a single point of contact in the top 500 based on the company's organization structure and operational policies. The executive and human resources departments are logical starting points.

Strategy and Primary Message: Corporations want to know how the Canyon Ranch experience will benefit their key performing employees. Position the experience as a health and wellness experience that will rejuvenate employees and their motivation to be effective and productive professionals. They will be reenergized. Promote the central message and be sure to communicate that Canyon Ranch handles everything and there is little investment other than the cost of the experience which will yield an appealing ROI through better performing executives.

Objective 1: By the end of the 12-month campaign, have on-site visits with 150 of the Fortune 500 companies.

Tactic 1: Send digital communications, make personal calls, and meet with higher probability prospects.

Tactic 2: Provide a complimentary one-night stay to a designated decision-making so that she/he experiences Canyon Ranch.

Tactic 3: Follow-up with a telephone call and email with all prospective representatives, and, if possible, their potential visitors focusing on their needs.

Objective 2: By the end of the 12-month campaign, open accounts where at least 3–5 executives from 50 of the Fortune 500 stay at Canyon Ranch within 12 months of the campaign.

Tactic 1: Offer one complimentary visit for every specified number purchased packages to Canyon Ranch.

Tactic 2: Follow-up after the visit with a telephone call and email focusing on their experience and needs.

Tactic 3: Seek approval and implement a link to Canyon Ranch with the host client company. The link or content should focus on the central message as it relates to meeting individual client needs. Possibly provide testimonials. Praise the client company for providing the Canyon Ranch experience to its community.

Tactic 4: Monitor the progress of achieving corporate client marketing benchmarked objectives.

Travel Agents and Agencies

There are approximately 105,000 travel agents in the United States alone. Of those, 3,000–5,000 thousand are luxury vacation/destination agents. Eighteen percent of Canyon Ranch's referrals are from such travel agents.

Strategy and Central Message: Convey the central message to travel agents including additional information that may integrate with the travel agency services. Messaging will emphasize the benefits to the travel agency including commission structure; integration of agency services to include the resort; and co-advertising and promotional activities. The commission structure will take two forms: 1) The commission paid in dollars or 2) Payment in kind, which the agent would receive a stay credit at the Canyon Ranch Resort equal to 120% of the commission. Additionally, Canyon Commission would refer clients seeking a travel agent to affiliate agencies.

Objective 1: By the end of the 12-month campaign, travel agency referrals from existing relationships will increase by 20%.

Objective 2: By the end of the 12-month campaign, new travel agency affiliations will increase by 25%.

The tactics apply to existing and new agency affiliations.

Tactic 1: Develop a co-advertising and promotional plan for Canyon Ranch and its travel agency affiliates.

Tactic 2: Email all prospect and existing affiliate travel agencies about the new initiative centering on health and healing services at Canyon Ranch. Launch three email blasts over a 6-week period.

Tactic 3: Cold call all prospect and existing affiliate travel agencies as a follow-up to the second email blast. Describe the innovative health and healing services as well as the new incentive packages.

Tactic 4: For major travel agency affiliations, offer a complimentary overnight stay highlighting the health and healing department.

Tactics 5: Monitor and assess travel agency referral developments.

V. Scheduling and Budgeting

Because wellness services are in demand year-round, the campaign will adopt a continuous scheduling strategy as demonstrated in the Gantt chart located in Figure 14.7.

A complete Gantt chart contains all tactical costs.

Master Schedule and Budget

Table 14.1 is a partial master schedule and budget. The CPM is $3554. Keep in mind that the costs include updating the website and developing and maintaining a social media presence and blog. If the complete master schedule and budget were developed, then some of those costs would be allocated to prospective client targeting.

Indicate the cost basis for calculating CPM.

Contingency Fund

The contingency allocation is $25,000.

VI. Evaluation

Overall Benchmarked Objectives

(Any outcomes that fall within 2–3 percentage points of the overall benchmark objectives are considered a success. The actual outcome percentages would be listed here in the objective format.)

Action Plan Benchmarked Objectives

(Any outcomes that fall within 2–3 percentage points of the each action plan benchmark objectives are considered a success. The actual outcome percentages would be listed here in the objective format.)

Partial Public Relations Campaign Master Budget and Schedule for 1/1/19 to 12/31/19

Gantt Chart

Name	Begin date	End date
⊟ ▪ Objective 1: Achieve 90% knowledge of health and healing services for ...	1/1/19	12/31/19
▫ Redesign the Canyon Ranch website	1/2/19	1/2/19
▫ Develop and implement a mobile app	1/2/19	1/2/19
▫ Develop and implement blog	1/2/19	12/31/19
▫ Create and maintain social media presence	1/2/19	12/31/19
▫ Email blast to existing female customers	1/1/19	3/1/19
▫ Follow-up email blast, with a hardcopy mailer	3/2/19	4/2/19
▫ Run ongoing email and texting tracking studies	1/1/19	12/31/19
⊟ ▪ Objective 2: 25% increase in health and healing sales from existing fem...	1/1/19	12/31/19
▫ Personal selling paired guests	1/1/19	12/31/19
▫ Suggest personalized plan	1/1/19	12/31/19
▫ Benchmark tracking	2/28/19	12/31/19

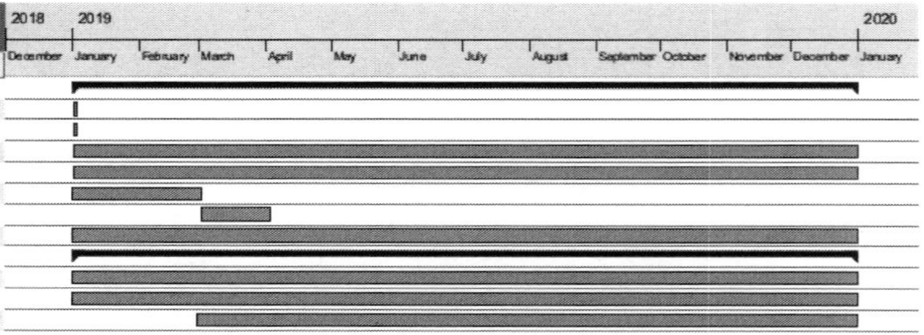

Figure 14.7 Partial Gantt Chart Schedule

Table 14.1 Partial Public Relations Campaign Master Budget and Schedule for 1/1/19 to 12/31/19

Public: Women from Affluent Households in the USA totaling 12 million[a]

Objective 1: From 1/1/19 to 12/31/19, achieve 90% knowledge of health and healing services for existing female customers.

Tactic description:[a]	Dates	Public Exposures	Forecasted total tactic cost
Redesign the Canyon Ranch website	1/2/19	–	$1,500[b]
Develop and implement a mobile app	1/2/19 1/2/19–12/31/19 1/2/19–12/31/19 1/1/19–3/1/19	10,000	$7,500[c]
Develop and implement blog		5,000	$7,500[b]
Create and maintain social media presence: Facebook, Twitter, and Instagram email blast to existing female customers	3/2/19–4/2/19 2/28/19–12/31/19	20,000	$30,000[b]
		6375	$7,500[b]
Follow-up email blasts, with a hardcopy mailer		6375	$40,000
Run ongoing email and texting tracking studies		–	$1,125[b]
	Objective/Public subtotal	47,750	$95,125

Public: Women for Affluent Households in the USA totaling 12 million[a]

Objective 2: From 1/1/19 to 12/31/19, 25% increase in health and healing sales from existing female guests.

Tactic description:	Dates	Public Exposures	Forecasted total tactic cost
Personal selling to individual guests paired win an expert based on CRM client data	1/2/19–12/31/19 1/2/19–12/31/19 2/28/19–12/31/19	2,000	$20,000
			$105,000
Develop and suggest a personalized plan for services and products		15,000	$10,000
Track benchmark objective progress on an ongoing and regular basis		–	
	Objective/Public subtotal	17,000	$135,000
	Partial campaign total	64,750	$230,125

[a] The focus of this partial schedule and budget are the existing Canyon Ranch Lenox women customers. The news media action plan is directed to new customers.

[b] The social media function for the entire campaign is the responsibility of a single full-time social media manager; 75% of these costs are allocated to existing women customers and 25% are charged to existing men customers.

[c] This is a 75%/25% allocation like the second footnote.

Advertising Value Equivalency

The post-campaign, assessed final version of the plansbook contains the advertising value equivalency evaluation.

VII. Conclusion

The goal of this 12-month promotional campaign is to primarily increase sales in the U.S. market of Canyon Ranch's health and healing services at the Lenox location by integrating the spa, fitness, and salon services and the hotel as a total healthy/wellness vacation experience while maintaining the total brand saliency within the allocated budget.

By the end of the campaign, awareness and knowledge of Canyon Ranch's health and healing services will increase to 90% of its existing customer list; health and healing services sales will increase by 30% and overall sales grow by 5%; and there will be a 5% increase in new visits and a 15% jump in repeat visits.

VIII. References

(This section contains references that support the plansbook.)

IX. Appendix

(This section contains the activity briefs for each tactic.)

Summary of Key Concepts

- A plansbook contains a public relations campaign.
- A typical plansbook is 10–75 pages with a duration of 6–24 months.
- The executive summary, situational analysis, strategy, action plans, schedule/budget, and evaluation are the standard components of a public relations campaign plans.
- Parts of the plansbook are interdependent thus providing the big picture of the campaign.
- Cost per thousand and advertising value equivalency are financial tools available to determine cost-efficiencies and return on investment approximations for public relations campaigns.

Key Terms

Chapter Questions

14.1   What is the typically length of a public relations plansbook?

14.2   What period does a public relations campaign cover?

14.3   What is an executive summary?

14.4   Describe a situational analysis.

14.5   When defining a public, what information is collected?

14.6   What comprises a public relations plansbook strategy?

14.7   What does a campaign goal address?

14.8   What is the central message?

14.9   What is an action plan?

14.10   Describe benchmarked objective.

14.11   What is a tactic?

14.12   Typically, how many tactics does an objective have?

14.13   Usually, how many objectives does an action plan have?

14.14   Define scheduling strategy.

14.15   What plays a role in media selection and other related decisions?

14.16   Define cost per thousand.

14.17   Define AVE.

14.18   What is an activity brief?

Note

1 A short or truncated plansbook is 10-12 pages. Other plansbooks contain more information about strategy, reasoning, and tactics, which extend the length to 35-40 pages. A full and extensive plansbook, including implementation guidelines, can reach 150 pages. Campaign duration and the nature of the appendices affect the length.

References

Diggs-Brown, B. (2012). *Strategic public relations, an audience focused approach*. Boston, M.A.: Wadsworth.

Hawthorne, J. (2013). Fantasy fragrance messaging celebrates 10 years of Britney. *PR Week, November, 45*. Retrieved from http://www.prweek.com/article/1274222/fantasy-fragrance-messaging-celebrates-10-years-britney .

Part VII

Cultural Factors

Chapter 15

Culture, Diversity, and Inclusion

*Surely whoever speaks to me in the right voice, him or her I shall follow, as the water follows the
moon, silently, with fluid steps anywhere around the globe.*

(Walt Whitman, 1900, p. 308)

Learning Objectives

To:

- Know demographic trends and the changing face of society.
- Understand that diversity is about race, age, sex, gender, disabilities, ethnicity, background, lifestyle, socio-economic status, culture, and other differences.
- Describe what is culture.
- Know what is the difference between tolerance and acceptance.
- Understand diversity and equality.
- Understand and describe what are inclusion and multiculturalism.
- Understand the barriers and challenges to diversity and inclusion.
- Understand and describe diversity and requisite variety in public relations.
- Know best practices for a culture of diversity.

Introduction

Before moving to global public relations in the next chapter, we will first examine diversity, inclusion, culture, and multiculturalism. With the advent of new technologies, social media, and social movements that show promise for a more integrated and communicative world, understanding cultural diversity and inclusion are vital to reaching many stakeholders both locally and internationally.

The face of society continues to change. According to the World Population Prospects The 2017 Revision, by the end of 2017, the global population will reach at least 7.6 billion with people concentrated in Asia and Africa and the balance of the world accounting for nearly 24% of the population. By 2030, the anticipated global population will reach 8.6 billion. Population growth rates remain high and will continue to do so for the foreseeable future especially in the economically least developed countries. Longevity is increasing across the world particularly in Africa where there are pockets of younger populations. Globally, the numbers of men and women are nearly even.

The 2017 Revision Report indicated that between 1950 and 2015, Europe and North America accepted the largest number of international migrants. Africa, Asia, Latin America, and the Caribbean were the major sources of people migrating to other countries. This pattern will continue through 2050 (United Nations, 2017).

As the United Nation report reveals, population trends continue to shape our society, suggesting the importance of the roles of diversity and inclusion in our multicultural world and how we communicate in that world. A commitment to maintaining a diverse talent pool, while being socially responsible, also provide additional opportunities to reach more and diverse stakeholders.

The public relations sector has had its struggles adopting this strategy. In a 2001 study by Hon and Brunner (2001), approximately one-third of public relations practitioners indicated that their company was aware of diversity issues, but did little about it. Another third indicated that their organization was genuinely committed; yet efforts were slow moving. Opposite views represent the final third. Some revealed that there was no interest in addressing diverse issues; whereas, others expressed a deep commitment to it. These conditions persist today and require attention (Berger, Meng, & Heyman, 2017; Wilson, 2016).

A 2015 study by The National Black Public Relations Society, Inc. found that 62% of respondents indicated that their organizations do not have any black men in communication leadership roles and 37% do not have any black women in similar positions (Ford & Brown, 2015). Other studies revealed similar findings.

Last, men dominate senior management and leadership positions in public relations firms and departments. In a review of research findings, Bardhan (2017) found that: (1) White public relations managers believe that diversity and inclusion efforts were successful; whereas, non-white public relations professionals did not think that efforts were effective. (2) Less than 50% of firms and corporations have diversity and inclusion directors. (3) There are limited definitions of diversity. (4) There are few pipelines to executive positions for persons of color and Latino(a)s. (5) LGBTQ work environments were largely restrictive (Bardhan, 2017).

What Are Diversity and Inclusion?

Let us define what are diversity and inclusion.

> The concept of **diversity** (and inclusion) encompasses acceptance and respect. It means understanding that each individual is unique, and recognizing our individual differences. These can be along the dimensions of race, ethnicity, gender, sexual orientation, socio-economic status, age, physical abilities, religious beliefs, political beliefs, or other ideologies. It is the exploration of these differences in a safe, positive, and nurturing environment. It is about understanding each other and moving beyond simple tolerance to embracing and celebrating the rich dimensions of diversity contained within each individual.
>
> (University of Oregon, Diversity Initiative, 2017)

Figure 15.1 The Glass Ceiling Can Be Subtle. Can You Think of Examples?

Figure 15.2 Although not Always Apparent, Barriers to Diversity and Inclusion Can Be Formidable

Diversity alone is a condition in which an environment consists of people from different backgrounds and cultures. Diversity is based on race, ethnicity, gender, sexual orientation, socio-economic status, age, physical abilities and attributes, religious beliefs, political beliefs, or other ideologies. Moreover, national origin and perceived behaviors such as different lifestyles, speech accents, culturally based practices and values constitute diversity. In short, diversity encompasses all factors that make us different from others.

A diverse community is a shared community comprising the characteristics of different communities (Hon & Brunner, 2000). A shared community may be larger than constituent communities, but not necessarily so. For instance, the United States is a large, shared community consisting of many communities or stakeholder groups. On the other hand, the British Parliament is a relatively small community comprised of communities that populate an entire country.

Diversity starts with having representatives of diverse groups, organizations, or other types of social structures. Often legal requirements guide hiring practices, which is an easily measurable outcome. Yet, a diverse culture is more than hiring quotas. It includes tolerance. **Tolerance** is a permissive attitude toward those persons who are different. And still, diversity goes beyond tolerance to acceptance.

Acceptance is thinking, feeling, and behaving in a manner respecting and consistent with diversity. The uniqueness of each individual matters. It is the recognition and understanding of individual differences and the nurturing of these differences. Acceptance is understanding each other and embracing and celebrating the enriching nature of diversity. This acceptance happens in small one-on-one relationships, in small groups, in large groups, in organizations, in sectors of society, and in an entire society.

Acceptance is an attitude; it is internal. The acceptance of behaviors that are different move us to celebrate diversity and inclusion. **Inclusion** involves actions associated with

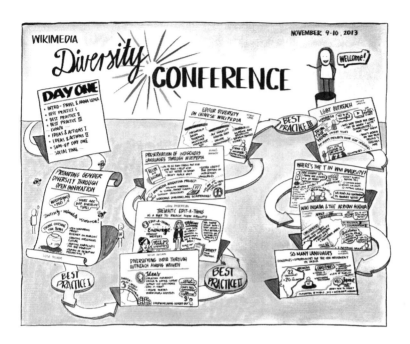

Figure 15.3 Diversity Covers Many Aspects of Life and Influences Many People in Many Ways

Figure 15.4 One World, One People, Diverse Perspectives

Figure 15.5 The Process of Diversity and Inclusion Involves Steps. First, there Is a Representative Diverse Group in the Organization. Second, there Is Tolerance for Diversity. Third, there Is Acceptance of Diversity. Fourth, Acceptance Requires Inclusion Behaviors, as Demonstrated in the Mission Statement, Policies, and, if Appropriate, the Existence of a Designated Compliance Officer.

the acceptance of diverse beliefs and values. In sum, diversity is the guiding principle of inclusion. Inclusion occurs through programs designed to support and integrate diverse individuals in a group or organizational culture (Hon & Brunner, 2000). Once this occurs, a multicultural organization will thrive. Figure 15.5 illustrates the progression from representation to celebrating **multiculturalism**.

A successful diversity and inclusion program results in a **multicultural environment**, which is an environment where diverse cultures live and thrive together contributing to each other's well-being and the overall organizational mission.

Culture

Culture is the cumulative deposit and passing down of knowledge (everything learned), experience, beliefs, values, attitudes, meanings, language, communication (ways of interacting) hierarchies, religion, artifacts, and material objects acquired by generations of a group of people through individual and group existence and behaviors (Samovar & Porter, 1994). A culture may be national, regional, local, or organizational. Cultures overlap and share characteristics. In the next chapter, we will examine cultural differentiators.

A multicultural environment supports and integrates more than one culture. Diversity is inherent in multiculturalism. There are varieties of subcultures as well. For instance, not all gay people are progressive or share the same buying habits. Moreover, diversity and inclusion pertain to all socio-economic groups and political perspectives. Individuals from the same socio-economic segment also have an array of political preferences There is no one catch all designation.

Strong Organizational Cultures

Deal and Kennedy (2000) posit that strong organizational cultures consist of four elements. The first is **Values**. These are the basic organizational beliefs which form the core of a culture. They are supported and diffused throughout the organizational hierarchy. For example, Ford launched an ad campaign in 1981 with the slogan, "Ford is Job #1." Ford employees wore pins and posted signs with this slogan. Job #1 indicated that Ford was about manufacturing the highest quality vehicles.

Second, a strong organization includes **Heroes**. Heroes personify values and serve as a tangible source of inspiration. They are known by virtually all organizational members and provide role models for how one should conduct oneself. Steve Jobs was the exemplar hero at Apple. He developed the "Apple" culture centered on constant innovation.

Figure 15.6 All Sorts of People, All Sorts of Views

Organizational members follow systematic and regularized routines. In a strong culture, these constitute **Rites and Rituals**, which are behaviors that orient organizational members to the ways of the culture. The annual Apple meeting is an example. Awards ceremonies and team exercises are instances of rites and rituals.

Last is the **cultural network**, which is a network of people and the key source of informal communication within the organization apart from the formal structure. People maintain different roles in these networks.

There are **Storytellers**, who interpret what they observe in the organization and create a narrative passed on to members to orient themselves to the culture by shaping their perceptions and expectations. Often the stories are about organizational legends or heroes.

Priests are the guardians of organizational values. They know the history of the organization. They can interpret organizational situations in the context of beliefs, values, and past practices. They advise members in the case "of defeat, frustration, and disappointment" (Deal & Kennedy, 2000, p. 89).

Whisperers are those members who have access to the influential people in the organization. They often informally convey messages to senior management.

Gossipers know and communicate all the intriguing scuttlebutt in the organization, placing their own spin on events. Organizational members take this information for what it is-gossip and entertainment.

Spies provide valuable information to senior management daily. They are the informal eyes and ears of those at the top of the hierarchy.

Administrative staff possess all sorts of information and knowledge about an organization, some of which is gossip and some of which accurately describes the inner workings of the organization. They know who are the go-to individuals for specific situations.

Last, there are **cabals**. A cabal is a group of two or more persons who covertly meet to serve a common purpose. Cabals advance organizational culture internally as well as serve as a protection mechanism. They provide strength and backing through their members. A cabal can be a professional organization such as the Public Relations Society of America, a union, or an informal group.

According to Deal and Kennedy (2000), a strong culture acts in two important ways. First, it is a guide of informal norms that specify how people should behave and, second, it enables people to feel positive about what they do so that organizational members work productively and effectively. Understanding and incorporating aspects of a strong culture where there are opportunities to effectuate positive change or reinforce existing behaviors, all contribute to the organization's mission.

Cultural Relativism

Cultural relativism holds that an understanding of a person's beliefs, values, and practices exists by knowing an individual's culture. It is based on the perspective that the world is relative. No one culture has a monopoly on the truth or what is "best." Cultural perspectives exist in relation to the persons that comprise the culture. Of course, what is acceptable in one culture may not be in another. The environment's legal, moral, and ethical norms and expectations mediate the interaction of individuals from diverse cultures.

Cultural Ethnocentrism

Contrary to cultural relativism, there is **cultural ethnocentrism**. This is the belief that one's culture is superior to others. It extends to judgments about other cultures predicated on the values, beliefs, and standards of one's own culture particularly concerning language, customs, religion and other practices. In short, one's culture filters views of the world.

This view discourages diversity and inclusion and often leads to groupthink (Janis, 1982). **Groupthink** is the belief that one's group or culture is unquestionable and infallible. Groupthink centers on three characteristics:

1   There exist overestimates of the group or culture's influence and morality.
2   The group is closed-mindedness and resists challenges.
3   There is a strong tendency toward uniformity.

Deal and Kennedy's elements of a strong culture, if not well-managed, can reinforce groupthink at the expense of diversity and inclusion.

Figure 15.7 Groupthink is Self-Perpetuating

Figure 15.8 For Groupthinkers, What One Doesn't Know, Doesn't Hurt

Think about This . . .

In a 2016 *PR Week* op/ed piece entitled "Diversity and Inclusion in PR: The world won't wait for us," Renee Wilson discusses diversity and the public relations industry's lackluster effort to support it. Clients communicate to their public relations firms the need to include talent with heterogeneous backgrounds.

Research has found that a diverse workforce is more productive. In short, this means that having more (diverse) options than required to solve a problem assures that an optimal response is available to address the challenge. This is especially the case in creative communities where inclusion fosters innovative thoughts and ideas.

Demographic trends support diversity and inclusion. Wilson reported that, by 2020, half or more of U.S. children will be part of a minority segment of the population. Of course, besides pragmatic considerations, we should do it because it is the socially responsible thing to do.

Ask yourself: Can you think of specific examples or hypothetical cases where supporting diversity and inclusion benefits public relations efforts? Think of this question from the perspective of different stakeholders, cultures, and global public relations campaigns.

Wilson, R. (2016). Diversity and Inclusion in PR: The world won't wait for us. *PR Week*, June 22. Retrieved from www.prweek.com/article/1396460/diversity-inclusion-pr-world-wont-wait-us.

Diversity Is about Equality

As people, we strive for equality, which includes respecting the dignity of those who are different. In a multicultural organization, people feel that they belong, fit in, have value, and can make meaningful contributions to the organization. At the same time, there is respect for and value ascribed to individuality.

Equal opportunities apply to many parts of our individual and collective lives including the social, work, and economic areas. However, people perceived as different often face challenges in society and in the workplace. The Equal Employment Opportunity Act Affirmative Action and the Americans with Disabilities Act are laws enacted to encourage diversity and inclusion. However, laws alone do not guarantee diversity and inclusion.

Structural and relational barriers to inclusion confront organizations. Structural barriers are unintentional and built into the organization. Examples are a lack of formal mentoring programs or insufficient diversity and inclusion training. Relational barriers occur at the individual relationship level especially in the informal structure of the organization such as feelings of prejudice and acts of discrimination.

Structural Barriers

Structural barriers are obstacles to diversity that are inherent in an organizational system. Often the failure lies in lack of the development, implementation, and follow-up of a comprehensive diversity and inclusion program that integrates the formal and informal aspects of an organization. The following considerations cover programmatic areas that often fall

"We must have miscommunicated. The remodel was supposed to be a contemporary."

Figure 15.9 Assumptions about Others Leads to Miscommunication and Misunderstanding

short (Appelbaum, Walton, & Southerland, 2015; Berger, Meng, & Heyman, 2017; Ford & Brown, 2015; Groeneveld & Verbeek, 2012; Public Relations Coalition, 2005).

- The organizational mission and values statements do not explicitly address diversity and inclusion.
- Lack of communication limits the degree to which top management is committed to diversity and inclusion. Moreover, often allocated resources to promote diversity are insufficient.
- There is no designated individual to oversee the diversity and inclusion program. This poses a host of problems including a lack of follow-up and advocacy for diversity programs.
- Human resource recruitment efforts do not coordinate organizational needs and diversity goals.
- There is a lack of meaningful mentorship programs for minority employees.
- There is a lack of regularly available quality training and skills workshop for minority members.
- Quality and regularly available and scheduled organization-wide diversity and inclusion training is in short supply.

Relational Barriers

Relational barriers are obstacles to diversity that are based on interpersonal dynamics. They are individual responses to diversity and inclusion. Responses take the form of thoughts, feeling, and behaviors toward others. Let's cover some barrier-related practices.

Stereotyping is the behavior of ascribing characteristics to all members of a group, while not recognizing individual differences. For instance, a manager may believe that all Asians are highly competent at all things mathematical or that certain cultural groups are overly emotional. Stereotyping often leads to prejudice.

Prejudice is a negative attitude toward individuals based on his/her cultural identity and others' perceptions about those identities (Eagly & Chaiken, 1993). These negative

Figure 15.10 Active Listening Can Reduce Relational Barriers

thoughts and feelings lead to exclusion behaviors. **Discrimination** is observable behavior resulting from someone who is prejudiced (Miller, 2012).

Stereotyping, prejudice, and discrimination reinforce ethnocentric beliefs. **Ethnocentrism** is the belief that one's ethnic background is superior to others and thus other cultures are largely irrelevant. This process marginalizes people viewed as different and often precludes them from opportunities to participate in the informal network and communication structure where valuable organizational information, contacts, and other resources are available.

Diversity and Inclusion in Public Relations

Multiculturalism in the public relations industry is a combination of two conditions operating in unison. Diversity hires provide agencies and organizations with practitioners who represent, know, and understand the diverse communities and markets with whom they identify. To understand publics is to know them.

This approach requires requisite variety. **Requisite variety** means that to optimally address an issue, an organization must possess resources that are equal to or greater than those inherent in the issue – than those that created the issue. Put differently, to effectively address situations, individuals, groups, or organizations with the greatest flexibility choices are needed. An organization must have diversity equal to or greater than the diverse environment in which it acts. The Law of Requisite Variety is not domain specific. It applies to any context where interaction takes place whether in the biological, physical, or social sciences.

For example, consider a situation in which one of two consulting firms develops a comprehensive public relations strategy and plan. One firm's core competency is social media strategy and the other is the big picture. The latter firm is likely to receive the contract. The big picture firm is more flexible because it has more to offer. Although easily

Figure 15.11 Multiculturalism Has Its Benefits

understood, in practice, requisite variety is challenging to implement because of limited resources, complex situations, and personal relationships between and among practitioners.

Research supports the benefits of requisite variety. In a 2013 study by the Center for Talent Innovation, Hewlett, Marshall, Sherbin, and Gonsalves (2013) examined diversity and inclusion in the global marketing industry. Of those companies that had a strong culture of inclusion, 48% reported improved market share as opposed to 33% for those without strong diversity and inclusion programs. Demonstrating a similar pattern, 46% reported capturing new markets compared to 27%. Inclusion culture organizations reported greater opportunities to express views and opinions. Respondents perceived that the organization heard and recognized their ideas.

These benefits extend to other areas as well. Requisite variety links to competitive advantage. Cox and Blake (1991) as well as numerous other researchers found that diversity and inclusion provide an organization with a competitive advantage in the areas of costs, resource acquisition, marketing, creativity, problem-solving, and organizational flexibility (Mor-Barak & Cherin, 1998; Sabattini & Crosby, 2008; Sabharwal, 2014; Stewart & Johnson, 2009).

Some Multicultural Challenges that Face Public Relations Practitioners

This section highlights some specific challenges to cultural understanding. These considerations also apply to external and internal publics. We will briefly describe paralanguage, status markers, translation vs. interpretation, and gestures.

In some languages, paralanguage influences the meaning of oral communication. **Paralanguage** is everything associated with speech in conjunction with the actual words, phrases, and sentences. Paralanguage includes posture, eye contact, hand gestures, and pronunciation involving as volume, syllable emphasis, tempo, pauses, and accent. The audio component is vocal paralanguage. So, where words are usually concrete, paralanguage is open to interpretation. Nuanced changes in articulation can change meaning, which varies by language and culture. In sum, paralanguage extends the meaning of words beyond the dictionary definitions, thus providing greater language flexibility and speech diversity.

Some cultures contain **status markers**, which are indicators that someone is privileged. They come in many forms such as level of eye contact during a meeting, how someone bows before another, and hand gestures. One kind of status marker involves language usage. In some cultures, a respected person is addressed in the third person while interacting. For example, "Would your majesty like a cup of tea?" refers to the person or queen in this case by speaking directly to the individual in the third person. To address the person directly by saying "Would you like a cup of tea?" is inappropriate. I recall when I was on a flight to Italy with my mother and aunt. There was a nun sitting next to me. In Italian, I offered her some peanuts by addressing her in the second person "Would you like some peanuts?" rather than "Would she like some peanuts?" The literal translated is awkward, but the context makes the meaning and intention clear. In any case, my aunt corrected me and I never forgot the role of status markers again!

In addition to the spoken word of a country, some nations or cultures have more than one (official) language. For example, Canada has two official languages: English and French. In Canada, many instances of the written word are in both languages.

There is also the issue of translation vs. interpretation. **Translation** is the process of converting the corresponding meaning of *written* words in one language to one or more

Figure 15.12 Learn How Cultures Communicate

other languages or dialects. **Interpretation** is the *oral* translation of a discussion including interpreting paralanguage. Each function requires similar and different skills, training, and knowledge. A language expert usually is a translator or interpreter. Ideally, translators and interpreters are: (1) knowledgeable of the general subject at hand; (2) familiar with the cultures from which the translation/interpretation occurs, (3) well versed in the vocabulary of the languages, and (4) clear and concise.

In both cases, an understanding of cultural and language nuances is important. For example, the Italian expression "un uomo in gamba" literally means "a man in leg" loosely meaning a well-traveled, experienced, and wise person. One of the meanings for the word "nick" in American English is a small cut. In British English, it is a verb meaning "to steal."

Across cultures, many gestures have different meaning. **Gestures** are nonverbal forms of communication. In Nigeria and Greece, waving one's hand is insulting. Pointing with the index finger is impolite in the Middle East and China. Folded arms over one's chest is disrespectful in Fiji. Bowing to a lesser degree to your host implies superiority in Japan. The list goes on and on. Clearly, in intercultural communication, vigilance is a virtue because there are many opportunities for miscommunication and misunderstanding.

Diversity and Inclusion Best Practices in Organizations

A culture of inclusion empowers, promotes belonging, and conveys the value of respect toward associates. At the same time, diversity and inclusion encourage individuality by advancing professional development, creativity, and innovation in the workplace. As internal diversity keeps pace with external issues, public relations organizations will maximize their effectiveness through the synergies of diversity.

Suggested relational and structural best practices follow. They are by no means exhaustive, but simply provide a sampling of effective practices.

Pless and Maak (2004), presented the following relational behaviors:

- Showing respect and empathy;
- Recognizing others as different but equal;
- Showing appreciation for different voices, e.g. by:
  - listening actively to them,
  - trying to understand disparate viewpoints and opinions, and
  - integrating different voices into the ongoing cultural discourse;
- Practicing and encouraging open and frank communication in all interactions;
- Cultivating participative decision-making and problem-solving processes and team capabilities;
- Showing integrity and advanced moral reasoning, especially when dealing with ethical dilemmas; and
- Using a cooperative/consultative leadership style (Pless & Maak, 2004, p. 140).

There are several structural level best practices.

1 Top management should affirm its commitment to diversity and inclusion by explicitly communicating it as well as by providing sufficient resources. This commitment represents the mission and values statements.
2 There is a person designated to coordinate and oversee the program on a regular basis, who is committed to a culture of diversity.
3 The organization's diversity and inclusion commitment should inform recruitment and promotion efforts.
4 There are fair and equal salary and bonuses implementation for all organizational members.
5 Develop and implement detailed career track and succession plans.
6 Develop and implement mentoring and networking programs. Structure a formal network program to be as effective at the informal one.
7 Create team-based projects comprised of diverse organizational members across functional and other areas so that individuals understand the unique needs of the various units.
8 Offer workshops about diversity and inclusion regularly in-person and online.
9 Include a regular evaluation of the program in the organization's annual report and social responsibility reports.
10 Coordinate and integrate the above to maximize effectiveness.

Summary of Key Concepts

- Changing global demographics provide opportunities for a multicultural workforce.
- Diversity and inclusion are more than just quotas.
- Diversity and inclusion provide organizations with a multitude of opportunities both internally and externally as well as being socially responsible.
- Requisite variety makes an organization flexible and highly responsive.

- There are structural and relational barriers to diversity and inclusion.
- There are language and communication challenges that cause miscommunication and misunderstanding.
- Best practices can go a long way to create inclusion.

Key Terms

Acceptance 363
Administrative staff 366
Cabals 366
Culture 365
Cultural ethnocentrism 371
Cultural networks 366
Cultural relativism 367
Discrimination 371
Diversity 362
Ethnocentrism 367
Gestures 373
Gossipers 366
Groupthink 367
Heroes 365
Inclusion 363
Interpretation 373
Multicultural environment 365

Multiculturalism 365
Paralanguage 372
Prejudice 370
Priests 366
Relational barriers 370
Requisite variety 371
Rites and rituals 366
Spies 366
Status markers 372
Stereotyping 370
Storytellers 366
Structural barriers 369
Tolerance 363
Translation 372
Values 365
Whisperers 366

Chapter Questions

15.1   Why is an understanding of multiculturalism important today?

15.2   By the end of 2017, where will the global population be concentrated?

15.3   By 2030, what is the projected global population?

15.4   What areas accepted the largest number of immigrants between 1905 and 2015?

15.5   Is there a lack of diversity and inclusion in public relations especially at the upper levels of management?

15.6   What is diversity?

15.7   Can diversity exist within a minority group and provide a hypothetical example?

15.8   Define tolerance.

15.9   Define acceptance.

15.10   What is inclusion?

15.11   What is multiculturalism?

15.12   What are the steps of diversity and inclusion?

15.13   Define culture and name two of them.

15.14   What are the four elements of Deal and Kennedy's strong culture framework?

15.15   In Deal and Kennedy's social network element, who are the players?

15.16   What is cultural relativism?

15.17   Define cultural ethnocentrism.

15.18   Define groupthink.

15.19   Define structural barriers to diversity and inclusion.

15.20   Define relational barriers to diversity and inclusion.

15.21   What is stereotyping and provide an example?

15.22   What is prejudice and offer an example?

15.23   What is discrimination and provide an example?

15.24   Define ethnocentrism.

15.25   Define requisite variety.

15.26   What is paralanguage and offer an example?

15.27   Define status marker and provide an example.

15.28   What is the main difference between translation and interpretation?

15.29   Define gestures and provide an example.

15.30   How might you apply Deal and Kennedy's strong organizational culture elements to reduce barriers to diversity and inclusion?

References

Appelbaum, L., Walton, F., & Southerland, E. (2015). *An examination of factors affecting the success of under-represented groups in the Public Relations profession*. The City College of New York.

Bardhan, N. (2017). *Trends in D&I research and trade press discourse*. The Plank Center for Leadership in Public Relations, 1–15. Retrieved from http://plankcenter.ua.edu/wp-content/uploads/2016/07/PR-industry-DI-trends-and-research-highlights.pdf.

Berger, B. K., Meng, J., & Heyman, W. (2017). Gender differences deepen, leader–employee gap remains and grade slide, *Plank Center Report Card 2017 on PR leaders*, 1–8.

Cox, T. H., & Blake, S. (1991). Managing cultural diversity: Implications for organizational competitiveness. *Academy of Management Executive, 5*(3), 45–56.

Deal, T. E., & Kennedy, A. A. (2000). *Corporate Cultures: The rites and rituals of corporate life*. New York: Basic Books.

Eagly, A. H., & Chaiken, S. (1993). *The psychology of attitudes*. New York: Harcourt Brace College.

Ford, R., & Brown, C. (2015). *State of the PR industry defining & delivering on the promise of diversity*. White paper for The National Black Public Relations Society, 1–14. Retrieved from www.instituteforpr.org/state-pr-industry-defining-delivering-promise-diversity/.

Groeneveld, S., & Verbeek, S. (2012). Diversity policies in public and private sector organizations: An empirical comparison of incidence and effectiveness. *Review of Public Personnel Administration, 32*, 353–381.

Hewlett, S. A., Marshall, M., Sherbin, L., & Gonsalves, T. (2013). *Innovation, diversity, and market growth*. New York: Center for Talent Innovation.

Hon, L. C., & Brunner, B. (2000). Diversity issues and public relations. *Journal of Public Relations Research, 12*(4), 309–340.

Janis, I. L. (1982). *Groupthink: Psychological studies of policy decisions and fiascoes*. Boston, MA: Houghton Mifflin.

Miller, K. (2012). *Organizational Communication: Approaches and processes*. Boston, MA: Wadsworth.

Mor-Barak, M. E., & Cherin, D. (1998). A tool to expand organizational understanding of workforce diversity. *Administration in Social Work, 22*, 47–64.

Pless, N. M., & Maak, T. (2004). Building an inclusive diversity culture: Principles, processes, and practice. *Journal of Business Ethics, 54*, 129–147.

Public Relations Coalition (2005). *Focus on diversity: Lowering the barriers, raising the bar*. Public Relations Coalition 2005 Summit.

Sabattini, L., & Crosby, F. (2008). Overcoming resistance: Structures and attitudes. In K. M. Thomas (Ed.), *Diversity resistance in organizations* (pp. 273–301). New York: Lawrence Erlbaum.

Sabharwal, M. (2014). Is diversity management sufficient? Organizational inclusion to further performance. *Public Personnel Management, 43*(2), 1–21.

Samovar, L. A, & Porter, R. E. (1994). *Communication between cultures.* Belmont, CA: Wadsworth.

Samovar, L. A., Porter, R. E., & McDaniel, E. R. (2011). *Intercultural Communication: A reader.* Boston, MA: Cengage Learning.

Stewart, M. M., & Johnson, O. E. (2009). Leader–Member exchange as a moderator of the relationship between work group diversity and team performance. *Group & Organization Management, 34,* 507–535.

United Nations. (2017). *World Population Prospects: The 2017 Revision: Key findings and advance tables.* New York: New York City: United Nations.

University of Oregon. *Diversity Initiative.* Retrieved from http://gladstone.uoregon.edu/ ~asuomca/diversityinit/definition.html.

Whitman, W. (1900). *Leaves of Grass.* Philadelphia, PA (p. 308). David McKay.

Wilson, R. (2016 June). *Diversity and inclusion: The world won't wait for us.* PRWeek.com. Retrieved from www.prweek.com/article/1396460/diversity-inclusion-pr-world-wont-wait-us.

Chapter 16

Global Public Relations

The limits of my language mean the limits of my world.

(Ludwig Wittgenstein, 1922, p. 5)

Learning Objectives

To:

- Describe the three major reasons for the importance of global public relations.
- Understand what are multicultural, multinational, international, and global organizations.
- Describe what is global public relations.
- Understand and explain Hofstede's cultural dimensions.
- Describe how language can affect the way people think.
- Understand and describe ethical practices throughout the world.
- Understand how various environments impact the function of public relations.
- Explain the role and importance of activism to public relations.

Introduction

There are three major reasons contributing to the value of global public relations and strategic communication. First, the ease with which people can travel across countries spurred by relatively inexpensive modes of transportation has provided opportunities to interact and learn about people from around the world. According to the World Bank, in 2015, there were 1.36 billion international trips (The World Bank Group, 2017).

Second, the division of the global economy into organized regions of comparative advantage in which geographical areas specialize in certain economic activities owing to low costs and innovations, such as manufacturing in the Far East and professional services in North America, contribute to a highly interdependent world economy. In fact, as reported by the Woodrow Wilson International Center for Scholars (2009), the increased focus on innovation in Europe, China, India, and other areas assures constantly changing comparative advantages.

Last, the advent of social media points to the importance of global communication. People throughout the world are aware of what is happening in the far corners of the planet, participate in and support world events through social media, and learn what others experience. Social media serves as the communication hub and has facilitated regional social movements such as the Arab Spring, MoveOn.Org, Tea Party, Midwest Academy,

Figure 16.1 Communication Binds the World

Oxfam, various political candidates fundraising, and many other organizations, some of which started as movements, keeping the world aware through their activism efforts.

The common thread of these three trends is communication. In a world in which peoples are becoming more interdependent through physical or virtual connections, communication is the glue that binds us. Increased trade of all sorts, political coalitions, global causes, and the free flow of information continue to reinforce these relationships. Global organizations and public relations shape and play an important role in people communicating and shaping agendas on a worldwide scale.

What exactly does it mean to be global? Keep in mind that there are different levels of what constitutes a global organization (Stohl, 2001). A **multicultural** organization is one in which the organization primarily identifies with one country, but recognizes the value of a culturally diverse and inclusive workforce. Colleges and universities, Starbucks operating locally, and IBM are examples of multicultural organizations.

Next, there are **international organizations**. They have little to no foreign investments. They simply export and import products. They have no staff, warehouses, or sales offices in other countries. Walmart, Starbucks, and Spencer's are examples of international companies.

A **multinational** company focuses on national identity. It conducts business across multiple nations, manages a multinational workforce, and has global customers. A multinational organization invests in other countries; however, it does not coordinate product offerings in each country. Research and development take place in the country where the headquarters are located. Marketing focuses on adapting products and services to each individual local market. General Motors and Intuit are multinational companies.

Finally, we have a **global** organization. This type of company identifies as a global organization and being part of a global community rather than identifying with any single nation. Global organizations maintain worldwide operations necessary to produce, distribute, and market their brands. The organizational members are more important than any national loyalty. Direct foreign investment is typical. The organization has centralized decision-making.

Figure 16.2 Global Organizations Have Many Opportunities and Challenges.

The parent company conducts research and development. BMW is an example of a global company. Many of its ad campaigns emphasize "Made by BMW" rather than "Made in Germany." Other examples are Lenovo, Kellogg, Microsoft, ExxonMobil, BP, and Coca-Cola.

As we can see, as an organization moves from multicultural to global, its identification becomes widely defined.

How do these designations relate to what is global public relations? **Global public relations** is a process involving efforts to communicate directly or indirectly with publics and stakeholders across national boundaries and from different cultures to convey messages that are informative, persuasive, and activate target behavior through various tactics and activities. Global public relations faces geographical, cultural, political, legal, socioeconomic, and communication challenges that are unique in many ways (Culbertson & Jeffers, 1993). We will touch upon these challenges in this chapter.

What follows is a discussion of the various contextual factors relevant to the practice of global public relations. There are cultural, language, ethical, economic, political, legal, media, and activism considerations. These areas of concern constitute the situational analysis.

Cultural Dimensions

Hofstede (2010) developed a well-known framework for classifying national cultures. Based on his classification system, country segmentation occurs according to degree of power distance, individualism, masculinity, uncertainty avoidance, long-term orientation, and indulgence. The indexed categories are meaningful as a measure of comparison between two or more countries. The website: https://geert-hofstede.com/countries. html allows for country comparisons. What follows is a description of each component. Figure 16.4 summarizes the dimensions.

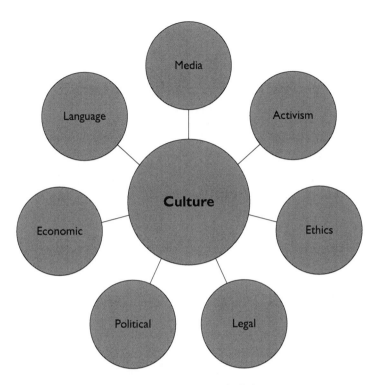

Figure 16.3 The Environments of Global Public Relations

Power Distance

Power distance is a cultural measure that indicates the degree to which the less power-ful members of a society anticipate and accept an unequal distribution of power in their society. Power can be political, economic, social, and religious. Cultures that accept a high degree of power distance accept a hierarchical power order. The acceptance of intrusion of various societal authorities into their lives as the natural order of things is unquestioned. This power dynamic is typically associated with centralized authority in which there is acknowledgment of a leader and disagreement is implicit at most.

On the other hand, those societies that possess a low degree of power distance, do not tolerate intrusion and question authority. These environments support distributed decision-making, delegation of authority and power, decentralized organizations, and local concerns. American citizens are less tolerant of intrusive authority compared to Portugal and South Korea.

Individualism (as Opposed to Collectivism)

High **individualistic** countries are places that possess a preference for loosely knit social structures. People are competitive and individualistic. The expectation is to focus on oneself and one's family. These societies encourage individual achievement and the questioning of authority and social issues.

Low levels of individualism represent **collectivism**, which is typically a tightly knit society that values cooperation and collective agreement. In exchange for loyalty, the larger social order cares for individuals and their relatives. People view themselves as part of something greater than themselves. This culture cherishes wisdom. These people frown upon negative feedback and lack of cooperation. The United States is high in individualism; whereas, Portugal and South Korea are relatively low and display more collectivist characteristics.

Masculinity (as Opposed to Femininity)

Competition, achievement, material acquisitions, heroism, assertiveness, and material rewards characterize a **masculine** culture. Opportunities, risks, and individual goal-setting drive these individuals.

The converse is femininity, which exemplifies cooperation, modesty, caring for the weak, and quality of life. Relationships and meaning are important as well as maintaining a work–life

Figure 16.4 Hofstede's Cultural Dimensions

balance. Negotiation, collaboration, and input from all levels drive success in this culture. The United States represents a more masculine society compared to Portugal and South Korea.

Uncertainty Avoidance

Uncertainty Avoidance is the degree to which individuals feel uncomfortable with uncertainty and ambiguity. The issue is how societies manage uncertainty. Cultures that demonstrate strong uncertainty avoidance support rigid codes of belief and behavior. They are intolerant of nonconformity. Unspoken cultural expectations typify this culture. Nations that possess weak uncertainty avoidance, display more flexibility in their attitudes and beliefs. To these people, titles are unimportant and results take precedence over process. Portugal and South Korea are less tolerant of uncertainty compared to the United States.

Long-Term Orientation (as Opposed to Short-Term Normative Orientation)

Nations that are **long-term oriented** are pragmatic. These cultures encourage thrift and modern education to prepare for the future. Solving problems in new and innovative ways are common. By the same token, cultures that are short-term focused seek to keep time-honored traditions and norms. Members of this type of society deem change to be suspicious. They have strong convictions. They treasure values and rights. South Korea has a long-term orientation. On the other hand, Portugal and the United States are more short-term focused.

Indulgence (as Opposed to Restraint)

Indulgence cultures center on personal achievement and satisfaction. Enjoying life and having fun are paramount. These individuals tend to be optimistic, engage in free speech, and focus on personal happiness. They value debate, feedback, and a work–life balance.

Low levels of indulgence activities are associated with societies that demonstrate restraint. These cultures suppress gratification and manage it with strict social norms. Controlled, they engage in rigid behaviors. They prefer to be formal and express displeasure in private. Portugal and South Korea are less prone to indulgences compared to the United States.

Sapir-Whorf Hypothesis: A Way of Looking at Language

Effective global communication requires understanding the culture of the audience. It requires understanding the language of the culture. The **Sapir-Whorf Hypothesis** is a framework for seeing the connections between how members of a culture think, feel, behave, and communicate in their world. According to the theory,

Human beings do not live in the objective world alone, nor alone in the world of social activity as ordinarily understood, but are very much at the mercy of the particular language which has become the medium of expression for their society. It is quite an illusion to imagine that one adjusts to reality essentially without the use of language and that language is merely an incidental means of solving problems of communication or reflection. The fact of the matter is that the 'real world' is to a large extent unconsciously built on the language habits of the group. No two languages are ever sufficiently similar to be considered as representing the same social reality. The worlds in which different societies live are distinct worlds, not merely the same world with different labels attached. We see and hear and otherwise experience very largely as we do because the language habits of our community predispose certain choices of interpretation.

(Whorf, 1956, p. 134)

Although it has critics, the hypothesis posits the influence of language on people. If this is indeed the case, then we can understand how members of a culture perceive the world by knowing their language and its structure. For example, Americans talk about time in different contexts. Maintaining a schedule is important and a key to success in the business world. It is central to American life and manifests itself in different contexts. Conversationally, people talk about physical distance in temporal terms. For instance, someone who asks how far is the local grocery store is likely to receive an answer such as "It's a 15-minute drive."

The Pirahã Tribe of the Amazon Rainforest has a language that only accommodates the present tense. Everything exists in the present for them. When something is no longer perceived, then it ceases to exist. The Pirahã have no need for history or remembering the past or telling stories. They are existential beings and live their lives as such.

As we can see, the effects of language on cognitions and behaviors are complex. Nonetheless, the characteristics of language tell us something about a society and what it values. The next section examines culture in a broader context.

Ethical Practices

Organizations such as the Center for Public Integrity, PR Watch, and Corporate Watch posit that public relations is essentially a propaganda arm of company marketing departments. Public relations advances its goals through lobbying and the spinning of stories in a manner that presents organizations in a favorable light. From a global perspective, national culture influences public relations ethics. Let's look at the practices of bribery and payments for news coverage.

Transparency International's 2011 Bribe Payers Survey (Hardoon & Heinrich, 2011) questioned more than 3,000 business executives in the world's largest 28 economies about their perceptions of business bribery. The study reported the top five countries whose companies were likely to be engaged in bribery overseas; the first listed as the most likely of all 28 nations, were:

Russia (1st)
China (2nd)
Mexico (3rd)
Indonesia (4th)
United Arab Emirates (5th).

The top five countries whose companies were least likely to engage in bribery in other countries were:

Netherlands (1st)
Switzerland (2nd)
Belgium (3rd)
Germany (4th)
Japan (5th).

The study found characteristics associated with the bribery index scores. Bribery among companies is just as likely as bribery between companies and public officials. Second, since 2008, there has been no change in perceptions about bribery. Third, expectations of bribery in a company's home country affects bribery activity overseas. If bribery is common at home, then the likelihood of those companies engaging in such behavior overseas is greater. Fourth, linked to the third point, the home country's laws about bribery affect overseas practices. Last, bribery is most prevalent in the public works and construction industries.

Commissioned by the Institute for Public Relations, The International Public Relations Association (Kruckeberg & Tsetsura, 2003) developed and tested an index that assessed the likelihood of "cash for news coverage" paid to newspaper media. The index ranked 66 countries from high ranking, indicating the payment is nonexistent to low ranking, denoting the increased existence of payment for media coverage. The countries selected were based on their "global economic and political importance and—to some extent—the availability of reliable data for variables in the index" (p. 3).

The highest ranked nations were:

Finland (1st)
Denmark (2nd)
New Zealand (3rd)
Switzerland (4th)
Germany (5th).

The lowest ranked nations were:

Pakistan (62nd)
Bangladesh (63rd)
Vietnam (64th)
Saudi Arabia (65th)
China (66th).

The Center for International Media Assistance monitors and collects data about media bribery.

Economic Environment

The economic climate shapes public relations activities based on the nature of the marketplace (Duhe & Sriramesh, 2009; Sriramesh & Vercic, 2009). The following questions examine the economic system.

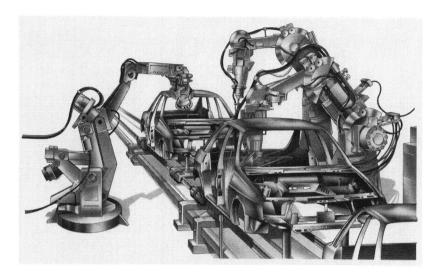

Figure 16.5 Knowing How Economic Trends Impact People Is Important

1   What is the primary purpose of the economy? Is it open to the outside world? If so, what are the key constraints? Is it in transition?
2   What is the level of economic development?
3   How sophisticated is the economic infrastructure? Can it support public relations efforts? Are roads, the power grid, other forms of transportation, the labor force, and technologies adequate and scalable?
4   What is the extent of the private sector's influence on public policy?
5   What is the relationship between industry and the public sector?
6   To what extent are specific sectors regulated? What might be the effect on public relations?
7   What role do unions and collective bargaining play in the economy?
8   Is corporate social responsibility valued? Who is primarily responsible for the welfare of the public?
9   What is the poverty rate?

Political and Legal Environments

The political and legal environments impact and set parameters on public relations activities. Sriramesh and Vercic (2009) suggest the following considerations which comprise the political context in which public relations operates.

1   What is the political structure? Is it democratic, authoritarian, theocratic, totalitarian, or some other form?
2   Are diverse political perspectives and parties allowed?
3   Are people allowed to express their political views?
4   What role do governmental institutions play in the political process? Are there checks and balances?

5   Do advocates have opportunities to impact public policies?
6   How influential and independent is the judiciary system?
7   Is the media regulated and, if so, how so?

The following three examples speak to Point 7.

Three Examples

Some public relations and advertising practitioners call for the standardization or centralization of strategy and planning – a one size fits all perspective. They emphasize cost-effectiveness, degree of control, and the opportunity to create unified brand equity. The assumptions are that everyone embraces consumerism, wants better lives for themselves and their families, and wants to be "appealing" (Frith, 2003). Yet, is this homogenization of cultures approach an effective public relations strategy?

According to Frith (2003), five major political systems dominate the world. They are the libertarian-capitalist (United States), socialist-capitalist (Great Britain, much of Europe, Australia, and Canada), authoritarian-capitalist (Brazil, Thailand, Mexico, and Malaysia), sectarian-authoritarian capitalist (Saudi Arabia and Iran), and totalitarian-semi-capitalist (Vietnam and China).

These systems manage advertising and public relations differently. In the United States, the advertising industry is largely self-regulated. In Great Britain, much of Europe, Australia, and Canada, regulators direct their efforts to encourage responsible advertising and public relations. In Brazil, Thailand, Mexico, and Malaysia, regulations assure that marketing communications is consistent with the sociocultural and political systems of the country. Saudi Arabia and Iran control the media so that they maintain standards in line with social control and religious rules. Last, Vietnam and China allow advertising that does not place the government in a negative light.

Keep in mind that cultures and the introduction of different ways of conducting business change including evolving regulatory practices. With that said, let's delve into the regulatory worlds of Japan, Vietnam, and Malaysia (Frith, 2001, 2003).

In Japan, for the most part, the advertising and public relations sectors are self-regulated. Japanese culture places importance on saving face and peer reliance. It is a strong culture that shows disdain for violations of norms and cultural expectations. Advertisers comply with custom and implicit rules predicated upon Japanese cultural values and beliefs. Advertisers who violate these cultural norms are shamed, which is a powerful form of punishment in Japan. For example, challenging competitive brands must be indirect because not doing so violates codes of respect and decency.

Currently, the Japan Advertising Review Organization, a self-regulatory body, polices all advertising in Japan. The structure has become more formalized over the years. It investigates claims about unjustifiable charges and misleading representations in ads, which potentially do not abide by the provisions of the Japanese Consumer Protection Fundamental Act.

Vietnam (Frith, 2001) requires multinational companies to establish alliances whether a joint-venture or joint-partnership with domestic companies to assure the preservation of Vietnamese identity and culture in the marketplace. Other regulations protect the Vietnamese national language and culture. For instance, all ads must be in Vietnamese and must be consistent with the country's public morals and customs. Ads must portray

Figure 16.6 Political Institutions Impact Organizations and Their Activities

Vietnamese lifestyles and not those of other countries. The country forbids sexually explicit or suggestive ads. These regulations exist today.

Malaysia maintains a strong religion-based system of advertising regulation. It is a multicultural society that allows international advertising firms to operate. In 1977, The Advertising Standards Advisory, an independent body in Malaysia, regulated advertising practices. Ads must reflect Malaysian culture and identity as well as be "legal, decent, honest, and truthful" (Frith, 2003, p. 200). There is a proscription on ads offensive to religion, either explicitly or implicitly. Commercials, which regulators must approve, cannot present foreign cultural values, beliefs, and symbols. The government requires all commercial production to take place in Malaysia.

Think about This . . .

In a 2016 article entitled, "Updating the Generic/Specific Theory of International Public Relations: More Factors to Consider When Practicing in New Markets" published on the *Institute for Public Relations* website, Alaimo discusses a study that she conducted in which she interviewed 74 global public relations practitioners from 31 countries. The goal of the study was to learn what global public relation strategies were used and what factors came into play when strategizing and planning.

The framework of the study was Verčič, Grunig, and Grunig's Generic/Specific Theory which holds that political-economic systems, cultures, extent of activism, levels of development, and media systems inform the practice of public relations in a new country.

Alaimo added two additional factors to the mix: social expectations and local influencers. Social Expectations – local peoples' expectations of organizations vary in different countries and even within countries. Local Influencers – opinion leaders, who can be critical to the success of a public relations campaign, vary by country and culture, as well as within countries. These considerations help practitioners identify key publics and design appropriate messages important to the success of the campaign.

Ask yourself? Can you think of sharp contrasts between two countries? Are there similarities as well? Think about specific examples.

Alaimo, K. (2016). Updating the generic/specific theory of international public relations: More factors to consider when practicing in new markets. *Institute for Public Relations.* Retrieved from www.instituteforpr.org/updating-genericspecific-theory-international-public-relations-factors-consider-practicing-new-markets/.

Media Environment

The media is a key public and critical to the flow of information. They provide publicity through news coverage and issue engagement. Although there are similarities, the role of media varies across national boundaries. Sriramesh and Vercic (2009) conceptualize media in three clusters.

Media control

1   Are the media part of the private or public sector? If it is public, is it directly or indirectly controlled by the government?
2   Are various media outlets associated with a specific political party or theocracy?
3   What is the degree of editorial freedom?
4   What is the media infrastructure? What is the level of competition?
5   What is the role of media in the country? Generally, are they perceived as credible?
6   Are the laws that protect the media effective?
7   Do the media practitioners have professional standards? Are they accredited? Are they self-regulated or does government play a central role in managing them?
8   Are there any public relations professional associations? If so, what role do they play in public relations?

Media diffusion

1   Do the media effectively inform the public? Are there barriers? If so, what are they?
2   Which medium platforms are most effective and popular, especially digital media?
3   Does the national infrastructure support media activities?
4   What is the penetration of media vehicles in society?
5   What is the illiteracy rate?

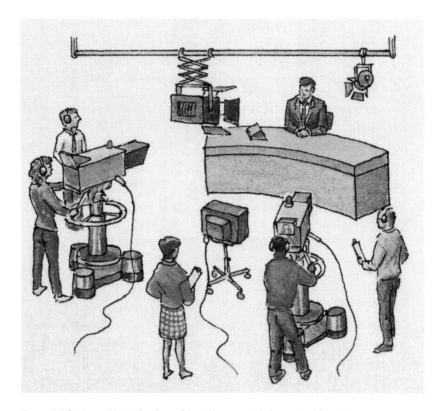

Figure 16.7 News Media Perform Surveillance and Information Functions

Media access

1   What percentage of the population has access to media?
2   Are there gatekeepers between the media and organizations? If so, what are these relationships?
3   How do the media prefer to operate when acquiring and disseminating information?

The responses to these questions will provide valuable information necessary for public relations planning.

Activism

Kim and Sriramesh (2009) define **activism** as:

> The coordinated effort of a group that organizes voluntarily in an effort to solve problems that threaten the common interest of members of the group. In the process of problem solving, core members of the group attract other social constituents or publics, create and maintain a shared collective identity among members for the time

being, and mobilize resources and power to influence the problem-causing entity's decision or action through communicative action such as education, negotiation, persuasion, pressure tactics or force.

(p. 82)

This description equates with the definition of a public. In an open society, the role of activism plays an important role in shaping public opinion. The degree to which businesses practices ethical behavior, the economic structure, the political and legal environment, and the media situation impacts activism and, at the same time, activism influence these factors. With these considerations in mind, the interaction between public relations and activism necessitates addressing the following questions.

1   What has been the role of activism in the past? Has it been effective?
2   Currently, what is the nature of activism? Does it involve nongovernmental organizations? Does it involve special interest groups?
3   What tools do organizations use to address activism directed at them?
4   What level of technology do activists use?

Why All of These Environmental Questions?

Activism can thrive in conducive cultural, economic, political, legal, and media environments. Public relations is a boundary spanning endeavor. In other words, it relies on the two-way flow of information and exchange of ideas in a give and take dynamic. Activism is the mechanism that creates this dynamic and the necessary conditions for public relations to exist. Pluralistic societies and "freedom of the press" are conditions required for public relations to flourish. The answers to all the questions put forth above in the environmental

Figure 16.8 Passionate Activists Are a Potent Force in Society

sections paint a picture of a society, what kind of public relations exists in that society, and what public relations *can* exist in that society.

A Few Examples

United Kingdom. The United Kingdom consists of Great Britain and Northern Ireland. These people are generally skeptical and suspicious. British communication makes use of irony and understatement. Arguments bring issues to the public forefront. There is a great deal of freedom of speech to the point where some subcultures find it disconcerting. The British public relations sector thrives in this environment. The culture is sophisticated and sensitive to an array of messages.

Italy. Local communities are important in Italy. In northern Italy, the nuclear family lives together. However, in southern Italy, the extended family often resides together. Impressions are important to Italians. Appearance conveys status. In line with appearances, Italians prefer face-to-face contact. They typically are extremely expressive communicators. They tend to be loquacious, eloquent, emotional, and demonstrative. The local newspapers are a valued source of information for them. In Italy, public relations is viewed as supporting marketing and advertising. During the 1990s a series of public relations scandals plagued Italy leading to an increase in professional standards and regulation.

Germany. Germans value privacy and individualism. The society is moving toward an information and knowledge-based economy, which is conducive to messaging, information, and public relation in general. There are essentially two cultures within Germany. First, there are those individuals who subscribe to the traditional structure of family and relationships in which men and women assume traditional roles. Then there are those more individualistic people who do not fit the traditional roles, many of whom reside in single family households. Within the growing second group, there is less homogeneity. Public relations activities targeting this group are more effective.

Sweden. Transparency is important in Sweden. Openness and no censorship are critical and valued, especially in the media. Swedes are egalitarian and humble. They speak softly and calmly. Swedish culture values expressing gratitude and not taking anything for granted. They believe that virtue stands in the middle. Swedish culture does not promote competition. They are punctual and agenda driven. The Swedish culture values direct and explicit communication. Swedes are suspicious of public relations because they equate it with manipulation and propaganda. They prefer the term strategic communication.

Russia. Russians perceive public relations as the propaganda arm of those in power, particularly individuals in political positions. This has become known as "Black PR." On the other hand, "White PR" is associated with ethical, symmetrical public relations. In Russia, information dissemination is fractured and lacks a national focus. This may be due to media self-censorship because of governmental pressure to manipulate them. Moreover, what constitutes public relations in Russia varies. To some, it is marketing, advertising, or propaganda. Different groups within the country value different aspects of public relations.

China. China has over 1.3 billion people. The Chinese view foreign visitors as representing their nationality rather than as individuals. Communication is formal, especially when interacting with someone of higher rank. Chinese people prefer face-to-face meetings. There is a separation between business tasks and social activities. There is no discussion of business during meals and social events.

Although often associated as a marketing function, public relations in China is new and constantly changing. The growth of public relations in China is attributable to an increase

Figure 16.9 Cultures are Diverse, but They Also Share Similarities. What Are Some Similarities?

in state-owned media outlets, advances in communication technologies, and international trends. Virtually all the demand for public relations comes from the private sector adapting Western methods and realizing the importance of corporate image building. Occasionally, the Chinese government has commissioned public relation agencies on an ad hoc basis to manage issues or mitigate negative publicity.

India. India has over 1.2 billion people, second only to China. Family values are important in India. Family relationships permeate business and professional life. The business environment is largely paternalistic. Indian culture has a caste system in which people are born into a social class that also impacts their personal and professional lives. The four major groups are: Brahmins, Kshatriyas, Vaishyas, and Shudras. Brahmins are teachers and intellectuals; Kshatriyas are the military and political leaders; Vaishyas are the business people; and Shudras are regular workers. With a labor force over 510 million, the Indian economy is experiencing rapid growth exceeding 7% per annum. Respecting a person's personal space is important in India. Communication is often implicit, including gestures and vocal paralanguage. Although new to India, the competition among public relations firms is intense and there is some trending toward specialization.

Global Public Relations Best Practices

Effective internal communication supports a successful public relations campaign focused on external publics. Implementing best practices increases the likelihood of desirable outcomes.

The following practices are by perspective, communication, and organizational interaction (Some of them are adopted from Conrad & Poole, 2012; Kealey, 2000; and Wilcox, Cameron, Ault, & Agee, 2005).

Perspective

1   Learn about the culture in question.
2   Be nonjudgmental of other's values, beliefs, and attitudes.
3   Recognize the influence of one's own perceptions and knowledge.
4   Avoid ethnocentric thinking and behavior. Sometimes, there is more than one way to look at or do something.
5   Be empathic in both thinking and feelings, which will increase one's understanding of organizational members from other cultures.
6   Be flexible about deadlines. In some culture, time has different meaning and is not as important as it is in other countries.
7   Know that understanding another culture's customs is not always clear; thus, be able to tolerate ambiguity and differences. For example, during a weekend conference, American and Canadian employees of the same company were asked what gave them the most job satisfaction. The American employees mentioned increased company profits and the Canadian employees reported customer satisfaction. At this weekend meeting, they were all invited to attend a Boston Celtics basketball game. The American employees did not understand why their Canadian counterparts were not as excited as they were about the event. Later, a Canadian employee commented that hockey is to Canadians what basketball, football, and baseball are to Americans.
8   Discover commonalities with members of the host country. People that share something in common, may very well share other things in common.

Communication

1   Verbally and nonverbally, communicate respect for the culture of the host nation. In some cases, languages have nuanced differences such as the different versions of English or Spanish. Being mindful of these differences and conveys an appreciation of the host culture and people.
2   Demonstrate that a speaker is important by being a good listener (do not simply hear) and clearly communicate any concerns to the speaker.
3   When communicating, be clear but sensitive to customs. It is better to have too many details rather than too few and risk miscommunication.
4   When there is the opportunity, use multiple forms of communication. This mitigates misunderstanding.
5   Some cultures tend to be emotional when communicating, while others are less so and rely only on the presentations of facts and evidence. Do not misinterpret an emotional exchange as confrontational or an unemotional response as apathy.
6   Some cultures communicate indirectly, which requires an interpretation of the message. Implicit communication is often cultural and does not represent indecisiveness or an attempt to obfuscate. Asian cultures practice implicit communication. Read between the lines and respond accordingly.

7   In some cultures, form takes precedent over function. In many cultures, interacting is social with a small fraction of time devoted to the "purpose" of the meeting. This is typically the case in Arab cultures. Be patient when interacting in such situations.

8   The term "multinationals" has a disparaging connotation in some cultures. Use more collegial expressions for organizational members from other countries.

9   Avoid using culture specific terms that can be confusing such as blue-collar, white-collar, high-five, and so forth.

10   Try to avoid using abbreviations and acronyms (e.g. TGIF, or OMG).

Organizational

1   The level of infrastructure and development of public relations can vary by organization and country. Plan accordingly.

2   Generally, a global organization has a longer chain of command (red tape) than one with a less expansive reach. Be flexible and plan accordingly.

3   With all the communication technologies and tools available, global teams are often more practical and allow for diverse perspectives. Take advantage of these viewpoints. Note that individuals may work in different time zones, which affects live-meeting availability.

Summary of Key Concepts

- Global public relations is increasingly important because of greater global transportation, economic competitive advantage, and advances in communication technologies.
- The degree to which companies are global is based on whether they are multicultural, multinational, international, or global.
- Global public relations is complex owing to various environmental factors.
- Levels of power distance, individualism, masculinity, uncertainty avoidance, long-term orientation, and indulgence define and differentiate a country.
- A nation's language can affect how its people perceive, think, and feel about situations and issues.
- Countries develop reputations about their ethical practices which impact how their companies conduct business overseas.
- Public relations requires certain conditions to flourish.
- The level of activism influences public relations.
- Best practices optimize public relation effectiveness.

Key Terms

Chapter Questions

16.1   What are the three major contributing factors to growth in global public relations?

16.2   Define a multicultural organization and provide an example.

16.3   What is a multinational company and offer an example?

16.4   Define an international organization and provide an example.

16.5   What is a global company an offer an example?

16.6   What is global public relations?

16.7   What environments play a role in shaping public relations in a country?

16.8   What is power distance and provide an example?

16.9   Define a highly individualistic society and offer an example.

16.10   What is a masculine country and offer an example?

16.11   What is uncertainty avoidance and provide an example?

16.12   Define a long-term orientation culture and offer an example.

16.13   Define indulgence as a cultural attribute and offer an example.

16.14   Define the Sapir-Whorf Hypothesis and provide an example.

16.15   What characteristics are associated with bribery in countries?

16.16   Provide three questions about a country's economic environment that are relevant to public relations.

16.17   Provide five questions about a country's political and legal environments that are relevant to public relations.

16.18   What are the five major political systems that dominate the world? Provide examples of countries.

16.19   Provide six considerations about a country's media environment that are relevant to public relations.

16.20   Define activism.

16.21   Provide four questions about a country's activism environment that are relevant to public relations.

16.22   Why are the various environments important to activism and public relations?

16.23   Indicate eight global public relations best practices.

References

Alaimo, K. (2016). Updating the Generic/Specific Theory of International Public Relations: More Factors to Consider When Practicing in New Markets. *Institute for Public Relations.* Retrieved from www.instituteforpr.org/updating-genericspecific-theory-international-public-relations-factors-consider-practicing-new-markets/.

Conrad, C., & Poole, M. S. (2012). *Strategic organizational communication in a global economy.* Malden, MA: Wiley-Blackwell.

Culbertson, H. M., & Jeffers, D. W. (1993). *Social, political, and economic contexts in public relations: Theory and cases.* Routledge Communication Series. New York: Routledge.

Duhe, S. C., & Sriramesh, K. (2009). Political economy and public relations. In K. Sriramesh & D. Vercic (Eds.), *The global public relations handbook: Theory, research, and practice* (pp. 22–46). New York: Routledge.

Frith, K. T. (2001). Cultural regulation and advertising in ASEAN: an analysis of Singapore and Vietnam. In B. Moeran (Ed.), *Asian media production* (pp. 75–88). London: Routledge Curzon Press.

Frith, K. T. (2003). International Advertising and Global Consumer Culture. In K. Anokwa, M. Salwen, & C. Lin (Eds.), *International communication: Concepts and cases* (pp. 190–204). Belmont, CA: Wadsworth Publishing.

Hardoon, D., & Heinrich, F. (2011). *Bribe payers index 2011*. Berlin: Transparency International.

Hofstede, G., Hofstede, G. J., & Minkov, M. (2010). *Cultures and organizations: Software of the mind*. New York City: McGraw-Hill.

Kealey, D. L. (2000). A study of Canadian technical advisors overseas. Canadian Foreign Service Institute. Department of Foreign Affairs and International Trade.

Kim, J. N., & Sriramesh, K. (2009). Activism and public relation. In K. Sriramesh & D. Vercic (Eds.), *The global public relations handbook: Theory, research, and practice* (pp. 79–100). New York City: Routledge.

Kruckeberg, D., & Tsetsura, K. (2003). *International index of bribery for news coverage*. Gainesville, FL: Institute for Public Relations. Retrieved from www.instituteforpr.org/files/uploads/Bribery_Index_2003.pdf.

Sriramesh, K., & Vercic, D. (2009). A theoretical framework for global public relations research and practice. In K. Sriramesh & D. Vercic (Eds.), *The global public relations handbook: Theory, research, and practice* (pp. 2–21). New York City: Routledge.

Stohl, C. (2001). Globalizing organizational communication. In F. M. Jabin & L. L. Putnam (Eds.), *The new handbook of organizational communication: Advances in theory, research, and methods* (pp. 323–375). Thousand Oaks, CA: Sage.

The World Bank Group. (2017). *International tourism, number of departures*. Retrieved from https://data.worldbank.org/indicator/ST.INT.DPRT.

Whorf, B. L. (1956). *Language, thought, and reality*. Ed. J. B. Carroll. New York: Wiley.

Wilcox, D. L., Cameron, G. T., Ault, P. H., & Agee, W. K. (2005). *Public relations: Strategies and tactics*. New York: Allyn & Bacon.

Wittgenstein, L. (1922). *Logico-philosophical treatise*. New York: Harcourt, Brace.

Chapter 17

Women in Strategic Communications

On my own I will just create, and if it works, it works, and if it doesn't, I'll create something else. I don't have any limitations on what I think, I could do, or be.

(Oprah Winfrey, Forbes, 1995, p. 70)

Introduction

I had the fortunate opportunity to interview and profile five incredibly dynamic and successful women in careers where public relations or strategic communication play an important role. Their backgrounds and professions vary, but they share similarities as well. They are in the business of connecting with publics and stakeholders in different ways.

Their individual and professional stories serve to inspire the student practitioner about what is achievable in the field of public relations and, more broadly, strategic communications. These professionals are Carmen Baez, founder of PRxPR Fund and former President of DAS Latin America-Omnicom Group; Carlie Danielson, Strategy Lead at fuseproject; D. Josiane Lee, Recruitment Outreach Officer at the U.S. Department of State; Karen van Bergen, Chief Executive Officer of Omnicom Public Relations Group; and Lily Vautour, Social Media Manager at Boston Children's Hospital. Let's learn about these remarkable women and what they do. I hope they spark you as they did me!

Carmen Baez: Engendering Intrapreneurship on a Global Scale

Carmen Baez founded and leads PRxPR, a non-partisan, private, no-overhead fund dedicated to rebuilding Puerto Rico after the destruction brought by Hurricane Maria. Ms. Baez was President of Diversified Agency Services (DAS) Latin America-Omnicom Group located in New York City. She was responsible for Mexico, Central America, the Caribbean, and South America markets focusing on all areas of marketing, including advertising, public relations, healthcare communication, customer relationship management, events, promotional marketing, branding, and research firms. Her clients were in the entertainment, financial services, high tech, telecommunications, and travel industries. Prior to DAS Latin America, she was managing partner of Baez-Zahorsky and President of Rapp Collins Worldwide. Carmen holds a bachelor's in marketing communication and an honorary doctorate from Simmons University. She served on numerous boards including Simmons University Board of Trustees and is currently a member of the Board of the Puerto Rico Conservation Trust.

Ms. Baez was a consultant for Omnicom Group from 1994 to 1996. From 1997 to 2013, she served as President of DAS Latin America Omnicom where she developed Omnicom's presence in Latin America including the United States Latina/o markets. At the time, Omnicom Group had virtually no operations or affiliates in Latin America. She found, vetted, and acquired companies that were a good fit for the Omnicom Group. Additionally, she collaborated with communications professionals to build marketing communications awareness through the establishment of professional associations, networks, affiliations, a host of other activities, and the introduction of best practices designed to improve support for marketing communications in the Latin American market.

Carmen developed a growth strategy that fell into three buckets. First, she had to grow DAS in her massive territory. She found new partners through acquisitions and exclusive affiliations. Second, she had to assure that DAS and its partners were profitable. Although she was not involved with day-to-day operations, Carmen provided strategic guidance such as best practices and access to various businesses that might contribute to cost-efficiencies. Like Omnicom, she embraced an "intrapreneurship" for working with member organizations in which the various Omnicom firms behaved as independent entities while under the organization's umbrella. She provided support and various resources to firms who knew their markets and how best to develop them. To paraphrase Carmen, *Intrapreneurship is the DNA of Omnicom* (C. Baez, personal interview, October 30, 2017). The third bucket was business development. She connected partners with potential clients through Omnicom's extensive global network. For example, Carmen was the single point of contact for Procter and Gamble (P&G) in Latin America. This meant that should any Procter and Gamble division require any marketing communications services in Latin America, they would consult Carmen, who would connect them with a partner that would meet their needs. This process served P&G, the local partner, and DAS.

By 2013, DAS Omnicom had ownership in or affiliations with 100 of the largest marketing communication firms in the region. Moreover, the marketplace became aware of the value of having a professional marketing communications industry and support infrastructure. For example, Porter Novelli Brazil grew from 30 to 350 employees. Presently, DAS Omnicom comprises over 200 companies with 700 offices in 71 countries.

Over the years, Carmen Baez observed the marketing communications industry increasingly fueled by technology involving precise and timely assessment through analytics and cost-efficient planning and execution in a dynamic marketplace. This led to marketing communications organizations constantly reinventing themselves in the wake of shifting business models and new ways to communicate. She likens the industry as, "Constructing an airplane while it's flying 1,000 miles per hour" (C. Baez, personal interview, October 30, 2017).

I found a 2013 article containing segments of an interview with Carmen Baez. Cristina Martinez asked her what advice would she give individuals seeking a career in communications. Carmen responded, "Learn collaboration and at least the fundamentals of talent management. Be humble and be nice. Remember, the people you see on your way up, will see you on your way down" (Martinez, 2013, March 5, para 15–16). Carmen has found tremendous reward working and collaborating with professionals in her field. She especially enjoyed discovering marketing communications intrapreneurs and with them building their enterprise and the public relations industry in their respective areas.

Since retiring from DAS, Carmen has focused on perfecting the art of beach bumming. In addition to her PRxPR work, she spends eight months of the year on the beach at her homes in Puerto Rico and Cape Cod, Massachusetts.

Carlie Danielson: Bringing Ideas to Life through Strategy

Carlie Danielson is Strategy Lead at fuseproject in San Francisco. Some of her clients are Samsung and PayPal. Prior to fuseproject, Ms. Danielson was Senior Analyst at Marshall Strategy where she served clients such as U.C. Berkeley, U.C. San Francisco, Caltech, Georgetown University, Blackboard, VMware, and LinkedIn. She held various communications roles prior to transitioning to the strategy and design industry. Carlie earned her bachelor's degree from Georgetown University and a masters in integrated marketing communication from Northwestern University, as well as a certificate in social marketing from the University of South Florida.

As a brand strategist at Marshall Strategy, Carlie incorporated research to develop extensive brand strategies drawing on her critical thinking skills to connect the dots uncovering the big picture. In her words, "The process was abstract and, at times, an academic exercise because the outputs of our work were not tangible" (C. Danielson, personal interview, September 21, 2017). Although achieving a litany of successes, she needed something more, which she found at fuseproject.

At fuseproject, new clients tend to be small start-ups focused on physical technologies, many coming from the MIT Idea Lab. Other clients are existing large companies in the software, and hardware industries. As strategy lead, Carlie ensures that user needs are top-of-mind throughout the design process from product and service development to the creation of the big selling idea. Design strategy starts after profiling market segments including identifying user needs and wants. To paraphrase Carlie: *We test ideas before bringing them to life. Whether it is a product or service, I see to it that a good idea moves to physical propagation. And, at some point during the latter half of this process, the client starts developing marketing strategies* (C. Danielson, personal interview, September 21, 2017). Depending on client needs, Carlie's teams provide product mark-ups or examples of visual messaging, which serve as strategy-based guides.

Research from informal searches to qualitative ethnographies, to trend analysis inform her design decision-making. Carlie deploys marketing research firms to run ethnographic studies targeting specific market segments sometimes collecting information from interviews; journals, in which study participants record their activities, purchasing habits, and items that they keep at home; and shadowing individuals who exemplify the market segment. These types of studies gather behavioral information about target market members in their natural environments. She distills research findings into actionable guidelines so that graphic, industrial, and user-oriented designers develop products likely to do well in the marketplace. To gauge effectiveness and inspire future design, Carlie encourages her clients to conduct marketing assessments at key milestones. Although her clients target an array of diverse populations, the focus is moving more and more towards Millennials and aging populations, two segments with growing purchasing power.

At Marshall Strategy, she primarily developed brand strategies. At fuseproject, her strategy work supports the development of graphic, digital, and industrial design; and requires understanding and connecting with consumers at an emotional level. Her satisfaction comes from positive consumer and industry analyst feedback about the products and service she helped develop as well as knowing that consumers buy and own these products. Carlie further thrives on the human connection between her and her professional teams of graphic, digital, and industrial designers, who bring a diversity of ideas to the product development table. As she enthusiastically put it: "Working across disciplines, everyone learns new things and new ways of looking at these things" (C. Danielson, personal interview, September 21, 2017). Her clients, the consumers, and colleagues provide her with an enriching career, and, the same time, she delivers tremendous value to them. She clearly is passionate about her work.

Carlie Danielson knows the reification process. She takes ideas and brings them to life. She embraces the abstract and makes it concrete. Her design achievements have become part of people's lives, which is what drives her. In the future, she plans to continue these connections in new and exciting ways.

D. Josiane Lee: Building Relationships through Outreach Public Relations

D. Josiane "Josie" Lee is a Recruitment Outreach Officer at the U.S. Department of State. She travels nationwide to high schools, colleges, and universities to promote opportunities at the Department of State and Foreign Service. Ms. Lee served in various U.S. Embassies and Consulates in the Bureau of Consular Affairs and Human Resources in Germany, Peru, Addis Ababa, and Ethiopia. She holds two bachelor's degrees, one in human resources administration from the University of Phoenix and a second in accounting and international business management from Agitel Superior School of Technology in Abidjan, Republic of Côte d'Ivoire. She also earned her Professional Certificate in Human Resources Management/Personnel Administration from the HR Certification Institute.

Josie Lee was born and raised in the Republic of Côte d'Ivoire, which is a country of 24 million inhabitants located on the Atlantic coast of West Africa. Her story at the U.S. Department of State began in 2006 when her spouse joined the U.S. Foreign Service and received notice that he would serve in Canada. She left her position in the pharmaceutical industry to support her family. During this time, she became acquainted with the Department of State Family Members employment program, a program designed to encourage family members of the foreign service to apply and work for the State Department, which she did and has thrived there for over the last 8 years, traveling extensively as well as accepting assignments at the State Department headquarters in Washington, D.C.

Currently, she is one of ten recruitment outreach officers and 16 domestic diplomats in residence at the State Department, an organization with nearly 70,000 members in Washington and at 275 embassies and consulate offices worldwide. Her charge is to identify and establish relationships with talented candidates for Foreign Service Officer, Foreign Service Specialist, and Civil Service positions as well as internship opportunities at home and abroad.

There is no typical day for Josie. Her duties are wide ranging. She hosts the State Department booth at career fairs; holds information sessions; visits high schools, colleges, and universities; organizes discussion panels with civil servants and foreign service employee for visiting students; assists public relations in granting interviews; arranges tours for media representatives; and maintains a social media presence. A key attribute to her success is flexibility and a desire to share what the State Department offers someone committed to serving her country. Josie often shares her success story, her experiences representing the United States overseas, and how she is living her dream of being in public service and doing good.

Much of Ms. Lee's activities are public relations functions. She maintains relationships with several internal and external stakeholders. Through the various exchange programs offered by the State Department, she establishes and maintains relationships with high school students. This program exposes students to international affairs and different cultures with the intention to generate interest in the foreign service. Moreover, the career services offices at universities and colleges are also stakeholders where outreach provides employment opportunities and internship openings. Josie and her colleagues mentor college and university students keeping track of their progress and providing internship and other State Department opportunities to them. Upon graduation from college, she guides them to career opportunities while looking for "good fits."

Josie as well as the State Department are committed to diversity and inclusion. To paraphrase her: *Because the State Department is the face of America, we are committed to having our people represent the changing demographics of our country both domestically and abroad* (D. J. Lee, personal interview, January 19, 2017). She reaches out to various organizations to inform them of career opportunities. She and her team members have built relationships with People of Color, Latina/o, Asian, Native American, LGBTQ, Veterans and other groups. She also focuses on outreach to women who are MBAs, physicians, other healthcare professionals, engineers, and IT specialists.

Josie's commitment to inclusion extends to her internal stakeholders. She facilitates affinity groups for employees with different backgrounds and perspectives. These groups network, are aware of career opportunities and openings, have mentors, and share experiences and expertise.

Over the last 12 years, Josie Lee has seen two major changes that she has come to embrace. In the past, foreign service recruitment focused on older, experienced individuals seeking a career change. In a labor market with ever increasing private sector competition for talented human capital, the State Department directs outreach toward younger, just out of college professionals. This leads to the second major shift, which is the growth and usage of social media to communicate, share information, and build networks. Just as younger people grew up exposed to social media, the State Department sees platforms such as Facebook, Twitter, Instagram, LinkedIn, and others as outreach and relationship building tools.

Josie is passionate about sharing her story and how others can achieve their career dreams. Her goal is to make others aware of the opportunities at the State Department. In the future, she sees herself doing foreign service tours of duty sharing American values and culture, learning about new cultures, and helping those in her capacity as a diplomat. When she retires, she wants to mentor women to empower them to achieve their potential through education and knowledge acquisition; she wants to help them achieve their dreams.

Karen van Bergen: Follow Your Intuition and See Challenges as Opportunities

Karen van Bergen is the CEO of Omnicom Public Relations Group, employing over 6,300 public relations specialists in over 385 offices throughout the world with headquarters in New York City. Prior to Omnicom, Ms. van Bergen served as CEO and Senior Partner at Porter Novelli as well as Senior Vice-President at FleishmanHillard. Additionally, she's held numerous top leadership positions at McDonald's Europe including Chief of Staff to the President and Vice-President for Corporate Affairs. She also held executive management and directorship positions at The Coca-Cola Company, Outboard Marine Corporation, and Van Luyken Public Relations. She is listed on PRWeek's Power List for 2013–2017, including the number one ranking in 2017, the first woman to ever achieve that rank. Karen was named PRWeek's Hall of Femme for 2016 and received the PR Professional of the Year award in 2016. Karen earned a master's degree in law and political science at Leiden University, the Netherlands.

Karen started her career at Van Luyken Public Relations and Public Affairs, at the time, the largest public relations firm in the Netherlands. At the age of 25, she made a plan to open a new office for the agency in Brussels, securing commitment from three clients to serve as the office's starting revenue foundation. The office was profitable from the start. Karen used her education in political science and law to navigate the political landscape and provide strategic counsel to her clients. According to her, "With the rise of the EU, it was an exciting time to introduce strategic communications innovations" (K. van Bergen, personal interview, December 5, 2017). She learned the value of developing new and creative solutions to challenges.

Karen left Van Luyken to start her own consultancy. She was highly successful, but she missed the interpersonal interaction that made her thrive at the agency level. As a water sports enthusiast, she accepted a position at Outboard Marine Corporation, a global producer of motor boats, engines, and accessories, as Director of Corporate Affairs. Men dominated the industry and as a woman, Karen was underestimated. She mastered the product and brand lines, enabling her to help the company outmaneuver the competition and build good relations with all stakeholders. However, the company hit difficult times. Throughout, Karen helped the company communicate openly and transparently, assuring that all stakeholders were aware of the company's position.

After leaving Outboard Marine, Karen spent the next 7 years with McDonald's in Europe, building the European government relations function and the company's Brussels office. Initially, her peers viewed the move with skepticism. At the time, McDonald's was not a popular name in Brussels. Karen built positive brand equity by focusing on a balance between food and healthy lifestyle, facilitating transparency, promoting sustainability, and building awareness of the food and restaurant industries through the development of a trade association called the European Modern Restaurant Association, which brought together leaders from quick service restaurant chains who then worked together on joint priorities.

Karen's success led to her promotion to Director of Marketing, Communications, and Government Relations for McDonald's Central Europe and Central Asia, based in Vienna. For those markets, McDonald's represented a free democratic and open market society and, for the most part, new restaurant locations were welcomed by governments and consumers. Initially, Karen was the only woman on the region's McDonald's board. She was responsible for creating and expanding the entire marketing apparatus for the company, which often entailed spending weeks at a time in central European and central Asian countries. She enjoyed the people and highly talented workforce. Being responsible for the entire marketing function was a new experience in which she thrived and was highly successful.

Karen left McDonald's for the Coca-Cola Company in the Netherlands, where she served as director of corporate affairs, building that department from scratch. After two years, she returned to McDonald's Europe as Assistant Vice President of Corporate Affairs. Her continued successes led her to promotion to Vice President of Corporate Affairs and Chief of Staff to the President of McDonald's for Europe, which comprised four regions. She continued to build relationships between and among stakeholders and encouraged an environment of collaboration, diverse thinking, and innovation. As Chief of Staff she had the opportunity to engage more on the business strategy and operations side.

During her more than 13 years at McDonald's, the quick service chain experienced significant growth. Karen described her time at McDonald's as a "love affair." She was and still is passionate about the McDonald's brand. Her time at the company gave her a foundation of business knowledge that has served her well in future roles. In Karen's words, "At McDonald's Europe, I learned to focus on what you can do, not on what you can't do" (K. van Bergen, personal interview, February 26, 2018).

Karen's next position was senior vice president and regional director for the Netherlands, Central and Eastern Europe for FleishmanHillard. Karen led the creation of the integrated OneVoice for Philips cross-agency team. She then served as global lead for the team, with the goal of helping to change perception of Philips as a consumer electronics company to that of a health and wellness company with global audiences.

After her work at FleishmanHillard, Karen became managing director at Porter Novelli, also an Omnicom company, in New York City. After 6 months, she was named CEO. At Porter Novelli, Karen led a significant turnaround for the agency, focusing on talent acquisition.

In 2016, after three years at the helm of Porter Novelli, Karen was named CEO of the newly created Omnicom Public Relations Group (OPRG), overseeing 20 public relations and public affairs agencies within Omnicom. In her role as CEO, she focuses on bringing best-in-class teams and innovative offerings to clients, facilitating collaboration between OPRG agencies, and providing a best place to work for talent. The agencies within OPRG offer a full range of client services including the growing areas of reputation management, crisis management, and influencer relations. Omnicom's breadth and depth provides many opportunities for talent to develop and enrich their careers and gain new professional experience. As in her previous leadership positions, Karen focuses on and excels at unifying teams around shared vision of goals and putting talent at the center.

Karen's professional in-house and agency life has provided her with invaluable insights that she gladly shares with aspiring public relations practitioners. First, she advises young professionals to trust and follow their gut. It is what got her where she is today. Second, embrace challenges. Develop positive self-imagery and "know that you can be good at it, then, dive into it, make it happen, solve it" (K. van Bergen, personal interview, February 26, 2017). Third, create a network. Besides keeping a pulse on what is happening in the world of business, it is an opportunity to seek advice from those with specific expertise. Networking can also be a source for career opportunities. Fourth, always speak up, voice your views, and contribute to the dialogue. Unless you do so, no one will know what you are thinking or see the value you can contribute. Last, give back to society. Mentor others when the opportunity arises and engage in social causes. To paraphrase Karen, giving back offers such tremendous reward and personal satisfaction.

Karen is proud to point out that Ketchum, one of the top five public relations firms in the world, recently promoted agency partner and president Barri Rafferty to global CEO. Ms. Rafferty is the company's first woman CEO and the first female CEO of a top five PR agency.

Karen strives to provide an intrapreneurial environment where she gives colleagues the support to be successful through encouraging independent thinking, innovation, and professional career growth. She sees her future as continuing to create a vision and continuing to motivate capable people to achieve that vision. She moves forward in her role as enterprise leader welcoming challenges and discovering opportunities leading to success.

Lily Vautour: Connecting with Internal and External Stakeholders through Social Media

Lily Vautour manages social media at Boston Children's Hospital (BCH), which, is the highest rated children's hospital in America (*U.S. News and World Report*, 2017). She develops social media and community engagement strategies as well as oversees their execution. Strategy involves patient stakeholders as well as internal group-related duties such as employee social media training and education. Ms. Vautour is also responsible for managing, organizing, and distributing social media analytics on a monthly, quarterly, and annual basis to various stakeholders. Prior to her role at BCH, she worked at SHIFT Communications where she developed a range of public relations-related skills. Lily earned her bachelor's in public relations from Boston University and her M.B.A. from Simmons College. She also is a Big Sister at the Big Sister Association of Greater Boston.

She started as the sole tactician developing content and monitoring social media communication at BCH to growing the "social" function becoming, in fact, the hospital's social media manager overseeing one full-time social specialists as well as interns. She and her team are responsible for communicating and building relationships with internal and external stakeholder groups, *which involve internal communication, media relations, and social media across the enterprise* to paraphrase Lily (L. Vautour, personal interview, September 27, 2017). This involves the coordination with all BCH social media contact points with publics especially patients and their families. She manages 40 social media channels targeting hospital-wide audiences as well as specific publics.

Linked to BCH's goal, Ms. Vautour is also responsible for developing the annual social media strategy and plan, which currently comprise five buckets: (1) support the hospital's reputation, (2) grow patient volume and mobilize physicians, (3) engage, train, and mobilize employees, (4) support the patient experience, and (5) strengthen social fundraising efforts. These strategic social media objectives collectively encompass internal and external stakeholders.

To grow the positive reputation of the hospital, Lily assures that social media shares quality and consistent content more than 30 times per day. Social media shares inspiring patient stories, healthcare innovations, new research, and highlights staff. These communications take place using earned media, blogs, videos, photos, and graphics, while adhering to best practices.

Related to this objective, she runs clinical trial Facebook recruitment ads to increase study participation, which has been challenging in the past. Being able to recruit study participants is a requirement to conducting vanguard research that ultimately improves the lives of children.

Additionally, the interaction between healthcare provider and patient contributes to the hospital's reputation. Lily provides physicians and other healthcare specialists with guidelines for communicating with patients suggesting where there are opportunities for enriching interaction. Affinity groups and special interest groups are publics that support BCH's reputation and mission. Lily establishes and maintains relationships with their social media administrators especially in areas where common and coordinated interests benefit all those concerned. These efforts contribute to BCH's positive brand equity as well.

The second bucket is growing patient volume and mobilizing physicians. In addition to the standard advertising and communications campaign, social media plays an important role by being responsive, empathetic, and understanding of patient needs especially during often trying times. BCH shares positive and upbeat stories of patients and provides support and advice to them and their families. Physicians are engaged and responsive to patient families guided by best practices developed by Lily and her team.

Healthcare provider interaction with patients and their families affects reputation and ultimately patient volume. BCH employee training about best practices for communicating with stakeholders via social media enhances the quality of interaction, which leads to the third objective-engage, train, and mobilize employees. The social media team publishes 1–2 internal articles per month offering best practices that help balance engagement with patients and their families and social media policy compliance. The department also runs social media training for 50 different groups throughout BCH and consults about numerous other social media practices.

Fourth, the three buckets described above support the patient experience. Patient support occurs in different ways. First, timely responses to patient and family posts are important and indicate that BCH's healthcare providers care and understand. Second, the hospital establishes and maintains special patient and family-based groups to support very specific needs using social media platforms. Families share their experiences and BCH healthcare professionals provide responses to questions and comments. Additionally, social media increase collaboration with various patient care services and operations.

The fifth bucket focuses on strengthening social fundraising efforts. As per policy, the social media department is required to provide fundraising with 30% of content time on Facebook. Lilly assures that fundraising efforts and results are aptly covered.

According to Lilly, the key to making social media a strategic partner at the table is the ability to demonstrate quantifiable results. Realizing the importance of social media public relations' return on investment, she deploys several kinds of assessment analytics and currently uses number of appointments, telephone calls, click-throughs, and social engagements as general measures of effectiveness.

For Ms. Vautour, social media collectively is a cost-efficient and timely mechanism to effectively communicate and interact with internal and external stakeholders. Social media can enhance morale and strengthen an organizational culture.

She is passionate about what she does. Heading social media at BCH is her dream job. Lilly wants to continue evolving at BCH and making a positive impact on children's lives as well as contribute to the hospital's goals. She sees social media as playing a more dominant role across the enterprise and hopes to be a key player in making it happen.

Conclusion

These professional women have no typical work day. However, what their positions share is the need to be flexible and to adjust to dynamic circumstances. They also personally have similar attributes. They have a sense of humor, they are high energy, possess an incredible level of knowledge in their areas of expertise, love and are passionate about what they do, and they are highly intelligent. Self-determination Theory, covered in Chapter 3, is a framework for describing highly motivated individuals. It is based on four characteristics associated with what people do. Individuals who have a degree of control over their activities, are competent at what they do, enjoy human relationships and interaction, and find their responsibilities enjoyable are self-determined and highly motivated. These women demonstrate these qualities. I thank them for setting time aside for these informative and insightful interviews.

References

Baez, C. (October 30, 2017). *Personal interview.*

Danielson, C. (September 21, 2017). *Personal interview.*

Forbes, B. C. (1995). *Forbes, Volume 156, Issues 6–10.* New York: Forbes.

Lee, D. J. (January 19, 2017). Personal interview.

Martinez, C. (2013, March 5). *Unboxed Conversations: Latin America PR legend, Carmen Baez.* Retrieved from: www.prosek.com/unboxed-thoughts/unboxed-conversations-latin-america-pr-legend-carmen-baez/ .

U.S. News Announces the 2017–2018 Best Children's Hospitals. (2017, June 27). Retrieved from: www.usnews.com/info/blogs/press-room/articles/2017-06-27/us-news-announces-the-2017-2018-best-childrens-hospitals.

Van Bergen, K. (December 5, 2017). *Personal interview.*

Van Bergen, K. (February 26, 2018). *Personal interview.*

Vautour, L. (September 27, 2017). *Personal interview.*

Glossary

Acceptance is thinking, feeling, and behaving in a manner respecting and consistent with diversity. It is accepting that everyone is unique. It is the recognition and understanding of individual differences and the nurturing of these differences. Acceptance is understanding each other and moving beyond tolerance to embrace and celebrate the enriching nature of diversity that is within everyone.

Accomplishments is one of the VALS' three expressives or drivers of human motivation.

Accreditation in Public Relations (APR) is designed for experienced public relations professionals. APR certifies a public relations professional's status as current with best practices, public relations developments, and competencies.

Accreditation in Public Relations and Military Communication (APR+M) is geared to improve the practice of military public affairs. Like the APR, it facilitates ongoing professional development that is easily transferred to civilian public relations.

Achievers as a VALS type, achievers are motivated to accomplish things; thus, they are goal driven. They are committed to career and family. Their social lives focus on family, worship, and work. They are conventional people who live conservative lives.

Action plan is a course of action directed at a specific public. Each plan contains the description of the public, specific benchmarks, a customized version of the central message, and specific tactics to be deployed.

Action plan objectives apply to the public relations plans for a specific public.

Active public is a group that is highly immersed in the situation possessing extensive knowledge of an issue whether or not they support the message.

Activism is the coordinated effort of a group that organizes voluntarily to solve problems that threaten the common interest of members of the group. In the process of problem solving, core members of the group attract other social constituents or publics, create and maintain a shared collective identity among members for the time being, and mobilize resources and power to influence the problem-causing entity's decision or action through communicative action such as education, negotiation, persuasion, pressure tactics or force.

Activity brief provides details about each tactical activity such as execution dates, target public information, messaging content, images, storyboards, scheduling, and assures that the tactic is appropriate for the campaign goal.

Administrative costs are one of three groups of costs associated with a public relations campaign. These costs are general administrative expenses.

Administrative staff possess all sorts of information and knowledge about the organization, some of which is gossip and some of which accurately describes the inner workings of the organization. They know who are the go-to individuals for specific situations.

Adversarial stakeholder   are active publics who oppose the public relations message. They are the opposition, resistant to change and concessions, and are typically defensive.

Advertising   or paid messaging is typically one-way messaging and short term, geared toward selling brands, products, and services.

Advertising value equivalency (AVE)   is a method to estimate gross return on investment. The AVE places an advertising dollar value on outcomes owing to public relations efforts, especially media coverage after deducting the costs of facilitating such coverage.

Advisory-only   public relations consulting does not obligate management to follow any advice provided by the practitioner.

Advocate stakeholders   are active publics in support of the campaign message. They embrace the message and advocate for it.

Affective empathy   is the ability to feel what another person feels.

Affect-Reason-Involvement Model   is a suggested framework of human awareness that involves thinking and feeling. Issue involvement is based on the amount of thinking and feeling about an issue.

Affects   are feelings, emotions, and moods.

Alliance   is an informal and loosely structured relationship between or among organizations.

Altruism   "Out of the kindest of your heart, would you please let me go and not give me a ticket, please." "Please join me in volunteering to help those in need. It's the right thing to do for all of us." These are appeals to altruism.

American Marketing Association (AMA),   established in 1937, is one of the largest marketing associations in the world, comprising over 30,000 professional and academic members. Membership consists of marketing professionals, organizations, academics, and students.

Amotivation   is the absence of motivation.

Analytics   is an encompassing and multidimensional field that uses mathematics, statistics, predictive modeling, and machine-learning techniques to find meaningful patterns in recorded data.

Animated banners   are digitially-based advertisements that have a fixed number of loops in GIF format. Audio is available. Product banners demonstrate features. They tend to have higher click-through rates.

Annual report   contains information about a company or other type of organization including the names of officers, their salaries, financial statements, narratives about the company's performance, social responsibility statement, and independent auditor's certification about the veracity of the report.

Apathetic public   knows that the problem exists, but considers it unimportant.

Apathetic stakeholders   are the apathetic publics. They either do not care or do not acknowledge the problem's existence.

Application   is a type of message that concentrates on communicating service or product stakeholder usage.

Argument   is a claim supported by warranted evidence.

Assertion   is a statement not supported with evidence.

Assistant moderator   aids a focus group moderator and takes thorough notes, operates the recording device (video/audio or only audio), sets up the physical or virtual meeting place, addresses coordination, responds to unexpected interruptions, and keeps track of time.

Asymmetric public relations   provides publicity, one-sided facts, or an appeal with evidence to support a specific position that is short term, eliciting a desired response to an existential issue.

Attention   is attending to a message.

Attitude   is a predisposition toward an object, issue, or person. It is the acceptance or rejection of that object, issue, or person.

Attributes and benefits   are messages that center on the characteristics and benefits of an issue. The issue may be a position, service, product, or brand.

Attitudinal decision stage   is the point where a person begins to evaluate a message and options.

Attitudinal inertia   is the resistance to attitude change because of a strongly held attitude, belief, or associated value.

Audience   is a group of people exposed to a media message at a given time. They are usually larger than the number of members constituting a target public.

Audio news release   is a sound bite news story for radio news media.

Audioblog   is an audio-based blog. See blog for definition.

Auto-communication   occurs when message senders are affected by the messages that they convey.

Autonomy   is a perceived sense of control over aspects of one's life.

Average frequency   is the average number of message exposures per person.

Aversive stimulation   "I am taking your cell phone away from you until you do your homework every night." "Until everyone completes the reimbursement paperwork correctly, there will be no reimbursements." These are examples of such stimulation.

Aware public   are groups that know an issue and its relevant consequences. However, they are not organized to act on the issue. They have knowledge of the problem and are involved to the extent that they recognize the problem.

Awareness   is knowing about a topic.

Backing   is reinforcement that assures the legitimacy of the warrant.

Baseline   is the starting point of an objective before the campaign intervention. It serves as a reference point from which to develop the anticipated outcome of an objective.

Behavioral decision stage   is the behavior associated with the information processing of an issue.

Behavioral objectives   are behavioral outcomes.

Behavioristic segmentation   categorizes publics predicated on behaviors or behavioral response to a message. Depending on the situation and issue, responses vary. The number of instances of behavioral compliance of an appeal, the status of the person complying, the readiness stage, and, in the case of marketing, product or brand loyalty are all components of behavioristic segmentation.

Beliefs   are what one holds to be true.

Believers   as a VALS type, are motivated by their ideals. These are conservative and conventional individuals with concrete beliefs based on traditional, established codes for family, religion, community, and country.

Benchmark   is part of an objective. It is the anticipated outcome.

Benchmarked objective   is an expected quantitative outcome that includes a timeline and identified public.

Blog   is a web page usually on a host site maintained by an individual or party for regularly posting content in a specified format. Posts include opinions, commentaries, thoughts, and ideas, or an unfolding situation. Most blogs offer news and content on a specific subject, while others are essentially personal journals.

Bloghood   are blogs located in the same geographical area. See blog for definition.

Blogroll   is a list of links to other blogs and sites located on the blog homepage.

Boards   are places where pins are available for viewing on Pinterest. Users collect and organize pins on these boards. Boards can be about any subject. Users can comment on pins and boards.

Borrowed interest   draws attention and interest to the message by the person, object, or idea, which is the main driver of the appeal.

Brand ambassador   is a change agent compensated to hold and present a position.

Brands,   according to Lovemarks, are respected, but lack an emotional connection with the consumer.

Brand specialists   are practitioners who are mostly technicians, but sometimes perform supervisory duties. They possess less experience than those fulfilling management roles. They are often involved with company brands, corporate image, or building the organizational brand with internal stakeholders.

Brochure   is an organizational publication that focuses on a topic of interest.

Budget   consists of the financial resources necessary to implement a specific public relations campaign.

Buyable Pins   are about purchasable products on Pinterest.

Buyer's remorse   is the guilt felt by a consumer for purchasing a product or service.

Cabals   are groups of two or more persons who covertly meet to serve a common purpose. Cabals advance a position within an organization as well as serve as a protection mechanism. They provide strength and backing through their members.

Campaign   is the development and implementation process by which systemic public relations tactics serve the achievement of objectives designed to reach a goal that addresses an issue.

Canadian Public Relations Society (CPRS),   founded in 1948, is an association that practices public relations in Canada and abroad.

Case study analysis   is an intensive examination, using multiple sources of evidence (which may be qualitative, quantitative or both), of a single entity bounded by time and place. Usually it is associated with a location. The "case" may be an organization, a set of people such as a social or work group, a community, an event, a process, an issue, or a campaign.

Celebrity endorsement   is a comment by a celebrity who supports an issue that an organization promotes.

Census data   are information derived from an entire public or population.

Central idea   is the conceptualization of a central message.

Central message   is the key message that appeals to stakeholders. The big selling idea, central thesis, or central motif of the campaign are other terms for the central message.

Centralized organization   is one for which predictable or repeated processes exist. This type of organization is conducive to hierarchical structures in which decision-making and communication follow the hierarchy.

Certificate in Principles of Public Relations   demonstrates a fundamental level of competence desirable for entry level public relations practitioners

Change agent   is a compensated "opinion leader." Such a person may be a brand ambassador.

Charisma   is a basis of credibility consisting of personality attributes, energy level, and general likability. Charismatic individuals usually can affectively and cognitively empathize with audience members thus increasing their persuasiveness.

Circadian Rhythms   are 24 hour internally activated physiological cycles experienced by many forms of life including human beings.

Circulation   is the number of subscribers to a periodical.

Claim   is an argued statement. It is what we ask the audience to believe or agree to supported by evidence.

Closed setting   option requires that prospective members ask to be added to a group by a member to the group.

Clustering sampling   draws sampling units from natural clusters such as geopolitical locations like states, company departments, neighborhood blocks, people who shop on certain days, and so forth. The clusters are mutually exclusive and collectively exhaustive subpopulations.

Coalition   is a formal and structured relationship between or among organizations.

Code of Conduct   is the set of behaviors associated with a code of ethics.

Code of Ethics   articulates the philosophical values of an organization.

Code of Ethics Pledge   is a commitment required of all PRSA members, which is a declaration of members' pledge to conduct themselves in a manner consistent with the PRSA's Code of Ethics.

Cognitions   are thoughts.

Cognitive dissonance reduction   occurs when one experiences discomfort from an inconsistency between what one thinks, feel, values, or beliefs and one's actions. The reduction happens when there is an adjustment between the action and the thought, feeling, value, or belief that restores consistency.

Cognitive Dissonance Theory   states that individual mental representations of a person's values, beliefs, attitudes, basis for decision-making, commitments, and behaviors operate and tend to exist in a state of harmony with one another. Disharmony causes psychological discomfort and motivates the person to take action that restores harmony within the person's mental schema. The techniques for returning to harmony can take several forms known as cognitive dissonance reduction.

Cognitive empathy   is the ability to think what someone else is thinking.

Cohort study   is a type of tracking study that focuses on a similar group of individuals who share a specific experience during the same time.

Collectivism   is the degree to which cultures are cooperative and less competitive.

Command-authority   allows the legal department to edit or change content to meet legal liability concerns with or without the consent of public relations.

Compared to competition   is messaging that emphasizes comparisons with the organization's major competitors, which can extend across categories of choices.

Compensation and benefits communication   function involves all matters about pay and benefits.

Competence   is based on education/training and/or experience. In Self-determination Theory it is the need to be good at doing something.

Competitive-comparison   is budgeting based on the amount of spending by competing organizations for similar campaigns. The comparison can be with the main competitors, all competitors, or only those that are most like the organization. Armed with this information, the practitioner can decide whether to match, increase, or decrease spending.

Compliance gaining strategies are techniques used to persuade an individual or group to think a certain way or to engage in a target behavior. CGS can be short or long-term oriented involving interpersonal or nonpersonal relationships.

Compounded blogs are blog posts that have increased traffic and engagement over time.

Comprehension is the understanding of something such as information or an issue.

Compulsory-advisory exists when the decision-makers must listen to the public relations professional.

Concurring-authority is when the approval of public relations takes place before messaging occurs. If there are differences between the communication creator and public relations professional, no action occurs. Only upon agreement can messaging transpire. In cases of trademark and other content of a proprietary nature, sometimes the legal department must approve the content. Johnson & Johnson and its many divisions follow this approach.

Connections are two-way relationships between two people on LinkedIn. Connected parties see each other's shares and updates on their homepages.

Consideration set of behaviors are the behaviors that one would consider when responding to an issue.

Consonant element is the basis for reconciliating cognitive dissonance.

Constituents are groups (such as voters) that an organization serves and to whom the organization is ethically and legally responsible.

Consumer kit is a press kit about a product or brand.

Content analysis examines communication content.

Contingency fund is set aside and available in case there are campaign adjustments. This may occur if any initial tactics were ineffective or if an unexpected opportunity presents itself.

Continuous maintains the same consistent schedule throughout the year such as promoting laundry detergent, food staples like milk and bread, and awareness of the importance of taking medications regularly according to the prescribed time.

Convenience sampling is a type of sampling based on selecting sampling units that are readily available.

Co-op Only Budgeting primarily operates in a corporate setting. It centers on limiting the budget size to cooperative (co-op) advertising support dollars from a vendor such as a manufacturer and an intermediary.

Corner peel banner partly displays (also called peel banners, page peels, or magic corners) in the corner of a web page. Once the user moves the mouse over the animation peel in the top corner (usually the right), the animation peels over the web page displaying the entire ad. These types of banner ads are not annoying to most viewers.

Corporate social responsibility (CSR) messaging centering on corporate social responsibility communication as a process that inherently concentrates on the good deeds performed by an organization relative to its various stakeholders.

Cost per thousand (CPM) is a calculation that permits us to compare costs per 1000 exposures of the message in different communication channels or in total.

Cost–benefit analysis is budgeting that compares the cost of the campaign to the estimated anticipated outcomes or benefits. This method optimizes benefits in relation to associated costs.

CPRS Canadian Public Relations Society Accreditation in Public Relations is the CPRS public relations professional accreditation offered to individual practitioners.

Creative road map   is the central message.

Credibility   is believability and supported by message source trust, competence, and charisma.

Crisis communication   presents an issue, problem, or disruption that triggers negative stakeholder reactions which can impact the organization's reputation, business, and financial strength.

Crisis   consists of unplanned events that have the potential to disrupt normal organizational operations and endanger the mission.

Crisis management   is a reactive approach to an out of control problem often laden with uncertainty.

Cross-sectional study   involves collecting data from a sample at a single point in time. It is a snapshot in time.

Crowdfunding   focuses on generating funding for an endeavor through investments or donations.

Crowdideation   engages parties to develop ideas and innovations about an issue, product, or service.

Crowdlaboring   concerns recruiting individuals, groups, or organizations to engage in some action such as volunteering for a social cause.

Crowdsourcing   is taking a function once performed by employees and outsourcing it to an undefined (and generally large) network of people in the form of an "open call" to some form of action. It is about building knowledge and engagement through a group response to a call for action to address a situation or achieve a goal.

Crowdvoting   generates support such as "Likes" or "votes" for a position on an issue.

Cultural barriers   are cultural items that can be misinterpreted resulting in hindered communication.

Cultural ethnocentrism   is the belief that one's culture is superior to others. It extends to judgments about other cultures predicated on the values, beliefs, and standards of one's own culture particularly concerning language, customs, religion and other practices.

Cultural networks   are the key informal mode of communication within the organization apart from the formal structure.

Cultural relativism   holds that a person's beliefs, values, and practices should be understood in the context of the individual's culture. It is based on the perspective that the world is relative. No one culture has a monopoly on the truth or what is "best."

Cultural symbol   messaging can be presented by creating a new or using an existing cultural symbol, which is usually a person, object, or idea that represents what stakeholders value and believe and linking it to the appeal.

Culture   is the cumulative deposit and passing down of knowledge (everything learned), experience, beliefs, values, attitudes, meanings, language, communication (ways of interacting) hierarchies, religion, artifacts, and material objects acquired by generations of a group of people through individual and group existence and behaviors.

Cut   is the transition or change from one camera sequence or shot to another.

Data   are the facts or evidence used to support or prove the claim.

Debt   "I've given you rides in the past. Now, I need you to return the favor." "When you needed time off, I was always accommodating. Now I need you to work this weekend." This is an appeal based on reciprocity.

Decentralized organization   are organizations in which individuals have greater discretion and decision-making options, as well as increased opportunity for two-way communication with others in lateral positions, in higher management/leadership roles, and the rank and file.

Deindividualization is a condition in which group cohesiveness dominates individual freedom of expression and identity.

Demographic segmentation is segmentation based on gender, age, educational background, marital status, ethnicity, religion, race, occupation, position within organization, functional position, position/job within an organization, income, and the like.

Deontological ethics are ethics informed by morality, values, and beliefs.

Dependent variable is influenced by the independent variable.

Descriptive analytics discovers, describes, and detects patterns and trends in the data.

Diffusion of innovations is the adoption curve and rate for how people accept and/or use an innovation whether it is an idea, belief, product, brand, service, or some behavior.

Digital observations require a device rather than an individual to record observations. Observation may include video or audio recordings, Internet traffic and behavior, eyes-on-screen tracking, response latency devices, vehicle traffic counters, devices that record individual physiological responses, and so forth.

Discrimination is observable behavior resulting from someone who is prejudiced.

Disguised observations is when the participants in a study are unaware that they are observed for the intended purpose of the study.

Disproportionately stratified sampling is all stratum sample sizes are equal regardless of their known proportions in the population.

Dissonant element is the disagreement point in cognitive dissonance.

Diversity encompasses acceptance and respect. It means understanding that everyone is unique, and recognizing our individual differences. These can be along the dimensions of race, ethnicity, gender, sexual orientation, socio-economic status, age, physical abilities, religious beliefs, political beliefs, or other ideologies. It is the exploration of these differences in a safe, positive, and nurturing environment. It is about understanding each other and moving beyond simple tolerance to embracing and celebrating the rich dimensions of diversity contained within everyone.

Dormant stakeholder stakeholders are not ready to become involved. They may be unaware of the issue. The degree of knowledge varies, but is not at a point where it increases engagement. As a latent public, they may not know how to deal with the problem or they may think that it is not a concern. They might require more information including content that addresses barriers to involvement.

Drop-down banner enables viewers to choose which site area to visit before clicking through.

Early adopters in diffusion of innovation are respected people who place great value in being respected. This group represents 13.5% of the population. This group consists of a high percentage of opinion leaders. They also have high social status, financial resources, greater education, and are vanguard in many of their views.

Early majority in diffusion of innovation are deliberative. This is one of the two largest groups comprising 34% of the population. Late majority wait significantly longer than the innovators and early adopters before adopting an innovation. Because they are thoughtful in decisions to adopt, they require time and adopt just before the average person does so.

Earned media are acquired through public relations attempts to manage and communicate with various traditional and social media with the intention of obtaining favorable media coverage.

Effective communication   reduces uncertainty. It is the overlap of the sent message with the received message. The greater the overlap, the less miscommunication or misunderstanding.

Emotions   are not thoughts, but feelings. They are intense, directed, and short-lasting.

Employee recruiter   is a role in which the practitioner recruits potential employees through social media. This person shares information about the appeal of the organizational culture.

Environmental Monitoring Attention Cycle   is a 60–90 second attention cycle. After this period, individuals break attention and then refocus to continue attending to the stimulus (i.e. video).

Environmental scanning   is the acquisition and use of information about events, trends, and relationships in an organization's external (and internal) environments, the knowledge of which would assist management in planning the organization's future course of action.

Esteem needs   are needs that relate to self-esteem. They are one's self-assessments.

Ethical relativism   suggests that ethics and their priority shift in time and under different circumstances.

Ethics   are the moral principles governing or influencing professional conduct. They comprise a system of acceptable beliefs that control professional behavior. Ethics are also the rules of conduct or moral principles of an individual or a group.

Ethnocentrism   is the belief that one's ethnic background is superior to others and thus other cultures are largely irrelevant.

Evergreen release   is a human-interest video news release.

Evoked set of behaviors   are behaviors that come to mind when considering an issue. They are not necessarily the actions that the person would take as in the case of a consideration set.

Execution   refers to how objectives are achieved. They are the individual messages, ads, events, or other activities associated with realizing the objectives.

Executive summary   is a one-page summary of a public relations campaign plan that accompanies the plansbook and is located at the front of the plan.

Exhibitions   are trade shows that target publics.

Experiencers,   as a VALS type, are driven by self-expression. They are young, impulsive, and enthusiastic about new possibilities. They like variety, excitement, enjoying the new, the offbeat, and the risky. Their activities include exercise, sports, and social activities.

Experiment   is a study centered on exposing participants to a treatment, manipulation, or stimulus to measure the effect of the experimental condition.

Experimental design study   introduces a condition in a laboratory or field (natural) setting and tests to determine whether the condition affects the study participants in some way. Thus, the study focuses on the presence or absence of a condition and establishes whether there is a cause and effect relationship at least in the short term.

Explicit communication   is written, visual, and/or in audio form. Explicit messaging is clear leaving little room for interpretation.

Exposure objectives   are outcomes that expose stakeholders to a message. They are about the number of stakeholders exposed to the campaign message. Traditionally, they were measured as number of news article clippings, mentions on the radio or broadcast television, and event attendance for example. Today, social media play an important role in effectuating message exposure such as the number of Facebook friends, Twitter followers, email list, LinkedIn connections, media impression, and various online content analysis.

Exposure is an instance in which a message is displayed to an individual.. It does not necessarily indicate that a person will attend to it. However, it is a required condition for message attention.

Extension is a type of software application that increases functionality.

Extemporaneous speech is a form of public speaking where there is general outline preparation of what will be presented; however, the delivery is not verbatim.

External information sources are external sources of information used in environmental scanning.

External regulation according to Self-determination Theory is motivation that is extrinsic or external to the person.

External stakeholders are external publics such as customers, vendors, competitors, distributors, wholesalers, banks, franchisees, government regulators, media, voters, trade associations, labor unions, nongovernmental organizations (NGOs), SIGs, and any other group who affect the organization and/or who are impacted by the organization.

External validity, also called generalizability, assures that research results from the sample can be generalized to the entire public of interest.

Extinction refers to the termination of a habit.

Extraneous variable is an external variable and not part of the study, but may influence the study in some way.

Extrinsic motivation is caused by an external source and is not innate.

Extrovert, according to the MBTI, is a person who is outgoing and tends to think out loud. Extroverts are comfortable in crowds of strangers and enjoy introducing themselves to strangers. American culture values extroversion.

Facebook groups are smaller communities within Facebook. These parties share common interests and express their views. They center on a common cause, issue, or activity to organize and plan, discuss issues, and share content.

Facebook page allows public figures, businesses, organizations, fans, and other entities to create an authentic and public presence on Facebook.

Facebook profile is a web page that contains a personalized description of the person and shared images, stories, content, and experiences. The profile owner can post his/her status and life events on a timeline.

Fact sheet, given to reporters, summarizes the key points about an event, issue, product, or organization.

Fads are merchandise that appeal to emotions where interest passes in time

Fan status is a one-sided relationship with news communicated to the fan from a Facebook page. Content from the fan's profile does not flow to the page.

Fave Fave is a mark for a photo that is liked. The photo owner is notified that the picture has been marked as a fave (favorite) and then it is added to the person's fave folder where it can be viewed any time.

Fear appeal is a persuasive message to effectuate behavior that attempts to arouse fear through the threat of an existential danger or harm.

Feeler, according to the MBTI, is a decision-maker who considers the consequences of a decision on people.

Femininity from a cultural perspective are places where cooperation, modesty, caring, and quality of life are encouraged

Field experiment   is an experiment that occurs in a natural setting.

Finish to Finish   is a schedule in which a tactic cannot end before the preceding one ends, but it may end later.

Finish to Start   is a schedule in which a tactic cannot start before its predecessor ends. It also can start later than the end of the previous tactic.

Fixed panel banner   appears on the website. The panel (measuring 336 x 860 pixels) rolls to the top and bottom of the page as the user scrolls up and down.

Flighting   is a schedule in which messaging transpires only at certain times of the year because of the seasonal nature of an issue (or product) such as selling snow blowers, selling Cadbury Easter eggs, and recruiting volunteers to work at various summer festivals.

Floating banner   appears after a viewer first lands on the web page. It then floats on or around the page for up to 30 seconds or more. These banners may move over a desired mouse click location sometimes hindering accessibility to page content thus frustrating visitors. They have a high click-through rate.

Focal element   is the point of contention in cognitive dissonance.

Focus group   is a qualitative study in which a small group of participants discuss an issue. The researcher moderates the session.

Follower   status allows one who follows a profile to see posts without having a two-sided relationship or friend's status. It is a type of "fan" setting for personal profiles.

Formal opinion leaders   are leaders in professional positions such as tax assessors, safety engineers, physicians, or union leaders. They are in structured roles of authority.

Formal research   is a planned and systematic approach to research which follows an established set of procedures.

Formative evaluation   describes how the information gathered during the summative phase benefits future campaigns.

Fragile self-esteem   requires the validation of others.

Frame   is presenting a message in a way involving some aspects of a perceived reality and making them more salient in a communicating context to promote a problem definition, causal interpretation, moral evaluation, and/or treatment recommendation for the item (or issue) described.

Frequency   is the number of message exposures a person receives.

Friends   are those individuals with profiles who are accepted into one's Facebook social network.

Gantt chart   is a horizontal bar chart designed as a management tool to coordinate, track, and manage the flow of tasks from start to completion.

Gatekeepers   are those news professionals who decide which stories are covered. They are editors and news producers.

Geographic segmentation   is defining a group based on physical location such as city, county, state, region, facility where someone works, department, company division, or some other boundary.

Gestures   are nonverbal forms of communication.

Global Communication Certification Council (GCCC) Certification Programs evaluate the business communication skills and knowledge and experience of applicants. There is a required screening application process. Those who are approved, take a certification examination. The areas covered are: Ethics, Strategy, Analysis, Context, Engagement, and Consistency. There is also an ongoing maintenance component requiring periodic testing.

Global objectives apply to all the campaign's publics.

Global organization identifies as a global organization and being part of a global community rather than identifying with any single nation.

Global public relations is a process involving efforts to communicate directly or indirectly with publics and stakeholders across national boundaries and from different cultures to convey messages that are informative, persuasive, and activate target behavior through various tactics and activities. Global companies face geographical, cultural, political, legal, socioeconomic, and communication challenges that are unique in many ways.

Glocalization is a global strategy with a local focus on execution.

Goal is a general statement of purpose. It is what the public relations campaign will attain or accomplish in relation to the issue under consideration.

Gossipers know and communicate all the intriguing scuttlebutt in the organization, placing their own spin on events.

Group-level messaging applies to messaging groups who have a shared interest or other commonality.

Groupthink is the unquestionable belief that one's group or culture is infallible, is always "right."

Halo effect is a type of cognitive bias in which a favorable assessment of a person in one area extends to other areas.

Hamburger icon is three short horizontal lines that represent a menu. It is located on the top right of the mobile website.

Handbook is an organizational publication that focuses on a topic of interest.

Handling fee is the cost for purchasing and managing the various aspects of the campaign.

Hardcore loyalty is always being loyal or devoted to a single organization.

Heroes personify values and serve as a tangible source of inspiration. They are known by virtually all organizational members and provide role models for how one should conduct oneself.

Heuristic processing is a type of information and evaluation processing that is not comprehensive and utilizes a limited amount of information relying on mental shortcuts and simple rules to make evaluations.

Heuristic Systematic Model is an information processing framework that explains how people receive and process persuasive messages. Message processing is done either heuristically or systematically.

High group cohesiveness is a high degree of group closeness and identity.

Human communication is the process by which a sender encodes and transmits information received and decoded by a receiver. The information received may or may not be intentional.

Iconic signs are artifacts of an object. In other words, they are explicit representations of something such as a photo or drawing of someone identified as a person. For instance, a picture of a red rose, is a red rose.

Identified regulation is external motivation in which a person identifies with the behavior because it has value.

Image campaigns promote an organization's reputation often by communicating the company's good deeds and corporate citizenship.

Implicit communication is indirect, more complex and influenced by an individual's perceptual filters. An organization's policies, practices, and operations convey directly and sometimes indirectly what it values.

Impressions   are the number of times a message is received (or delivered to a person or household) during a period.

Impromptu speech   requires no preparation.

Inclusion   is the actions associated with diverse beliefs, values, and acceptance.

Independent variable   is a predictor because it predicts or influences another variable namely the dependent variable.

Indexical sign   is an image that resembles some aspect of reality. Indexical signs provide a physical trace to a cause and effect relationship in many but not all cases. Their influence on individuals is based on their connection to the person's life experiences. For example, a bullet hole indicates that a gun was discharged, smoke is an index of fire, tire tracks on a road suggest that a vehicle drove on the road, and a weathervane provides the direction of the "invisible" physical wind.

Individualism   is the degree to which cultures are competitive and individualistic.

Individual-level messaging   provides an appeal geared to the identified individual using tactics such as personal emails, telephone calls, personal meetings, and private messaging through the various social media platforms.

Indulgence   is a cultural measure of the degree to which individuals value and engage in activities that provide personal satisfaction and happiness.

Informal opinion leaders'   influence is based on their personal relationships with followers. The relationships are informal, social, and less structured than formal ones.

Informal research   is less complex and less structured than formal research. It is usually exploratory, and typically it is not conducive to measurement.

Information objectives   are outcomes that create awareness and knowledge about an issue through repeated contact so that there is message recall. Measurement occurs through awareness and recall survey data collection in which the individual is asked whether she or he recalls the item. An average public member is exposed to a message 3–10 times before it is remembered.

Information processing   is the mental processing of thoughts, feelings, and moods sometimes resulting in an evaluation.

Innovators   are those individuals who are the first to use an innovation. Further, as a VALS type, they are successful, complex, in-charge people with high self-esteem. They possess all three primary motivations, which may exist at different levels. They have abundant resources.

Instrumental values   are goal driven values that affect our modes of behavior. They are important to us and guide our lives as well as lead to terminal values or goals.

Integrated communication   includes all communication, internal as well as external, that is highly interdependent, coordinated, and consistent.

Integrated marketing communication   includes public relations, advertising, personal selling, and anything else concerned with messaging and selling the product, service, or brand. It is integrated because it represents consistent or related messaging with all communication contact points in the marketplace.

Integrated regulation   results from the most autonomous extrinsic motivation. This type of motivation requires the identification and congruence of a person's values and beliefs with the target behavior.

Intention to act   is psychological conation. It is an intention to act.

Internal communication audit   is internal research regarding some aspect of the organization and its stakeholders. The focus is on discovering communications effectiveness and perceptions and behaviors of internal stakeholders about an issue.

Internal communicator has technical and managerial duties. Typically, this practitioner has roughly the same number of years of experience as the brand specialist. This person is concerned with employee morale, motivation, and a variety of internal communications. Much of his/her communication is face-to-face.

Internal information sources are internal sources of information used in environmental scanning.

Internal organizational action relates to appeals directed at organizational members and can come in many forms covering a wide range of topics. Some central messages may be persuasive such as convincing employees to make charitable contributions to increasing the number of volunteer hours per month to aid a social cause. Other messaging may focus on increasing employee morale or productivity.

Internal social media practitioner in this role writes content for the organizational intranet and internal social media. Employee engagement measurement occurs via likes, shares, comments, and other metrics. The public relations practitioner informs employees of key developments and social events designed to maintain morale, productivity, and motivation.

Internal stakeholders are groups within an organization. They can be employees, contract workers, or volunteers. For example, sale associates, customer service representatives, members of a specific department, line supervisors, managers, division heads, and so forth.

Internal validity assures that what is intended to be measured is in fact measured. This can become challenging when measuring concepts such as intrinsic or extrinsic motivation, brand loyalty, or love.

International Associations of Business Communicators (IABC), formed in 1970, has more than 102 chapters worldwide consisting of over 10,000 members in more than 60 countries. As the name reveals, the primary focus is internal public relations practiced globally. IABC allows members to connect to a global communication network, stay informed about emerging trends and best practices, learn from top experts, gain recognition for members' outstanding work and join a community of communication professionals around the world who are striving to be the best in the profession.

International organization identifies with more than one country each with distinct cultures and ways of operating.

International Public Relations Association (IPRA), established in 1955, has over 10,000 members worldwide. To quote the association website: "Today, IPRA is a worldwide organization with members in both established and emerging countries. It is governed by a geographical representative Board and run by a Secretariat in the UK. IPRA represents individual professionals, not agencies or companies. IPRA is recognized as an international non-governmental organization by the United Nations and has been granted consultative status by the Economic and Social Council (ECOSOC)."

Interpretation is *oral* translation including interpreting paralanguage.

Interstitial banner opens in a new browser window as the destination page loads. They often contain large images, a streaming presentation, and extra applets that enhance the use of display, graphics, and human interaction.

Intrinsic motivation is that which originates from within an individual. This motivation fulfills a person's basic psychological needs.

Introjection regulation is a type of motivation that has been partially internalized, but the individual does not consider it part of the integrated self. The behavior avoids guilt and shame.

Introvert, according to the MBTI, is a person who does not think out loud. Introverts prefer an agenda beforehand so that they can process information in advance. They are comfortable around small groups of people who they know. They prefer not to socialize with strangers.

Intuitive, according to the MBTI, is a strategist, a leader. This is a big picture person who integrates the various aspects of an endeavor and inspires organizational members to what they can achieve. He/she is a visionary and future-oriented.

Innovations are ideas, objects, ways of doing things, and so forth characterized as new or novel approaches to addressing conditions in the environment.

Issue is the public relations campaign problem or opportunity.

Issues management is a long-term proactive and systematic approach that monitors, anticipates degree, and evaluates issues that could impact the organization positively or negatively.

Jingle is catchy music such as the Kit Kat "Give me a break" short song, which also is associated with a central message, tagline or slogan, and issue.

Judger, according to the MBTI, value order, planning, and decisive decision-making. He prefers information for decision-making presented in bullet form and will not hesitate to decide on an issue. Judgers do not let decisions linger.

Judgmental sample consists of experts. For example, if a study goal is to predict when a cure for cancer will likely occur, the researcher may ask the top leading oncologists and oncological researchers in the world.

Key publics are of paramount importance for a public relations campaign. They are those publics whose support is required to achieve the public relations goal.

Keyword density is the amount of keyword content expressed as a percentage of the total web page words.

Knowledge is more than awareness and understanding about an issue. It includes the ability to successfully apply what is understood.

Lab experiment is an experiment conducted in a controlled setting.

Laboratory setting is a controlled setting usually to conduct an experiment.

Laggards are those persons who are the last to adopt an innovation.

Late majority are persons who adopt an innovation after the average person. A high degree of skepticism and caution exists towards the innovation. Peer norms play an important role in adoption. Individuals in this group generally have below average social status, limited financial resources, are in communication with others within their group, and have little opinion leadership.

Latent content analysis examines the underlying meaning of words in a message.

Latent public is a group of individuals that know the issue exists, but they do not see it as a problem or opportunity. Latent publics have little knowledge and low levels of involvement. The objective with this public is to increase knowledge and engagement.

Learning stage is the period in information processing when an individual understands an issue.

Legality is the extent to which behaviors abide by the laws of a society. Society's institutions such as the legislature and executive branches of government or religious authorities construct or affect laws within their domain of influence.

Like is an expression of favorability.

Liking behavior examples are: "You've done well in school and have been a go-getter. When do you plan to visit graduate schools and plan for the GREs?" You take an employee to lunch and praise her contribution to the company's mission. On the way back from lunch, you ask her to head a new task force because she can get it done right.

Linklog   is a blog consisting of short posts with links to other blogs. See blog for definition.

Liveblog   is a blog post occurring in real-time. See blog for definition.

Lobbyist   is a person who attempts to influence the voting on legislation or the decisions of government officials by meeting directly with officials or staff to make a case.

Longitudinal study   is research that occurs over the long term involving data from multiple time periods.

Long-term orientation   is the degree to which people are long-term focused, planning for the future and making sacrifices over the short-term.

Love/Belonging Needs   is the third level of needs in Maslow's Hierarchy.

Lovemarks   is a framework for classifying a product or brand based on the amount of love (positive emotions) and respect (assessed quality) for it. The system classifies items or issues by low and high levels of these two consumer assigned properties.

Loyalty   is devotion to a product, service, brand, or cause. It has three parts. First, loyalty requires a favorable attitude toward the organization. Second, repeated pro-organizational behavior is a component of loyalty. For instance, a repeated action would be donating to a specific charity every year. Last, those loyal toward an organization are advocates of that organization.

Makers,   according to VALS, focus on self-expression. They communicate to the world about themselves and their experiences by building a house, raising children, and repairing a car. They are practical individuals, who have constructive skills and believe in self-sufficiency. They have traditional families, do practical work, and engage in physical recreation. Makers are suspicious of innovations and big business. They respect government and organized labor.

Manifest content analysis   examines the occurrences of words in a message.

Manipulation check   is a test used to determine whether an experimental condition was sufficiently salient.

Manuscript speech   is reading a speech word for word from a podium or teleprompter.

Market maven   is an opinion leader about financial markets.

Market segment   is a specific defined market of consumers or potential customers for a product, brand, or service.

Marketing campaigns   communicate with consumers to sell goods, services, and brands.

Masculinity   is the degree to which cultures are oriented toward competition, achievement, material acquisitions, heroism, assertiveness, and material rewards for success. Opportunities, risks, and individual goal-setting drive individuals.

Maslow's Hierarchy Needs Theory   is a motivation framework based on the fulfillment of physical, psychological, and self-actualizing needs.

Mass-level messaging   is communication that does not differentiate individuals or groups.

Mat release   is a video news release ready-for-broadcast.

MBTI (Myers-Briggs Type indicator)   is a typology based on personality as represented by four mental habits.

Media advisory   or media alert informs the news media of forthcoming newsworthy events. Unlike a news release, the advisory describes the accommodations available to news media professionals during the event such as photography and filming opportunities including lighting and sets, but does not include the level of topic information provided in a release. The journalists or reporters must attend the event to get the "scoop."

Media alert   or media advisory informs the news media of forthcoming newsworthy events. Unlike a news release, the advisory describes the accommodations available to news media professionals during the event such as photography and filming opportunities including lighting and sets, but does not include the level of topic information provided in a release. The journalists or reporters must attend the event to get the "scoop."

Media kit   consists of materials about an issue or organization to support an organization's position. It goes to news media outlets or is accessed online depending on the content. It is in hardcopy and more often is available in digital form on an organization's website. It contains a cover letter, which previews its contents, news releases, fact sheets, and other items such as background information, product information, the benefits of products and services, demonstrated product usage, product samples, images, schedules, brochures, reports, newsletters, promotional materials, and any other material germane to the issue and situation.

Media objectives   are special objectives because they serve a key purpose. They relate to exposing the message to stakeholders, thereby creating awareness through publicity.

Media specialist/manager   is involved with technical as well as managerial tasks. This practitioner has extensive experience. Her/his primary focus is external stakeholders especially the news media. This person also consults with senior management about key stakeholders. He also provides some strategic planning inputs especially about news media.

Memorized speech   is simply a speech presented from memory.

Meta-messaging   is everything associated with a message that contributes to meaning. It is the message (text, images, audio, and video), channel of communication, and context of the message including the source, topic, mode of delivery, and any other characteristic associated with the message.

Mixed research design   simply incorporates more than one study design.

MMS   denotes Multimedia Messaging Service for texting. Messages can be longer including media rich content such as pictures, video, and/or audio content.

Moderator   is the facilitator of a focus group session.

Month-to-month budgeting   is based according to what resources are available rather than by a long-term, planned approach. This technique is common in organizations that view public relations as an expense rather than as an investment in the future.

Moods   are affects that are relatively long lasting, not as intense as emotions, and not focused on something.

Moral appeal   examples are "It is morally wrong for you not to do your best in college especially when your parents are paying for your education." "We have a responsibility to be informed voters keeping society and our follow human beings in mind when voting."

Morale and satisfaction communication   (function) provides effective follow-up and responsive communication between and among organizational members.

Morality   is one's personal sense of what is "right" and what is "wrong."

Motigraphics   is a method to discover, define, and measure human motives and desires.

Motives   are situationally based reasons for moving us to certain thoughts, feeling, and/or actions.

Motivation   causes action after stimulus exposure.

Multicultural environment   is a place where people from diverse cultures live and thrive together.

Multicultural organization   is an organization that primarily identifies with one country, but recognizes the value of a culturally diverse and inclusive workforce.

Multiculturalism is an environment where diverse cultures live and thrive together contributing to each other's well-being and the overall organizational mission.

Multinational organization centers on national identity. It conducts business across multiple nations, manages a multinational workforce, and has global customers.

Multisnap allows Snapchat users to record up to 60 seconds posted in six 10-second snaps.

Mutual understanding reduces uncertainty. There is a shared subjective/objective reality.

Native video upload is uploading a video directly in a social media site as opposed to linking it from such sources as YouTube.

Natural system are collectivities (an organization) whose participants are pursuing multiple interests, both disparate and common, but recognizing the value of perpetuating the organization as an important resource. The informal structure of relations that develops among participants provides a more informative and accurate guide to understanding organizational behavior than the formal.

Naturalistic setting refers to data collection that occurs in a natural setting where the phenomenon takes place.

Need for autonomy refers to a need to have control over one's life.

Negative altercating "You tell Mike to explain to his children when he punishes them because only a callous person would not do so." "Not signing the green petition is irresponsible and the act of someone who does not care for future generations."

Negative expertise "If one does not graduate from a reputable college with a STEM degree, one will have difficulty finding a well-paying position." "Employees who don't participate in the workshop will have difficulty justifying why they should be promoted."

Negative interpersonal relatedness "If you are the only member of your family not participating in the charity dinner, your family might think less of you?" "If you don't stand up to the polluters, what will your neighbors and family think of you?"

Negative self-feeling "If you are the only member of your family not participating in the charity dinner, your family might think less of you and how then will you feel?" "If you don't stand up to the polluters, will you be able to live with yourself?"

Neuroplasticity is a physical process in the brain in which it reorganizes itself by forming new neural connections throughout life. This is usually due to normal learning or learning in response to brain damage.

News release is a story given to gatekeepers for coverage in local, regional, national, and international news media, which may be reported to the public as submitted to the gatekeeper. The practitioner submits general and specialty topic news releases to the relevant editors, news directors, reporters, newspapers, magazine, radio stations, and television stations.

Newsletter is an informal publication in hardcopy or digital format designed to provide information to stakeholders at regular intervals.

Nonprobability sampling is the selection of sampling units not based on randomization techniques.

Objective-Based Budgeting starts with the campaign's overall objectives, followed by the tactics needed to achieve the objectives.

Objectives answer the four Ws of a public relations campaign. Who do we want to target? What do we want to achieve and to what degree? When will it be done?

Observational research   is the observation, collecting, and recording of data from people, objects, and events in a systematic manner by human and/or digital methods. The observer does not question any people. Personal observation, digital observation, audit, content or interaction analysis, and trace analysis are the major methods of observation.

Ongoing evaluation   monitors and assesses the campaign underway so that any ineffectiveness tactics detected are rectified in time to make a difference.

Online media relations   role comprises tasks and responsibilities such as developing relationships with opinion leaders including media professionals. The person in this role also pitches stories to news media representatives as well as establishes a presence on social media.

Open system   is an organization centered on independent activities linking changing stakeholder groups, both internal and external to mutual benefit. The internal groups are dependent on continued interaction with the external environments where they operate.

Opinion editorial   is opinion content sent to a news media outlet gatekeeper espousing an issue or position. Editorials can be letters to the editor or a submission to the op-ed page. Public relations practitioners write editorials for others who sign the piece. Editorial pieces appear in local, regional, national, or international newspapers, magazine, radio, television, and online.

Opinion leaders   are an intervening public. That is, they pass the public relations message along to larger publics through such channels as blogging. They are trusted experts in a chosen field. Opinion leaders support, are neutral, or oppose an issue.

Opportunity–cost analysis   is a budgeting approach related to objective-based budgeting, guided by previously accepted objectives. It weighs the costs associated among alternative tactics to achieve specified objectives. The intent of this method is to attain objectives in a cost-effective manner.

Organic public relations   is transactional public relations created, developed, and changed at the grassroots or user level.

Organization   is a structured environment in which individuals are divided by job tasks grouped and coordinated in the service of a mission. The structure includes work specialization, departments, a hierarchy of authority, a specified number of individuals who report to supervisors, and a designated decision-making authority.

Organizational development and change   communication is a function of internal communication.

Organizational communication   is a process through which people, acting together, create, sustain, and manage meanings through verbal and nonverbal signs and symbols within a context.

Organizational culture   is the collected deposit, passing down, and learned knowledge (history), experience, beliefs, values, attitudes, meanings, lexicon, communication (ways of interacting), hierarchies, artifacts, and material objects acquired by an organization during the fulfilling of its mission during its collective existence.

Organizational equity   is the reputation of the organization.

Orientation and indoctrination communication   in an internal communication function in which communication exposes new employees to the procedures and practices of the company.

Outcome   is the indirect or direct influence on one or more publics that occurs because of public relations efforts. Anticipated outcomes are measurable objectives included within an allocated budget. This means that cost efficiencies are part of planning.

Owned media are public relations' issue coverage and messaging owned by a public relations organization.

Pacing is the number of cuts in a video of a given size.

Paid media are public relations coverage paid by an organization.

Panel study entails collecting data from the same sample over time whether they are persons, devices, records, or some other type of data source.

Paralanguage is everything associated with speech in conjunction with the actual words, phrases, or sentences. Paralanguage includes posture, eye contact, hand gestures, and how words are spoken such as volume, syllable emphasis, tempo, pauses, and accent.

Parasocial relationship is when someone follows another in the media, and learns a great deal about the person. The person extends emotional energy, interest, and time, and the object of attention is unaware of the person's existence.

Pass-along rate is the number of total readers exposed to the magazine (passed from person to person who are typically not subscribers). For example, although a dentist's office subscribes to a single copy of a magazine, many patients read it. Pass-along rates range from 2 to 6. In other words, 2 to 6 people read the magazine.

Past-spending is budget planning based on similar previous campaign budgets, employing the same benchmarks and objectives and assuming successful outcomes. In the interim, adjustments can be made to account for the rate of inflation.

Perceiver, according to the MBTI, requires a thorough review of detailed information and research to make the "perfect" decision. Perceivers sometimes become trapped in nuances and are viewed as procrastinators.

Percentage-of-sales is the most common budgeting method utilized by organizations that market products and/or services. It is based on a percentage of a previous sales period, revenues, donations, or profit so that the budget connects directly to sales or profitability.

Personal observations are recorded interactions with study participants.

Personnel costs are one of three groups of costs associated with a public relations campaign. They include cost allocation for permanent staff, hired consultants, and/or freelancers to perform specialized duties. The number of hours estimated and assigned to a project or campaign are multiplied by the billable hourly rate.

Person-to-person administered survey is directly administered in-person. The survey interview can be mediated by technology such as digital devices using applications such as Skype, Google Plus, and many other platforms.

Persuasion is an attempt to influence the attitudes of others and may include a call to action.

Persuasion objectives are outcomes that form or shape attitudes toward an issue by using some form of persuasion based on rationale and/or emotional considerations.

Persuasive communication influences the attitudes of others and may include a call to action.

Physiological Needs are basic needs required for human existence.

Picked for You Pin are recommended pins based on a board a user creates on Pinterest.

Pinning, which is often associated with Pinterest, allows individuals to share images across social media.

Pins are visual bookmarks consisting of images and/or video about a topic that link or are uploaded to a Pinterest board.

Pitch letter   draws attention to an event. Sent to an editor or producer, it often accompanies a media advisory or fact sheet. The personalized letter justifies why an event warrants news coverage by emphasizing its novelty or relevance to the audience.

Plansbook   comprises an entire public relations campaign including the situational analysis, strategy, tactical plans, and eventually the post-campaign evaluation and reflection.

Platform   is software (and sometime hardware) interfaced with other independent applications.

Plug-in   interface is a specific application to a platform or other application to extend software capabilities.

Podcast   is a recorded audio program such as a radio show, lecture, or book reading that is available on the Internet for download and listening using a digital device.

Policing role   involves monitoring organizationally related social media for appropriateness and professional (and favorable) presentation of the organization's image.

Policy maker   develops policies and guidelines for how organizational members utilize social media, which involves feedback from multiple departments, thus, it involves boundary spanning.

Policy/operations managers   have technical responsibilities owing to duties including managing and developing strategic plans.

Political campaigns   are communication campaigns directed at electing a political candidate and/or supporting specific issues.

Population   are all the possible members of a group.

Pop-under banner   displays after the browser window closes according to a fix size, which makes identifying with the previously visited page less likely.

Positioning statement   is a general statement of how an organization wants its stakeholders to view an issue or organization.

Positioning strategy   is the rationale for how an organization wants its stakeholders to view an issue or organization.

Positive altercating   "A student who appreciates the sacrifice made by his/her parents to pay for college, will not hesitate to do his/her best in school." "Anyone who cares about the future and people will without a doubt sign the green petition because it is the responsible thing to do."

Positive expertise   "Because one graduates from a reputable college with a STEM degree, finding a highly desirable job that pays well will be relatively easy." "Employees who participate in the workshops will be career fast-tracked in the company."

Positive interpersonal relatedness   "Your family will think very highly of you for participating in the charity dinner" "By standing up to the polluters, your neighbors and family will know that you care about the community."

Positive self-feeling   "You will feel a sense of pride and accomplishment because you played a major role in organizing the charity dinner." "You will have a tremendous feeling of reward because you stood up to the polluters."

Post-purchase cognitive dissonance   is also buyer's remorse. It is a condition of inconsistent thoughts, feelings, beliefs, or values relative to the purchase of a product or service. The inconsistency causes psychological discomfort.

Post-test   is the means by which data are collected after the source of data is exposure to an experimental condition

Power distance   is a cultural measure that indicates the degree to which the less powerful members of a society accept and expect the unequal distribution of power in their society. Power can be political, economic, social, and religious.

Predictive analytics   utilizes data to develop models that forecast future behaviors and events.

Pregiving   is when a person invites a neighbor to lunch with the hope that he will be invited to a dinner party at that neighbor's home, for example. A person buys charity cookies from a colleague's child hoping that the colleague will reciprocate in the future.

Prejudice   is a negative attitude toward individuals based on his/her cultural identity and others' perceptions about those identities.

Prescriptive analytics   combines descriptive and predictive analytics and adds data-driven decision-making to the mix, including calculating the probabilities of success for alternative courses of action and risk evaluation.

Press agent   finds unusual news angles and planning events that draw media attention.

Press Agent/Publicity Model   focuses on creating evocative publicity with the intention that the relevant public will receive and embrace the public relations message.

Press tour   is a visit and tour of an organization.

Pre-test   is a baseline measurement established before exposure to a treatment.

Pre-testing evaluation   involves gauging reactions to a message or some aspect of the campaign prior to launching it.

Pre-testing   is testing the effectiveness of a message on a sample of a public before used in the campaign.

Price and quality   are messages that emphasize quality for the price. The benefits of compliance outweigh the costs.

Priests   are the guardians of organizational values. They know the history of the organization. They can interpret organization situations in the context of the beliefs, values, and past practices.

Primary research   involves collecting data for analysis.

Probability sampling   is the selection of sampling units based on some type of random sampling.

Problem   is the difference between a desired situation and the actual situation.

Process   is a systematic sequence of actions that produce something or achieve a targeted end. Most of the results are intentional, but some are unintentional.

Products,   based on Lovemarks, draw little consumer attention and usually involve pragmatic items such as bread, milk, and so forth.

Product class   messaging is based on comparing similar benefits derived from competing different types of products.

Product or service user and affiliation   messaging aims to create a link between the stakeholder and the organization whether it is a product, brand, service, or affiliation. The goal is to establish and strengthen the stakeholder's identification with the organization.

Product recall   is an appeal that requests the return of a product for various reasons such as defective parts in the item especially when continued product usage could result in injury. Depending on the nature of the recall, the message may have components addressing not only the product recall, but procedures and support to successfully executive the recall.

Production and program costs   directly relate to the public relations campaign communication activities other than practitioner-related personnel costs. They are all that goes into messaging including what it costs to design, produce, and disseminate messages including the costs of event planning, management, and execution.

Professional Certified Marketer in Digital Marketing   is an AMA certification that assesses competence in: Metrics & Conversions, Social & Community, Email Marketing, User Interface & Experience, Online Advertising, SEO, and Content Marketing.

Program   addresses a few objectives linked to a goal on an ongoing basis. It typically focuses on a single public or stakeholder group.

Project   is a single public relations task such as developing a news release, a Twitter page, a video news release, planning an event, and so forth.

Promise   "If you do well in school, I will buy you your dream cell phone." "If you take on this additional responsibility for the next year, I will advocate for your promotion citing this additional work."

Promoted pin   are pins marketed to users based on their Pinterest interests.

Propaganda   attempts to persuade based on an appeal unsupported by sound reasoning and/or evidence presented objectively.

Proportionately stratified sampling   requires that the number of groups within a sample represent their proportion in the target population.

PSA (public service announcement)   is messaging that focuses on the public good. They come in different formats, but typically take the form of audio (radio) spots or video for impact. They are pre-recorded and produced for broadcast or they are spot announcements in which the talent delivers the PSA live. They normally run 30 to 60 seconds. Medium vehicles such as radio, television, and cable stations donate air time to PSAs.

Psychographic segmentation   centers on defining publics according to lifestyle, values, beliefs, attitudes, and personality characteristics.

Public Information Model   is a one-way communication approach. It deploys news releases and other techniques to distribute information. Generally, there is less concern for drawing attention and extensive news coverage. The goal is to disseminate information to stakeholder groups in a managed manner. Formal research is not part of the process.

Public   is an active stakeholder group.

Public relations   is a managed, researched, and planned process involving efforts to communicate directly or indirectly to publics of one or more persons or groups to inform, persuade, and/or to urge a call to action through various paid or unpaid messaging tactics.

Public relations research   is a set of techniques and principles for systematically collecting, recording, analyzing, and interpreting data that can inform decision makers about public relations including outcome evaluation, the organization itself, and the environments in which public relations operates.

Public Relations Society of America (PRSA),   founded in 1947, is the largest public relations association and has a global presence. It reports a membership of more than 30,000.

Public Relations Student Society of America (PRSSA)   is the student branch of the PRSA. PRSSA has more than 300 chapters consisting of more than 11,000 students and advisers located in the United States, Argentina, Colombia, and Peru.

Public service announcement (PSA)   is messaging that focuses on the public good. It comes in different formats, but typically take the form of audio (radio) spots or video for impact. It can be pre-recorded and produced for broadcast or be a spot announcement in which the talent delivers the PSA live. It normally runs 30 to 60 seconds. Medium vehicles such as radio, television, and cable stations donate air time to PSAs.

Public setting   allows anyone to join a group.

Publicist   is a professional who deals with the placement of a client's stories in the news media. Publicists also advise about other client communications.

Publicity   is a type of news or other media coverage about an issue not sponsored by the public relations organization. The organization has no control over the content, where it appears, or whether it is positive or negative.

Publics are individuals or organizations with shared interests and attributes. A public mobilizes or self-organizes around an issue.

Puffery overstates product performance.

Pulsing is a schedule that is continuous with spikes (a combination of continuous and flighting) such as promoting issues or products that are regularly used, but more so during certain times of the year like during political campaigns, new model year vehicles, and efforts to raise charitable donations during specified holidays.

Push-down banner expands to almost a full screen upon loading a page. Some publishers require the ad to collapse after a certain time (usually 7 to 10 seconds). The viewer may then click to re-expand the banner and read the content. Other website hosts allow the advertiser to keep the ad expanded, requiring the viewer to click to collapse it.

Qlog is a question-based blog. See blog for definition.

Qualifier is a statement that limits the strength of a claim. It presents the claim to be generally true with some realistic exceptions.

Qualitative research is planned and systematic. It does not involve statistics or numbers, but, at most, may include some basic tabulations.

Quantitative research is the exemplar of formal research. It involves statistics or applied mathematics used specifically for analyzing sample data. A sample consists of data derived from small groups of people or sources that are representative of the larger population of interest.

Quota sampling is a special case of judgmental sampling involving two stages. First, categories of characteristics serve as the basis for groups. Second, sample characteristics have quotas that are representative of the public in general.

Rational system is an organization that is highly formalized in pursuit of organizational goals and its mission. In a rational organization, the formal hierarchy provides the structure and formal mechanisms that are consequential.

Reach is the number of a public's members exposed to a message over a specified amount of time.

Red tape is a term that has a negative connotation. It refers to the perception of an overabundant number of steps or requirements necessary to operate in some way.

Reification is the process of taking something abstract and making it concrete or measurable.

Relatedness need, in Self-determination Theory, is the innate need to relate to others for the sake of doing so.

Relational barriers are obstacles to diversity that are based on interpersonal dynamics.

Reliability provides statistical consistency.

Repositioning is changing how an organization wants its stakeholders to view an issue and/or organization.

Requisite variety means that to optimally address an issue, an organization must possess resources that are equal to or greater than those inherent in the issue – than those that created the issue.

Research goal is what we intend to achieve by conducting a study. Issues inspire the development of research goals and informed decision-making.

Reservation is the rebuttal or acknowledgment of counterarguments to a claim. Think of it as a special type of qualifier.

Return on investment (ROI) is the profit derived from an investment in public relations efforts after cost is deducted.

Risk management   identifies and develops plans for responding to uncertain situations that, as yet, have not become issues that impact an organization.

Rites and rituals   are behaviors that orient organizational members to the ways of the culture.

ROI-AVE   is the closest standardized metric for placing a gross financial value on public relations efforts after the costs of related public relations activities are deducted.

Rotating banners   switch between two pages every 10–15 seconds. They are for high traffic sites. The refresh content is appealing, which gives publishers more impressions to sell.

RSS feed   provides new posts and updates from sources in the feed.

Safety Needs   consist of the desire to stay free from danger and environmental threats.

Sample   is a representative smaller group of a larger population under study

Sample data   are pieces of information collected from a small group of a specific population.

Sampling frame   is a source of data such as specific telephone lists, email lists, Facebook friends, Twitter followers, LinkedIn connections, voter lists, type of registration list, property ownership list, all the machinery output records from a manufacturing facility, or list of companies.

Sampling   is the activity associated with selecting sampling units from a population under study.

Sampling unit   is the individual source of data such as a person.

Sapir-Whorf Hypothesis   is a framework for seeing the connections between how members of a culture think, feeling, behave, and communicate in their world.

Scan™   is a continuous, multidisciplinary process that globally harvests seminal events in the chaotic external environment in which businesses operate. In successive steps, the Scan process identifies underlying currents likely to have an impact on future developments. Scan strives to provide early alerts about emerging issues that so far haven't found recognition in the business community.

Scheduling strategy   is the systematic placement and frequency of messaging using one or more communication channels to achieve campaign objectives within the specified timeline.

Scrolling banner   causes the ad to scroll through banner space like a billboard every 10–30 seconds.

Secondary research   is data previously collected for analysis. Some secondary data are summarized.

Secret setting   requires the prospective Facebook member to be added by an existing member. Only current or former group members can see a secret group's home page.

Secure self-esteem   is self-esteem based on one's own assessment and not contingent upon the evaluation of others. It is associated with task-involved activities.

Self-Actualization Needs   is the highest level of needs in which individuals aspire to achieve their full potential and become complete individuals.

Self-administered survey   is when invited respondents complete the surveys in their own time. They are given the survey or access to it. Participants answer questions using any of the following formats: hardcopy (which is returned via mail), text message, email, email or text message-linked, or web-based surveys using services such as Qualtrics and Zoomerang.

Self-concept   is one's self-description. It is not evaluative.

Self-Determination Theory is a framework for explaining human motivation based on the fulfilment of three basic and fundamental needs.

Self-esteem is how one feels about oneself after self-assessment.

Self-expression is, according to the VALS framework, one of the basic motivations.

Senior public relations management/leadership individual is a consultant to the organization, has extensive experience, and participates in strategic decision-making. The consultant spans boundaries (reaches out to various groups) by engaging both internal and external stakeholders. Some responsibilities involve organizational image, product and services positioning, and public relations campaign evaluation.

Sensors, according to the MBTI, are tacticians, operators, line supervisors, and managers. These people are detail-oriented and focus on implementing operational plans.

Search engine optimization (SEO) denotes search engine optimization. It is an approach to optimize the visibility of web pages as well as make user searches as relevant as possible.

Service fee is the cost assigned to the internal "client." These figures are analyzed along with the budgets of all departments or profit centers to assess organizational costs and contributions.

Setting is the environment in which an experiment takes place.

Shared media is publicity with a focus on sharing as the key mode of distribution.

Sign is any mark, bodily movement, symbol, token, etc., used to indicate and to convey thoughts, information, comments, etc.

Signage is outdoor and indoor signs that communicate the public relations campaign message.

Simple random sample is a method for selecting sampling units in which every sampling unit has an equal chance of selection.

Situation is a public relations environment such as the market for products, financial institutions, and legislative branches of state and federal governments in which the public relations issue exists.

Situational analysis is the information gathering phase of the public relations planning process.

Situational context is a major cause of groupthink.

Sleeper effect is a delayed increase in the impact of a salient persuasive message because of doubts in the source's credibility. Over time, as the connection between a message and source weakens, the audience member remembers the content and embraces the message without thinking about the source.

Slogan is a catch phrase using between one and a few words that capture the essence of the central message. It is fluid and changes over relatively short periods of time because it pertains to a brand, product, campaign, or limited area of an organization.

SMS is the Short Message Service protocol used for text messaging. Messages are 70–160 characters. Longer messages split into smaller parts.

Snap are self-destructing messages, photos, and videos on Snapchat.

Snowball sampling involves selecting an initial group of participants using random sampling techniques. The initial participants, in turn, identify other target public members for recruitment. This process continues until a sufficient number of individuals participate. Snowball sampling is utilized when the target public is small, unique, and/or recruitment is extremely difficult.

Social bookmarking   comprises social media sites that maintain lists of web addresses by subject from "all" users for future access.

Social campaigns   involve social issues such as domestic violence awareness and reporting, raising funds for disabled veterans, breast cancer awareness and support, Habitat for Humanity, Oxfam (global social justice and food for the poor), and many more.

Social influencers   are informal opinion leaders. Their influence is based on perceived or actual relationships.

Social listening and analytics   involve monitoring and interpreting social media communications and trends including deploying analytics.

Social media   are digital platforms that afford people, groups, communities, and organizations to not only communicate but also to interact in a dynamic and transactional way that allows for the creating and sharing of information, knowledge, beliefs, values, and opinions through informal and/or formal dialogue. In short, social media provide a place where stakeholders communicate; collaborate; educate and learn; and/or entertain.

Social media influencer   is a type of opinion leader who exerts influence in social media spaces. This person, group, or organization is perceived as a trusted and objective third party. The basis of influence may be emotional, and/or cognitive relying on the party's level of expertise or topic knowledge.

Social media tactics   are the specific activities deployed to achieve public relations objectives. Developing these tactics requires an understanding of social media platforms and what they offer users.

Social media technician's   role develops and implements public relations tactics such as writing news releases and blog posts.

Social network   is a place where parties connect much of which is online.

Source credibility   is another term for believability.

Special interest group (SIG)   is a community within a larger organization who shares an interest in advancing a specific area of knowledge. Community members cooperate and often produce solutions within their particular expertise as it relates to an issue.

Specialty periodical   can take the form of magazines, trade journals, and organizational magazines. Some examples are *Motor Trend*, *Aviation Week & Space Technology*, *Money*, *The Chronicle*, *Consumer Reports*, *America's Civil War*, *The African Executive*, *Le Commerce du Levant*, *FinanceAsia*, and *New Civil Engineer*.

Spies   provide valuable information to senior management daily. They are the informal eyes and ears of those at the top of the hierarchy.

Split loyalty   is loyalty to more than one organization.

Stage-of-Life-Cycle Budgeting   is based on the progression of an issue and used in conjunction with objectives.

Stakeholders   can be individuals or organizations. In either case, they comprise a group with shared characteristics. Stakeholders have ongoing relationship with an organization.

Start to Finish   a schedule in which a tactic cannot end before the preceding one starts, which may end later.

Start to Start   a schedule in which a tactic cannot start until the preceding tactic starts, but it does not have to be at the same time because they are interdependent tactics.

Statistics   is a type of applied mathematics used specifically for analyzing sample data.

Status markers   are indicators that someone is privileged. They come in many forms such as level of eye contact, how someone bows before another, and hand gestures.

Stereotyping is the behavior of ascribing characteristics to all members of a group, whether accurate, while not recognizing their individual differences.

Stimulus is an experimental condition, treatment, or manipulation.

Storyboard consists of key scene shots framed in drawing or photo format; direction for camera angles, types of cuts, transitions, and sound effects; and a voice script. The size of the storyboard varies based on the video length. For example, 8 to 12 frames are standard for a 30–60 second production. Movies contain hundreds of storyboard frames.

Storytellers interpret what they observe in the organization and create a narrative passed on to members to orient themselves to the culture by shaping their perceptions and expectations.

Strategic communication is systematic and planned through strategy and consistent messaging in the environments where an organization operates.

Strategy is the reasoning behind and overall framework of a public relations plan including goals, objectives, and a central message.

Stratified random sampling segments of the publics into sub publics or strata based on homogeneous characteristics that are important to the study. These characteristics are stratification variables and have different levels. Once the strata (and level) combinations are determined for each subgroup, then a representative sample is drawn from each.

Strivers, as a VALS type, are driven by achievement. This fun-loving public is trendy and attracted to fads. They seek peer approval. Money and materialism define their success. Strivers typically do not possess a sufficient amount of financial resources to meet their desires.

Structural barriers are obstacles to diversity that are inherent in an organizational system.

Structural faults are structures in an organization that hinder the communication of information; thus, decisions become less informed, and careless.

Structured observation is a specific method of observation.

Study design is the strategy and plan that specifies the methods for collecting and analyzing data.

Stuffing is repeating the keywords in a web page many times to the point that it is spamming.

Subjective Budgeting is based on practitioner expertise and/or experience. This type of budgeting considers objectives, but is subjective. The practitioner who sets this budget often uses features from other budgeting techniques.

Subjective norms are how we perceive others (e.g. peers, friends, family members, and professionals) and how society expects us to behave.

Subreddit is a smaller discussion forum community within a larger Reddit group.

Summative evaluation determines whether the campaign was successful by comparing the benchmarked objectives with the actual outcomes.

Survey design is based on questionnaires given to a sample to complete in order to analyze responses and uncover potential phenomena or patterns.

Survivors, as a VALS type, are just that, survivors. This public has few resources and perceives the world as too fast and rapidly changing. Their focus is more on Maslow's lower level needs such as safety and security. Typically, they do not have any primary motivation. Survivors tend to be cautious.

Symbols are arbitrary conventions such as stop signs or words.

Symbolic sign　is an arbitrary convention such as a stop sign or word. Providing that a person has knowledge of the symbol, its meaning is largely straightforward. Sometimes a word has multiple definitions that give way to an array of meanings.

Symmetric public relations　is communication that is socially responsible and considers the positions of the various publics in a free-flow of information and give-and-take. Communication is transparent, relational, and long term.

Syntactic indeterminacy　indicates that meaning ascribed to an image is implicit and subjective.

Systematic processing　is the comprehensive and analytic processing of information.

Systematic random sampling　is an approach to selecting sampling units in which every item has a known and equal chance of selection as in the case of the simple random approach. However, the methodology varies and is more complex than simple random sampling. This method overcomes some of the pitfalls of simple random sampling because sampling units are selected from the full range of the population or sampling frame, which more closely represents the entire public.

Tactic　is a tool, task, or activity pursued to achieve an objective that is associated with a public relations' goal, strategy, or objective.

Tagging　is the act of identifying photos or some other content by placing key descriptive terms in the metadata part of a photo.

Tagline　captures the essence of an entire organization, everything it does, and/or all its brands. It encapsulates the mission and identity of the organization in one to a few words.

Target behavior　is a desired behavior owing to a public relations' call to action.

Teaser video　is a shorter segment of an actual video, which draws attention, spikes curiosity, and increases traffic to the full videos.

Teleological　ethics is based on the impact of behaviors on people. Positive effects are deemed ethical and negative influences are viewed as unethical.

Terminal values　are about desired goals toward end states of existence.

Text network analysis (TNA)　is a method used to analyze larger amounts of text and distill meaning from words in relation to other words, clusters of words, and the entire text under examination.

The Global Alliance for Public Relations and Communication Management　consists of the world's major public relations and communication management associations and institutions. These organizations represent approximate 160,000 practitioners and academics around the world.

Themed events　are conferences, annual meetings, celebrations, workshops, dinners, recruitment fairs, contests, and competitions.

Theory　explains some phenomenon (e. g. individual or group behavior), the causes of the phenomenon (e. g. response to a persuasive appeal), and the likelihood of the phenomenon reoccurring.

Theory of Beliefs, Values, and Attitudes　posits that behaviors are based on attitudes shaped by core values and beliefs.

Theory of Planned Behavior　posits that attitudes toward behaviors, subjective norms, and perceived behavioral control together shape an individual's behavioral intentions and actual behaviors.

Theory of Reasoned Action　posits that behaviors are based on attitudes shaped by core values and beliefs including subjective norms.

Thinkers,　as a VALS type, are primarily motivated by ideals. They are satisfied, mature, and comfortable in their lives. As the name suggests, they reflect on their lives and society. Thinkers value order, knowledge, and responsibility. Many of them are well educated and informed about the world.

Third person effect   is a condition in which a person thinks that a predicted behavior cannot happen to him/her, but to someone else. The person thinks he is far removed from a negative event or effect.

Threat   "If you fail that test, then you will not be able to use the car." "If the project is not completed on time, there may be lay-offs."

Tolerance   is a permissive attitude toward those persons who are different.

Toulmin Model of Argumentation   is a usable and useful framework for constructing a persuasive argument about an issue.

Trackback   is a tool in a post that informs the owner of a site that linked him/her in a post.

Tracking study   involves collecting data over time from the same people or replacing those who leave the study with others from the same sampling frame.

Transactional public relations   is shaped by the interaction of the publics with the organization. All parties take ownership and thus there is an increased likelihood of engagement and commitment by these publics.

Translation   is the process of converting the corresponding *written* word meaning or ideas in one language to one or more other languages or dialects.

Transtheoretical Model of Behavioral Change   is a theory of behavior based on change over time. It is a system for behavior change or action starting from before the action is considered to its completion. It is applied to a single event, action, or behavior over time. The process involves six stages which are Precontemplation, Contemplation, Preparation, Action, Maintenance, and Termination.

Treatment   is an experimental condition, manipulation, or stimulus.

Trolling   is an activity in which the primary purpose is to post disparaging content about an individual or organization to cause anger or to damage the party's reputation.

Trustworthiness   is a dimension of source credibility. It is demonstrated through the source's reputation or through personal experience.

Tumbleblog   is a media rich blog. See blog for definition.

Tweet   is a short blog post limited to 280 characters or less. It can include links and images, which can be tagged.

Two-Way Asymmetric Model   works to persuade stakeholders to embrace a specific attitude or behavior using one-sided arguments.

Two-Way Symmetric Model,   which is the most ideal and optimistic framework of public relations, employs communication between all publics involved. Back and forth negotiation results in mutual understanding, resolved conflicts, and long-term agreement that respects the positions of all concerned publics.

Uncertainty avoidance   is the degree to which individuals feel uncomfortable with uncertainty and ambiguity.

Undisguised observation   is a method of observation in which the participants are aware that they are being observed.

Unicast banner   usually runs in a pop-up window playing a video like a television commercial, up to 30 seconds. They generate a high click-through rate.

Unique selling proportion   is messaging that makes an offer in which, in return for purchasing the product or service, the purchaser will receive a specified unique benefit that is not available from the competition. This process extends across different contexts in which an appeal is presented and a decision is made in response.

Unit-of-Sales Budgeting is a variation of the percentage-of-sales technique. It is based on the number of units sold. For example, for each unit sold or for each volunteer recruited, a set amount of funds is committed to the campaign for the subsequent year.

Unstructured observation does not have restrictions. The observer sees and records what is detected.

User kit is a press kit about a product or brand.

Uses and Gratifications Theory focuses on understanding why and how people, groups, and society in general actively seek out and use media to satisfy needs. It is an audience-centered approach focused on psychological and social reasons why people use media.

VALS is a typology of people based on individual's primary motivation. One or more of three self-expressive motivations drive people. They are ideals, achievement, and self-expression. People identify with them. They also serve as the basis from which people make sense of the world. There are eight general types.

Values are what we hold dear; they are fundamental to ourselves as human beings. At the organizational level, they are basic beliefs that form the core of what we hold dear; they are fundamental to ourselves as human beings.

Values expressive, according to the VALS framework, is a basic type of motivation. People have a desire to express what they value.

Variable is something that can be measured and changes or varies, such as age, attitude, belief, or some behavior.

Video b-rolls are unedited video shots and sound bites related to a news topic.

Video consists of motion graphics and audio. Some video are animations or rely heavily on special effects.

Video news release is a video formatted news release. It typically is 30 to 90 seconds long with narration, interviews, and other information.

Virtual reality is where users are exposed to a virtual world, usually through the use of a headset. Some headsets simulate places and conditions throughout the world that otherwise would be inaccessible to most people. Stories unfold in a virtual world that provides an audio-visual compelling presence supporting or opposing an issue.

Vlog is a video-based blog. See blog for definition.

Warrant is the reasoning or logical connection between a claim and its supporting data. It is the satisfaction of the relationship between the claim and the data.

Whisperers are those members who have access to the influential people in an organization. They often informally convey messages to senior management.

Wiki is akin to an online, collaborative encyclopedia that specializes in a general or specific topic.

Within-subjects' design is a study method that measures the same sample more than once and compares the measurements to uncover changes within the person over time.

XXL box banner is a colossal sized (468 x 648 pixels or more) ad used by prominent advertisers for brand effectiveness. This massive advertisement can comprise several pages and video.

Zero-Based Budgeting starts from zero. Resources are allocated based on prioritized objectives and tactics within those objectives. Once resources are exhausted, less important objectives or tactics are eliminated from the budget.

Public Relations Campaign Plansbook Checklist

CAMPAIGN TITLE:	
CHECKOFF	*REQUIREMENT*
	EXECUTIVE SUMMARY
	Table of Contents
	Situational Analysis
	Brief History and Description of the Organization, Situation, & Issue
	Issue Definition
	Competitive Idea Analysis
	Profile/Definition of Publics
	Strategy
	Public Relations Goal
	Central Message (including slogan/tagline)
	Complete Overall Benchmarked Objectives
	Action Plans for Each Public
	Define Public for Messaging
	Key Message
	Public Benchmarked Objectives
	Tactics (including timeline)
	Scheduling
	Scheduling Strategy (reasoning included)
	Gantt Chart
	Master Schedule & Budget

(continued)

(continued)

CAMPAIGN TITLE:	
COMPLETE	REQUIREMENT
	EXECUTIVE SUMMARY
	Table of Contents
	Budget
	Budget Strategy (type)
	Budget for Personnel, Administration, & Production
	Costs per Thousand Analysis
	Contingency Allocation
	Evaluation
	Ongoing over timeline
	Overall Benchmarks
	Action Plans' Benchmarks
	Advertising Value Equivalency
	Post-Campaign
	Overall Benchmarks
	Action Plans' Benchmarks
	Advertising Value Equivalency
	Conclusion
	References
	Appendix

Appendix C

Case Studies

Burger King Branding in Japan

Introduction

Campaign: Burger King "We Love 'Big'"

Burger King is a quick service (fast food) restaurant chain. It has 13,000 restaurants in 79 countries. Sixty-six percent are in the United States and 99% are privately owned. Many of its international locations are in Europe, Oceania, and East Asian countries such as Japan, Singapore, Taiwan, and South Korea. Recently, it entered the Indian market. To maintain expansion, Burger King relies on different franchising options. Typically, it is the responsibility of the franchisees to keep the individual restaurants modern and clean. Burger King invests in seating arrangements, décor, equipment, and other items that impact the consumer experience. This case study is about the launch of the Burger King Big King burger in Japan.

Japan is a very important market for us, and one that we have great growth plans for in the future, said Burger King Chief Executive John Chidsey, in Tokyo for the countdown ceremony where a jazz band played. A giant firecracker went off and glittery streamers filled the air as the doors opened (Associated Press, 2007, para. 9).

During the time of this case, 10% of Burger King restaurants in Japan were franchise owned. The company hopes to increase that to 70%. Despite limited resources Burger King Japan has been successful and anticipates continued success moving forward.

The Challenge for Burger King

The McDonald's Big Mac has iconic status in Japan cemented by strong brand loyalty over the years. Burger King had to make people aware of the Big King and attract Big Mac customers. Burger King had fewer than 93 restaurants in Japan, while McDonald's had 3,000. In fact, the chain was struggling to compete with much bigger rivals in Japan. The company hoped to have 200 restaurants in Japan by the end of 2017.

Competition between hamburger chains is intense. The challenging competitive mix involves *gyudon* beef bowl chains, ramen and soba noodle shops, and even convenience stores make it challenging to break through the market. Fast food restaurants need to localize their products for Japanese tastes. Because of these barriers to entry, Burger King withdrew from the Japanese market in 2001, as did several other U.S.-based burger chains including Carl's Jr. and Wendy's (Nagata, 2015, para. 7).

New York-based Bareburger opened its first store in Tokyo on July 19, 2015 while Florida-based Carl's Jr. re-entered the market in the fall and Shake Shack, also from New

York, planned to enter the Japanese market. Having more rivals means "we will have to compete for a limited pie. Thus, I'd rather have fewer rivals," Murao said (Nagata, 2015, para. 14).

Moreover, Burger King's brand recognition was limited to the Tokyo metropolitan area. Awareness was low in other areas of the country.

Additionally, profitably operating a Burger King in high traffic cities is nearly prohibitive in Japan owing to the cost of real estate. This was challenging for price conscious restaurants.

The McDonald's chicken incident negatively impacted many quick service food chains last July and August of 2014. However, sales have slowly recovered.

Product Line

When Burger King was opened, the first restaurant menu included basic hamburgers, desserts, French fries, milk shakes and soft drinks. In 1957, Burger King introduced the "Whopper Sandwich" to its menu. This hamburger that is just a quarter pounder has become synonymous with the brand name and therefore the new restaurants were even named "Whopper Bars."

In 1979, a special Sandwich line was introduced and later the breakfast product line was offered. In the later years, Mini Muffins and French toast sticks were added to the menu. With the expansion of various outlets in different regions the menus were somewhat localized to adhere to regional tastes and religious beliefs.

Fast-food items such as Texas Double Whopper, Mushroom sandwiches and Swiss cheese have been rotated in the menu on and off over time. At present **bacon cheeseburger, hamburger, coffee, juice, cookies, whopper junior, French fries of medium size, chicken tenders, onion rings, soft drink and a shake** are served to the customers (Bhasin, 2018, para. 2–4).

"Burger King Japan says its strength is the taste of its food and menu range, and the right mix of local offerings and recipes that are popular globally" (Nagata, 2015). To develop tasty foods for the market, the company modified its buns to include more water to match the taste of the Japanese consumers, who the company reported have less saliva compared to other people. Additionally, Burger King's prices are high enough to signal the quality of products, but sufficiently low so that customers are willing to pay for it.

Publics

The key public consisted of Big Mac customers and fans. Other customers were the market in general public as well as the news media.

The Strategy

Burger King launched the We Love "Big" campaign focusing on promotions. A key strategy component was to make consumers associate the word "big" with Burger King by converting any items that were big in size or had the word "big" in them into unique game coupons redeemable at Burger King for discounts on hamburgers.

Based on the classic Japanese word association game "Ogiri," players provide the simplest and most logical answer in response to a question or topic. For example, for consumers, "big" equates with Burger King, or the Big King burger. Any customers that submitted the coupon and answer at Burger King restaurant would receive a discount on the Big King, which made the paid price comparable to the Big Mac. This contest received a substantial amount of publicity. Customers not only submitted the coupon, but brought into the restaurants empty Big Mac boxes, McDonald's receipts, and albums by the American rock band Mr. Big, or a tall friend, among other items to qualify for the discount so that anything large could become a media vehicle for Burger King.

Additionally, Burger King's product line in Japan varied. One product was a black burger dyed with tomato powder and a brand new black burger with deep-fried eggplant. Another version had black buns, black cheese, and black sauce. The burgers appeared unappetizing in real life.

Because of a small promotional budget, these odd colors burgers were meant to draw attention to the brand through grass roots buzz and media coverage, which proved effective. Major media organizations in the United States and Japan, including *Business Insider, The Wall Street Journal, Time, Forbes,* and *The Japan Times* covered the uniquely colored sandwiches and customers posted hundreds of photos of the burgers online.

Results

The We Love "Big" campaign created huge media buzz and was a major trend across various social media platforms for several weeks in Japan. As reported in an article by Faaez Samadi (2016, para. 10–11):

> In total, 66,000 "big" items were brought to Burger King stores during the campaign, which ran from January to December 2015. Moreover, in a survey of 106 customers, 70% said they preferred the Big King to the Big Mac.
>
> All of this led to a 116% growth in sales compared to the previous year, with estimated media exposure worth US $3.3 million, making We Love "Big" Burger King's most successful campaign to date in Japan.

Assignment

Using this case material as a starting point, develop a public relations strategy and plan for Burger King Japan. How would you win over Big Mac devotees to Burger King? Conduct an online search for additional information and facts including news stories, social media, YouTube, and other sources. Keep in mind that the cultural, economic, political, legal, and media environments play a role in determining the degree of activism and public relations in a given country. Considering the effective tactics deployed by Burger King, what would you change or incorporate in your strategy and plan today? Consult the campaign checklist located in the appendix and think about the following questions.

1   Who are the major Burger King Japan publics and why?
2   How would you measure engagement of the major Burger King market segment?
3   How would you address Burger King's challenges?
4   What additional tactics would you deploy not mentioned in the case? Be specific and think about social media and other tactics while considering Burger King's promotional successes.

References

Associated Press. NBCNews.com. (2007, June 8). *Burger King back in Japan after 6-year hiatus.* Retrieved from www.nbcnews.com/id/19106828/ns/business-us_business/t/burger-king-back-japan-after--year-hiatus/.

Bhasin, H. (2018, January 15). *Marketing mix of Burger King.* Retrieved from www.marketing91.com/marketing-mix-of-burger-king/.

Nagata, K. (2015, July 28). *Burger King to press ahead with expansion despite increasing competition.* Retrieved from www.japantimes.co.jp/news/2015/07/28/business/corporate-business/burger-king-press-ahead-expansion-despite-increasing-competition-ceo/.

Samadi, F. (2016, January 29). *Case study: How Burger King took a bigger bite out of Japan.* Retrieved from www.prweek.com/article/1381379/case-study-burger-king-took-bigger-bite-japan.

CVS: Promoting Recruitment and Retention

The Situation

Over the period 2014–24, the labor will grow an anticipated 5%, while the expected labor force growth rate of the 65- to 74-year-old age group is 55%, and the growth rate of the 75-and-older age group will be 86%. Most of this growth comes from the Baby Boomers generation, those born between 1946 to 1964. Some of the Boomers expect to work after they qualify for Social Security retirement benefits.

Between 1970 and 2000, workers 55 years old and older constituted the smallest segment of the U.S. labor force. However, during the 1990s, the older worker labor force share began to increase, while younger workers are on the decline. In 2003, the older age group no longer had the smallest share. The United States Bureau of Labor Statistics predicts that by 2024, the American labor force will grow to approximately 164 million people, which will include 41 million people aged 55 years and older, and 13 million are expected to be aged 65 and older (Toossi & Torpey, 2017).

People are working later in life for several reasons. First, they are healthier and have a longer life expectancy than previous generations. Second, they are more educated, which increases their likelihood of staying in the labor force. Third, some older people prefer to stay active and engaged. Fourth, for some people, work adds meaning to their lives. Fifth, there are flexible schedule work options available. Sixth, Boomers have a strong work ethic that they carry into retirement. Last, changes to Social Security benefits and employee retirement plans, along with the need to save more funds for retirement, make continued work a necessity.

Introduction to CVS and the Issue

CVS Pharmacy is a subsidiary of the American retail and health care company CVS Health, headquartered in Woonsocket, Rhode Island, U.S.A. CVS is an acronym for its original name, Consumer Value Stores. Founded in Lowell, Massachusetts in 1963 CVS Pharmacy is the largest pharmacy chain in the United States. In 2017, CVS revenues were $155 billion. The chain has over 240,000 employees and maintains nearly 10,000 retail stores. It is the seventh largest corporation in the United States.

CVS sells prescription drugs and a wide assortment of general merchandise, including over-the-counter drugs, beauty products and cosmetics, film and photo finishing services, seasonal merchandise, greeting cards, and convenience foods through its CVS retail stores and online at CVS.com. Moreover, CVS offers healthcare services at more than 1,100 Minute Clinics (medical clinics), as well as diabetic care services at its Diabetes Care Centers. Most of these clinics are at the CVS retail stores.

CVS, like many organizations, faces the challenge of finding competent and reliable workers, whether pharmacists, technicians, or those in other positions. By 2024, 25% of the U.S. labor force will be 55 years old or more. CVS anticipates that at least 25% of its workers will be over 55 years old by that year. The company is actively engaged in attracting and recruiting prospective employees 55 and older. CVS's efforts to recruit mature workers and create a multigenerational culture started during the mid-2000s.

According to David Casey, Vice President of Workforce Strategies and Chief Diversity Officer for CVS Health,

Mature workers play an integral role in the culture at CVS Health by providing increased experience, dependability, and a desire to learn new skills. Some have been with the company for decades, while others joined our team more recently as a second or third career . . . We know that 90 percent of Americans aged 65 and older are using at least one prescription drug a month, and 40 percent use at least five. So, as we see the baby boomer generation age, having colleagues across the company who can personally relate to these customers and patients is a differentiator for us.

(Recruiting Mature Workers, 2017)

Challenges for CVS

CVS faces image challenges in its efforts to recruit and retain quality employees. Several controversies and negative publicity have tarnished its credibility.

- During 2005, some Boston area CVS stores made prescription errors going back to 2002. In February 2006, the Massachusetts Board of Pharmacy announced that the non-profit Institute of Safe Medication Practices would monitor all Massachusetts CVS stores for two years.
- A federal grand jury returned an indictment charging bribery, conspiracy, and fraud concerning former CVS executives, John R. Kramer and Carlos Ortiz, for allegedly paying off a Rhode Island State senator to act as a "consultant." The senator, who pled guilty, had received $1,000 per month, tickets to golf and sporting events, and compensation for travel to Florida and California. A jury trial acquitted Kramer and Ortiz in May 2008.
- In 2009, a CVS location in Austin, Texas was sued and ordered to pay the federal government $2.25 million in a HIPAA Privacy Case. The U.S. Department of Health and Human Services Office for Civil Rights and the Federal Trade Commission found that CVS did not appropriately dispose of sensitive patient information or provide the required training on records disposal to its employees. This was the second incident; CVS paid a fine of nearly $400,000 for the first episode in 2007.
- In February 2008, CVS settled a large civil lawsuit for engaging in deceptive business practices. The company agreed to a $38.5 million multi-state settlement. CVS had misinformed physicians by telling them that that patients or health plans would save money if patients changed to certain brand-name prescription drugs. The only financial beneficiary of the switch was CVS's and other pharmacy management programs, which kept discounts and rebates that should have been passed along to the patient or health plan. "The settlement prohibits Caremark from requesting prescription drug switches in certain cases, such as when the cost to the patient would be higher with the new prescription drug; when the original prescription drug's patent will expire within six months; and when patients were switched from a similar prescription drug within the previous two years" (Levick, 2008).
- During October 2010, CVS was ordered to pay $77.6 million in fines from a lawsuit for improper control of the selling of pseudoephedrine, which is an ingredient used to make methamphetamine.
- In 2011, the Department of Justice held that CVS pharmacies in Sanford, Florida ordered enough Oxycodone painkillers to supply a population eight times the city's size. The CVS city locations averaged 137,994 pills a month per location.

Other pharmacies in Florida averaged 5,364 oxycodone pills per month. The incident was reported in USA Today.

- Like other pharmacies, CVS sold cigarettes after criticism from many health groups. The company's position was that their internal research discovered that ceasing cigarette sales would not change smoking behavior. However, under intense pressure, in February 2014, CVS announced that it would stop selling cigarettes and other tobacco products at its retail stores. A Forbes magazine article cited that the change in heart corresponded with CVS's decision to change its corporate name from CVS/Caremark Corp. to CVS Health.

Publics

Prospective mature employees, aged 55 years and older is the key public. However, presenting CVS as a desirable place of employment requires reaching other publics such as the public, shareholders, customers, current employees, news media, and present mature employees. These publics contribute to positive brand equity by having a favorable image of CVS and sharing that perception with other stakeholder groups.

Recruitment and Retention Goal and Objectives

CVS is committed to hiring and retaining mature employees; therefore, the impression of CVS in the communities it serves provides labor to its stores is vitally important. The goal is to recruit and retain mature employees. However, before this happens, there are objectives that must be met.

- Establish CVS as a corporate leader in workforce development;
- Position CVS as an attractive employer to workers age 55+;
- Gain exposure for the mature worker initiative and other innovative CVS workforce programs targeting seniors; and
- Build brand equity for CVS in markets such as the Northeast and other regions where the company has grown through acquisitions.

To meet this goal and these objectives, a public relations team met each year to set goals, objectives, and strategies as well as plan for the subsequent year.

Tactics to Recruit and Retain Mature Employees

There are two sets of tactics required to achieve the two-faceted goal: (1) recruit and (2) retain reliable and capable mature employees. CVS first established an internal program to retain and encourage mature worker engagement through the "Talent Is Ageless" initiative. This and other programs served to highlight CVS's commitment to hiring experienced and valued mature employees.

Retention

Many organizations seek younger employees with digital skills so that they operate in cost-efficient ways. Arguably, some employers push out older workers. Raises, which were once routine, vanished, accompanied by a reduction in responsibilities and poor evaluations. By the same token, some organizations promote innovative programs for older employees because they do not wish to lose their experience, their rapport with customers, and their ability to mentor younger workers. CVS falls in the latter group.

Talent Is Ageless Mature Worker Hiring Program

The "Talent is Ageless" program cultivates public and private partnerships at the local, state, and national level with the intention to recruit mature workers into all areas of CVS's business. Some national partnerships were the American Society on Aging, Experience Works, AARP, National Council on Aging, and the Senior Community Service Employment program. As reported on the CVS website, the program continues to focus on three priorities:

Compassionate, Caring People

As a pharmacy innovation company, we are compassionate and caring, offering our colleagues opportunities for personal and professional growth and developing strong loyalty with our community partners, customers, clients and patients. We are driven by the strong belief that helping people on the path to better health is not only a social responsibility but a way to achieve long-term growth and economic success. We help individuals unlock their own full potential and capabilities. As we attract a new talent pool, we also help break the cycle of poverty and build resilience.

Working Together

Working Together is a vital part of the Talent Is Ageless program. CVS Health is closely tied with industry thought leaders, and partners regularly with federal, state and local government agencies. These strong workforce partnerships help us meet today's demands and prepare for tomorrow's talent needs. We have ongoing partnerships with organizations that include the American Society on Aging, National Caucus and Center on Black Aging, Inc., and the Network of Jewish Human Service Agencies.

In addition, our partnerships with academic institutions, such as the Sloan Center on Aging & Work at Boston College, provide insights into current and future trends, and we work with community colleges to create relevant offerings to our mature workforce.

Discovering You!

All CVS Health employees have the opportunity to further their careers through education. By way of the "Discovering You!" training module, mature employees can put their newly acquired skills and knowledge to work and inspire their colleagues to do the same.

(*Talent is Ageless*, 2017, para. 3–6).

Additionally, CVS offers a "snowbird" program in which several hundred pharmacists and other employees from Northern states are transferred each winter to pharmacies in Florida and other warmer states (CVS/pharmacy Receives Top Honor for Mature Worker Initiatives, 2007). Suzanne Fontaine, 66, a certified pharmacy technician at a CVS in New England, said she would have retired years ago if the company had not let her work during the winter months at a CVS store in Naples, Florida, where she and her husband have a home. Ms. Fontaine helped with the extra retail business that spiked during the winter months as well as trained and mentored new employees.

Another initiative is the Alternate Work Arrangements program, which centers on helping mature workers remain in the workplace with modifications that include: telecommuting, flextime, job sharing, reasonable accommodations, and compressed work weeks. As Casey put it, "By looking for new ways to integrate the wants and needs of mature workers into our culture, we can ensure that everyone has a place within our company" (*Recruiting Mature Workers*, 2017, para. 7).

Recruitment

Retention messaging links to recruitment communication because awareness about retention and the attractive programs and commitment to keep mature employees is likely to influence those who consider and apply for a position in the first place. What follows are the key tactics and activities for reaching and creating knowledge about CVS's commitment to hiring and keeping mature workers.

News Media

News releases with a pitch letter about a national worker trend story can lead to positive publicity. After CVS submitted stories on CVS Caremark's mature worker initiatives to *The Christian Science Monitor*, *Time*, and the *Boston Globe*, other media outlets approached CVS requesting information so that they could cover such stories. CVS also provided video news releases. The news media presented the stories from a unique angle suited to meet their audience's preferences. CVS reached out to multiple designated market areas across the country presenting these stories to many news medium outlets.

Partnering

To increase exposure to CVS's initiatives, the company collaborated with AARP. The company leverages itself as an AARP Featured Employer to tie the CVS stories to the larger workplace trend. Two studies came out in late 2005 that made the case for older workers in the marketplace. "The Business Case for Workers Age 50 plus" study dismissed the fallacy that mature workers cost more than younger workers to maintain. Another was the Boston College Center on Aging and Work's Study. It concluded that Baby Boomer employees would not stop working entirely and that flexible schedules will keep them working. Both studies were attention getters for presenting CVS's mature employee recruitment and retention programs.

In addition, CVS collaborated with state and federal workforce agencies to provide employment services and training to underserved communities. Nation-wide, thousands of people accessed meaningful employment opportunities. CVS also reached out to schools, churches, universities, faith-based organizations, and community groups to hire mature people from diverse backgrounds.

Open Lines of Communication

A dialogue was maintained between stores and the public relations team. Stores were reminded to email employee stories on a regular basis.

Sometimes one tidbit of information isn't newsworthy on its own, but when added to information received from other field staff, it turns into an interesting trade story for the media. During the past several years, my field staff has recognized the value in sending ideas to the (ad) agency, and now they regularly send ideas to Weber Shandwick without any prompting.

(PR News Editors, p. 22)

Results

CVS's outreach to recruit mature employees had a limited budget. Yet, it was successful. During its first year of implementation in 2006, 38 articles covered CVS recruitment efforts. It resulted in 37 million media impressions as well. Additionally, the initiatives received significant online exposure in leading national, regional, and trade outlets. During 2006 and 2007, the campaign received more than 200 million media impressions.

Because of the public relation outreach campaign, CVS/ pharmacy also grew its mature worker program from fewer than 300 employees to more than 1,000 in 2006. Additionally, current employees, customers, and shareholders became more aware of CVS as a leader in workforce development.

The CVS public relations staff realized that workforce trends reporting had broad appeal with news media gatekeepers. Reporters who covered business, employment, education, retail, and social issues were also interested in the workforce stories, which provided personal relevance and an interesting perspective. All of this was done on a relatively small budget with high advertising equivalency value.

Assignment

Using this case material as a starting point, develop a public relations outreach strategy and plan to recruit and retain mature CVS employees. How would you create a favorable impression of CVS? How would you address its negative publicity? Conduct an online search for additional information and facts including news stories, social media, YouTube, and other sources. Considering the effective tactics deployed by CVS, what would you change or incorporate in your strategy and plan today? Consult the campaign checklist located in the appendix and think about the following questions.

1 Who are the major CVS publics and why?
2 How would you measure engagement of the major CVS stakeholder groups?
3 Identify and address any challenges.
4 What are the key objectives?
5 What additional tactics would you deploy not mentioned in the case? Be specific and think about social media and other tactics.
6 What additional tactics might you deploy directed at the media?
7 What specific partnering arrangements and events might contribute to the goal?

References

CVS/pharmacy Receives Top Honor for Mature Worker Initiatives. (2007, March 9). *Retrieved from:* https://cvshealth.com/newsroom/press-releases/cvspharmacy-receives-top-honor-mature-worker-initiatives.

Levick, D. (2008, February 15). Caremark Settles States' Probe. *Hartford Courant.* Retrieved from https://en.wikipedia.org/wiki/CVS_Pharmacy.

PR News Editors. (Fourth Edition). PR News Top 100 Case Studies in Public Relations. *PR New Press.*

Recruiting Mature Workers. (2017, August 9). Retrieved from https://cvshealth.com/about/diversity/recruiting-mature-workers.

Talent Is Ageless. (2017, August 9). Retrieved from https://cvshealth.com/about/diversity/talent-is-ageless-mature-workers.

Toossi, M., & Torpey, E. (2017, May). Older workers: Labor force trends and career options. *Bureau of Labor Statistics: Career Outlook.* Retrieved from www.bls.gov/careeroutlook/2017/article/older-workers.htm.

Deepwater Horizon Case Study in Crisis Communication

Introduction

Deepwater Horizon was a deep water, semi-submersible offshore drilling rig owned by Transocean, which is one of the world's largest offshore drilling contractors based in Vernier, Switzerland. The company has offices in 20 countries, including Switzerland, Canada, United States, Norway, Scotland, India, Brazil, Singapore, Indonesia and Malaysia. In 2001, Hyundai built the Deepwater Horizon in South Korea. Its registration was Majuro, Republic of the Marshall Islands with a population of 28,000. BP, a British-based global oil company, signed a contract to lease the rig from Transocean for three years for deployment in the Gulf of Mexico. The crew, gear and support vessels were additional costs. The Deepwater Horizon was known for drilling the deepest hole in history, which was over 35,000 feet and under nearly one mile of water. The rig was legendary for its performance and drilling achievements.

Typically, Transocean owns, operates, and sometimes leases rigs to customers such as large oil companies as was BP in this case. Leases range from one to five years. A third company, Halliburton provides specific services, equipment, and supplies such as the cement intended to secure the drilled well and prevent leaks. In short, BP was the client. Transocean and Halliburton were BP's oil service vendors.

On April 20, 2010, while drilling in the Gulf of Mexico off the southeast coast of Louisiana, an uncontrollable blowout caused an explosion on the rig that killed 11 crewmen and was visible 40 miles away. An uncontrollable fire ensued. Two days later, the Deepwater Horizon sank leaving the well gushing at the seabed and causing the largest oil spill in U.S. waters.

Rig Design

The Deepwater Horizon was a fifth-generation mobile offshore drilling unit, designed to drill underwater wells for oil exploration and production. In 2010, the Deepwater Horizon was one of 200 deep water offshore rigs capable of drilling in waters deeper than 5,000 feet. In 2002, Transocean upgraded the rig with the "e-drill" monitoring system so that technical personnel based in Houston, Texas received real-time drilling data from the rig and could transmit maintenance and troubleshooting information.

Advanced systems played a key role in the rig's operation, from pressure and drill monitoring technology and automated shutoff systems to modelling systems for cementing. The OptiCem cement modelling system, used by Halliburton in April 2010, played a critical role in the cement slurry mix and support decisions, which became a focus of the subsequent investigation of the explosion.

The rig's estimated cost was $340 million. It was insured for $560 million to cover replacement and salvage costs.

The Incident

The well was in the final stages of completion at the time of the accident. Its injected cement casing was hardening and the rig was scheduled to move to its next job as a semi-permanent production platform at another site 50 miles off the coast of Louisiana.

According to press accounts, certain safety documentation and emergency procedure information, including documentation about the incident was absent. For example, the number of required monthly inspections performed varied over time. Although this was common because circumstances such as weather and movement preclude inspections, the inspections were carried out as required for the first 40 months, but after that only 75% were documented. Each of these inspections lasts up to two hours.

During its lifetime, the Deepwater Horizon received five citations for non-compliance, four of which were in 2002 (safety, including the blowout preventer) and the other in 2003 (pollution related). A sixth citation in 2007 related to non-grounded electrical equipment. According to a drilling consultant reviewing the information, the overall safety record was "strong," which by all accounts was corroborated by other sources.

At 9:45 pm on April 20, 2010, a geyser of seawater erupted from the marine riser onto the rig shooting 240 feet into the air followed by the eruption of a slushy combination of drilling mud, methane gas, and water. The gas component of the slushy material quickly transitioned into gaseous state and then ignited into a series of explosions resulting in a firestorm. The blowout preventer safety mechanism failed to activate. The final mechanism to prevent an oil spill, a device known as a blind shear ram, activated but failed to plug the well.

At the time of the explosion, there were 126 crew on board; seven were employees of BP, 79 of Transocean, and there were employees of various other companies involved in the operation of the rig, including Anadarko, Halliburton and M-I SWACO. Eleven workers died during the initial explosion. During the evacuation, injured workers were airlifted to medical facilities. After approximately 36 hours, Deepwater Horizon sank. The remains of the rig were located resting on the seafloor approximately 5,000 feet deep at that location 1,300 feet northwest of the well. The oil spill continued until July 15 when the well was permanently capped.

Issue

The issue was complex. There are four components to it: The initial incident in which 11 workers died and others were injured. Second, the spill was not immediately under control, but had to be stopped as soon as possible. Third, BP's reputation was called into question because of its past safety performance record and reports of the backup systems failing. Last, how the company manages the current situation considering its past operational performance will impact its financial situation notwithstanding the financial consequences of the spill per se.

Publics

Local, state, and federal authorities.

The news media.

Victims and families of victims.

Local residents.

Environmental groups and other NGOs.

Major shareholders and banking institutions.

BP's Response

BP initially declared that the accident was not its fault. BP representatives blamed their oil service contractors: Transocean and Halliburton. They further denied the extent of the environmental damage. For instance, the company initially informed reporters that the rig was leaking 1,000 barrels of oil per day. The actual amount was 5,000 barrels per day. Even after this information was brought to light, a BP spokesman downplayed the leak to between 1,000 and 5,000. Their position appeared arrogant and callous.

In the past, BP was well known for its public relations, both positive and negative. Launched in 2000, its "Beyond Petroleum" rebranding campaign earned kudos and accolades from the public relations community. Its critics saw the campaign as greenwashing. Because of the Deepwater Horizon accident, BP experimented with new ways to get its message out in addition to official statements, press releases, and morning-show interviews with mixed results. But it appeared to be having more success with social media. However, prior to the accident, BP CEO Tony Hayward had slashed the company's public relations budget to cut costs. At the time of the incident, consultants and inexperienced BP staffers advised him.

Hayward's lack of public relations understanding manifested in a series of insensitive comments he made. He walked the beaches in the Gulf wearing an expensive starched white shirt. During one of his visits to the shore, he said, "There's no one who wants this thing over more than I do. You know, I'd like my life back." Hayward did not understand the influence of the media or the public's perception of a foreigner in south Louisiana.

Additionally, BP Chairman Carl-Henric Svanberg said that BP cared about the "small people" affected on the Gulf Coast. This reference contributed to the larger narrative of a foreign company with a history of industrial accidents damaging the Gulf Coast environment while only showing concern about the event's impact to the company. It was apparent that BP did not have a public relations strategy.

The public reviewed the Gulf of Mexico oil spill as BP's oil spill. This was further reinforced by President Obama's and the Environmental Protection Agency's reference to the BP oil spill.

To mitigate the negative publicity, BP ran a multimillion-dollar national TV ad featuring Hayward. He stated, "We will make this right" and promised that BP would clean up every drop of oil. The shoreline would be restored to its original state. Essentially the message was to trust BP because they would correct the situation. This happened as the oil was gushing into the Gulf, which questioned the company's statement that everything was under control. President Barack Obama responded by saying that the money spent on the ads should have gone to cleanup and to compensate devastated fisherman and small business owners.

BP's social media was effective. The company updated the public on Facebook, Twitter, Flickr, and YouTube about capping the spill, clean-up in the Gulf, and restitution. Social media also allowed BP to respond quickly to any rumors or errors in media coverage. It also became an outlet for people to vent their anger and frustrations. Social media became a way for BP to gain direct access to the public bypassing news media. On the BP website, visitors found pictures, videos, and maps that tracked the spill and clean-up also serving as a channel to communicate directly with stakeholders.

During the beginning of the crisis, BP and government officials held daily in-person briefings with media in a Q&A format. As time passed, BP officials increasingly resorted to teleconferences with reporters and limited the Q&A sessions. In Houston, BP PR officials discouraged reporters going directly to their engineers and other managers for information. In fact, BP spokesperson Robert Wine wrote in an email to The Associated Press that media visits to the BP Houston offices were strictly controlled and sparingly arranged by design.

BP also bought website pop up ads when people searched for information about the oil spill on Google and Yahoo. The ads, linked to BP's own oil-response sites, appeared above or to the right of other search results. BP claimed that the ads were to help people living along the Gulf coast find people and information quickly and effectively. Critics suggested that they were there to steer searchers away from negative BP press.

Based on the prospect of billions of dollars in law suits, BP's stock prices in the United States and Europe dropped to their lowest point since the mid-1990s. Company spokespersons responded by saying that they were unaware of any reason that justified the stock price change.

Assignment

Using this case material as a starting point, develop an alternative public relations strategy and plan for BP. In other words, how would you address from a public relations perspective the Deepwater Horizon Crisis? Conduct an online search for additional information and facts including news stories, social media, YouTube, and other sources. Consider what was done and what you would change or incorporate in your strategy and plan today. Consult the campaign checklist located in the appendix and think about the following questions.

1 What should have been BP's public relations (crisis communication) goals?
2 In order of priority who were the BP key publics and why?
3 Identify a central message to address the accident.
4 What tactics would you suggest that BP deploy and why?

Dubai International Motor Show: Media Coverage and Promotions

Introduction

In 2017, the Dubai International Motor Show held its annual event at the Dubai World Trade Centre. For the last 14 years, it has been the largest international automotive show across the Middle East and North Africa. The venue brings together worldwide manufacturers, distributors, automotive industry specialists, key-buyers, and many driving enthusiasts to experience exclusive car launches, interactive demonstrations, and other activities.

The number of global and regional launches at the 2017 exhibition surpassed the previous high of 157 in 2015. There were dedicated pavilions for every driving passion, from supercars and custom bikes to highly specialized vehicles. The key show features were:

- 550+ cars and bikes
- 100+ global and regional car premiers
- 15+ supercar brands
- 10+ concept cars
- 108,000+ visitors from more than 70 countries
- 1,000+ global medium outlets
- Over 85,000 square meters of exhibition space featuring the world's top manufacturers.

Show-Related Transportation Services

Dubai Metro

The Dubai Metro's red line "World Trade Centre Station" served the exhibition center. Parking was available on the Red Line at Rashidiya, Nakheel Harbour & Towers, and on the Green Line at Etisalat.

Taxi Service

Taxis are affordable in Dubai and operated by RTA through five companies (denoted by different color roofs). All RTA taxis are metered at the same rate, except the "pink" ladies-only cabs for which there is a small surcharge. Only women drive pink cabs, which are only accessible to women and families. In a 2017 interview, Ammar Bin Tamim, Director of Dubai Taxi, told Reuters, "Our society is conservative and our women do not want to ride with men alone at night or when they arrive at the airport at two or three in the morning" (Saadeh, 2007, para. 3).

At the show location, there are two taxi drop-offs sites: opposite Ibis Hotel and in front of Zabeel Hall entrance. The taxi pick-up point is located opposite Ibis Hotel. Taxi-sharing is likely to be in operation during peak periods.

Transportation Card

"Nol" cards are offered as a convenient method of payment for transportation services. With the card, visitors can pay for the Dubai's Metro, buses, water buses, and parking.

Situational Analysis

The high-end automotive market in the Middle East is growing and is very competitive. The Dubai International Motor Show is an important event. Positive media coverage is an effective marketing approach to reach the market segment of upper middle and upper income consumers. Therefore, it is important to know what content the media report. For media outlets, a larger audience translates into selling advertising space for more money.

During the 2013 exhibition, one of the exhibitors, Jaguar Land Rover (JLR), decided to conduct research about media coverage for the show, and particularly about JLR and its key competition's media coverage before, during, and post show. The research was to aid in:

- assessing the relative visibility of the JLR brands compared to the competition;
- comparing favorable coverage JLR brands against the competition;
- identifying the geographical reach features of the media coverage;
- discovering the depth and breadth of overall media coverage in the area and coverage on JLR and its competition;
- determining to what degree JLR and its competition were covered in the context of the show;
- learning which product attributes of JLR and its competitors were given positively in coverage; and
- assessing media coverage of JLR's new C-X17 concept vehicle.

The Current Media Landscape

News outlets in the Middle East and North Africa covering the automotive sector and relevant market segment are abundant. Many of the magazines and newspapers are available online. The following is a list of medium vehicles.

Websites:

- Al Badia
- Almuraba.net
- AMEinfo
- Auto-Data.net
- Autos Middle East and Africa
- Carsworld.ae
- Crankandpiston.com
- Mawater Arabia
- MyUAEguide
- Opulence Asia
- Readme.ae
- Rijal
- RoadSafetyUAE

Newspapers, Weeklies, and Magazines:

- *AL YAQZA*
- *Alam Attijarat*
- *Alam Elsyarat Magazine*

- *Alroeya*
- *Amlak Real Estate Newspaper*
- *AMWAL Newspaper*
- *Arab Motor World*
- *Arab Motors Magazine*
- *Auto Middle East*
- *Automobile*
- *Autozone Magazine*
- *BESPOKE*
- *BodyShop News*
- *Business Emirates Magazine*
- *CarBook Magazine*
- *Durrah Magazine*
- *East Springs*
- *Elite Living Africa*
- *English Automotive Magazine*
- *FACT*
- *FIRST AVENUE*
- *Forbes Middle East*
- *Gulf Auto Zone (GAZ)*
- *Khaleej Times*
- *Maqina*
- *Ohlala*
- *Petrolhead Arabia*
- *Russian Emirates Magazine*
- *Saneou Al Hadath*
- *Saudi Auto*
- *Sport Auto*
- *TeknoTel*
- *Tharawat Magazine*
- *The Billionaire Magazine*
- *Top Performance*
- *TRENDS*
- *WEALTH*
- *YallaMotor*

Television:

- B4U Aflam
- B4U Plus
- BBC Top Gear Middle East
- Bloomberg Businessweek Middle East
- BodyShop News International
- CATV
- Sky News Arabia

Results

For the 2017 Dubai International Motor Show, the JLR's public relations program directed at garnering favorable media coverage proved successful.

1   JLR was among the top three most discussed brands in nine of the 14 tracked markets. Comments by a senior company representative boosted the volume and prominence of the brand's coverage.
2   More than 50% of articles mentioning Jaguar or Land Rover featured the brands in the headline, with 25% of all such articles exclusive to JLR brands.
3   The C-X17 was well received, appearing in the greatest number of articles for the brand, and winning praise for its styling, innovation and desirability.
4   Although BMW and Audi were placed ahead of both Jaguar and Land Rover in terms of visibility, marketers were able to explain the reasons behind this (the launch of a revolutionary hybrid sports car and a successful communications campaign in the region, respectively), which would help inform the client's future communications strategy (Salient Insight, 2014, para. 9–12).

Assignment

Using this case material as a starting point and considering the JLR results, develop a public relations strategy and plan for the *entire* 2019 Dubai International Motor Show focusing on the news media as *the key public*. How would you promote the show to journalists/consumers? Conduct an online search for additional information and facts including news stories, social media, YouTube, the show website, and other sources. Keep in mind that the cultural, economic, political, legal, and media environments play a role in determining the degree of engagement. Discover the tactics that previous Dubai International Motor Shows deployed. Would you change or incorporate any in your strategy and plan today? Consult the campaign checklist located in the appendix and think about the following questions.

1   Who are the major Dubai International Motor Show publics and why?
2   How would you measure awareness, attitude, and level of engagement of the major publics?
3   Since the key markets for the show are the Middle East and North Africa, what cultural factors would you consider when implementing a public relations plan in these countries?
4   What media research and information are required to develop an effective plan?
5   Consider developing objectives and benchmarks based on the stated primary goal – strong positive media coverage.
6   What tactics would you deploy to achieve the goal? Consider social media, press kits, and interviews.
7   To target the key stakeholders and achieve the campaign goal, what information must be known and understood to develop an informed strategy and plan?

References

Saadeh, D. (2007, June 13). Pink for ladies, red for gentlemen-taxis in Dubai. *Reuters Lifestyle.* Retrieved from https://www.reuters.com/article/us-emirates-taxi/pink-for-ladies-red-for-gentlemen-taxis-in-dubai-idUSL1331205520070613 .

Salient Insight. (2014). JLR Dubai International Motor Show. *International Association for the Measurement and Evaluation of Communication.* Retrieved from https://amecorg.com/case-study/jlr-dubai-international-motor-show-jaguar-land-rover-mena/ .

Equifax: Crisis Communication and Credibility

Incident

During December 2016, an Equifax online security expert detected that a portal for employees only could be accessible by everyone with an internet connection. The site was vulnerable to a basic forced browsing bug. The expert tested the vulnerability and could download the personal data of hundreds of thousands of Americans in approximately 10 minutes. The expert reported the vulnerability.

During May to July 2017, Equifax experienced a security breach that allowed access to the private information of millions of American and foreign consumers including their names, birth dates, social security numbers, and financial information. According to Equifax, the company became aware of the breach on July 29. Throughout this period, security experts gained access to Equifax's servers and reported the security vulnerabilities to the company. Despite receiving these warnings, the portals remained open until six months later at the end of July. Breach analysis suggested multiple breach sources.

During September 2017, Bloomberg News reported that Equifax experienced a "major breach of its computer systems" that occurred during May–July 2017. This intrusion exposed the records of more than 145 million or 44% of American consumers (initially Equifax underreported the number of affected consumers by 5 million), upwards of 44 million British residents, and 8,000 Canadians. The company began notifying a small number of business customers. Equifax commissioned Mandiant to address the vulnerabilities. The news media reported it as one of the largest online security breaches in history.

Additionally, approximately 14,000 consumers and more than 100 staff members of Equifax Argentina had their personal data accessed by anyone who entered "admin" as both the username and password for one of its online systems. Furthermore, on the same day that Equifax announced the large security breach, the company removed its official mobile apps from the Apple App Store and from Google Play because they detected security flaws. During October 2017, The Work Number, a website operated by Equifax's TALX division, was hacked, exposing the salary histories of tens of thousands of employees at many U.S. companies.

Following the announcement of the May–July 2017 breach, Equifax's actions received criticism. The company did not reveal whether PINs and other sensitive information were compromised. It did not explain the delay between its discovery of the breach in July and its public announcement in early September.

Equifax shares dropped 13% in early trading the day after the public became aware of the breach. Because of the breach, several parties sued Equifax. In one suit, the plaintiffs sought $70 billion in damages, which was the largest class-action suit in U.S. history. Many media outlets urged consumers to request a credit freeze to reduce the impact of the breach.

As we will see below, Equifax public relations professionals faced major challenges, some of which were more complex because of ill-conceived initial responses.

Challenges

Some of Equifax's challenges to corporate image centered on the major breach, involved the following challenges.

1 In September 2017, Richard Cordray, the director of the Consumer Financial Protection Bureau (CFPB), authorized an investigation into the data breach on behalf of affected consumers. However, in November 2017, Mick Mulvaney replaced Cordray. He subsequently stopped the probe. Under Mulvaney, the CFPB also rebuffed bank regulators at the Federal Reserve Bank, Federal Deposit Insurance Corporation, and Office of the Comptroller of the Currency who offered to assist with on-site examinations of the credit bureaus.

2 Three top Equifax executives sold $2 million of their personal holdings of company shares days after the company discovered the breach but more than a month before publicizing the breach. The company indicated that the executives, including the chief financial officer, John Gamble, had no knowledge that the breach occurred at the time they sold their stock. On September 18, Bloomberg reported that the U.S. Justice Department opened an investigation to determine whether they violated insider trading laws.

3 Equifax suffered from negative publicity owing to court cases. The Federal Trade Commission (FTC) twice fined Equifax for violating the Fair Credit Reporting Act. In 2000, the company received a $2.5 million fine for blocking and delaying phone calls from consumers trying to get information about their credit. In 2003, the FTC sued Equifax for the same reason and settled with the company, which paid a $250,000 fine.

In July 2013, a federal jury in Oregon awarded $18.6 million to Julie Miller of Marion County against Equifax for violations of the Fair Credit Reporting Act. Equifax merged her credit reports with another person with a different Social Security number, date of birth, and address. Miller contacted Equifax repeatedly in writing and over the telephone, yet Equifax did not delete dozens of false collection accounts from Miller's credit report. Consequently, Miller's reputation and her credit rating were damaged. The award comprised $18.4 million in punitive damages and nearly $200,000 in compensatory damages. In 2014, a federal judge reduced the award to $1.62 million.

In 2014, Kimberly Haman from St. Louis sued Equifax and Heartland Bank for reporting she was dead. In April 2014, God Gazarov claimed that the company erroneously reported him as having no credit history because of his unusual first name. He sued Equifax in New York federal court. There have been numerous other law suits against Equifax.

4 On October 13, 2017, the U. S. Internal Revenue Service suspended a $7.2 million contract with Equifax because of the breach and ongoing negative publicity.

Equifax Response

Some of Equifax's responses to the breach only made an already difficult situation more challenging for the company's public relations team.

In a September 15 press release and six weeks after the company became aware of the breach, Equifax reported the details of the intrusion, potential consequences for consumers, and the company's response. The release responded to criticisms regarding Equifax's initial response to the incident and announced the immediate departures and replacements of its Chief Information Officer and Chief Security Officer. Equifax stated that the reporting delay was due to the time needed to discover the scope of the breach. The statement noted that it hired Mandiant on August 2 to internally investigate the breach. However, Equifax did not inform the public that they reported the breach to federal and various state authorities. The company did note that it was collaborating closely with the FBI about the breach.

Equifax reported that a flaw in Apache Struts facilitated the breach. A patch for the vulnerability was released on March 7; however, the company failed to apply the security updates before the attack occurred approximately two months later. The portals also maintained an insecure network design such as insufficient segmentation, inadequate encryption of personally identifiable information, and ineffective breach detection mechanisms.

Three days after Equifax revealed the May–July 2017 breach, Congressperson Barry Loudermilk (R-GA), who received thousands of campaign dollars from Equifax, introduced a bill in the U.S. House that would reduce consumer protections concerning credit bureaus. This included capping "potential damages in a class action suit to $500,000 regardless of class size or amount of loss." The bill also eliminated all punitive damages. Following public outcry from consumer advocacy groups, Loudermilk delayed consideration of the bill until after a full and complete investigation into the Equifax intrusion.

On September 28, 2017, the new Equifax CEO, Paulino do Rego Barros, Jr., responded to criticism of Equifax by promising that the company would allow every consumer the option to control access to their personal credit data from early 2018. This would be at no charge to the consumer.

After revealing the intrusion, Equifax offered a website (www.equifaxsecurity2017.com) for consumers to learn whether they were victims of the breach. The website had many traits in common with a phishing website such as being hosted on a domain not registered to Equifax, it had a flawed TLS implementation, and it ran on WordPress, which was unsuitable for high-security applications. These issues led Open DNS servers to classify it as a phishing site and block access. Additionally, to learn whether their data were compromised, members of the public needed to use the Equifax website. To do so, required that they provide a last name and six digits of their social security number. The website results appeared randomly generated resulting in inaccurate information.

Further, free credit monitoring and identity theft protection were offered to consumers who used the website. In exchange for revealing whether their information was compromised and for receiving the protection, consumers were required to waive their right to participate in any class action law suit against Equifax and curb their legal options to the breach to an arbitration process that limited their consumer rights. Eventually, the arbitration clause disappeared from the equifaxsecurity2017.com website.

Timeline

Feb 14	Apache notifies of the Struts vulnerability
Mar 6	Apache releases a fix for the vulnerability
Mar 7	Exploit-DB made an exploit available
May 14	The day the breach occurred according to an Equifax statement
Jul 29	Equifax detects the breach
Jul 30	The patch was deployed
Aug 1	CFO and President of U.S. Information Solutions sells shares

(continued)

(continued)

Aug 2	President of Workforce Solutions sells shares
Sep 7	Equifax announces the breach
Sep 8	Stakeholders criticized Equifax for the TrustID forcing users to waive their right to a class action lawsuit and New York Attorney General Eric Schneiderman demands the removal of the language. Equifax share price is down 13.7% since Sep 7.
Sep 9	Equifax twitter account accidentally and repeatedly directs users to phishing site
Sep 15	Equifax shares are down 34.58% following the breach announcement CSO and CIO announce retirement "effective immediately"
Sep 26	CEO announces retirement and takes a $90,000,000 payout
Oct 2	Equifax raises the number of affected U.S. consumers to 145.5 million and adds 8000 Canadians
Oct 3	Equifax CEO blames a single individual for the breach
Oct 10	Equifax announces 44 million UK records compromised, of which 14.5 million contain names and dates of birth, and 700,000 contain sensitive information
Oct 12	Equifax announces it has removed malicious software from its Credit Assistance site
Nov 3	Equifax announces it found no wrong doings in the three executives share trades.

Note: The case does not discuss all the events in the timeline.

Assignment

Using this case material as a starting point, develop an alternative public relations strategy and plan for Equifax. In other words, how would you address from a public relations perspective the Equifax consumer data breach crisis? Conduct an online search for additional information and facts including news stories, social media, YouTube, and other sources. Considering Equifax's tactics, what was effective and what would you change or incorporate in your strategy and plan today? Consult the campaign checklist located in the appendix and think about the following questions.

1   When should have Equifax have revealed the breach?
2   Would full transparency have been pragmatic and effective? Explain.
3   What is the role of credibility in this type of situation and why is it important?
4   Should Equifax have acknowledged that the company ignored the warnings from the security experts?
5   In order of priority who were Equifax's key publics and why?
6   Identify a central message and key objectives to address the breach?
7   What tactics would you suggest that Equifax deploy and why?

IBM: An Evolving Brand

Introduction

IBM, a 105-year-old company operating in 170 countries and comprised of 377,000 employees worldwide, set out to move the company from hardware and software services to a cognitive solutions, analytics, and cloud platform company branded as IBM Cognitive Build (aka Cognitive Business or Watson), building on Smarter Planet and digital technologies globally.

So, what can Watson do? It uses artificial intelligence. Watson can optimize a company's online display advertising using predictive customer analytics. Additionally, cognitive computing can be used in advertising to generate creative ideas and copy, assist in image selection, and enhance filming. Other applications include Watson Food Advisor (IoT – internet of things), which helps health organizations and governments in their campaigns for a healthy life style including easily measuring and regularly monitoring levels of sugar in diabetic individuals or persons with heart disease. Watson also monitors the levels of minerals and vitamins, which integrates with Chef Watson, an application that proposes healthy recipes. Other applications include assisting farmers when they should irrigate crops and monitoring and maintaining remote equipment such as elevators in tall buildings. Watson monitors thousands of data points to predict failure points and notifies and schedules routine and ad hoc maintenance.

The implementation of the transformative Cognitive Build focus requires a critical and major alignment and redefinition of the IBM workplace culture. It requires the staff to assume disruption, adopt innovative and new work approaches, and serve as the catalyst for changing the culture at IBM through the mobilization of an internal engagement and communications team.

IBM's Internal Response

In a PRWeek article (PRWEEK, 2017) the following was reported:

In the spring of 2016, IBM designed a learning-by-doing experience to educate its staff about cognitive business. More than 275,000 employees joined an 88-day journey across five stages, embracing next-generation work methods, including agile development and IBM Design Thinking, among others.

The goal was to create a "do tank" where IBMers would collaborate to propose a problem and its cognitive possibility, and immediately form a team to design a prototype.

The best work advanced to the next stage, where teams – using IBM build bars – worked on transformative ideas. Using ifundIT (an internal crowdfunding tool), IBMers received 2,000 "ifundIT dollars" to kick-start the best prototypes. The top 50 teams advanced to the Outthink Challenge, where 100 staffers pitched their prototype to IBM's CEO, senior leaders, industry executives, and clients.

Results were exceptional. More than 72% of employees participated in the challenge, and nearly 10% of the projects are being adopted by the business for additional development – both for clients, as well as internally. More than half of participating staffers are now infusing new methods in their work practices.

Overall, 8,361 cognitive build teams were formed worldwide; and 2,704 teams' cognitive solutions passed feasibility reviews and entered crowdfunding stage.

"This was highly aspirational," said one observer. "They achieved huge success."

A Sampling of Employee Comments at the Time of Cognitive Build Implementation

The following is feedback from employees at the time of the Cognitive Build Launch:

- Global business exposure and a good place to start a career. Lots of good people and managers, and there was once an ethos in the company.
- No job security ever. The intent of the company is to treat full-time people like contractors. Politics growing as the same senior people get the opportunities, so you are in or you are out. Benefits decreasing. No longer good for families. Constant layoffs that never seem to affect the top layer. Stopping employees from taking vacation by giving them so much work that it's impossible. Forget any opportunity if you . . .
- Be up front, transparent and truthful. Create a "high performance culture with focus on nurturing skills not just watch out for yourself."
- Disapproves of CEO.
- You get to work with smart people on cool projects. Opportunity is always available if you want to try something new or volunteer for as stretch project. The education at IBM is online and obtained at events. You can learn so much in a short time.
- The company is transforming so fast that it is difficult to understand where you should focus. The best benefit of IBM was working from home, however this is going away to a very few limited offices across the US. The accomplished individual contributors are being let go and replaced with millennials.
- The worst policy at IBM is allowing managers to block an employee from taking a new position at IBM. If an employee has found a new opportunity allowing the manager to make them stay after 12 months of service to them is a bad choice. The true measure of a good manager/leader is that people flock to them. If a manager's team is trying to leave them it should reflect on the manager's ability to inspire and load balance . . .
- Great people and products.
- Advice to Management: Respect for the individual, treatment of employees, provide leadership.
- Flexible work schedule is a significant benefit.
- Scope and scale is a challenge for work/life balance.
- Flexibility, nice people, good salary package.
- Low chances to promote, the tasks are separated into many teams, you get to do only a small part of the process.
- Very smart people that are trying to maintain forward momentum.
- Interesting work and innovations that matter. Good technology. Good benefits. Good espoused values, corporate social responsibility. Decent pay, values diversity.
- High stress, back to the office movement from telecommuting. Jobs moving offshore. Layoffs have become part of the culture.
- Should care about employees more.
- Great flexibility working at IBM.
- Not a great place to be early in your career.
- Career opportunities, employee benefits, flexible working.
- None come to mind.
- High quality colleagues, team rigor for new innovations and emerging business models.

- Great new Design agency and workshops for offerings. Push employees to stay continually educated on latest technologies and trends, examples: Think Fridays, Cognitive Build contest with far flung teaming opportunities, free Company Online courses.
- Still too many layoffs, culling down employee population due to transition.
- Losing some great people due to some managers that aren't listening.
- Advice to Management: Don't be tied to old overly conservative metrics for M&As – we lose out on opportunities. Keep investing in future tech, be bold.

IBM's External Response

The brand realignment is the third in 20 years for IBM and includes an investment at least as large as the seven-year Smarter Planet effort, which incorporated 100 TV spots and several hundred print ads. As reported by Kate Kaye in AdAge (2015):

"We will apply at least that amount behind the Cognitive Business idea behind Watson," said Jon Iwata, IBM's senior VP marketing and communications, who would not provide campaign budget numbers. "As we did with Smarter Planet, we will roll this out globally and it will continue and gain a great deal of momentum in the coming months." The initiative was developed in conjunction with IBM's longtime agency of record, Ogilvy & Mather.

The company teased the concept last night during Monday Night Football on ESPN with spots featuring the computerized voice of IBM's Watson chatting with former "Jeopardy!" champ Ken Jennings and folk rock legend Bob Dylan.

"We wanted to go kind of big" said Iwata of the TV launch and buy.

"My analysis shows your major themes are that time passes and love fades," states Watson, IBM's data-parsing system, in an unlikely conversation with the music icon. "That sounds about right," responds Mr. Dylan, a prolific songwriter known for his lyrical prowess, in one of three :30 ads.

IBM began to realize that the message of Smarter Planet – basically that computing is and will be integral to everything, as manifested in innovations such as smart power grids and connected cars – is no longer a differentiator for the business, explained Iwata. The emerging pattern, as harnessed and fostered by its Watson technology, is that these super computing capabilities can be built into anything digital because they live in the cloud.

Today's fascination with artificial intelligence and big data analytics was another indicator that the company should turn the page on Smarter Planet. "This will resonate strongly with not only our current clients but . . . companies and decision makers and software developers who aren't currently IBM clients," said Iwata of Cognitive Business.

"We wanted to get ahead of that," he said. "I think of these as branded points of view, and they underpin our advertising but they're a lot more than that."

IBM has based an array of data management and analytics services tailored to industries from retail to healthcare on the Watson technology. The cognitive computing system ingests data – such as medical data, media research, or Bob Dylan lyrics – at a rapid pace, learning and optimizing its analytics and language skills with each new bit of information.

The Cognitive Business strategic brand platform follows IBM's e-business initiative of 1995, which was followed by its Smarter Planet branding launched in 2008. Since Smarter Planet was introduced, IBM has developed new industry-specific ways for business clients to use Watson's cognitive computing system, highlighted by partnerships like North Face for e-commerce, Nielsen for media planning, and Memorial

Sloan Kettering for oncology research, for example, in addition to enabling mobile app developers to access the technology.

As part of its ongoing quest to turn Watson into a continuously learning entity resembling the human brain, IBM acquired Merge Healthcare in August; the company provides medical imaging processing. When IBM announced the purchase, it suggested that Merge's technology would help Watson "see."

The new Cognitive Business brand strategy is intended to guide not only marketing communications, but how the company's salespeople interact with clients, and how it recruits new talent. Staff will learn about the initiative and find training tools such as videos and infographics on IBM's personalized internal online and mobile university called Think Academy.

The *New York Times* and *Wall Street Journal* featured an 8-page insert promoting Cognitive Business. Digital efforts included display, paid search, and social media ads that complemented the print insert and television spots.

"Digital is not the destination but the foundation for a new era of business," read the insert. "We call it cognitive business, and IBM Watson is the platform."

Assignment

Using this case material as a starting point, develop an internal or external public relations strategy and plan for IBM's evolving brand, Cognitive Build. Conduct an online search for additional information and facts including news stories, social media, YouTube, and other sources. Keep in mind that the cultural, economic, political, legal, and media environments play a role in determining the degree of activism and public relations in a given country. Considering the effective tactics deployed by IBM, what would you change or incorporate in your strategy and plan today? Consult the campaign checklist located in the appendix.

From an internal communication perspective, think about the following questions.

1   Who are the major IBM internal publics and why?
2   How would you measure internal cultural realignment success? Consider engagement and social media as well as innovation.
3   How would you address employee feedback? Explain your recommendations.
4   What objectives and benchmarks would you consider concerning internal stakeholders?

From an external communication perspective, think about the following questions.

1   Identify key publics or market segments.
2   What would be the basis of your segmentation?
3   Would your central message vary by market segment? Explain.
4   Would you build relationships with all stakeholders? If not, why?

References

Best in internal communications 2017. (2017, March 12). *PRWEEK*. Retrieved from www. prweek.com/article/1427576/best-internal-communications-2017.

Kaye, K. (2015, October 6). Tangled up in Big Blue: IBM replaces smarter planet with . . . Bob Dylan. Launches cognitive business campaign with Monday night football spots. Retrieved from http://adage.com/article/datadriven-marketing/ibm-replaces-smarter-planet-cognitive-business-strategy/300774/.

Knowing the Consumer and Promoting the iPhone **X**

Introduction

Apple Inc. is an American multinational technology company headquartered in Cupertino, California, that designs, develops, and sells consumer electronics, computer software, and online services. The company's hardware products include the iPhone smartphone, the iPad tablet computer, the Mac personal computer, the iPod portable media player, the Apple Watch smartwatch, the Apple TV digital media player, and the HomePod smart speaker. Apple's software includes the macOS and iOS operating systems, the iTunes media player, the Safari web browser, and the iLife and iWork creativity and productivity suites, as well as professional applications such as Final Cut Pro, Logic Pro, and Xcode. Its online services include the iTunes Store, the iOS App Store and Mac App Store, Apple Music, and iCloud.

Apple is the world's largest information technology company by revenue and the world's second-largest mobile phone manufacturer after Samsung. On August 2, 2018, Apple became the first U.S. company worth $1 trillion. The company employs 123,000 full-time employees, as of September 2017, and maintains 499 retail stores in 22 countries, as of December 2017. It operates the iTunes Store, which is the world's largest music retailer. As of January 2016, more than one billion Apple products are actively in use worldwide.

Apple's worldwide annual revenue totaled $229 billion for the 2017 fiscal year. The company enjoys a high level of brand loyalty and has been repeatedly ranked as the world's most valuable brand. However, it receives significant criticism regarding the labor practices of its contractors, and its environmental and business practices, including anti-competitive behavior . . .

(Apple, Inc., Wikipedia, 2018)

One of Apple's most successful products to date is the iPhone. Currently, the iPhone moved from the iPhone 7 and iPhone 7 Plus to the iPhone 8 and iPhone 8 Plus, while concurrently introducing the iPhone X (pronounced "10"). Although both were introduced on September 12, 2017 at the Big Apple event, they were available at different dates to allow the consumer to consider both models before making a phone purchase. The iPhone 8, starting at $699, was available for shipment September 12 and the iPhone X, starting at $999, was available September 15. The iPhone X has no home button and an edge-to-edge ultra-high-resolution screen. Owing to strong demand, it quickly sold out and backlogged. During this period, the company's total market stock value approached $1 trillion.

iPhone X Features

The iPhone X has a 5.8-inch Super Retina HD display, 12MP wide-angle and telephoto cameras, Face ID, a A11 Bionic chip, and wireless charging, which functions with Qi-certified chargers. Additionally, storage capacity is available in 64 GB and 256 GB sizes.

The display is the OLED Multi-Touch. The HDR display is 2436 x 1125-pixel resolution at 458 ppi. The contrast ratio is 1,000,000: 1 with True Tone display and P3 wide color. There are also 3D Touch and 625 cd/m2 max brightness features.

The phone's height is 5.65 inches, width is 2.79 inches, and depth is .30 inch. It weights 6.14 ounces. Like many Apple products, it is splash, water, and dust resistant. It has a long battery life (21 hours talk time, 12 hours internet use, 13 hours video playback, 60 hours audio playback, and up to 50% charge in 30 minutes), lithium-ion rechargeable battery, and wireless and other charging modes.

The iPhone X's video recording features are: 4k video recording at 24 fps, 30 fps or 60 fps; 1080p HD recording at 30 fps or 60 fps; optical image stabilization for video; optimal zoom and digital zoom up to 6x; slo-mo video support for 1080p at 120 fps or 240 fps; and time-lapse video for stabilization. The front camera offers the TrueDepth camera; 7MO photos; f/2.2 aperture; retina flash; wide color capture for photos and live photos; 1080p HD video recording; portrait mode; portrait lighting; and Animoji.

The iPhone X offers Bluetooth features; Wi-Fi calling; video calling (FaceTime); audio and video playback; and Siri (voice command).

The iPhone X is available through the following carriers: AT&T, Sprint, T-Mobile, Virgin Mobile, and Verizon.

Since the announcement, and release, of the iPhone X, facial recognition has quickly become a topic of household conversation. Apple took technology that previously existed in niche markets or academic domains and introduced it to popular culture (amid great expectation). And while the key feature is a security function and phone unlocking function, a device that recognizes faces is clearly a powerful technology with vast communication implications.

Research reveals that 90% of personal communication is nonverbal. Up to this point, we have mimicked facial expression using emojis and LOLs to compensate for not being able to share emotion in our digital interactions. The iPhone X's facial recognition capability is indicative of Apple's awareness that the consumer wants an experience which represents human interaction and communication.

Product Distribution

The iPhone X has a highly effective retail distribution system. The iStores are Apple owned stores with knowledgeable service people. They take extraordinary care to provide customers with assistance, which enhances the experience of buying and servicing an iPhone. Second, there are high-end stores, located in malls. Buying from these stores is a pleasant experience. These stores purchase the iPhones from distributors rather than Apple directly. Third, Apple products are available online at many sites such as eBay, Flipkart, or Amazon. Apple also helps consumers find these stores at the nearest location. Last, there is the second-hand market. This is substantial owing to the brand's durability and the status attached to it. eBay is a major site for the sale of second-hand iPhones.

Situational Analysis

Product Research

Apple conducted marketing research to glean insights about its market segments. The basis of the research were the 15–20 years, 20–25 years, 25–45 years, and 45 years and older age groups. One social usage study involved high school and college aged participants. To discover business application and social/personal use, the researchers drew a sample of 25–45 years old persons. In another study, the 45 years and older participants developed a plan to market the iPhone X to a senior segment.

Survey-based research via an email campaign through portals such as iTunes and other online applications developed for the iPhone and interviews in Apple stores were used. Researchers hoped to uncover the "social cool" and "business cool" factors of the iPhone X. The study also sought feedback about iPhone X features. Online users designed their ideal iPhone using adaptive conjoint analysis.

The following are some of the marketing research findings:

- There is a small market segment who wants to pay more for a better product. In technology, this segment pays more to be the first to have the newest. In nontechnological products, the segment's interest derives from exclusivity to be the first to experience the brand's features. Both perspectives pay a premium to be the first users.
- The iPhone separates into two segments:

  o *iPhone 8 segment*. These are customers who want improvements, but do not like risks. They want the proven product because it has a track record. For instance, they want the traditional fingerprint sensor and are critical of the new Face ID. They prefer the old LCD screen technology over the new OLED.

  o *iPhone X segment*. Some people enjoy new and innovative tools. They are future oriented and sometimes wish to acquire exclusive products. Some are opinion leaders and enjoy the recognition as product experts. This market segment will pay more to maintain their status.

Competitive Advantage

Apple has several advantages over its competitors:

1 Superior technology products – MacBook and iWatch are clearly leaders in their market space because of the OS and technology used.
2 Brand equity – Apple has repeatedly taken the top spot for its brand equity and has a cult following over many years.
3 Revenue over time – Apple has deep pockets due to its high margins.
4 R&D – A major competitive advantage of Apple is the amount it spends on R&D, keeping its eyes on the future rather than the present.

SWOT Analysis

Strengths

Augmented Reality (AR): The iPhone X's AR capacities make it appealing to marketing campaigns that demonstrate product features and usage.

Brand awareness: Apple is well known for cool things and technological innovations.

Compatibility: The iPhone X is cross-compatible with all Apple products such as iTunes and many software tools which provide upgrade ability.

Ease-of-Use: The all-new touch screen interface recognizes multi finger gestures, behaving similarly to the human hand.

Innovative: The iPhone X has an innovative touch screen. It also has many functions of other mobile products all in one single device

Price: iPhone X is considered reasonably priced according to its key market segments.

Quality: It has a scratch resistant screen, it is durable, it has a light metallic finish, and it includes a software suite resistant to computer viruses.

Opportunities

Increasing demand and expansion to new market segments: As technology advances and smart phones get cheaper Apple will attract more consumers and get users to upgrade to the iPhone X.

Partnerships: Apple can partner with many powerful global mobile phone companies to increase iPhone X penetration, which reduces costs in marketing and increases revenue through long-term agreements and economies of scale.

Upgradeable: The iPhone X software allows new features that take advantage of the touch screen ability. Future versions will be hardware upgrade enabled.

Weaknesses

Image: Arguably, the Apple brand is new to the business people market and does not have a reputation as being compatible with the corporate world.

Price: Owing to lack of economies of scale, the iPhone X is pricy starting at $999, which may postpone some consumers from purchasing the unit in anticipation of a price reduction.

User Interface: The touch screen interface suffers from the problem of "gorilla arm," which is when a person using a vertical or standing touchscreen experiences fatigue or the arm starts to hurt because of the awkward positioning that is required to use the device.

Threats

Difficulty expanding into Asian market: There is less interest and media coverage in Asia since smartphones are better known and widely used.

Downward pricing pressure: The iPhone X is a high-end phone even among the other iPhone models. Market smart phone prices will fall when other companies undercut the price of the iPhone X.

Increased competition: Smart phones are easier to produce now. More companies may enter the market. Competitors and Apple contractors can circumvent patent laws to create similar devices.

Global Environment

Economic Situation

Economic growth worldwide is slow. Market potential is decreasing, yet, it is higher than other industries in the Telecom sector.

Socio-Cultural Situation

Consumers rely more and more on smart phones to help organize and manage their lives. With a more educated world, more people are open to ideas, innovation, and willing to change their behaviors. Perception of technological advances and devices are positive worldwide. Furthermore, acceptance of imported products in some countries is growing.

TECHNOLOGICAL SITUATION

Access to technology in the world is increasing. The internet, its potential usages, and access to information is growing. Think about the Arab Spring movement fueled by Twitter. These advances are possible because of the infrastructure buildup such as more fixed phone lines capacity and satellite access. Moreover, advanced cell phone technology, lower priced phones, and less expensive service plans allow more people access to information, social media, and communication tools. Technological linkages among cities, universities, colleges, hospitals and other institutions are increasing connectivity via smart phones.

COMPETITIVE SITUATION

Although there are thousands of cell phone producers in the world, only 15 large companies compete on a global basis.

iPhone **X** Marketing Objectives

- First-year Objective: 2% market share (reach unit sales of 445,000) for the U.S. and U.K. markets.
- Second-year Objective: 10% market share.
- Measure awareness/attitude and provide any required adjustments to the marketing campaigns as necessary.

iPhone **X** Target Market Considerations

- **Primary customer market segment** is the middle and upper income professionals who need the iPhone X to coordinate their busy schedules and communicate with colleagues, friends, and family.
- **Secondary consumer market segment** is high school, college, and graduate students who need a portable multi-functional device.
- **Primary business market segment** is large cell phone service providers, AT&T, Verizon, Sprint, and Cellular One and large enterprise software firms where information is critical to the end user.
- **Secondary business market segment** is mid-size corporations that want to assist managers and keep employees in communication and provide them with access to critical data on the go.

For the consumer market, existing customers were targeted and included: 1) Music lovers who used iTunes, 2) Professionals or even teenagers who owned iTablets, MacBook, and other gadgets used by anyone irrespective of age, and 3) Consumers who use other Apple products and services such as Apple TV, iWatch, iBooks, and Apple Pay.

Public Relations Strategy

Differentiate the iPhone X ("Say hello to the future" tagline) from other cell phones in the market without cannibalizing the current Apple line perhaps complementing cell phone models. iPhone has created a unique position in the market, with its many differentiating factors. Its new models always have a new tagline. For example, the iPhone 6 tagline is "The only thing that has changed is everything." Such positioning promotes not only the iPhone 6, but the entire brand. iPhone promotions demonstrate how the world is changing with each iPhone.

Launch events are dramatic for iPhones. For instance, the launch of the wireless charging feature drew consumer attention. Social media, YouTube, and other social media are some platforms highly utilized by Apple to talk about the iPhone X's distinctive features including its strong resale value. With its unique value proposition, the iPhone X sets the standard in the product category and has no close competitor, especially to the loyal customer base.

Rather than providing iPhone X units to experts and journalists for their review, Apple gave the product to a group of YouTube video bloggers first. The company wanted the reviewers to focus on the fun features of the device rather than reporting on product specs and technical capabilities. The YouTube influencers in fact welcomed the device and displayed its features. Showing the iPhone X features in video made the reviews more exciting and easier to understand.

This approach served multiple purposes, First, initial positive reviews created "blindly optimistic" feelings that drown out any later complaints about technical issues. Second, YouTubers helped Apple reach younger and more diverse audiences. In fact, most of the video stars who reviewed the iPhone X were younger and Latino, which might explain why the videos trended in almost all countries despite iPhones being less popular than the trending suggested.

Messaging consisted of the following attributes:

- integrated Apple message of revolutionary communications and audio/visual experience (augmented reality features) together in all media advertisements;
- emphasized the iPhone touch screen functionality;
- emphasized Apple brand prominently and associated the iPhone with its groundbreaking lineage;
- messaging was attention getting, professionally produced, original, and tasteful;
- a remarkable TV ad featured the iPhone X, which rivaled the legendary 1984 ad; and
- messaging maintained brand awareness and positive attitude.

Media Coverage

In a 2017 article published by Macworld, Michael Simon wrote:

But Apple's main motivation with all these iPhone X promotions is to focus on its fun features rather than specs. That's plain to see in the YouTube videos that were heavy on entertainment and light on examination. But even the transitional outlets focused more on Face ID and the new design rather than battery benchmarks and speed tests. Apple needs the core features of iPhone X – buttonless navigation, hands-free unlocking, and yes, the notch – to become ingrained in its culture even before most people are able to buy one. And even before iPhone X releases, Apple is already laying the groundwork for it to take over.

But whether Apple sells more iPhone Xs in the holiday quarter than iPhone 8s isn't the issue. It's about impressions. When iPhone X was first announced, the reaction was somewhat muted. There were concerns about Face ID. People wondered if it was worth such a premium over iPhone 8 Plus. Some even started questioning whether Apple "all screen" claim was even accurate.

But that too plays right into Apple's marketing strategy. Apple knew there would be questions about iPhone X. But with one fell swoop of first impressions, Apple dispelled all naysaying. Face ID works. The screen is amazing. And it's worth the extra money if you can afford it.

Even if you don't buy an iPhone X today, tomorrow, or next month, Apple has planted the seed of desire. It doesn't matter if you watched Booredatwork's videos, read Matthew Panzarino's review, or followed Recode's discontent. People who were already going to buy an iPhone X really want one now. But more importantly, a whole group of people who normally might not care about an iPhone launch weekend will go to the Apple Store this weekend to get a glimpse of the new iPhone. They'll try it out. They'll tweet out pics. And they'll tell their friends that they need to go see it too (Simon 2017, para. 7, 11–13).

Assignment

Using this case material as a starting point, develop a public relations strategy and plan for the iPhone X launch. How would you approach opinion leaders to promote the iPhone X? Conduct an online search for additional information and facts including news stories, social media, YouTube, and other sources. Considering the effective tactics deployed by Apple, what would you change or incorporate in your strategy and plan today? Consult the campaign checklist located in the appendix and think about the following questions.

1   Who are the major iPhone X market segments and why? Would you consider other potential segments for future sales? If so, why?
2   How would you measure awareness, attitude, and level of engagement of the major iPhone X segments?
3   Would you develop a competitive benefit analysis matrix (table) to better understand the iPhone X compared to its major higher-end competitive models? If so, develop a matrix.
4   What are the iPhone X's weaknesses and how would you respond to them?
5   What additional tactics would you deploy not mentioned in the case?

References

Apple, Inc. (2018). *Wikipedia*. Retrieved from https://en.wikipedia.org/wiki/Apple_Inc.
Simon, M. (2017). How Apple's unconventional iPhone X marketing strategy will make you want one at any cost. *Macworld*. Retrieved from www.macworld.com/article/3235955/iphone-ipad/apple-iphone-x-strategy.html.

Museum of London: A Study in Engagement

Introduction

"The Museum of London is an award-winning, charitable institution funded by a variety of organisations and individuals including the City of London Corporation and GLA" (Museum of London, About us, 2018, para. 1).

The museum comprises chronological galleries containing original artifacts, models, pictures and diagrams that emphasize archaeological discoveries, the city of London, urban development and London's social and cultural life. Many displays are interactive and there are activities for all ages. Fragments of the Roman London Wall are visible outside the museum.

The museum has two locations: The Museum of London, which will relocate to West Smithfield, Farringdon by 2022, and a newer site at Museum of London at Docklands. The museum intends to raise awareness for both sites especially at the London Wall location, where the building is not easily visible to the public, as well as bolster support for the West Smithfield move.

The museum completed a £20 million redevelopment in May 2010, which was the largest investment since opening in 1976. The renovations included the new City Gallery featuring large street level windows along London Wall as well as an illuminated showcase for the Lord Mayor's State Coach, which operates on the street each November for the Lord Mayor's Show. Today, over one million visitors tour the displays and showcases annually.

The Challenge

In March 2015, the museum announced that it would move its London Wall presence to a new location at the West Smithfield General Market Building, with an anticipated opening date of 2022. The new location is in a historic area, which offers cathedral-sized space and is next door to a famous meat market. The site offers scalability and many opportunities for the museum to link itself to the history of London.

Reasons for the move included the claim that the current site is difficult for visitors to find, and that by expanding, from 17,000 square meters to 27,000, a greater proportion of the Museum's collection can be placed on display. The cost of the move is estimated to be approximately £70 million. Plans for the vacated site include making it the permanent home for the London Symphony Orchestra.

Officials state that the museum wants to involve Londoners and visitors incorporating the city and its history by giving people the means "to participate as citizens in all sorts of new ways." The museum intends to display many more objects in a more meaningful way.

According to officials,

> We believe London is the world's greatest city and we are uniquely placed to tell its story, but only if we have a showcase worthy enough. So our ambition is to do this at the heart of a new cultural hub in the City of London with outstanding links to the rest of London and the world, and in doing so we will become one of London's top five most visited museums.
>
> (West Smithfield, London's Showcase, 2018, para. 3).

The future site buzzes with activity 24 hours per day, 7 days per week. During the day, there are commuters. At night, the market draws traffic as well as the night club crowd.

The challenge is to determine how to involve people and successfully engage them with what the Museum of London offers. Specific questions that require answers are: How does and will the museum engage people and draw them to visit? Should the museum open evenings or 24 hours a day? Should more retailers be encouraged to open shop in the local community at the new location to increase traffic?

Goal and Objectives

The museum's public relation plan goal is to increase awareness, engagement, and visits to its locations, hoping to bring visits to more than 2 million per year once the new site opens.

The Museum of London's public relations strategy is based on the following main objectives:

- determine the level of museum awareness and knowledge;
- expose more people to their message;
- increase awareness and knowledge about the museum and what it offers;
- link what the museum offers to London heritage; and
- increase engagement and visits to the museum.

Understanding the level of awareness and knowledge of the museum among its stake-holders are critical to developing an effective public relation strategy and plan. Andrew Marcus, the Director of Communications at the museum, stated, "As the Museum of London looks towards a future in West Smithfield, our communications will become ever more sophisticated so that people get to know that the Museum of London is the Museum of Londoners" (Smith, 2017, para. 2).

Target Publics

There are eight target publics based on psychographic and behavioral data:

- cultural connoisseurs – the middle- and upper-class cultured individuals;
- London insiders – social influencers and columnists who write about different aspects of London and culture;
- day trippers – people who seek recreational activities to do for the day;
- self-developers – these are persons who desire personal development and growth through learning and new experiences;
- experience seekers – simply, these are visitors who seek new experiences and may be single visit guests;
- learning families – these are older family members who share an interest in learning;
- kids first families – primary caregivers that wish to educate their children about history and culture, especially theirs, as well as provide entertainment and recreational options;
- school-age children – these students visit the museum through school efforts as part of their education and recreation;

The educational objectives' creative dimension will need to combined educational and recreational aspects of the museum to accommodate the relevant publics.

Research

Initial Research

As noted in the objectives section, an informed and effective strategy and plan requires an understanding of the issue, situation, and stakeholders, which are all discovered during the situational analysis phase of strategy and plan development.

Making use of a research firm, the museum conducted a 10,000 U.K. resident survey, which collected data about demographics, lifestyles, opinions, attitudes, values, belief systems, and media habits. This approach provided information that would inform the creative strategy and tactics development, as well as determine the channels of communication (periodicals, social media, television, and so forth) for the identified publics.

Ongoing Research

Some planned research, such as tracking studies, were ongoing during the campaign. One involved monthly and quarterly data collection from a nationally representative sample of 1,000 respondents. The goal of this research program was to monitor changes in museum awareness and perceptions about the museum's relocation.

Another assessment program centered on content analysis of news and educational-based social media coverage of the museum. This approach monitors the student and educationally/recreational-related objectives as they progress throughout the campaign.

Additionally, rather than the traditional advertising value equivalency (AVE) metric, the museum combined public relations spending, reach, and the number of visitors to calculate and identify ratios such as the cost per thousand reached, cost per thousand visitors, and the number of visitors per £1 spent.

Some data were collected after key media coverage or events were measured against key performance indicators such as trends owing to the museum's communications activities, museum exhibitions, and directly and indirectly related news stories.

According to Laura Bates, the Public Relations Manager at the Museum of London,

> We use it to see message cut-through and work out if they need to be tweaked or if we need to focus on a different message for the next month/quarter. The communications team primarily works with two of the Museum's wider business objectives: to reach more people and to become better known.
>
> To do this effectively, we need to gauge our successes and if we're reaching the right people through the right medium. We've worked closely with Cision to share our audience research, target media, key messages and visitor number information so we can accurately track the links between our media relations and what that means for our KPIs. Using the monthly and quarterly reports, we know exactly what works and doesn't work and can have a fast insight into our media landscape.
>
> In particular, the awareness surveys about our impending move directly affect the ongoing communications work towards the move and shaping the strategy.
>
> We report on awareness, top stories, message cut-through, volume and these stats are shared widely. The awareness surveys are becoming ever more important as we plan to move to a new home in West Smithfield and have put more resources into promoting the Museum of London Docklands.

(Hender, 2016, para. 32–35)

Results

To date, the promotional campaign has yielded the following results.

- Despite the overall reach falling slightly short, more than 75% of each stakeholder group was reached. The cost per thousand people reached was £0.49.
- Seventy-four percent of coverage was about the central message, which was more than the targeted 40%.
- Coverage appeared in 12 of the top media outlets, against a benchmark of 9.
- Social media engagement increased by 60% from 2016 to 2017.
- Visitor numbers increased and there was a statistically significant association between media coverage (especially social media), and visitors.
- The cost of public relations activity for each thousand visitors was £72.
- Awareness of the museum's planned relocation increased from 34% in March 2016 to 47% by December 2016.
- Support for the relocation rose from 39% to 49%.

Future Opportunities

The ongoing evaluative research guides future communications. Quarterly assessment informs the relocation. In fact, the assessments provide the public relations staff with opportunities for future targeting.

For example, there was a significant gap between the level of awareness of the relocation among young adults and how supportive they were about the move. Only 15% of 18–24-year-olds surveyed supported the relocation; yet, of those aware of the reason for the move, support jumped to 67%. This finding suggests the importance of raising awareness of the relocation to generate support among this demographic.

Assignment

Using this case material as a starting point, develop a public relations strategy and plan for the Museum of London, focusing on the move to West Smithfield. How would you approach journalists/patrons to promote the move? Conduct an online search for additional information and facts including news stories, social media, YouTube, and other sources. Keep in mind that the cultural, economic, political, legal, and media environments play a role in determining the degree of activism and public relations in a given location. Considering the effective tactics deployed by the museum, what would you change or incorporate in your strategy and plan today? Consult the campaign checklist located in the appendix and think about the following questions.

1   Who are the major Museum of London publics and why?
2   How would you measure awareness, attitude, level of engagement, and knowledge of the move in the major museum publics?
3   How would you address the Museum of London's ongoing evaluative research areas requiring attention?
4   Although this case primarily addresses the London market in the United Kingdom, what factors would you consider when implementing a public relations plan for the museum targeting all of Europe, especially tourists visiting London?
5   What additional tactics would you deploy not mentioned in the case?

References

Hender, P. (2016). Museum of London. *AMEC*. Retrieved from https://amecorg.com/case-study/museum-of-london-paul-hender/.

Museum of London. (2018). *About us*. Retrieved from www.museumoflondon.org.uk/about-us.

Smith, R. (2017, August 10). The Museum of London appoints Pagefield to deliver six-figure relocation brief. *PRWeek*. Retrieved from www.prweek.com/article/1441662/museum-london-appoints-pagefield-deliver-six-figure-relocation-brief.

West Smithfield. London's Showcase. (2018). Museum of London. Retrieved from www.museumoflondon.org.uk/about-us/our-organisation/west-smithfield.

Real Estate Public Relations: Three Examples, One Case Study

This case study involves developing a hypothetical public relations campaign based on the information about the three cases described. The three real estate cases are as follows (Schneider Associates, 2018). The first involves positioning renovated rental property as an ideal residential community, as well as promoting its new renovations, residents, and staff. The second centers on gaining town approval for re-zoning a 109-acre corporate campus in Marlborough, Massachusetts, USA. The last case is about the launch of a luxury resort and driving awareness among potential buyers. These situations address key issues when marketing real estate projects: relaunch and positioning; re-zoning and outreach; and lead generation through a promotional theme.

First is a review of the real estate promotional tools available followed by a description of the basic re-zoning process.

Real Estate Promotional Toolkit

There are many tools available to the public relations practitioner who promotes real estate projects. Many of the tactics focus on local audiences, particularly the media, regulators, and potential or existing customers. Some involve zoning advocacy as well. The following highlights key tactics adopted from the inMotion Real Estate Media website (2017) and Schneider Associates (2018).

Launch Individual Property Websites. Commercial property websites beyond the real estate company website listing is required. It serves as a digital hub for the property marketing efforts and communicates the property's value, which engages website visitors.

Targeted Email Lists. Through such services as Constant Contact and MailChimp, personalized email lists are built and maintained that focus on prospective customers and their unique requirements. Email addresses come from the company website, manual storage, blogs, lead capture pages, and customer relations management data sites.

Share Content on Social Media. Social media marketing is an effective way to build brand awareness and drive traffic to property websites. Social dialogue sparks conversation and fosters connections with potential customers and partners. Twitter, LinkedIn, and Facebook are the most relevant social networks for commercial real estate.

Garner Press Coverage. Building relationships with opinion leaders, journalists, real estate influencers, and bloggers is important. Media coverage increases property awareness and generates positive attitude toward the broker and property thus adding credibility to listings.

Search Engine Optimization (SEO) for Your Properties' Websites and Home Page. Search engine visibility drives interest and traffic such as potential tenants, brokers, and investors to your website. Related to SEO, Google AdWords is an acquisition channel that draws leads through paid display ads.

Advertise and Post Your Listings on Commercial Real Estate Listing Sites. Commercial real estate sites are an effective way to generate visibility for a purposeful audience. Some sites are: 42Floors, RealMassive, Rofo, Commercial Café, Truss, Brevitas, Crexi, Quantum Listing. OfficeSpace, OffMarket, Commerical MLS, The SquareFoot, and many more.

Advertise in Trade Journals. Thousands of potential investors, brokers, and other industry leaders read daily commercial real estate trade journals and online publications. Advertising increases exposure to relevant audiences whether locally, state-wide, regionally, nationally, or internationally.

Display and Window Signage. Eye-catching banners, monument signs, and window graphics visually showcase properties and draw traffic.

Property-related events. Memorable, exciting events that capture media coverage are effective and can provide content for future marketing efforts. For instance, photos of events can be shared on social media and the property website. The content holds interests and continued engagement as well as lends credibility to the client, property, and broker. News releases, video release, and media advisories promote the event. A post-event release reinforces the event and property's value.

Networking and Long-term Relationships. Whether with clients, regulators, construction and other professional services, or brokers, real estate projects and effective promotions require relationships and industry contacts especially at the local level.

Ongoing Updates. If perceived as transparent, major real estate and development projects maintain credibility. Regularly updating and providing news about the company, property, and major developments, establishes transparency and creditability. Updates can occur across platforms such as social media, blogs, the company website, and property website. Timely information serves potential tenants, investors, and brokers. Additionally, offering useful insights, industry trends, and expert advice creates trust and added-value.

Re-Zoning Considerations

Re-zoning property usage plays an important role in real estate and the viability of development projects. The following are the key steps involved in the re-zoning process and may vary contingent upon circumstances and jurisdiction.

Step 1: Informal Counseling with Planning and Zoning

This counseling allows the development staff and the applicant to review various issues as part of the re-zoning process. Items discussed include the zoning ordinances that relate to or impact the land use proposal. Informal discussions may occur at the department counter, over the phone, or in person.

Step 2: Re-zoning Pre-Application Meeting

This meeting, which assists in filing complete applications, is the first opportunity to review the re-zoning procedures and submittal requirements.

Step 3: Submitting Re-zoning/Special Permit Application

Applicants for re-zoning submit all information listed in the re-zoning checklist.

Step 4: Notifying and Sending First Neighborhood Notification Letter

The first neighborhood notification letters explaining the re-zoning request and all appropriate review and comment opportunities are mailed to all property owners within a set distance from the project site, all neighborhood associations registered with the city that are within a set radius of the site, and all other statutory party notifications. The letter typically has other specific content such as procedural and timeline requirements depending on regulations.

Step 5: Authority's Review of Application

A municipal staff member assigned to the re-zoning application serves as the primary reviewer and principal point of contact. The staff person examines existing and proposed land uses and how the request fits in with other city goals and policies. This official communicates with the applicant and may request additional information or have questions.

Step 6: Neighborhood Meeting

The re-zoning applicants meet with the local community to hear their concerns and respond accordingly. The date, time, and location of the meeting must be well-publicized.

Step 7: Re-zoning Post-Application Meeting

The staff share formal recommendations/stipulations with the developer, reviews zoning and development issues, and address local residents' concerns during this meeting.

Step 8: Notification and Sending Second Neighborhood Notification Letter

This notification includes additional authorities in some capacity such as the planning committee and commission, zoning hearing officer, and City Council hearing dates, times, and locations, as well as local residents and organizations.

Step 9: Posting Sign on Property

The property signs notify the public of the next steps and meeting information.

Step 10: Other Authorities' Input.

Any authority recommendations are forward to the zoning commission.

Step 11: Zoning Hearing Officer Action – Public Hearing

During this public hearing, the re-zoning application is reviewed and either approved, approved with stipulations, denied, or denied and approved differently than requested, or continued. Typically, there is an appeal process option.

Step 12: Planning Commission Action – Public Hearing

Any revisions are resubmitted at this time for action. The resubmitted re-zoning application is reviewed and either approved, approved with stipulations, denied, or denied and approved differently than requested, or continued. There is an appeal option at this stage as well.

Step 13: City Council Action – Public Hearing

At this hearing the local elected council members approve or deny the re-zoning application.

Case 1: Positioning Renovated Rental Property

Metropolitan Properties of America (MPA) invested over $20 million to renovate 919 apartments and construct a new recreation center at Granada Highlands in Malden, Massachusetts. MPA positioned the property as an ideal residential community, with refurbished units, a welcoming residents' community, and a staff second to none. MPA wanted to be perceived as a respected long-term neighbor in Malden, through building long-term relationships with the city's political and municipal leadership. A well-publicized reception served as the centerpiece of the company's public relations campaign.

A Comprehensive Media Relations and Community Engagement Campaign

MPA developed a media relations and community engagement campaign to draw attention to the Granada Highlands property, new ownership and management, and MPA's commitment to the community. The campaign included the following tactics.

- media pitches centered on improvements at Granada Highlands and in the city of Malden;
- a bylined article from MPA President, Jeffrey Cohen, which ran in print and online in three city outlets, emphasizing his local ties, working relationship with the city, and his investments in the community's future;
- a planned, promoted, and facilitated "thank you reception" and media event at the Granada Highlands amenity center;
- a speaking program, photo opportunities, amenity center hours, apartment tours included in the reception, as well as lunch for all guests;
- many leaders of the Malden community such as the city's mayor, two state representatives, chief of police, fire chief, city councilor, director of public works, and other prominent individuals attended the reception;
- visuals of the event were captured for outreach usage on social media.

Results

Granada Highlands experienced an increase in rental applications. The event and press coverage cemented a positive and lasting relationship between MPA and Malden municipal and political officials.

As part of the media relations campaign, seven media outlets covered the reception and reported on MPA's larger investment in revitalizing Granada Highlands resulting in more than 2.5 million impressions. The Boston Globe's coverage further facilitated interest in living at Granada Highlands.

Case 2: Gaining Town Approval for Re-Zoning

Atlantic Management developed and implemented a strategic advocacy outreach campaign to re-zone its 109-acre *Forest Park* corporate campus in Marlborough, Massachusetts. The campaign involved introducing an all-in-one, mixed-use zoning concept to city residents and legislators to help gain City Council approval, which took place over several public meetings.

The Marlborough Hills project planned to transform the outdated Forest Park, vacant business park into centers featuring commercial office, retail, residential, hotel, and pedestrian spaces.

Advocacy Outreach Campaign

The public relations plan promoted the project to municipal government officials, local stakeholders, and the media. Messaging highlighted the financial benefits of re-zoning, as well as the unique aspects of the real estate plan that city officials would likely favor including regular interactions with city officials, abutters, town residents, and the news media.

To keep the community and opinion leaders engaged, Atlantic developed and distributed information packets, presentation boards, FAQ documents, PowerPoint presentations, infographics, a comprehensive summary of the economic development report, and talking points for Atlantic representatives.

Local print; local business and trade publications; online content; and broadcast media; covered outreach efforts resulting in more than 900,000 impressions for Atlantic Management and the Marlborough Hills proposal.

Results

After endorsements from the Planning Board and Urban Affairs committees, the Marlborough City Council unanimously approved the Forest Park re-zoning to include residential, retail, hotel, and office uses.

Case 3: The Launch of a Luxury Resort Aimed at Driving Awareness Among Potential Buyers

RiverWalk at Loon Mountain in Lincoln, New Hampshire is a luxury resort. RiverWalk developed a public relations campaign with the goal to increase awareness among potential buyers by focusing on lead generation and conversions to sales.

All of the RiverWalk luxury condominium suites are available for deeded ownership and can be purchased as traditional whole ownership, seasonal ownership (winter or summer) or fractional ownership for families that visit our region less often. Studio, one, two, and three bedroom suites are available fully furnished with full kitchens.
(River Walk, How Does Ownership Work, 2018, para. 1)

According to RiverWalk, owners experience extreme convenience, special private check-ins, owners' club access, private parties and activities, wine clubs, private permanent lockers, full property management, optional rental management opportunities, and other amenities.

Centerpiece Event and Unique Central Message

RiverWalk held an event centered around a unique message, which garnered media coverage and facilitated lead generation. The launch theme (Gatsby-liked) was about the roaring 1920s when the grand hotels of New Hampshire were at the height of their popularity. This approach highlighted RiverWalk at Loon Mountain as a luxury resort. Art-deco style invitations, event materials, and vehicles from the era maintained the theme. Sales pitches told the historical story of the property and created buzz around RiverWalk's commitment to preserving the best of the past while developing a luxurious resort with modern amenities.

Results

The event resulted in substantial local, state, and Massachusetts media coverage, a spike in bookings, and over $1 million in sales in the three days following the event. Moreover, event prospect activities identified several qualified leads for outreach and engagement.

Print, online, and broadcast outlet coverage included:

- New Hampshire 1 Television
- Manchester Union Leader
- New Hampshire Public Radio
- New Hampshire Business Review
- NewHampshire.com
- SnoCountry.com
- InsidetheGate.com.

Assignment

Using this case material as a starting point, develop a public relations strategy and plan for a hypothetical real estate developer who requires re-zoning advocacy. How would you approach opinion leaders and the news media to promote and garner support for the development? Where are there advocacy opportunity points in the re-zoning process? Conduct an online search for additional information and facts including news stories, social media, YouTube, and other sources about such promotions. Considering the effective tactics deployed in the three real estate cases, what would you incorporate in your strategy and plan today? Consult the campaign checklist located in the appendix and think about the following questions.

1   Who are the major stakeholder groups and why? Do they vary from the re-zoning stakeholder groups? If so, why?
2   How would you measure attitude, knowledge, and level of engagement in stakeholders?
3   What are the key counterarguments to real estate development projects and how would you address them?
4   Explain the crucial relationship between the local public and authorities in this type of public relations issue.
5   What additional tactics would you deploy not discussed in the cases?

References

How does ownership work? (2018). *RiverWalk*. Retrieved from www.riverwalkresortatloon. com/ownership.

How to create a commercial real estate marketing plan. (2017, November 20). *inMotion Real Estate Media*. Retrieved from www.inmotionrealestate.com/resources/how-to-create-a-commercial-real-estate-marketing-plan/.

Schneider Associates. (2018). *Real Estate Marketing and PR*. Retrieved from www.schneiderpr. com/expertise/real-estate/.

Starbucks: Promoting Through Social Media

Introduction

Starbucks Corporation is an American chain of coffee shops, founded in Seattle, Washington in 1971. As of 2017, the company operates 27,339 stores worldwide. Starbucks locations serve hot and cold drinks, whole-bean coffee, micro-grounded instant coffee, espresso, cafe latte, full- and loose-leaf teas, Evolution Fresh juices, Frappuccino beverages, La Boulange pastries, snacks, and local specialty items. Many stores sell pre-packaged food items, hot and cold sandwiches, and products including mugs and tumblers. The select "Starbucks Evenings" locations offer beer, wine, and appetizers. Local and chain grocery stores sell Starbucks-brand coffee, ice cream, and bottled cold coffee drinks.

In 2017, Starbucks annual revenues were nearly $23 billion. Operating income was over $4 billion and net income was nearly $3 billion. The company employs 240,000 people. Starbucks Corporation also has the following subsidiaries: Starbucks Coffee Company, Ethos Water, Evolution Fresh, Hear Music, La Boulange Bakery, Seattle's Best Coffee, Tazo, Teavana, and Torrefazione Italia.

Market Segments

The following segmentation description is adopted from a Barbara Bean-Mellinger article "Who Is Starbucks' Target Audience?" published in the *Chron* (2018).

High Income, High Spenders

Starbucks' key public are affluent or high income (at least $90,000). At the same time, consumers earning less have discretionary income and are willing to spend it on premium coffee drinks. They enjoy treating themselves to their favorite coffee and, sometimes, a breakfast sandwich, snack, or dessert.

While Starbucks also has regular customers who are black coffee purists, those people are not the company's target market. Starbucks seeks those consumers who are willing to spend $10 for a snack and beverage.

Urban, On-the-Go

Starbucks' customers are also urbanites. Many Starbucks are located in outlying areas that are considered suburbs of urban areas, but are often 60 miles or more from the city. They are busy people, who spend a great deal of time in their vehicles going from place to place, such as work, to their kids' sports activities, the store, or the gym. They have an urban attitude, even though they do not reside in the inner city. As suburbanites, they spend a lot of time waiting in traffic, which makes their coffee splurge welcome.

Technology Early Adopters

The target age of the Starbucks' market is 22 to 60 years, with the teen audience growing steadily. Starbucks' app for mobile orders and payments has been a success. The 50- and 60-year-olds use the app regularly. Since offering Wi-Fi in the stores in 2002, Starbucks' customers see the store as not just a stop, but as an "office" where they can set up their laptops and attend to business while sipping their favorite beverages.

Healthy(ish) Professionals

Most of Starbucks' customers consist of educated, white-collar professionals, who are well-informed including knowing the latest trends about health. Starbucks offers teas and tea concoctions, specifically decaffeinated tea, green teas, wellness tea, mixtures such as Royal English Breakfast Tea, latte, and Teavana bottled blends. Starbucks bought Tazo and Teavana tea companies and Evolution Fresh for its line extensions.

Socially Conscious

Starbucks is a socially responsible "citizen." It is committed to protecting the environment and making a difference in the communities its cafés serve. For example, in 1995, it built its first LEED-certified store, which complied with green standards. Starbucks is also dedicated to sustainable coffee growing, open farmer support centers, a reduction of its carbon footprint, usage of recycled fiber cups, providing college opportunities to employees, opening stores in underserved and less affluent areas, and working to improve the surrounding communities where its shops operate.

Flexible to Change

Starbucks' publics are laid back but driven. They know that advancing in life requires adaptability and, like their favorite coffee store, they embrace the changes that come with growth and social dynamics. Change is viewed as an opportunity rather than a burden. The typical Starbucks' customer remains enthusiastic about what the future may bring.

Social Media Presence

Starbucks maintains the following social media presence.

- 37.32 million Facebook likes
- 6.56 million Twitter followers
- 2.98 million Instagram fans
- 2.86 million Google+ followers
- 160K Pinterest followers
- 32K YouTube subscribers.

Starbucks' approach to social media is as unique and appealing as the "social" environment the stores create for their customers. Let's look at Facebook, Twitter, Pinterest, and Instagram.

Facebook

The Starbucks social media management team does not post Facebook updates often. Of those that are posted, they were attention getting and facilitated engagement. The posts are a balance between being fun contests and helpful information for the java-loving crowd, while offering a subtle sales message to the customer.

Twitter

Starbucks has an interesting and unique approach to Twitter updates. Updates are infrequent, but strategic. The social team posts unique content and reaches out to customers to discuss their in-store or product experiences.

Tweets are directed at specific Twitter users who have "spoken" to Starbucks, sometimes with a complaint or negative feedback. The Starbucks social media practitioner checks in several times a day and encourages dissatisfied customers to contact the company for follow-up using Twitter-specific email addresses. This approach rectifies issues before they grow out of control.

Pinterest and Instagram

A major component of the retail coffee culture is presentation. For instance, decorated espressos and favored coffees are drunk in fancy designed cups. Starbucks' presentations are exceptional and provide eye-catching images for visually oriented social sites such as Pinterest and Instagram. "The company maintains several Pinboards featuring tea rituals, coffee gadgets, and soothing spaces to get cozy while you sip." Instagram displays an assortment of images about the coffee community and culture.

What Starbucks Knows about Social Media

Starbucks' goal is to develop a personal relationship with patrons. So far, the company seems to be succeeding.

New companies understand the intricate triangulation between consumers, a product, and social media, and how the three, when successfully managed, can increase a brand's profile and generate higher sales. In the case of Starbucks, nine out of ten people who use Facebook are either fans of Starbucks or know someone who is.

The real power of social media is that they allow companies to develop new products, and new revenue streams, by observing how customers interact with their product(s) and listening to their feedback, all to a degree that was previously unimaginable. It can also provide new avenues for bi-directional communication and deeper interaction with customers, fostering a closer relationship. An additional benefit is that agile companies can use these elements to more easily reposition a brand as a commercial environment changes.

Starbucks, for quite some time now, has been on the cutting of edge of incorporating digital marketing and social media into its operations, allowing it to almost seamlessly merge its brick and mortar stores with the numerous digital marketing channels available. The company has also been adept at developing relationships with its customers, using the latest technology and social media platforms. Starbucks is adamant when it says that the purpose of new technology is not just to improve its website or to process payments quicker for people who are waiting in line. It is really about getting in touch with its customers, and trying to better understand them so as to improve service levels and their experience with the brand. As a sign of its commitment, the company has reportedly taken all the money that it used to spend on traditional media outlets and shifted it into digital and social media marketing.

Starbucks is considered ahead of the curve when it comes to using social media as compared to other companies. "Starbucks was holding Facebook promotions before most restaurants even figured out this was a space they needed to be in," say Alicia Kelso, an editor-in-chief at Networld Media Group. The company's first large-scale social media campaign was back in 2009, when it offered U.S. customers a free pastry when they purchased a drink before 10:30 a.m. One million people took advantage of the offer.

Experts believe that when it comes to using digital marketing and social media, there are certain rules of etiquette that should be respected. One important principle would be to engage with your customers on their own terms and to the degree that they want to be engaged with. "Pushing" an ad in this digital age really does not work, especially with millennials who were basically born into a world of social media. Today, the expectation for many is that they will "invite" a brand or product into their lives, while at the same time actively resisting something that was "forced" upon them. An example of a normally sure-footed company getting this wrong comes from Apple. In September of 2014, Apple announced that it was making U2's latest album available for free to users of iTunes users. What people did not realize was that the album was also going to be forcibly downloaded to their iPhones and iPods, which many saw as a violation of their privacy. After metaphorically being "thrown under the bus" by Apple, the band's lead singer Bono was forced to issue an apology. The failed stunt reportedly cost Apple $100 million.

Starbucks, however, is extremely adept at engaging with its customers and fans in that it first gets "permission" before interacting with them. One way it has done this is by developing a huge social media presence involving 50 million people who have agreed to join Starbucks' communities on such sites as Facebook, YouTube, Twitter, Google+, and Instagram. Another way that Starbucks has managed to get invited into people's lives is through its mobile payment app (which people must download). This ingenious little app allows people to order and pay for their favorite Chestnut Praline Frappuccino without having to wait in line. It is currently the most popular wallet app in the U.S., with higher usage levels than even PayPal. Once again, in all of the above cases, Starbucks has permission to interact with the audience.

Additionally, Starbucks engages with its customers and builds brand recognition through competitions. For instance, the company put up new advertising posters in six major cities in the U.S. and people had to take a picture of them and Tweet them, with winners receiving a store gift card worth $20. The success of the campaign allowed Starbucks to amplify its message through social media. The value of the interest that it generated was far greater than the actual cost of the promotion. Starbucks stated that the impact of the marketing campaign was "the difference between launching with millions of dollars versus millions of fans."

In an ingenious example of using social media to execute "ads" in real-time, Starbucks took full advantage of a massive snow storm that hit the Northeastern United States in February of 2013. As temperatures dropped, and the snow started piling up, Starbucks began showing pictures of people holding nice warm mugs of coffee on its social media pages. The ads were formatted in such a way that when people did online searches about the storm, Starbucks' photos of people drinking coffee would also show up in the results as well.

Another way that Starbucks actively engages with its customers is through its "MyStarbucksIdea.com" site. Here, people can leave their thoughts, ideas, and opinions as to how Starbucks can improve its business. A reported 500,000 people have done just that. The site summarizes all of the ideas and then ranks and clearly presents them according to different categories. As a sign that the company truly listens to its customers, it then tells people which ideas are seriously being thought about and which ideas have already been implemented.

A criticism from some quarters, oddly, is that Starbucks does not update the content of its various social media platforms quickly enough. This is countered with the argument that the company is more concerned with the quality of its content, rather than the quantity or frequency of posts. Maybe this is a good thing. For the most part, Starbucks has been able to avoid any serious controversy from its digital marketing efforts. One small exception would be a Twitter campaign during Christmas of 2012 in the U.K. In it, Starbucks implored people to "spread the cheer." People who responded implored the company to "pay its taxes" (the company was facing accusations at the time that it was unfairly avoiding U.K. taxes).

Starbucks famously describes its vision of reaching its customers as "one neighborhood, one person, and one cup at a time." It would appear that through the effective use of digital marketing and social media, it is doing just that (McNamara and Moore-Mangin, 2015).

Starbucks Social Media Strategy

Keeping customers is great. With more than 27,000 stores in over 65 countries, many coffee drinkers know about Starbucks. These days, the company's challenge is to maintain its loyal customers: favorable attitude toward Starbucks, repeat purchases, and brand advocacy so that the competition does not gain a foothold by mimicking its offerings.

The Starbucks social media team is highly effective at offering customer service and a local coffee drinking experience on a large scale through its social media channels. The company gives customers individual attention, which encourages brand loyalty and repeat business.

Coffee is for socializing. Drinking coffee is a social activity, which is the focus of Starbucks' social media efforts. People love to "meet" over coffee, bring each other coffee, swap stories about coffee such as trying and talking about different kinds and flavors, and bringing the acquisition of coffee into their morning routines. Social media complements this dynamic where people share the coffee-drinking experience. Starbucks has capitalized on this process to their success.

Consistent branding. No matter what social media platform deployed, the Starbucks "feel" is there. Their social channels have the same look, feel, and tone similar to their stores. The content is consistent and informed by the company's mission, central message, and goals. Starbucks' attention to detail and customer-centered messaging makes their public relation the exemplar of best practices.

Conclusion

In addition to all that Starbucks does, a key component is the retail experience; it is a social experience in a place that people can unwind. Starbucks' social media efforts extend this experience to the digital world where customers can discuss, be informed, and order coffee. The only Starbucks benefit not available is receiving an order through one's digital device's screen.

Assignment

Using this case material as a starting point, develop a public relations social media-based strategy and plan for Starbucks. Would you approach opinion leaders to promote the Starbucks' brand? Conduct an online search for additional information and facts including news stories, social media, YouTube, and other sources. Keep in mind that the cultural, economic, political, legal, and media environments play a role in determining the degree of activism and public relations in a given country. Considering the effective tactics deployed by Starbucks, what would you change or incorporate in your strategy and plan today? Consult the campaign checklist located in the appendix and think about the following questions.

1   Who are the major Starbucks market segments and why? Would you consider other potential segments? If so, why?
2   How would you measure social media awareness, attitude, and level of engagement in the major Starbucks segments?
3   Who are Starbucks' major competitors and why? Consider developing a competitive benefit analysis matrix (table).
4   Develop a central message for Starbucks' social media efforts. Explain why it will be effective.
5   What objectives might you establish and why?
6   What additional tactics would you deploy not mentioned in the case?

References

Bean-Mellinger, B. (2018, March 14 Who Is Starbucks' Target Audience? *Chron.* Retrieved from http://smallbusiness.chron.com/starbucks-target-audience-10553.html.
McNamara, T., & Moore-Mangin, A. (2015, August 3). Starbucks and social media: It's about more than just coffee. *EContent.* Retrieved from www.econtentmag.com/Articles/Editorial/Commentary/Starbucks-and-Social-Media-Its-About-More-than-Just-Coffee-103823.htm.

The Skoda Global Campaign and the Role of Data

Introduction

This case study is about Skoda Auto and specifically the Kodiaq (pronounced Kodiak) SUV. Skoda Auto, more commonly known as Skoda, is a Czech automobile manufacturer founded in 1895 under the company name Laurin & Klement. Its headquarters are in Mladá Boleslav, Czech Republic. In 2016, the Kodiaq was rolled out globally. Although global in nature, this case features content from marketing efforts in the United Kingdom and India.

In 1925, Laurin & Klement was acquired by Skoda Works, which itself became state owned during the days of the Communist government. After 1991 it was gradually privatized and, in 2000, Skoda became a wholly owned subsidiary of the Volkswagen Group.

Initially the company was meant to serve the role of VW Group's entry brand. Over time, however, the Skoda brand quality improved, with most models overlapping their Volkswagen counterparts on price and features, while eclipsing them on sales. In 2016, its total global sales reached 1.13 million cars, an increase of 6.8% annually, and profit rose by 6.5% (Wikipedia, 2017, para. 1–3).

In the United Kingdom, Skoda was the fourteenth best-selling brand with a 3% market share, which is greater than both Mazda and Mitsubishi. In Europe as a whole, Skoda maintains 4.3% market share, outselling Mazda, Hyundai, and Toyota. In Germany, Skoda is the seventh largest automobile brand with 5.6% market share. The Germans buy three times as many Skodas as they do Toyotas. In China, Skoda outperforms Mazda and BMW.

Situation Analysis

Skoda has been an underdog brand, but as the vehicles win awards, the company is experiencing increased sales and is thriving. The SUV segment is the fastest growing in Europe. It accounts for 13% of the United Kingdom market. Since 2010, SUV growth is 20% per year.

Kodiaq is the brand's first major inroad into this booming category. "We are conquering a new segment for the brand – and new customer groups," says Skoda CEO, Bernhard Maier. According to him, the target demographic is different, the message is different and the strategy must be different, too, if Skoda is to stand a chance of success (International Association for the Measurement and Evaluation of Communication, 2017).

The Product

From the Skoda Website (www.Skoda.co.United Kingdom/news/ the-Skoda-Kodiaq/):

The adventure begins: new Skoda Kodiaq to start from £21,495 which is available in gas and diesel models

13/10/2016

United Kingdom prices and specifications for the all-new Skoda Kodiaq have been announced ahead of its showroom debut early next year. Skodas first ever seven-seater SUV will start from just £21,495 (OTR) when ordering starts in November, and will be available from launch in four trim levels, five engine options, two and four-wheel drive, and a choice of manual or DSG transmission.

Milton Keynes, 13 October: Setting a new benchmark for value

The Kodiaq will be available in 24 different variants when order books open in November. The range comprises three familiar trims; S, SE and SE L along with a new Edition grade that celebrates the arrival of the brand's first ever seven-seater SUV.

S Model

The range starts with the S model that despite its entry level status and price tag of just £21,495 (OTR), is brimming with standard equipment. The specification list includes LED daytime running lights, 17-inch Ratikon alloy wheels, leather multifunction steering wheel and air-conditioning. S models also feature Front Assist, KESSY Go, Swing touchscreen infotainment system, DAB digital radio and SmartLink for seamless smartphone connectivity. The S model is available with a 1.4 TSI 125PS engine only.

SE Model

SE models are priced from £22,945 (OTR) and are available with a broad range of engine and transmission options (see table for availability). Standard specification includes 18-inch Elbrus alloy wheels, sunset glass, cruise control and rear parking sensors. Customers also benefit from a Bolero touchscreen infotainment system with eight-inch display, dual-zone climate control, rain and light sensors, and auto-dimming rear view mirrors. Seven seats are available as a £1,000 option in SE trim.

SE L Model

Further up the range, SE L models start from £28,595 (OTR) and feature a generous specification list. Among the equipment highlights are seven seats, which now become standard, powered tailgate, 19-inch Sirius alloy wheels, and Columbus navigation system with WiFi. Drive Mode Select, Alcantara upholstery, heated front seats, and full LED headlights are also included as standard on all SE L models.

Edition

Topping the range from launch is a new Edition trim grade. Created to showcase the Kodiaq's exceptional range of equipment, Edition models start from £30,695 (OTR). Standard equipment includes 19-inch Triglav alloy wheels, seven seats, leather upholstery, metallic paint, and chrome roof rails. Technology features include Lane Assist, High Beam Assist, wireless charging and phone box, and Blind spot detection.

Design

Fully integrating Skoda's celebrated design language, the Kodiaq's exterior neatly combines elegant lines, sporty contours, and a feeling of robustness. Built on the Volkswagen

Group's modular transverse matrix (MQB), the Kodiaq is 4,697 mm long, 1,882 mm wide, and 1,676 mm tall (including roof rails), while the wheelbase measures 2,791 mm.

Although the Kodiaq is a completely new model, it is unmistakably a Skoda. The styling is characterized by clear, precise, and clean-cut lines – typified by a distinctive, highly recessed shoulder line. Double horizontal lines on the front convey a feeling of protection and strength while the wide, three-dimensional radiator grille is framed on either side by a pair of raked double headlights.

The interior includes bold vertical elements, such as the four large air vents and the large display that splits the instrument panel into two equal sections for the driver and passenger.

While the Kodiaq is just 40 mm longer than the Octavia, it offers a larger-than-average interior for the SUV segment. The interior length is 1,793 mm, elbow room is 1,527 mm in the front, and 1,510 mm in the rear. Head room is 1,020 mm in the front and 1,014 mm in the rear.

Rear legroom measures up to 104 mm. The middle seat row can be folded 60:40, features individually adjustable backrests and can slide lengthways by 18 cm as standard. The third row of seats can be folded neatly into the floor space to create a larger load area. And with a volume of 720 to 2,065 litres (5-seater with the rear seats folded down), the Skoda Kodiaq offers the largest boot within its class.

As buyers have come to expect from Skoda, the Kodiaq is brimming with Simply Clever features designed to make life on board even easier. These include a new door-edge protection system that deploys automatically when opening the door. When shutting the door, the trim folds itself back in. In total, more than 30 Simply Clever features have been integrated into the new Kodiaq, seven of which are completely new.

New Levels of Connectivity

Skoda Connect and its two major features makes its debut in the Kodiaq: Infotainment Online services – that provide more information and real-time navigation details and Care Connect – that provides remote access as well as assistance.

Infotainment Online includes online traffic information, Google Earth, Google Street View, fuel prices, parking information, online news, weather information, and "My Points of Interest" services.

Care Connect features an eCall emergency call system triggered after an accident, along with a notification function for minor accidents as well as a breakdown call function. Care Connect includes proactive services. Upon activation, all the required data goes to the garage in a timely manner before a vehicle's service.

Also included is Care Connect Remote Access. Integrated with the Skoda Connect app, it accesses and controls additional services and allows the transfer of routes from home to the navigation system in the car.

Care Connect is free on all trim levels for the first year of ownership. The Infotainment Online includes satellite navigation systems.

Driver Assistance Systems

The new Kodiaq is available with the broadest range of driver assistance systems ever offered in a Skoda. These include new-to-brand systems such as Trailer Assist that can take over steering when going into reverse slowly. Additionally, while in reverse, the new Manoeuvre Assist actives and stops the SUV at obstacle detection.

The Area View system is also a first for the brand. Wide angle surround-view cameras located in the front and rear, as well as the door mirrors, display views of the area immediately surrounding the car on the infotainment screen. These include a virtual, top-down view, and 180-degree images to the front and rear.

Other systems integrated into the Kodiaq include Front Assist; City Emergency Brake (standard on all models); Adaptive Cruise Control (ACC); and Lane Assist, Blind Spot Detect and Rear Traffic Alert. Safety systems include Driver Alert, Emergency Assist (DSG only), Crew Protect Assist, Multi-Collision Brake, and Travel Assist with Traffic Sign Recognition.

Engines and Transmissions

The Kodiaq launches in the United Kingdom with a choice of five engines; three gasoline and two diesel. Power outputs range from 125PS to 190PS, with customers able to choose between two or four-wheel drive and manual or DSG transmissions. All engines feature Stop-Start system, brake energy recovery, and a powerful thermo-management system that contributes to low consumption.

The petrol line-up consists of two 1.4 TSI units, one with an output of 125PS and another with 150PS using Active Cylinder Technology. PS refers to horsepower. The former is available in two-wheel drive manual, while the 150PS version comes a manual 4x4 transmission, two-wheel drive DSG, and 4x4 DSG. The range-topping 2.0 TSI petrol unit delivers 180PS and drives through a seven-speed DSG 4x4 transmission. A DSG is a direct shift gearbox. It is two manual gearboxes working alternatively but enclosed inside one housing, and, therefore, it uses two clutches and two gear shafts to deliver power to the wheels.

The diesel line-up features a pair of 2.0 TDI units with outputs of 150PS and 190PS. The 150PS version offers a manual 4x4 transmission, two-wheel drive DSG, and 4x4 DSG, while the 190PS comes with a seven-speed DSG 4x4 transmission only.

The Kodiaq's all-wheel-drive system with electronic control delivers exceptional traction, stability, and driving safety in all conditions. At the heart of the system is an electronically controlled multi-plate clutch that operates intelligently and quickly. The control unit constantly calculates the ideal driving torque for the rear axle. The control system, which is dependent on driving status, eliminates loss of traction. When in overrun or at low load, drive is via the front axle, which saves fuel.

By a simple touch of a button (optional for the all-wheel-drive versions in combination with Driving Mode Select), the off-road mode activates. In this setting, the chassis, engine management, and brakes adjust their operation specifically to rough terrain by managing traction and deceleration. In off-road mode, Hill Descent Assist helps the driver safely master driving downhill over rough terrain by braking appropriately.

Reviews

The following are Kodiaq reviews from various markets.

> The Skoda Kodiaq has been in the news for quite some time. When it was first showcased last year, it was the personification of a new, bold, and evocative design language from Skoda and was the flag-bearer of the company's strategy with regards to SUVs in

general. Taking its name from a species of bear found in Alaska, the Kodiaq is the first ever seven-seater SUV from Skoda and the company believes that it will be something of a game-changer once it's launched in India. But it is not going to be easy. The Skoda Kodiaq will have to take on established rivals such as the Toyota Fortuner, Ford Endeavour, and Kodiaq's cousin, the Tiguan.

(Dutta, 2017a, para. 2)

The Skoda Kodiaq is based on the flexible MQB platform that underpins a host of offerings in the Volkswagen Group. That's why the VW Tiguan and the new Kodiaq share the same base and engine options as well. However, in VW's pyramid, Skoda emerges as a smaller brand over the parent group and this applies in pricing too. This means that the Kodiaq just might be cheaper than the Tiguan when it comes to India. While prices for the latter start at ₹26.56 lakh (ex-showroom), expect the Kodiaq to be cheaper by a little more than a lakh and just might start at ₹25 lakh, going up to ₹30 lakh for the range-topping version.

(Contractor, 2017, para. 3)

. . . pricing we think works best for the Skoda Kodiaq that will face competition from a host of offerings. The segment has two highly capable SUVs already including the Toyota Fortuner and Ford Endeavour, while more recently the Isuzu MU-X and VW Tiguan also joined the stable. Skoda then, will have to keep things competitive on the Kodiaq, with an aggressive starting price being one of them.

(Contractor, 2017, para. 4)

To be honest, there's nothing here that's going to make your jaw drop. Engines and gearboxes are shared elsewhere with the VW group, while the second row of seats slides back and forth, and the optional third row (a £1,000 extra on lower spec models) rise out of the boot floor. A full suite of driver assistance systems and Skoda Connect online capability tick all those de rigeur tech boxes, while the latest 8in glass-fronted infotainment system is impressively slick.

(Towler, 2017, para. 2)

The steering is accurate, light, and completely de-sensitised. In Sport mode it's accurate, slightly less light and remains de-sensitised, but also adopts a slightly rubbery feel. The chassis – tuned to be a little firmer than other Skodas – balances grip, roll, and ride comfort respectably, particularly with the optional adaptive dampers (DCC), but offers no enjoyment. The manual gearshift is light and slop-free, but DSG is a sensible addition.

(Towler, 2017, para. 8)

Most buyers opt for the 148bhp 2.0-litre diesel, which is gutsy enough to haul around seven people with little drama. However, the rival Kia Sorento delivers a welcome dollop of extra shove when you put your foot down – useful when overtaking or towing a caravan. To counter that, Skoda offers the Kodiaq with a 188bhp version of the same 2.0-litre diesel engine, which has similar acceleration to the Sorento, but it does push up the price considerably.

(*What Car Review*, Skoda Kodiaq, 2018)

. . . the Skoda Kodiaq looks promising and will come with a host of bells and whis-tles. The styling is impressive and quite sleek and urban as well, unlike its bulky rivals. The SUV will be a proper 7-seater with a foldable second and third row, while the feature list will include a touchscreen infotainment system with Apple CarPlay and Android Auto, as well as auto climate control, cruise control, and much more. The model will come to India via the CKD route and will be locally assembled.

(Contractor, 2017)

The Skoda Kodiaq has been launched in the country and is available in a single vari-ant priced at ₹34.49 lakh (ex-showroom, India). In this price bracket, you get a legit 7-seater SUV with a bunch of features and equipment, superb passenger comfort, and safety along with decent performance. The pricing does push the Kodiaq against the likes of the Audi Q3, BMW X1, and Mercedes-Benz GLA. Much like the Superb too then, the Kodiaq does offer more practicality against some of the more expensive SUVs in the same price bracket.

(Dutta, 2017b, para. 12)

The Challenge

- The Kodiaq is the automaker's first full-sized SUV, and, therefore, does not have a track record. Most manufacturers have had a full-size SUV for a while now. Some are excellent, some are well priced, and some handle very well.
- The Toyota 4Runner and Ford Endeavor are much larger and better off-roaders.
- The Volkswagen Tiguan shares the same underpinnings as the Kodiaq.
- The Kodiaq is not a typical rough and tough premium SUV. It is more of a soft-roader and designed to offer a comfortable daily city commute and highway driving.
- The cramped third row is suitable only for short trips when seating adults.
- Being a flagship model, the Kodiaq is expensive. Also, there is no air conditioning for the third row.
- Large SUVs look highly aggressive with a daunting road presence, but the Kodiaq does not. It has an urban sophisticated look, not meant for those who love intimidating SUVs.
- Kodiaq is a large SUV, but its 2.0L TDI engine is not powerful.
- The transmission does not transition between gears smoothly.

The Campaign

Campaign title: "Skoda Goes Off-Road for Success"

The goal of the public relations campaign was to generate enthusiasm and engagement for the Skoda Kodiaq. The target for Kodiaq registered inquiries was set at 125% of Skoda's previous most successful car launch. Media analysis played an integral role in developing, fine-tuning, and assessing the campaign, particularly since PR activity took place in near isolation from other integrated marketing communication efforts.

Strategy

Previously, Skoda relied heavily on advertising value equivalency (AVE) to prove success. However, since Kodiaq was Skoda's most important model launch to date, AVEs alone would not be sufficient. The campaign's success was based not only on media performance but linked to the core business objectives of awareness and positive attitude, registered inquiries, and sales. Analysis and assessment were ongoing throughout the campaign.

Planning for Success

Public relations practitioners identified the prominent topics, issues, and features that journalists and opinion leaders covered when reporting competitor brand roll-outs paying attention to the focus of media. They determined which points to use to present Kodiaq's strengths and minimize perceived weaknesses. A competitive benefit analysis compared the Kodiaq's pros and cons against the major competition in the eyes of the experts as well as the typical consumer. The Kodiaq had to stand out at auto shows. Armed with deep historical analysis and competitor benchmark data, Skoda planned its media relations strategy to optimize efforts.

To reach publics such as experts/journalists and consumers, the key channels of communication were researched to determine how best to reach these groups. As far as journalists were concerned, this would contribute to leveraging strong relationships as well as help to discover which communications tools would best reach them. Primary research used focus groups and survey data by Skoda's public relations agency Kindred to ascertain attitudes toward Skoda and the competition as well as other perspectives that would influence purchase behavior. For example, parent consumer focus groups determined what "ordinary" motoring meant to them. The research revealed that the school run was the most challenging trip that families undertook during the school day. This led to the "Extreme School Run" lifestyle campaign led by Kindred PR.

Execution

To assure that Skoda had the best chance of driving awareness and ultimately sales, the historic media insights contributed to a four-stage launch plan that included continuous analysis throughout the campaign.

1   **Geneva tease** – launch of concept car in March 2016
2   **Berlin standalone event** – launch of the car in September 2016
3   **Paris debut** – unveiling of the Kodiaq at the Paris Motor Show
4   **Special lifestyle campaign** – Extreme School Run aimed at families.

Data Driven Decision-Making

Data Informs a Successful Strategy

Analysis of previous auto show data revealed that they are becoming less appropriate for car launches due to the amount of competing noise. In a typical show, pre-show coverage accounts for 40% of total visibility. Consequently, feeding coverage before a show increases the likelihood that journalists are familiar with the product and thus offers auto manufacturers a distinct advantage.

Following a "tease" event in Geneva, the Kodiaq was introduced at a standalone event in Berlin in September 2016. With the Paris Motor Show scheduled for the following month, journalists had plenty of time to learn about the Kodiaq, which primed them to write about it in Paris. This strategy was effective: the Kodiaq had by far the most coverage compared to other vehicles at the Paris show. This was a fantastic achievement given the show's highly competitive nature.

Having achieved widespread appeal in Paris, the campaign then progressed to a lifestyle campaign aimed at their target audiences. Moving away from Skoda's traditional 55+ audience, the campaign focused on visually striking images in the an "Extreme School Run" campaign aimed at families.

Kindred PR conducted consumer research to ascertain how much of their lives families spend on the school run, including countries where families were most frequently delayed by flooding and livestock. These statistics informed the central message narrative.

Results

In line with other objectives, research showed that Kodiaq outperformed the SUV segment in both share of coverage and sentiment in the most critical areas for SUV buyers: space and versatility; price and running costs; and safety and handling. The Kodiaq dominated its competitors in all qualitative measures.

The Extreme School Run film was Skoda's best performing video of 2016, with at least 100,000 more Facebook views than any other competitor. In fact, the full video view completion rate for Extreme School Run was 95% more than the Skoda typical rate. Audience awareness was high, resulting in a 41% hike in traffic to the Skoda website during and after the execution of the Extreme School Run component of the campaign and Google search rankings increasing substantially.

Analysis showed that Skoda registered inquiries increased more than 33% of all model inquiries before the Kodiaq hit the showroom.

> The importance of the Kodiaq launch for Skoda cannot be underestimated. Simply put, it is the most important product launch in our 126-year history. PR played a critical role in giving the car the platform it needed to shine and deliver credibility.
> (Pietro Panarisi, Head of Public Relations, Skoda United Kingdom)

Assignment

Using this case material as a starting point, develop a public relations strategy and plan for the Kodiaq launch on a global basis focusing on Europe, India, and China. How would you approach journalists/consumers to promote the Kodiaq? Conduct an online search for additional information and facts including news stories, social media, YouTube, and other sources. Keep in mind that the cultural, economic, political, legal, and media environments play a role in determining the degree of activism and public relations in a given country. Considering the effective tactics deployed by Skoda, what would you change or incorporate in your strategy and plan today? Consult the campaign checklist located in the appendix and think about the following questions.

1   Who are the major Kodiaq publics and why?
2   How would you measure awareness, attitude, and level of engagement of the major Kodiaq publics?

3   Would you develop a competitive benefit analysis matrix (table) to better understand the Kodiaq compared to its major competitors? If so, develop a matrix.
4   How would you address the Kodiaq's weaknesses?
5   Although this case primarily addresses the Kodiaq market in the United Kingdom, what factors would you consider when implementing a public relations plan in all of Europe, India, and China?
6   What additional tactics would you deploy not mentioned in the case?

References

Contractor, S. (2017, August 10). Skoda Kodiaq: Price expectation in India. *CarAndBike*. Retrieved from https://auto.ndtv.com/news/Skoda-Kodiaq-price-expectation-in-india-1735629.

Dutta, K. (2017a, August 12). Skoda Kodiaq vs Toyota Fortuner vs Ford Endeavour vs Volkswagen Tiguan: Specifications comparison. *CarAndBike*. Retrieved from https://auto.ndtv.com/news/skoda-kodiaq-vs-toyota-fortuner-vs-ford-endeavour-vs-volkswagen-tiguan-specifications-comparison-1736817.

Dutta, K. (2017b, October 8) Skoda Kodiaq review. *CarAndBike*. Retrieved from https://auto.ndtv.com/reviews/Skoda-Kodiaq-first-drive-review-1755801.

International Association for the Measurement and Evaluation of Communication. (2017). *Skoda goes off-road for success*. Retrieved from https://amecorg.com/case-study/Skoda-goes-off-road-for-success-Skoda-United Kingdom-3/.

Skoda Kodiaq review. (2018). *What Car? Haymarket Media Group*. Retrieved from https://www.whatcar.com/Skoda/Kodiaq/estate/review/buying-owning/.

The adventure begins: New Skoda Kodiaq to start from £21,495 which is available is gas and diesel models. Retrieved from www.Skoda.co.United Kingdom/news/the-Skoda-Kodiaq.

Towler, A. (2017, April 5). Skoda Kodiaq review – Eminently practical, but is this new SUV enjoyable to drive? *EVO*. Retrieved from www.evo.co.uk/Skoda/18549/Skoda-Kodiaq-review-eminently-practical-but-is-this-new-suv-enjoyable-to-drive.

Wikipedia, (2017). *Skoda Auto*. Retrieved from https://en.wikipedia.org/wiki/%C5%A0koda_Auto.

UNICEF: A Study in Advocacy

Introduction

The United Nations Children's Fund (UNICEF), founded in 1946 with revenues of $5 billion, is a United Nations program headquartered in New York City. It provides humanitarian and developmental assistance to children and mothers in developing countries. "UNICEF works in 190 countries and territories to save children's lives, to defend their rights, and to help them fulfil their potential. And we never give up" (UNICEF for Every Child, What We Do, 2018, para. 2).

UNICEF developed and launched a public relations campaign that extended from 2014 to 2017 with the goal "to realize the rights of every child, especially the most disadvantaged," which is the focus of this case. This campaign was:

> **tied to the priorities of the UNICEF Strategic Plan** – using communication and public advocacy to realize organizational goals;
>
> **equity-focused** – putting the lives and rights of the most disadvantaged children at the heart of our messaging;
>
> **"glocal"** – setting global priorities, adaptable in local contexts, scaling up the most promising local solutions across the entire organization;
>
> **innovative** – embracing new ways of working to drive change for children;
>
> **integrated** – with new global brand and advocacy strategies (in development); and
>
> **measurable** – against key performance indicators to show impact (*Communicate to Advocate for Every Child: UNICEF's Global Communication and Public Advocacy Strategy, 2014–2017*, 2014).

Changing Landscape

Over time, society has evolved, demonstrating the following relevant major trends:

- Civil society has grown in size, reach, power and influence. Individuals are organizing, planning, and taking collective action as never before, shaping local and international priorities.
- Advances in digital technology have contributed to that shift by empowering individuals to seek and generate information, build virtual networks, and exchange experiences in real time.
- "Digital" is transforming the way individuals relate to each other, their communities and the world.
- The rise of social media has fed the growth and influence of social movements that defy geographic boundaries.
- Mobile information and communication technologies (ICT) are rapidly becoming one of the most important ways people connect and communicate.
- Communication is increasingly used to drive public advocacy, accountability, and responsibility (*UNICEF's Global Communication and Public Advocacy Strategy 2014–17*, 2014).

Changing Ways to Communicate

As reported in the *Communicate to Advocate for Every Child: UNICEF's Global Communication and Public Advocacy Strategy, 2014–2017* (2014), a changing world requires new ways to communicate and message stakeholders. UNICEF was dedicated to effectuating these communication and messaging changes, which heretofore were not the mainstay of the organization. All that was about to change starting with the developing and implementation of this campaign. Some of the key changes were:

From working to change policies . . .	To also working to change behaviors, social attitudes, and beliefs.
From primarily targeting governments, corps., and influencers . . .	To also powerfully communicating with the broad general public.
From primarily informing . . .	To inspiring by telling compelling stories.
From telling . . .	To also listening, conversing, and crowdsourcing (two- way communication).
From disseminating information . . .	To communicating to advocate, to drive change, and to move people to act.
From focusing mainly on print media . . .	To fully developing content for print, digital, mobile, and broadcast media.
From knowledge brokering . . .	To knowledge leadership.
From press releases . . .	To integrated communication strategies (which include traditional communication).
From "everything" . . .	To selected strategic priorities, communicated, and supported across the organization.
From partnership initiatives . . .	To a broader fueling of social engagement.

Key Stakeholder Groups

There were two key publics for this campaign. First, Youth and Millennials (ages 15–34), who are the world's future decision-makers, and Middle-class adults who are a growing audience conducive to engagement and advocacy.

Youth and Millennials: Thirty-two percent of the world's population are millennials and 1.4 billion of them live in 20 countries. Asia has the highest number of millennials and Africa has among the highest proportion of the group.

Middle Class: The middle class is educated, socially aware, and willing to support children's causes. They are an important public that supports, bolsters, and leads many social movements. The middle class is growing on every continent and in every country, except in North America. They are growing in East Asia and the Pacific, South Asia, the Middle East, North Africa, Latin America, and the Caribbean.

Objectives

1   Be the leading voice for children throughout the world especially those who are disadvantaged.
2   Reach 1 billion people around the world.
3   Engage 50 million people namely in the key publics to support and advocate for children.

Central Message

The central message contained the following motifs:

- Equity and rights are at the heart of messaging.
- UNICEF's communication and public advocacy campaign is global (including parallel branding and advocacy strategies), fully integrated, and adaptable at the local level – in high-, middle- and low-income countries.
- Communication and public advocacy focus on a call to action on behalf of children.
- Communication and public advocacy are people-focused.
- Communication and public advocacy deploy innovative approaches.

Strategic and Tactical Direction

For Objective 1: Be more strategic and create an emotional story; support messaging with evidence; provide rapid, authoritative, and proactive communication.

For Objective 2: Integrated digital communications; deploy broadcast and print media; establish new and stronger partnerships; overall, develop innovative channels of communication.

For Objective 3: Take a "Glocal" approach; leverage partnerships to mobilize and fuel social movements; utilize Goodwill Ambassadors and opinion leaders.

Assignment

Using this case material as a starting point, develop a public relations outreach and advocacy strategy and plan for UNICEF. Conduct an online search for additional information and facts including news stories, social media, YouTube, and other sources. Keep in mind that the cultural, economic, political, legal, and media environments play a role in determining the degree of activism and public relations in a given country. Considering the effective tactics deployed by UNICEF, what would you change or incorporate in your strategy and plan today? Consult the campaign checklist located in the appendix and think about the following questions.

1 Who are the major UNICEF publics and why?
2 What different environments must one consider when operating in different countries and why?
3 Based on the central message requirements, what would be an effective central message for the key stakeholders? Consider engagement and social media as well as innovation.
4 How would the central message vary by key stakeholder group? Explain your reasoning.
5 What are the key objectives? Fully develop them so that they serve as measurable benchmarks?
6 What metrics would you deploy to monitor, evaluate, and, if necessary, adjust the campaign as it progresses from 2014 to 2017?
7 What tactics would you utilize in 2018?
8 What approaches/ways might serve to increase engagement?

References

Communicate to Advocate for Every Child: UNICEF's Global Communication and Public Advocacy Strategy, 2014–2017. (2014). New York: UNICEF.

UNICEF. (2018). *For Every Child, What We Do.* Retrieved from www.unicef.org/what-we-do.

UNICEF's Global Communication and Public Advocacy Strategy 2014–17. (2014). New York: UNICEF.

Winnipeg CEO Sleepout: Building Support

Introduction

CEO Sleepout is a charity and social movement that raises awareness and money to fight homelessness and poverty throughout the world with organizations in the United Kingdom, South Africa, Canada, and the United States to name some areas. By sponsoring or being sponsored to sleep outside in the streets for a night, business executives raise funds for homeless people. Local charities that aid homeless people receive the proceeds.

The first CEO Sleepout in Canada occurred in 2011. CEOs, community leaders, and media representatives increased awareness about homelessness. Moreover, the participants raised over $100,000 with Change for the Better, a consultancy for social good and homeless employment programs. The event gained international media coverage and set in motion a CEO Sleepout 10-year plan to end homelessness involving support from the private and public sectors. In 2012, CEO Sleepout raised $119,000 and, in 2013, over $200,000 to help the homeless in the greater metropolitan Winnipeg area, a city of 800,000 people.

Throughout the years, some of the non-profits supported were Artbeat Studio, Graffiti Art programming, MacDonald Youth Service, Red Road Lodge, Siloam mission, and Union Gospel Mission. These programs assist people who are homeless through empowering them by providing a home and helping them keep it, offering support in dealing with life's challenges, and creating meaningful jobs that give them a sense of being part of a community.

To date, CEO Sleepout Winnipeg has raised over $900,000 and provided thousands of hours of gainful employment to those in need. To quote Rob Johnston, Royal Bank of Canada, Regional President, "Sleeping out certainly gave me an appreciation for how much opportunity we can extend to the homeless, to those who are underemployed or unemployed. We can do more, we need to do more, and this is a great beginning," (Downtown Winnipeg Biz, 2018, para. 1).

Goals

The Winnipeg chapter, like all CEO Sleepout locations, endeavors to inform, discuss, and engage with the downtown business community on homelessness and poverty issues, and, at the same time, provide financial supporting for work programs that directly empower the city's most vulnerable. Sleepout's goals are:

1   To educate the business community about the solutions to ending homelessness, such as providing access to housing and employment.
2   To engage and educate the business community, and to fundraise for homeless employment programs through hosting the Change for the Better CEO Sleepout.
3   To work with organizations like the Winnipeg Poverty Reduction Council to help influence policy regarding homelessness.

Serving as an exemplar,

Winnipeg Poverty Reduction Council brings together leaders from a variety of sectors to work collaboratively at addressing the underlying causes of poverty. WPRC's role has three components: to have and share knowledge about complicated issues, to use its influence to engage all sectors and communities, and to foster collaboration that breaks down silos, creates collective impact, and reduces poverty in Winnipeg.

(WPRC, About, 2008, para. 1).

In short, CEO Sleepout serves to not only to raise funds, but also to increase other forms of support and engagement among stakeholders such as influencing public policy; engaging in other forms of advocacy; encouraging private organizations to become involved in some way whether to provide jobs, volunteer, promote, donate, or sponsor related programs; as well as other creative ways. The goal is to build lasting relationships that extend to long-term efforts and success.

Stakeholders

CEO Sleepout has diverse stakeholder groups. They are news media, the public, partners, CEOs, sponsors, volunteers, the organizations that will hire people, and the local disadvantaged residents.

News media provide publicity and aid to increase awareness and engagement.

Increasing awareness, positive attitude, and involvement from the public can aid in multiple areas such as recruiting volunteers, donations, spreading the word, and awareness that influence publics crucial to the achievement of the movement's mission.

Partners take various forms such as other related non-profits, corporations, local business, opinion leaders, local celebrities, and local municipal governments.

Parties sponsor the CEOs sleepout. The quality and degree of their participating and promoting the event reflect their commitment to the cause. Sponsors take various forms such as individuals or organizations. Sponsorship contributes to good will and responsible citizenship.

Volunteers and their passion about the program can have a positive effect on the event and contribute to Sleepout spreading throughout the community.

Organizations that hire individuals and provide a nurturing place of employment are a critical public for this program. Moreover, the hours of employment provided is a measure of CEO Sleepout's success.

The people who directly benefit from the program is another public. They need to see Sleepout as credible. They must trust the program and perceive that it can serve their needs in a pragmatic and realistic manner.

The diverse publics provide challenges to central messaging. Although the central theme is the creative direction targeting all publics, it must speak to the uniqueness of each specific stakeholder group.

Criticism

CEO Sleepout Winnipeg is not without its detractors. During a recent event, protestors encircled Sleepout CEO participants handing out flyers to them. Some protectors dressed as members of the Downtown Watch and told the CEOs to "move along." They wanted the CEOs to experience what some individuals who live on the streets go through.

Other critics claim that the government cut taxes for CEOs, while, at the same time, decreasing funding for social programs. "Everything affects everything else. Most people on the street don't have anything at all, and they're taking more and more away from us," said Tiffany Mamakeesic, who spent time living in shelters.

Another criticism centered on the nature of the CEO Sleepout event. The CEOs were there for one evening. Their heated "quarters" included WiFi access. A security detail protected them from approaching street people. Detractors stated that it is hypocritical to have an event intended to help street people occur on the street yet deny access to street people. Critics claimed that persons affected by the issue should participate and contribute to the dialogue.

Additionally, some CEOs were criticized for blatantly using the Sleepout as a vehicle for self-promotion rather than focusing on homelessness and poverty.

Others pointed out that although well-intended, the CEO Sleepout events lack substantive dialogue about homelessness and how to combat it in the long-run. This point demonstrates the lack of knowledge about the full extent of Sleepout's impact. In fact, CEO Sleepout Winnipeg collaborates with Winnipeg Poverty Reduction Council, a non-profit with a deep understanding of the factors, dynamics, and many other aspects of homelessness and poverty in the community.

Assignment

Using this case material as a starting point, develop a public relations strategy and plan for the next Winnipeg CEO Sleepout launch. How would you approach journalists/consumers to promote the Sleepout? Conduct an online search for additional information and facts including news stories, social media, YouTube, and other sources. Keep in mind that the cultural, economic, political, legal, and media environments play a role in determining the degree of activism and engagement. Determine the tactics the Winnipeg CEO Sleepout deployed. Would you change or incorporate any in your strategy and plan today? Consult the campaign checklist located in the appendix and think about the following questions.

1   Who are the major CEO Sleepout publics and why?
2   How would you measure awareness, attitude, and level of engagement of the major Sleepout publics?
3   How would you address the Winnipeg CEO Sleepout criticisms?
4   Although this case primarily addresses the Winnipeg, Canada environment, what factors would you consider when implementing a public relations plan in other parts of the world where CEO Sleepout operates such as the United Kingdom and South Africa?
5   Consider developing objectives and benchmarks based on the stated Sleepout goals. This activity will require research.
6   What tactics would you deploy to achieve the Winnipeg CEO Sleepout goals?

References

CEO Sleepout: What about sleepout. (2018). *Downtown Winnipeg BIZ*. Retrieved from http://downtownwinnipegbiz.com/programs-services/homelessness-assistance/ceo-sleepout/.
Who we are: About. (2018). *Winnipeg Poverty Reduction Council*. Retrieved from http://wprc.ca/who-we-are/.

Index